Defeating Authoritarian Leaders in Postcommunist Countries

From 1998 to 2005, six elections took place in p
that had the surprising outcome of empowering tl
itarian incumbents or their designated successoɪ
Wolchik compare these unexpected electoral breɛ
elections that had the more typical result of maintaining authoritarian rule. They draw
three conclusions. First, the opposition was victorious because of the hard and creative work of a transnational network composed of local opposition and civil society
groups, members of the international democracy assistance community, and graduates of successful electoral challenges to authoritarian rule in other countries. Second,
the remarkable run of these upset elections reflected the ability of this network to
diffuse an ensemble of innovative electoral strategies across state boundaries. Finally,
elections can serve as a powerful mechanism for democratic change. This is especially
the case when civil society is strong, the transfer of political power is through constitutional means, and opposition leaders win with small mandates.

Valerie J. Bunce is the Aaron Binenkorb professor of government and interna-
tional studies at Cornell University, where she served as chair of the Department of
Government from 2001 to 2007. Since receiving her Ph.D. in political science at the
University of Michigan, Bunce has also taught at Lake Forest College, Northwestern
University, Central European University (Budapest), and the University of Zagreb.
She has served as president of the American Association for the Advancement of
Slavic Studies and as vice president of the American Political Science Association,
and she is a member of the American Academy of Arts and Sciences. Her articles have
appeared in the *American Political Science Review*, *Comparative Political Studies*,
Comparative Politics, *World Politics*, *International Organization*, the *American
Journal of Political Science*, the *British Journal of Political Science*, *Slavic Review*,
Communist and Post-Communist Studies, and *East European Politics and Societies*.
She is the author of *Do New Leaders Make a Difference? Executive Succession
and Public Policy under Capitalism and Socialism* and *Subversive Institutions: The
Design and the Destruction of Socialism and the State* and a coeditor of *Democracy
and Authoritarianism in the Postcommunist World*.

Sharon L. Wolchik is professor of political science and international affairs at The George
Washington University. She has served as director of the Russian and East European
Studies Program and the Masters in International Policy and Practice Program at the
Elliott School of International Affairs and is a member of the Institute for European,
Russian, and Eurasian Studies. She has served on the board of the American Association
for Slavic Studies and the Cold War International History Project and as chair of the
Board of the National Council for Eurasian and East European Research. She is the
author of *Czechoslovakia in Transition: Politics, Societies, and Economics* and is a coed-
itor of *Domestic and Foreign Policies in Eastern Europe in the 1980s*; *Women, State,
and Party in Eastern Europe*; *Women and Democracy: Latin America and Central and
Eastern Europe*; *Women in Power in Post-communist Parliaments*; *The Social Legacies
of Communism*; and *Central and East European Politics: From Communism to
Democracy*. She has authored articles in *Slavic Review*, *Comparative Political Studies*,
World Politics, *Studies in Comparative Communism*, the *Journal of Communist and
Post-Communist Studies*, and *East European Politics and Societies*.

Advance Praise for *Defeating Authoritarian Leaders in Postcommunist Countries*

"*Defeating Authoritarian Leaders in Postcommunist Countries* is a major contribution to debates on regime transition. Bunce and Wolchik make the paradigmatic case that opposition creativity, innovation, and ambition are central to successful democratization. The book also offers a refreshing take on democratic diffusion. Contrary to the 'high altitude' approach taken by so many studies, this book, based on primary research in at least eleven countries, shows us exactly how diffusion takes place and the array of domestic and external actors who play a critical role in its success or failure. This book will be of enormous interest to scholars of democratization and essential reading for those concerned with strengthening democratic institutions in the world today."

– Lucan A. Way, University of Toronto

Cambridge Studies in Contentious Politics

Editors

Mark Beissinger *Princeton University*
Jack A. Goldstone *George Mason University*
Michael Hanagan *Vassar College*
Doug McAdam *Stanford University and Center for Advanced Study in the Behavioral Sciences*
Suzanne Staggenborg *University of Pittsburgh*
Sidney Tarrow *Cornell University*
Charles Tilly (d. 2008) *Columbia University*
Elisabeth J. Wood *Yale University*
Deborah Yashar *Princeton University*

Ronald Aminzade et al., *Silence and Voice in the Study of Contentious Politics*
Javier Auyero, *Routine Politics and Violence in Argentina: The Gray Zone of State Power*
Clifford Bob, *The Marketing of Rebellion: Insurgents, Media, and International Activism*
Charles Brockett, *Political Movements and Violence in Central America*
Christian Davenport, *Media Bias, Perspective, and State Repression*
Gerald F. Davis, Doug McAdam, W. Richard Scott, and Mayer N. Zald, *Social Movements and Organization Theory*
Jack A. Goldstone, editor, *States, Parties, and Social Movements*
Joseph Luders, *The Civil Rights Movement and the Logic of Social Change*
Doug McAdam, Sidney Tarrow, and Charles Tilly, *Dynamics of Contention*
Sharon Nepstad, *War Resistance and the Plowshares Movement*
Kevin J. O'Brien and Lianjiang Li, *Rightful Resistance in Rural China*
Silvia Pedraza, *Political Disaffection in Cuba's Revolution and Exodus*
Eduardo Silva, *Challenging Neoliberalism in Latin America*
Sarah Soule, *Contention and Corporate Social Responsibility*
Sidney Tarrow, *The New Transnational Activism*
Ralph Thaxton, Jr. *Catastrophe and Contention in Rural China: Mao's Great Leap Forward Famine and the Origins of Righteous Resistance in Da Fo Village*
Charles Tilly, *Contention and Democracy in Europe, 1650–2000*
Charles Tilly, *Contentious Performances*
Charles Tilly, *The Politics of Collective Violence*
Stuart A. Wright, *Patriots, Politics, and the Oklahoma City Bombing*
Deborah Yashar, *Contesting Citizenship in Latin America: The Rise of Indigenous Movements and the Postliberal Challenge*

Defeating Authoritarian Leaders in Postcommunist Countries

VALERIE J. BUNCE
Cornell University

SHARON L. WOLCHIK
The George Washington University

CAMBRIDGE
UNIVERSITY PRESS

CAMBRIDGE UNIVERSITY PRESS
Cambridge, New York, Melbourne, Madrid, Cape Town,
Singapore, São Paulo, Delhi, Mexico City

Cambridge University Press
32 Avenue of the Americas, New York, NY 10013-2473, USA

www.cambridge.org
Information on this title: www.cambridge.org/9780521187251

First published 2011
Reprinted 2012 (twice)

A catalog record for this publication is available from the British Library.

Library of Congress Cataloging in Publication Data

Bunce, Valerie, 1949–
 Defeating authoritarian leaders in postcommunist countries /
 Valerie Bunce and Sharon Wolchik.
   p. cm. – (Cambridge studies in contentious politics)
 Includes bibliographical references and index.
 ISBN 978-1-107-00685-0 (hardback)
 ISBN 978-0-521-18725-1 (paperback)
   1. Former communist countries – Politics and government. 2. Democracy – Former
 communist countries. 3. Authoritarianism – Former communist countries
 I. Wolchik, Sharon L. II. Title. III. Series.
 JN96.A58B876 2011
 324.9171´7–dc22   2011003650

ISBN 978-1-107-00685-0 Hardback
ISBN 978-0-521-18725-1 Paperback

Contents

Figures and Tables

Acknowledgments

The idea for this book originated in a casual conversation between the two of us in early 2004. Val had been working on a project comparing variations in bargaining dynamics between central and regionally based political leaders in Georgia and Serbia. In the process of exploring why some regions were cooperative, others wanted more autonomy, and still others demanded independence, she noticed that both countries had experienced a surprising and similar event: elections that generated large-scale popular protests in response to fraud and that replaced long-serving authoritarian leaders with leaders of the opposition. When she mentioned this to Sharon, Sharon said that actually, the same thing (minus the protests) had happened earlier in Slovakia. Being "graduates" of 1989, we thought, "Here we go again." We decided it would be a great idea to put our heads together and analyze this dynamic. Of course, several more cases were added to the study – Ukraine in 2004 and Kyrgyzstan in 2005. As our study progressed, we came to see the connection between our original cases and developments in Croatia in 2000 and, as a prelude to the Slovak breakthrough, Bulgaria in 1990 and 1997 and Romania in 1996. We also decided that we did not want to fall into the trap of confining our attention to successful cases of electoral turnover – that is, elections where oppositions succeeded in their quest to replace authoritarian leaders or their anointed successors. Looking only at such cases would have been a problem because they are the clear exception to the rule in mixed regimes that straddle democracy and dictatorship. Variation in electoral results would also help us tease out important causal influences. Thus, we added elections in Armenia, Azerbaijan, and Belarus to the group. These elections look a lot like the successful ones, save for their outcomes.

Our enthusiasm for this study was boundless. However, we confess that this has not been an easy book to research and write. Among other things, tracking down key local and international participants in so many elections taking place in so many different countries and then interviewing them was not easy, especially because many of them have moved or taken new positions since the events we analyzed took place. Thus, this book took a great deal longer to research and to write than we expected. The writing was also difficult because we had a great deal of data, and we analyzed these elections in three ways. We carried out case studies of each one; we compared them to one another; and we treated them as events that were interconnected through a diffusion dynamic. Of course, how many academic books would get written if authors were better at predicting how much work they would actually require?

This book has also been a labor of love. In part, this was because after more than thirty years of friendship (beginning as graduate students at the University of Michigan), we decided that it was finally time to work together. Miraculously, the friendship survived – even when we did fieldwork together in Armenia and Azerbaijan! Indeed, it deepened. This book was also a trip down memory lane in another respect. We returned to an issue that had long preoccupied us before the collapse of communism led us to take up the new topic of democracy – that is, struggles against authoritarian rule. This project returned us both to our intellectual roots and, in those countries where democratic breakthroughs did not occur, to our early experiences in conducting fieldwork in nondemocratic settings. It also raised issues about authoritarianism that we had not considered during the communist era. A final rewarding aspect of this study was the opportunity to interview so many fascinating people. In both those countries where efforts to use elections to unseat semiauthoritarian leaders succeeded and those where they did not, we met amazing people who, in their dedication, courage, and willingness to persist in struggling against difficult odds, reminded us of the dissidents and independent intellectuals we had come to know under communism. It did not hurt, moreover, that the participants in these elections were in many cases very willing to share what was the most exciting political experience of their lives. They were eager to share their experiences, and we were privileged to listen. We want to thank them again for their generosity in sharing their time and insights with us.

Our "struggle," like that of the activists we interviewed, was not just long; it also owed its success to the contributions of a wide range of people. Thus, we have a long list of thank-yous. We can begin with our mentors at the University of Michigan, William Zimmerman and Zvi Gitelman. Our common intellectual grounding clearly made our collaboration easier, as our perspectives on the information we gathered and, more importantly, our standards for evaluating it were generally very similar. More recently, we are thankful to the Smith-Richardson Foundation, the International Center for Non-Violent Conflict, the Einaudi Center for International Studies and the Institute for the Social Sciences at Cornell University, and the Institute for European, Eurasian, and Russian Studies at the George Washington University for providing financial support and to the U.S. Department of State for inviting us to give lectures in Armenia. Residential fellowships at the Rockefeller Foundation's Bellagio Center and at the National Endowment for Democracy gave us much-needed time to carry out collaborative writing and also introduced us, particularly in the latter case, to numerous actors involved in our cases. In addition, we are grateful to Keti Nozadze, Aida Badalova, and Aaron Presnall at the Jefferson Institute, as well as to Oleksander Horin for helping set up interviews in Georgia, Azerbaijan, Serbia, and Ukraine, respectively; to Michael Varnum, Igor Logvinenko, and Sara Rzayeva for conducting interviews on our behalf in Croatia, Kyrgyzstan, and Azerbaijan, respectively; and to Melissa Aten, Cristine Cannata, Kallie Knutson, Nancy Meyers, Nawal Mustafa, David Szakonyi, Tsveta Petrova, and Sara Rzayeva for research and editorial assistance. We also received valuable feedback from presentations of our work at conferences organized by the Jefferson Institute (Charlottesville), the University of California at Irvine, Stanford University, Cornell University, the University of Florida, the University of Florence, and Dartmouth College. In addition, our study was enriched by reactions to our work at presentations we made in Baku, Yerevan, Moscow, Tbilisi, and Belgrade, and at Bergen, Berkeley, Cornell, Columbia, Duke, the Foreign Service Institute of the U.S. Department of State, The George Washington University, Georgetown, Harvard, Miami University of Ohio, the University of Michigan, the National Endowment for Democracy, Notre Dame, NYU in Prague, Johns Hopkins–SAIS, the University of British Columbia, the University of North Carolina, the College of William and Mary, and several panels at the annual meetings of the American Association for the Advancement of Slavic Studies and the American Political Science Association. Special thanks for reading the first draft of the manuscript (which was a good deal longer than this one) go to Mark Beissinger, Anna Grzymala-Busse, and Sidney Tarrow. We are especially grateful to Sidney Tarrow for his many contributions to this project from its inception to its completion, and in Val's case, for his intellectual and personal support since she joined the Cornell faculty two decades ago.

Our warmest thanks go to our families who supported us in this as in all of our endeavors. Ronald Herring, Nicholas Bunce-Herring, Leon and Olga Wolchik, Sharlene Wolchik, and John, Michael, Andrew, and Annie Varnum all played their roles in encouraging us and keeping us grounded, and it is to them that we dedicate this book.

PART I

THE PUZZLE

I

Breakthrough Elections

Mixed Regimes, Democracy Assistance, and International Diffusion

> While democracy must be more than free elections ... it also cannot be less.
>
> Kofi Annan[1]

> Eventful temporality recognizes the power of events in history ... and events may be defined as that relatively rare sub-class of happenings that significantly transform structures....
>
> William Sewell[2]

From 1998 to 2005, a wave of electoral defeats of authoritarian leaders swept through postcommunist Europe and Eurasia. This surprising run of opposition victories began with the Slovak election in 1998, when Mikuláš Dzurinda, the candidate of the democratic opposition, succeeded in forming a government and thereby ended the assault on democracy mounted by his predecessor, Vladimír Mečiar. Two years later, the Croatian Democratic Union, which had relied on autocratic methods to govern Croatia since its victory in the first competitive elections held in that country a decade earlier, finally lost power to the democratic opposition. The electoral "virus" then spread to neighboring Serbia. Here, popular protests following the September 2000 election for the Yugoslav presidency forced the long-serving dictator, Slobodan Milošević, to respect the verdict of the voters and transfer power to Vojislav Koštunica, the candidate of the liberal opposition. Georgia in 2003, Ukraine in 2004, and Kyrgyzstan in 2005 then joined the wave of electoral turnovers. All three of these elections featured developments similar to those that had taken place in Serbia – that is, popular protests in reaction to rigged elections and the empowerment of new political leaders and governing parties.

---

[1] Kofi Annan, quoted in Eric C. Bjornlund, *Beyond Free and Fair: Monitoring Elections and Building Democracy* (Washington, DC: Woodrow Wilson Center Press, 2004), 31.

[2] William Sewell, Jr., "Three Temporalities: Toward an Eventful Sociology," in *The Historic Turn in the Human Sciences*, ed. McDonald Tedrance (Ann Arbor: University of Michigan Press, 1996), 262.

PURPOSE AND PUZZLES

The purpose of this book is to analyze this remarkable run of democratizing elections in postcommunist Europe and Eurasia.[3] These elections are of interest for both empirical and theoretical reasons. First, they were undeniably important political events. At the very least these electoral breakthroughs by

---

[3] For other studies of this wave, see, for example, Mark Beissinger, "Structure and Example in Modular Political Phenomena: The Diffusion of Bulldozer/Rose/Orange/Tulip Revolutions," *Perspectives on Politics* 5:2 (June 2007), 259–276; Joshua Tucker, "Enough! Electoral Fraud, Collective Action Problems, and Post-Communist Colored Revolutions," *Perspectives on Politics* 5:3 (September 2007), 537–553; Joshua A. Tucker, "People Power or a One-Shot Deal? The Legacy of the Colored Revolutions Considered from a Collective Action Framework," paper presented at the annual meeting of the AAASS, New Orleans, LA, November 2007; Michael McFaul, "Transitions from Postcommunism," *Journal of Democracy* 16:3 (July 2005), 5–19; Michael McFaul, "Importing Revolution: Internal and External Factors in Ukraine's 2004 Democratic Breakthrough," in *Democracy and Authoritarianism in the Postcommunist World*, ed. Valerie Bunce, Michael McFaul, and Kathryn Stoner-Weiss (Cambridge: Cambridge University Press, 2010), 3–29; Amichai Magen, *Evaluating External Influence on Democratic Development: Transition*, CDDRL Working Paper No. 111, Center for Democracy, Development and the Rule of Law, Freeman Spogli Institute for International Studies, Stanford University (March 2009); Anders Åslund and Michael McFaul, *Revolution in Orange: The Origins of Ukraine's Democratic Breakthrough* (Washington, DC: Carnegie Endowment for International Peace, 2006); Joerg Forbrig and Pavol Demeš, eds., *Reclaiming Democracy: Civil Society and Electoral Change in Central and Eastern Europe* (Washington, DC: German Marshall Fund, 2007); Taras Kuzio, "Ukraine Is Not Russia: Comparing Youth Political Activism," *SAIS Review* 26:2 (Summer 2006), 67–83; Taras Kuzio, "From Kuchma to Yushchenko: Ukraine's 2004 Presidential Elections and the Orange Revolution," *Problems of Post-Communism* 52:2 (March/April 2005), 29–44; Taras Kuzio, "Civil Society, Youth, and Societal Mobilization in Democratic Revolutions," *Communist and Postcommunist Studies* 39:3 (September 2006), 365–386; Taras Kuzio, "The Orange Revolution at the Crossroads," *Demokratizatsiya* 14:4 (Fall 2006), 477–493; Taras Kuzio, "The Opposition's Road to Success," *Journal of Democracy* 16:2 (April 2005), 117–130; Taras Kuzio, "Regime Type and Politics in Ukraine under Kuchma," *Communist and Post-Communist Studies* 38:2 (June 2005), 167–90; Paul Kubicek, "Ukraine and the European Neighborhood Policy: Can the EU Help the Orange Revolution Bear Fruit?," *East European Quarterly* 41:1 (Spring 2007), 1–23; Paul D'Anieri, "Explaining the Success and Failure of Postcommunist Revolutions," *Communist and Postcommunist Studies* 39:3 (September 2006), 331–350; Valerie Bunce and Sharon L. Wolchik, "International Diffusion and Postcommunist Electoral Revolutions," *Communist and Post-Communist Studies* 39:3 (September 2006), 283–304; Valerie Bunce and Sharon L. Wolchik, "Bringing Down Dictators: The Diffusion of Democratic Change in Communist and Postcommunist Europe and Eurasia," paper presented at the Conference on Postcommunist Resilience, Dartmouth University, May 25–26, 2007; Valerie Bunce and Sharon L. Wolchik, "Promoting Democracy after Communism: Electoral Revolutions in Slovakia, Serbia, Georgia, Ukraine and Kyrgyzstan," paper presented at the Conference on Transnational Actors and Postcommunist Politics, Syracuse University, September 30–October 1, 2005; Valerie Bunce and Sharon L. Wolchik, "Democratizing Elections in the Postcommunist World: Definitions, Dynamics and Diffusion," *St. Antony's International Review* 2:2 (February 2007), 64–89; Valerie Bunce and Sharon L. Wolchik, "Transnational Networks, Diffusion Dynamics, and Electoral Revolutions in the Postcommunist World," *Physica A: Statistical Mechanics and Its Applications* 378:1 (May 1, 2007), 92–99; Valerie Bunce and Sharon L. Wolchik, "Favorable Conditions and Electoral Revolutions,"

the opposition terminated a trend in all six countries of growing authoritarianism over time, and at most they produced a veritable leap from authoritarianism to democracy. These elections also influenced political developments considerably beyond the borders of the six countries where authoritarian leaders lost power. For example, many of the symbols and much of the rhetoric of Ukraine's 2004 Orange Revolution resurfaced in the huge demonstrations against Syrian control that took place in Lebanon in March 2005 and nearly three years later in both the campaigns preceding the Kenyan presidential election and the protests that followed.[4] In addition, many of the strategies used by the opposition in Ukraine in 2004 and earlier by students in Serbia from 1998 to 2000 were deliberately redeployed by opponents of the Mugabe regime in Zimbabwe and by students in Venezuela opposing the 2007 constitutional amendments proposed by President Hugo Chávez.[5] Protests against irregular elections in Togo and Ethiopia in 2005 and Mexico in 2006 also seem to have been influenced by the precedent and by some of the practices of successful challenges to official election results that took place in Serbia, Georgia, and Ukraine.[6] Finally, the mass demonstrations against electoral fraud that broke

Journal of Democracy 17:4 (October 2006), 5–18; Lincoln Abraham Mitchell, *Uncertain Democracy: U.S. Foreign Policy and Georgia's Rose Revolution* (Philadelphia: University of Pennsylvania Press, 2009); Jonathan Wheatley, *Georgia from National Awakening to Rose Revolution: Delayed Transition in the Former Soviet Union* (Aldershot, UK and Burlington, VT: Ashgate, 2005); Cory Welt, "Regime Weakness and Electoral Breakthrough in Georgia," in *Democracy and Authoritarianism in the Postcommunist World*, ed. Valerie Bunce, Michael McFaul, and Kathryn Stoner-Weiss (Cambridge: Cambridge University Press, 2010), 115–188; Scott Radnitz, "A Horse of a Different Color: Revolution and Regression in Kyrgyzstan," in *Democracy and Authoritarianism in the Postcommunist World*, ed. Valerie Bunce, Michael McFaul, and Kathryn Stoner-Weiss (Cambridge: Cambridge University Press, 2010), 300–324; Scott Radnitz, "What Really Happened in Kyrgyzstan?," *Journal of Democracy* 17:2 (April 2006), 132–146; Matthew Fuhrmann, "A Tale of Two Social Capitals: Revolutionary Collective Action in Kyrgyzstan," *Problems of Postcommunism* 53:6 (November/December 2006), 16–29; and Ray Jennings, *Serbia's Bulldozer Revolution: Evaluating Internal and External Factors in the Successful Democratic Breakthrough in Serbia*, CDDRL Working Paper No. 105, Center on Democracy, Development and the Rule of Law, Freeman Spogli Institute for International Studies, Stanford University (March 2009).

[4] Julia Choucair, *Lebanon's New Moment*, Carnegie Endowment for International Peace Policy Outlook (March 2005), http://www.carnegieendowment.org/files/PO14.Choucair.FINAL.pdf; Max Rodenbeck, "A New Lebanon?," *New York Review of Books* 52:7 (April 28, 2005), 28–32.

[5] Neil MacFarquar, "Huge Demonstration in Lebanon Demands End to Syrian Control," *New York Times*, March 15, 2005, www.nytimes.com/2005/03/15/international/middleeast/15lebanon.html; Simon Romero, "Students Emerge as a Leading Force against Chavez," *New York Times*, November 19, 2007, www.nytimes.com/2007/11/10/world/americas/10venez.html; Choucair, *Lebanon's New Moment*; Michael Wines, "Grass-Roots Effort Aims to Upend Mugabe in Zimbabwe," *New York Times*, March 27, 2005, www.nytimes.com/2005/03/27/international/27zimbabwe.html; Michael Wines, "Tough on Togo, Letting Zimbabwe Slide," *New York Times*, April 10, 2005, www.nytimes.com/2005/03/27/international/27zimbabwe.html; and see *Izvestiia*, "Bashkiry privezli v mosvu "oranzhevuiu" revoliutsiiu," *IsvestiiaRU*, August 4, 2008, www.izvestiia.ru/community/article1552736.

[6] James C. McKinley, Jr., "In a Presidential Tone, Calderon Rejects Recount," *New York Times*, July 14, 2006, www.nytimes.com/2006/07/14/world/americas/14calderson.read.html;

out in June 2009 in Iran following the presidential election bore a family resemblance to the postelection protests that took place in the postcommunist world from 2000 to 2008. In fact, Ayatollah Khameini, a strong supporter of the incumbent and declared victor in that controversial election, Mahmoud Ahmadinejad, drew an explicit parallel between the Iranian protests against electoral fraud and those that had brought an end to the Shevardnadze regime six years earlier in Georgia.[7]

These elections are also of interest because they pose some fascinating puzzles for specialists in comparative and international politics. Why and how did these electoral breakthroughs take place? While it can be argued that electoral defeat is always a possibility when authoritarian leaders allow competition for office, the fact remains that the norm in these countries, as more generally in mixed regimes, has been for incumbent authoritarians to win rather than lose elections.[8] This is not surprising. Authoritarian incumbents command far more resources than the opposition, and oppositions in contexts that combine authoritarian politics and competitive elections tend to be divided, disputatious, and thus ineffective. At the same time, citizens in such systems tend to be either relatively supportive of the regime or, if not, unlikely to transfer their votes to the opposition. On the one hand, why bother to vote for the opposition if it cannot win power? On the other hand, why support opposition parties and candidates when they have shown themselves time and again to be more interested in bickering with each other, collaborating with the regime, running lackluster campaigns, and/or boycotting elections than in identifying issues of concern to the electorate and mounting collaborative, ambitious, and therefore credible electoral challenges to authoritarian rule?

A second and related puzzle focuses on the pattern of these electoral breakthroughs. Why do we see such similar developments in so many countries in one region within such a short span of time? Here, we are struck by the

---

Michael Kamber, "In an Untamed Tide of Violence, Bystanders Die," *New York Times*, May 5, 2005, www.nytimes.com/2005/05/05/international/africa/05togo.html.

[7] See Nazila Fathi, "Iran's Top Leader Dashes Hopes for a Compromise," *New York Times*, June 20, 2009, A1, A7.

[8] See, especially, Andreas Schedler, ed., *Electoral Authoritarianism: The Dynamics of Unfree Competition* (Boulder, CO: Lynne Rienner Publishers, 2006); and Andreas Schedler, "Sources of Competition under Electoral Authoritarianism," in *Democratization by Elections – A New Mode of Transition?*, ed. Staffan Lindberg (Baltimore: Johns Hopkins University Press, 2009), 179–201; Marc Morjé Howard and Philip G. Roessler, "Liberalizing Electoral Outcomes in Competitive Authoritarian Regimes," *American Journal of Political Science* 50:2 (April 2006), 365–381; Nicolas Van de Walle, "Meet the New Boss: Same as the Old Boss: The Evolution of Political Clientelism in Africa," in *Patrons, Clients and Policies: Patterns of Democratic Accountability and Political Competition*, ed. Herbert Kitschelt and Steven I. Wilkinson (Cambridge: Cambridge University Press, 2007), 50–67; Grigore Pop-Eleches and Graeme Robertson, "Elections and Liberalization in the Postcommunist World," unpublished paper, Princeton University and University of North Carolina, September 2009 and Philip G. Roessler and Marc Morjé Howard, "Post Cold War Political Regimes: When Do Elections Matter?," in *Democratization by Elections – A New Mode of Transition?*, ed. Staffan Lindberg (Baltimore: Johns Hopkins University Press, 2009), 101–127.

parallels between the cross-national spread of electoral challenges to authoritarian rule and the spread of popular protests in the same region a decade
earlier that led to the collapse of communism. Is there something special about
this part of the world that encourages popular mobilizations against authoritarian rule?⁹ This question leads in turn to a more basic issue highlighted
by the geography and timing of the breakthrough elections. Was the clustering of these electoral shifts a matter of similar circumstances giving rise to
similar, but nonetheless separate, political dynamics, or, as phrases such as
"wave" and the "spread of electoral change" seem to imply, a more interconnected cross-national dynamic, wherein the defeat of authoritarian rulers in
one country influenced similar electoral turnarounds in the neighborhood?¹⁰

Third, how can we account for the variations in democratic progress that
followed the empowerment of the opposition? While these pivotal elections
ended a dangerous episode of de-democratization in Slovakia, they had the
different, but even more dramatic, effects in Croatia and Serbia of replacing
nearly overnight long-standing authoritarian regimes with democratic orders.
In Ukraine, democratic progress after the 2004 election was considerable but,
as in Serbia, was accompanied by continuing conflicts among the winners,
as well as between the winners and losers in the parliamentary and presidential elections that followed the pivotal 2004 election for the Ukrainian
presidency.¹¹ Finally, the 2003 election in Georgia and the 2005 election in
Kyrgyzstan, while leading to the removal from power of long-serving authoritarian leaders, produced a more checkered record with respect to improvements in civil liberties and political rights.¹²

A final puzzle requires us to look beyond our six pivotal electoral episodes
and ask why these elections led to turnover, whereas other elections failed to
do so – a contrast that it is necessary to explore if we are to develop a compelling explanation of why these electoral shifts occurred and why they moved
from state to state. Here, two sets of instructive cases come to the fore. One is

⁹ For parallels and differences between these two rounds of democratic change, see Valerie
  Bunce and Sharon Wolchik, "A Regional Tradition: The Diffusion of Democratic Change
  under Communism and Postcommunism," in *Democracy and Authoritarianism*, ed. Michael
  McFaul and Kathryn Stoner-Weiss (Cambridge: Cambridge University Press, 2009), 30–58.
¹⁰ See Mark Kramer, "The Dynamics of Contagion in the Communist Bloc and the Impact
  on Regime Survival," paper presented at the Conference on Postcommunist Resilience,
  Dartmouth University, May 25–26, 2007; Lucan Way, "The Real Causes of the Color
  Revolutions," *Journal of Democracy* 19:3 (July 2008), 55–69; and Valerie Bunce and Sharon
  L. Wolchik, "Getting Real about 'Real Causes,'" *Journal of Democracy* 20:1 (January 2009),
  69–73.
¹¹ McFaul, "Importing Revolution"; Sonja Licht, "Serbia between Autocratic and Democratic
  Transition: A Case Study," paper presented at the Project on Democratic Transitions,
  Seminar II: Lessons Learned and Testing Their Applicability, Foreign Policy Research
  Institute, Philadelphia, February 22–24, 2007; and Maurizio Massari, "Do All Roads Lead
  to Brussels? Analysis of the Different Trajectories of Croatia, Serbia-Montenegro and Bosnia-
  Herzegovina," *Cambridge Review of International Affairs* 18:2 (July 2005), 259–273.
¹² See, for example, Radnitz, "A Horse of a Different Color"; Welt, "Regime Weakness and
  Electoral Breakthrough"; and Mitchell, *Uncertain Democracy*.

TABLE 1.1. *Case selection*

Country	Date of Election	Type of Election	Result
Croatia	2000[a]	Presidential	Turnover
Georgia	2003	Parliamentary[b]	Turnover
Kyrgyzstan	2005	Parliamentary[b]	Turnover
Serbia	2000[a]	Presidential	Turnover
Slovakia	1998	Parliamentary[c]	Turnover
Ukraine	2004	Presidential	Turnover
Armenia	2003[a]	Presidential	Continuity
Armenia	2008	Presidential	Continuity
Azerbaijan	2003	Presidential	Continuity
Azerbaijan	2005	Parliamentary[b]	Continuity
Belarus	2006	Presidential	Continuity

[a] Both parliamentary and presidential elections were held in this year.
[b] Parliamentary elections held in mixed presidential/parliamentary system.
[c] Parliamentary elections held in parliamentary system.

the earlier elections that took place in our six countries – elections that often occurred in circumstances similar to those that had led to electoral turnover, but that had, with the exception of Slovakia, the invariable result of producing a defeat for the opposition. Just as analytically illuminating is another group of elections – that is, those in Armenia in 2003 and 2008, Azerbaijan in 2003 and 2005, and Belarus in 2001 and 2006. In all of these cases, authoritarian incumbents or their anointed successors won power despite striking similarities between these elections and those that had resulted in a transfer of power from authoritarians to democrats. For example, in these three countries as in Serbia in 2000, Ukraine in 2004, and Kyrgyzstan in 2005, regimes had become more repressive in the years leading up to the elections; oppositions had succeeded in forming coalitions in order to improve their prospects for winning office; and rigged elections had been followed by large-scale popular protests contesting the official results.

In the chapters that follow, we address these four questions by comparing eleven elections and the political and economic evolution of the nine regimes in which these elections took place (see Table 1.1). Our answers are based upon six years of research that involved conducting more than 200 interviews in Baku, Berlin, Belgrade, Bratislava, Ithaca, Kyiv, Lviv, Moscow, New York, Oxford, Philadelphia, Tbilisi, Washington, D.C., Yerevan, and Zagreb with participants in and analysts of both the elections that led to the defeat of authoritarians and those that failed to do so. Thus, we interviewed members of the U.S. and European democracy assistance community; U.S. ambassadors and their staffs; local academic specialists and journalists; and members of a wide range of political parties, social movements, and civil society organizations (a list of our interviewees may be found in the Appendix). In addition, we benefited from interviews conducted on our behalf by Sara

Rzayeva in Azerbaijan, Michael Varnum in Zagreb, and Igor Logvinenko in Kyrgyzstan and from commentaries on these elections and our interpretations of them in roundtables organized on our behalf in Belgrade, Charlottesville, and Yerevan.[13] Finally, we made use of a variety of other materials written by academics, policy makers, and journalists, along with public opinion surveys, statistical compendia, and other documents provided by political parties, civil society organizations, international organizations, and a range of private and public European and U.S. democracy assistance organizations. While all this written information was useful, it was the interviews that gave us the greatest insights into what happened, why, and how.

In the remainder of this chapter, we set the stage for our analysis of electoral continuity and change. We begin by identifying four major debates in comparative and international politics that we will address throughout this study. One involves competing views on the potential for democratic change in regimes that combine authoritarian politics and competitive elections. Another focuses on the controversial question of whether elections can serve as key sites for democratic change. Yet another highlights divergent perspectives on the cross-national diffusion of democracy, and a final debate concerns the question of whether the United States can and should promote democratic change abroad. We end the chapter by laying out our approach, defining key terms, and previewing the chapters that follow.

THEORETICAL DEBATES ABOUT MIXED REGIMES

The third wave of democratization has led to the proliferation of what have been variously termed gray, mixed, hybrid, electoral, or competitive authoritarian regimes, that is, regimes that have the distinctive profile in comparison to full-scale democracies and dictatorships of combining elements of both types of political systems.[14] Depending upon the definition

---

[13] We also benefited from reactions to our analyses of these events in talks given at the College of William and Mary, the University of Notre Dame, Harvard University, The University of British Columbia, University of California at Berkeley, Indiana University, University of Michigan, The George Washington University, Cornell University, Dartmouth College, Duke University, The University of North Carolina, University of Florida, Georgetown University, Johns Hopkins University – SAIS, Stanford University, New York University in Prague, and the American University in Baku, Azerbaijan, as well as at the Foreign Service Institute of the U.S. Department of State and the Woodrow Wilson International Center for Scholars in Washington, DC; the University of Florence, Villa Serbelloni, Bellagio, Italy; the Jefferson Institute (Charlottesville and Belgrade); the Institute for the Social Sciences in Moscow; and meetings of the American Political Science Association and the American Association for the Advancement of Slavic Studies.

[14] See, for instance, Larry Diamond, "Thinking about Hybrid Regimes," *Journal of Democracy* 13:2 (April 2002), 21–35; Steven Levitsky and Lucan A. Way, "The Rise of Competitive Authoritarianism," *Journal of Democracy* 13:2 (April 2002), 51–65; and Steven Levitsky and Lucan A. Way, "Competitive Authoritarian Regimes: The Evolution of Post-Soviet Competitive Authoritarianism 1992–2005," paper presented at the conference Why Communism Didn't Collapse: Understanding Regime Resilience in China, Vietnam, Laos, North Korea and

used, such regimes now constitute between 25 and 30 percent of all regimes in the world today.[15]

Although these kinds of regimes differ from one another in their precise mixture of authoritarian and democratic politics, they nonetheless share two core characteristics. One is that elections in such political settings are regular and competitive, but take place on an uneven playing field that favors authoritarian incumbents over opposition parties and candidates. The other is that these kinds of regimes are much more likely than either democracies or dictatorships to be located in weak states and to change regime types from one year to the next.[16] Mixed regimes, in short, are notable for their instability.

Analysts of these regimes, however, disagree not just about what these kinds of polities should be called, but also about why they have become so prevalent, why they evolve in different ways over time, and whether they are best understood as temporary formations or regimes in their own right. All these issues will be addressed throughout this book because all of the elections of interest took place in such regimes. However, there is a final and more fundamental point of contention among analysts that needs to be highlighted here. This is the very different readings by scholars of what motivates authoritarian leaders to "decorate" their regimes with seemingly democratic institutions, and what these explanations imply in turn about the likelihood of more authentic democratic politics in the future. For analysts who focus on democratization and who specialize in regions of the world where transitions from authoritarian rule have produced at least some examples of fully democratic orders, the usual argument is that mixed regimes reflect an uneasy compromise between democrats and authoritarians in which neither side is sufficiently powerful to dictate its preferred rules of the political game. This "rough balance," according to this view, in addition to the global diffusion of democratic norms and the decisions by international financial institutions and Western governments to tie aid to democratic progress, plays a role in "forcing" authoritarian leaders and their allies to risk their tenure in office and thus their control over the system by holding regular and competitive elections.[17] Because of the gap between their democratic rhetoric and their often illiberal practices and because of their exposure to possible defeat as a result of electoral competition, therefore, authoritarian leaders in mixed systems are inherently vulnerable to challenges mounted by leaders of the democratic opposition. These considerations have led some scholars to conclude that the

Cuba, Dartmouth College, Hannover, NY, May 25–26, 2007; Marina Ottaway, *Democracy Challenged: The Rise of Semi-Authoritarianism* (Washington, DC: Carnegie Endowment for International Peace, 2003); and Roessler and Howard, "Post Cold War Political Regimes."

[15] Diamond, "Thinking about Hybrid Regimes."

[16] Roessler and Howard, "Post Cold War Political Regimes"; David Epstein, Robert Bates, Jack Goldstone, Ida Kristensen, and Sharyn O'Halloran, "Democratic Transitions," *American Journal of Political Science* 50:3 (July 2006), 551–569.

[17] See, especially, Andreas Schedler, ed., *Electoral Authoritarianism*, and Schedler, "Sources of Competition."

very existence of mixed systems indicates authoritarian weakness and that the institutions that go along with that weakness provide opportunities for subsequent democratic progress.[18]

A very different interpretation of these regimes, however, has been put forward by analysts who specialize in the study of authoritarianism and who focus on parts of the world where authoritarian regimes have been very successful in resisting the global shift to democratic governance.[19] Rather than assuming vulnerability, these scholars proceed from the opposite assumption. In particular, they argue that authoritarian leaders in mixed regimes are in fact quite resourceful, that democratic oppositions and civil society groups are often relatively weak, and that the introduction of democratic reforms, such as competitive elections, reflects not so much growing domestic and international pressures on authoritarians to embrace some aspects of democracy as strategic decisions on the part of powerful leaders to enhance their control over the system. According to this analytical perspective, leaders add selected democratic features to the polity in order to expose, divide, and thereby weaken regime opponents; calibrate alliances; fine-tune patronage networks; and, more generally, solve the information problems that are built into the authoritarian political enterprise.[20] At the same time, democratic

---

[18] Also see Roessler and Howard, "Post Cold War Political Regimes," and Pop-Eleches and Robertson, "Elections and Liberalization."

[19] See, especially, James H. Rosberg, "Roads to the Rule of Law: The Emergence of an Independent Judiciary in Contemporary Egypt" (Ph.D. dissertation, Political Science Department, MIT, 1995); Ellen Lust Okar, "Divided They Rule: The Management and Manipulation of Political Opposition," *Comparative Politics* 36:2 (January 2004), 159–179; Ellen Lust Okar, "Opposition and Economic Crises in Jordan and Morocco," in *Authoritarianism in the Middle East: Regimes and Resistance*, ed. Marsha Pripstein Posusney and Michelle Penner Angriste (Boulder, CO: Lynne Rienner Publishers, 2005); Ellen Lust Okar, "Legislative Elections in Hegemonic Authoritarian Regimes: Competitive Clientelism and Resistance to Democratization," in *Democratization by Elections – A New Mode of Transition?*, ed. Staffan Lindberg (Baltimore: Johns Hopkins University Press, 2009), 226–245; Lisa Blaydes, "Authoritarian Elections and Elite Management: Theory and Evidence from Egypt," unpublished manuscript, April 2008; Pauline Jones Luong, *Institutional Change and Political Continuity in Post-Soviet Central Asia: Power, Perceptions, and Pacts* (Cambridge: Cambridge University Press, 2002); Jennifer Gandhi and Adam Przeworski, "Cooperation, Cooptation, and Rebellion under Dictatorships," *Economics & Politics* 18:1 (March 2006), 1–26; and Peter Solomon, "Courts and Judiciaries in Authoritarian Regimes," *World Politics* 60:1 (October 2007), 122–145. And see the criticisms of the democracy "bias" offered by Jason Brownlee, "Low Tide after the Third Wave: Exploring Politics under Authoritarianism," *Comparative Politics* 34:4 (July 2002), 477–498; Marsha Pripstein Posusney, "Enduring Authoritarianism: Middle East Lessons for Comparative Theory," *Comparative Politics* 36:2 (January 2004), 127–138; and Lisa Anderson, "Searching Where the Light Shines: Studying Democratization in the Middle East," *Annual Review of Political Science* 9 (2006), 189–214.

[20] See note 19 and Ronald Wintrobe, "Dictatorship: Analytical Approaches," in *The Oxford Handbook of Comparative Politics*, ed. Carles Boix and Susan C. Stokes (Oxford: Oxford University Press, 2007), 363–396; and Mancur Olson, "Dictatorship, Democracy, and Development," *American Political Science Review* 87:3 (September 1993), 567–576.

reforms, such as competitive elections, carry other benefits that are thought to solidify, rather than undermine, authoritarian rule. For example, such reforms can appease the international community and, in the process, reduce external pressures for "real" democratic change and maintain the inflow of international development assistance. Even when it includes democracy assistance, moreover, the support extended by the international community can have the perverse effect of strengthening authoritarians – by providing more patronage to the regime and forging the dependence of civil society groups on a flush authoritarian state.[21]

Thus, scholars disagree sharply about whether democratic reforms are introduced by authoritarian leaders from a position of weakness or strength and whether such reforms, once introduced, expand or contract opportunities for democratic change. Just as curious is the equally divergent understanding of what a pattern of growing authoritarianism in such regimes means for future political trajectories. On the one hand, the obvious interpretation could be the correct one – that is, that repressive regimes are more powerful and more likely to endure. On the other hand, repression can also communicate the very different message to ordinary citizens, and especially to opposition groups, that the leader is becoming weaker and must resort to more draconian measures in order to safeguard his power.[22] This alternative interpretation of increased repression would seem to apply particularly well to mixed regime settings, where at least some opportunities exist for expressing dissatisfaction and where the very instability of the regimes, as noted earlier, would seem to tempt opponents and even allies to imagine alternative political futures.

THE IMPORTANCE OF ELECTIONS

Scholars also disagree about the role of elections in promoting democratic change. Many analysts minimize their importance, for a variety of convincing reasons. For example, skeptics argue that, by placing so much emphasis on elections, whether in the context of established, but new, democracies or countries emerging from dictatorship and/or internal war, the international community all too easily reduces democracy and democratic progress to the holding of competitive elections.[23] As Thomas Carothers has elaborated in his study of international democracy assistance, the problem is that promoters of democracy

[21] Amaney A. Jamal, *Barriers to Democracy: The Other Side of Social Capital in Palestine and the Arab World* (Princeton, NJ: Princeton University Press, 2007).

[22] And see Diamond, "Thinking about Hybrid Regimes."

[23] Fareed Zakaria, *The Future of Freedom: Illiberal Democracy at Home and Abroad* (New York: W. W. Norton & Co., 2003); Thomas Carothers, "The End of the Transition Paradigm," *Journal of Democracy* 13:1 (January 2002), 5–21; Paula Pickering, *Peacebuilding in the Balkans* (Ithaca, NY: Cornell University Press, 2008), 91–92. But also see Mitchell, *Uncertain Democracy*, for a more nuanced discussion of this issue.

... have tended to hold very high expectations about what the establishment of regular, genuine elections will do for democratization. Not only will elections give new post-dictatorial governments democratic legitimacy, they believe, but the elections will serve to broaden and deepen political participation and the democratic accountability of the state to its citizens. In other words, it has been assumed that in attempted transitions to democracy, elections will be not just a foundation stone but a key generator over time of further democratic reforms.[24]

Other analysts have added to these concerns about the "fallacy of electoralism"[25] by highlighting the variable functions that elections can serve, many of which are far from supportive of democratic change. For example, especially when they are relatively novel exercises that have been introduced in regimes lacking a democratic history, competitive elections may be understood by publics not as opportunities to choose among candidates and thereby exercise their democratic rights but, rather, as more ritualistic processes that allow them to express political support for incumbents, reinforce existing group solidarities, and participate in patronage networks.[26] Moreover, as noted earlier, elections can serve some decidedly undemocratic functions, especially in mixed regimes. At the very least, elections – which have become in recent years the "autocrat's latest fashion"[27] – can confer on authoritarian governments a patina of enhanced legitimacy.

Because elections have variable results, moreover, they cannot be understood as playing a consistent role in democratic development.[28] The advantages of incumbency usually translate into continuity, rather than change in leadership, whether elections are free and fair or whether they are rigged. In addition, even when the constitution requires term limits, authoritarian leaders have often found ways to circumvent this constraint – by changing the constitution, by appointing successors who are closely tied to them, or by adding to the second option occupation of another office that allows them to exercise power and monitor their successor.[29] While a familiar indicator of democratic progress, we must remember, electoral turnover does not always support democratic development. Throughout history, elections have served

[24] Carothers, "The End of the Transition Paradigm," 8.

[25] To borrow from Terry Karl, "The Hybrid Regimes of Central America," *Journal of Democracy* 6:2 (April 1995), 72–87.

[26] Frederic Charles Schaffer, *Democracy in Translation: Understanding Politics in an Unfamiliar Culture* (Ithaca, NY: Cornell University Press, 1998).

[27] Jason Brownlee, *Authoritarianism in an Age of Democratization* (Cambridge: Cambridge University Press, 2007), 42.

[28] See, for example, Jan Teorell and Axel Hadenius, "Elections as Levers of Democracy: A Global Inquiry," in *Democratization by Elections – A New Mode of Transition?*, ed. Staffan Lindberg (Baltimore: Johns Hopkins University Press, 2009), 77–100.

[29] Kristin McKie, "The Politics of Adopting Term Limits in Sub-Saharan Africa," paper presented at the Annual Meeting of the American Political Science Association, Boston, MA, August 29, 2008.

as sites for democratic breakdown, not breakthrough, whether because they bring authoritarians to power or because threatening electoral results encourage authoritarians to suspend the democratic rules of the game.[30]

These issues lead to a final and more fundamental concern about attributing too much democratic influence to elections. As Jason Brownlee has argued, analysts overstate the impact of even those elections, such as the defeat of Marcos in the Philippines in 1986, that are widely viewed as making sharp breaks with dictatorial rule.[31] Such electoral shifts, he argues, have been long in the making and say more about the structure of power and the fragmentation of the coalition supporting the dictator than they do about the role of elections as instruments of democratic change. Dorothy Solinger has drawn a similar conclusion in her comparative study of the transitions from long-standing one-party regimes that took place in the 1999 election in South Korea and the 2000 elections in Taiwan and Mexico:

> These opposition victories should be regarded not simply as the product of a finally freed-up, democratically expressed public will, but as the outcome of a lengthy process of unraveling of single party domination, first unleashed long before the decision to allow 'limited elections' and then given a critical boost by the perhaps necessary result of those elections, a split in the ruling party.[32]

By contrast, there are a number of analysts who argue in favor of elections as causal agents in democratic development. They make this claim for a number of reasons. One is the fact that, while democracy cannot be reduced to elections, elections nonetheless seem to preface significant improvements in democratic performance, even when other influences are taken into account and even under quite varying structural conditions.[33] Moreover, one recent study of elections in Africa has argued that repeated elections are associated with improvements in democratic performance, and several studies of trends in regime change in the postcommunist region have concluded that elections serve as the best (though far from perfect) predictor of democratic progress.[34]

---

[30] Nancy Bermeo, *Ordinary People in Extraordinary Times: The Citizenry and the Breakdown of Democracy* (Princeton, NJ: Princeton University Press, 2003).

[31] Brownlee, *Authoritarianism in an Age of Democratization.*

[32] Dorothy Solinger, "Ending One-Party Dominance: Korea, Taiwan, Mexico," *Journal of Democracy* 12:1 (January 2002), 30. Also see Beatriz Magaloni, *Voting for Autocracy: Hegemonic Party Survival and Its Demise in Mexico* (Cambridge: Cambridge University Press, 2006) on the Mexican election of 2000.

[33] Axel Hadenius and Jan Teorell, "Pathways from Authoritarianism," *Journal of Democracy* 18:1 (January 2007), 143–156, and Teorell and Hadenius, "Elections as Levers of Democracy."

[34] Staffan I. Lindberg, *Democracy and Elections in Africa* (Baltimore: Johns Hopkins University Press, 2006); M. Steven Fish, "Democratization's Prerequisites," *Post-Soviet Affairs* 14:3 (July–September 1998), 212–247; Valerie J. Bunce, "Sequencing Political and Economic Reforms," in *East-Central European Economies in Transition*, ed. John Hardt and Richard Kaufman (Washington, DC: Joint Economic Committee, Congress of the United States, 1994), 46–63; Valerie Bunce, *Subversive Institutions: The Design and the Destruction of Socialism*

Also relevant are the facts that democratic progress seems to be more likely in competitive authoritarian regimes than in regimes where electoral competition is disallowed, and that democratic performance seems to improve in those states where oppositions have been more successful in winning seats in parliament.[35] Finally, there is a widespread consensus that electoral change can matter a great deal. Turnover in leadership and governing coalitions, for example, is associated, even in competitive authoritarian regimes, with a deepening of democracy, reduced corruption, greater legitimacy of the system in the eyes of the citizenry, and perceptions among citizens that democracy itself has been consolidated.[36]

These are suggestive findings, but they leave open the question of *why* elections would play an important role in democratic development. Here, two lines of argument come into play. One possible reason is that, especially in new democracies, citizens tend to define democracy and measure regime performance by focusing on the quality of elections.[37] Thus, because democratic procedures matter to citizens, they are willing, even in highly repressive regimes, to register their dissatisfaction with corrupt electoral practices. In this way, elections are both symbols of democracy and mechanisms for demanding – and realizing – democratic change.

The other reason why elections themselves might matter draws upon the work of social movement theorists, who argue that a key factor explaining waves of contentious politics is a shift in "the political opportunity structure," which has been defined by Sidney Tarrow as "consistent – but not necessarily

and the State (Cambridge: Cambridge University Press, 1999); Valerie J. Bunce, "Global Patterns and Postcommunist Dynamics," *Orbis* 50:4 (Fall 2006), 601–620; Pop-Eleches and Robertson, "Elections and Liberalization in the Postcommunist World."

[35] Devra Moehler and Staffan Lindberg, "Narrowing the Legitimacy Gap: The Role of Turnovers in Africa's Emerging Democracies," unpublished manuscript, Oct. 11, 2007; Jason Brownlee, "Harbinger of Democracy: Competitive Elections before the End of Authoritarianism," in *Democratization by Elections – A New Mode of Transition?*, ed. Staffan Lindberg (Baltimore: Johns Hopkins University Press, 2009), 128–147; Roessler and Howard, "Post-Cold-War Political Regimes."

[36] Valerie Bunce, "The Return of the Left and Democratic Consolidation in Poland and Hungary," in *The Communist Successor Parties of Central and Eastern Europe*, ed. András Bozóki and Jon Ishiyama (New York: M. E. Sharpe, 2002), 303–322; Devra Moehler and Staffan Lindberg, "Narrowing the Legitimacy Gap"; Levitsky and Way, "Competitive Authoritarian Regimes"; Anna Maria Grzymała-Busse, *Rebuilding Leviathan: Party Competition and State Exploitation in Postcommunist Democracies* (Cambridge: Cambridge University Press, 2007); Valerie Bunce and Sharon L. Wolchik, "Mixed Regimes in Postcommunist Eurasia: Tipping Democratic and Tipping Authoritarian," in *Hybrid Regimes: International Anchoring and Domestic Dynamics in Post-Soviet States*, ed. Elena Barcani (Florence, Italy: European Press Academic Publishing, 2010), 57–86.

[37] Russell J. Dalton, Doh L. Shin, and Willy Jou, *Popular Conceptions of the Meaning of Democracy: Democratic Understanding in Unlikely Places*, Center for the Study of Democracy Paper 07–03 (May 18, 2007), http://repositories.cdlib.org/csd/07–03; Michael Bratton and Eric C. C. Chang, "State-building and Democratization in Sub-Saharan Africa: Forwards, Backwards or Together?," *Comparative Political Studies* 39:9 (November 2006), 1059–1083.

formal, permanent or national – dimensions of the political environment that either encourage or discourage people from using collective action."[38] While opportunity structures can be understood in static terms, they can also be seen as dynamic in the sense that actors can create new opportunities for change as well as exploiting existing ones. In fact, one of the most important aspects of elections is that they have the ability to combine both understandings of the political opportunity structure. Elections can be ideal sites for expanding opportunities for mobilization while lessening the familiar constraints on collective action. This is because elections are infrequent, scheduled, and therefore empowering political events, and because they have clear and widely visible beginnings, endings, and outcomes. They also provide a regular forum for, and thus regular expectations of, popular participation. They serve as moments for rendering a verdict on regime performance, and they hold open the possibility, admittedly often remote, of changes in politicians and policy. Elections also expand opportunities for contentious politics, whether in the streets or at the ballot box, because they combine pressures to choose with high political stakes. Finally, especially in elections viewed as critical turning points, campaigns typically engage not just political parties but also civil society organizations, the former focused on winning power and the latter on getting key issues onto the agenda.

For all of these reasons, therefore, it is far from surprising, as Doug McAdam and Sidney Tarrow have recently observed, that "social movements and elections are not discrete and separate events, but mutually constitutive forms of politics that often interact to shape the prospects for both short and longer-term social/political change."[39] It is precisely this natural affinity between the two that explains why elections and protests often go together and why elections, as a result, may be understood as political processes that expand opportunities for democratic change.[40]

Does all this mean that we should take the further step of arguing that elections should be considered a *mode* of democratic transition?[41] The claim here is that if elections lead to the defeat of dictatorships and shape subsequent regime trajectories, then they should be added to the familiar list of approaches to democratic transition that typically includes pacting among

---

[38] Sidney G. Tarrow, *The New Transnational Activism* (Cambridge: Cambridge University Press, 2005), 23.

[39] Doug McAdam and Sidney Tarrow, "Ballots and Barricades: On the Reciprocal Relationship between Elections and Social Movements," paper presented at the conference *Hot Models and Hard Conflicts*: The Agenda of Comparative Political Science in the 21st Century, a symposium in honor of Hanspeter Kriesi, Center for Comparative and International Studies, Zurich, Switzerland, June 26, 2009, 2.

[40] Guillermo Trejo, "The Political Foundations of Ethnic Mobilization and Territorial Conflict in Mexico, 1975–2000," in *Federalism and Territorial Cleavages*, ed. Ugo Amoretti and Nancy Bermeo (Baltimore: Johns Hopkins University Press, 2004) 355–386; Tucker, "People Power or a One-Shot Deal?"; Mark R. Thompson and Philipp Kuntz, "Stolen Elections: The Case of the Serbian October," *Journal of Democracy* 15:4 (October 2004), 159–172.

[41] See Lindberg, ed., *Democratization by Elections*.

elites and between elites and key groups, such as labor, and, on the basis of more recent studies, mass mobilization.[42]

DIFFUSION OF DEMOCRACY

This study will also engage debates about the diffusion of innovation. We understand diffusion to be a process whereby new ideas, institutions, policies, models, or repertoires of behavior spread geographically from a core site to new sites, whether within a given state (as when the movement of new policies invented in one political subunit spreads to other subunits within a polity) or across states (as with the spread, for example, of public sector downsizing or nongovernmental organizations).[43] A number of studies have argued in concert that the spread of democracy around the world, whether during the Third Wave or during earlier periods in history, is a consequence of international diffusion.[44] As evidence for their interpretation, analysts have pointed to the

[42] See, for example, Valerie J. Bunce, "Rethinking Recent Democratization: Lessons from the Postcommunist Experience," *World Politics* 55:2 (January 2003), 167–192; Peter Ackerman and Adrian Karatnycky, *How Freedom Is Won: From Civic Resistance to Durable Democracy* (New York: Freedom House, 2005); Peter Ackerman and Jack Duvall, *A Force More Powerful: A Century of Nonviolent Conflict* (New York: St. Martin's Press, 2000); and Leslie Anderson and Lawrence C. Dodd, *Learning Democracy: Citizen Engagement and Electoral Choice in Nicaragua, 1990–2001* (Chicago: University of Chicago Press, 2005).

[43] See, for example, the pioneering work of Jack Walker, "The Diffusion of Innovation among the American States," *The American Political Science Review* 63:3 (September 1969), 880–890; and Zvi Y. Gitelman, *The Diffusion of Political Innovation: From Eastern Europe to the Soviet Union*, Sage Professional Papers in Comparative Politics, Vol. 01–027 (Beverly Hills, CA: Sage Publications, 1972); along with Ackerman and DuVall, *A Force More Powerful*; Doug McAdam and Dieter Rucht, "Cross-National Diffusion of Movement Ideas: The American 'New Left' and the European New Social Movements," *The Annals of the American Academy of Political and Social Sciences* 528:1 (July 1993), 56–74; David Strang and Sarah Soule, "Diffusion in Organizations and Social Movements: From Hybrid Corn to Poison Pills," *Annual Review of Sociology* 24 (August 1998), 265–290; Sada Aksartova, "Civil Society Promotion or Global Organizational Diffusion? U.S. Civil Society Assistance for the FSU," paper presented at the annual meeting of the Eastern Sociological Society, Washington, DC, May 17–20, 2005; Chang Kil Lee and David Strang, "The International Diffusion of Public-Sector Downsizing: Network Emulation and Theory-Driven Learning," *International Organization* 60:4 (October 2006), 883–909; Beissinger, *Nationalist Mobilization*; Daniel Brinks and Michael Coppedge, "Diffusion Is No Illusion: Neighbor Emulation in the Third Wave of Democracy," *Comparative Political Studies* 39:4 (May 2006), 463–489; John Markoff, *Waves of Democracy: Social Movements and Political Change* (Thousand Oaks, CA: Pine Forge Press, 1996); Tarrow, *The New Transnational Activism*; Donatella Della Porta and Sidney G. Tarrow, *Transnational Protest and Global Activism: People, Passions, and Power* (Lanham, MD: Rowman & Littlefield, 2005); Doug McAdam, Sidney G. Tarrow, and Charles Tilly, "Comparative Perspectives on Contentious Politics," in *Ideas, Interests and Institutions: Advancing Theory in Comparative Politics*, second edition, ed. Mark Lichbach and Alan Zuckerman (Cambridge: Cambridge University Press, 2009), 260–290; and Mario Diani and Doug McAdam, eds., *Social Movements and Networks: Relational Approaches to Collective Action* (Oxford: Oxford University Press, 2003).

[44] See, for instance, Brinks and Coppedge, "Diffusion Is No Illusion"; Harvey Starr and Christina Lindborg, "Democratic Dominoes Revisited: The Hazards of Governmental

pronounced tendency of new democracies to "bunch" across time and space, with transitions from authoritarianism to democracy demonstrating strong regional effects. Thus, when one or several states within a region experience democratic change, neighboring countries tend to follow suit.

While persuasive in some respects, these arguments are nonetheless problematic. First, there is a very large literature on transitions to democracy that emphasizes two issues that would seem to call into question the role of diffusion dynamics in democratic change. One is the central role of domestic preconditions and struggles in democratic development, and the other is the uneven nature of international effects on democratic transitions.[45] Second, studies of the diffusion of democracy leave some important questions unanswered and thereby weaken their case for diffusion. In particular, it is unclear what exactly is being diffused – the idea of democracy, democratic institutions, or processes that undermine authoritarian rule or empower democrats. It is also unclear *how* the innovation in question (however defined) moves from one locale to another. Is the process largely a matter of demonstration effects, with similar contexts inviting emulation; characteristics of the innovation itself, such as modularity, that make it unusually amenable to cross-national transfer; or the impact of networks, local or transnational in form, that are responsible for defining and then transferring similar ideas, practices, and institutions across state borders? All of these "mechanisms" and processes supporting the movement of change are well represented in the large literature on diffusion, and they serve, at the same time, as major sources of disagreement about how cross-national diffusion – of democracy or, for that matter, of new ideas, policies, organizational forms, institutions, products, and norms – takes place.[46]

Transitions, 1974–1996," *Journal of Conflict Resolution* 47:4 (August 2003), 490–519; Kristian Skrede Gleditsch and Michael Ward, "Diffusion and the International Context of Democratization," *International Organization* 60:4 (October 2006), 911–933; Barbara Wejnert, "Diffusion, Development, and Democracy, 1800–1999," *American Sociological Review* 70:1 (February 2005), 53–81; Beth Simmons, Frank Dobbin, and Geoffrey Garrett, eds., *The Global Diffusion of Markets and Democracy* (Cambridge: Cambridge University Press, 2008); and Markoff, *Waves of Democracy.*

[45] See, for example, Guillermo A. O'Donnell, Philippe C. Schmitter, and Laurence Whitehead, *Transitions from Authoritarian Rule: Latin America* (Baltimore: Johns Hopkins University Press, 1986); Laurence Whitehead, "Three International Dimensions of Democratization," in *The International Dimensions of Democratization: Europe and the Americas*, ed. Laurence Whitehead (Oxford: Oxford University Press, 2001), 3–25; and Richard Youngs, *International Democracy and the West: The Roles of Governments, Civil Society, and Multinational Business* (Oxford: Oxford University Press, 2005).

[46] See, in particular, Aksartova, "Civil Society Promotion or Global Organizational Diffusion?"; Beissinger, *Nationalist Mobilization* and "Structure and Example"; Johanna Bockman and Gil Eyal, "Eastern Europe as a Laboratory for Economic Knowledge: The Transnational Roots of Neoliberalism," *The American Journal of Sociology* 108:2 (September 2002), 310–352; Brinks and Coppedge, "Diffusion Is No Illusion;" Mario Diani, "Introduction: Social Movements, Contentious Actions and Social Networks: From 'Metaphor' to Substance?," in *Social Movements and Networks: Relational Approaches to Collective Action*, ed. Mario

It is surprising that students of diffusion have had so little to say about the what, how, and why questions associated with the cross-national spread of democratic change. Silence on these questions seems to reflect what Wade Jacoby has termed a "high altitude" problem built into many studies of diffusion.[47] Thus, analysts are often too removed from the dynamics on the ground to identify the processes and the people involved. While the lack of sustained attention to these issues is a good reason to put such questions on the agenda for future work, it also has a more immediate cost. In the absence of information about what is driving the dynamic, diffusion could very well be an illusion.[48] The observed cross-national similarities in democratic change and the compressed time span within which they occur could reflect a series of parallel, but unconnected, responses to similar situations, or such similarities could speak to the intervention of a powerful international actor intent on orchestrating similar changes in a group of weaker states. In either case,

Diani and Doug McAdam (Oxford: Oxford University Press, 2003), 1–20; Gitelman, *The Diffusion of Political Innovation*; Marco F. Giugni, "Explaining Cross-National Similarities among Social Movements," in *Globalization and Resistance: Transnational Dimensions of Social Movements*, ed. Jackie Smith and Hank Johnston (Lanham, MD: Rowman and Littlefield, 2002), 13–30; Juliet Johnson, "Two-Track Diffusion and Central Bank Embeddedness: The Politics of Euro Adoption in Hungary and the Czech Republic," *Review of International Political Economy* 13:3 (August 2006), 361–386; Margaret E. Keck and Kathryn Sikkink, *Activists beyond Borders: Advocacy Networks in International Politics* (Ithaca, NY: Cornell University Press, 1998); Lee and Strang, "The International Diffusion of Public-Sector Downsizing"; Judith Kelley, "Assessing the Complex Evolution of Norms: The Rise of International Election Monitoring," *International Organization* 62:2 (April 2008), 221–255; Beth Simmons and Zachary Elkins, "The Globalization of Liberalization: Policy Diffusion in the International Political Economy," *American Political Science Review* 98:1 (February 2004), 171–189; Strang and Soule, "Diffusion in Organizations and Social Movements"; McAdam and Rucht, "Cross-National Diffusion"; Gregory M. Maney, "Transnational Structures and Protest: Linking Theories and Assessing Evidence," in *Globalization and Resistance: Transnational Dimensions of Social Movements*, ed. Jackie Smith and Hank Johnston (Lanham, MD: Rowman and Littlefield, 2002), 31–50; Markoff, *Waves of Democracy*; McAdam, Tarrow, and Tilly, "Comparative Perspectives on Contentious Politics"; Rebecca Kolins Givan, Kenneth M. Roberts, and Sarah A. Soule, eds., *The Diffusion of Social Movements: Actors, Mechanisms, and Political Effects* (Cambridge: Cambridge University Press, 2010); Sidney G. Tarrow, *Power in Movement: Social Movements and Contentious Politics* (Cambridge: Cambridge University Press, 1998); Sidney G. Tarrow, "From Lumping to Splitting: Specifying Globalization and Resistance," in *Globalization and Resistance: Transnational Dimensions of Social Movements*, ed. Jackie Smith and Hank Johnston (Lanham, MD: Rowman and Littlefield, 2002), 229–250; Tarrow, *The New Transnational Activism*; Porta and Tarrow, *Transnational Protest and Global Activism*; Kurt Weyland, "Theories of Policy Diffusion: Lessons from Latin American Pension Reform," *World Politics* 57:2 (January 2005), 262–295; Gillian Wylie, "Social Movements and International Change: The Case of Détente 'From Below,'" *International Journal of Peace Studies* 4:2 (July 1999), http://www2.gmu.edu/programs/icar/ijps/vol4_2/wylie.htm; Charles Tilly and Sidney Tarrow, *Contentious Politics* (Boulder, CO: Paradigm Publishers, 2006); and Wejnert, "Diffusion, Development, and Democracy."

[47] Wade Jacoby, "Inspiration, Coalition and Substitution: External Influences on Postcommunist Transformations," *World Politics* 58:4 (July 2006), 623–651.

[48] To borrow from Brinks and Coppedge, "Diffusion Is No Illusion."

the horizontal dynamic implied in the very idea of diffusion – that is, the movement of an innovation from one site to others – would be absent. What makes selection among these alternative interpretations even more difficult is the reliance in many diffusion studies on evidence that establishes commonalities among sites that enhance their joint receptivity to importing the same innovation.

This study is well positioned to address two other aspects of diffusion that have received insufficient attention. Diffusion in practice is always more complex than the mere spread of a particular innovation across time and space. In particular, there are always sites, even quite similar ones and ones that are located close to the original site, that resist adoption of the innovation in question; innovations always change when making their cross-national journey; and waves of change invariably come to an end. The question in all these instances is why diffusion is always both uneven and finite – a question that is inextricably linked to the whether and (if so) how issues associated with establishing diffusion. For example, we can hardly generate a compelling explanation of why innovations travel unless we can also say something about the itineraries not taken.

The puzzle of the uneven nature of diffusion also reminds us of a definitional issue. The work on diffusion rarely draws a distinction between two types of innovation: those that are more modest and involve relatively circumscribed modifications of the status quo versus those that are more ambitious and threatening because they constitute fundamental challenges to the prevailing distribution of power. After all, it is one thing to introduce, for instance, a new pension system (though such changes certainly threaten vested interests) and quite another to carry out activities committed to the defeat of incumbent dictators and their allies. In the latter situation, the innovations involved would be expected to call forth extraordinary resistance on the part of a regime and its allies, whether we focus on the internal politics of states or the cross-national spread of electoral confrontations with authoritarian rule.[49] As a result, it would seem reasonable to expect that the diffusion of politically charged innovations, such as new strategies for removing authoritarians from power, would require the presence of not just one but several supportive mechanisms.

[49] On resistance to democratic change in this region, see, for example, Vitali Silitski, "Contagion Deterred: Preemptive Authoritarianism in the Former Soviet Union," in *Democracy and Authoritarianism in the Postcommunist World*, ed. Valerie Bunce, Michael McFaul, and Kathryn Stoner-Weiss (Cambridge: Cambridge University Press, 2010), 274–299; Regine A. Spector and Andrej Krickovic, "The Anti-Revolutionary Toolkit," unpublished manuscript, University of California, Berkeley, Department of Political Science and Institute for International Studies, March 7, 2007; Graeme P. Herd, "Colorful Revolutions and the CIS: 'Manufactured' Versus 'Managed' Democracy?", *Problems of Post-Communism* 52:2 (March/April 2005), 3–18; and National Endowment for Democracy, *The Backlash against Democracy Assistance: A Report Prepared by the National Endowment for Democracy for Senator Richard G. Lugar, Chairman, Committee on Foreign Relations, July 8, 2006* (Washington, DC: National Endowment for Democracy, 2006).

INTERNATIONAL DEMOCRACY PROMOTION

A final debate that will figure prominently in this book is one that is distinctive in spanning the worlds of academics, policy makers, and democratic activists. This is the question of whether the United States can and should play an active role in supporting democratic change abroad.[50]

This issue lies at the center of this study for a simple reason. The United States (along with other international actors) played an important role in *all* of the elections analyzed in this book. The involvement of the United States in these elections is not surprising. While always sharing the stage with other foreign policy goals, such as national security and access to markets and energy, and often being overshadowed by them, support for democratic change abroad has nonetheless had a long history in U.S. foreign relations.[51] For the purposes of this study, however, there were two developments that secured a key role for democracy assistance in U.S. foreign policy. One was the strong commitment of Ronald Reagan to supporting democratic change abroad and the founding in 1983 of the National Endowment for Democracy and its associated organizations, including the National Democratic Institute, the International Republican Institute (as it is currently called), the Center for International Private Enterprise, and the American Center for International Labor Solidarity (its current title). The other was the end of the Cold War – an event that prompted a sharp increase in U.S. democracy aid. For example, from 1990 to 2003 the United States provided democracy assistance to 165 countries, and from 1990 to 2004 the outlays on these programs by the United States Agency for International Development (USAID) grew by a factor of six.[52]

---

[50] See, for example, Zoltan Barany and Robert G. Moser, eds., *Is Democracy Exportable?* (Cambridge: Cambridge University Press, 2009); James Traub, *The Freedom Agenda: Why America Must Spread Democracy (Just Not the Way George Bush Did)* (New York: Farrar, Straus, and Giroux, 2008); and Michael McFaul, *Advancing Democracy Abroad: Why We Should and How We Can* (Lanham, MD and Stanford, CA: Rowman and Littlefield/Hoover Institution, 2010).

[51] See, for example, Michael Cox, John Ikenberry, and Takeshi Inoguchi, *American Democracy Promotion: Impulses, Strategies and Impact* (Oxford: Oxford University Press, 2000); Jonathan Monten, "The Roots of the Bush Doctrine," *International Security* 29 (Spring 2005), 112–156; Paul Drake, "From Good Men to Good Neighbors, 1912–1932," in Abraham Lowenthal, ed., *Exporting Democracy: The U.S. and Latin America* (Baltimore: Johns Hopkins University Press, 1991), 3–40; Gregory Dombar, "Supporting the Revolution: America, Democracy, and the End of the Cold War in Poland, 1981–1989" (Ph.D. dissertation, Department of History, The George Washington University, 2008).

[52] See Andrew Green, "Democracy and Donor Funding: Patterns and Trends," *Woodrow Wilson Center Eastern European Studies Newsletter* (September–October 2007); Andrew T. Green and Richard D. Kohl, "Challenges of Evaluating Democracy Assistance: Perspectives from the Donor Side," *Democratization* 14:1 (February 2007), 151–165; and Steven F. Finkel, Anibal Pérez-Liñán, Mitchell A. Seligson, and Dinorah Azpuru, *Effects of US Foreign Assistance on Democracy Building: Results of a Cross-National Quantitative Study, Final Report*, USAID (January 12, 2006), Final Report Version #34, 26.

The growth in U.S. democracy assistance has, not surprisingly, prompted some compelling criticisms of such aid. One set of concerns centers around the normative argument that states do not have the right to intervene in the domestic politics of other states. This is precisely the tack that Russian analysts have taken, for example, when analyzing the "color revolutions" in the Soviet successor states. As Vyacheslav Nikonov, the president of the Moscow-based Politika Foundation, has argued: "In Ukraine (in 2004) we are seeing yet again the implementation of an American 'velvet revolution' plan or, rather, a special operation to replace a regime that does not suit the U.S., a process that had already been successfully tested in 'banana republics' and was then transferred to the countries of Eastern Europe and Georgia."[53] Aleksandr Kniazev, another Russian political analyst, has offered a similar diagnosis of the "Tulip Revolution" in Kyrgyzstan in 2005: "If it were not for the constant interference of the United States in the internal affairs and the political processes in Kyrgyzstan, the opposition would not have mounted a revolution, and the administration of Akayev would have remained in power."[54]

A second set of concerns is more empirical in nature. Some studies of U.S. democracy assistance have concluded that these programs (together with development aid) have been co-opted by powerful international actors in order to pursue their own agendas.[55] Moreover, democracy assistance has been shown to have perverse consequences. For example, despite the best of intentions, external democracy aid can create fragile, dependent, and unrepresentative civil society and opposition groups, and it can destabilize regimes and governments as a result of how decisions about democracy assistance are made and implemented. Thus, some target states have paid a high price for rigid advice that is insensitive to local contexts; the inconsistent foreign policy priorities of the United States; high rates of personnel turnover within the democracy assistance community; lack of coordination and even conflicts among international democracy promoters; and the inefficiency of the foreign aid bureaucracy. Moreover, as Philip Roessler has argued, democracy assistance can weaken states when authoritarian leaders decide to demonstrate their democratic credentials to external donors by subcontracting responsibility for repression to nonstate actors. In addition, providing democracy aid to authoritarian regimes can empower authoritarians rather than democrats

---

[53] Quoted in Herd, "Colorful Revolutions and the CIS," 5.

[54] Aleksandr Knyazev, *Gosudarstvennyi perevorot: 24 Marta 2005g v Kirgizii* (Moscow: Europa, 2005). Also see Alexander Kots, "'Politics: A KP Investigation.' Interview with Sergei Markov, Centre for Political Studies, Director," *Komsomolskaya Pravda*, February 27, 2007, printed in *Johnson's Russia List*, March 4, 2007, BBC Monitoring; Markoff, *Waves of Democracy*; and Alison Kamhi, "The Russian NGO Law: Potential Conflicts with International, National and Foreign Legislation," *International Journal for Not-for-Profit Law* 9:1 (December 2006), 1–16.

[55] See, for example, Janine Wedel, *Shadow Elite: How the World's New Power Brokers Undermine Democracy, Government, and the Free Market* (New York: Basic Books, 2009); and Nicolas Guilhot, *The Democracy Makers: Human Rights and the Politics of Order* (New York: Columbia University Press, 2005).

because of corruption and the transfer of resources to pro-regime civil society groups. Finally, by pressing for democratic change in one state, the United States can encourage authoritarians in neighboring states to protect themselves by becoming even more repressive.[56]

These are compelling criticisms. However, there is another side to this story. First, there is growing evidence that democracy is superior to dictatorship in a number of important areas. For example, democracies are more respectful of human rights; they are less likely to make catastrophic mistakes; and they have a stronger record than dictatorships with respect to economic growth, infant mortality rates, and providing a higher material quality of life.[57] Second, it has been argued that because international norms have changed, powerful states do have the right to intervene in the domestic politics of other states when these interventions involve the defense of human rights, democracy, and free and fair elections.[58] In addition, there are a number of analyses that conclude, unlike the studies cited earlier, that international democracy assistance programs have in fact had some positive influence on democratic development. For

---

[56] On these negative effects, see, for instance, Laurence Jarvik, "NGOs: A New Class in International Relations," *Orbis* 51:2 (Spring 2007), 217–238; Jamal, *Barriers to Democracy*; Sarah E. Mendelson, "The Seven Ingredients: When Democracy Promotion Works," *Harvard International Review* 26:2 (Summer 2004), 86–87; Philip G. Roessler, "Donor-Induced Democratization and the Privatization of State Violence in Kenya and Rwanda," *Comparative Politics* 37:2 (January 2005), 207–227; Andrew Ng, "Accompanying the King: Building a Democratic Governance State in Morocco" (honors thesis, Department of Government, Cornell University, April 16, 2007); Sarah L. Henderson, "Selling Civil Society: Western Aid and the Nongovernmental Organization Sector in Russia," *Comparative Political Studies* 35:2 (March 2002), 139–167; Alexander Cooley and James Ron, "The NGO Scramble: Organizational Insecurity and the Political Economy of Transnational Action," *International Security* 27:1 (Summer 2002), 5–39; Kristina Kaush and Richard Youngs, *Algeria: Democratic Transition Case Study*, CDDRL Working Paper No. 84, Center for Democracy, Development and the Rule of Law, Freeman Spogli Institute for International Studies, Stanford University (August 2008); Andrew Wilson, *Virtual Politics: Faking Democracy in the Post-Soviet World* (New Haven, CT: Yale University Press, 2005); Chrystia Freeland, *Sale of the Century: Russia's Wild Ride from Communism to Capitalism* (New York: Crown, 2000); Randall Stone, *Lending Credibility: The International Monetary Fund and the Postcommunist Transition* (Princeton, NJ: Princeton University Press, 2002); Janine R. Wedel, *Collision and Collusion: The Strange Case of Western Aid to Eastern Europe, 1989–1998* (New York: St. Martin's Press, 1998); Jaba Devdariani, *Building Democracy in Georgia: The Impact of International Assistance*, Discussion Paper No. 11, International Institute for Democracy and Electoral Assistance (May 2003); William Easterly, "The Cartel of Good Intentions: The Problem with Bureaucracy in Foreign Aid," *Journal of Policy Reform* 5:4 (2002), 223–250; and Walt Bogdanich and Jenny Nordberg, "Democracy Undone: Back Channels versus Policy; Mixed U.S. Signals Helped Tilt Haiti toward Chaos," *New York Times*, January 29, 2006, http://query.nytimes.com/gst/fullpage.html?res=9C01E3DE1E3FF 93AA15752C0A9609C8B63&sec=&spon=&pagewanted=all.

[57] For a helpful summary of these studies, see McFaul, *Advancing Democracy Abroad*, 25–70.

[58] Martha Finnemore, *The Purpose of Intervention: Changing Beliefs about the Use of Force* (Ithaca, NY: Cornell University Press, 2003). However, also see Nicolas Guilhot, *The Democracy Makers: Human Rights and the Politics of Global Order*, (New York: Columbia University Press, 2005).

instance, statistical studies of democracy assistance provided by the European Union, the Organization of American States, and the United States Agency of International Development have demonstrated their important contributions to democratic progress in, respectively, Eastern and Central Europe, Latin America, and, in the case of USAID, around the globe, especially with respect to electoral assistance.[59] This conclusion, moreover, is also supported in some recent case studies of democratic transitions, albeit with the caveat that local influences are usually paramount.[60]

This leads to a final and more general point. Critics of international democracy assistance can exaggerate the claims made by supporters of these policies. In fact, there is a consensus among many analysts that such assistance has had positive effects, but largely at the margins.[61] This conclusion is based in part

[59] Milada Anna Vachudova, *Europe Undivided: Democracy, Leverage, and Integration after Communism* (Oxford: Oxford University Press, 2005); Milada Anna Vachudova, "Democratization in Postcommunist Europe: Illiberal Regimes and the Leverage of the European Union," in *Democracy and Authoritarianism in the Postcommunist World*, ed. Valerie Bunce, Michael McFaul, and Kathryn Stoner-Weiss (Cambridge: Cambridge University Press, 2010), 82–106; Richard Youngs, *The European Union and the Promotion of Democracy* (Oxford: Oxford University Press, 2002); Youngs, *International Democracy and the West*; Jon C. Pevehouse, *Democracy from Above: Regional Organizations and Democratization* (Cambridge: Cambridge University Press, 2005); Finkel, Pérez-Liñán, Seligson, and Azpuru, *Effects of US Foreign Assistance on Democracy Building*; and Steven Finkel, Anibal Pérez-Liñán, and Mitchell A. Seligson, "The Effects of U.S. Foreign Assistance on Democracy Building, 1990–2003," *World Politics* 59:3 (April 2007), 404–439.

[60] See, for example, Michael McFaul, "Ukraine Imports Democracy: External Influences on the Orange Revolution," *International Security* 32:2 (Fall 2007), 45–83; Antoinette Handley, "The World Bank Made Me Do It? Domestic and International Factors in Ghana's Transition to Democracy," paper presented at the Evaluating International Influences on Democratic Development Authors' Workshop, Center for Democracy, Development and the Rule of Law, Stanford University, March 5–6, 2009; Jennings, *Serbia's Bulldozer Revolution*; A. David Adesnik and Sunhyuk Kim, *If At First You Don't Succeed: The Puzzle of South Korea's Democratic Transition*, CDDRL Working Paper No. 83, Center for Democracy, Development and the Rule of Law, Freeman Spogli Institute for International Studies, Stanford University (July 2008); and Magen, *Evaluating External Influence on Democratic Development*.

[61] Carothers, "The End of the Transition Paradigm;" Thomas Carothers, *Aiding Democracy Abroad: The Learning Curve* (Washington, DC: Carnegie Endowment for International Peace, 1999); Thomas Carothers, "Misunderstanding Gradualism," *Journal of Democracy* 18:3 (July 2007), 18–22; Thomas Carothers, "The 'Sequencing' Fallacy," *Journal of Democracy* 18:1 (January 2007), 12–27; Thomas Carothers, *Critical Missions: Essays on Democracy Promotion* (Washington, DC: Carnegie Endowment for International Peace, 2004), and Thomas Carothers, *Revitalizing Democracy Assistance: The Challenge of USAID*, Carnegie Report (October 2009). Also see Devdariani, *Building Democracy in Georgia*; Giorgi Meladze, "Civil Society: A Second Chance for Post-Soviet Democracy: A Eurasianet Commentary," *Eurasianet*, September 5, 2005, http://www.eurasianet.org/departments/civilsociety/articles/eav090605.shtml; National Research Councils of the National Academies, Committee on Evaluation of USAID Democracy Assistance Programs, *Improving Democracy Assistance: Building Knowledge through Evaluations and Research* (Washington, DC: National Academies Press, 2008); James Wertsch, "Georgia as a Laboratory for Democracy," *Demokratizatsiya* 13:4 (Fall 2005), 519–535; McFaul, "Ukraine Imports Democracy"; Vachudova, *Europe Undivided*, and Vachudova, "Democratization

on the common assumptions shared by international democracy promoters and local democracy activists that domestic politics "trumps" international influences and that external aid is effective only in receptive contexts – that is, in settings where citizens are demanding democracy and partnerships can be forged between external democracy promoters and local political activists.

This argument is also based upon careful readings of how international democracy promotion actually works on the ground. A good example is a recent book by Lincoln Mitchell, who worked for the National Democratic Institute in Georgia when the Rose Revolution took place.[62] Mitchell argues that, while the U.S. helped define the form of the confrontation with the Shevardnadze regime that took place in 2003, and while it played a key and longer-term role (along with the European Union and private foundations, such as the Open Society Institute) in supporting civil society, its participation in the removal of Shevardnadze from power was nonetheless modest. This is because the United States had been a long-time supporter of the regime, to the point of exaggerating its local support and its accomplishments, and because U.S. democracy assistance often took the form of being "confused and directionless"[63] and was based on a strategy that was "neither consistent nor ambitious."[64]

Are critics correct that U.S. democracy assistance is dangerous and indefensible, or are supporters of such aid correct that international democracy support can contribute in modest ways to democratic progress? Our analysis of breakthrough elections in postcommunist Europe and Eurasia provides an ideal opportunity to address this question. This is in part because of the approach we have adopted. By comparing nine countries and eleven elections and by controlling as well for electoral results, we are able to strike a balance between tracing complex dynamics on the ground and drawing conclusions that can be generalized. At the same time, our interviews with a wide range of participants in these processes help us assess the relative influence of local actors, Western democracy promoters (including private foundations), and regional democracy activists.

Equally helpful for evaluating the impact of U.S. democracy aid is the regional focus of this book. The postcommunist region has in fact played a central role in U.S. efforts to advance democratic change abroad. For instance, from 1990 to 2003, 33.2 percent of USAID democracy and governance allocations went to postcommunist Europe and Eurasia; 23.6 percent to Latin America and the Caribbean; 19.5 percent to Africa; 10.9 percent to the Middle

in Postcommunist Europe"; Mitchell, *Uncertain Democracy*; Finkel, Pérez-Liñán, Seligson, and Azpuru, *Effects of US Foreign Assistance on Democracy Building*; Finkel, Pérez-Liñán, and Seligson, "The Effects of U.S. Foreign Assistance on Democracy Building, 1990–2003"; Adesnik and Kim, "If At First You Don't Succeed"; Magen, *Evaluating External Influence on Democratic Development*.

[62] Mitchell, *Uncertain Democracy*.
[63] Ibid., 116.
[64] Ibid., 126.

East and the Mediterranean; and 10.4 percent to Asia (with the remainder going to Portugal and Ireland, along with Oceana).[65] Just as indicative of the importance of this region is another indicator: USAID spent $5.77 million (in 1995 dollars) per country on democracy assistance in the twelve successor states to the Soviet Union versus $2.36 million per country (also 1995 dollars) in Latin America and $1.29 million per country in Africa.[66]

THE DESIGN OF THIS STUDY

Our analysis of the wave of democratizing elections in the postcommunist world from 1998 to 2008 proceeds from several core premises. First, to draw on William Sewell, we embrace the idea of an "eventful" political science – in our case, the importance of the elections themselves and all the activities that went along with them. These include decisions on the part of oppositions about whether to go it alone or collaborate with one another, actions of civil society groups (including youth movements), candidate selection, campaigns, voter registration, electoral procedures, voter turnout, election monitoring, tabulation of the results, and the reactions of candidates, citizens, and the international community to the official results. In our view, while developments leading up these contests were important, so were the details of each of these elections.

Second, these elections deviated from "politics as usual." They involved an unusually rich brew of actors, activities, and organizations, and they included an array of domestic, regional, and international actors and organizations. As a result, understanding what happened and why requires us to resist the temptation, so prevalent in studies of political change, to treat outcomes as somehow inevitable and to base our conclusions on as broad a range of data as possible. The final point is particularly important. Many of the actors involved had strong incentives to portray what happened in certain ways, and many of the questions of interest in this study require us to make difficult calls. It is perilous but necessary, for example, to draw conclusions about whether international assistance was decisive in these electoral breakthroughs.

Our final premise follows from the first two. Comparisons among cases is the best approach to analyzing questions, such as the ones of interest in this study, that focus on complex domestic and international processes of change involving multiple actors, movements, organizations, and national sites. Such comparisons, however, will lead to compelling conclusions only if the following conditions are met: 1) the number of cases is small enough to explore important details, but large enough to introduce sufficient variation in both causes

---

[65] As calculated from the data provided by Finkel, Pérez-Liñán, Seligson, and Azpuru, *Effects of US Foreign Assistance on Democracy Building*, and a slight revision of the chart they present on page 28.

[66] As calculated from ibid., page 32 – which treats the three Baltic states as a separate category.

and consequences; 2) case selection facilitates controls through the methods of either similarity or difference; 3) the cases analyzed vary, depending upon the question at hand, and; 4) cases are treated not just as separate, but also as potentially related (given diffusion effects).

KEY TERMS

One term that figures prominently in this study is *democratizing elections*. We use this term to connote a subset of elections that meet two conditions. One is that they take place in political contexts where the opposition is out of power, and where authoritarian incumbents use a variety of antidemocratic methods in order to maintain political control. The other is that, despite these constraints, the opposition nonetheless succeeds in winning office. Thus, because authoritarians leave office – the very fact of turnover – and oppositions pledge to provide a more authentic democracy than their predecessors, these elections share the common feature of expanding opportunities for democratic change. Whether they actually do so and in which ways, however, is an empirical question.

By using the term "democratizing elections," we have avoided using the more familiar terms for these pivotal elections, that is, *electoral* or *color revolutions*.[67] In our view, it is highly misleading to use the rather sensationalist "term revolution." Definitions of "revolution" vary, but most definitions emphasize the existence of dual sovereignty; significant levels of violence and mass mobilization; regime and state collapse; and the eventual construction of stronger states and certainly new regimes and social orders.[68] While the electoral confrontations in Serbia, Georgia, and Ukraine, in particular, exhibited in a superficial way a few of these revolutionary features (such as high levels of popular mobilization and the multiplication of sovereignty through competing vote tabulations), even these cases diverged in most respects from common understandings of what revolutions entail.

However, there is an additional reason why we favor the term "democratizing elections" over "electoral revolutions." The latter characterization introduces several biases into the analysis. One is that it sets extremely high expectations for what "should" follow these electoral breakthroughs, thereby generating,

---

[67] See, for example, Mark Beissinger, "Promoting Democracy: Is Exporting Revolution a Constructive Strategy?," *Dissent* 53:1 (Winter 2006), 18–24, and Beissinger, "Structure and Example"; Menno Fenger, "The Diffusion of Revolutions: Comparing Recent Regime Turnovers in Five Post-Communist Countries," *Demokratizatsiya* 15:1 (Winter 2007), 5–28; Charles Fairbanks, "Revolution Reconsidered," *Journal of Democracy* 18:1 (January 2007), 42–57; Theodor Tudoroiu, "Rose, Orange and Tulip: The Failed Post-Soviet Revolutions," *Communist and Post-communist Studies* 40:3 (September 2007), 315–342; Joerg Forbrig and Pavol Demeš, eds., *Reclaiming Democracy*; and Bunce and Wolchik, "Favorable Conditions and Electoral Revolutions" and "Getting Real about 'Real Causes.'"

[68] Theda Skocpol, *States and Social Revolutions* (Cambridge: Cambridge University Press, 1979); Charles Tilly, *From Mobilization to Revolution* (New York: McGraw-Hill, 1978); Jeff Goodwin, *No Other Way Out: States and Revolutionary Movements, 1945–1991* (Cambridge: Cambridge University Press, 2001).

almost by definition, assessments that invariably emphasize the limits of change and the constraints on democracy, while casting serious doubt on the importance of these electoral shifts and, more generally, electoral outcomes. The other bias is that the term *color* or *electoral revolutions* has been used in quite political ways. Just as some participants in these elections like to use the term to dramatize their accomplishments, so authoritarians, eager to defend their power against the "electoral virus," adopt the terminology of revolution in order to accomplish two self-serving objectives: to persuade allies, oppositions, and citizens that such electoral challenges are both unnatural, because they result from the illegitimate interventions of "outsiders," and dangerous, because they produce political chaos. It was precisely such arguments, for example, that we encountered repeatedly in Armenia not just from representatives of the regime, but also from college students, journalists, and even leaders of opposition parties. The emphasis on political order is particularly appealing in countries such as Armenia, but also in Azerbaijan and, for that matter, in China and Russia, where there are widespread fears of instability as a result of painful recent experiences with chaotic politics and poor economic performance.

The second conceptual issue involves our characterization of regime types. As noted earlier in this chapter, there is a significant cottage industry devoted to the classification of regimes that straddle democracy and dictatorship.[69] In this book, we use the term "mixed regimes" to refer to regimes that, like all the regimes of interest in this study and like a large number of regimes around the world, combine two traits: competitive elections and authoritarian political leadership. Beyond this core commonality, however, these regimes differ from one another in whether their elections are free and fair or whether they are rigged – and in displaying variations between these two poles – and in how far their leaders go in pursuing other aspects of the authoritarian agenda, such as controlling the media, harassing civil society groups, and centralizing political power in the executive.

Some of these political differences are highlighted in Table 1.2, where we compare Nations in Transit scores for our nine countries in the two years preceding the pivotal elections. It is evident in this table, for example, that while corruption scores tend to be relatively high among our cases, with the exception of Slovakia (see column 5), scores on civil society, the independence of the media, and the quality of electoral procedures diverge substantially. In Table 1.3, we continue our comparison by applying economic as well as additional political measures to our cases. Once again, it is clear that the elections of interest in this study have taken place in a wide range of political and economic contexts. For example, at the time of their pivotal elections, the per

[69] See, for example, Levitsky and Way, "The Rise of Competitive Authoritarianism" and "Competitive Authoritarian Regimes"; Diamond, "Thinking about Hybrid Regimes"; Ottaway, *Democracy Challenged*; Howard and Roessler, "Liberalizing Electoral Outcomes in Competitive Authoritarian Regimes"; and Roessler and Howard, "Post-Cold-War Political Regimes"; and Carothers, "The End of the Transition Paradigm."

TABLE 1.2. *Elections and democratic performance. The assessments in this table are two-year average scores preceding the electoral breakthroughs. For example, for Armenia in 2003, the scores for 2001 and 2002 were averaged.*

Country (Year)	NIT	CS	IM	EP	Corruption
Armenia (2003)	4.83	3.50	4.75	5.50	5.75
Armenia (2008)	5.68	3.50	5.68	5.75	5.75
Azerbaijan (2003)	5.59	4.50	5.68	5.75	6.25
Azerbaijan (2005)	5.55	4.48	5.68	5.88	6.25
Belarus (2001)	6.25	6.00	6.75	6.75	5.25
Belarus (2006)[a]	6.59	6.75	6.75	6.88	5.89
Croatia (2000)	4.36	3.50	4.88	4.25	5.25[b]
Georgia (2003)	4.46	4.00	3.68	4.75	5.38
Kyrgyzstan (2005)	5.67	4.50	6.00	6.00	6.00
Serbia (2000) [c]	5.67	5.18	5.13	5.25	6.25
Slovakia (1998)[d]	3.80	3.25	4.25	3.75	N/A
Ukraine (2004)	4.82	3.68	5.50	4.25	5.88

[a] The scores for "after" include only results from 2007, as the scores for 2008 are not yet available.

[b] Scores for 2000/1999. Scores for 1998 not available.

[c] Score for 1999/2000. Score for 1998 not available.

[d] Score for 1997. Scores for 1996 not available.

Note: NIT = Nations in Transit Democracy Score; CS = Civil Society; IM = Independent Media; VA = Voice and Accountability; EP = Electoral Process.

Source: Freedom House, *Nations in Transit* (New York: Freedom House, 2007, 2006, 2005, 2004, 2003, 2002, 2001, 2000, 1998, 1997).

Note on methodology: Nations in Transit Democracy scores are an average of political rights and civil liberties scores, with 7 indicating most repressive and 1 indicating most free. The remaining categories are based upon the same range.

capita GDP of Croatia was six times that of Armenia and Georgia; the Slovak regime provided more extensive civil liberties and political rights to their citizens than, say, Kyrgyzstan or Belarus; and presidential power was far greater in Azerbaijan and Kyrgyzstan than in Croatia.

Is this variation a problem? We would argue that it is in fact analytically advantageous. This is because, in being able to combine similarities among our cases (for example, with respect to the communist past, recent statehood, and the joining of electoral competition with authoritarian political leadership) with areas of political and economic difference, we are in a strong position to explore in a systematic way why electoral outcomes varied and why after electoral turnover democratic progress also varied.

ORGANIZATION AND ARGUMENTS

The book is divided into three parts. In the next chapter, we develop a series of hypotheses about why elections in mixed regimes would be more or less likely

TABLE 1.3. *Economic and political variations among regimes*

Country	GDP per Capita (US $)	Economic Growth (%)	Border Conflicts	Freedom House Scores	Voice and Accountability	Presidential Power	Corruption
Armenia	522.2/740.3	11.4	Yes	4/4	−0.52	16	5.75
Azerbaijan	312.9/760.5	11.2/26.4	Yes	6/5	−0.82	18	6.25
Belarus	1035.4/1042.8	4.7/9.9	No	6/6	−1.35	21	5.25
Croatia	4029/4371.1	0.8	No	4/4	−0.29	9	5.25
Georgia	534.6/741	5.1	Yes	4/4	−0.58	13	5.50
Kyrgyzstan	330.6/434.5	7.0	No	6/5	−0.96	16.4	6.00
Serbia	1730.4/2319.2	0.05	Yes	5/5	−1.11	N/A	6.25
Slovakia	3615.7/3935	5.35	No	2/4	+0.28	4	N/A
Ukraine	721.5/1053.3	7.2	No	4/4	−0.66	13	5.75

Note on methodology: GDP per capita scores include data for 1995 and for the year prior to the election. For countries with multiple elections, data for 1995 and for the year prior to the first election are included. Economic Growth scores are an average of the two years prior to the pivotal election. Where there were multiple elections, scores are reported for both. Freedom House scores comprise political rights/civil liberties based on a scale of 1–7, with 1 indicating most free and 7 indicating most unfree. Scores are taken from the year prior to the pivotal election. In cases where there were multiple pivotal elections, the scores from the first elections are used. Voice and Accountability and Rule of Law scores are measured on a scale of +2.5 to −2.5. Higher scores correspond to better governance. In cases where there were multiple pivotal elections, the scores from the first elections are used. For Presidential Power scores, higher scores represent higher levels of presidential power. In cases where there were multiple pivotal elections, the scores from the first elections are used. Nation in Transit Corruption scores are based on a range of 1 to 7, with 7 indicating most corrupt and 1 indicating least corrupt. In cases where there were multiple pivotal elections, the scores from the first elections are used.

Sources: European Bank for Reconstruction and Development, "Economic Statistics and Growth," www.ebrd.com/country/sector/econo/ stats/index.htm; Freedom House, "Comparative Scores for All Countries from 1973 to 2006,"/Freedom House, www.freedomhouse. org/uploads/fiw/FIWAllScores.xls), and Freedom House, *Freedom in the World 2008*, www.freedomhouse.org/uploads/fiwo8launch/ FIWo8Tables.pdf); Daniel Kaufmann, Aart Kraay, and Massimo Mastruzzi, "World Governance Indicators, 1996–2006," World Bank, http://info.worldbank.org/governance/wgi2007/home.htm; Freedom House, *Nations in Transit* (New York: Freedom House, 2007, 2006, 2005, 2004, 2003, 2002, 2001, 2000, 1998, 1997).

to lead to the empowerment of the democratic opposition. These hypotheses are divided into three groups. The first two are based on the familiar distinction between the vulnerability of the regime as a consequence of its institutional characteristics and long-term political and economic trends, on the one hand, and shorter-term developments that are associated with the elections themselves, on the other. This distinction between long-term and short-term influences, and thus between structure and agency, is a familiar one in comparative research.[70] The third set of hypotheses is less familiar. Thus, we will stake out new terrain by introducing a third causal possibility with respect to electoral stability and change: the role of international diffusion in these elections and alternative mechanisms driving this dynamic.

In Part II, we provide the raw data for our analysis by carrying out a series of case studies. We begin in Chapter 3 by analyzing the politics and economics surrounding the Slovak election in 1998 and the Croatian election in 2000. These two electoral breakthroughs are grouped together because they took place at the beginning of the wave, with Slovakia playing what could be termed a pioneering role in this process, and because they resulted from the deployment by the opposition of very similar approaches to winning power.

Chapters 4 and 5 are devoted to case studies of the 2000 election in Serbia and the 2004 election in Ukraine, respectively. What is important about the Serbian case is that it was in that country that the ensemble of innovative electoral strategies deployed in Slovakia and Croatia was first applied in a relatively repressive regime, and where it also for the first time confronted rigged elections. As a result, the strategies for winning power had to be amended to include large-scale popular protests following the election to force the incumbent president, Slobodan Milošević, to admit defeat and leave office. The Ukrainian case is also of particular interest because of certain similarities with the Serbian case – for instance, a relatively authoritarian regime and exceptionally large-scale protests following the election. However, there were also some differences between these two electoral breakthroughs – for example, less campaigning on the part of the United States in Ukraine to bring about regime change and the greater importance in Ukraine of a charismatic leader who had defected from the regime and who became the candidate of the opposition.

In Chapter 6, we compare Georgia and its pivotal election in 2003 to Kyrgyzstan and its 2005 election. These countries are paired for a simple reason. The breakthrough elections took a very different form in these two cases than in the other cases we examine. Both of the elections were for parliament in a presidential system, and they were used by oppositions to force the incumbent, who was not up for reelection, to leave office.

---

[70] For a helpful discussion of this contrast and the trade-offs associated with each approach, see Herbert Kitschelt, "Accounting for Postcommunist Regime Diversity: What Counts as a Good Cause?," in *Capitalism and Democracy in Central and Eastern Europe: Assessing the Legacy of Communist Rule*, ed. Grzegorz Ekiert and Stephen C. Hanson (Cambridge: Cambridge University Press, 2003), 49–88.

We close Section II by comparing three countries – that is, Armenia, Azerbaijan, and Belarus – where elections held in 2003 and 2008, 2003 and 2005, and in 2006, respectively, had the more typical outcome for mixed regimes: the defeat of the opposition. Our goal in this comparison is the same as in the earlier chapters – that is, to explain electoral outcomes by focusing on the interplay among regime context, economic and political trends, international democracy assistance, and electoral dynamics. However, what makes this chapter crucial to our project is that it provides cases where similarities in many key variables, including popular protests and united oppositions, failed to be converted into a victorious opposition.

In Section III, we use the data presented in the earlier chapters, along with other data, to answer the questions posed earlier in this chapter. In Chapter 8, we merge our case studies of successful and failed attempts to remove authoritarian leaders in order to provide a rigorous test of the hypotheses that we laid out in Chapter 2. Here, we discover that many of our hypotheses fail to differentiate clearly between our two sets of elections – for instance, trends in political protests, leadership turnover, opposition cohesion, democratic development, and external democracy assistance. By contrast, innovative electoral strategies used by the opposition, such as ambitious campaigns and voter registration and turnover drives, emerge as the most powerful explanation.

In Chapter 9, we follow up this finding about the impact of these electoral strategies – which we term the *electoral model* – by analyzing its invention, its core components, and the key political functions it served in mixed regimes. As we will discover, this ensemble of innovative electoral techniques was very much a work in progress that owed part of its existence to campaign practices in the United States and part of its design to successful struggles against authoritarian rule in such far-flung locations as the Philippines, Chile, Nicaragua, Bulgaria, Romania, and Slovakia. What made this approach so effective and therefore so popular among democratic activists around the world were four things. One was its remarkable ability to use elections – a cornerstone of democratic politics – to exploit the vulnerabilities of authoritarian leaders. Another was its capacity to expand public support of the opposition. In addition, this bundle of electoral strategies was easy to transport to new places, and it was relatively open to revision in keeping with changing local conditions.

In Chapter 10, we analyze the spread of these electoral strategies within the postcommunist region as a case of the cross-national diffusion of innovation. We identify three factors that served as the drivers of the diffusion dynamic: the easy transportability of the innovative electoral tool kit; perceptions among key domestic and international actors that local conditions in a number of states in the region were similar and similarly ripe for political change; and the invention, implementation, and cross-national transfer of the electoral model by an ambitious transnational network composed of Western democracy promoters, local oppositions and civil society groups, and regional democracy activists.

In Chapter 11, we return to our comparison of our nine countries and eleven elections in order to explain variations in democratic progress after both types of electoral outcomes. As we will discover, just as all the countries where electoral breakthroughs took place made some democratic progress (and usually a great deal), in Armenia, Azerbaijan, and Belarus regimes became far more repressive. As a result, the "democracy gap" between our two sets of cases widened considerably after these elections. Second, three factors were critical in explaining why some electoral turnovers were more supportive of subsequent democratic change than others: the long-term development of civil society and the politics of the turnover itself. Thus, what explains the checkered democratic progress of Georgia and Kyrgyzstan, in contrast to the far more significant democratic improvements in the other four cases of electoral turnover, was the relative weakness of civil society in these two countries, the opposition's use of extra-constitutional processes to remove authoritarian leaders from office; and large electoral mandates in the presidential elections that quickly followed the parliamentary contests. These three distinctive characteristics in turn translated into less competitive politics after the breakthrough elections. As a result, there were fewer societal and institutional constraints on the new presidents who took power in Georgia and Kyrgyzstan.

In Chapter 12, we summarize our conclusions and use them to reenter the debates that we outlined earlier in this chapter. Thus, we argue that mixed regimes, even when they seem to be weakening and when their leaders are unpopular, are nonetheless capable of erecting formidable barriers to democratic change. As a result, oppositions and their local and international allies need to take extraordinary measures to win power. Second, one extraordinary measure that they have taken and that has demonstrated its ability to remove authoritarian leaders from power is the adoption by the opposition of an innovative set of electoral strategies that include, for example, forming a united front among opposition parties, forging close alliances between the opposition and civil society groups, and carrying out ambitious nationwide campaigns and voter registration and turnout drives. These strategies solve a number of problems for the opposition, ranging from getting citizens to vote (and vote for them) to providing the incentives and the sites for popular protests after the election, should the incumbent lose but refuse to vacate office. Third, elections can be understood, therefore, as a mode of transition. Fourth, the cross-national diffusion of the innovative ensemble of electoral strategies explains the clustering across time and space of the breakthrough elections that took place in postcommunist Europe and Eurasia from 1998 to 2005. However, precisely because electoral turnover in mixed regimes is so threatening to incumbents, their allies, and the regime they control, multiple drivers of diffusion were required. The spread of the electoral model and its success in producing opposition victories, in short, was far from easy or automatic. Finally, we close the book by arguing that the United States played a powerful and positive role in these cases of electoral change. However, the impact of the United States depended upon its participation in a transnational network supporting free and fair elections; the key role of regional "graduates" of these electoral breakthroughs who took their experiences "on the road"; and the hard and often both tedious and dangerous work of ordinary citizens, civil society organizations, and opposition parties and candidates in the countries involved. Electoral change, in short, was hard-won, and it grew out of a deeply collaborative enterprise between domestic and international actors.

2

Electoral Stability and Change in Mixed Regimes

One of the most striking features of the 'late period' of the third wave has been the unprecedented growth in the number of regimes that are neither clearly democratic nor conventionally authoritarian.

Larry Diamond[1]

All of the elections of interest in this book took place in mixed regimes – that is, regimes that combine authoritarian politics with competition for political office. Our nine regimes also share a common past. Armenia, Azerbaijan, Belarus, Croatia, Georgia, Kyrgyzstan, Serbia, Slovakia, and Ukraine had all been republics nested within federal states during the communist era, and each one of these republics became an independent state in the early 1990s as a consequence of the collapse of communism and the dissolution of the Soviet Union, Yugoslavia, and Czechoslovakia. At the same time, however, these regimes were also very different from one another. For example, it was common practice in some of these countries but not in others for elections to be rigged; the media were relatively free to operate in some cases, but muzzled in the rest; and one leader had ruled since independence in Croatia, Serbia, and Kyrgyzstan, whereas turnovers in leadership had taken place in the remaining members of the group.[2]

---

[1] Larry Diamond, "Thinking about Hybrid Regimes," *Journal of Democracy* 13:2 (April 2002), 25.

[2] One reason why we used the broader term, "mixed regimes," rather than, say, "competitive authoritarianism" is the analytical leverage we gain as a result of being able to vary the extent to which election procedures are irregular. By contrast, many studies of these regimes "in the middle" restrict their focus to cases where elections are rigged. See, for example, Steven Levitsky and Lucan Way, *Competitive Authoritarianism: Hybrid Regimes after the Cold War* (Cambridge: Cambridge University Press, 2010); Joshua Tucker, "Enough! Electoral Fraud, Collective Action Problems, and Post-Communist Colored Revolutions," *Perspectives on Politics* 5:3 (September 2007), 537–553; and Philipp Kuntz and Mark Thompson, "More than Just the Final Straw: Stolen Elections as Revolutionary Triggers," *Comparative Politics* 41:3 (April 2009), 253–272.

The purpose of this chapter is to explore these and other differences among mixed regimes and to generate a series of hypotheses about why opposition parties and candidates might succeed in defeating authoritarian incumbents or their anointed successors. We begin our discussion by identifying a series of factors that set the stage for the elections and that could have influenced their outcomes – in particular, institutional characteristics of the regime, such as its level of democratic development, and long-term political and economic trends, such as patterns of political protest and economic performance. We then turn our attention to more short-term factors that are directly associated with electoral politics – for instance, variations in types of elections, electoral assistance provided by external actors, and electoral strategies. We then conclude the chapter by introducing a third group of hypotheses that builds on the idea of the importance of electoral strategies in explaining electoral results, but that proceeds from a new premise – that is, that these elections were related rather than separate events. Once we introduce this possibility, some new hypotheses present themselves that focus our attention on the factors that encourage or discourage cross-national diffusion.

REGIME VULNERABILITY

Many analysts approach the question of why leaders lose power – whether through elections or by other means – by assuming that structural and institutional influences are paramount and focusing, as a consequence, on the strength of the regime at the time the electoral season begins. According to this view, the central issue in these elections is whether regimes were ready to fall. Elections, therefore, are less important in and of themselves than as sites that register regime strength. This understanding of elections and the causes of electoral turnover – which also resonates with the discussion in Chapter 1 about the limits of elections more generally as independent variables – has been summarized succinctly by Jason Brownlee: "Elections provide an arena for political contestation, but they are not an independent causal factor."[3]

The key issue, therefore, is identifying variables that contribute to the regime's capacity to defend and enhance its power. One such factor is institutional: the weight of democratic and authoritarian features in the political system at the time the elections are held.[4] Here, one would expect more

---

[3] Jason Brownlee, *Authoritarianism in an Age of Democratization* (Cambridge: Cambridge University Press, 2007), 32. Also see Lucan Way, "The Real Causes of the Color Revolutions," *Journal of Democracy* 19:3 (July 2008), 55–69; Lucan Way, "Authoritarian State Building and the Sources of Regime Competitiveness in the Fourth Wave: The Cases of Belarus, Moldova, Russia, and Ukraine," *World Politics* 57:2 (January 2005), 231–261; and Levitsky and Way, *Competitive Authoritarianism*. Also see Dorothy Solinger, "Ending One-Party Dominance: Korea, Taiwan, Mexico," *Journal of Democracy* 12:1 (January 2002), 30–43.

[4] Also see Nicolas Van de Walle, "Meet the New Boss: Same as the Old Boss: The Evolution of Political Clientelism in Africa," in *Patrons, Clients and Policies: Patterns of Democratic Accountability and Political Competition*, ed. Herbert Kitschelt and Steven I. Wilkinson (Cambridge: Cambridge University Press, 2007); and Jason Brownlee, "Harbinger of

democratic systems to be more vulnerable, because they provide a more level playing field for political competition. Thus, just as more democratic contexts deny the incumbent authoritarian regimes the institutional tools they need to control citizens, civil society organizations, the media, and opposition groups, so they provide more resources to opposition parties and more opportunities for them to mount major and successful electoral challenges.[5] In addition, all else being equal, it can be argued that citizens are more predisposed to support the opposition in more democratic political settings. In that context, they can be more confident that their votes will count, and the opposition is more likely to have accumulated a track record showing its ability to win elections and govern the country. Citizens in less repressive regimes are also less likely to face reprisals for supporting the opposition.

However, we must recognize at the same time that the opposition is more likely to have won power in the past in more democratic systems and, therefore, more likely to be burdened by a negative record in office. A good example of this problem is the 1997 election in Bulgaria – an election that has not been included in the group compared in this book, but that nonetheless played an influential role, as we will discover in later chapters, in the spread of electoral change in this region. This election was held because an economic crisis and increasingly violent anti-regime protests had made it impossible for the Socialist-led government to continue in office.[6] According to Avis Bohlen, the U.S. ambassador in Bulgaria during this period, the Bulgarian opposition was extremely slow to join these protests (whereas the unions, in particular, were engaged from the beginning) and to recognize their potential for forcing early elections and thereby giving the opposition a chance to return to office.[7] They were slow in part because they were so divided, and their divisions had played a key role in their inability earlier to form a sustainable government. At the same time, when the 1997 election was finally held, turnout was extremely low. This reflected, on the one hand, the dissatisfaction of

Democracy: Competitive Elections before the End of Authoritarianism," in *Democratization by Elections: A New Mode of Transition*, ed. Staffan Lindberg (Baltimore: Johns Hopkins University Press, 2009), 128–147.

[5] Brownlee, "Harbinger of Democracy"; Andreas Schedler, "Sources of Competition under Electoral Authoritarianism," in *Democratization by Elections: A New Mode of Transition*, ed. Staffan Lindberg (Baltimore: Johns Hopkins University Press, 2009), 179–201.

[6] See Tsvetlana Petrova, "A Postcommunist Transition in Two Acts: The 1996–1997 Anti-Government Struggle in Bulgaria as a Bridge between the First and Second Waves of Transition in Eastern Europe," in *Democracy and Authoritarianism in the Postcommunist World*, ed. Valerie Bunce, Michael McFaul, and Kathryn Stoner-Weiss (Cambridge: Cambridge University Press, 2010), 107–133.

[7] Interviews with Avis Bohlen, Washington, DC, November 15, 2006, and Ivan Krastev, Berlin, July 27, 2005. However, as Scott Carpenter, the director of the International Republican Institute in Bulgaria at that time, argued in the interview we conducted with him in Washington, DC, on April 9, 2009, the opposition played an early and important role in the protests and was quite ready to press for new elections and to compete effectively in them. We are more persuaded, however, by the first interpretation, given trends in voter turnout and public opinion.

the Bulgarian public with the incumbent communists and, on the other, their skepticism about the ability of the opposition to govern effectively and deal with a cascading economic crisis.[8]

When viewed from this vantage point, oppositions that have never won power have some decided political advantages. This was certainly the case, for example, with the two presidents who succeeded Slobodan Milošević in Serbia: Vojislav Koštunica and Boris Tadić. The popularity of both of these men when they assumed office was greatly enhanced by two interrelated aspects of their political past: their failure to accumulate much of a political track record and the absence of any ties to the Milošević regime. At the same time, a positive track record, albeit one that falls short of occupying the top political office, can also have payoffs. Here, Mikheil Saakashvili in Georgia (who had served briefly as the minister of justice under Shevardnadze) and Viktor Yushchenko in Ukraine (who had served for a short time as prime minister under Kuchma) are two cases in point. They succeeded in staking out positions independent of the regime, yet also demonstrated that they were capable policy makers.

We can also add a temporal dimension to the arguments about democratic development and political competition. Here, we confront two competing hypotheses. On the one hand, if we assume that fear about the costs of supporting the opposition and pessimism about the prospects for leadership change are key considerations, then a trend away from democracy and in the direction of greater political repression should encourage electoral continuity – if for no other reason than the translation of these considerations into low turnout and demobilization of the opposition and its supporters. However, as Larry Diamond has suggested, increased repression can improve the prospects for electoral change – for example, by making citizens and opposition groups more angry and more aware of the costs of the regime as well as more able to identify a common enemy. While signals in the admittedly murky political environment of mixed regimes are always hard to read, repression can also be read as an indication that political leaders have become increasingly nervous about their hold on power.[9]

---

[8] Also see Venelin I. Ganev, *Preying on the State: The Transformation of Bulgaria After 1989* (Ithaca, NY: Cornell University Press, 2007). On strikes in hybrid regimes, see Graeme Robertson, "Managing Society: Protest, Civil Society, and Regime in Putin's Russia," unpublished manuscript, University of North Carolina, Department of Political Science, 2008.

[9] Diamond, "Thinking about Hybrid Regimes." These arguments also appear in studies of protest dynamics under conditions of repression. See Francisco Ronald, "After the Massacre: Mobilization in the Wake of Harsh Repression," *Mobilization: An International Journal* 9:2 (June 2004), 107–126; and Jay Lyall, "Pocket Protests: Rhetorical Coercion and the Micro-Politics of Collective Action in Semi-Authoritarian Regimes," *World Politics* 58:3 (April 2006), 378–412. Finally, this is a central claim put forward by analysts who argue on behalf of the effectiveness of nonviolent conflict in authoritarian regime settings. See Peter Ackerman and Jack Duvall, *A Force More Powerful: A Century of Nonviolent Conflict*, 1st Palgrave paperback ed. (New York: St. Martin's Press, 2000).

There are also two other dynamics associated with increased repression that are harder to nail down. An upsurge in repressive activities can violate the informal norms that have developed around what constitutes acceptable and unacceptable behaviors on the part of the authoritarian leader. Thus, regime allies, opposition leaders, and ordinary citizens can be emboldened to challenge the power of the leader for the simple reason that he has gone "too far." At the same time, repression can interact with the principal-agent problem in more authoritarian regimes by encouraging lower-level officials to overread signals from the top and thereby take increasingly extreme actions against citizens. These actions, in turn, can lay the groundwork for mobilizations against authoritarian rule – at the ballot box and in the streets.

Regimes are also more vulnerable when they have been less able to centralize and institutionalize their powers. We recognize that these aspects of regime capacity are very hard to measure and therefore quite susceptible, especially in more structural accounts, to a biased reading that rests on knowing a particular outcome and working backward from that point. Here, we are reminded of an observation by John Glenn: "In hindsight successful challengers often misinterpret events so as to make their success inevitable, and history is not kind to failed challenges – so that often less is known about these attempts."[10] Indeed, it is precisely because of these problems that we have adopted certain research strategies in this study – in particular, comparing the elections of interest to earlier ones; exploring the impact of a variety of factors, some of which were relatively short-term; and adding to the study cases where seemingly similar contexts and electoral efforts had the very different consequence of producing electoral continuity, not change.

All that recognized, however, we can imagine a range of indicators of regime institutionalization that, while imperfect, at least tap into some aspect of this very loaded term. Thus, stronger regimes are those in which incumbents rule through a well-established party – which is one reason (but only one and perhaps not the key cause, since such regimes also tend to have an ideological base and an ambitious agenda of transformation) why these types of authoritarian regimes tend to be more durable than others.[11] Moreover, well-institutionalized regimes would seem to be those that are more successful in preventing defections from the ruling circle – though this factor is very hard to isolate because it can indicate rather than cause regime crises. The importance of unity has been captured in the observations of one palace informant interviewed by Ryszard Kapuściński in his remarkable study of the fall of Haile

---

[10] John Glenn, *Framing Democracy: Civil Society and Civic Movements in Eastern Europe* (Stanford, CA: Stanford University Press, 2001), 224.

[11] Barbara Geddes, "Authoritarian Breakdown: Empirical Testing of a Game Theoretic Argument," paper presented at the Annual Meeting of the American Political Science Association, Atlanta, GA, September 1, 1999. Also see Benjamin Smith, "Life of the Party: The Origins of Regime Breakdown and Persistence under Single Party Rule," *World Politics* 57:3 (April 2005), 421–451.

Selassie. Thus, recalling when popular protests began to spread in Ethiopia, one interviewee sketched out a particular defection dynamic, wherein:

> ... slowly, gradually, three factions appear in the Palace. The first, the Jailers, are a fierce and inflexible coterie who demand the restoration of order and insist on arresting the malcontents, putting them behind bars, beating and hanging them.... A second faction coalesces, the Talkers, a coterie of liberals: weak people, and philosophizers, who think that one should invite the rebels to sit down at a table and talk.... Finally, the third faction is made up of Floaters, who are the most numerous group in the palace. They don't think at all, but hope that like corks in water they will float on the waves of circumstance.[12]

Other indicators of institutionalization of power could include a divided opposition that has repeatedly failed to win power; demobilized citizens; and political leaders who have enjoyed long tenure. The assumption underlying the final distinction is that durable rule has important advantages for incumbents, including the construction of large patronage networks that fan out from the leader. Thus, long tenure generates strong disincentives for defection, whether by members of the ruling circle or by ordinary citizens.[13] At the same time, however, the opposite can be hypothesized. Long tenure can be associated with the fraying of networks as a consequence of their overuse and with the gradual redistribution of power from principals to agents in bureaucratic entities, such as authoritarian systems, that feature incomplete and asymmetric information.[14]

It is also plausible to expect that economic performance affects regime survival – in two ways. One is that poor performance depletes public support for the regime. The other is that slower growth in the economic resources available to the regime, especially in countries where corruption is extensive, undercuts the ability of leaders to maintain their patronage networks.[15]

---

[12] Ryszard Kapuściński, *The Emperor* (New York: Vintage International/Random House, 1983), 125.

[13] See, for example, Anna Grzymała-Busse, *Rebuilding Leviathan: Party Competition and State Exploitation in Postcommunist Democracies* (Cambridge: Cambridge University Press, 2007).

[14] It was precisely the long-term costs of the structure of the Soviet state, for example, that was used to explain its eventual disintegration. See, for example, Steven L. Solnick, *Stealing the State: Control and Collapse in Soviet Institutions* (Cambridge, MA: Harvard University Press, 1999); and Valerie Bunce, *Subversive Institutions: The Design and the Destruction of Socialism and the State* (Cambridge: Cambridge University Press, 1999).

[15] See Henry E. Hale, "Democracy or Autocracy on the March? The Colored Revolutions as Normal Dynamics of Patronal Presidentialism," *Communist and Post-Communist Studies* 39:3 (September 2006), 305–329; and Henry E. Hale, "Regime Cycles: Democracy, Autocracy, and Revolution in Post-Soviet Eurasia," *World Politics* 58:1 (October 2005), 133–165. Also see Michael Bratton and Nicolas Van De Walle, "Popular Protest and Political Reform in Africa," *Comparative Politics* 24:4 (July 1992), 419–422; and Van de Walle, "Meet the New Boss." A more nuanced analysis of economic influences on electoral outcomes is provided by Beatriz Magaloni, who, in her study of the decline and then departure

Corruption, of course, is a pervasive problem in most mixed regimes. For example, in 2002 – that is, on the eve of the Rose and Orange Revolutions – 84 out of 102 countries in the world ranked above Georgia and Ukraine, respectively, on Transparency International's Corruption Perception Index.[16]

We can now close this discussion of structural and institutional influences on electoral outcomes by shifting our focus from largely domestic sources of regime capacity to international influences. Here, we would suggest that a key issue is whether the United States supports the regime, and whether the country in question has received substantial democracy assistance from the United States, the European Union, and private foundations located in the West. One can argue that more vulnerable regimes are those that are not supported by the United States and that have been under long-term pressure to democratize by the international community. Such pressure, for example, does not just provide support for oppositions and civil society groups; it also signals to a variety of domestic audiences, including supporters as well as opponents of the regime, that major international actors place a premium on democratic progress. This leads to high expectations about the assistance the international community will provide not just before and during confrontations between the regime and its opponents, but also in the event that opponents of the regime actually win power and begin introducing new policies. These signals, however, are often muddy, and they are very easy for oppositions and their local allies to misread. This is because major powers and their foreign aid bureaucracies operate on the basis of competing and ever-changing policy priorities. As we will discover in Chapter 7, it was only after the 2005 elections that the opposition in Azerbaijan finally realized that the United States was not a strong or consistent ally.

In addition, international assistance, whether in the area of democratic or economic development, can work against the improvements it seeks by buttressing authoritarian regimes through the transfer of resources, solidifying ties between the regime and groups dependent on it, and enhancing the regime's claim that it is obviously "open."[17] Moreover, such support does not necessarily translate into the vibrant civil society that is understood to support

---

of the PRI in Mexico, assesses long-term and shorter-term consequences of economic performance; the distribution of benefits to supporters and opponents after elections; and the role of various economic logics, including evaluations of personal economic situations versus those focusing on the overall health of the economy. See Beatriz Magaloni, *Voting for Autocracy: Hegemonic Party Survival and Its Demise in Mexico* (Cambridge: Cambridge University Press, 2006).

[16] As reported in Transparency International, *Corruptions Perceptions Index 2002*, at http://www.transparency.org/policy_research/surveys_indices/cpi/2002. Accessed February 22, 2010.

[17] On the politics of foreign aid after the Cold War, see Stephen Knack, "Does Foreign Aid Promote Democracy?," *International Studies Quarterly* 48:1 (2004), 251–266; and Clark C. Gibson and Barak D. Hoffman, "Can Foreign Aid Help Produce Democracy? A Political Concessions Model of Africa's Transition Period," unpublished manuscript, University of California, San Diego, 2007.

democratic change. Sarah Henderson's observation about the Russian case is applicable throughout much of the postcommunist world:

> ... foreign aid designed to facilitate the growth of civil society has inadvertently had the opposite effect. Rather than fostering horizontal networks, small grassroots initiatives, and ultimately, civil development, foreign aid contributes to the emergence of a vertical, institutionalized, and isolated (though well-funded) civil community.[18]

At the same time, U.S. pressures on regimes can produce a rally-around-the-flag phenomenon, as we saw in Serbia immediately following the NATO bombing campaign in 1999. While Milošević's support eventually fell, his popularity in the wake of Western military action proved to be very frustrating to the Serbian opposition. More generally, authoritarian regimes have often mobilized domestic support by arguing that less dramatic forms of international intervention in their domestic politics, such as the provision of democracy and development assistance, violate state sovereignty. This is a claim, for example, that Chinese, Russian, and (since June 2009) Iranian political leaders have repeatedly made in order to justify their use of authoritarian methods at home, including crackdowns on protesters and civil society groups. It is also an argument that they conveniently forget when they try to influence the politics of other states by, for example, exporting Confucian Institutes (as in the case of China), controlling their energy sectors (as Russia does in the case of Armenia), and buying up their media (as with Russia in the case of Kyrgyzstan).[19]

IT'S THE ELECTIONS, STUPID

These predictions about regime durability as a result of the institutional design and their structural assets and deficits, however, overlook a critical consideration. Although weak regimes are by definition more politically vulnerable than stronger regimes, even quite weak regimes have been able to endure, even in the face of long-term economic decline and protracted protests.[20] The durability of even very unpopular regimes is not terribly surprising – for several reasons. First, just as strong international support for weak regimes

---

[18] Sarah L. Henderson, "Selling Civil Society: Western Aid and the Non-Governmental Organization Sector In Russia," *Comparative Political Studies* 35:2 (March 2002), 140.

[19] Valerie Bunce and Karrie Koesel, "Dictatorships in Collaboration: Russian and Chinese Efforts to Stop Democratic Change," paper presented at the Midwest Political Science Association meeting, Chicago, April 22–24, 2010; and *The Backlash against Democracy Assistance: A Report Prepared by the National Endowment for Democracy for Senator Richard G. Lugar, Chairman, Committee on Foreign Relations, United State Senate*, June 8, 2006, www.ned. org/docs/backlash06.pdf.

[20] It was precisely this dual defection that sealed the fate of Haile Selassie – see Kapuściński, *The Emperor*. On the latter point, see Adam Przeworski, "The Man of Iron and the Men of Power in Poland," *Political Science*, 15:1 (Winter 1982), 15–31.

can prolong them, as can continued support by the military and the police (as was the case for most of the Central and Eastern European members of the Soviet bloc during the communist era), so the absence of a realistic political alternative to the regime can have a similar effect.[21] This is one reason why the rise of Solidarity in Poland in 1980 had such powerful effects, not just in that country, but throughout the Soviet bloc. Solidarity represented a clear alternative to the Polish United Workers Party, and a year and a half later martial, but not "party," law was declared (in part because a substantial portion of the Communist Party membership had joined Solidarity), thereby clearly testifying to how much that movement had accumulated power and how successful it had been in identifying a viable successor to the status quo. In addition, Solidarity did not disappear with the jailing of its leaders, but rather remained on the Polish scene until communism departed nine years later. During that period, moreover, new opposition groups formed that invented new repertoires of protest – for example, the Orange Alternative, which influenced, at least in name, the Orange Revolution that took place in neighboring Ukraine twenty years later.[22] The key insight here is that citizens can reject their regime, but they are much more likely to act on these feelings if they are able to imagine a new regime on the horizon.

Even in regimes that seem to be vulnerable, moreover, oppositions still have a hard time predicting how citizens will react to a sudden expansion in opportunities for political change. This even seems to be the case, for example, when regimes try to steal elections. As Tea Tutberidze, a member of the Liberty Institute in Georgia and an activist in the demonstrations that broke out following the 2003 Georgian elections, confessed in our interview with her: "Georgian society took us by surprise."[23] Elections in Georgia, after all, had never met the standard of being free and fair, yet Georgian citizens, while sometimes mounting political protests, had rarely done so in response to fraudulent elections. The same degree of uncertainty about what citizens would do in response to electoral fraud, moreover, was voiced by a number of opposition group respondents in the interviews we conducted in Serbia in April 2005.

The important distinction between weakened regimes and regimes that actually fall leads to a second set of hypotheses that focus not on structural, institutional, and other factors predating the elections, but rather on characteristics of the elections themselves. Here, we build on four arguments presented in Chapter 1 that link elections to democratic development. One is that elections have often served as key contributors to democratic progress;

[21] Przeworski, "The Man of Iron and the Men of Power in Poland."

[22] Padraic Kenney, *A Carnival of Revolution: Central Europe, 1989* (Princeton, NJ: Princeton University Press, 2003).

[23] Interview in Tbilisi, Georgia, October 13, 2005. Also see Marshall Ganz, "Why David Sometimes Wins: Strategic Capacity in Social Movements," in *The Psychology of Leadership: New Perspectives and Research*, ed. David M. Messick and Roderick M. Kramer (Mahwah, NJ: Lawrence Erlbaum Associates, 2004).

another is that elections, rather than, say, civil liberties, are understood by citizens in countries outside the West as the defining feature of democracy; and a third is that turnover in leadership and governing coalitions (that is, leadership change that does not come about as a result of passing the baton, because of the death of the leader or term limits, to an ally) is consistently associated in competitive authoritarian regimes with subsequent democratic progress. Finally, a number of studies have argued in concert that elections feature conditions unusually conducive to the outbreak of political protests.[24] The question then becomes: why would some elections in competitive authoritarian regimes function as agents of political change?

One distinction we can draw is between national elections that place the incumbent or an anointed successor on the ballot versus elections that do not (as in parliamentary elections held in presidential systems). In the former instance, it is much easier for the election to become a verdict on the regime and for oppositions to focus their efforts. Henry Hale has provided another helpful distinction among elections. He has argued that elections vary in the extent to which they are able to promise continuity in patronage opportunities. Thus, elections are more likely to lead to an opposition victory when there is a designated successor running for office (as opposed to an incumbent) or when a president in the context of parliamentary elections is – as, for example, was the case of both Akaev in Kyrgyzstan in 2005 and Shevardnadze in Georgia in 2003 – a lame duck who is rapidly approaching the end of his tenure.

The electoral factor that has received the most attention, however, is the unity of the opposition. As Nicholas van de Walle has observed, "Opposition cohesion is often described as a prerequisite for successful regime transitions. As long as the incumbent strongman is able to keep the opposition divided, it is argued, his hold on power is safe."[25] While there is strong support for

---

[24] See, for example, Staffan Lindberg, *Democracy and Elections in Africa* (Baltimore: Johns Hopkins University Press, 2006); Andreas Schedler, "The Contingent Power of Elections," in *Democratization by Elections – A New Mode of Transition?*, ed. Staffan Lindberg (Baltimore: Johns Hopkins University Press, 2009), 179–201; Jan Teorell and Axel Hadenius, "Elections as Levers of Democracy? A Global Inquiry," in *Democratization by Elections – A New Mode of Transition?*, ed. Staffan Lindberg (Baltimore: Johns Hopkins University Press, 2009), 77–100; Valerie Bunce, "Sequencing Political and Economic Reforms," in *East-Central European Economies in Transition*, ed. John Hardt and Richard Kaufman (Washington, DC: Joint Economic Committee, Congress of the United States, 1994), 46–63; Valerie Bunce, "Global Patterns and Postcommunist Dynamics," *Orbis* 50:4 (Fall 2006), 601–620; Russell Dalton, Doh Shin, and Willy Jou, *Popular Conceptions of the Meaning of Democracy: Democratic Understandings in Unlikely Places*, Center for the Study of Democracy (May 18, 2007), http://escholarship.org/uc/item/2j74b860; Tucker, "Enough! Electoral Fraud and Collective Action Problems in Post-Communist Colored Revolutions"; Guillermo Trejo, "The Political Foundations of Ethnic Mobilization and Territorial Conflict in Mexico, 1975–2000," in *Federalism and Territorial Cleavages*, ed. Ugo Amoretti and Nancy Bermeo (Baltimore: Johns Hopkins University Press, 2004), 355–386; and Levitsky and Way, *Competitive Authoritarianism*, 32.

[25] Nicolas van de Walle, "Tipping Games: When Do Opposition Parties Coalesce?," in *Electoral Authoritarianism: The Dynamics of Unfree Competition*, ed. Andreas Schedler (Boulder,

this argument in quantitative studies of competitive authoritarian regimes, there are rival interpretations, given endogeneity problems, of what is actually driving the relationship. Thus, as van de Walle has suggested, when regimes weaken, opportunities for defeating them improve, and oppositions, as a result, have greater incentives to collaborate with each other.[26] Rather than standing alone as a causal agent, in short, this factor seems to lead us back to many of the indicators of regime strength that we discussed earlier in this chapter.

We can now close our discussion of electoral factors by drawing four more distinctions. One is the contrast between fair and fraudulent elections. The latter are understood, because of their advantages for surmounting constraints on collective action, to be unusually conducive to popular mobilization against the regime.[27] Second, the more engaged the international community is with the quality of democracy and the quality of elections, the greater the likelihood that the democratic opposition will win.[28] The critical insight here is that such attention – and the money that usually goes along with it – carries a clear signal to both the regime and opposition groups that important international actors are defining the election as a test of the regime, and that they are likely to impose limits on the lengths to which regimes can go in order to insure victory. Such limits can include large-scale international election-monitoring missions, which can expose fraud as it is happening and, less obviously,

CO: Lynne Rienner Publishers, 2006), 77; Marc Morjé Howard and Philip G. Roessler, "Liberalizing Electoral Outcomes in Competitive Authoritarian Regimes," *American Journal of Political Science* 50:2 (April 2006), 365–381.

[26] See, especially, Nicolas Van de Walle, "Tipping Games" and "Meet the New Boss." In addition, see Vladimir Gelman, "Political Opposition in Russia: A Dying Species?," *Post-Soviet Affairs* 21:3 (July–September 2005), 226–246; and Karen Dawisha and Stephen Deets, "Political Learning in Post-Communist Elections," *East European Politics and Societies* 20:4 (November 2006), 691–728. In our interviews, however, this line of argument was in fact repeatedly challenged, as we will discuss later in this book – for example, by Isa Gambar, chairman of the Musavat Party, and Fuad Mustafayev, chairman of the National Movement Party in Azerbaijan (interviews in Baku, March 7, 2007). Just as they believed that unity could reduce their ability to win power because it would encourage more extreme actions on the part of the regime to undermine the opposition and go to greater lengths to steal the election, so they argued that a more vulnerable regime can tempt oppositions to go it alone in order to monopolize the benefits from winning office.

[27] Mark Thompson and Philipp Kuntz, "Stolen Elections: The Case of the Serbian October," *Journal of Democracy* 15:4 (October 2004), 159–172; Thompson and Kuntz, "More than Just the Final Straw," 253–272; Mark Thompson, *The Anti-Marcos Struggle: Personalistic Rule and Democratic Transition in the Philippines* (New Haven, CT: Yale University Press, 1995); and Tucker, "Enough! Electoral Fraud, Collective Action Problems, and Post-Communist Colored Revolutions." However, Frederic Charles Schaffer has offered a new perspective on this question. See Frederic Charles Schaffer, *The Hidden Costs of Clean Election Reform* (Ithaca, NY: Cornell University Press, 2008).

[28] See Valerie Bunce and Sharon L. Wolchik, "Favorable Conditions and Electoral Revolutions," *Journal of Democracy* 17:4 (October 2006), 5–18; and Steven E. Finkel, Anibel S. Pérez-Liñán, and Mitchell A. Seligson, "The Effects of U.S. Foreign Assistance on Democracy-Building, 1990 to 2003," *World Politics* 59:3 (April 2007), 404–439.

encourage citizens to vote in larger numbers and use their ballots to express their true preferences.[29] Third, we would expect elections that feature charismatic opposition leaders to be more likely to lead to leadership turnover.

ELECTORAL STRATEGIES

A final aspect of elections that might account for variations in their results is differences in the strategies that oppositions use to win power. In established democracies, explanations of who wins and who loses often rest on comparisons of the quality of the campaign each candidate runs. One would expect electoral strategies to play an even more important role in mixed regimes. As Larry Diamond reminds us: "While an opposition victory is not impossible in a hybrid regime, it requires a level of opposition mobilization, unity, skill, and heroism far beyond what would normally be required for victory in a democracy."[30]

What kinds of strategies would seem to be the most likely to yield payoffs for the opposition? Most obviously, the formation of an electoral bloc would have the advantages of concentrating voter choices and signaling to citizens that the opposition has a strong commitment to winning and the capacity to govern effectively. These are not trivial achievements. Oppositions lose elections in mixed regimes in part because citizens have grown very cynical about an opposition that has a long history of internal divisions, corruption, and showing little interest in the issues that are of particular concern to the electorate.

Other electoral strategies that would seem to maximize opportunities for an opposition victory include, for example, the establishment of close ties between opposition parties and civil society groups; significant pressures placed on the regime by local and international actors to reform electoral procedures; and ambitious campaigns mounted by the opposition and their allies to win popular support, register voters, and get out the vote. Finally, oppositions are more likely to be victorious when they have the technical know-how and the resources to carry out public opinion polls, election monitoring, exit polls, and parallel vote tabulation.[31]

We hypothesize, therefore, that oppositions are more likely to win office when they mount sophisticated and energetic electoral campaigns. It is precisely this argument that has been used to explain why and how opposition parties and their allies managed to defeat the referendum in Chile that was

[29] See, especially, Susan D. Hyde, "The Observer Effect in International Politics: Evidence from a Natural Experiment," *World Politics* 60:1 (2007), 37–63.

[30] Diamond, "Thinking about Hybrid Regimes," 24.

[31] Hyde, "The Observer Effect in International Politics"; Larry Garber and Glenn Cowan, "The Virtues of Parallel Vote Tabulations," *Journal of Democracy* 4:2 (April 1993), 95–107; and Eric Bjornlund, *Beyond Free and Fair: Monitoring Elections and Building Democracy* (Washington, DC: Woodrow Wilson Center Press, 2004). Interview with Larry Garber, April 9, 2010.

proposed by the Pinochet regime in 1988 and to defeat as well authoritarian leaders in the presidential elections that were held in the Philippines in 1986, Panama in 1989, and Nicaragua in 1990.[32] In all of these cases, the outcome of the election (and the referendum) took regimes, oppositions, citizens – and, for that matter, the United States – by surprise. Moreover, in all four cases creative and hard-fought electoral struggles paved the way for transitions from dictatorship to democracy.

Is it merely tautological, however, to hypothesize that oppositions win when they make a significant effort to win? At the very least, could we not argue, to echo our earlier discussion, that the causal factor in play here is the vulnerability of the regime? The logic here is that oppositions would be more willing and able to run ambitious campaigns if they thought their chances of winning power were relatively good.

This interpretation could certainly be correct – and it is one that we will be evaluating throughout this book. However, there are some good reasons to take seriously the hypothesis that differences in opposition strategies explain differences in electoral outcomes. First, we in fact know very little about the role of electoral campaigns in mixed regimes. Just as structural accounts of electoral stability and change in mixed regimes pay little heed to the issue of electoral efforts, so studies that focus more on the relationship between electoral dynamics and electoral outcomes pay little attention to the kinds of strategies we have just outlined.[33] Thus, it remains an open question whether such efforts make a difference. Second, regime strength is very hard to read, especially in mixed regimes. As a result, it might not make sense to assume that opposition leaders will calibrate their campaign strategies in accordance with their readings of their electoral prospects. These predictions are all the more difficult to make and to link with campaign strategies given some other considerations. One is that in many mixed regimes, winning an election is one thing and being allowed to take office another. Moreover, the electoral strategies we have outlined are demanding and, in repressive political contexts, dangerous. They can also be very expensive – a consideration that returns us to our earlier

[32] See, for example, Ackerman and Duvall, *A Force More Powerful*, Chapters 7, 10; Garber and Cowan, "The Virtues of Parallel Vote Tabulations"; Mary Racelis, "New Visions and Strong Actions: Civil Society in the Philippines," in *Civil Society Aid and Democracy Promotion*, ed. Marina Ottaway and Thomas Carothers, (Washington, DC: Carnegie Endowment, 2000), 159–190; Mark Thompson, *The Anti-Marcos Struggle*; Brownlee, *Authoritarianism in an Age of Democratization*, Chapter 3; Bjornlund, *Beyond Free and Fair*; David Altman, Sergio Toro, and Rafael Piñeiro, *International Influences on Democratic Transitions: The Successful Case of Chile*, CDDRL Working Paper No. 86, Center for Democracy, Development and the Rule of Law, Freeman Spogli Institute for International Studies, Stanford University (July 2008); interviews with Patrick Merloe, Washington, DC, April 30, 2009; Scott Carpenter, Washington, DC, April 9, 2009; Harry Barnes, Philadelphia, February 24, 2007; and Larry Garber, Washington, DC, April 9, 2010.

[33] Teorell and Hadenius, "Elections as Levers of Democracy"; Grigore Pop-Eleches and Graeme Robertson, "Elections and Liberalization in the Postcommunist World," unpublished manuscript, Princeton University and University of North Carolina, September 2009.

discussion of international democracy assistance.[34] Finally, if we assume (as many do) that ambitious electoral efforts have political payoffs, then why do oppositions so rarely mount them? We have already suggested several reasons. They are expensive and dangerous; they are very time-consuming; and they require a great deal of technical expertise. Here, we must remember that these kinds of campaigns, while familiar to Western audiences, are unprecedented in the postcommunist region. When combined, these considerations suggest that oppositions would be willing and able to run ambitious campaigns only under quite specific and therefore unusual circumstances.

INTERNATIONAL DIFFUSION

Thus far, we have mentioned several kinds of contexts that might encourage oppositions to run sophisticated campaigns. For example, because some mixed regimes are more democratic than others, they provide more opportunities for oppositions to be independent, active, and innovative. However, the financial and technical burdens imposed by implementation of these strategies, in combination with the enormously appealing precedents set for oppositions in mixed regimes by the political upsets that took place in the Philippines, Chile, Panama, and Nicaragua from 1986 to 1990, suggest a very different line of argument. To what extent did these new and ambitious strategies for winning power *diffuse* from Latin America and Southeast Asia to the postcommunist region and, within the postcommunist region, from Eastern and Central Europe to the Soviet successor states?[35]

The cross-national and cross-regional diffusion of innovative electoral techniques would seem to explain, among other things, the unusual pattern of these electoral breakthroughs – that is, the fact that so many electoral turnovers took place in so many mixed regimes in the postcommunist region within such

[34] See, especially, Thomas Carothers, *Critical Missions: Essays on Democracy Promotion* (Washington, DC: Carnegie Endowment, 2004); and Thomas Carothers, *Revitalizing Democracy Assistance: The Challenge of USAID*, Carnegie Report, Carnegie Endowment for International Peace (2009).

[35] On diffusion and its drivers, see, for example, Doug McAdam and Dieter Rucht, "Cross-National Diffusion of Movement Ideas: The American 'New Left' and the European New Social Movements," *The Annals of the American Academy of Political and Social Sciences* 528:1 (July 1993), 56–74; David Strang and Sarah Soule, "Diffusion in Organizations and Social Movements: From Hybrid Corn to Poison Pills," *Annual Review of Sociology* 24 (August 1998), 265–290; Chang Kil Lee and David Strang, "The International Diffusion of Public-Sector Downsizing: Network Emulation and Theory-Driven Learning," *International Organization* 60:4 (October 2006), 883–909; Mark Beissinger, *Nationalist Mobilization and the Collapse of the Soviet State* (Cambridge: Cambridge University Press, 2002); Daniel Brinks and Michael Coppedge, "Diffusion Is No Illusion: Neighbor Emulation in the Third Wave of Democracy," *Comparative Political Studies* 39:4 (May 2006), 463–489; Mario Diani and Doug McAdam, eds., *Social Movements and Networks: Relational Approaches to Collective Action* (Oxford: Oxford University Press, 2003); Johanna Bockman and Gil Eyal, "Eastern Europe as a Laboratory for Economic Knowledge: The Transnational Roots of Neoliberalism," *The American Journal of Sociology* 108:2 (September 2002), 310–352.

a short span of time. This interpretation is all the more compelling because most of the electoral breakthroughs took place in countries with shared borders. In addition, this region has long functioned as an antechamber for the cross-national spread of popular protests.[36] Finally, oppositions in this part of the world are quite inexperienced with electoral politics. It seems unlikely, therefore, that they would be in a position to devise, or implement, the elaborate strategies political parties in the West took many decades to develop.

If the hypothesis is correct that international diffusion and not the other factors we noted earlier explains our electoral breakthroughs, then what is driving the spread of these electoral techniques? Here, we can bring our discussion of competing hypotheses to a close by mentioning several possible drivers of diffusion as suggested by the literature on international diffusion. One is demonstration effects. The argument here is that appealing innovations that are adopted in one site embolden actors in other sites to press for similar kinds of changes. This was a common explanation, for example, for the spread of popular protests against communism in Eastern Europe and the Soviet Union from 1987 to 1999.[37] A second argument is that these electoral strategies spread because of the hard work and, indeed, the growth and spread of transnational democracy promotion networks.[38] Finally, innovations, such as new electoral strategies, could spread because they are modular and thus easy to transfer, or because of what sociologists term "structural isomorphism" – that is, the availability of a large number of similar and similarly receptive sites.[39]

It is important to test these competing hypotheses about the diffusion of innovative electoral strategies among mixed regimes not just because they identify the causal model involved, but also because of a broader consideration. A convincing claim about the role of international diffusion rests, among other things, on being able to pinpoint the innovation (and not just its consequences) and the mechanisms driving the cross-national spread of that innovation. In order to do this, one is required, as we have done in this study, to avoid the temptation to analyze these events from afar and thereby ignore interactions of individual actors and institutions, both domestic and international, on the ground.

---

[36] Zvi Y. Gitelman, *The Diffusion of Innovation from Eastern Europe to the Soviet Union*, Sage Professional Papers in Comparative Politics series, Vol. 3 (1972).

[37] See, especially, Beissinger, *Nationalist Mobilization.*

[38] See, especially, Bookman and Eyal, "Eastern Europe as a Laboratory."

[39] See, especially, Sidney Tarrow, *Power in Movement: Social Movements and Contentious Politics*, 2nd ed. (Cambridge: Cambridge University Press, 1998), 38ff.; Mark Beissinger, "Structure and Example in Modular Political Phenomena: The Diffusion of Bulldozer/ Rose/Orange/Tulip Revolutions," *Perspectives on Politics* 5:2 (June 2007), 259–276; Sada Aksartova, "Civil Society Promotion or Global Organizational Diffusion? U.S. Civil Society Assistance for the FSU," paper presented at the annual meeting of the Eastern Sociological Society, Washington, DC, May 17–20, 2005; and Sada Aksartova, "Civil Society from Abroad: U.S. Donors in the Former Soviet Union" (Ph.D. dissertation, Department of Sociology, Princeton University, 2005).

CONCLUSIONS

The purpose of this chapter has been to identify factors that could account for electoral continuity and turnover in regimes that combine authoritarian politics with competition for political office. We have explored three sets of hypotheses, each of which proceeded from different core assumptions about what drives political change. While the first group focuses on the electoral effects of institutional factors and long-term political and economic trends, the second group highlights the impact of shorter-term influences that are associated with the elections themselves. Finally, we developed a series of hypotheses that were based on the argument that the cross-national diffusion of innovative electoral strategies explains why some oppositions in the region were successful in winning power, whereas others were not.

In the next two parts of the book, we test these hypotheses. Thus, in Part II, we provide "raw data" in the form of case studies of each of our elections and the regimes in which they took place. In Part III, we combine our cases and follow up the core distinction drawn in this chapter by analyzing our group of eleven elections as separate events and then as developments that were linked to one another through the process of cross-national diffusion.

PART II

CASE STUDIES

3

The 1998 Elections in Slovakia and the 2000 Elections in Croatia

The Model Solidifies and Is Transferred

I Vote, Therefore I Am

Civic Campaign poster, Slovakia, 1998

I want to live in a normal country.

Croatia, 2000

This chapter and the four that follow set the empirical stage for analyzing why elections in mixed regimes in postcommunist Europe and Eurasia have had such different effects. In this chapter we focus on the 1998 elections in Slovakia and the 2000 elections in Croatia, which were the beginning of the wave of electoral turnovers in the postcommunist world. In contrast to the cases we analyze in later chapters in this section, these elections were largely free and fair, and electoral mobilization was sufficient, as a result, to bring about a transition from semi-authoritarian rule to rule by the democratic opposition. We devote particular attention to the Slovak case, as it was in Slovakia that the set of innovative electoral strategies, tactics, and tools – which we have termed the *electoral model* of regime change – was first elaborated fully in the postcommunist world. Once these proved successful, the Slovak case was quite influential in the electoral confrontations that followed the Slovak precedent – not just in Croatia in 1999–2000, but also in Serbia, Georgia, Ukraine, Kyrgyzstan, and even in Armenia, Azerbaijan, and Belarus. Because elements of the strategies and tactics that proved successful in Slovakia and later in Croatia were present in the 1996 elections in Romania, and because the protests and elections in Bulgaria in 1996–97 had a large influence on the strategies and tactics later elaborated in Slovakia, we begin this chapter with a discussion of those events.

Key findings that this chapter illustrates include a) the importance of unity of the opposition and the difficulty of achieving it; b) the realization on the part of NGO leaders that they could retain their nonpartisan orientation and still be active in political life; c) the value of cooperation between the opposition and civil society organizations in inspiring citizens and getting out the vote; d) the significance of both optimism and planning in mobilizing citizens; and e) the utility of using sophisticated electoral strategies and tactics. These two cases also highlight the important role played by outside actors and document the beginning of the transnational coalition of outside actors that was to be active in subsequent cases.

EARLY PRECEDENTS: ROMANIA AND BULGARIA

The elections in Romania in 1996 and the protests and elections in Bulgaria in 1996 and 1997 occurred in countries that according to Freedom House had relatively stable political rankings over the course of the first half of the 1990s and, in the case of Bulgaria, a poorly functioning but fully democratic state. We include discussion of these events because, along with the 1990 election in Bulgaria, they provided examples and techniques that were important to the transfer of what we have termed the electoral model to Slovakia, where it was first fully elaborated in the postcommunist region.[1]

The 1996 elections in Romania represented the first real break at the national level with the communist past. After the ouster and execution of Nicolae Ceauşescu in 1989, a group of second-rank Communist Party leaders formed a coalition and won the first competitive presidential election. Thus, although the Communist Party was outlawed, in fact former communists remained in power. Marginalized by Iliescu's Party of Social Democracy (PDRS), the Romanian political opposition suffered from internal divisions that made it an ineffective political competitor in the 1990 and 1992 parliamentary elections. In 1996, however, this situation changed. Aided by the party-building activities of the International Republican Institute, which had openly confined its party-building and campaign techniques training sessions to the Social Democratic Union (which was less true of such activities in other countries that joined the wave of electoral change), the opposition coalition won the November 3 parliamentary elections. After this victory, leaders of the Socialist Democratic Union and the Democratic Convention agreed to support Emil Constantinescu against Iliescu in the second round of the November presidential elections. Focusing on endemic corruption, the declining standard of living, and the need for reforms to ensure the rule of law and speed privatization, the opposition also capitalized on the frustration of many citizens with the continued dominance of communist-era officials.[2] As in later democratizing elections, the victory of the Romanian opposition in national elections in 1996 was preceded by its strong showing in local elections.[3]

---

[1] We will devote more attention to the 1990 Bulgarian election in Chapters 9 and 10.

[2] See Vladimir Tismaneanu, "Electoral Revolutions," *Society*, 35:1 (November/December 1997), 61–65; and Vladimir Tismaneanu and Gail Kligman, "Romania's First Postcommunist Decade: From Iliescu to Iliescu," *East European Constitutional Review* 10:1 (Winter 2001), 76–96.

[3] Tismaneanu, "Electoral Revolutions," 63; Michael Shafir, "Romania's Road to 'Normalcy,'" *Journal of Democracy* 8:2 (April 1997), 144.

The opposition's victory has been explained by some as an election that was "not so much won by the opposition parties with skillful campaigning or attractive candidates as lost by the ruling party,"[4] owing particularly to the lack of economic reform. This view, which highlights the importance of the vulnerability of the regime, a factor that will also figure in some of our subsequent analyses, is consistent with the interpretation of the victory of the opposition in 1996 as in part a protest vote.[5]

However, the success of the opposition in attracting support in 1996 also reflected other factors whose importance will be evident in the four chapters that follow: the active support of part of the NGO community, increased participation by young people, and a growing popular desire for fundamental change. As in many other postcommunist countries, the NGO sector grew very rapidly in Romania after the end of communism.[6] Most of these organizations focused on providing social services or meeting local needs, and most of the NGOs that engaged in advocacy were supported by outside donors such as the United States Agency for International Development (USAID). As the 1996 elections approached, civic advocacy groups formed their own coalitions. One of the best known of these, the Pro-Democracy Association, which was supported by and whose activists were trained by the National Democratic Institute (NDI), provided numerous volunteers to monitor elections and also organized training for members of parliament. Using its thirty-five offices throughout the country, it organized an "If You Don't Vote, You Can't Complain" campaign to encourage citizens to vote. The association also developed voter education materials and a handbook for election monitors, worked with the media, and trained 5,000 election monitors. Other NGOs, including Lado and the Foundation for Pluralism, engaged in similar activities.[7] Several NGOs, including the Civic Alliance and the Association of Former Political Detainees of Romania, joined the opposition CDR coalition. Such organizations and activities, it is important to recognize, were virtually absent from earlier elections in Romania. In this sense, the 1996 election was unique not only in its outcome, but also in the strategies the opposition and civil society groups deployed.

Compared to the highly organized, focused, and innovative campaigns the civic sector organized in Slovakia in 1998 and the other democratizing elections we will examine, the campaign to mobilize citizens to vote in Romania was rather low-key. Voter turnout was considerably higher than in the local elections in 1996, although at 76 percent for the parliamentary elections and 75.9 percent for the presidential elections, it was not significantly greater

---

4 Thomas Carothers, *Aiding Democracy Abroad: The Learning Curve* (Washington, DC: Carnegie Endowment for International Peace, 1999), 325.
5 Tismaneanu, "Electoral Revolutions," 62.
6 International IDEA, *Democracy in Romania: Assessment Mission Report* (Stockholm: International IDEA, 1997), 88.
7 Dan Petrescu, *Report: World Bank NGO Stock-Taking in Romania*, World Bank Resident Mission in Romania Report (November 9, 1998), 3.

than in comparable elections in 1990 and 1992.[8] However, together with the regime's mistakes, the unity of the political opposition, and the growing desire of the population for change, support by the NGO community and especially the votes of younger, better-educated citizens helped put the opposition over the top. The realization on the part of civil society activists that they could be political without being partisan was critical for the successful defeat of the former communists. This revelation, in turn, had an important influence on Slovak NGO activists when they began thinking about the upcoming 1998 parliamentary election and when they met with their Romanian and Bulgarian counterparts at the Vienna airport in November 1997.

Activities by the NGO sector were also critical in Bulgaria in 1996 and 1997, where mass protests by trade unions, students, NGOs, and the center right opposition succeeded in defeating the socialist candidate for president in November 1996 and bringing about early parliamentary elections, which the opposition won, in 1997. As a result, Bulgaria, which had made significant progress in democratization but had lagged in moving to the market, espousing instead a "third way," turned decisively toward economic reform and integration into Europe.[9]

As in Romania, there was no clear break with the communist past following the formal end of communism in Bulgaria. Instead, the former communists, renamed the Bulgarian Socialist Party (BSP), won the June 1990 parliamentary elections. These elections were important for later electoral challenges in the region because they saw the first introduction to the post-communist region of elements of what would eventually coalesce as the electoral model. As part of the efforts of the international democracy promotion community – in particular, the International Republican Institute, Freedom House, and the National Democratic Institute – to ensure free and fair elections, NDI brought leaders of the successful campaign to defeat Ferdinand Marcos in the Philippines in 1986, the National Citizens' Movement for Free Elections (NAMFREL), to Bulgaria to consult with the Bulgarian opposition. The idea here, as it was in similar efforts in Chile in 1988, was to use NAMFREL as a "learning delegation" that would enhance the effectiveness of civil society and opposition parties in Bulgaria.[10] USAID provided support for

[8] Shafir, "Romania's Road to 'Normalcy,'" 149.
[9] Tsvetlana Petrova, "A Postcommunist Transition in Two Acts: The 1996–1997 Anti-Government Struggle in Bulgaria as a Bridge between the First and Second Waves of Transition in Eastern Europe," in *Democracy and Authoritarianism in the Postcommunist World*, ed. Valerie Bunce, Michael McFaul, and Kathryn Stoner-Weiss (Cambridge: Cambridge University Press, 2009), 107–133; Venelin I. Ganev, *Preying on the State: The Transformation of Bulgaria after 1989* (Ithaca, NY: Cornell University Press, 2007); and interviews with Avis Bohlen, Washington, DC, November 15, 2006; Scott Carpenter, Washington, DC, April 9, 2009; Ivan Krastev, Berlin, July 27, 2005; and Patrick Merloe, Washington, DC, April 30, 2009.
[10] Interviews with Scott Carpenter, Washington, DC, April 9, 2009; Patrick Merloe, Washington DC, April 30, 2009; Larry Garber, Washington, DC, April 9, 2010; and Kenneth Wollack, Washington, DC, May 12, 2010.

the first use of exit polls and parallel vote tabulation procedures in elections in the postcommunist region.[11]

Although the opposition United Democratic Front (UDF) defeated the communists in 1991, the communists once again came to control the national government as a result of the 1994 elections. In contrast to the situation in Romania in 1996 and the cases we examine in the rest of this section, the protests that led to the victory of the opposition in the April 1997 elections in Bulgaria were based more on economic issues than on lack of progress in establishing and adhering to the procedures of democratic government. Moreover, in Bulgaria protests precipitated elections rather than following them. However, the Bulgarian example had an important influence on the Slovak election in 1998.

As a result of the economic policies of the former communist government that came to power in 1994, Bulgaria experienced an acute economic crisis in 1996, including hyperinflation and the collapse of the currency. Gross national product fell by 9 percent in 1996, and average monthly salaries declined from $118 to $12.[12] Faced with the disastrous results of the left's economic policies, the unions, students, and NGOs – and, though somewhat belatedly, the opposition parties – organized a series of peaceful demonstrations.[13] As the economic crisis deepened, students, workers, and pensioners made use of unusual tactics such as occupying buildings and, drawing on a tactic used by the Polish opposition in the 1980s, staging a mock funeral for the country. They also threatened to barricade roads. Union and student association leaders organized a twenty-four-hour national strike in December that drew 953,000 participants calling for the resignation of the cabinet, early elections, and assistance to citizens who could not afford heat or food.[14] Originally reluctant to support the unions' calls for mass protest, the leaders of the opposition UDF eventually took a role in leading the protests after they were assured, in part by U.S. Ambassador Avis Bohlen, of outside support.[15]

Other external actors also played a role in the resignation of the socialist government in Bulgaria and the agreement to hold new elections in April 1997, including Western governments, foundations, and NGOs, which had been supporting the development of civil society and political parties since the end of communism. Petar Stoyanov also received assurances of support from U.S. and European leaders. The IMF, by its refusal to grant the government

[11] Interviews with Scott Carpenter, Washington, DC, April 9, 2009; and Patrick Merloe, Washington, DC, April 30, 2009.
[12] See Nikolai Vasilev, *Bitkata Za Bulgariia: Poslednoto Desetiletie Na XX Vek* (Bulgaria: Litse, 2002), as cited in Tsvetlana Petrova, "A Postcommunist Transition." See also Venelin I. Ganev, "Bulgaria's Symphony of Hope, " *Journal of Democracy* 8:4 (October 1997), 125–139.
[13] Avis Bohlen saw the opposition as slow to participate in these protests; Scott Carpenter saw them as engaged from the beginning.
[14] See Petrova, "A Postcommunist Transition," 15, 20, for these and other examples.
[15] Interview with Avis Bohlen, Washington, DC, November 15, 2006.

a stabilization loan in November 1996 and its announcement in early 1997 that it would negotiate only with a stable government, further undermined the legitimacy of socialist rule and thereby aided the opposition.[16]

NGO activists in both of these countries used some of the techniques, such as street theater, that had been used in the communist period in Poland and later in Yugoslavia.[17] They also used techniques that were new to the region and would prove decisive in later contests. Two of the most important of these were vote-monitoring regimes and parallel vote tabulation – techniques that first came to the region in the Bulgarian election of 1990 as the National Democratic Institute from the U.S. brought techniques used in the electoral experiences of both Latin America and the Philippines in the 1980s to the region. A second critical element of these electoral confrontations and protests was the fact that civil society groups, which had generally eschewed "political" activity in the postcommunist world, were active participants. Although their activities were only loosely coordinated, and their reach (apart from the unions in Bulgaria) more or less limited to the capitals and large urban areas, their leaders and members were important actors in the campaigns that brought about change.

A third feature of these developments that provided an important example for activists in the region was the involvement of youth, although, unlike the case of Slovakia and many of the other cases we will examine, no nationwide organization of young people or campaign directed at them emerged in either country.[18] In Bulgaria, student leaders were inspired by the three-month-long protests from late 1996 to early 1997 against Milošević's attempt to steal local elections in Serbia. Several visited Belgrade and then used some of the same tactics, such as street theater, marches, and humor, that had been deployed by student protesters there.[19] Student leaders, along with union leaders, also played a key role in asking U.S. democracy promotion organizations for assistance in the 1990 elections.[20]

[16] Petrova, "A Postcommunist Transition." See Ronald H. Linden, *Norms and Nannies: The Impact of International Organizations on the Central and East European States* (Lanham, MD: Rowman & Littlefield Publishers, 2002); and Milada Anna Vachudova, *Europe Undivided: Democracy, Leverage, and Integration after Communism* (Oxford: Oxford University Press, 2005).

[17] Padraic Kenney, *A Carnival of Revolution: Central Europe, 1989* (Princeton, NJ: Princeton University Press, 2003); Valerie J. Bunce and Sharon L. Wolchik, "A Regional Tradition: The Diffusion of Democratic Change under Communism and Postcommunism," in *Democracy and Authoritarianism in the Postcommunist World*, ed. Valerie Bunce, Michael McFaul, and Kathryn Stoner-Weiss (Cambridge: Cambridge University Press, 2009), 30–58.

[18] Shafir, "Romania's Road to 'Normalcy,'" 149.

[19] Petrova, "A Postcommunist Transition," 22; Evgenii Dainov, Mihail Nedelchev, Teodora Gandova, Svetlana Lomeva, Maria Bakalova, Mira Yanova, and Zornitsa Velchev, *The Awakening: A Chronicle of the Bulgarian Civic Uprising of January–February 1997* (Sofia: Democracy Network Program, 1998).

[20] Interviews with Larry Garber, Washington DC, April 9, 2010; and Patrick Merloe, Washington, DC, April 30, 2009.

Finally, in both of these cases, participants in the international democracy assistance community played an important role. This role was particularly evident in Romania, where IRI activists openly supported the opposition on the grounds that the regime did not need its assistance, an orientation that led the U.S. ambassador to request their departure in March 1996.[21] In Bulgaria, the U.S. ambassador's assurance of Western support was a factor in the opposition's decision to take leadership of the protests, and U.S. and other Western actors provided long-term support for the development of civil society organizations. Change in these governments was not a high priority for the U.S. or most European governments.[22] Outside democracy promoters were also less active (especially in Romania) than they would be in other countries in this study. However, it is in these cases that many of the actors and institutions, as well as some of the strategies and techniques, that will become important once the electoral model is fully articulated, arrive on the scene.

SLOVAKIA AND CROATIA ON THE EVE: THE CONTEXT

Slovakia under Vladimír Mečiar and Croatia immediately after Franjo Tudjman's death shared a number of characteristics. Both were new states created from federations that, although differing radically in the amount of power they allowed their lower units, failed to satisfy their constituent parts. Citizens in both countries had therefore had significant conflicts with a larger ethnic group that they perceived to have dominated their fortunes during much of the interwar and communist periods. In Croatia, these struggles were complicated in major and tragic ways by the wars and ethnic cleansing that accompanied the breakup of Yugoslavia.

As a result, the transition from communism and a planned economy to democracy and the market was complicated significantly in both countries by issues related to the nature and boundaries of the nation. Given this fact, it proved easy for ambitious leaders to use the nationalist card to consolidate their power and to fracture and demobilize the political opposition. Vladimír Mečiar and Franjo Tudjman both made use of this card, although in Mečiar's case, nationalism was only part of a broader populist approach that also called for changes in economic policy.[23]

Economic issues contributed to growing disillusionment with both the Mečiar and Tudjman regimes. Although economic performance in Slovakia remained relatively robust under Mečiar's rule, the shift to the market produced major economic dislocations and a rapid decline in industrial production

[21] See Michael J. Jordan, "Iliescu's foes say US envoy meddling in Romania Vote," *Christian Science Monitor*, vol. 88, issue 223 (October 11, 1996), p. l, lc for a brief discussion of tensions between the ambassador and IRI officials.

[22] Interview with Daniel Calingaert, Washington, DC, July 19, 2005.

[23] There is a vast literature on the breakup of Czechoslovakia and Yugoslavia. See Valerie J. Bunce, *Subversive Institutions*; and Karen Henderson, "The Slovak Republic: Explaining Defects in Democracy," *Democratization* 11:5 (December 2004), 133–155.

and incomes in the early postcommunist period. Since much of Slovakia's industrialization had occurred only under communism, many of the former Czechoslovakia's largest, most inefficient enterprises, including the arms industry, were located there. Unemployment rates rose very rapidly, reaching 13.1 percent in 1995; unemployment fell somewhat in 1996, but rose to 12.5 percent in 1998.[24] By 1998, the state budget deficit had reached a record level, and net foreign debt grew significantly.[25]

In Croatia, the war and the country's international isolation under Tudjman took a predictable toll on the economy. As importantly from a political perspective, the end of the war did not spur sustained economic growth. GDP grew at 5.9 percent in 1996 and 6.8 percent in 1997, but fell precipitously to 2.5 percent in 1998 and -0.9 percent in 1999. Growth increased to 2.9 percent in 2000, but voters going to the polls in January 2000 had experienced a very difficult economic period. Similarly, unemployment, which declined from 14.5 percent in 1995 to 9.9 percent in 1997, began to increase again, reaching 13.5 percent in 1999 and 15.7 percent in 2000.[26] Prices increased dramatically, while real wages remained at the same levels as in the 1980s. As Sharon Fisher notes, economic issues were the main concern of voters on the eve of the 2000 elections.[27]

There were also important similarities in Slovakia's and Croatia's relationships to the international community. The Tudjman government faced ongoing and serious criticism from the EU, the Council of Europe, and the United States for its role in the wars with Serbia and Bosnia and its policies toward the Serb minority and returning refugees. It also came under increasing pressure to cooperate with the International Tribunal at The Hague in turning in indicted war criminals. As Dejan Jović notes, "Croatia ended the decade of the 1990s in unofficial isolation, and with no formal agreements with the EU."[28] A Croatian political scientist in an interview in 2005 put it more bluntly: "Europe didn't want to touch us and there was an

[24] World Bank Data and Statistics: Slovak Republic, http://go.worldbank.org/UZFFK6I940.
[25] See Marek Jakoby, Eugen Jurzyca, Peter Pažitný, Igor Polonec, Oľga Reptová, and Eduard Žitňanský, "The Economy of the Slovak Republic," in *Slovakia 1998–1999: A Global Report on the State of Society*, ed. Grigorij Mesežnikov, Michal Ivantyšyn, and Tom Nicholson (Bratislava: Institute for Public Affairs, 1999), 198–232; Sharon Fisher, John Gould, and Tim Haughton, "Slovakia's Neoliberal Turn," *Europe-Asia Studies* 59:6 (September 2007), 987–989.
[26] World Bank Data and Statistics: Croatia, http://go.worldbank.org/PA8DYK9N90.
[27] Sharon Fisher, *Political Change in Post-Communist Slovakia and Croatia: From Nationalist to Europeanist* (New York: Palgrave Macmillan, 2006), 99. See Alex Bellamy, "Croatia after Tudjman: The 2000 Parliamentary and Presidential Elections," *Problems of Post-Communism* 48:5 (September 2001), 20. See Siniša Kušić, "Croatia: Advancing Political and Economic Transformation," *Journal of Southeast European & Black Sea Studies* 6:1 (March 2006), 67, for a brief overview of economic policy under Tudjman.
[28] Dejan Jović, "Croatia and the European Union: A Long Delayed Journey," *Journal of Southern Europe and the Balkans* 8:1 (April 2006), 86.

overall bad mood. The changes we thought would happen after the end of the war didn't happen."[29]

Although considerably less isolated than Croatia, Slovakia under Mečiar also suffered from negative feedback from the international community, due to the regime's discriminatory policies toward the Hungarian minority and the Roma, as well as its persistent violation of the civil liberties and political rights of the opposition. In late 1997, only 13 percent of respondents felt that Slovakia was in a good position internationally; 48 percent, by way of contrast, evaluated Slovakia's international position negatively.[30] U.S. and European leaders made it increasingly clear, as U.S. Ambassador Ralph Johnson stated in July 1997 and as the NATO and EU summits in that year confirmed,[31] that Slovakia would not get into the EU or NATO as long as Mečiar was in office. They nonetheless continued to be engaged with and active in Slovakia, particularly with the NGO community, but also with the government.

The desire of leaders in both countries for membership in the EU created an additional tool that could be used by outside actors to encourage democratic development. This factor was particularly important in Slovakia, initially a candidate for the first round of enlargement of the EU and NATO, but kicked off the fast track by Mečiar's misuse of power.[32] Although many citizens in Croatia aspired to membership in these organizations, the impact of the wars and the lingering issue of cooperation with The Hague made negotiations to join the EU and NATO a more distant goal.[33]

At the same time, the political climate differed in the two cases. Although the political regime in the late communist period was much harsher in Slovakia than it had been in Croatia, there was an initial period of democratization in Slovakia immediately after the fall of communism when Public Against Violence, as the Civic Forum in the Czech Lands, won a landslide victory in the June 1990 parliamentary elections and began the process of moving to a democratic system. Vladimír Mečiar's break with Public Against Violence in April 1991 and the subsequent victory of his Movement for a Democratic Slovakia (HZDS) in the 1992 elections thus initiated a period of de-democratization.[34] In Croatia, Tudjman quickly emerged as the dominant figure in the context of the breakup of Yugoslavia, eclipsing the democratically oriented intellectuals who resurrected old political parties or began new ones in the early 1990s and

[29] Interview with Ivan Grdešić, Zagreb, May 21, 2005.
[30] Zora Bútorová and Martin Bútora, "Slovensko a svet," in *Slovensko pred voľbami. Ľudia – názory – súvislosti*, ed. Zora Bútorová (Bratislava: IVO, 1998), 82–97.
[31] Geoffrey Pridham, "Complying with the European Union's Democratic Conditionality: Transnational Party Linkages and Regime Change in Slovakia, 1993–1998," *Europe-Asia Studies* 51:7 (November 1999), 1221–1244.
[32] See Vachudova, *Europe Undivided*; but see Karen Henderson, "The Slovak Republic," for the argument that the desire for EU membership was minimal in the 1998 elections.
[33] See Vachudova, *Europe Undivided*.
[34] See Henderson, "The Slovak Republic," for the argument that the foundations of democracy in Slovakia were basically sound throughout this period.

the civil society groups that, in some cases, had their roots in the late communist period. Tudjman was thus less constrained in the early to mid-1990s than was Mečiar. As a popular military figure leading a nation at war, he was able to deflect challenges to his rule by pointing to the threat the nation faced. It was only after the Dayton Agreement brought an end to the war in Bosnia in 1995 that opposition groups could really call his leadership into question. Mečiar, on the other hand, had been ousted by the political opposition in 1991 and again briefly in 1994 before returning to office after the parliamentary elections in September of that year. Although he easily won these elections, he continued to face substantial, although disunified and often ineffective, opposition.[35] Put simply, Slovak politics was a good deal more competitive than Croatian politics prior to the breakthrough elections.

Slovakia and Croatia also differed from each other in the path and direction the regime was taking on the eve of the elections. In Slovakia, Vladimír Mečiar's use of extra-parliamentary means to resist the opposition and parliamentary means to consolidate his power after President Kováč's term ended in March 1998 and to change the electoral law, among other actions, was accompanied by an escalation of violence against those who challenged his power. In Croatia, with Tudjman's illness and subsequent death in late 1999, repression decreased, and space for opposition activity increased as his successors cast about for the best way to move forward.

Despite these differences, cooperation between the more united political opposition and the NGO sectors resulted in the defeat of the incumbent governments in both countries. In Slovakia, Mečiar's party continued to receive the largest share of votes cast (27 percent); however, this share, together with that of his former coalition partners, the Slovak National Party (9.1 percent) and the Association of Slovak Workers (which, with 1.3 percent of the vote, fell below the threshold needed to seat deputies in parliament), was not sufficient to form a ruling majority, and Mečiar ceded victory to the opposition. The Slovak Democratic Coalition, which won 26.3 percent of the vote, then formed a governing coalition with the Party of the Hungarian Coalition (SMK), which received 9.1 percent, the Party of Civic Understanding (SOP), which polled 8.0 percent, and the Party of the Democratic Left (SDL), which received 14.7 percent.[36]

---

[35] See Fisher, *Political Change in Post-Communist Slovakia and Croatia*, Chapter 7, for an overview of political developments in both countries in the 1990s.

[36] There is a sizeable literature on the 1998 elections. See Grigorij Mesežnikov, Michal Ivantyšyn, and Tom Nicholson, eds., *Slovakia 1998–1999: A Global Report on the State of Society* (Bratislava: Institute for Public Affairs, 1999), 65–81; Martin Bútora, Grigorij Mesežnikov, and Zora Bútorová, eds., *Slovenské voľby '98: Kto? Prečo? Ako?* (Bratislava: Inštitút pre verejné otázky, 1998); Soňa Szomolányi, *Kľukatá cesta Slovenska k demokracii* (Bratislava: STIMUL – Centrum informatiky a vzdělávání FIFUK, 1999); Matthew Rhodes, "Slovakia after Meciar: A Midterm Report," *Problems of Post-Communism* 48:4 (July 2001), 3–13; David Reichardt, "Democracy Promotion in Slovakia: An Import or an Export Business?," *Perspectives: Central European Review of International Affairs* 18 (Summer 2002), 5–20; Martin Bútora and Zora Bútorová, "Slovakia's Democratic Awakening,"

In Croatia, the opposition SDP-HSLS coalition earned 47.02 percent of the vote; the four-party coalition consisting of the Croatian Peasant Party, the Croatian National Party, the Istrian Democratic Assembly, and the Liberal Party garnered 16.55 percent of the vote, defeating Tudjman's Croatian Democratic Union (HDZ), which received 30.46 percent of the vote in elections to the lower house of parliament. The victory of the opposition was completed in the presidential elections of January 24 when the HDZ's candidate, Mate Granić, came in third behind Stipe Mesić of the Croatian National Party, who received 41 percent of the vote in the first round, and Dražen Budiša of the Croatian Social-Liberal Party, who won 28 percent. Thus, the second round of the election, in which Mesić defeated Budiša by a vote of 56 percent to 44 percent, was between two opposition candidates.

In the rest of this chapter, we will first examine the Slovak case, which represented the first full articulation of the model of using elections to oust a semi-authoritarian or "illiberal" leader, in the postcommunist world. We will then analyze the way the Slovak experience was transferred to Croatia.

THE SLOVAK DEMOCRATIC COALITION AND OK'98

In the 1998 parliamentary elections, a unified political opposition and a massive citizens' campaign mounted by civil society groups succeeded in ousting Vladimír Mečiar from power and ending the period of de-democratization that had occurred under his rule.[37] As prime minister of Slovakia first when it was still part of the Czechoslovak federation and again after independence, Mečiar made good use of the opportunities privatization provided to ensure his support among the beneficiaries of the process. He exercised considerable control over the media and had a great deal of influence in the police and security forces. Although his abuses of power were not as frequent or as costly as those of many semi-authoritarian leaders, Mečiar also engaged in his share of dirty tricks and antidemocratic behavior. These ranged from the kidnapping of then President Kováč's adult son and his transport across the border to Austria, where he was wanted for fraud, to the firebombing of the car of the main inspector investigating this incident. His government also verbally harassed prominent figures in the opposition and, as in the beating of Christian Democratic member of parliament František Mikloško in September

---

Journal of Democracy 10:1 (January 1999), 80–95; and Martin Bútora, "OK'98: A Campaign of Slovak NGOs for Free and Fair Elections," in *Reclaiming Democracy: Civil Society and Electoral Change in Central and Eastern Europe*, ed. Joerg Forbrig and Pavol Demeš (Washington, DC: German Marshall Fund, 2007), 21–52.

[37] See Martin Bútora, Miroslav Kollár, and Grigorij Mesežnikov, eds., *Slovakia 2005: A Global Report on the State of Society* (Bratislava: Institute for Public Affairs, 2000); Soňa Szomolányi and Grigorij Mesežnikov, eds., *Slovakia: Parliamentary Elections 1994: Causes–Consequences–Prospects* (Bratislava: Friedrich Ebert Foundation, 1995); and Soňa Szomolányi and John A Gould, eds., *Slovakia: Problems of Democratic Consolidation* (Bratislava: Slovak Political Science Association and Friedrich Ebert Foundation, 1997).

1995, with force. Mečiar also concentrated the power of the prime minister and the president in his own hands after President Kováč's term expired in March 1998 and tried to skew the 1998 elections in his own favor by creating a single electoral district in all of Slovakia and increasing the percentage of the vote needed by coalitions in order to seat deputies on the eve of the elections. As the result of these actions, Slovakia, which had received a score of 2 for political rights and 3 for civil liberties, as well as a ranking of "free" from Freedom House in 1994 and 1995, received a score of 4 for civil liberties while retaining its ranking of 2 for political rights, but dropped to being labeled "partly free" in 1996 and 1997.

THE OPPOSITION UNITES

As in the other cases we discuss, the decision of leaders of the fragmented and often fractious Slovak opposition to unite to contest the 1998 parliamentary elections was a critical element in ending Mečiar's rule. Stung by Mečiar's ability to defeat them when they ran individually in the parliamentary elections in 1994, leaders of several opposition parties began in 1997 to discuss the formation of a coalition to contest the 1998 elections.[38] These efforts built on the informal "blue coalition" that the center-right Christian Democratic Movement (KDH), Democratic Party (DS), and Democratic Union (DU) had established in late 1996, which had been active in the effort to have a referendum on direct election of the president. After prolonged negotiations, the parties settled on the then relatively unknown Mikuláš Dzurinda of the Christian Democratic Movement to lead the coalition. This choice would prove inspired, as Dzurinda emerged as a charismatic leader whose youth and energy were important in gaining support for the coalition, especially among young people. These parties were joined by the Green Party (SZS) and the Social Democratic Party of Slovakia (SDSS) and formed the Slovak Democratic Coalition in July 1997. The Hungarian Party (SMK) and the Party of the Democratic Left (SDL) agreed to cooperate with the SDK in late 1997, as did the newly formed Party of Civic Understanding (SOP) in April 1998.[39]

The unification of the opposition was an important step in Slovakia, but it would not have been enough by itself to defeat Mečiar. Both election results and public opinion polls, including one conducted on behalf of IRI in 1997, documented the fact that Mečiar had a stable core of loyal, generally older, less-educated, and often female supporters who could be counted on to vote

---

[38] Interview with František Mikloško, Bratislava, June 7, 2007.
[39] See Tim Haughton and Marek Rybář, "All Right Now? Explaining the Successes and Failures of the Slovak Centre-Right," *Journal of Communist Studies and Transition Politics* 20:3 (September 2004), 115–132; Grigorij Mesežnikov, "Domestic Politics," in *Slovakia 1998–1999: A Global Report on the State of Society*, ed. Grigorij Mesežnikov, Michal Ivantyšyn, and Tom Nicholson (Bratislava: Institute for Public Affairs, 1999), 13–64, especially 41–62, for discussions of the development of the Slovak party system prior to 1998.

and to vote for him.[40] Although the turnout rate for the 1994 parliamentary elections was fairly high in Slovakia (75.7 percent),[41] turnout among the youngest voters was low (about 20 percent),[42] and public opinion surveys indicated that many voters, particularly young voters, were either undecided or did not plan to vote in 1998. A large turnout of voters, especially young and first-time voters, who were likely to vote for the opposition, was critical if Mečiar was to be defeated. Civil society groups, including those that organized Civic Campaign '98 (OK'98), which informed citizens of the issues, encouraged them to vote, and mobilized new voters were thus an extremely important part of the electoral model as it was implemented in Slovakia.

CIVIL SOCIETY ORGANIZATIONS AND ACTIVITIES

In Slovakia, OK'98 and other NGO efforts could build on the already high degree of development and self-organization of the NGO sector. Mečiar's domination of the sphere of partisan politics for nearly a decade led many of the most able and energetic people in Slovakia to be active in nongovernmental organizations. These activists faced serious handicaps because of legislative restrictions on the activities of NGOs as well as funding problems. The Mečiar regime also fostered a set of so-called parallel organizations, that is, NGOs that received their funding from the government and supported it.[43]

Reflecting on the success of the campaign in 1999, participants stressed the importance of their previous experiences in working with the public or in local government as well as the knowledge they had of each other through informal links and previous cooperation as key elements in their ability to mount a successful campaign in 1998.[44] In addition to its coordinating committee, founded in 1994, and its annual conferences, the NGO sector also benefited from the activities of the Slovak Academic Information Agency-Service Center for the Third Sector (SAIA-SCTS) and its network of regional centers that disseminated information throughout the NGO sector, published the monthly *Nonproft*, and managed the Changenet website.[45] The NGO

[40] See, for example, Zora Bútorová, Jan Hartl, and Sharon L. Wolchik, "Citizen Attitudes in Slovakia," FOCUS, December 1994, and the results of a poll that IRI commissioned FOCUS to conduct in 1997. See also Kevin Deegan Krause, "Slovakia's Second Transition," *Journal of Democracy* 14:2 (April 2003), 65–79, on citizens' political attitudes and values.

[41] International IDEA, Voter Turnout: Slovak Republic, http://www.idea.int/vt/countryview.cfm?country=SK.

[42] Ol'ga Gyárfášová, in Nadácia pre občiansku spoločnost', *Rock Volieb '98 Campaign: Report on Activities and Results – 1998 Slovak Parliamentary Elections* (Bratislava: Nadácia pre občiansku spoločnost', 1999), http://www.wmd.org/documents/RockVoliebGOTV.pdf.

[43] See Ruth Hoogland DeHoog and Luba Racanska, "The Role of the Nonprofit Sector amid Political Change: Contrasting Approaches to Slovakian Civil Society," *Voluntas: International Journal of Voluntary and Nonprofit Organizations* 14:3 (September 2003), 263–282.

[44] Reichardt, "Democracy Promotion in Slovakia."

[45] Pavol Demeš, "The Third Sector and Volunteerism," in *Slovakia 1998–1999: A Global Report on the State of Society*, ed. Grigorij Mesežnikov, Michal Ivantyšyn, and Tom Nicholson (Bratislava: Institute for Public Affairs, 1999), 354–355.

sector had developed a large core of activists who trusted each other. Some of them had participated in the activities of what Martin Bútora, one of the founders of Public Against Violence, and later head of the Institute of Public Affairs and Slovak ambassador to the U.S., described as "islands of creative deviance" during the communist period.[46] These features led the head of the Democracy and Governance Division of USAID in Slovakia to rate the Slovak NGO sector "'as one of the strongest in the region,' ... there is more unity here than in any other country, also the most organized leadership, and the sector is effective because of [these factors]."[47]

Activists in the third sector were thus well equipped to play a role in mobilizing opposition to Mečiar in 1998. Previous campaigns, such as the "SOS" campaign against the law on foundations in early 1996, common action in the failed referendum of 1997, and the Walk Across Slovakia in June 1997, provided dress rehearsals for 1998.[48] Journalists and editors, actors and others in the cultural sphere, and university and secondary students also mounted joint protests in 1997.[49]

A final feature of the third sector in Slovakia that would prove important was the existence of think tanks – such as the Institute for Public Affairs, the Slovak Foreign Policy Association, SPACE, MESA, and Focus – with the expertise needed to conduct sophisticated sociological research and public opinion polls that played a key role in identifying potential supporters and opponents of the regime. Leaders of the third sector were also very well connected in the West and skilled in dealing with international donors and actors.[50]

The importance of preexisting links was evident in the formation of OK'98, or Civic Campaign '98. Slovak NGO leaders began discussing their role in the elections in the summer of 1997 and determined at the fifth NGO conference in October that they would take an active role in the campaign. Nevertheless, although participants adopted a resolution supporting efforts to increase citizens' information about conditions for democratic elections and requesting the presence of international observers, many NGOs, particularly those that received government funding, expressed misgivings about the politicization of NGO activities.

NGO strategies were influenced by the activities of international donors, who also began to focus on the need to increase citizens' participation in politics in light of the upcoming elections. In November, at the annual meeting

---

[46] Martin Bútora and Pavol Demeš, "Tretí sektor, dobrovoľníctvo a mimovládné neziskové organizácie," in *Slovensko 1996. Súhrnná správa o stave spoločnosti a trendoch na rok 1997*, ed. Martin Bútora (Bratislava: IVO, 1997), 79–99.

[47] Dehoog and Racanska, "The Role of the Nonprofit Sector amid Political Change," 269.

[48] Martin Bútora and Grigorij Mesežnikov, eds., *Slovenské referendum '97: zrod, priebeh, dôsledky* (Bratislava: IVO, 1997), especially 137–152.

[49] See Martin Bútora and Pavol Demeš, "Občianske organizácie vo voľbách 1998," in *Slovenské voľby '98: Kto? Prečo? Ako?*, ed. Martin Bútora, Grigorij Mesežnikov, and Zora Bútorová (Bratislava: Inštitút pre verejné otázky, 1998), 132–133.

[50] See Bútora and Demeš, "Tretí sektor, dobrovoľníctvo a mimovládné neziskové organizácie."

of the European Foundation Center in Brussels, representatives of the Civil Society Development Foundation, the Open Society Foundation, and the Foundation for a Civil Society, which were part of the Slovak Donors' Forum, met with representatives of major foreign donors active in Slovakia, including the Charles Stewart Mott Foundation, the German Marshall Fund of the United States, the Westminster Foundation, the Rockefeller Brothers' Fund, Tara Consultants, and the EU, to discuss the role of NGOs in the elections.[51] At that meeting, Slovak NGO leaders learned that financial support would be available if they developed a clear plan for a campaign. This message was repeated at the Vienna airport in December 1997 at a meeting of Slovak activists and political leaders, organized by U.S. democracy promoters, with NGO activists from Bulgaria and Romania who had been involved in the pivotal elections of 1996 and 1997 in their countries.[52]

At this meeting analysts and participants from Bulgaria and Romania shared their views on factors that had led to the victory of the opposition in their countries. Ivan Krastev of the Center for Liberal Strategies in Sofia, for example, noted that in Bulgaria, NGO activists and think tank personnel came to see the role of civil society organizations as preventing the government from convincing people that no change was possible. As part of this role, they focused on the message that: "1) there is an alternative, 2) change is possible, and 3) change is possible only through participation in the process, i.e., voting."[53] Luminiţa Petrescu highlighted the role that NGOs in Romania played in transforming the country's " 'inhabitants' into 'citizens'."[54] Working groups discussed plans for Slovak NGOs to be involved in election monitoring and for fleshing out the call made at the October conference for NGOs to be involved in training the media, identifying issues, and educating citizens about the electoral process. Participants discussed parallel vote counting and domestic election monitoring. A suggestion was also made that a "network" or "alliance" be developed to act as a clearing house for NGO efforts.[55] As OK'98 leaders later recounted, the Vienna airport meeting was crucial, for it reinforced the idea, which some NGO activists had begun to espouse earlier, that NGOs could be involved in mainstream political life without violating their commitment to the principle of nonpartisanship.

---

[51] Adriena Richterová, Alena Pániková, and Jana Kadlecová, "Coordination of Donors and the Role of the Donors' Forum in Slovakia OK'98 – Campaign of Slovak NGOs for Free and Fair Elections," unpublished manuscript, 1.

[52] Interviews with Pavol Demeš in Washington, DC, and Bratislava, February 2005, June 2005; Jan and Lenka Surochak, Bratislava, June 2005 and June 2006; and Wendy Luers, New York, April 2008.

[53] "Workshop Summary: Non-Governmental Organizations and the Democratic Process: An East-East Exchange of Experience," summary of the international workshop held in Vienna, Austria, December 15, 1997, sponsored by the Bulgarian Center for Liberal Strategies, the Foundation for Civil Society, the Open Society Foundation Bulgaria, the German Marshall Fund of the United States, and the C. S. Mott Foundation.

[54] Ibid., 3, 7.

[55] Ibid., 9.

The plan for a campaign to encourage citizens to vote that became OK'98 (Civic Campaign '98) was conceptualized over the Christmas holiday by Pavol Demeš, previously foreign minister of Slovakia and an advisor to President Kováč, who was a leader in the self-organization of the third sector and served as its spokesperson.[56] This draft was then refined at a meeting of NGO leaders at the Institute for Public Affairs in Bratislava in January 1998. The preparatory committee established at that time elaborated plans for a broad-based campaign to focus attention on the upcoming parliamentary elections and encourage citizens to vote in large numbers. The campaign was based at NOS, the Foundation for Civil Society, and was led on a day-to-day basis by an executive committee consisting of Šarlota Pufflerová, director of the Minority Rights Foundation, who served as spokesperson for the campaign, and longtime civic activists Pavol Demeš and Andrej Bartosiewicz.[57]

In contrast to earlier campaigns, the organizers of OK'98 agreed to adopt a positive rather than defensive or negative approach[58] as Bulgarian activists had stressed at the Vienna meeting, noting that a negative approach would discourage people and dissuade them from voting.[59] The OK'98 logo itself was meant to reinforce a positive message: in addition to standing for "civic campaign," it also was meant to counter fears citizens might have about voting and the outcome of the elections by reassuring them that everything would in fact be "OK."

A large number of NGOs throughout the country organized activities as part of the campaign. These included voters' meetings with candidates; training sessions for leaders of political parties and candidates to discuss ways of reaching voters; and a massive information campaign that distributed leaflets, brochures, T-shirts, and other items bearing the campaign's distinctive logo.

The campaign also included activities directed particularly at young voters, whom public opinion polls indicated would be likely to vote for the opposition coalition – if they voted at all.[60] The most significant of these were carried out as part of the Rock the Vote (*Rock volieb*) campaign organized under the direction of the Foundation for a Civil Society (*Nadácia pre občiansku spoločnosť*), a partner of the Foundation for a Civil Society in the United States. FCS staffers began discussing the need for civic education in September 1997 and met with representatives of the American Rock the Vote organization and IRI personnel, who had conducted a campaign to get young voters

---

[56] Pavol Demeš, ""Návrh do diskusie pre MVO, Občianská koalicia '98 (OK 98)," internal memo of MVO of OK'98, January 1998.

[57] OK'98, "Vyhlásenie občianskej kampane OK'98," one-page proclamation, Zvolen, March 3, 1998.

[58] Excerpts from interviews with Pavol Demeš and Hana Hanúsková in Oľga Berecká, Natália Kušnieriková, and Dušan Ondrušek, *NGO Campaign for Free and Fair Elections: OK '98 – Lessons Learned* (Bratislava: Centrum prevencie a riešenia konfliktov, 1999), 14, at www.partners-intl.org/case_studies/Supp%20Materials/Slovakia-OK98.doc.

[59] Berecká, Kušnieriková, and Ondrušek, *NGO Campaign for Free and Fair Elections*, 38.

[60] IRI poll, Bratislava, 1997.

to participate in the May 1997 referendum. They also conducted focus groups and surveys of young people in April 1998 and, in June 1998, invited four Bulgarians from the Political Academy for Central Europe (PACE) with experience in organizing NGO activities to get out the vote to spend three days in Bratislava to discuss *Rock volieb*'s planned structure and strategies.[61] IRI commissioned monthly polls to track public opinion and consulted with *Rock volieb* organizers throughout the campaign.[62]

Rock volieb organizers used rock concerts by popular musicians and bands in Bratislava and other cities, TV spots in connection with the "I Vote, Therefore I Am" (*"Volím, teda som"*) campaign in cooperation with Hlava 98, appearances on TV talk shows, radio interviews, press conferences and releases, and a "Voter Awareness" bus tour to convince young Slovaks that voting was not just a civic duty but somehow part of a young, hip lifestyle. Activists passed out educational materials explaining how to vote and why voting was important, as well as stickers, pencils, and, in what would become a common feature of democratizing elections, three times as many T-shirts as originally planned. The group also distributed materials in Hungarian.

The success of these and other efforts by organizations such as the Council of Youth of Slovakia, the European Association for Student Rights, and the Forum of Student Solidarity was evident in the over 80 percent turnout rate for first-time voters. The significance of this turnout rate is evident if we compare these results to the participation of young voters in the 1994 elections, for example, when an estimated 20 percent of voters age eighteen to twenty-five voted. Research conducted in late 1997 indicated that 40 percent of voters age eighteen to twenty-four either did not plan to vote or did not know whom to choose.[63] The calculation that young people, if they did vote, would vote for the opposition also proved to be correct. Thirty-one percent of first-time voters supported the Slovak Democratic Coalition (SDK); an additional 8 percent voted for the Hungarian Party, 13 percent for the Party of Civic Understanding (SOP), and 18 percent for the Party of the Democratic Left, the other parties that formed the new government in 1998. In contrast to the overall results, which gave Vladimír Mečiar's HZDS 27 percent of the vote, only 11 percent of first-time voters supported HZDS.[64]

[61] This group included Mikhail Berov, who was involved in the 1996 GOTV campaign, as well as Dimitar Dimitrov, who was a member of the Central Election Commission in Bulgaria. See Nadácia pre občiansku spoločnosť', *Rock Volieb '98 Campaign: Report on Activities and Results – 1998 Slovak Parliamentary Elections* (Bratislava: Nadácia pre občiansku spoločnosť', 1999), http://www.wmd.org/documents/RockVoliebGOTV.pdf.

[62] *Rock Volieb '98 Campaign: Report on Activities and Results.*

[63] From polls conducted by FOCUS as reported in *Rock Volieb '98 Campaign: Report on Activities and Results,* 2–3.

[64] *Parlamentné volby '98. Výskum pre International Republican Institute* (Bratislava: FOCUS, 1998), as cited in footnote 2 in Martin Bútora and Zora Bútorová, "Slovakia's Democratic Awakening," *Journal of Democracy* 10:1 (January 1999), 82. See also Vladimír Krivý, "Volebné výsledky," in *Slovenské voľby '98: Kto? Prečo? Ako?*, ed. Martin Bútora, Grigorij Mesežnikov, and Zora Bútorová (Bratislava: Inštitút pre verejné otázky 1998), 245–260; and

After the elections, campaign organizers highlighted the importance of cooperating with other organizations and using every opportunity to get into the media, as well as remaining nonpartisan and working with experts to define issues and make the message and the campaign's products professional. Reflecting on how these activities contributed to an atmosphere that was very different from that of "normal" election campaigns in Slovakia, they also noted that "Fun stuff is important," including the production of T-shirts and cultural events such as concerts, and advised others who might emulate their campaign to "be trendy" and to find a simple logo and name for the campaign that people would remember.[65]

Young people, involved both as targets of and as activists in the civic campaign,[66] also used less orthodox techniques in some cases. There were several groups of university students that focused on delegitimizing and ridiculing Mečiar and his regime. Not officially associated with OK'98, they nonetheless helped to activate young people.

OK'98 also included a media element. Although Mečiar had a great deal of control over the broadcast media, which reported on the campaign in a highly partisan way,[67] the owner of TV Markíza, a private station that had the highest audience ratings, supported the campaign and aired information about its activities, as well as the spots aimed specifically at young voters that were also shown in movie theaters.[68] Rádio Twist and Rádio Ragtime, both of which had significant audiences among young people, aired information on the campaign. The activities of OK'98 were also presented objectively by many of the daily print media, with the exception of the pro-Mečiar *Slovenská Republika* and some of the regional dailies.[69] Part of the approach to the media also involved countering the numerous attacks on the campaign by the government

---

Oľga Gyárfášová and Miroslav Kúska, "Vývoj volebných preferencií a analýza volebného správania," in *Slovenské voľby '98: Kto? Prečo? Ako?*, ed. Martin Bútora, Grigorij Mesežnikov, and Zora Bútorová (Bratislava: Inštitút pre verejné otázky 1998), 261–276. See Oľga Gyárfášová, Miroslav Kúska, and Marián Velšic, "Prvovoliči a voľby 1998: volebné správanie, motívy hlasovania," in *Slovenské voľby '98: Kto? Prečo? Ako?*, ed. Martin Bútora, Grigorij Mesežnikov, and Zora Bútorová (Bratislava: Inštitút pre verejné otázky, 1998), 277–288.

[65] Berecká, Kušnieriková, and Ondrušek, *NGO Campaign for Free and Fair Elections*, 26–27.

[66] Valerie J. Bunce and Sharon L. Wolchik, "Youth and Postcommunist Electoral Revolutions: Never Trust Anyone Over 30?," in *Reclaiming Democracy: Civil Society and Electoral Change in Central and Eastern Europe*, ed. Joerg Forbrig and Pavol Demeš (Washington, DC: German Marshall Fund, 2007), 191–204.

[67] See MEMO 98 monitoring report as reported in Berecká, Kušnieriková, and Ondrušek, eds., *NGO Campaign for Free and Fair Elections*, 38; Andrej Školkay, "Médiá a politická komunikácia v predvolebnej a volebnej kampani," in Martin Bútora, Grigorij Mesežnikov, and Zora Bútorová, *Slovenské voľby '98: Kto? Prečo? Ako?* (Bratislava: Inštitút pre verejné otázky, 1998), 167–196.

[68] Bútora and Demeš, "Občianske organizácie vo voľbách 1998."

[69] Berecká, Kušnieriková, and Ondrušek, *NGO Campaign for Free and Fair Elections*, 39.

and media loyal to it.[70] Civic groups, including MEMO98, played an important role in monitoring the media. Organized by the Helsinki Citizens Association and the Association for the Support of Local Democracy in 1997, MEMO monitored broadcast and print media for three months prior to and during the election campaign and publicized its results in daily newspapers as well as in its own information bulletins. Other groups, such as the Slovak Union of Journalists, also conducted media monitoring.[71] A final area of OK'98's activity focused on the mechanics of free and fair elections. Campaign activists worked to obtain permission for international election observers from the OSCE and also to place citizens on the commissions that supervised the elections. Civic Eye (*Občianske oko*), for example, organized efforts to monitor the elections and trained over 1,700 monitors.[72]

One important aspect of the campaign was its focus on activity outside the capital. Regional coordinators worked with OK'98 organizers in Bratislava to try to reach voters in all parts of the country. As in the capital, local and regional activists built on previously established networks in some cases. In southern Slovakia, for example, local activists had started clubs to involve citizens in politics a year before the elections. Some of these then founded civic associations that participated in the campaign.[73]

The trade unions and churches were also active during the pre-election period. Leaders of the Confederation of Trade Unions, which had approximately 100,000 members in 1997, nearly a third of all potential voters, decided to become engaged in the pre-election campaign.[74] As Darina Malová notes, union leaders, angered by the government's violation of the tripartite agreement that brought unions, the government, and employers together by

[70] See Školkay, "Médiá a politická komunikácia v predvolebnej a volebnej kampani," 167–196; Zuzana Mistríková and Richard Rybníček, "Pôsobenie regionálnych a lokálnych elektronických médií pred voľbami 1998," in *Slovenské voľby '98: Kto? Prečo? Ako?*, ed. Martin Bútora, Grigorij Mesežnikov, and Zora Bútorová (Bratislava, Inštitút pre verejné otázky, 1998), 197–208; Vladimír Krivý, "Regionálny monopol STV a výsledky volieb," in *Slovenské voľby '98: Kto? Prečo? Ako?*, ed. Martin Bútora, Grigorij Mesežnikov, and Zora Bútorová (Bratislava, Inštitút pre verejné otázky, 1998), 209–212; Simona Bubánová, "Financie a reklama vo volebnej kampani 1998," in *Slovenské voľby '98: Kto? Prečo? Ako?*, ed. Martin Bútora, Grigorij Mesežnikov, and Zora Bútorová (Bratislava, Inštitút pre verejné otázky, 1998), 213–216; and Martin Vystavil, "Voľby 1998 a Internet," in *Slovenské voľby '98: Kto? Prečo? Ako?*, ed. Martin Bútora, Grigorij Mesežnikov, and Zora Bútorová (Bratislava, Inštitút pre verejné otázky, 1998), 235–244.

[71] See Školkay, "Médiá a politická komunikácia v predvolebnej a volebnej kampani."

[72] See Bútora and Demeš, "Občianske organizácie vo voľbách 1998," 134–136; and Darina Malová, "Od váhania k premyslenej stratégii: Konfederácia odborových zväzov SR vo voľbách 1998," in *Slovenské voľby '98: Kto? Prečo? Ako?*, ed. Martin Bútora, Grigorij Mesežnikov, and Zora Bútorová (Bratislava: Inštitút pre verejné otázky, 1998), 142–149, for the role of unions.

[73] Myrtil Nagy in Berecká, Kušnieriková, and Ondrušek, *NGO Campaign for Free and Fair Elections*, 32.

[74] Malová, "Od váhania k premyslenej stratégii," 139.

unilaterally adopting a law about wages, mobilized their members to vote; organized discussions with political parties, interest groups, and other actors in civil society; and conducted a media campaign.[75]

NGO and union leaders repeatedly emphasized the nonpartisan nature of their involvement in the election campaigns[76] and opened their events to participants and voters from all parties. However, candidates for Mečiar's party and his allies, as well as their supporters, generally did not take advantage of these opportunities.[77] Some of the materials distributed to citizens through OK'98 also identified the policies of the Mečiar government as the source of the country's main problems and disclaimed opposition responsibility for them.[78] The message thus implicitly supported the opposition parties. It was also clear from the beginning of the get-out-the-vote campaign that increased turnout would benefit the political opposition and disadvantage Mečiar.

Similarly, the many informal links that existed between leaders and activists in the NGO sector and the opposition political parties facilitated communication, if not coordination of NGO and party activities. Outside actors sometimes also played a role in this regard. As the result of their party-building activities and role in supporting the unification of the opposition, for example, IRI officials in Bratislava had extensive contact with opposition party leaders. IRI also sponsored surveys that provided information useful to both NGOs and more partisan actors.

Contact between the opposition and NGOs also took place through more formal channels. Representatives of the Coordinating Committee of the Third Sector participated in the Democratic Roundtable of opposition parties and NGOs that met prior to the election and freely criticized the government.[79] Established, in the words of Martin Bútora and Zora Bútorová, to "prevent electoral fraud and to secure a smooth transfer of political power after the election," the roundtable also facilitated communication between the two sectors. Pavol Demeš notes the importance of these links:

> It was precisely this alliance between the political parties, the NGOs, independent media, unions, and a part of the churches, that led to the fall of the Mečiar regime. In some cases it involved an implicit unwritten alliance of actors professing the same values and prepared to defend them together. In the case of the Democratic Roundtable, it involved the public, visible and purposeful uniting of pro-democratic forces. It was at once evident that this

---

[75] Ibid., 146–148.

[76] Interview with Šarlota Pufflerová, Bratislava, June 2008; interview with Jan and Lenka Surotchak, Bratislava, May 2005.

[77] Interview with Šarlota Pufflerová, Bratislava, June 2008.

[78] Vystavil, "Voľby 1998 a Internet."

[79] See Bútora and Demeš, "Občianské organizácie vo voľbách 1998," 132; and Martin Bútora and Pavol Demeš, "Civil Society Organizations in the 1998 Elections," in Martin Bútora, Grigorij Mesežnikov, Zora Bútorová, and Sharon Fisher, *The 1998 Parliamentary Elections and Democratic Rebirth in Slovakia* (Bratislava: Institute for Public Affairs, 1999), 163.

kind of institutionalized association of leaders of representative democracy and actors in participatory democracy was prepared to defend the democratic course of the elections.[80]

As was the case with *Rock volieb*, Slovak NGO and party activists introduced activities that were not commonly used in electoral campaigns in Slovakia, many of which would be emulated in later democratizing elections. Thus, in addition to the positive messages that predominated in campaign and voter awareness materials, both sets of actors emphasized activities that would engage citizens and bring abstract issues of national politics down to a personal level. One of the most noteworthy of these was the fifteen-day March Across Slovakia that brought approximately 300 participants through more than 1,000 towns and villages to highlight the importance of the election and distribute literature that informed citizens about voting procedures but also emphasized some of the problems the country faced.[81] SDK leader Mikuláš Dzurinda rode a bicycle through Slovakia and also took a well-publicized trip on a steam-powered train.[82] Coalition leaders participated in countless face-to-face meetings with voters and citizens' forums. Together with the techniques discussed earlier, these activities, which may appear commonplace to citizens used to competitive democratic elections, were decidedly not "politics as usual." They were designed to catch the attention of citizens who had become apathetic about politics and to convince them that voting – and, in the case of the coalition, voting for the opposition – was worthwhile and would produce positive change.

At the same time, while unusual, the activities of the NGO sector, as well as of the opposition political parties, were clearly "within system" activities – that is, they were legal and respected the principles of the Slovak constitution and legal system. They were also nonviolent. In contrast to the situation in the cases we will discuss in the next chapter, there was never any real fear expressed, either by opposition leaders or by leaders of OK'98, that Mečiar would not leave office if he lost the election or that he would use violence to remain in office. He had, after all, left the post of prime minister peacefully (if temporarily) in 1991 and again in 1994 when parliament forced his resignation. NGO leaders had had some contact with "allies" in the police, who were, however, replaced by Mečiar.[83] But, while the opposition and NGO leaders feared that Mečiar would try to manipulate the election in order to stay in power, they did not believe he would resort to force to do so. Nor, perhaps because of the extensive preparation for vote monitoring and exit polls conducted by the Tenega Foundation, were there any plans to protest stolen elections, or any formal contingency plans regarding what to do if Mečiar

---

[80] See Bútora and Demeš, "Občianske organizácie vo voľbách 1998," 137.

[81] See OK'98 and Gemma 93, "Voľby 98, Cesta pre Slovensko," election pamphlet (Bratislava: IVO, 1998).

[82] Fisher, *Political Change in Post-Communist Slovakia and Croatia*, 158.

[83] Interview with Šarlota Pufflerová, Bratislava, May 2008.

did not leave office.[84] Šarlota Pufflerová, spokeswoman for OK'98, noted in an interview that it was clear that, in such a case, despite the lack of a concrete plan by the NGO sector, "it would have been something like the Velvet Revolution: People would have been very sure what to do. It was clear after November 1989 that it was too much: people were waiting to see what would happen. After what happened in Prague and when they saw it on the TV, it was just in the air, people went out into the streets." Stating that the "whole 98 campaign was predicated on the ideas of 89, the elixir of 89, although it was never said," Pufflerová continued, "on our side it was imminently clear: if something like that [a stolen election or refusal to leave office] happened, who could stop us?"[85]

By way of contrast, Mečiar's campaign and that of the Slovak National Party (SNS), which was also part of the government, were decidedly politics as usual. Relying on references to Slovak nationalism and using primarily standard campaign techniques such as rallies and Mečiar's weekly TV interviews, the Movement for a Democratic Slovakia's campaign also tried to discredit the opposition and OK'98 activists with accusations (by now standard in Slovak public life) that they were not sufficiently patriotic and were in effect tools of outside powers. SNS slogans and symbols also portrayed the party as the defender of Slovakia against all threats.[86]

THE ROLE OF OUTSIDE ACTORS

As in the other democratizing elections we will discuss, the successful outcome of the 1998 elections in Slovakia was due largely to the actions of domestic actors. As a report on the NGO campaign prepared in November 1998 by three Slovak participants notes, "While technical know-how was mostly transferred from abroad, the major portion of the third-sector effort to increase citizen participation in 1998 was developed in-country on an ad-hoc basis reflecting local conditions and experience in working with the community."[87] However, the United States and other outside actors played a key role in this effort, first, by supporting the long-term development of civil society, which provided the foundation for OK'98 and other activities, and engaging in party-building activities, and, second, by providing funding for many of the activities the NGO sector used in the campaign.[88] The fact that many of the efforts of NDI

---

[84] Interviews with Šarlota Pufflerová, Bratislava, June 2008; Pavol Demeš, Washington, DC, June 2006; Lindsay Lloyd, Washington, DC, November 16, 2006; and Jan and Lenka Surotchak, Bratislava, May 2005.

[85] Interview with Šarlota Pufflerová, Bratislava, May 2008.

[86] See Fisher, *Political Change in Post-Communist Slovakia and Croatia*, 156–166, for a brief discussion of the campaign. See Grigorij Mesežnikov, ed., *Vol'by 1998 Analýza volebných programov politických strán a hnutí* (Bratislava: IVO, 1998), for party platforms.

[87] Richterová, Pániková, and Kadlecová, "Coordination of Donors."

[88] Interviews with Wendy Luers, New York, April 2008; Carl Gershman, Washington, DC, May 14, 2010; Barbara Haig, Washington, DC, May 14, 2010; and Roger Potocki, Washington, DC, May 7, 2010. Also see Reichardt, "Democracy Promotion in Slovakia."

in particular in Slovakia in the years preceding the 1998 election focused on party and civil society development outside the capital was also helpful.[89]

Actors from the United States and other countries were instrumental in encouraging the NGO sector to define a concrete strategy for getting out the vote in the 1998 elections.[90] As noted earlier, they also were critical in convincing activists in the NGO sector that they could legitimately be political without being partisan. In addition to the Vienna airport meeting, for example, the Mott Foundation, the German Marshall Fund, the Open Society Foundation in Bulgaria, and the Foundation for a Civil Society supported a December 1997 meeting between Slovak NGO leaders and Bulgarian and Romanian activists whose organizations had been established with the help and funding of Western organizations, including NDI,[91] and provided the resources for Bulgarian activists to spend three days in Bratislava consulting with the organizers of the *Rock volieb* campaign.

Outside actors also played a central role by funding the activities of OK'98 and other civic initiatives in 1998. Operating through a Donor's Forum with the cooperation of several embassies, funders elaborated a system to coordinate and expedite funding of election-related activities by NGOs.[92] Private funders, in particular, had established a pattern of informal communication at regular meetings a year and a half before the founding of the Donors Forum in 1997. In 1998, the Forum provided a total of approximately $43 million in grants.[93]

Although other actors were also involved,[94] the United States was clearly the most important outside player. Since Slovakia had already been graduated from SEED funding administered by USAID, U.S. funding was administered by the Foundation for a Civil Society, which distributed approximately $3,005,000 to the NGO sector between 1993 and 1998.[95] As John Glenn notes, the United States supplied approximately 40 percent of all the aid foundations provided to support democracy and election assistance between 1994 and 1998.[96] The

---

[89] Interviews with Robert Benjamin, Washington, DC, April 9, 2010; and Kenneth Wollack, Washington, DC, May 12, 2010.

[90] Interviews with Pavol Demeš, Washington, DC, June 2006; Wendy Luers, New York, April 2008; Carl Gershman, Washington, DC, May 14, 2010; Barbara Haig, Washington, DC, May 14, 2010; and Roger Potocki, Washington, DC, May 7, 2010.

[91] Richterová, Pániková, and Kadlecová, "Coordination of Donors," 2; and interviews with Roger Potocki, Washington, DC, May 7, 2010; and Kenneth Wollack, Washington, DC, May 12, 2010.

[92] During the course of the campaign, fifty-eight of the ninety projects submitted to the Donors' Forum, amounting to approximately $875,000, were funded. Richterová, Pániková, and Kadlecová, "Coordination of Donors," 2, 5.

[93] Demeš, "The Third Sector and Volunteerism," 350.

[94] Ibid., 351–352, for amounts of grants in 1998.

[95] Personal communication from Lenka Surotchak, director, The Pontis Foundation (successor to Nadácia pre občiansku spoločnosť), September 22, 2008.

[96] See J. K. Glenn, "Civil Society Transformed: International Aid to New Political Parties in the Czech Republic and Slovakia," *Voluntas: International Journal of Voluntary and Nonprofit Organizations*, 11:2 (June 2000), 167. Glenn notes that international aid to new political parties in Slovakia was "nearly nonexistent" prior to the breakup of Czechoslovakia (173).

importance of this financial support cannot be overemphasized. Although the form the campaign took and its ultimate success reflected domestic conditions and actions, NGO leaders openly admit that the campaign could not have taken place without outside funding.[97] Similarly, when asked why there was no campaign in 2002 to get out the vote and support democratically oriented parties, NGO leaders had a simple but eloquent answer: "No means [i.e., money]."[98]

Outside actors, including IRI and NDI, also reinforced the decision of the political opposition to unify by, for instance, bringing the leaders of the parties in the Slovak Democratic Coalition to Washington to meet with officials soon after its formation. They also fostered political party development. Representatives of the Slovak National Party (SNS) did participate in some of IRI's activities and used IRI-sponsored public opinion polls to define their message in the campaign.[99] However, in practice, since they were the main parties that participated, although all were invited, the opposition particularly benefited from outside efforts to encourage them to make use of new, more active campaign techniques. These included door-to-door campaigning, strengthening local party organizations, and providing opportunities for voters to meet candidates in citizens' forums, voters' meetings, and on such unorthodox occasions as the March Across Slovakia or the bicycle trip Mikuláš Dzurinda made through parts of the country.[100]

Although most of the activities of OK'98 were devised by the NGOs that carried them out, outside actors also played a role in suggesting and refining certain tactics and activities. The results of the poll conducted at the behest of IRI in 1997, for example, led to the campaign's focus on young voters. Similarly, *Rock volieb* was modeled on the U.S. Rock the Vote campaign and, although modified for Slovak conditions, used many of the same techniques.[101] Planned before OK'98 came into being, the idea of using a Rock the Vote–style campaign to motivate youth was in fact first suggested by a young American volunteer with the Foundation for a Civil Society.[102] OK'98's headquarters was based in NOS (*Nadácia pre občiansku spoločnosť*), the Slovak successor to the Foundation for a Civil Society, which previously had administered USAID's Democracy Network and NGO development initiatives. Although most activities relied on local expertise,[103] outside actors brought in foreign experts to consult on issues such as media and vote monitoring.

[97] Interviews with Pavol Demeš, Washington, DC, June 2006; and Šarlota Pufflerová, Bratislava, June 2008.
[98] Interview with Šarlota Pufflerová, Bratislava, June 2002.
[99] Fisher, *Political Change in Post-Communist Slovakia and Croatia*, 159.
[100] Interviews with Lindsay Lloyd, Bratislava, May 1997 and Washington, DC, June 2006; and Jan Surotchak, Bratislava, May 2005; John K. Glenn, "Civil Society Transformed."
[101] Interview with Lenka Surotchak, Bratislava, May 2005.
[102] Interviews with Wendy Luers, Washington, DC, June 1998; and Lenka Surotchak, Bratislava, May 2005.
[103] OK'98, "Záznam pracovného stretnutia koordinačnej skupiny OK 98," unpublished minutes of Coordinating Committee meeting, March 24, 1998.

Finally, as mentioned earlier in this chapter, outside actors, including EU officials and U.S. Ambassador Ralph Johnson, played a role in signaling the costs of Mečiar's reelection with respect to Slovakia's admission to European and transatlantic institutions.

THE LESSONS OF OK'98

After the success of OK'98, numerous participants reflected on the lessons the campaign might provide to others. A report prepared by the Center for Conflict Resolution, Partners for Democratic Change, for example, drew explicit lessons for others who might want to use the OK'98 model. Many of the campaign's problems, the report noted, developed as the result of the ad hoc, informal nature of the campaign's origins. Thus, lack of clear lines of authority, difficulties with communication, personality conflicts, and different perspectives on how to achieve the campaign's goals complicated the work of the coordinating committee and organizations that participated in the campaign.[104] Articulating and implementing the agreed-upon principle to be political but nonpartisan was a particularly difficult task. As Peter Németh observed, "the mechanisms of non-partisanship were followed, but beliefs of people were partisan toward the opposition."[105]

Asked about the applicability of their experiences to other situations, participants in OK'98 stressed the need to take local conditions into account. The remarks of Juraj Mesík were typical:

> I think much depends on the cultural context. I don't have an idea whether something like this could be possible in Ukraine or any other country, for example, Croatia. But this experience could be interesting to people in other countries who would like to start a campaign of this kind.... individual tools that we used can be relevant for them while the overall situation does not have to be applicable.... the only thing we can do is to give them inspiration.... it will definitely be possible to use our experience but we don't know how much of it they can use; they have to find out themselves.[106]

Slovak activists stressed the importance of their earlier meetings with NGO representatives in Bulgaria and Romania. As Marek Kapusta stated,

> ... it showed us the way, the light appeared at the end of the tunnel and I think that vision was fundamental for OK'98 efforts. Because I think that at the beginning only (a) very few... believed it's possible, and that something could really be changed by our activities and exactly that positive example of Romania and Bulgaria. The bare fact that it is possible, that it has been done in three countries already, is a fascinating thing, I think.[107]

---

[104] Interview with Šarlota Pufflerová, Bratislava, June 2007.
[105] Berecká, Kušnieriková, and Ondrušek, *NGO Campaign for Free and Fair Elections*, 31.
[106] Ibid., 51.
[107] Ibid., 52.

Peter Németh concurred, noting that

> it would have been very difficult to apply something in Slovakia, it was more
> of encouragement, sort of, "Look it is nothing crazy, it can be done, people
> do it, let's do it our way," that moment when the barrier breaks.... it is proba-
> bly about bringing the idea and then making people understand it is the time
> for them to do something.[108]

Activists identified training election observers, OK'98, media monitoring,
MEMO98, and get-out-the-vote techniques such as *Rock volieb, Hlava* 98, rock
concerts, video clips, discussion forums, and the use of leaflets and posters as
elements that could be copied with slight modification, but warned that other
aspects, such as cooperation and the forming of coalitions, could not be.[109]

The success of the opposition and NGO sector in defeating Mečiar in the
1998 elections made Slovakia a powerful example in the next case we will
examine: Croatia. Many Croatian activists, especially in the NGO sector, as
well as outside supporters explicitly looked to the Slovak example as they
contemplated the use of the 2000 elections to remove Tudjman's successors
from power.

THE SLOVAK EXAMPLE MOVES TO CROATIA

The next opportunity in the "neighborhood" to use elections to replace a semi-
authoritarian leadership with democratic leaders occurred in Croatia in early
January 2000. The Croatian opposition and NGO community clearly were
inspired by what happened in Slovakia as they planned for the 2000 elections,
particularly when the death of the long-serving authoritarian leader, Franjo
Tudjman, in late 1999 and the disarray in his party, the Croatian Democratic
Union (the HDZ), that followed created significant local opportunities for
change. Other conditions in Croatia also seemed favorable, including increasing citizen disaffection with Tudjman's policies, the lack of change after the
end of the war, Croatia's international isolation, high levels of corruption
and cronyism, and the country's poor economic situation. As in Slovakia,
these factors combined to create a readiness for change on the part of many
citizens and an opportunity for the opposition to take advantage of these
desires.[110]

It was also critical that many citizens felt it was time to move to a new
stage of politics and, thus, new leaders. The war was over, and Croatia was
independent. Since Tudjman had been the key player in these developments, a
successor to him, one who would identify and implement a new political and
economic agenda, was widely welcomed. Thus, it is not surprising that public

---

[108] Ibid.
[109] Ibid., 52–53.
[110] Joerg Forbrig and Pavol Demeš, eds., *Reclaiming Democracy: Civil Society and Electoral
       Change in Central and Eastern Europe* (Washington, DC: German Marshall Fund, 2007).

opinion polls, including those sponsored in 1998 by IRI at the behest of the U.S. ambassador, William Montgomery, documented decreasing support for Tudjman in the last years of his rule.

The growth of support for the opposition was evident in the elections of 1995. Tudjman's HDZ not only failed to increase its share of the vote substantially but in fact lost 2.53 percent, despite the recapture of Krajina six weeks earlier.[111] Although Tudjman did not allow the opposition to take office, the victory of the opposition in the city council elections in Zagreb in 1995 also demonstrated growing strength. By June 1999, 71 percent of those surveyed and even higher proportions of young voters believed it was time for a change.[112]

THE OPPOSITION COALESCES

In Croatia, some members of the opposition had been active during the communist era, when the more liberal conditions in Yugoslavia had allowed intellectuals a good deal of freedom. Often experienced in and sometimes educated in the West, these intellectuals continued their activities after independence. Despite Tudjman's dominance of political life, leaders of opposition parties had some freedom to articulate policies different from those of the governing party. However, with the advent of the war, they had relatively little success in defining the terms of the debate or in gaining popular support. Once Tudjman gained power as the result of competitive elections in 1990, the HDZ dominated parliamentary elections until 2000.

Political leaders in Croatia note that the opposition had in fact lived together in opposition for ten years and that, as a result, many of the leaders of different parties knew each other well and, in some cases, were on friendly terms.[113] Discussions about uniting for the elections had begun, in fact, before Tudjman's death. These efforts intensified when the six main opposition parties issued a joint draft of the election law in September 1998[114] and, in November, agreed to form a coalition government and formed two electoral coalitions. The first of these, the Coalition of Four, included the Croatian Peasants' Party (HSS) and the smaller Croatian People's Party (HNS), the Liberal Party (LS), and the Istrian Democratic Congress (IDS). The two main opposition parties, the Social Democratic Party (SDP) and the Croatian Social Liberal Party (HSLS), formed a separate Coalition of Two.[115]

---

[111] Bellamy, "Croatia after Tudjman," 20. Also see Lenard J. Cohen, "Embattled Democracy: Postcommunist Croatia in Transition," in *Politics, Power and the Struggle for Democracy in South-East Europe*, ed. Karen Dawisha and Bruce Parott (Cambridge: Cambridge University Press, 1997), 69–121.

[112] Irvine, "From Civil Society to Civil Servants."

[113] Interview with Ivan Grdešić, Zagreb, May 21, 2005.

[114] Sharon Fisher and Biljana Bijelić, "Glas 99: Civil Society Preparing the Ground for a Post-Tudjman Croatia," in *Reclaiming Democracy: Civil Society and Electoral Change in Central and Eastern Europe*, ed. Joerg Forbrig and Pavol Demeš (Washington, DC: German Marshall Fund, 2007), 61.

[115] See Bellamy, "Croatia after Tudjman," for the campaigns of the HDZ and the opposition.

CIVIL SOCIETY IN CROATIA

Tudjman's successors, like Mečiar in Slovakia, faced a growing and increasingly active civil society. Civil society groups formed in Croatia in the 1970s and 1980s, although not to the same extent as in neighboring Slovenia. In the 1980s, women's groups were particularly active.[116] As in the rest of Yugoslavia, civil society groups had more opportunities to organize and faced fewer limitations on their activities than existed in other communist states. Tudjman's rise to power and the war reduced both interest in civil society organizations and their room to maneuver. However, numerous groups that had been active in the more liberal conditions of communist Yugoslavia persisted. Antiwar groups and organizations working with refugees and minorities joined earlier women's and human rights groups. After 1995, civic society groups, as well as the political opposition, began to revive, as did the media and the trade unions.[117]

During the period immediately preceding the 2000 elections, both the number and the activities of NGOs grew rapidly.[118] Citizens groups, such as Citizens Organized to Monitor Voting (GONG), the Civic Coalition for Free and Fair Elections (Glas 99), and women's groups were particularly active prior to and during the election campaign.[119] As in Slovakia in 1998, these elections marked a turning point for Croatia's NGO sector, as it was the first time that NGOs had entered the "real" political arena.

Founded in February 1997, GONG grew out of a joint monitoring initiative organized by a number of human rights groups for the April 1997 elections. Prevented from observing the 1997 elections, activists monitored polls for Croatian refugees in the elections for the federal government in Bosnia. GONG activists registered as an NGO in 1998 and, as the result of the Croatian Constitutional Court's decision that independent observers should be allowed to participate in all phases of the elections, monitored local elections in Osijek in 1998.[120]

GONG's efforts to have its draft regarding domestic election observers included in the new election law in 1999 proved useful for its later activities in 2000, as the lobbying effort and petition drive it organized made people all

---

[116] Sabrina P. Ramet, *Gender Politics in the Western Balkans: Women, Society, and Politics in Yugoslavia and the Yugoslav Successor States* (College Park: Pennsylvania State Universtiy Press, 1998); and Fisher, *Political Change in Post-Communist Slovakia and Croatia.*

[117] Fisher and Bijelić, "Glas 99," 56.

[118] Freedom House, *Nations in Transit 2003: Democratization in East-Central Europe and Eurasia* (New York: Freedom House, 2004), 8.

[119] See Jill Irvine, "From Civil Society to Civil Servants: Women's Organizations and Critical Elections in Croatia," *Politics & Gender* 3:1 (March 2007), 7–32; Fisher and Bijelić, "Glas 99"; Lynn Carter, Jill Irvine, Eugene Lin, Bruce Kay, and Ann Phillips, "USAID/Croatia Democracy and Governance Activities Impact on Political Change: 1995–2000," unpublished report for USAID, October 2002. Interview with Peter Novotný, Washington, DC, February 24, 2010.

[120] "About Gong," GONG website, http://www.gong.hr/page.aspx?PageID=6.

over the country aware of the organization and mobilized new volunteers.[121] GONG activists were involved in the process that led to the formation of GLAS 99, but did not join the coalition's get-out-the-vote campaign so as not to jeopardize the neutrality of their observers in the elections.[122]

GONG initiated its "We the Citizens Are Observing" campaign for the 2000 elections in June 1999 and established thirteen regional offices in July to recruit and train election monitors. Approximately 5,600 monitors affiliated with GONG monitored the 2000 elections, covering approximately 65 percent of all polling spots. GONG also assisted with parallel vote tabulation (PVT).[123] In addition to training observers, GONG used posters, brochures, and flyers to educate observers and citizens about election procedures. GONG also organized training for other monitoring organizations, including CeSID (in March in Croatia) and Otpor activists (in August in Montenegro) from Serbia, Montenegro, Bosnia and Herzegovina, Kosovo, and Central Asia.[124]

GONG's monitoring activities were supplemented by those of a coalition of NGOs that organized a broad civic campaign modeled explicitly on OK'98. Officially the Civic Coalition for Free and Fair Elections, the group was known as Glas ("Voice" or "Vote") 99. As in Slovakia, this campaign played a large role in the opposition's victory by educating and mobilizing undecided and, particularly, young and urban voters.

As Sharon Fisher and Biljana Bijelić note, there were several attempts to bring NGOs together around common campaigns as well as other activities in 1995 and 1996, but these did not lead to the development of a coordinating body with an articulated structure and regularly scheduled meetings as had occurred in Slovakia.[125] The idea of a joint NGO campaign that developed into Glas 99 was introduced by Slovak activists brought to Croatia at the initiative of the U.S. ambassador to Croatia, William Montgomery, and was modeled specifically on the experience of OK'98 in Slovakia.[126] At a meeting organized in February 1999, representatives of women's and other civic organizations, together with representatives of USAID, began plans to emulate OK'98 in Croatia. Activists then had a number of meetings with Slovak "graduates" of the campaign in Slovakia.[127] Slovak NGO activists traveled

[121] Suzana Jašić, "Monitoring the Vote in Croatia," *Journal of Democracy* 11:4 (October 2000), 161–162.
[122] Jašić, "Monitoring the Vote in Croatia," 162; Carter, Irvine, Lin, Kay, and Philipps, "USAID/ Croatia Democracy and Governance Activists."
[123] GONG, *GONG: Parliamentary Elections, Croatia, January 2 and 3, 2000, Preliminary Report*, Zagreb, January 4, 2000, 1, at http://www.gong.hr/download.aspx?f=dokumenti/ Clanci/Report2000.pdf.
[124] Aleksandra Kuratko, Anela Resanovic, and Suzanna Jašić, "GONG, Annual Report 2000," GONG, Zagreb, 2001, http://www.gong.hr/download.aspx?f=dokumenti/2000_GONG_ Annual_Report.pdf.
[125] Fisher and Bijelić, "Glas 99," 59–60. Our discussion draws heavily on this source.
[126] Interview with Pavol Demeš, Washington, DC, 2006.
[127] Fisher and Bijelić, "Glas 99," 62; interviews with Marek Kapusta, Bratislava, May 2002; Jan Surotchak, Bratislava, May 2001; Pavol Demeš, Washington, DC, 2006.

to Croatia to work with their Croatian counterparts as they designed their campaign and organized numerous training workshops in Croatia. *Rock volieb*'s Marek Kapusta was particularly active. In the words of a young GONG activist, "Kapusta was everywhere in Croatia."[128]

Several NGOs discussed ways of being active in the elections in the spring of 1999, and thirty-five groups eventually united to form Glas 99. As in the case of OK'98, the main goal of Glas 99 was a voter education and get-out-the-vote campaign. Targeted at youth, women, pensioners, and environmental activists, each aspect of the campaign was run by a separate organization. As in Slovakia, the campaign focusing on youth was particularly crucial. Run by a newly formed Union of Nongovernmental Organizations, the youth campaign employed many of the same techniques used in Slovakia, including TV spots by popular musicians and humorous as well as informative brochures and pamphlets. As Sharon Fisher notes, the campaign aimed at women drew on the previous experiences of twenty-seven women's organizations that had worked together in 1995 and 1997 and focused on issues of particular interest to women.[129]

Although tactics were obviously adapted to reflect Croatian conditions, the role of the Slovak example was thus crucial in the development of the NGO campaign in Croatia. Just as the successful mobilizations of the NGO sectors in Romania and Bulgaria had inspired Slovak activists at the Vienna airport meeting in November 1997, so the Slovak success in ousting Mečiar and the central role the NGO community played in this outcome were critical in inspiring Croatian NGO activists to mount their own "GOTV" campaign.

THE ROLE OF OUTSIDE ACTORS

As in Slovakia, outside actors played an important role in the development of cooperation among the political opposition and in encouraging the NGO sector to be actively involved in the election. Although European actors were also involved, the United States took the lead in these activities. For many of the U.S. democracy promoters involved, a key aspect of the Croatian (as well as the Slovak) situation was the presence of a well-developed NGO sector.[130]

In 1998, IRI brought six opposition leaders to Washington to meet with Secretary of State Madeleine Albright and other officials.[131] U.S. Ambassador William Montgomery was also actively involved in supporting the effort to bring about political change. In contrast to the situation in Romania, where the U.S. ambassador had forced IRI to leave, as he felt it was behaving in a partisan way, Ambassador Montgomery (who had been the U.S. ambassador to Bulgaria from 1998 to 2000 and who had consulted with Avis Bohlen, then

---

[128] Interview with Alan Vojvodić, Zagreb, May 16, 2005.

[129] Fisher and Bijelić, "Glas 99," 64–65, 66.

[130] Interviews with Robert Benjamin, Washington, DC, April 9, 2010; Larry Garber, Washington, DC, April 9, 2010.

[131] Interview with Vesna Pusić, Zagreb, May 15, 2005.

U.S. ambassador to Bulgaria) requested that IRI begin working with opposition party leaders in Croatia by taking them to Slovakia to meet with OK'98 leaders.[132] As in Slovakia, IRI sponsored polls that helped identify voters' concerns and shape the opposition's approach to the elections.[133] These polls showed that cooperation within the opposition would pay off and, together with disappointment in the results of the 1997 local elections and victory in a by-election in Dubrovnik in October 1998, shored up unity among the opposition coalition. NDI and IRI activists urged party leaders to make better use of volunteers, allow more citizen input into their platforms, and focus on grassroots events to bring leaders into "continuous contact" with voters. U.S. activists also played an important role in urging parties to reach out to previously uninvolved constituencies such as young people, women, and, in the Croatian case, the elderly.

As in Slovakia, outside actors played a critical role in funding both monitoring organizations and NGO coalitions such as Glas 99. USAID provided financial support for GONG, and the group's monitors were trained by NDI.[134] NDI organized a series of workshops on campaign structure and organizations, the role of election monitoring, and recruitment of volunteers for GONG in July 1999 and workshops in all thirteen regional offices on recruiting monitors and retaining activists.[135] USAID and the Open Society Institute were Glas 99's largest financial supporters. The U.S. role in this respect was particularly significant and amounted to over $5,200,000.[136]

In the Croatian case, we see the network of "graduates" of civic movements that succeeded in defeating undemocratic or semiautocratic leaders thicken. Just as Bulgarian and Romanian activists proved to be very important as inspirations and practical advisors in Slovakia, so Slovak "graduates" of OK'98 played a key role in bringing new electoral strategies and techniques to Croatia – a process encouraged in part by geographical proximity and commonalities in language. This influence was most evident in the NGO sector and its campaign to mobilize citizens to vote, but the successful unification of the Slovak opposition was also a useful example for opposition political parties in Croatia, as it showed what unity could achieve, as well as providing a practical illustration of techniques that had helped the opposition win.

CONCLUSION

As we have seen in this chapter, the new strategies and tactics of both the opposition and NGOs in Bulgaria and Romania inspired the NGO sector in Slovakia to mount what proved to be a successful citizens' campaign

---

[132] Irvine, "From Civil Society to Civil Servants."
[133] Bellamy, "Croatia after Tudjman."
[134] Fisher and Bijelić, "Glas 99," 62.
[135] Jašić, "Monitoring the Vote in Croatia," 161, 164.
[136] Fisher and Bijelić, "Glas 99," 67.

that, together with a unified opposition, ended a dangerous episode of de-democratization and set the country firmly on a democratic path. The elaboration of a successful set of electoral strategies and techniques, encouraged and supported by outside democracy promoters in Slovakia, would in turn prove to be very important to future developments in the postcommunist world. It was the Slovak experience in the form of a specific model for winning elections that was consciously transported, first to Croatia and then, with modifications to fit local conditions, to other postcommunist mixed regimes. The victories of the opposition, which came about as the result of mobilizing citizens in the course of election campaigns in partly free countries, in turn had an impact in 2000 in Serbia, where, as we will discuss in Chapter 4, domestic actors were already engaged in opposing Milosevic and his policies. In both of these cases, outside actors played critical roles in urging the opposition to coalesce and the NGO sector to become involved; they also contributed by funding civil society activities during the campaigns, as well as by supporting earlier, longer-term programs to support civil society development and train party leaders.

4

Defeating a Dictator at the Polls and in the Streets

The 2000 Yugoslav Elections

Mečiar was Mother Theresa in comparison with Milošević.

Otpor activist[1]

Milošević made citizens of Serbia stoop so low that we had to use protest and even violence to make him leave office after he was defeated in the election.

Boris Begović[2]

In the last chapter, we analyzed the 1998 election in Slovakia and the 2000 election in Croatia.[3] These elections were of interest in part because they were so similar. For example, while the incumbents had used authoritarian methods to rule, and these methods had included tinkering with electoral districts and rules in ways that served their reelection interests, the 1998 election in Slovakia and the election that took place two years later in Croatia were largely free and fair. Moreover, international democracy promoters made significant contributions to both of these elections, and in both cases the opposition succeeded, in direct contrast to its past behavior, in forming a united front that ran an unusually ambitious and effective political campaign with the aid of a coalition of NGOs.

In this chapter, we continue our discussion of the remarkable run of democratizing elections in the postcommunist region by analyzing the defeat of Slobodan Milošević in the Yugoslav elections of September 2000. We have devoted an entire chapter to this event for the simple reason that this election served as a turning point in the wave of electoral turnovers that took place from 1998 to 2005 in postcommunist Europe and Eurasia. Just as it

---

[1] Quoted in Pavol Demeš and Joerg Forbrig, "Civic Action and Democratic Power Shifts: On Strategies and Resources," in *Reclaiming Democracy: Civil Society and Electoral Change in Central and Eastern Europe*, ed. Joerg Forbrig and Pavol Demeš (Washington, DC: German Marshall Fund, 2007), 189.

[2] Interview in Belgrade, April 14, 2005.

[3] We thank Marijana Trivunovic and Ray Jennings for reading an earlier version of this chapter.

was highly unlikely that the leader of Yugoslavia would be defeated, so it was unlikely in the event of such a defeat that he would actually leave office. This is because Yugoslavia was a more repressive regime than Croatia and especially Slovakia at the time of the electoral challenges to authoritarian rule, and because Slobodan Milošević, as a result, was willing and able to go to much greater lengths to stay in power – for example, by stealing elections, blocking international democracy assistance, and using violence against the opposition, civil society groups, and citizens. Milošević's removal from power, therefore, was remarkable for the simple reason that it was so hard for local and international opponents of the regime to accomplish.

We begin our analysis of the 2000 election in Serbia with a puzzle: how did Milošević stay in power throughout the 1990s, despite multiple rounds of competitive elections, political protests, and wars? Our answer is that he constructed a mixed regime that was extraordinarily successful in neutralizing domestic and international challenges to his rule. We then identify two sets of changes that opened Yugoslavia up to democratic change. One was a shift, beginning in 1997, in the domestic politics of the regime and the opposition and in U.S. policy toward the Milošević regime. The other was more short-term in nature: the rapid, yet careful, deployment by the opposition and its domestic and international allies, once Milošević suddenly called for early elections in the summer of 2000, of an innovative set of electoral strategies that resembled in many ways the very strategies that the Slovak and then the Croatian opposition had put to such good use in their defeat of authoritarian rulers. While the first set of changes made the regime more vulnerable, it was the second set of actions that converted vulnerability into actual political defeat.

DOMINATION IN THE FACE OF DISASTER

Slobodan Milošević ruled Serbia for fourteen years, beginning with his selection in 1987 as the leader of the Serbian League of Communists (at a time when Yugoslavia was still a communist-governed state composed of six republics and two autonomous provinces) and ending in October 2000, when Vojislav Koštunica, the candidate of the Democratic Opposition of Serbia, was elected to become his successor as president of the country (which at that time was still called Yugoslavia). Between these two events, Milošević was elected twice in competitive elections to serve as the president of Serbia (1989 and 1992). Once he completed his second term in that position and faced the prospect of having to leave office as a result of the term limits imposed by the 1990 Serbian Constitution, which he largely wrote, Milošević then set his sights on a new office: the Yugoslav presidency.[4] This office was easy to win,

---

[4] Kristin McKie, "The Politics of Adopting Term Limits in Sub-Saharan Africa," paper presented at the annual meeting of the American Political Science Association, Boston, MA, August 29, 2008.

because the Yugoslav parliament was responsible for filling the post, and supporters of Milošević had the votes to select him as the president. However, term limits on that position, mandated by the Yugoslav Constitution, led him in the summer of 2000 to push through the federal parliament a series of constitutional changes that, among other things, converted the Yugoslav presidency into a popularly elected post, thereby freeing him to seek reelection when his final term expired in 2001. Because of fears about another winter of severe heating shortages throughout the country and the calculation that he would catch the opposition by surprise, while continuing to capitalize on its divisions, Milošević then called for early elections to take place in September 2000. It was these elections that brought his long tenure as head of Serbia and then Yugoslavia to a close.

What is remarkable about this story is not that Milošević managed to stay in power for fourteen years by rewriting constitutions, winning a few competitive elections, and, when necessary, switching offices while using each one to exercise executive authority. Such actions are in fact far from unusual for autocratic leaders who govern mixed regimes. Rather, what is surprising is that Milošević managed to sustain his preeminent political position in Yugoslavia and in Serbia during these fourteen years in particular. During his early years in power, Communist Party hegemony collapsed not just in Yugoslavia but also in the rest of Central and Eastern Europe as well as in the Soviet Union; the Yugoslav as well as the Soviet and Czechoslovak states dissolved, and the Cold War international order ended. Thus, the very domestic and international structures that had long defined and defended the communist experiment in Yugoslavia crumbled while Milošević was serving as head of the Serbian branch of the League of Communists and then as the president of Serbia.

His tenure in office also witnessed a number of other dramatic and de-stabilizing events. These included, for example, the introduction of competitive politics throughout Yugoslavia;[5] wars in Croatia and Bosnia-Herzegovina from 1991 to 1995 that were aided and abetted by the Yugoslav government and that produced in their wake 200,000 deaths and millions of displaced citizens; and Western imposition of sanctions against Serbia. Finally, in the spring of 1999 Serbian repression in Kosovo prompted NATO to launch a seventy-eight-day bombing campaign in Serbia that led to the formation of an international protectorate (and eventually an independent state) in Kosovo, a province that had been attached to Serbia. Continued Serbian domination over Kosovo, which the NATO bombing had ended, was an issue that had long been used by Milošević as a rallying point for Serbian nationalism and as the foundation for his claim to rule.

[5] For example, forty-four parties competed for power in the first competitive elections in Serbia in 1990. See Dušan Pavlović, "Polarizacija stranačkog sistema nakon 2000 godine," in *Političke stranke u Srbiji. Struktura I funkcionisanje*, ed. Zoran Lutovac (Beograd: Friedrich Ebert Stiftung/Institut društvenih nauka, 2005), 76.

Not surprisingly, these cataclysmic developments were in turn responsible for an implosion of the Serbian economy during the 1990s. By 2000, for example, a heavy defense burden drained the economy of productive capital investment, and unemployment, high throughout the 1990s, ranged (according to various estimates) from 27 to 40 percent.[6] During the first half of the 1990s, Serbia achieved the dubious distinction of registering the highest-ever recorded rate of inflation in the world since such figures had been formally tabulated,[7] and the Serbian economy by the second half of the 1990s was estimated to have shrunk to 40 percent of the size it had been a decade earlier.[8] Mounting corruption also contributed to the Serbian economic crisis. Despite the "end" of communism, Serbia had remained a socialist economy throughout the 1990s, which was a particular problem, given the combined effects of Western sanctions and the unchallenged rule of Milošević, his family, and his allies in the Socialist Party. Thus, public officials, including the prime minister and the speaker of parliament, were also heads of major companies that functioned as monopolies in key sectors, such as the provision of energy products, and the licensing of all enterprises depended upon permission granted by the state and, thus, on maintaining close connections to the Socialist Party and its satellites, such as the neocommunist party headed by Milošević's wife, Mirjana Marković.[9] At the same time, the wars plus Western sanctions had generated market dynamics that gave considerable power to those who could control and manipulate shortages, capitalize on weak state boundaries, and dominate illegal trade.[10] While much of this money benefited Milošević and his allies personally, it was also used, some have argued, to fund the government during a time of considerable national economic shrinkage.[11]

---

[6] Sarah Birch, "The 2000 Elections in Yugoslavia: The 'Bulldozer Revolution'," *Electoral Studies* 21:3 (September 2002), 499–511.

[7] Not even Zimbabwe under Mugabe surpassed Yugoslavia in the early 1990s. See Sebastien Berger, "Zimbabwe Inflation Second Worst in History," *Telegraph*, November 13, 2008, http://www.telegraph.co.uk/news/worldnews/africaandindianocean/zimbabwe/3451873/Zimbabwe-inflation-second-worst-in-history.html.

[8] See Boris Begović and Boško Mijatović, *Four Years of Transition in Serbia* (Belgrade: Center for Liberal-Democratic Studies, 2005); interview with Boris Begović, Belgrade, April 14, 2005.

[9] See Gabriel Partos, "Serb Killings Linked to a Corrupt Government," April 26, 2000, http://news.bbc.co.uk/1/hi/world/Europe/727052.stm; Ray Jennings, *Serbia's Bulldozer Revolution: Evaluating Internal and External Factors in the Successful Democratic Breakthrough in Serbia*, CDDRL Working Paper No. 105, Center for Democracy, Development and the Rule of Law, Freeman Spogli Institute for International Studies, Stanford University (March 2009).

[10] See also Charles King, "The Benefits of Ethnic War: Understanding Eurasia's Unrecognized States," *World Politics* 53:4 (July 2001), 524–552; Peter Andreas, "Criminalizing Consequences of Sanctions: Embargo Busting and Its Legacy," *International Studies Quarterly* 49:2 (June 2005), 335–360; Peter Andreas, *Blue Helmets and Black Markets: The Business of Survival in the Siege of Sarajevo* (Ithaca, NY: Cornell University Press, 2008).

[11] Our thanks to Marijana Trivunovic for this insight.

YUGOSLAVIA AS A MIXED REGIME

How, then, did Milošević succeed in maintaining his power in the face of the disintegration of the regime and the Yugoslav state, competition for political power, war, and economic implosion? The easy response is: political repression. However, that answer is based upon a misreading of Serbian politics during the 1990s.[12] First, until 1997, as we will discuss, Milošević in fact practiced a relatively soft form of authoritarian rule. On the one hand, he limited civil liberties (but in an inconsistent way), harassed opposition parties and nongovernmental organizations (also inconsistently), and exerted control over the media and electoral procedures and outcomes. Moreover, he weakened the Serbian and Yugoslav parliaments by limiting their powers while filling these bodies with his allies; placed limits on the pluralization of Serbian politics and rule of law; and centralized the powers of the presidency (first in Serbia and then in Yugoslavia) while exploiting its institutional ties to the police, the security forces, the Yugoslav military, and the Serbian mafia along with Serbian banks and enterprises. He linked this formal network, in turn, to informal chains of economic and political dependencies that radiated outward from himself, his family, and the Socialist Party and amended the constitution, as noted earlier, in ways that served his political interests while dividing and weakening those who would challenge his power.[13] Finally, he used tanks to crush an antiwar revolt that took place in 1991.

However, it is still fair to argue that, especially during the period before 1997, Yugoslavia was in fact a mixed regime, rather than a dictatorship.[14] Thus, Milošević did respect the constitution, at least formally – which is why he went to the trouble of changing offices and offering constitutional amendments. Moreover, all twelve of the national-level elections that were held in the 1990s were competitive and, despite rigged elections beginning in 1992, became more competitive over time. For example, his Socialist Party won 46 percent of the vote in the 1990 republican elections, but by 1997 the figure had fallen (even with the "coalition of the left" competing for power) to 34 percent.[15] As a result, beginning in 1992, Milošević was forced to form

---

[12] Vitali Silitski, "Is the Age of Post-Soviet Electoral Revolutions Over?," *Democracy at Large* 1:4 (September 2005), 8–10.

[13] Vladimir Goati, *Stabilizacija Demokratije Ili Povratak Monizmu: "Treća Jugoslavija" Sredinom Devedesetih* (Podgorica: Unireks, 1996); Pavlović, "Polaricacija stranackog system a nakon 2000 godine"; Dušan Pavlović, "Serbia during and after Milošević," unpublished manuscript, September 27, 2004; Dušan Pavlović, *Akteri I modeli: ogledi o politici u Srbiji pod Miloševićem* (Beograd: Samizdat Free B92, 2005); M. Steven Fish, "Stronger Legislatures, Stronger Democracies," *Journal of Democracy* 17:1 (January 2006), 5–20.

[14] Goati, *Stabilizacija Demokratije Ili Povratak Monizmu*; Pavlović, "Polaricacija stranackog system a nakon 2000 godine"; Pavlović, "Serbia during and after Milosevic."

[15] Vladimir Goati, "The Nature of the Order and the October Overthrow in Serbia," in *Revolution and Order: Serbia after October 2000*, ed. Ivana Spasić and Milan Subotić (Belgrade: Institute for Philosophy and Social Theory, 2001), 47; and see Srećko Mihailović, "Political Formulae for the Perseverance and Change of Regime in Serbia," in *Revolution and*

coalition governments.[16] While it is true that these elections "bestowed a kind of procedural legitimacy on Milošević, while underscoring the weakness of his opponents,"[17] they nonetheless provided opportunities for the opposition to contest power and even in some cases to become part of the government.

Leaders of the democratic opposition, moreover, played a visible role in the politics of Serbia and Yugoslavia during this era. Thus, the man who became the victor in the presidential election of September 2000, Vojislav Koštunica, had been a major voice in parliament from 1990 to 1997. The co-leader of the 2000 opposition electoral effort, Zoran Djindjic, had also been a member of parliament during that period and was elected mayor of Belgrade in 1996. Vuk Drašković, the leader of the Serbian Renewal Party and the coleader, along with Djindjic, of an opposition coalition that won power in local elections in 1996, became a member of the government in 1997.

At the same time, there were always pockets (hard-won and hard-maintained) of political autonomy in Serbia, including some independent media. Indeed, an active civil society was a fixture of the Milošević regime and dated back to the communist era, when Serbia had been among the most liberal republics in the Yugoslav federation.[18] In addition, public protests were a relatively common feature of Serbian politics in the 1990s, as they had been in the 1980s. For example, major demonstrations against the regime organized by students, opposition parties, military reservists, and such opposition groups as the Belgrade Circle, the Center for Anti-War Action, and Women in Black took place in 1991, 1992, 1996 to 1997, and 1999.[19]

The 1996 to 1997 protests were particularly important, largely because of the precedents they set in both a positive and negative sense for future mobilizations against the Milošević regime.[20] First, they were unusually large and long-lasting. Second, they demonstrated that members of the opposition could work together – though Zajedno ("Together"), the coalition of opposition parties that formed to contest the 1996 elections, was misnamed in several respects. For example, it did not by any means include all of the

Order: Serbia after October 2000, ed. Ivana Spasić and Milan Subotić (Belgrade: Institute for Philosophy and Social Theory, 2001), 59–72 and Table 1, 66.

[16] See especially Pavlović, *Akteri I modeli: ogledi o politici u Srbiji pod Miloševićem*, Chapter 2; Pavlović, "Polarizacija stranačkog sistema nakon 2000 godine," 223; Mihailović, "Political Formulae," 66.

[17] Mark R. Thompson and Philipp Kuntz, "Stolen Elections: The Case of the Serbian October," *Journal of Democracy* 15:4 (October 2004), 164–165.

[18] See Goati, "The Nature of the Order and the October Overthrow in Serbia," and Goati, *Stabilizacija Demokratije Ili Povratak Monizmu*.

[19] See, in particular, Nancy L. Meyers, "Vreme Je! It's Time! Mobilization and Voting for Regime Change: The Serbian Elections of 2000" (Ph.D. dissertation, Department of Political Science, The George Washington University, 2009).

[20] See, especially, Mladen Lazić and Liljana Nikolić, *Protest in Belgrade: Winter of Discontent* (Budapest and New York: Central European University Press, 1999); interview with Nenad Konstantinović, Belgrade, April 15, 2005; and comments by Milan St. Protić at the Roundtable in Belgrade, April 13, 2005.

opposition parties or their leaders, and opposition unity was transitory in that the coalition broke up several months after the protests ended. Third, 1996 to 1997 was the first time that both students and opposition parties (but not workers)[21] protested at the same time, albeit in largely parallel fashion. Fourth, the protests, in part because of pressures from the international community and, more importantly, from the Serbian Orthodox Church, succeeded in forcing Milošević to allow opposition parties to take the offices they had won in the 1996 local elections. Fifth, the geography of the protests, like the geography of the election itself, demonstrated for all to see that the core components of Milošević's political constituency – that is, smaller towns outside of the capital – were showing signs of defecting from the Socialist Party to the opposition. Finally, in another preview of what was to happen immediately after the September 2000 elections, the stimulus for the protests was electoral fraud.[22] As Florian Bieber notes, "The concrete event of election fraud turned out to be more effective than the more serious, but less tangible devastation of the economy and society and the wars in Bosnia and Croatia."[23] Lazić and Nikolić agree: "The arrogant and obvious forgery of electoral results ... abruptly released the frustrations the middle classes had been accumulating for years: this one act revealed to them how deep the problem of Serbian society was."[24]

STRATEGIC INTERACTIONS: REGIME AND OPPOSITION

Repression, therefore, is not a good explanation of why the Milošević regime endured – a line of argument that is further weakened by the fact that, as we will demonstrate later in this chapter, it was precisely when he became more repressive that Milošević's hold on power declined. Rather, a better explanation of why Milošević was able to endure, despite all these challenges and an abysmal record in office, focuses on the strategic side of politics, that is, the relative effectiveness of the strategies adopted by Milošević compared to those of the democratic opposition and the impact of these strategies, in turn, on the voting behavior of Serbian citizens.

To turn to the first point: when Milošević assumed the leadership of the Serbian party apparatus and then the presidency of Serbia in the second half of the 1980s, Serbia was in political and economic turmoil. On the table and subject to acrimonious debate not just within the League of Communists, but also within the relatively large Serbian opposition and among ordinary

[21] See Lazić and Nikolić, *Protest in Belgrade.*
[22] Thompson and Kuntz, "Stolen Elections."
[23] Florian Bieber, "The Serbian Transition and Civil Society: Roots of the Delayed Transition in Serbia," *International Journal of Politics, Culture, and Society* 17:1 (Fall 2003), 84.
[24] Lazić and Nikolić, *Protest in Belgrade*, 16; also see Thompson and Kuntz, "Stolen Elections"; Joshua A. Tucker, "Enough! Electoral Fraud, Collective Action Problems, and the Second Wave of Post-Communist Democratic Revolutions," *Perspectives on Politics* 5:3 (September 2007), 535–551.

citizens, were not only old issues drawn from the "cauldron of Yugoslav historical controversies,"[25] but also new issues of immediate and major importance. These issues included the future of the socialist experiment and the Yugoslav state; the advisability of economic and political liberalization in Serbia and, more generally, in Yugoslavia; the definition of the Serbian nation and its rights and boundaries; and the relationship between Serbia, on the one hand, and other republics and provinces within Yugoslavia, especially those containing sizeable Serbian minorities, on the other. Milošević responded to this complex array of issues and the searing divisions they generated within Serbian politics – in direct contrast, for example, to the consensus developing in Slovenia at the same time around an independent state, democracy, capitalism, and integration with Europe – by claiming to be a reform communist who supported political and economic change, who would defend the Yugoslav state against republican leaders bent on its dissolution, and who would be willing and able to stand up for the Serbian nation, whether in Serbia or in neighboring republics.[26] Milošević, therefore, was the proverbial example (though rare in actual fact in the region) of the communist who, recognizing the threats imposed by the dissolution of the communist order, opted nearly overnight (and helped along by audience reactions to a speech given in Kosovo) to redefine himself as a nationalist.

Thus, he sidestepped needed political and economic reforms that would have necessarily undermined his rule and that of the Socialist Party and, instead, played up threats to the nation, using minority populations and other republics as scapegoats. In the process, he built a "bunker" mentality among many elites and publics in Serbia and launched a series of wars in order to protect the nation from existential threats. As a result, Milošević built a strong base of support not just among members of the Serbian League of Communists, who saw him as the defender of their monopoly over politics and economics, and among many Serbian intellectuals, who were in some cases still attached to the Yugoslav experiment and in other cases very receptive to his defense of the Serbian nation, but also, more generally, among the citizens of Serbia (particularly in rural areas and small towns) who feared the disintegration of their way of life and their state.

[25] Veljko Vujacic, *Reexamining the Serbian Exceptionalism Thesis*, Berkeley Program in Soviet and Post-Soviet Studies, Working Paper Series, Spring 2004, 12.

[26] See, for instance, Vujacic, "Reexamining the Serbian Exceptionalism Thesis"; Veljko Vujacic, "From Class to Nation: Left, Right, and the Ideological and Institutional Roots of Post-Communist 'National Socialism,'" *East European Politics and Societies* 17:3 (August 2003), 359–392; Bieber, "The Serbian Transition and Civil Society"; Vladimir Ilić, *"Otpor" in or Beyond Politics: Helsinki Files Vol. 5* (Belgrade: Helsinki Committee for Human Rights in Serbia, 2001); Goati, *Stabilizacija Demokratije Ili Povratak Monizmu*; V. P. Gagnon, *The Myth of Ethnic War: Serbia and Croatia in the 1990s* (Ithaca, NY: Cornell University Press, 2004); Eric Gordy, *The Culture of Power in Serbia: Nationalism and the Destruction of Alternatives* (College Park: Pennsylvania State University Press, 1999); Valerie Bunce, *Subversive Institutions: The Design and the Destruction of Socialism and the State* (Cambridge: Cambridge University Press, 1999).

Milošević also benefited from his ability to claim the *center* of the Serbian elite political spectrum – a location that allowed him the luxury of being a more popular and certainly less risky political choice than the alternatives. On the one hand, in contrast to the democratic opposition, he was more supportive of the nation in words and deeds, more respectful of the communist experience, and less likely to expose Serbia to the unknowns of radical and destabilizing economic and political reforms. On the other hand, in contrast to nationalist extremists, such as Vojislav Šešelj (who headed a paramilitary force and the Radical Party), Milošević had in fact contributed to a liberalization of Serbian politics (or at least gone along for the ride), carried out actions that demonstrated his commitment to defending the nation, and used rhetoric that stopped short of advocating the wholesale extermination of all the enemies, real and imagined, of Serbia.[27]

The other reason why Milošević was able to stay in power over the course of the 1990s was the failure of those who opposed him, both outside and within Serbia, to mount effective challenges to his power. On the international side of the equation, we can point to the inability of the United States and members of the European Union to respond in a forceful and consistent manner to the aggressive actions Milošević took in the neighboring republics and then states of Croatia and Bosnia-Herzegovina from 1991 to 1995. Instead, as Ray Jennings has aptly summarized, Western "diplomatic relations with Milošević were schizophrenic."[28] Indeed, even when the war in Bosnia ended with the Dayton Peace Accords in 1995, the West, if anything, became more supportive of Milošević, given his role as a signatory and key enforcer of the Accords. This was a bitter pill for the Serbian opposition to swallow, especially when the West stood by while hundreds of thousands of Serbian citizens took to the streets for three months from 1996 to 1997 to protest the fraudulent local elections that had taken place in 1996. The NATO bombing of Serbia for seventy-eight days in 1999 constituted yet another chapter in this story. While demonstrating the international isolation of Serbia and foreclosing any possibility of continued Western toleration of the regime, these actions also primed domestic support for Milošević in the short term at a time when the opposition was beginning to view the regime as increasingly vulnerable.[29]

If the West was divided and often demobilized when confronting the Milošević regime, so was the Serbian opposition. Part of the problem was differences in ideology, though arraying the opposition at that time with respect

[27] See Pavlović, *Akteri I modeli: ogledi o politici u Srbiji pod Miloševićem*, 76; Mihailović, "Political Formulae," on Serbian voting behavior; and Bieber, "The Serbian Transition and Civil Society," on the Serbian opposition.

[28] Jennings, "Serbia's Bulldozer Revolution," 6.

[29] For Richard Miles, the chief of mission in the American embassy in Belgrade at the time, the bombing campaign served as the turning point in U.S. – Yugoslav relations during the Milošević era (interview in Washington, DC, September 25, 2009). However, the short-term effects in fact strengthened Milošević's political position at home – as observed by Milan St. Protić at the Roundtable organized by the Jefferson Institute in Belgrade, April 13, 2005.

to ideological differences is devilishly difficult.[30] However, the larger problem that surfaced repeatedly in our interviews was the existence of personality conflicts, which contributed to "nasty actions that in turn prevented coalition formation."[31] In addition, opposition leaders inherited from the communist era a political culture that lacked any understanding of – or much experience with – collaboration in pursuit of political power or any sense of the important role of democratic oppositions in tracking and responding to public opinion when mobilizing political support or shaping ideas on public policy.[32] As Gregory Simpson and Daniel Calingaert, both of whom worked for the International Republican Institute in Serbia (and in other countries in the region, including Bulgaria), put it: while Serbia was blessed at the time of transition with a large and experienced opposition as a result of the liberal character of Yugoslavia during communism, the opposition nonetheless had a pronounced tendency to "prefer posturing over power."[33] The opposition was also self-defeating in another way. As Vesna Pešić, a longtime leader of civil society organizations opposing the war, succinctly summarized a key problem: "Opposition leaders were much more interested in keeping people out, rather than bringing people in."[34]

These deficiencies were only exacerbated by the difficult choices Milošević dictated to the opposition – choices that helped him co-opt some of his opponents while keeping others divided, disputatious, and, as a result, demobilized.[35] Thus, the opposition in Yugoslavia did not just have understandable disagreements about such complicated questions as the extent of actual outside threats to the Serbian nation and whether war was the appropriate response to such threats or could in fact be better understood as their cause. They were also undermined by a familiar game leaders play when national security is in doubt. Milošević labeled those who criticized the regime either unpatriotic Serbs or, worse yet, "foreign agents" (as both Zoran Djindjic and Vojislav Koštunica, for example, were labeled during the 1996 to 1997 protests).[36]

However, there was a more general problem that the Yugoslav opposition repeatedly faced during the Milošević years. By their very nature, mixed regimes are good at preempting strong challenges to their power. While such

---

[30] See Ilić, "Otpor"; Bieber, "The Serbian Transition and Civil Society"; and Pavlović, "Polaricacija stranackog system a nakon 2000 godine."

[31] Interview with Marko Blagojević, Belgrade, April 11, 2005.

[32] Interviews with Marko Blagojević, Belgrade, April 11, 2005; Suzana Grubješić, Belgrade April 12, 2005; and Srdjan Bogosavljević, Belgrade, April 13, 2005.

[33] Interviews with Gregory Simpson, Belgrade, April 13, 2005, and Charlottesville, November 9, 2007; and Daniel Calingaert, Washington, DC, July 19, 2005; Pavlović, "Polaricacija stranackog system a nakon 2000 godine"; Bieber, "The Serbian Transition and Civil Society."

[34] Interview with Vesna Pešić, Belgrade, April 14, 2005.

[35] See, especially, Ilić, "Otpor"; Bieber, "The Serbian Transition and Civil Society"; Gagnon, *The Myth of Ethnic War*; and Gordy, *The Culture of Power in Serbia*.

[36] See Damjan de Krnjević-Mišković, "Serbia's Prudent Revolution," *Journal of Democracy* 12:3 (July 2001), 96–110.

regimes are vulnerable, as many have noted, because they expose themselves to competition for political office, they also fortify themselves by presenting the opposition with an unusually long menu of competing political options. For example, should they participate in elections or boycott them? Should they join the government or oppose it? Should they support anti-regime protests or maintain distance from these actions? As a result, oppositions find it extraordinarily difficult to forge a consensus about the strategies they should use to counter the regime. In this sense, "fake" democracies tend to be Janus-faced.[37] They provide opportunities for change, but at the same time prevent exploitation of these opportunities by fragmenting opposition forces.

Thus, it is far from surprising, especially in view of the earlier points about opposition culture and the personalities involved, that the leaders of the twenty or so democratic opposition parties of Serbia found it very easy to disagree with each other. This is precisely what we saw throughout the 1990s in the cases of Vuk Drašković and his Serbian Renewal Party, Zoran Djindjic and his Democratic Party, and Vojislav Koštunica and his Democratic Party of Serbia. Indeed, the latter two parties formed because of a split in 1992 between Djindjic and Koštunica over such questions.

THE PUBLIC PROBLEM

Thus, clever strategies on the part of Milošević and the strategic failings on the part of the opposition maintained Milošević in power. However, just as important for Milošević's tenure in office were four other considerations that focus our attention on the role of Yugoslav citizens in sustaining the regime. One was the fact that Milošević avoided facing voters from 1992 to 2000, which made it hard for voters to focus their attention on the costs of his rule and translate those sentiments into votes for the opposition. As Dušan Pavlović has summarized the problem: "With direct elections, Serbs would have realized sooner what Milošević really was: a former communist apparatchik and a third-rate banker with a 'strong affinity' for corruption."[38] Second, voting in Serbia throughout much of the 1990s was strongly affected by the national question – to the benefit of Milošević and his close allies – and by the ingrained communist-era habit (helped, no doubt, by continuity in rule by the Socialists) of viewing elections as rituals held for the expression of regime support in general and support of the incumbent nationalist-socialist bloc in particular. Elections, in short, were not understood by Serbian citizens as exercises in retrospective voting, with pocketbook issues playing the decisive role in voter choices, and they were not viewed as contests asking publics to select among politicians and policies.[39] Another factor was that nonvoters, whose numbers

---

[37] Here we are borrowing from Andrew Wilson, *Virtual Politics: Faking Democracy in the Post-Soviet World* (New Haven, CT: Yale University Press, 2005).

[38] Pavlović, *Akteri I modeli: ogledi o politici u Srbiji pod Miloševićem*, 5.

[39] See, especially, the analyses by Ilić, "Otpor"; Mihailović, "Political Formulae"; Pavlović, *Akteri I modeli: ogledi o politici u Srbiji pod Miloševićem*; and Pavlović, "Polarizacija

grew over the course of the decade as a result of citizen perceptions of electoral fraud as well as election fatigue, were far more likely to oppose Milošević than those who voted.[40] While in practice less and less favorable to Milošević over time, therefore, electoral tallies over the course of the decade – which resulted more and more in fraudulent elections – increasingly exaggerated the size of his support.[41]

Finally and most importantly: Milošević's losses were *not* the opposition's gains. In fact, the Serbian electorate viewed the opposition in very negative ways. They were fully aware of the personal rivalries and disagreements about strategy within the opposition, and they had seen some opposition leaders collude with the regime. They recognized that elections were stolen, but nonetheless resented the fact that the opposition often engaged in electoral boycotts. They also saw little evidence of a distinctive stance toward the problems, nationalist and economic, that confronted Serbia on the part of the opposition.[42] The opposition was widely seen, in short, as divided, corrupt, and incompetent. For example, a survey conducted in December 1999 found that less than one-quarter of all respondents in Serbia thought that the opposition would be able to form a coalition in the coming election.[43]

The unpopularity of the Serbian opposition, even on the eve of the 2000 breakthrough elections, is a point that needs to be highlighted, because the same was also the case for most of the other oppositions analyzed in this book. Public distrust and dislike of the opposition, in turn, call into serious question an assumption that is central to many strategically oriented analyses of the "color revolutions" – that is, that when citizens are angry at the regime, they transfer their support in nearly automatic fashion to the opposition. Whether they then act on these changing sentiments depends, of course, on whether the obstacles to collective action can be surmounted.[44]

By contrast, one can argue that several difficult steps must be taken if popular dissatisfaction with the government in mixed regimes is to translate into a victory for the opposition. In particular, people must think that voting is a meaningful way to signal this dissatisfaction, believe that their votes will count, and support the opposition when they vote. In the Serbian and Yugoslav cases, while public opinion surveys indicated by the second half of the 1990s that citizens were becoming increasingly dissatisfied with the regime, the other preconditions for an opposition victory were not in place.

stranačkog sistema nakon 2000 godine." Their observations are supported by "Election Orientation of the Citizens of Serbia in 1999–2000," http://www.bbnet.pluznikov.co.rs/bdnet/elections/eng/lutovac.htm (accessed October 1, 2009). A summary of public opinion and voting data was also provided by Milan Nikolić, Belgrade, April 12, 2005.

[40] "Election Orientation."

[41] Also see Ilić, "Otpor"; and Mihailović, "Political Formulae."

[42] Pavlović, "Polaricacija stranackog system a nakon 2000 godine."

[43] "Election Orientation."

[44] See, for example, Tucker, "Enough!"; and Lucan Way, "The Real Causes of the Color Revolutions," *Journal of Democracy* 19:3 (July 2008), 55–69.

Thus, while Milošević was losing ground even with Serbs from small towns and cities (and he had never won an election, for example, in Belgrade), he was not by any means losing ground *to* the opposition. This was not a zero sum game where voters were forced to choose between two players, with rejection of one meaning selection of the other. People are not required to vote; they do not have to choose the opposition if they reject the incumbent; and they do not have to defend their choice in the streets. What this discussion suggests is that, while Milošević was politically vulnerable in certain ways by the end of the 1990s, he was nonetheless quite likely to remain in power, if only because of the continuing problems of the opposition and its lack of appeal for voters; the failure of so many protests over the course of the 1990s to dislodge him; and, more generally, his proven record of surmounting one political and economic obstacle after another over the course of his career.

From 1997 to 1999, however, three important changes took place in Serbia and abroad that shifted politics on the ground in favor of the removal of Milošević from power. One was Milošević's decision to tighten his authoritarian hold over Serbian politics – a decision that, ironically, had the opposite effect. Second, two new civil society organizations were formed from 1997 to 1998 that were well situated to contest Milošević's hold over Serbian society and over Serbian and Yugoslav elections. The first was an organization committed to free and fair elections, the Center for Elections and Democracy (CeSID), and the second was the student movement, Otpor ("Resistance"). Finally, beginning in 1998, U.S. policy toward Yugoslavia began to shift in a significant way.

THE IRONIC CONSEQUENCES OF HARD-LINE POLITICS IN SERBIA, 1998 TO 1999

The eighty-day protests that took place from 1996 to 1997 in Serbia had the path-breaking effect of forcing Milošević to accept the defeat of the Socialist Party in the 1996 local elections and thereby allow the victorious opposition to take office in fourteen of the most important towns in Serbia.[45] However, soon after this bow in the direction of a more pluralistic politics, Milošević made it clear that he was intent on replacing the "incomplete autocracy" of the past (to borrow from Florian Bieber)[46] with a much more complete version. Thus, from 1998 to 1999 he pushed through new laws that severely circumscribed freedom of the press, civil society groups, the autonomy of universities (even closing down the University of Belgrade in 2000), and the political and financial independence of local governments.

Second, from 1998 through the summer of 2000, his regime launched increasingly violent attacks not just on its enemies – that is, NGOs, the media, and opposition parties – but also on its purported friends, such as individuals

[45] de Krnjević-Mišković, "Serbia's Prudent Revolution."
[46] Bieber, "The Serbian Transition and Civil Society."

who were members of the governing alliance.[47] For example, from 1999 to 2000 the Serbian police took between 1,700 and 2,000 members of the youth movement Otpor into custody for questioning.[48] One survey of 600 members of Otpor indicated that nearly one-half of the total membership of the organization had been detained at some point by the police.[49] The police also regularly confiscated their equipment and literature. During the same period, there were several assassination attempts against Vuk Drašković, the leader of the Serbian Renewal Party and a co-leader of the protests that took place from 1996 to 1997, yet thereafter a periodic member of coalition governments in Serbia. Moreover, at least twenty political murders occurred in Serbia from 1998 to 2000, including that of Slavko Ćuruvija, a prominent journalist, and in 2000 alone (before the elections), those of three major political figures: Živorad Petrović, the director of JAT (Yugoslav Airlines); Pavle Bulatović, the defense minister; and, on the eve of the elections, Ivan Stambolić, Milošević's mentor, the former head of the Serbian League of Communists (until Milošević pushed him aside in 1987), and a former president of Yugoslavia in the 1980s.[50] The final murder was the most significant, because Stambolić was seen by Milošević as the primary challenger to his power – a perception that spoke volumes, among other things, about his habit of underestimating the democratic opposition, including in 2000 the eventually victorious Democratic Opposition of Serbia.[51]

These actions have led Vladimir Goati, an astute longtime analyst of Serbian and Yugoslav politics, to date 1998 as a turning point in the nature of the Serbian political regime under Milošević. As Goati explained:

> Democratic institutions – political parties, parliament, multiparty elections – were introduced in Serbia in 1990, so it would be an oversimplification to call this order authoritarian. At the same time, Serbia's political order did not ensure an 'equal arena' for mutual contest to all political parties, so therefore it cannot be called democratic either. Hence, the order in Serbia was most accurately classified as being of the pseudo-democratic type analyzed by Larry Diamond.[52] This definition held until 1998, when the regime started increasingly to resort to violence against opposition parties, independent media and NGOs. In this way, the type of order was essentially changed: pseudo-democracy degenerated into a pure authoritarian order.[53]

While ostensibly limiting the room for political maneuver in Serbia and thereby undercutting the ability of opposition parties and civil society groups

---

[47] Goati, "The Nature of the Order and the October Overthrow in Serbia."

[48] See Goati, "The Nature of the Order and the October Overthrow in Serbia," and Ilić, "Otpor," for estimates.

[49] Ilić, "Otpor."

[50] Partos, "Serb Killings Linked to a Corrupt Government."

[51] Our thanks to Marijana Trivunovic for making this point.

[52] Larry Diamond, "Thinking about Hybrid Regimes," *Journal of Democracy* 13:2 (April 2002), 21–35.

[53] Goati, "The Nature of the Order and the October Overthrow in Serbia," 45.

to challenge Milošević's rule, the hardening of the regime nonetheless had a series of effects that undermined Milošević's hold on politics. First, repression in this instance undercut popular support of the regime – as was also the case in Slovakia under Mečiar (see Chapter 3) and in Ukraine under Kuchma (see Chapter 5). Citizens were alienated by the wave of repressive legislation from 1998 to 2000 and its violation of constitutional principles; the constant crackdowns on the media and various civil society groups and opposition parties; the upsurge in political murders; and growing evidence that Milošević had manipulated electoral outcomes (which was particularly apparent in the 1998 Serbian presidential election). At the same time, Serbian publics drew a particular – and easily overlooked – conclusion from these developments. This lesson was succinctly summarized by Nenad Konstantinović, a leader of Otpor: "The rising despotism of the Milošević regime testified to his growing desperation." Indeed, once the police in their campaign against Otpor began to arrest students as young as thirteen, as Konstantinović elaborated in the interview we conducted with him, Serbian citizens started to rally in support of the youth movement and to view the Milošević regime as increasingly "ridiculous" and "embarrassing."[54]

Thus, it was not just what Milošević and his allies did and the degree to which their actions violated political norms; it was also that these actions revealed and contributed to the weakness, rather than the strength, of the regime. As a result, in a series of surveys conducted throughout 1999 by the Center for Political Studies in Belgrade and summarized in an interview we conducted with its director, Milan Nikolić,[55] an easy majority of Serbian citizens rejected the nationalist rhetoric that was foundational for Milošević's political mandate. These shifts in public opinion, especially when combined with the concerns discussed earlier, led 80 percent of the survey respondents to express opposition to Milošević – a percentage that crystallized on the eve of the NATO bombing of Serbia in the spring of 1999 and that, after a temporary rally-around-the-flag detour, returned by the fall of that year.[56]

Growing repression from 1998 to 2000 also cut into the support of the very groups upon which the survival of the regime depended: the police, the security forces, and the military. In contrast to his earlier years in power when the enemies of Serbia were conveniently located outside of the country, which made it easier to construct a case against them, by 1998 the enemies of the people had become the people themselves. By pressing the security forces, the police, and the military to take much more aggressive actions against Serbian citizens, who were after all exercising the freedoms guaranteed by the constitutions of Serbia and Yugoslavia, Milošević to some extent set the stage for a deregulation of the coercive monopoly that had served as the foundation of his

[54] Interview with Nenad Konstantinović, Belgrade, 2005.
[55] Interviews with Milan Nikolić, Belgrade, April 12, 2005; Kenneth Wollack, Washington, DC, May 12, 2010; Barbara Haig and Carl Gershman, Washington, DC, May 14, 2010.
[56] Also see the data summarized by Pavlović, *Akteri I modeli: ogledi o politici u Srbiji pod Miloševićem*, 1.

rule. By all accounts, many members of these organizations were becoming increasingly uncomfortable with their new job descriptions, especially given the contrast between the respect for the constitution and political niceties characteristic of Milošević's earlier years in office and the kinds of actions (to which they were a party) that took place beginning in 1998. Bearing down on Serbian citizens contradicted the familiar script of protecting the Serbian nation from its external enemies, and the actions against members of Otpor in particular were, as already noted, hard to justify, especially when very young people were the target. Thus, concerns about the wisdom and legitimacy of Milošević's war against his own people began to surface in increasingly visible ways in 1999 as the police began to interact more with Otpor, keep the flowers and the literature that members of the organization gave them, and listen to the message that they were also being victimized by the regime.

These developments, however, must be placed alongside other factors that remind us that, even by the end of the 1990s, the Milošević regime was still relatively strong. For example, there had in fact been few visible defections from the regime, and the ruling Socialist Party was fully intact. This situation was very different, as we will see in Chapter 6, from that of Georgia on the eve of the Rose Revolution and Kyrgyzstan on the eve of the Tulip Revolution. Finally, Milošević had demonstrated time and again his ability to survive strong political and economic challenges to his rule.

THE RISE OF OTPOR AND CESID

The period from 1997 to 1998 was also important because of the rise of two new civil society organizations that were to play a critical role in the 2000 elections and that grew out of widespread anger about the crackdown on the universities and Milošević's increasingly blatant interventions in Serbian elections. The first organization was Otpor ("Resistance"), which formed in 1998 partly in response to the student protests in 1996 and 1997 and which brought together in one organization Serbian middle school, high school, and college students sharing a common goal: opposing the Milošević regime because of its repressive actions, the international isolation of Serbia, and the destruction of economic opportunities for the young. What made Otpor so effective as a regime opponent was the long history of student protests in Serbia and the lessons drawn from that tradition, together with its sheer size, organizational depth, and geographical and generational reach.[57] For example, by 1999 Otpor had 60,000 members and 100 offices located throughout Serbia. It had a flat, rather than hierarchical, organizational structure that protected the organization as a whole from attacks on individual offices and leaders launched by the

---

[57] See Meyers, "Vreme Je! It's Time!"; and Olena Nikolayenko, "The Learning Curve: Student Protests in Serbia, 1991–2000," paper prepared for the eleventh annual Graduate Workshop, Kokkalis Program on Southeastern and East-Central Europe, Harvard University, February 12–13, 2009, http://www.hks.harvard.edu/kokkalis/gsw/2009/Leadership/Nikolayenko%20 Paper.pdf (accessed September 27, 2009).

authorities, and it was the first civil society organization in Serbia to reach the entire country, including minorities, such as the Hungarians in Vojvodina.[58] In addition, Otpor had at its disposal 70,000 mobile phones.[59]

Otpor was also very active in making connections with important individuals and groups in Serbia that were ignored by other opposition groups or that had ties to the regime – for example, in the first case, pensioner organizations and unions, and in the second, Dobrica Ćosić (the former Yugoslav president and the best-known defector from the regime), the Serbian Academy of Sciences, the Association of Dramatic Artists, and the Serbian Orthodox Church. At the same time, Otpor members were energetic, and their activities were daring, creative, and often entertaining. For example, in reaction to the regime's claim that they were lackeys of the West, Otpor members began wearing buttons claiming they were "foreign hirelings." They also made wide use of street theater that poked fun at Milošević and embraced the "poster mania" that we also saw in Slovakia in 1998. This – along with police actions taken against students as young as thirteen; the success Otpor had in making daily, concise anti-regime statements that they used the media to publicize; and their widespread use of popular cultural symbols and cell phones – made Otpor a very popular movement and one that police found extremely hard to contain. Unlike the democratic opposition, Otpor avoided big confrontations with the regime – though the opposition often felt that Otpor was unnecessarily provocative.[60]

Finally, beginning in 2000, Otpor turned its attention to calling for elections and encouraging, if not forcing, the Serbian opposition parties to work together to defeat Milošević. Thus, they invited leaders of the opposition to their first congress in February 2000 (which met at the same time as the congress of the Socialist Party), where seventy-six municipalities were represented. Otpor leaders then demanded, before the audience of activists and with the doors of the auditorium locked, that the leaders pledge themselves to full-scale collaboration with one another. Otpor, in short, became a formidable adversary. Its daily "happenings" demonstrated the limits of Milošević's power, and the movement's sole focus on ending Milošević's rule helped override the divisions within the opposition and the citizenry, especially connected to the issue of nationalism.

The other new organization was the Center for Elections and Democracy (CeSID), which was formed in 1997. If Otpor was full of spirited political amateurs using innovative techniques to organize opposition to the regime and undermine its political authority, CeSID was composed of sophisticated social scientists who were interested in using polling and reforms in electoral

---

[58] Interviews with Nenad Konstantinović, Belgrade, April 15, 2005; Ivan Marović, Washington, DC, October 14, 2004, and Belgrade, April 14, 2005; Mike Staresinic, Belgrade, April 15, 2005; and Srdja Popović, Oxford, March 2007. Also see Ilić, "Otpor."

[59] Interview with Vesna Pešić, Belgrade, April 14, 2005.

[60] Interviews with Daniel Calingaert, Washington, DC, July 19, 2005; and Richard Miles, Washington, DC, September 25, 2009.

procedures to accomplish the same objectives. Moreover, if Otpor did the hard work of exposing the vulnerabilities, the violence, and the illegitimacy of the regime, coining apt verbal and visual critiques of the regime that did much to crystallize popular resentment, and devising effective ways to join popular anger against the regime with a stronger sense that it could be resisted, if not ended, CeSID accomplished a series of different and equally challenging but complimentary tasks. In particular, despite the constraints imposed by the regime, CeSID put together a group of people who had the commitment and the skills to collect and monitor public opinion, improve the quality of voter lists while registering large numbers of new voters and distributing material explaining the voting process, and build the volunteer infrastructure necessary to mobilize voter turnout and monitor elections.[61]

Like Otpor, moreover, CeSID was very savvy about working with the media and early on established ties with similar organizations in neighboring countries, especially in Slovakia and Bulgaria, but also in Croatia. As a result, CeSID, like Otpor, was in a strong position to play a critical role in the 2000 elections. It was this organization, for example, that pressured the regime to reform voter lists and helped organize mass voter registration and turnout drives. CeSID also made sure that each polling station would be monitored (in this case, solely by local volunteers, since Milošević did not allow external monitoring) and that it had the organization and the local and international linkages, including access to a mainframe in Bulgaria, to collect vote totals from each precinct and tabulate vote totals quickly. In addition, this organization was responsible for getting voters to the polls in the last hours of the election. These actions were critical for the victory of the opposition, given disappointing trends in the geography of voter turnover and CeSID's painstakingly collected information about the spatial distribution of public preferences. Finally, CeSID held widely publicized press conferences that announced the results of the election even before the official results had been made public. It was the contrast between CeSID's figures and those offered by the regime that took Milošević by surprise and that forced him to claim victory and then change his mind and call for a second round of voting. In fact, the vote tabulation generated by CeSID, along with other election-related activities carried out by the opposition and by CeSID, Otpor, and other civil society groups, served as the key stimulus for Serbian citizens to take to the streets to demand that Koštunica be allowed to take office.[62]

SHIFTS IN U.S. POLICY

The final key development in 1998 was a major change in U.S. foreign policy.[63] The NATO bombing of Serbia in the spring of 1999 in response to Serbian

---

[61] Interview with Marko Blagojević, Belgrade, April 11, 2005.

[62] See, especially, Thompson and Kuntz, "Stolen Elections," on this dynamic.

[63] See Jennings, "Serbia's Stolen Elections"; also see interviews with James C. O'Brien, Washington, DC, November 16, 2006; Daniel Serwer, Washington, DC, November 17,

attacks on the rebellious province of Kosovo signaled the end of the Clinton administration's willingness to appease Milošević as a guarantor of the Dayton Peace Accords, leave management of the Balkan theater to the Europeans, and shelve, as a result, the issue of regime change in Serbia. As members of the administration and specialists on the region in Washington concurred, especially in view of the worsening situation in Kosovo and the failure to forge an agreement between the Albanian and Serbian leadership in Rambouillet in 1998, it was time to craft a new policy to counter Milošević's long success in keeping the Serbian opposition, the United States, and the EU divided and ineffective. Thus, while Madeline Albright began to depict Milošević as the "butcher of the Balkans" in 1998, discussions at the United States Institute of Peace in that year began to converge on the question of how to defeat Milošević.[64] Democratic change in Serbia, therefore, was increasingly seen as critical to stability in the Balkans. The reorientation of U.S. foreign policy that took shape from 1998 to the summer of 1999 was the result of very hard work on the part of individuals located in the State Department, the United States Institute of Peace, the National Endowment for Democracy, the National Democratic Institute, and the inner circles of the Clinton administration – for example, Daniel Serwer, Albert Cevallos, James C. O'Brien, Robert Gelbard, James Swigert, Kenneth Wollack, and James Dobbins. By the fall of 1999 two important developments had taken place. First, there was a sharp increase in the money the United States government allocated to the goal of supporting democratic change in Serbia, and this money was supplemented by private foundations, such as the Open Society Institute, Rockefeller Brothers, and Mott. While helpful in and of itself, this money also communicated to Serbian opposition forces that the West was now on their side.

Second, a formal group was formed within the Clinton administration that defined its mandate as one of supporting regime change in Serbia. While these longer-term shifts in thinking about the Milošević regime were influential, so was an unavoidable fact on the ground. In bombing Serbia, with the targets including Milošević's residence, U.S. and, more generally, Western policies toward the Serbian regime had to change – from tolerating the regime to mounting active opposition to it. Until the summer of 2000, however, the focus of U.S. activities was primarily on providing money and equipment to support pluralism in Serbia – for example, an independent radio and print media (including B-92, Studio B, Blic, Vijesti, Danas, NIN, and Vreme); political organizations, such as the Civic Alliance; and civil society organizations, such as Nezavisinost (an independent union), the Center for Anti-War Action, the Belgrade Center for Human Rights, the Association for Independent

---

2006; Robert Gelbard, Ithaca, NY, March 1, 2007; Roland Kovats, Budapest, May 24, 2006; Daniel Calingaert, Washington, DC, July 19, 2005; and Mike Staresinic, Belgrade, April 15, 2005.

[64] See Madeleine Albright, *Madam Secretary: A Memoir* (New York: Miramax Books, 2003); see also interviews with Daniel Serwer, Washington, DC, November 17, 2006; Robert Gelbard, Ithaca, NY, March 1, 2007; and James C. O'Brien, Washington, DC, November 16, 2006.

Electoral Media (ANEM), Otpor, CeSID, and a host of women's organizations. The United States also supported public opinion polls and sponsored regular donors' meetings, along with seminars held, for instance, in Budapest, Bratislava, and Berlin, but also in Washington, for members of opposition parties and Otpor.[65] In addition, organizations funded by the United States government, together with the Open Society Institute, facilitated contacts between Serbian parties and civil society organizations within the country, and between them, on the one hand, and their counterparts in Slovakia and Bulgaria in particular, but also in Croatia, on the other.

While impressive in their reach, these actions, along with the information on nonviolent conflict techniques provided by the Center for Non-Violent Conflict and books and pamphlets written by Gene Sharp, were relatively scattergun.[66] They were built on the assumption – perhaps more accurately, the hope – that a stronger opposition and civil society would somehow in and of itself lead to the removal of Milošević from power.[67] What they lacked, however, as James O'Brien astutely argued in our interview with him, was a "transition mechanism."[68] As we will see later, Milošević solved this problem by calling for early elections and placing himself on the ballot.

From the perspective of the opposition, U.S. assistance was welcome, but there was widespread recognition that the United States had been, to put it mildly, an unreliable political ally and one that had all too often engaged in clumsy and counterproductive interventions.[69] As Milan St. Protić, who was elected mayor of Belgrade in 2000, commented at a roundtable discussing the causes of the defeat of Milošević sponsored by the Jefferson Institute in Belgrade on April 13, 2005: "Why would we ever put much stock in the West?"

Thus, significant changes in the domestic and international context of the Milošević regime from 1997 to 2000 had the combined effect of making the regime more vulnerable than it had been in previous years. However, vulnerability is one thing, and the fall of a regime another. As we have noted previously, quite vulnerable regimes can endure for decades. Moreover, Milošević, we must remember, had accumulated a remarkable record of staving off powerful international and domestic challenges to his rule. Second, and also echoing an earlier observation: the defeat of an autocrat is one thing, and the victory of the democratic opposition another. The general rule in regime transitions over the past thirty years has been for authoritarian regimes to give way to new authoritarian regimes, not democracies.[70]

[65] Interviews with Kenneth Wollack, Washington, DC, May 12, 2010; Barbara Haig, Washington DC, May 14, 2010; and Carl Gershman, Washington, DC, May 14, 2010.
[66] See interviews with Ivan Marović, Washington, DC, October 14, 2004; and Srdja Popović, Oxford, March 2007.
[67] Interview with James C. O'Brien, Washington, DC, November 16, 2006.
[68] Interview with Daniel Serwer, Washington, DC, November 17, 2006.
[69] Interviews with Milan St. Protić, Belgrade, April 13, 2005; Aleksandra Vesić, Belgrade, April 15, 2005; Ivan Vejvoda, Belgrade, April 11, 2005; and Ivan Marović, Washington, DC, October 14, 2004.
[70] Axel Hadenius and Jan Teorell, "Pathways from Authoritarianism," *Journal of Democracy* 18:1 (January 2007), 143–156.

All of this is to suggest that, even by the summer of 2000, there were good reasons to predict that the Milošević regime would continue in power, and that even if it did fall, the democratic opposition would not become its successor. Although changes in Serbian and international politics from 1998 to 2000 put in place some enabling conditions for these outcomes, four key factors were conspicuously absent. One was the formation of a united democratic opposition. Another was the establishment of collaborative ties between civil society organizations and opposition parties. A third was a belief on the part of the population that they could defeat Milošević and that they could and should support the democratic opposition. Finally, also missing from the equation was a site for political action and a related set of political strategies able to address these deficits. What was needed, therefore, was an election in which Milošević exposed himself to the verdict of the voters. This is precisely what Milošević provided in September 2000.

MISSTEPS BY A MASTER

From June to July 2000, Milošević engineered a series of constitutional changes in the Yugoslav parliament that, among other things, transformed the Yugoslav presidency into a post filled through direct election. Because the office was in effect "new," Milošević was able to run for the presidency once again by circumventing the term limits that would have forced his retirement in 2001.[71] Milošević was willing to take the risks involved in facing a verdict of the voters for a simple reason: he did not view the election as a particularly risky endeavor. Just as he assumed that the opposition would remain divided (as they had demonstrated once again in the protests that had taken place in the fall of 1999), so he was imprisoned, like so many autocrats, by the lessons he drew from his long rule. For example, he had an enviable record of surmounting political and economic challenges to his power, both domestic and international, and he had seen the opposition coalesce periodically only to divide again. In addition, his growing isolation from political developments on the ground – a familiar cost of long tenure – made him quite naïve about the threats to his power detailed earlier.[72] At the same time, as Dušan Pavlović has argued, Milošević became addicted to elections, because of the ostensible mandate and the democratic sheen they provided to his rule.[73]

Milošević then took the surprising step in July of calling an early election, to be held on September 25. Here, three considerations came into play.[74] One was that he wanted to run for office while memories of the NATO bombing campaign were still relatively fresh. Second, he recognized that his popular support could decline over the course of the coming winter, given the prospect

[71] Dragan Bujosevic and Ivan Radovanovic, *The Fall of Milosevic: The October 5 Revolution* (New York: Palgrave Macmillan, 2003).
[72] See Bieber, "The Serbian Transition and Civil Society"; and Birch, "The 2000 Elections in Yugoslavia."
[73] Pavlović, *Akteri i Modeli.*
[74] Jennings, "Serbia's Stolen Elections."

of significant heating oil shortages. Finally, and using logic very much like that used by the Polish communists in the spring of 1989 when they called for semicompetitive elections in early June (and with results similar to what transpired in Serbia eleven years later), he assumed that the short period allocated for election campaign activity – that is, two months – would make it virtually impossible for the perennially divided opposition to coalesce and to run an ambitious political campaign. Indeed, for many of the same reasons, Milošević himself did not bother to mount much of a campaign. However, as Putin was to do in 2007 before the Russian parliamentary elections and as Nazarbayev was to do in Kazakhstan in 2005, he did go to the trouble of filling the shops with scarce items in the week leading up to the election.[75]

These decisions provided precisely what Western democracy promoters, democratic activists in neighboring countries, and opposition parties and civil society groups within Serbia needed to change the course of Serbian politics, that is, a site for action, an opportunity for close collaboration, and a "to do" list. As James O'Brien, the director of the U.S. government's effort to unseat Milošević, stated in his interview with us: "Milošević's decision to call an election and then place himself on the ballot was, from our point of view, a gift from the gods."[76] Very quickly, in part because the election was called at a time when a major meeting of the U.S. democracy promotion group was taking place in Budapest, a range of international players assembled to work together in support of electoral change in Serbia – in particular, groups funded by the U.S. government, such as Freedom House, the National Endowment for Democracy, and especially the International Republican Institute, the National Democratic Institute for Foreign Affairs, and the Center for International Labor Solidarity; private foundations based in the United States, such as the Open Society Institute (which had a relatively long-standing presence in Serbia), Mott, Rockefeller Brothers, and the International Center for Non-Violent Conflict; Western European organizations, including the Westminster Foundation and organizations based in Sweden and Germany; and the Canadian and Swedish embassies in Belgrade (which played coordinating roles, because the U.S. embassy had to shut down after the 1999 bombing campaign). A final set of participants were graduates of democratizing elections from Croatia and Slovakia, who were unusually influential in the endgame in Serbia because of their access to that country (which was critical in view of the departure, for example, of many Western- and especially U.S.-based international democracy assistance organizations in 1999), their established ties to groups within Serbia, and the instructive lessons they could pass on as a result of their own successful defeat of authoritarian leaders.[77]

---

[75] Birch, "The 2000 Elections in Yugoslavia." Interestingly enough, this was also common practice on the eve of elections during the communist era.

[76] Interview with James C. O'Brien, Washington, DC, November 16, 2006.

[77] Interviews with Nenad Konstantinović, Belgrade, April 15, 2005; Suzana Grubješić, Belgrade, April 12, 2005; and Roland Kovats, Budapest, June 14, 2005.

This international ensemble – or a transnational network of democracy promoters that first took shape in the 1998 Slovak election, as argued in the last chapter – immediately began work on a variety of fronts. For example, thanks to the infusion by foreign donors of more than $20 million, by late 2000 more than 150 rural and urban civic organizations were formed and collaborated in election-oriented activities.[78] More generally, international donors worked on building interest in the election and optimism about opportunities for political change among civil society groups throughout Serbia, while persuading them that a commitment to free and fair elections did not by any means violate their associational missions. Members of the international democracy promotion community also played a key role in forging ties between these civil society groups and opposition parties (which had been virtually nonexistent); worked with leaders of political parties in order to help them collaborate and fashion a sophisticated campaign that reached out to broad constituencies, whether defined in class, associational, or geographical terms; and supported an independent media, public opinion polls, rock-and-roll concerts, and the production and distribution of campaign literature, T-shirts, and placards. In addition, this network provided substantial funding and technical assistance to the two key civil society organizations that were discussed earlier: Otpor and CeSID. It was these two organizations that played a decisive role in convincing the public that Milošević could be defeated, that voting was the only way to accomplish this objective, and that the opposition was worthy of their support. They also pressed opposition parties to form and maintain a united front; carried out large-scale voter registration and turnout drives; and set up the elaborate organization needed to poll the public, monitor the election, collect the votes by precinct, tabulate the results quickly, and hold press conferences during and immediately after the election.

There is little doubt, then, that the international players involved in the September 25 election made significant contributions to the defeat of Milošević.[79] These contributions included, for example, a sharp increase in U.S. funding. To take the case of the National Endowment for Democracy (NED): in 1998, NED support to Serbia reached $310,830; in 1999, the figure was $969,750; and in 2000, NED provided $1,458,981 (a figure that underestimates actual allocations, because it leaves out substantial funds given, for example, to both Otpor and CeSID, to encourage voter registration and turnout in the December 2000 elections). Just as important with respect to the impact of international assistance was a clear signaling, so absent in the past, that the United States, members of the European Union, and countries bordering Serbia were taking a strong stand in support of free and fair elections. At the same time, however, it is clear that the result of the election – that is, a first-round but razor-thin victory by Vojislav Koštunica, who won

---

[78] Jennings, "Serbia's Stolen Elections," 4.
[79] Interviews with Roland Kovats, Budapest, June 14, 2005; and Robert Benjamin, Washington, DC, April 9, 2010; also see Jennings, "Serbia's Stolen Elections."

slightly more than 50 percent of the vote – would never have occurred without the creative, risky, and often tedious actions taken by local actors – that is, not just by civil society groups and opposition parties, but also by ordinary citizens of Yugoslavia. The implementation of the set of strategies and techniques that unseated Milošević in 2000, therefore, was a deeply collaborative venture that rested in the final analysis on the actions of citizens and political activists within Serbia in particular.

It was Otpor activists, for example, who gave flowers to the police, exposed the vulnerability of the regime, kept pressure on the opposition to remain united, facilitated the break between the regime and the Serbian Orthodox Church, and took the campaign against Milošević to all parts of Serbia. Otpor activists played key roles in the "Caravan of Celebrities" and the Get Out the Vote and Rock the Vote campaigns (the latter based directly on the Slovak experience). Otpor, together with Izlaz 2000, an umbrella organization of activists composed of about 150 NGOs and 25,000 to 30,000 volunteers, also played a critical role in giving publics the strong sense that their votes were important and that they could defeat Milošević, and these two organizations were also responsible for turning out large numbers of young people to vote.[80] It was these votes, as well as those of citizens who had stopped voting as a result of their disgust with the regime and stolen elections, that made the difference in the election.[81] Finally, as already noted, Otpor maintained pressure on the opposition to remain united – a strategy that had multiple benefits. As Jelica Minić and Miljenko Dereta[82] have argued: "The unity demonstrated by the democratic opposition ... led to a shift in public opinion, as ordinary citizens gained trust and confidence in the democratic opposition and warmed to the idea that political change could be achieved through elections." At the same time, opposition unity helped Western democracy promoters maintain their strong commitment to democratic change in Serbia. This is primarily because members of the international democracy assistance community are far more likely to maintain and even increase their support of the opposition and its allies when opposition parties and candidates have made a credible commitment to seeking office by forming electoral coalitions.[83]

CeSID, which also worked closely with Izlaz 2000, which was based upon the OK'98 campaign in Slovakia and the Glas99 organization in Croatia, made major contributions to many of these electoral efforts as well. For example, CeSID trained 10,000 election observers and assembled a network of 23,000 volunteers during the election in order to generate a "real" set of

[80] Ilić, "Otpor."

[81] Jelica Minić and Miljenko Dereta, "Izlaz 2000: An Exit to Democracy in Serbia," in *Reclaiming Democracy: Civil Society and Electoral Change in Central and Eastern Europe*, ed. Joerg Forbrig and Pavol Demeš (Washington, DC: German Marshall Fund, 2007), 79–100; Jennings, "Serbia's Stolen Elections."

[82] Minić and Dereta, "Izlaz 2000," 82.

[83] Lincoln Abraham Mitchell, *Uncertain Democracy: U.S. Foreign Policy and Georgia's Rose Revolution* (Philadelphia: University of Pennsylvania Press, 2009).

electoral results that could be placed alongside the official results announced by the regime. It was the visible and galvanizing contrast between the two that gave citizens throughout the country the proof they needed to demand that Milošević leave office. CeSID also exerted pressure on the election commission to improve the quality of voter lists; to be more representative in its membership; to tighten up its procedures; and to carry out its tasks in a more transparent fashion.

In the process of carrying out these ambitious activities, CeSID exposed two ironic aspects of what transpired during the 2000 elections. One was the fact that Serbian polling stations had long been required by law to post the number of votes outside the station. CeSID then allocated workers to every constituency to phone in the numbers, thereby making it harder for vote fraud to take place through the last-minute generation of new ballots. The other irony is that CeSID leaders were very worried about turnout by the late afternoon of voting day, and they were able to disperse their volunteers to targeted constituencies in order to get out the vote. This turned out to be critical, since it is likely that, in the absence of these efforts, none of the candidates for the Yugoslav presidency would have won the required 50 percent plus one vote to avoid a second round of the election, which would have pitted Milošević against Koštunica and given the regime several weeks to devise measures to ensure its ultimate victory.

The actions of individuals also mattered a great deal. For example, despite being head of a much larger party and despite an antagonistic relationship with Vojislav Koštunica, Zoran Djindjic decided to step aside and support Koštunica as the presidential candidate of the eighteen-party coalition that was formed to run against Milošević. Data in public opinion polls – which Djindjic followed closely, even after he became prime minister – showed that Koštunica was the more popular opposition candidate.[84] This was because he had suffered under communism (he was relieved of his teaching position in Belgrade in 1974 and refused to be reinstated in 1989); had lived a modest life; had taken principled stances during his tenure in parliament; and combined moderate nationalism with commitment to the rule of law. His purely outsider status made him, therefore, more like Mikuláš Dzurinda in Slovakia than like the former government ministers Mikheil Saakashvili of Georgia and Viktor Yushchenko of Ukraine. Djindjic also assumed (correctly), when deciding to throw his support to Koštunica, that a victory for the opposition in the presidential race would lead quickly to new parliamentary elections. These elections, in turn, held open the prospect of a major coalition victory and a role for him as prime minister. Thus, he would have an opportunity to tackle an issue of particular concern, that is, economic reform.[85] Despite Djindjic's decision to defer to Koštunica, however, the presidential race still featured five candidates.

---

[84] Interview with Srdjan Bogosavljević, Belgrade, April 13, 2005.
[85] Interviews with Suzana Grubješić, Belgrade, April 12, 2005; and Milan Pajević, Belgrade, April 11, 2005.

Djindjic also played two other key roles. He served as campaign manager for the opposition coalition – the Democratic Opposition of Serbia – in the September elections. By all accounts, the coalition's campaign was extraordinarily strong. This was in part because, in contrast to earlier campaigns by opposition candidates, and for that matter by Milošević as well, Koštunica was able to carry his message to all parts of Serbia. At the same time, Djindjic, along with several retired generals who were leaders of the opposition coalition, took on the difficult task of approaching Milošević's allies during the campaign, including the heads of Serbian State Security, the Federal Customs Administration, and the Yugoslav army.[86] These discussions, which were preliminary and were followed up in considerably more detail after the two sets of vote totals were presented, helped prepare the groundwork for the decision by the security forces to stand aside while popular protests forced Milošević to leave office on October 5.

In the final analysis, however, Milošević was defeated and removed from office because of the ordinary and extraordinary actions of citizens of the country.[87] As Sonja Licht observed, "In the course of the 2000 election people had lost every illusion about the Milošević regime."[88] As a result, they were willing to take a stand for free and fair elections; they voted in unusually large numbers; and they decided to take a chance on the opposition. At the same time, they were the ones who believed the figures CeSID had painstakingly, but quickly, generated. They then watched, beginning on the evening of the election, a struggle unfold between the opposition and the regime that involved Milošević's declaration of victory followed by his argument that no candidate had won a majority, thereby requiring a second round. What happened next was a general strike called by the opposition on October 2; preliminary indications that Milošević did not have full control over the media; and a sit-in strike in sympathy with the opposition demands for an immediate transfer of office mounted by the miners at the Kolubara coal mines, which provided approximately 70 percent of the energy in Serbia.[89]

It was at that point that Milošević's power began to erode in a visible way. He ordered his army chief of staff, General Nebojša Pavković (who was the son of a miner), to persuade the coal miners to stop their protest. However, the miners convinced Pavković that the use of force against them would produce a civil war. At the same time, General Momčilo Perišić, who had been fired by Milošević in connection with the crisis in Kosovo and who had been Pavković's predecessor, had already defected to the opposition and with the strike started a campaign of convincing members of the military that their duty in the crisis was to uphold the constitution and the rights of Serbian

---

[86] See Bieber, "The Serbian Transition and Civil Society"; Miloš Vasić, *Atentat na Zorana* (Beograd: Politika/B92/Vreme/Narodna knjiga, 2005), Chapter 1.

[87] Interviews with Boris Begović, Belgrade, April 14, 2005; Sonja Licht, Belgrade, April 12, 2005; Milan Nikolić, Belgrade, April 12, 2005; and Florian Bieber, Belgrade, April 11, 2005.

[88] Interview with Sonja Licht, Belgrade, April 12, 2005.

[89] Jennings, "Serbia's Stolen Elections," 6.

citizens.[90] The Yugoslav Constitutional Court, which was still fully under the control of Milošević, then declared that the presidential election would need to be rerun, which led the opposition to demand that Milošević either step down by October 5 – which he refused to do – or face a citizen-led mobilization on the federal building in Belgrade. Despite the increasingly repressive climate in Serbia and the failure of so many previous protests, estimates of 500,000 to a million citizens from throughout Serbia (or approximately 10 percent of the population) – in cars, bulldozers, tractors, horse-drawn wagons, and even on bicycle and on foot – converged on Belgrade to demand that Milošević hand over power to Koštunica. Both the police and the military, many sporting Otpor stickers on their helmets, stood by while Milan St. Protić, the newly elected mayor of Belgrade, led the charge on the parliament.[91] To convert to past tense two popular slogans used widely during the campaign against Milošević and then exported to Ukraine four years later: the efforts signaled that at last Milošević was finished (*"gotov je"*), and that it was time for him to leave (*"vreme je"*).

Why were these oppositions so large and so successful? One reason is that the Serbian opposition and many civil society groups were prepared for public protests. They had learned a great deal from popular mobilization and protest techniques used in the past, and many of them, particularly the leaders of Otpor, had been trained during the election and in earlier struggles in techniques of nonviolent conflict.[92] Preparations for protest also capitalized on linkages already made outside the capital and large cities – through the campaign and through the work of civil society organizations. Also beneficial was the fact that the election had already mobilized citizens. It is not just that protest cycles often correlate with electoral cycles, both in general and in Serbia in particular.[93] It is also that in the case of Yugoslavia after the

[90] See Jonathan Steele, Tim Judah, John Sweeney, Gillian Sandford, and Rory Carroll, "Beyond Milosevic," *The Observer*, October 8, 2000, News section, 17.

[91] Interviews with Marko Blagojević, Belgrade, April 11, 2005; and Nenad Konstantinović, Belgrade, April 15, 2005; and see de Krnjević-Mišković, "Serbia's Prudent Revolution"; Milan St. Protić, *Izneverena revolutiutsija: 5 Oktobar 2000*. (Beograd: Čigoja Publishers, 2005); Bieber, "The Serbian Transition and Civil Society"; Thompson and Kuntz, "Stolen Elections"; and Birch, "The 2000 Elections in Yugoslavia."

[92] See Peter Ackerman and Jack Duvall, *A Force More Powerful: A Century of Nonviolent Conflict* (New York: St. Martin's Press, 2000); Thomas Carothers, *Critical Missions: Essays on Democracy Promotion* (Washington, DC: Carnegie Endowment for International Peace, 2004); and interviews with Ivan Marović, Washington, DC, October 14, 2004; Srdja Popović, Oxford, March 2007; and Vesna Pešić, Belgrade, April 14, 2005.

[93] See Guillermo Trejo, "The Political Foundations of Ethnic Mobilization and Territorial Conflict in Mexico, 1975–2000," in *Federalism and Territorial Cleavages*, ed. Ugo Amoretti and Nancy Bermeo (Baltimore: Johns Hopkins University Press, 2004), 355–386; Doug McAdam and Sidney Tarrow, "Ballots and Barricades: On the Reciprocal Relationship between Elections and Social Movements," paper presented at the conference Hot Models and Hard Conflicts: The Agenda of Comparative Political Science in the 21st Century, a symposium in honor of Hanspeter Kriesi, Center for Comparative and International Studies (CIS), Zurich, Switzerland, June, 26, 2009.

September election, "the joyous victory celebration, when confronted with regime actions, evolved quickly and easily into public protests."[94] Central to that dynamic, of course, was the widespread belief that the "alternative" results generated by CeSID, with the help of Otpor and other civil society activists, were the *real* results of the election.

Thus, the relatively easy transition from expressing political preferences at the ballot box to doing so in the streets was facilitated in many respects by the groundwork laid by civil society groups and the opposition before and especially during the election. But can we argue that these protests were events orchestrated by the opposition and by their civil society allies? Here, our interviews, along with studies of what happened from September 25 to October 5, present a picture that suggests astute predictions and careful preparations, yet considerable spontaneity as well. For example, over the course of the campaign, Zoran Djindjic held a number of discussions with the military, the security forces, and key defectors from the regime about the likely scenario that Koštunica would win the election, Milošević would either declare victory outright or call for a second round of voting, and citizens from across Serbia would take to the streets to demand that Milošević admit defeat and transfer power to Koštunica. Moreover, there is evidence that Otpor and other civil society groups played a role in coordinating the protests. At the same time, however, once the votes were tabulated and CeSID quickly announced a narrow victory for Koštunica, events took on a life of their own and were far from predictable. Here, we refer, for example, to Milošević's surprisingly inconsistent public positions on the electoral results, the unexpected but galvanizing strike by the miners, the refusal of the military to follow Milošević's orders and "establish order," the unraveling thereafter of the regime's media monopoly and its control over the police and the security forces, and, finally, the surprisingly large number of citizens from all over Serbia who converged on Belgrade on October 5 to demand a transfer of power. In this sense, the massive popular protests that so quickly ended the Milošević era can be understood simultaneously as both premeditated and spontaneous actions.

CONCLUSIONS

In many respects, the defeat of Milošević in the 2000 Yugoslav presidential election resembled the dynamics that had foreshadowed earlier opposition victories in Slovakia and Croatia. For example, we find in all these cases an energetic, creative and collaborative effort by oppositions, civil society organizations, and international democracy promoters to bring democratic parties and their candidates to power. However, the Serbian case parted company with these earlier cases of electoral turnover in one important respect. Massive protests following the election were required to force Milošević to accept the victory (albeit razor-thin) of Vojislav Koštunica, the candidate of

---

[94] Interview with Suzana Grubješić, Belgrade, April 12, 2005.

the Democratic Opposition of Serbia. As we will discover in the three chapters that follow, after the Yugoslav events postelection protests became a standard feature of electoral confrontations between authoritarian incumbents (or their anointed successors) and the opposition in mixed regimes in postcommunist Eurasia. While some of these electoral struggles led, as they had in Serbia, to the empowerment of the opposition, as in Ukraine, Georgia, and Kyrgyzstan, others did not, as in Armenia, Azerbaijan, and Belarus.

5

Ukraine

The Orange Revolution

It was very frightening. For two days we thought the police or army might fire. We talked to the army men with helmets and said "don't fire on us," and slowly, one by one, they took off their helmets.

Marisa Shukost, citizen, Ivano-Frankivsk

"Razom nas bahato, Nas ne podolaty." Together we are many, We cannot be defeated.

Song on the Maidan, 2004, modeled after the
Chilean song "The People United Will Never Be Defeated"

As we have seen in the last chapter, in contrast to the orderly turnovers of power that took place in Slovakia and Croatia from 1996 to 2000, the defeat of Milošević in Serbia required not just an electoral victory, but also large-scale popular protests following the election. As we will discover in this chapter and the two that follow, the Serbian precedent proved to be quite influential. Thus, from 2003 to 2008, popular protests also took place following electoral confrontations between opposition parties and incumbent authoritarian regimes in Armenia, Azerbaijan, Belarus, Georgia, Ukraine, and Kyrgyzstan. While the protests failed to dislodge the incumbent in the first three cases, they succeeded in doing so in Georgia, Ukraine, and Kyrgyzstan.

This chapter analyzes the 2004 presidential election that pitted Viktor Yushchenko and his Orange Coalition against the anointed successor of Leonid Kuchma, Viktor Yanukovych. The dramatic events that followed the effort by Kuchma and his supporters to steal the 2004 elections unfolded over a period of more than a month and came to involve hundreds of thousands of ordinary Ukrainians in addition to political and NGO leaders. In the first round of the elections, in which numerous other candidates also ran, Victor Yushchenko, leader of the united opposition, won 41.96 percent of the vote and Victor Yanukovych, the chosen successor of Kuchma, won 41.37 percent. Widely anticipating fraud in the second round, held because no candidate had obtained 50 percent of the vote, civil society groups and the opposition began to mobilize for protest. When evidence of massive levels of fraud in the second round was reported by both domestic and international observers, the opposition and NGO community quickly organized protests in Kyiv that brought citizens from all corners of the country to support the opposition and call for new elections. These protests lasted until the second round of the election was rerun on December 26, after the Supreme Court had ruled on December 3 that the earlier second round was invalid and a new election had to be held. In that round, Yushchenko won 55 percent of the vote, compared to 44 percent for Yanukovych. The inauguration of Yushchenko as president on January 23, 2005, capped the victory of the Orange coalition. As with our earlier case studies, we will begin by setting the context of these elections in terms of political and economic developments, from the formation of an independent Ukrainian state on January 1, 1992, to the eve of the 2004 elections.

UKRAINIAN POLITICS AFTER INDEPENDENCE

The political evolution of Ukraine after the breakup of the Soviet Union in 1991 reflected the continued influence of communist-era politicians as well as that of the newly empowered but often severely divided opposition. It also was influenced by the country's distinctive ethnic composition, which was reflected in important regional differences in political values and perspectives.[1] In addition, Ukraine's leaders faced the need, common to all postcommunist countries, to move from a state-controlled economy to a market economy as well as the necessity, common to all the republics that had once comprised the Soviet Union, Czechoslovakia, and Yugoslavia, to consolidate Ukraine as an independent state.

As in many postcommunist states, and particularly those that arose from the Soviet Union, the first post-independence elite in Ukraine included representatives of the old *nomenklatura* from the Soviet era as well as leaders of Rukh, the Ukrainian Movement in Support of Perestroika that developed into a mass movement in the late 1980s, and other parties and movements that had pushed for independence. Leonid Kravchuk served as president from 1991 to 1994. Formerly head of the Ideology Department of the Communist Party, he nonetheless won 61.6 percent of the vote, compared to the 23.3 percent that Vyacheslav Chornovil, then head of Rukh, won in the December 1991 presidential elections. As in other successor states in the former Soviet

[1] Valerie Bunce and Sharon L. Wolchik, "Mixed Regimes in Postcommunist Eurasia: Tipping Democratic and Tipping Authoritarian," in *Hybrid Regimes: International Anchoring and Domestic Dynamics in Post-Soviet States*, ed. Elena Barcani (Florence, Italy: European Press Academic Publishing, 2010), 57–86; Stephen White and Ian McAllister, "Belarus, Ukraine (and Russia): East or West?," paper presented at the thirty-ninth annual convention of the American Association of Slavic Studies, New Orleans, November 15–18, 2007; Stephen White, Ian McAllister, and Margot Light, "Enlargement and the New Outsiders," *Journal of Common Market Studies* 40:1 (March 2002), 135–153.

Union, such as Belarus, Kazakhstan, Uzbekistan, and Turkmenistan, where there was no clean break with the communist past, many members of the former Communist Party apparatus assumed positions of power in independent Ukraine.

The political vacuum created by the loss of power of the Communist Party and the breakup of the Soviet Union, coupled with new opportunities to get rich quickly by controlling and stripping state enterprises and setting up new businesses in a largely unregulated economic climate, resulted in widespread abuses of power and self-enrichment by political officials. Large businessmen also played important political roles. As in Russia, enterprising individuals made enormous fortunes, particularly in the energy sector, very quickly. These oligarchs, as they came to be known, benefited from their connections with political leaders, in particular the president.[2]

As in many other postcommunist states, strong political parties were slow to develop in Ukraine. Parties tended to be centered around powerful individuals and served more to protect the fortunes of their founders than to advance any consistent ideology or political platform. The granting of lifelong immunity to parliamentary deputies contributed to this pattern, as many businesspeople not only sought to buy influence among politicians but to become deputies themselves in order to protect themselves from prosecution.[3] Not surprisingly, trust in political parties remained low in this situation.[4]

As president, Kravchuk took steps to limit press freedom and stifle criticism by the broadcast media and attempted to use force against those who opposed him. As Lucan Way notes, under Kravchuk there was a high degree of fragmentation of power within the executive branch and relatively little effective unity or coordination within the elite owing to open competition over property, wealth, and influence.[5] Although Ukrainian politics came to

---

[2] See Aslund Åslund, "The Ancien Regime: Kuchma and the Oligarchs," in *Revolution in Orange: The Origins of Ukraine's Democratic Breakthrough*, ed. Anders Åslund and Michael McFaul (Washington, DC: Carnegie Endowment for International Peace, 2006), 9–28; and Andrew Wilson, *Ukraine's Orange Revolution* (New Haven, CT: Yale University Press, 2006), 39–45, for lucid attempts to sort out the fast-changing positions of the main oligarchic groupings.

[3] See Åslund, "The Ancien Regime," 17–23; see also Taras Kuzio, "Ukraine: Muddling Along," in *Central and East European Politics: From Communism to Democracy*, ed. Sharon L. Wolchik and Jane L. Curry (Lanham, MD: Rowman and Littlefield, 2007), 339–370; and John T. Ishiyama and Ryan Kennedy, "Superpresidentialism and Political Party Development in Russia, Ukraine, Armenia and Kyrgyzstan," *Europe-Asia Studies* 53:8 (December 2001), 1177–1193.

[4] See Anna Makhorinkina, "Ukrainian Political Parties and Foreign Policy in Election Campaigns: Parliamentary Elections of 1998 and 2002," *Communist and Post-Communist Studies* 38:2 (June 2005), 251–267. See also Sarah Birch, *Elections and Democratization in Ukraine* (London: Macmillan, 2000); and Arthur H. Miller and Thomas F. Klobucar, "The Development of Party Identification in Post-Soviet Societies," *American Journal of Political Science* 44:4 (October 2000), 681, 684.

[5] Lucan Way, "Rapacious Individualism and Political Competition in Ukraine, 1992–2004," *Communist and Post-Communist Studies* 38:2 (June 2005), 194.

be dominated to a large extent by oligarchs, they were not united but rather competed among themselves for power.

The election of Leonid Kuchma – who had served as prime minister under Kravchuk from October 1992 to June 1993, when he was forced out – as president in 1994 raised hopes that Ukraine's transition to democracy and the market would begin in earnest. Elected in what were generally recognized as free and fair elections against a field of seven candidates with distinct platforms, Kuchma benefited from the fragmentation of the opposition and from the fact that the economy had begun to improve during his second term, as well as from Western support for his proposed reforms.[6] However, hopes that Kuchma would enact more fundamental economic and political reforms were soon disappointed. Instead, Kuchma continued to increase the power of the presidency, and the growth of a kleptocratic political elite continued unabated.

This was also the case for interconnections between the president and the country's new oligarchic elite.[7] The symbiotic relationship between the president and the oligarchs continued throughout his tenure. However, changes brought about by modernization and privatization, which led to increased competition among the oligarchs and within oligarchic "blocs," eventually led some businessmen to buck Kuchma's system. Oligarchs increasingly ran for parliament, and several were part of Yanukovych's government formed after the 2002 parliamentary elections. By the 2002 elections, several of the oligarchs switched their allegiance to the opposition, and several were elected as deputies on the list of Yushchenko's Our Ukraine bloc.[8]

As the result of these patterns, corruption became an increasingly salient feature of political and economic life in Ukraine. The prevalence of corrupt practices is evident in Transparency International's Corruption Perception Index for Ukraine, as well as in the World Bank's World Governance Indicators from 1996 to 2006. On the first index, according to which a score of 0 indicates a highly corrupt regime and 10 a highly clean one, Ukraine ranked 1.5 in 2000, 2.4 in 2003, and 2.2 in 2004.[9] On the second set of indicators, in which higher scores correspond to better governance, Ukraine was rated a – 1.00 in 2000, –.98 in 2002, –0.90 in 2003 and –.092 in 2004.[10] A survey of citizens conducted by IFES in Ukraine in September 2003 found similarly high perceptions of corruption. When asked to rate the extent of corruption in a variety

---

[6] See Taras Kuzio, "Kravchuk to Kuchma: The Ukrainian Presidential Elections of 1994," *Journal of Communist Studies and Transition Politics* 12:2 (June 1996), 117–144.

[7] Åslund, "The Ancien Regime," 10.

[8] See ibid. for a detailed discussion of the main oligarchic groups and the evolution of their political role under Kuchma. See also Kuzio, "Ukraine: Muddling Along."

[9] Transparency International, *Corruption Perception Index (1995–1997)*, http://www.transparency.org/policy_research/surveys_indices/cpi accessed February 22, 2009.

[10] Daniel Kaufmann, Aart Kraay, and Massimo Mastruzzi, *Governance Matters VI: Governance Indicators for 1996–2006*, World Bank Policy Research Working Paper No. 4280 (July 2007), at SSRN: http://ssrn.com/abstract=999979.

of institutions, over 60 percent of respondents rated the problem as serious or very serious in all six institutions listed (hospitals, schools and universities, the courts, customs, tax authorities, and the police). Most citizens also felt that officials in a variety of positions would misuse their positions for their own benefit or engage in other corrupt practices.[11]

In contrast to the situation in Serbia on the eve of Milošević's ouster, Ukraine experienced a period of economic growth prior to the 2004 elections. As a result of reforms that Yushchenko enacted while prime minister as well as more robust economic growth in Russia, GDP grew by 5.2 percent in 2002 and by 9.6 percent in 2003.[12] At the same time, this growth was not evenly distributed, and much of the population had not experienced improvement in their standard of living. On the eve of the first round of the presidential elections in October 2004, 75 percent of respondents rated the country's economic situation as bad or very bad, compared to 19 percent who thought it was good or very good, slightly better results for the regime than reported in a survey IFES had conducted in September 2003.[13] However, most Ukrainians were clearly still dissatisfied with the country's economy. Dissatisfaction was particularly great among rural residents and older respondents.[14] Thus, while Ukraine's economic growth during the early to mid-2000s is often cited by analysts who argue that the economic situation was not the dominant motive leading to support for the opposition and later protest, these results indicate that economic dissatisfaction was in fact widespread in Ukraine and, through its connection to attitudes about politics, contributed to the vulnerability of the regime. That recognized, however, it is also important to remember that public concerns about the economy had also been great throughout the 1990s, but had failed to lead to a change in political leadership.

As president, Kuchma made good use of his control of government resources in order to increase his power, reward his supporters, and disarm his opponents.[15] The 1999 presidential elections were marred by the widespread use of bribes and other resources at the disposal of the presidential administration to gain support and co-opt potential opposition as well as by the "accidental" death of the Rukh leader Vyacheslav Chernovil in an accident

---

[11] Rakesh Sharma and Nathan Van Dusen, *Attitudes and Expectations: Public Opinion in Ukraine 2003* (Washington, DC: International Foundation for Election Systems, 2004), http:// www.ifes.org/publication/1dc4195c92359e089b76566dcf2321e3/Ukraine_Survey_2003_ English.pdf. See also Wilson, *Ukraine's Orange Revolution*, 2–33.

[12] World Bank Data and Statistics: Ukraine, http://go.worldbank.org/GPPNM8A3No, accessed February 12, 2009.

[13] International Foundation for Election Systems (IFES), "Findings from Pre-Election Survey in Ukraine" (November 2004), 10. See Sharma and Van Dusen, *Attitudes and Expectations: Public Opinion in Ukraine 2003*, for September 2003 results.

[14] IFES, "Findings from Pre-Election Survey," 10.

[15] For an excellent empirical treatment of the issue of patronage in Ukraine, see Serhiy Kudelia, "Clients' Revolt? Explaining the Failure of Government's Patronage in Ukraine's 2010 Election," paper presented at the Workshop on Ukraine's 2010 Presidential Election: What We Learned?, The George Washington University, April 5, 2010.

with a truck. Kuchma also succeeded in intimidating all real opposition candidates, including Yushchenko, who was prime minister at the time, and preventing them from running, winning what Andrew Wilson has termed a "virtual election" against candidates who were sponsored by Kuchma and oligarchs who were at least temporarily loyal to him.[16]

Kuchma's harassment of and use of violence against the opposition also increased – a pattern that we also saw in the case of Milošević in Serbia at the end of his rule. Two examples of the regime's increasing reliance on violence stand out. The first of these was the kidnapping and beheading of Hryhoriy Gongadze, the journalist who began the internet newspaper *Ukrayinska Pravda*, in September 2000 after Kuchma had ordered his subordinates to "deal with" him. The release in late November 2000 of tapes made illicitly in Kuchma's office that revealed Kuchma's role in the murder of Gongadze led to a series of popular protests, including those led by Yulia Tymoshenko, until her arrest in February, and by the Ukraine without Kuchma movement established in December 2000.[17] These included a short-lived "tent city" set up in December and demonstrations that involved an estimated 20,000 to 30,000 people,[18] as well as the "Stand Up Ukraine" campaign begun in September 2002 on the anniversary of Gongadze's abduction, a campaign that previewed many of the tactics used in 2004 but that failed to gain mass support.[19]

A final example of the regime's use of violent means to try to prevent an opposition victory was the poisoning of Viktor Yushchenko by dioxin in the course of the 2004 election campaign. A good deal of controversy still remains over this event, in terms of who was responsible and when it actually occurred. The most commonly accepted version argues that Yushchenko was poisoned during a dinner meeting with Ihor Smeshko, head of the State Security Service, and his deputy, Volodymyr Satsiuk, which was arranged by David Zhvania. Zhvania was a businessman and member of parliament who joined Yushchenko's Our Ukraine coalition in 2002; he was one of his major contributors in 2004 and served as deputy chief of staff during the campaign and later manager in chief of logistics on the Maidan. The poisoning, which nearly proved fatal to Yushchenko, was widely publicized and backfired. It not only failed to remove Yushchenko from the campaign, but also, along with Kuchma's evident involvement in the earlier death of Gongadze, served as a powerful symbol for many citizens that the regime had gone too far. As in Serbia, where the jailing of young Otpor activists was for many people the final straw (especially since these actions were accompanied by a series of murders of important figures), so the regime's effort to eliminate the opposition's

[16] Wilson, *Ukraine's Orange Revolution*, 42–43.
[17] See Taras Kuzio, "Regime Type and Politics in Ukraine under Kuchma," *Communist and Post-Communist Studies* 38:2 (June 2005), 169; and see Wilson, *Ukraine's Orange Revolution*, Chapter 4 (particularly 153–154), for a partial transcript of the tape.
[18] Wilson, *Ukraine's Orange Revolution*, 58.
[19] Ibid., 60.

candidate contributed to the sense, captured by the youth movement Pora's name ("It's Time!"), that it was indeed time for a change of regime.[20] The poisoning of Yushchenko also supported the opposition's claim that Ukraine's government was a "criminal authority."[21]

Kuchma also acted to restrict the media. A 2003 report on the media in Ukraine by Human Rights Watch noted, in fact, that Kuchma was ranked among the ten worst enemies of the press worldwide in 1999 and 2001 by the Committee to Protect Journalists.[22] Pressure on journalists increased in 2002. In addition to attacks on journalists, the regime attempted to institute a more formal type of censorship by distributing guidelines – *temniky*, or themes – specifying how sensitive topics, such as news about opposition leaders and the activities of the opposition, was to be covered as well as which subjects were not to be covered at all. Most TV networks were either controlled by the government or in the hands of individuals, such as Kuchma's son-in-law, who were supportive of the regime. Prior to the 2004 elections, the regime reduced access to Radio Liberty's Ukrainian service and other Western radio.[23] Attacks on independent journalists continued after the November 2004 election round, particularly in the eastern parts of the country.[24] Thus, although Ukraine had a large number of print media, television and radio stations, and news agencies, freedom of the media was in fact quite restricted on the eve of the 2004 elections. As a result, the opposition as well as the NGO community in Ukraine had limited access to the media as a tool to reach citizens. This factor was explicitly taken into account by NGO leaders in planning election-related activities in 2004 and was one of the reasons for the focus on building a network of organizations to take information directly to voters.[25]

The regime also used the tax administration to target pro-opposition businesses and extorted contributions from businessmen who supported Kuchma to consolidate his power and weaken the opposition. The first tactic was sometimes accompanied by arrests and detentions of businessmen who were too independent or who supported other political actors; the second was used to finance election campaigns, including that of Yanukovych in 2004.[26]

---

[20] See ibid., 96–104, for a gripping if chilling account of the poisoning, as well as C. J. Chivers, "A Dinner in Ukraine Made for Agatha Christie," *New York Times*, December 20, 2004, http://www.nytimes.com/2004/12/20/international/europe/20ukraine.html, for an overview of several of the theories.

[21] In an interview in Kyiv in June 2007, Volodymyr Sivkovych, MP for the Party of Regions and head of a parliamentary committee set up to investigate the poisoning in 2004, disputed the linkage between Kuchma's administration and the poisoning but acknowledged its utility to the opposition in its efforts to portray the government as criminal.

[22] Human Rights Watch, *Ukraine: Negotiating the News: Informal State Censorship of Ukrainian Television*, Volume 15, Number 2(D) (New York: Human Rights Watch, 2003), 8, at http://www.hrw.org/sites/default/files/reports/Ukraine0303.pdf.

[23] See Human Rights Watch, *Ukraine: Negotiating the News.*

[24] Human Rights Watch, *News: Ukraine: Attacks on Press Aim to Stifle Debate*, Human Rights News (December 3, 2004), at www.hrw.org/english/docs/2004/12/04/ukrain9766.htm.

[25] As noted, for instance, by Nadia Diuk, interview, Washington, DC, February 2009.

[26] See Wilson, *Ukraine's Orange Revolution*, Chapters 3 and 4, for detailed accounts of such activities under Kuchma.

As in Serbia and Slovakia, Kuchma also used administrative/legal means to disadvantage and split the opposition and, in the 2004 elections, to try to ensure the victory of Yanukovych. These included the effort to change the constitution before the 2004 elections to reduce the powers of the presidency in favor of the prime minister and parliament, which failed by eleven votes in April 2004.[27] A compromise version of this measure was adopted in December.

The regime also had very well-elaborated plans to steal the 2004 elections. Kuchma packed the Central Election Commission with his supporters. The administration also mobilized its resources to pressure voters and to falsify the vote, planning to win by 3 percent in the second round.[28] Znayu (" I Know"), an NGO active in 2004 in helping citizens understand their electoral rights, discovered a government directive detailing the kinds of techniques to be used in the second round of the election and the number of votes for Yanukovych that were to come from each. Money was also provided for bribes. Way notes that if only half of the polling stations received money to influence the vote, the sum would have equaled $809 million.[29] If all else failed, the regime had what it thought would be a fail-safe backup: a secret computer server that filtered the results before they went to the Central Election Commission.[30]

As the preceding section has illustrated, Leonid Kuchma made use of a variety of tools – including violence, on occasion – to maintain and increase his hold on power. At the same time, there were limits on Kuchma's ability to consolidate his power. These included the constitutionally prescribed relative independence of the parliament, even when controlled by forces largely favorable to the president, and the ability of the opposition to access at least some media outlets. Despite harassment of the opposition and the many tools that control over the state gave Kuchma, he proved unable to eliminate all competition and consolidate a purely authoritarian system.[31]

These limits, as well as the growing power of certain business elites, who had been able to shift much of their capital out of the country and thus were better able to resist pressure from Kuchma, have led some analysts to argue that the Orange Revolution in fact came about as a result of the weaknesses of the Kuchma regime.[32] There are two problems, however, with this

---

[27] Kuzio, "Regime Type and Politics in Ukraine under Kuchma," 182–183.
[28] See Lucan Way, "Ukraine's Orange Revolution: Kuchma's Failed Authoritarianism," *Journal of Democracy* 16:2 (April 2005), 134–135; and C. J. Chivers, "How Top Spies in Ukraine Changed the Nation's Path," *New York Times*, January 17, 2005, http://www.nytimes.com/2005/01/17/international/europe/17ukraine.html.
[29] Way, "Ukraine's Orange Revolution,"136.
[30] See ibid.; see also Wilson, *Ukraine's Orange Revolution.*
[31] See Way, "Ukraine's Orange Revolution," for an interpretation that traces this inability to the fragmentation of the political elite after the end of communism and the distinctive role of parliament, which, due in large part to parliamentary immunity, provided a safe haven for opposition leaders and gave them a public platform. See also Kuzio, "Regime Type and Politics in Ukraine under Kuchma," and Wilson, *Ukraine's Orange Revolution*, 32–33 and Chapters 3 and 4, for analyses of Ukraine under Kuchma.
[32] Way, "Ukraine's Orange Revolution."

interpretation. One is that the Kuchma regime, once we take into account such considerations as the uninterrupted rule of former communists in independent Ukraine and the extraordinary preparations Kuchma and Yanukovych made to ensure victory in the 2004 elections, was in fact not that vulnerable. Second, as in the other cases of mixed regimes that straddled democracy and dictatorship that we examine in this book, what matters is less the vulnerability of the regime than the ability of the opposition and its allies to exploit these opportunities. Put simply, vulnerable regimes do not fall of their own accord. They have to be pushed, and in Ukraine, as in Serbia, the push was massive when it came. While in Serbia hundreds of thousands of people played a role in ending the Milošević era, in the much larger country of Ukraine the comparable figure was in the millions. A united opposition was also critical in both cases.

In addition, as in the other cases we have examined so far, the opposition and the NGO community engaged in a series of similar and similarly unprecedented electoral strategies in order to emerge victorious. These strategies were adapted to local conditions, including in Ukraine the country's large size and regional divisions as well as the presence of an outside actor, Russia, not active in the other cases we have examined. They also built on previous efforts by the opposition to unite and by NGOs to mobilize citizens.[33] While the role of the local business community and the Supreme Court was distinctive to Ukraine, two other factors – the unification of the opposition and the mobilization of citizens by civil society organizations – were similar to those we saw in Slovakia, Croatia, and Serbia.

OPPOSITION COHESION

To a much larger extent than in Serbia, the political opposition that united to lead the Orange Revolution was composed of experienced politicians, many of whom had been supporters or allies of Kuchma at some point. These included not only Victor Yushchenko, who had been prime minister under Kuchma from 1999 to 2001, but also Yulia Tymoshenko, Petro Poroshenko, and Oleksander Zinchenko. In fact, as Lucan Way has calculated, nearly 63 percent of the members of the group that led Yushchenko's movement in 2004 had been allied with Kuchma previously.[34] Numerous wealthy oligarchs, many of whom were also parliamentarians from Yushchenko's party, also had defected from Kuchma.[35] These businessmen, who came to feel that their own interests required a change in power, provided both access to TV coverage through Channel 5 – which, although received by only 40 percent of the population, nonetheless gave the opposition some media access – and funding,

---

[33] Interview with Joanna Rohozinska, Washington, DC, February 18, 2009.
[34] As calculated by Way, "Rapacious Individualism," 199.
[35] Ibid.

estimated to have been approximately $150 million, for advertising, rallies, and the orange paraphernalia that came to mark the campaign.[36]

Many of these actors broke with Kuchma during the period between 2000 and 2004. Thus, as in Georgia, though far less so in Serbia, Ukraine experienced defections from the ruling circle in the years leading up to the change of regime. There were also defections to the opposition at the last minute. Volodymyr Lytvyn, Kuchma's former head of administration, who was speaker of parliament in 2004–05, broke with Kuchma only in September 2004. These defections proved critical after the second round of the election, when parliament declared the second round invalid and called for a new election.[37] The city administration of Kyiv and important segments of the broadcast media also broke with the regime once the demonstrations started, as did the police and security forces, who did not take action to block access to the city as they had previously or use force on the protestors.

The process that led to the victory of the Orange Coalition in 2004 thus began prior to the 2002 elections. Installed as prime minister by Kuchma in 1999, Yushchenko began Ukraine's first serious economic reform program. The results of this process, which was interrupted by Yushchenko's removal as prime minister in April 2001, were nonetheless far-reaching. They accelerated the shift from state to private ownership and, as a result, led to greater competition among the oligarchs as emphasis shifted from stripping the assets of state firms or controlling those firms for private benefit to the issue of production.[38]

As in previous cases, the opposition and the NGO community had several trial runs prior to 2004. The most important of these was the 2002 parliamentary election, which saw the victory of Yushchenko's Our Ukraine bloc in the half of parliament elected by proportional representation. In a move that would foreshadow his decision to build a broad coalition in 2004, Yushchenko gained the support of all three groups that had grown out of Rukh. His coalition also included numerous businessmen, as well as some former Kuchma supporters, including Roman Bezsmertnyi, who later became Yushchenko's campaign chief, and Yuri Yekhanurov, who had served as deputy prime minister under Yushchenko.[39] Yulia Tymoshenko's Bloc of Yulia Tymoshenko (BYuTy), founded in December 2001, and Oleksander Moroz's Socialist Party also joined the opposition at this time.

Although these elections demonstrated the advantages of unity, they also gave the opposition a foretaste of the difficulties it would face and the tactics

[36] Ibid., 200; interview with Yulia Mostovaya, Kyiv, June 12, 13, 2007. Valeriy Chaly, deputy director of the Razumkov Center, also stressed the role of the new middle class, including middle-sized and small business owners, as an important source of the protest; interview with Valeriy Chaly, Kyiv, June 14, 2007.

[37] See Way, "Ukraine's Orange Revolution," 13.

[38] Åslund, "The Ancien Regime."

[39] See Wilson, *Ukraine's Orange Revolution*, 60–63, for more detail.

the regime would use in the 2004 presidential elections. As in 1999, Kuchma again made use of bribery and violence to try to divide and demobilize the opposition. State organs, including the tax authorities, were misused against opposition candidates and supporters, as were other forms of intimidation, including arrests and beatings. The regime also tried to rig the elections, but, constrained by exit polls and a parallel vote count organized by the Democratic Initiatives Foundation with funding from the embassies of the United States, Italy, the UK, Sweden, and the International Renaissance Foundation, among others, Kuchma engaged in what has been described as "by local standards ... fairly limited fraud."[40]

Yushchenko's Our Ukraine received 23.6 percent of the vote, Yulia Tymoshenko's bloc 7.3 percent, and Moroz's Socialist Party of Ukraine 6.9 percent of the vote. Thus, together the three opposition parties gained just one seat short of a majority, 112 of 225, of the parliamentary seats elected by proportional representation.[41] In elections for the other half of the seats in the parliament, for which candidates were elected by the first-past-the-post majoritarian system, however, the opposition did far less well, winning only 45 of 225 seats. Using by now familiar tactics, Kuchma eventually won defectors from the opposition and gained control of parliament again. However, as Wilson notes, the 2002 elections were a "huge psychological breakthrough," because they showed the vulnerability of the regime. They also showed the opposition the advantages of unity and the lengths to which the regime would go to maintain control.

As the 2004 elections approached, the opposition put the lessons of 2002 to good use. Yushchenko and Tymoshenko agreed to unite in the Syla Narodu ("Force of the People") coalition for the election. Tymoshenko agreed not to run for president, and her bloc agreed to support Yushchenko's campaign. Oleksander Moroz, whose Socialists were one of the few political parties with grassroots organizations, ran for president in the first round but, in exchange for Yushchenko's agreement to support an increase in the role of parliament and posts in the government, agreed not to oppose Yushchenko in the second.[42]

Under the direction of Roman Bezsmertnyi and Oleh Rybachuk, the Yushchenko campaign staff elaborated a strategy, already evident to some degree in 2002, of portraying themselves as agents of change who would return Ukraine to the proper path. As in 2002, Our Ukraine somewhat downplayed Ukrainian nationalism, particularly of the West Ukrainian variety, and emphasized a positive message. Evident in the choice of orange as the

---

[40] Ukrainian Helsinki Human Rights Union, "Nine National Exit Polls of the Democratic Initiatives," October 23, 2007, http://www.helsinki.org.ua/en/index.php?id=1193136368, accessed February 2, 2009. See also Wilson, *Ukraine's Orange Revolution*, 67.

[41] See Wilson, *Ukraine's Orange Revolution*, 66–67.

[42] Kerstin Zimmer and Oleksiy Haran, "Unfriendly Takeover: Successor Parties in Ukraine," *Communist and Post-Communist Studies* 41:4 (December 2008), 551.

color of the movement, rather than the traditional blue and yellow, this choice was meant, in Andrew Wilson's words, to "emphasize an all-national, value-based campaign, which was overwhelmingly peaceful and a little bit jolly."[43] Yushchenko's campaign staff, as we will discuss later in this chapter, also initiated contact with the police, intelligence, military, and security forces to lay the groundwork for cooperation should the regime try, as was widely expected, to steal the elections. As in the earlier cases we have discussed, they were aided greatly in their efforts by the activities of the NGO community, which mobilized to prevent or minimize fraud by organizing election monitoring and exit polls, and made elaborate plans to protest if fraud occurred. NGOs also took the lead in efforts to get around impediments posed by the regime's control of most media.

CIVIL SOCIETY AND CITIZENS' MOBILIZATION

Citizens' attitudes toward politics and political institutions reflected the trends already discussed. Many had low levels of interest in politics, political efficacy, and trust in government leaders or institutions.[44] Taras Kuzio notes, for example, that by August 2002, over 70 percent of citizens surveyed wanted Kuchma to leave office early, and over 50 percent wanted him to be impeached.[45] By early 2003, only 7 percent of Ukrainians surveyed did not believe that change was necessary in Ukraine.[46] By spring 2004, approximately 56 percent of citizens surveyed believed that Ukraine was moving in the wrong direction.[47] The low regard in which the populace held the regime is perhaps best reflected in a study that Taras Kuzio cites, conducted by the Ukrainian Academy of Science in April 2004, that found that a higher percentage (16 percent) of respondents trusted astrologers than trusted the president (13 percent).[48]

Ukrainians were also pessimistic concerning the likelihood of free and fair elections. Over 70 percent of those polled in 2003, for example, did not believe there would be free and fair elections in 2004.[49] An even higher proportion lacked confidence in Kuchma (97 percent). A poll commissioned by

---

[43] Wilson, *Ukraine's Orange Revolution*, 73.

[44] But see also Arthur H. Miller, Thomas F. Klobucar, and William M. Reisinger, "Establishing Representation: Mass and Elite Political Attitudes in Ukraine," in *Ukraine: The Search for a National Identity*, ed. Sharon L. Wolchik and Volodymyr Zviglyanich (Lanham, MD: Rowman and Littlefield, 1999); and Miller and Klobucar, "The Development of Party Identification in Post-Soviet Societies," 684, for a somewhat different view.

[45] Reported in *Dzerkalo Tyzhnia*, August 15, 2002, as cited in Taras Kuzio, "Everyday Ukrainians and the Orange Revolution," in *Revolution in Orange: The Origins of Ukraine's Democratic Breakthrough*, ed. Anders Åslund and Michael McFaul (Washington, DC: Carnegie Endowment for International Peace, 2006), 43.

[46] Poll cited in *Ukrayinska Pravda*, March 11, 2003, as cited by Kuzio, "Regime Type and Politics in Ukraine under Kuchma,"184.

[47] Poll results cited in Kuzio, "Everyday Ukrainians and the Orange Revolution," 49.

[48] Poll results cited in ibid., 55.

[49] "People Don't Match Reforms," *Zerkalo Nedeli* 14 (439), April 18, 2003, 12, 18.

IFES (the International Foundation for Electoral Systems) in September 2003 found similar results: 55 percent of respondents thought that the 2002 elections had been unfair or very unfair, and 47 percent of respondents did not have much confidence that the 2004 elections would be fair. Nearly 70 percent disagreed that voting gives citizens influence over decision making, and 78 percent disagreed with the notion that people like themselves could influence the government.[50]

The majority of Ukrainians were also dissatisfied with the economic and political situation of Ukraine just prior to the 2004 elections. Approximately 75 percent, for example, were very or somewhat dissatisfied with the country's economic situation, and nearly similar percentages (71 percent) were either very or somewhat dissatisfied with the political situation.[51] Respondents were similarly pessimistic about the outcome of the election, as 50 percent felt that it was very or somewhat unlikely that the elections would be free and fair.[52] Nearly 60 percent of Ukrainians surveyed on the eve of the 2004 elections felt that Ukraine was not a democracy, as opposed to 23 percent who thought it was. Over twice as many respondents in the western part of Ukraine (76 percent) as in the East (34 percent) did not believe Ukraine was a democracy. Belief that Ukraine was democratic was linked to the respondents' economic situation and increased with economic well-being.[53]

Although many Ukrainians remained dissatisfied and disillusioned with politics, there were some important changes in public opinion prior to the 2004 elections. Levels of interest in politics, for example, remained similar in October 2004 to those in 2002 and 2003 (59 percent of respondents were very or somewhat interested),[54] but there was a marked increase in the number who said they had enough information to make a wise choice in voting (from 18 percent in 2003 to 41 percent in October 2004). The increase in belief that voting provided a means of influencing decision making was even more striking, rising to 47 percent in October 2004 from 24 percent in September 2003. Belief in the efficacy of voting was particularly strong in the West of the country (72 percent).[55]

At the same time, however, it is important to recognize that, as in the other cases we have examined, lack of support for the incumbent government and belief in the need for change did not translate automatically into support for the opposition in Ukraine. In mid and late 2003, a majority of Ukrainians indicated that they did not know the views of the opposition, and most of those respondents were not interested in learning more about them.[56] Similarly, only 33 percent of those surveyed in April 2003 supported the opposition,

---

[50] Sharma and Dusen, *Attitudes and Expectations: Public Opinion in Ukraine 2003.*
[51] IFES, "Findings from Pre-Election Survey in Ukraine," 9, 10, and 12.
[52] Ibid., 6.
[53] Ibid., 17.
[54] Ibid.
[55] Ibid., 4.
[56] Kuzio, "Regime Type and Politics in Ukraine under Kuchma," 184.

compared to 15 percent who supported the government.[57] All opposition leaders except Yushchenko had higher negative ratings than positive ratings in polls conducted in mid-2003.[58] A poll commissioned by IFES in September 2003 found similar results.[59]

Despite their distrust of politicians and disaffection from political life, widespread doubts concerning the likelihood of free and fair elections, and low expectations that voting made a difference, most Ukrainians polled in September 2003, including 79 percent of those who were dissatisfied with the current situation, compared to 90 percent of those who were satisfied, indicated that they would vote in the 2004 elections.[60] Ninety-two percent of those polled in October 2004 indicated that they were either very likely (79 percent) or likely (13 percent) to vote in the presidential elections.[61]

The task for the opposition, then, was to turn widespread popular dissatisfaction and desire for change into, first, a willingness to try to change the situation by actively participating in political life, at least as voters, and second, since voting turnout levels for national elections had generally been high prior to 2004, support for the distrusted and relatively little-known opposition. As Vladimir Chaly, the deputy director of the Razumkov Center in Kyiv, noted in an interview with us, "The most important part of the strategy [of Yushchenko's campaign staff] was to convince people that Yushchenko *could* win," particularly after he had to reduce his campaign activity for two months after his poisoning.[62]

Part of the responsibility for mobilizing voters to vote and to vote for the opposition fell to the political opposition, as part of its campaign to win office. But, as in the other cases we have analyzed, the opposition was helped to achieve this goal in Ukraine in indispensable ways by civil society groups. As in Slovakia, the political opposition was fortunate in that it could rely on a relatively robust civil society that included a variety of organizations active throughout the country. As in Slovakia and even more so in Serbia it also benefited from the energetic efforts of young people, organized in this case into two groups, both of which claimed the same name, Pora ("It's Time"). Civil society groups in Ukraine also drew on previous campaigns and experiences with protest, as well as on contact with outside actors, to shape their campaigns.

As in many other postcommunist countries, the development of a free associational life in independent Ukraine had its roots in the country's earlier traditions of voluntary organizations and had begun to take shape in the last years of the Soviet Union. In contrast to many other republics in the Soviet Union, Gorbachev's policy of *glasnost'* was not immediately introduced in Ukraine,

[57] Ibid.
[58] Ibid., 184–185.
[59] Sharma and Dusen, *Attitudes and Expectations: Public Opinion in Ukraine 2003.*
[60] Ibid.
[61] IFES, "Findings from Pre-Election Survey in Ukraine," 5.
[62] Interview with Valeriy Chaly, Kyiv, June 14, 2007.

due to the fact that Volodymyr Scherbytsky, a hard-liner, remained head of the Ukrainian Communist Party until 1989. He was replaced by Volodymyr Ivashko, a known moderate, who then allowed a number of groups outside the control of the Communist Party to develop. The best-known of these included Rukh (the Popular Movement in Support of Perestroika), the group that led the movement for Ukrainian independence, which was founded in 1989.[63] A variety of other groups also developed during the period just prior to the breakup of the Soviet Union, including student and environmental groups.[64]

Aided by external support, particularly from the United States, Ukraine's civil society burgeoned after independence. In 2001, 25,490 associations and charities and an additional 8,000 informal groups were registered, although only half of these were functional.[65] By 2003, there were over 30,000 nongovernmental organizations.[66] Most of these were local groups, and many dealt with educational, social, or charitable issues, or provided services. Few, therefore, had direct political concerns or played an advocacy role. These patterns, of course, were also typical of our other cases.[67]

As Nadia Diuk, vice president, Programs for Europe and Eurasia, Africa, Latin America and the Caribberan at the National Endowment for Democracy, notes, however, as in Slovakia and Serbia, the 1990s also saw the development of two kinds of NGOs that proved to be significant in the events of 2004: independent think tanks and groups that focused on monitoring elections and providing citizens with information about public issues.[68]

[63] See Marta Dyczok, *Ukraine: Movement without Change, Change without Movement* (Amsterdam: Harwood, 2000), 5; and Sarah Birch, *Elections and Democratization in Ukraine* (London: Macmillan, 2000), 41, for discussions of the late Soviet period in Ukraine; see Nadia Diuk and Adrian Karatnycky. *The Hidden Nations: The People Challenge the Soviet Union* (New York: Morrow, 1990), for an early discussion of Rukh.

[64] See Nadia Diuk, "The Triumph of Civil Society," in *Revolution in Orange: The Origins of Ukraine's Democratic Breakthrough*, ed. Anders Åslund and Michael McFaul (Washington, DC: Carnegie Endowment for International Peace, 2006), 69–84, for a lucid analysis of the development of civic society in Ukraine; see also Diuk and Karatnycky, *The Hidden Nations*, 80–96.

[65] Svitlana Kuts, Alex Vinnikov, Leo Abramov, Vasyl Polyiko, Maxym Filiak, Lyuba Palyvoda, and Julia Tyhomyrova, *Developing the Roots of Civil Society in Ukraine: Findings from an Innovative and Participatory Assessment: Project on the Health of Ukrainian Civil Society, A Preliminary Report on the Civicus Index on Civil Society Project in Ukraine*, Civicus Index on Civil Society Occasional Papers, vol. 1, no. 10 (August 2001), 10–12.

[66] Vladyslav Kaskiv, Iryna Chupryna, and Yevhen Zolotariov, "It's Time! Pora and the Orange Revolution in Ukraine," in *Reclaiming Democracy: Civil Society and Electoral Change in Central and Eastern Europe*, ed. Joerg Forbrig and Pavol Demeš (Washington, DC: German Marshall Fund, 2007), 130.

[67] Sarah Elizabeth Mendelson and John K. Glenn, *The Power and Limits of NGOs: A Critical Look at Building Democracy in Eastern Europe and Eurasia* (New York: Columbia University Press, 2002); Sarah Henderson, *Building Democracy in Contemporary Russia: Western Support for Grassroots Organizations* (Ithaca, NY: Cornell University Press, 2006); Laurence Jarvik, "NGOs: A New Class in International Relations," *Orbis* 57:2 (Spring 2007), 217–238.

[68] See Diuk, "The Triumph of Civil Society."

The first, which included the Center for Economic and Political Studies of Ukraine, established in 1994 and known as the Razumkov Center for its founder, Oleksander Razumkov, a former deputy secretary of the National Security and Defense Council of Ukraine, played an important role as an alternate source of information and helped counter the government's control of much of the media. In the 2004 elections, the Center's surveys provided information about popular opinion to Yushchenko's team. The Center also conducted exit polls and parallel vote counts.[69] *Ukrayinska Pravda*, the internet newspaper that Hrihoryi Gongadze helped establish in 2000 along with Olena Prytula (who continued to run the paper following Gongadze's murder), served a similar function and was particularly important in disseminating information after the early rounds of the 2004 election. The second group of organizations, some of which had received Western support since the early or mid-1990s, focused on civic education and election-related activities. The Committee of Ukrainian Voters, which trained election observers and had been active in all elections since 1994, and the Democratic Initiatives Foundation, which began using exit polls in the 1998 elections and, together with other groups, had foiled the government's plans to falsify the results of the 2002 elections, were particularly important in 2004.

According to USAID's NGO Sustainability Index, Ukraine's third sector rated 3.9 (on a scale of 1 to 7, 1 being the most advanced) in 2003 and 3.8 in 2004, scores that were both improvements over the 2002 score of 4.0.[70] Freedom House, by contrast, saw a slight decline in Ukrainian civil society's well-being between 2003, when it was rated 3.50, and 2004, when it received a score of 3.75.[71] These scores are in fact close and indicate a civil society at a middle level of sustainability. An IFES survey conducted just prior to the first round of the 2004 election found that 77 percent of respondents were not members of any civic organization. However, there was an increase between September 2003 and October 2004 in respondents' awareness of what an NGO was, if not of an NGO active in their area.[72]

Influenced in part by the Slovak and Bulgarian examples, Ukrainian NGOs began to cooperate more closely. Numerous Slovak "graduates" of OK'98 began working in Ukraine in the early 2000s, including Peter Novotný of Civic Eye and Pavol Demeš, then European director of the German Marshall Fund of the United States.[73] As in our earlier cases, the NGO community had

[69] Interview with Valeriy Chaly, Kyiv, June 14, 2007.

[70] U.S. Agency for International Development, *2002–2004 NGO Sustainability Index for Central and Eastern Europe and Eurasia*, http://www.usaid.gov/locations/europe_eurasia/dem_gov/ngoindex/index.htm.

[71] Freedom House, *Nations in Transit 2003* (New York: Freedom House, 2003); Freedom House, *Nations in Transit 2004* (New York: Freedom House, 2004).

[72] IFES, "Findings from Pre-Election Survey in Ukraine," 20.

[73] Interviews with Peter Novotný, Washington, DC, February 24, 2010; Nadia Diuk, Washington, DC, April 3, 2010; Pavol Demeš, Washington, DC, and Bratislava, May 2005; and Jan Sutorchak, Bratislava, May 2005. Also see Diuk, "The Triumph of Civil Society," 74, for the suggestion that the Bulgarian example may also have played a role.

some experience in cooperating prior to the 2004 elections. The Freedom of Choice Coalition, which was founded in 1999 and contributed to the opposition's victory in the half of parliament chosen by proportional representation in 2002, illustrated the value of a coordinated approach, and several NGO coalitions developed between 2002 and 2004.[74] These included the "Ukraine without Kuchma" campaign founded in reaction to Gongadze's death in 2000 and a number of other protest actions led by the group "Rise, Ukraine!" in Kyiv in September 2002 and March 2003.[75] Similarly, many of the activists in Pora, and particularly in Black Pora, were students who had participated in a 1990 strike calling for the resignation of one of Ukraine's top leaders or in a two-month strike in Lviv over nonpayment of student stipends.[76]

As the 2004 elections approached, several NGOs that had worked together between 2002 and 2004 under the guise of the Democracy League formed the New Choice 2004 coalition. Nadia Diuk, who was involved in funding a variety of NGOs and other democracy-building efforts in Ukraine beginning in the early 1990s, argues that the nongovernmental sector was in fact "far ahead in its strategies for parliamentary elections" in which they would have very limited access to the broadcast and other media.[77]

The activities of the Committee of Ukrainian Voters illustrate this strategy. From its founding in 1994, the Committee had grown to be one of the few national civic organizations in Ukraine. Devoted to educating citizens about their rights in its early years, this group held citizens' meetings and prepared printed materials designed to encourage citizens to become informed about their choices. The Committee, which monitored the 1998 and 2002 elections, also monitored the efforts of state authorities to marginalize the opposition and influence the results of the 2002 parliamentary elections in favor of pro-presidential parties.[78] In 2004, the committee's network of activists was ready to mobilize people to go to Kyiv when it became evident that the regime had falsified the election results.[79] As the 2004 elections approached, the Committee of Ukrainian Voters began, along with other NGOs, to prepare to mobilize its members to vote and, if necessary, to take to the streets to protest electoral fraud. University students and other young people were particularly active in the work of these groups.

As in Slovakia, Serbia, and Georgia, a number of youth organizations were formed prior to the 2004 elections. Pora, which developed two wings, Yellow Pora and Black Pora, is the best known of these groups. Chysta Ukraina ("Clean Ukraine"), Znayu ("I Know"), Studentska Khyvilya ("Student Wave"),

[74] Diuk, "The Triumph of Civil Society," 74.
[75] Taras Kuzio, "The Opposition's Road to Success," *Journal of Democracy* 16:2 (April 2005), 117–130.
[76] Interview with Jaroslavl Prytula, Lviv, August 3, 2005.
[77] Diuk, "The Triumph of Civil Society," 76.
[78] Nadia Diuk and Myroslava Gongadze, "Post-Election Blues in Ukraine," *Journal of Democracy* 13:4 (October 2002), 157–166.
[79] Interview with Jaroslavl Prytula, Lviv, August 3, 2005.

and several others also played important roles. Chysta Ukraina provided printed materials, had a web site, and helped monitor elections; one of its leaders also served as the chief coordinator of the training camp that Pora ran. Pora documents credit Chysta Ukraina as the source of the second-largest group, after Pora itself, of participants in demonstrations and protests.[80] Founded by Dimitro Potekhin in 2004 with funding amounting to $1 million from the US–Ukraine Foundation and approximately $50,000 from Freedom House,[81] Znayu attempted to remain nonpartisan and focused on distributing information about voters' rights. Znayu activists also oversaw the publishing of 12,000 copies of Gene Sharp's book on nonviolent conflict, supported by Sharp's foundation. Focusing on voter education and measures to prevent fraud through work with those responsible for vote counting, Znayu developed a network of volunteers in the regions that included three regional offices with thirty coordinators in each region. Znayu activists also cooperated with Pora on a number of actions prior to the election, particularly with Black Pora activists, who had originally had no links to political parties or movements, in contrast to Yellow Pora.[82] In contrast to these initiatives, which were nonpartisan, Studentska Khyvilya was organized by Yushchenko's campaign headquarters to mobilize youth to support Yushchenko. Its activists organized a "Student Assembly" supporting him in Kyiv in mid-October, served as election monitors, and distributed stickers and other information.[83]

Important as these groups were, Pora was clearly the youth group that contributed most to the victory of the Orange forces. So-called Black Pora was inspired by Otpor in Serbia and used a variety of tactics to challenge the government directly in order to point out its flaws and misdeeds. Founded by activists in Lviv and later led by veterans of earlier struggles including the "Ukraine without Kuchma" and "For Truth" movements of the early 2000s, Black Pora made its first public appearance at the end of March 2003 with the symbol of a ticking clock. By preference and in order to avoid infiltration, Black Pora activists rejected any formal organization or hierarchy.[84] They also used humor and direct confrontation with government officials to demonstrate that the government was vulnerable. In the words of the Black Pora activist Andriy Kohout in an interview in 2007,

> Before 2003, fear of the government and the police grew among people. After 2004, this fear was broken, and we showed that the government was not strong. We [Black Pora] made use of happy street actions making fun of the regime and government. The government and police detailed us and called

[80] *A Case Study of the Civic Campaign PORA and the Orange Revolution in Ukraine,* December 6, 2005, at www.pora.org.ua/eng/content/view/2985/325, 16.
[81] Wilson, *Ukraine's Orange Revolution,* 75.
[82] Interviews with Dmytro Potekhin, Kyiv, June 13, 2007; and Kataryna Botanova, Kyiv, June 13, 2007.
[83] *A Case Study of the Civic Campaign PORA,* 16.
[84] See Wilson, *Ukraine's Orange Revolution,* 74, and also ibid.

us terrorists. But all could see that we weren't. It showed the government's actions to be absurd. We laughed at many things the government did.[85]

At the same time, Kohout noted, their goal was always to defend people's vote and prevent the government from stealing the election. "What we did," he noted, "was funny. But our statements were serious."[86]

Noting that the first actions of his group occurred before the adoption of the Pora name and symbol, Kohout also emphasized the role that training sessions in fund raising, working with people and the media, and how to protect their own rights organized in February and March 2004, which brought together Serbs from Otpor and activists from Georgia as well as Belorusian activists from the youth group Zubr, played in the group's development. When asked what the "graduates" of earlier movements provided that was useful, Kohout stated in regard to the Georgians and Serbs: "what we mainly took from them was that we could do it.... If they did it, we could do it." He also noted that they learned a number of "technological" things from these actors, including the principles, which also corresponded to their own values and experiences, of nonviolence and a "leaderless" movement without hierarchy or a single center.[87]

Yellow Pora, which claimed to be inspired more by OK'98 in Slovakia, had its roots in the Freedom of Choice coalition that Yellow Pora's leader, Vladislav Kaskiv, had helped found in 1999. This coalition, which received Western funding to monitor the elections in 2002 and 2004, had close links to Yellow Pora through Kaskiv and a number of other Yellow Pora activists. Founded in Uzhhorod in April 2004, Yellow Pora's main goal was to ensure free and fair elections. Using a yellow clock as their symbol, Yellow Pora activists were originally concentrated in Kyiv and prior to the protests cooperated more closely with Yushchenko's campaign staff, and in particular with Roman Bezsmertnyi, who helped coordinate Pora's actions with those of the Yushchenko campaign, than Black Pora activists did.[88]

A number of similarities between the activities and organization of Yellow Pora and those of OK'98 in Slovakia immediately stand out. Thus, although widely thought of as an organization, or as two groups, in fact Pora billed itself as a "united initiative of hundreds of NGOs" that involved numerous volunteers and groups and implemented a wide variety of projects.[89] The rhetoric used by Yellow Pora's leaders also bears a strong resemblance to that of OK'98 activists.[90] As in Slovakia, Pora organized its activities in regional

---

[85] Interview with Andriy Kohout, Kyiv, June 14, 2007.
[86] Ibid.
[87] Ibid.
[88] Interviews with Vladyslav Kaskiv, Kyiv, June 13, 2007; Andriy Kohout, Kyiv, June 14, 2007; Dmytro Potekhin Kyiv, June 13, 2007; and Kataryna Botanova, Kyiv, June 13, 2007.
[89] See Kaskiv, Chupryna, and Zolotariov, "It's Time! Pora and the Orange Revolution in Ukraine," 132.
[90] Ibid.

groups. By September 2004, there were 72 regional centers that included approximately 150 mobile groups all over the country. There was also a national center in Kyiv.

In contrast to OK'98, however, in which older leaders of the NGO sector and think tanks founded the campaign and also organized many of its actions, the chief activists of Pora were students. Led by older veterans of the student movement in the 1990s,[91] the Ukraine without Kuchma movement and the All Ukrainian Public Resistance Committee for Truth (Za Pravdu), Pora, like Otpor in Serbia and Kmara in Georgia, attracted students from universities to secondary and even elementary schools.[92] Writing in 2006, Pora's leaders identified a "male, 18 to 20 years of age and a student in his first or second year of university," as the typical Pora activist.[93] The main nationwide youth organizations and organizations for students in higher education were among the eighty groups that pledged to support Pora between March and April 2004.[94] All told, an estimated 20,000 people were members of the two Poras, which agreed in August 2004 to cooperate.[95]

The tactics Pora used combined those used successfully elsewhere with those with roots in the 1990s student movement in Ukraine and illustrate the way in which aspects of the electoral model were adapted to local conditions in Ukraine. Thus, Pora activists drew on a repertoire of actions, including hunger strikes, demonstrations, rallies, picketing and, in 2004, a tent city, derived from earlier organizing and protest experience. They also, however, made use of many of the tools used by OK'98 and Otpor activists in particular, including the effort to "brand" their activities by using strong symbols, unifying slogans that changed as the stage of the campaign changed, and pamphlets, T-shirts, and other paraphernalia to identify supporters and create a sense of common purpose. The use of the clock set to eleven and the name Pora ("Time" or "It's (High) Time!") were part of this effort, as were the various slogans used in the campaign, including "I vote, therefore I am," a slogan also used in Slovakia. Activists also used door-to-door canvassing and other methods to encourage people to vote. Vladyslav Kaskiv explicitly recognized the influence of the Slovak experience on Yellow Pora's organization and tactics in an interview with us in Kyiv in 2007: "How did the Slovaks help us? In 1999, Pavol Demeš came to help us technologically to set up the Freedom of Choice Coalition. He helped us plan what to do. We gave our products to him for commentary and suggestions." Kaskiv noted other informal links with "graduates" from Georgia and Slovakia and the "Devin International" that linked them in an informal network. He also highlighted the role that

---

[91] Interview in Lviv, August 2007; interview with Vladyslav Kaskiv, Kyiv, June 13, 2007.
[92] See Kaskiv, Chupryna, and Zolotariov, "It's Time! Pora and the Orange Revolution in Ukraine," 132–134.
[93] Ibid., 133.
[94] Ibid.
[95] Wilson, *Ukraine's Orange Revolution*, 74–75.

"graduates," including Ivan Marović and others from Otpor, played in acting as consultants and sharing their experiences at training camps.[96]

To a greater extent than in either Slovakia or Serbia, NGO activists in Ukraine relied on the internet and cell phones to get their message to the public and to coordinate their activities. These technologies were particularly important in Ukraine due not only to the regime's control of many standard media, but also to the size of the country and the greater geographic dispersion of the population outside the capital.

Some of these techniques were given practice runs in connection with the mayoral elections in Mukachevo in April 2004, where, despite the presence of the OSCE, local authorities used violence, intimidation, and blatant fraud to ensure the "victory" of the pro-government candidate. Pora activists established a tent city and distributed the results of the parallel vote count and exit polls that NGOs conducted. They also presented the "winner" with a prison diet and displayed photos of the violence at polling stations at Kyiv–Mohyla Academy in Kyiv. After parliamentary hearings, the mayor resigned.[97] Pora activists also refined their techniques and tested methods, including door-to-door canvassing, used to get out the vote in Slovakia, as well as organizing mass protests, during two elections in Central and Eastern Ukraine. Vladyslav Kaskiv noted that "[a] key element during this phase was the testing of different formats of information and education activity, such as the 'hand to hand' and 'door to door' methods that also proved effective for increasing voter turnout in the OK'98 campaign in Slovakia."[98]

Many of these techniques were evident in the months leading up to the election. Beginning in September 2004, Pora launched an information and education campaign under the slogan "It's Time to Think," following its "It's Time to Stand Up" campaign designed to activate young people in August. In October, the slogans shifted to "It's Time to Vote" and "It's Time to Control," an action undertaken in connection with the Freedom of Choice Coalition to monitor voting lists and remind local authorities of their liability for violations of the election law.[99] Borrowing a page from dissidents in Poland under communism and from Otpor in Serbia, Pora activists also used humor and satire to draw attention to their activities and to the deficiencies of the regime.[100]

---

[96] Interview with Vladyslav Kaskiv, Kyiv, June 13, 2007.

[97] Kaskiv, Chupryna, and Zolotariov, "It's Time! Pora and the Orange Revolution in Ukraine," 137.

[98] Ibid.; see also Pavol Demeš and Joerg Forbrig, "Pora! It's Time for Democracy in Ukraine," in *Revolution in Orange: The Origins of Ukraine's Democratic Breakthrough*, ed. Anders Åslund and Michael McFaul (Washington, DC: Carnegie Endowment for International Peace, 2006), 85–102, for a remarkably similar account of the development and activities of Pora.

[99] Kaskiv, Chupryna, and Zolotariov, "It's Time! Pora and the Orange Revolution in Ukraine," 138.

[100] See ibid., 139, for reference to the performance that ridiculed the egging of Yanukovych in Ivano-Frankivsk in October 2004.

Under the banner of Pora, NGO leaders organized a wide variety of actions, including information campaigns and other efforts to mobilize Ukrainians to vote. Given the regime's control of information, Pora was particularly important in providing alternative information directly to voters. In the course of 2004, Pora activists engaged in many of the same activities that OK'98 had used in Slovakia. These included distributing 40 million copies of printed materials and holding over 750 regional actions and 17 mass rallies. This wing of Pora also trained activists to monitor the elections.[101] Pora's leaders estimate that their publications and actions reached approximately twenty-five million people, or half the population of Ukraine.[102]

Yellow Pora also played a key role in preparing for protests in the event that the regime tried to steal the election, as it was widely, and accurately, believed it would, and in setting up the 15,000-person tent city in Kyiv and smaller tent cities elsewhere in Ukraine.[103] These preparations intensified after more than 150 Pora activists were arrested and charged with terrorist acts, and criminal cases were brought against the organization for alleged possession of explosives and against individual activists for a variety of trumped-up crimes in October 2004. After these arrests, Pora emphasized the student character of its organization and also established strike committees at universities and schools throughout the country.[104]

Once the protests were underway on the Maidan, NGO activists and the Yushchenko campaign staff also made greater use of a variant of the mass rock concerts held in Slovakia as part of the Rock the Vote campaign (and later in Serbia) by bringing in popular cultural figures to entertain and inspire the crowd. These efforts built on the earlier use of concerts and other public events to create awareness of the campaign and to motivate young people in particular to participate in its activities.

Unlike Otpor in Serbia, which most local and external analysts view as central to the successful ouster of Milošević in 2000, opinions differ on how important Pora was in Ukraine's election campaign prior to the protests on the Maidan. IRI official Brian Mefford, for example, in a June 2007 interview in Kyiv, argued that Pora's legend grew after the 2004 election and that there was very little coordination between Pora and the political campaign of the opposition prior to the Maidan; he also stated that Pora played little role in the campaign itself and did not participate in the get-out-the-vote campaign.[105] Yulia Mostovaya, the editor of one of Ukraine's most influential weeklies, however, noted that the "role of Pora was not a small one, because for the first time youth and students self-organized and became examples, role

---

[101] Ibid., 127.

[102] Demeš and Forbrig, "Pora! It's Time for Democracy in Ukraine," 94.

[103] Kaskiv, Chupryna, and Zolotariov, "It's Time! Pora and the Orange Revolution in Ukraine," 127.

[104] Ibid., 140.

[105] Interview with Brian Mefford, Kyiv, June 12, 2007.

models for youth – so to be interested in politics became cool, fashionable."[106]
Volodymyr Horbach, of the Institute for Euro-Atlantic Cooperation founded
by Boris Tarasiuk, who worked for a year for Pora, noted that Pora "wasn't
the engine, but without it, it would have been difficult to do it.... Pora was the
revolutionary technology, though not the cause."[107]

Irrespective of one's judgment of the role Pora played in getting out the vote,
the group was well situated to act after the first round of the elections. Pora
activists immediately issued materials questioning the results of the first round
on October 31 and, in early November, established tent cities on the square
outside Kyiv–Mohyla University in Kyiv and in several other cities. Yellow
Pora activists pitched the first twenty-five tents on the evening of November
21, and Pora activists, as well as those of other youth groups, were critical
once protests began.

The activities of Black Pora, led by veterans of the Ukraine without Kuchma
campaign, were influenced to a greater extent by the approach of Otpor and
Kmara and focused on discrediting the regime. At the August 2004 nationwide meeting of NGOs, Black Pora leaders argued for a more spontaneous,
less organized "anticampaign" to play up the problems Kuchma's regime
had created. Black Pora activists used a variety of tactics to challenge the
government directly in order to point out its flaws and misdeeds. Despite the
division between the two groups and clashing claims about who came first,
activists from the two groups cooperated, particularly after protests broke
out.[108] Black Pora activists also participated in the training camps and other
activities designed to increase the number of activists for the later stages of the
campaign, including the camp at Yevpatoria in August 2004 that focused on
ways to mobilize citizens, election monitoring, interaction with the media and
law enforcement, internal communication, and nonviolent methods.[109] Slovak
"graduates" of OK'98, including many young activists, played a key role in
these sessions as in the overall elaboration of the campaign's strategy.

As in Serbia and, although not as overtly, in Slovakia, civil society groups
began to cooperate with the political opposition prior to the 2004 elections.
Despite its claims of nonpartisanship,[110] Yellow Pora in particular had strong
connections to Yushchenko's campaign staff. These connections were strengthened after police repression against Pora activists in the process of preparing
for protests in the fall of 2004. Endorsed by the Freedom of Choice coalition, whose headquarters later served as Pora's base of operations, Pora leaders began working closely with Victor Yushchenko's campaign staff and other
figures in the Syla Narodu ("Force of the Nation") coalition in mid-October in

---

[106] Interview with Volodymyr Horbach, Kyiv, June 12, 2007.
[107] Ibid.
[108] Demeš and Forbrig, "Pora! It's Time for Democracy in Ukraine," 91–92.
[109] Ibid., 92; and Kaskiv, Chupryna, and Zolotariov, "It's Time! Pora and the Orange Revolution
    in Ukraine," 138.
[110] See Kaskiv, Chupryna, and Zolotariov, "It's Time! Pora and the Orange Revolution in
    Ukraine"; and interview with Kaskiv, Kyiv, June 13, 2007.

preparation for mass protest.[111] As the protests on the Maidan developed, Pora activists, who organized themselves according to the principles of the Ukrainian Cossacks, took a leading role, in cooperation with Yushchenko's staff, in organizing life in the tent city and, along with other youth activists, finding food and accommodations for those who came to the Maidan from other cities and regions. Pora was also responsible for blockading the parliament, the presidential office, and other power centers and, in the view of some, for preventing the bloodshed that likely would have resulted had protestors succeeded in storming the presidential administration building by stopping the protestors.

The ability of the opposition and civil society leaders to mobilize the population rested in large part on preparation.[112] Although get-out-the-vote campaigns were a large part of the earlier work of many civic groups and of the political opposition, these activities were in some sense less important than they had been in Slovakia and Serbia, as Ukrainians had voted in relatively high proportions in earlier national elections, and, as indicated earlier, public opinion surveys indicated that large proportions planned to vote in 2004.[113] In contrast to our other cases, therefore, it was as important to get voters information that would lead them to support the opposition as it was to encourage them to vote.[114] Thus, a good portion of the early activities of NGOs focused on providing objective information that differed from that found in the largely regime-controlled mass media. As noted earlier, and as in Serbia, the opposition and civil society leaders began preparations to monitor and publicize election fraud as well as to conduct mass protest before the elections themselves began. These included not only training activists in the techniques of nonviolent resistance, but also stockpiling tents and other equipment that would be needed for protests in Kyiv.[115] Once the regime behaved as they expected it would in the second round of the elections, earlier preparations to monitor the vote and report fraud proved to be crucial. The presence of election monitors at polling stations and the ability to conduct parallel vote tabulation and exit polls, and to get these results to the public, allowed the opposition to quickly demonstrate the regime's attempt to steal the election. The strike committees set up by students and Pora's regional network were also important in mobilizing citizens to travel to Kyiv to protest.

As citizens began to mass on the central squares in Kyiv, and protestors began traveling to Kyiv from other regions by bus, train, and *marshrutkas*, the minibuses that had become an important part of public transportation

[111] Demeš and Forbrig, "Pora! It's Time for Democracy in Ukraine," 98, 95; Kaskiv, Chupryna, and Zolotariov, "It's Time! Pora and the Orange Revolution in Ukraine," 140–141.
[112] Interviews with Roman Bezsmertnyi, Kyiv, June 15, 2007; and Miroslav Soldat, Lviv, August 3, 2005.
[113] See International IDEA, Voter Turnout, http://www.idea.int/vt/index.cfm; and IFES Election Guide, http://www.electionguide.org/.
[114] Interviews with Jaroslavl Prytula, Lviv, August 3, 2005; and Orest Danchewsky, Lviv, August 4, 2005.
[115] Interviews with Roman Bezsmertnyi, Kyiv, June 15, 2007; and Nadia Diuk, April 2, 2010.

throughout the country, the protests took on a more spontaneous character. Popular response soon outran the expectations of the opposition and civic activists, as people used whatever means available to get to the Maidan. Cell phones and the internet were important tools in this process, for they allowed activists and participants to spread word of the protests before the official media began covering the growing demonstrations.[116] As the crowds swelled in Kyiv, preparation again paid dividends, as Pora and other groups were ready to help organize daily life on the Maidan.

Reflecting on the spirit evident on the Maidan, Yulia Mostovaya, the editor of the dual language weekly *Dzerkalo Tyzhnia* or *Zerkalo Nedeli*, noted in an interview in Kyiv in June 2007,

> A great number of people found the greatest adventure of their lives. Our girls approached the Donetsk mob and neutralized it, those machos who came with their egos, strong men: they were met with smiles, flowers, meals.... the Maidan was an amazing combination of the best you can find in people – human kindness, mutual assistance, support, and mainly, the very strong belief in their rightness, because their rights were threatened.[117]

Horbach, reflecting on the 2004 protests, noted that

> those who went to the Maidan were fighting for their own civil rights.... it was not a social but a citizens' revolution. It was not a revolution of the poor or the hungry; it was a revolution of full and self-made people who reacted to the violation of their right to vote.... they looked into themselves first of all to say it is enough ... we don't like that [the attempt to steal the election] and it has to be stopped.[118]

The experiences of the middle-aged wife of a Uniate priest from the west Ukrainian city of Ivano-Frankivsk illustrate the nature of the process for many citizens. At the market when she received a cell phone call from her daughter, then a university student in Kyiv, informing her that she was participating in the demonstrations on the Maidan, she left her husband a message and immediately, without returning home, got on a bus for Kyiv, a city she had never before visited.[119]

OTHER ACTORS: BUSINESS, THE SECURITY FORCES,
THE COURT, AND PARLIAMENT

Several other domestic actors also played important roles in the outcome of the 2004 elections, including the business community, the security forces, and

---

[116] Interview with Marisa Shukost, Smerechka, August 1, 2005; Kuzio, "The Opposition's Road to Success," 127–128; Michael McFaul, "Ukraine Imports Democracy: External Influences on the Orange Revolution," *International Security* 32:2 (Fall 2007), 45–83.

[117] Interview with Yulia Mostovaya, Kyiv, June 12, 13, 2007.

[118] Interview with Volodymyr Horbach, Kyiv, June 12, 2007.

[119] Interview with Marisa Shukost, Smerechka, August 1, 2005.

the courts. As noted earlier, the takeover of state enterprises that occurred soon after the end of the Soviet Union was followed by more extensive privatization of enterprises in the late 1990s and early 2000s.[120] As a result of this growth of the private sector, numerous businessmen amassed sizeable fortunes, some of which they transferred abroad in the face of harassment by the regime. By 2002, several of these figures, commonly referred to as oligarchs, threw their lot in with the opposition. In addition to running on opposition lists for parliamentary seats, they became an important source of funds for the opposition. Their role in this regard was extremely important in 2004.

As we will discuss later in this chapter, outside actors, including the U.S. government and foundations as well as numerous European governments and foundations, played a very important role in supporting the development of political parties in Ukraine after independence and in supporting the long-term development of civil society groups. There is some dispute over their role in funding the campaign to inform and energize citizens to vote and later to protest, or the tent city and protests on the Maidan. The accepted wisdom put forward by activists such as Pora's leaders claims, for example, that outside support for these activities was minimal and accounted for only approximately 130,000 Euros of the estimated 1.2 million Euros in cash spent on Pora's activities and campaign.[121] This claim, while narrowly correct, may in fact understate the role of outside funders significantly, as Pora itself notes that most of "[t]he administrative structure and human resources of PORA largely derived from the qualified staff and organizational resources of existing nongovernmental organizations, in particular, those belonging to the Freedom of Choice Coalition" as well as policy think tanks and student organizations.[122] Clearly, outside sources had been and in many cases continued to be important sources of funding for many of the NGOs in the coalition. Nonetheless, Pora's leaders claim that it was a combination of large and medium-sized businessmen who provided most of the resources for their activities in 2004, including the tent city and protests on the Maidan.[123] Many of these businessmen had been student activists in the early 1990s and provided contributions in kind, estimated to have equaled in excess of five million Euros. Numerous other Ukrainians, including particularly the citizens of Kyiv, also contributed after the protests started by bringing food, warm clothes, and blankets to the protesters, as well as by providing services such as transportation and housing.[124]

The police and intelligence/security forces also played an important role in the outcome of the Orange Revolution. Together with the decision of Kyiv's city council to reject the results of the fraudulent second round and thus in

---

[120] Åslund, "The Ancien Regime."

[121] *A Case Study of the Civic Campaign PORA*, 18.

[122] Ibid., 17.

[123] Ibid., 18. Also see Rosaria Puglisi, "Primary Consumers of Globalization: Oligarchs and Foreign Policy Orientations in Ukraine," paper presented at the eighth annual meeting of the Society for the Study of the Diffusion of Democracy, Florence, Italy, June 14, 2008.

[124] See McFaul, "Ukraine Imports Democracy," for an analysis that agrees that most funding came from domestic Ukrainian sources.

effect signal that the city would be open to protestors, the decision of the security forces not to try to block access to the city by blockading the roads and stopping train access or to use force on the demonstrators was obviously key to the growth of the demonstrations. The opposition had systematically tried to counter the regime's efforts to portray opposition and civil society activists as "terrorists" who made violent threats against the police as well as the regime by maintaining regular contact, going through the proper channels for organized events, and seeking to convince the police that Yushchenko would win and that they would be held accountable for any disregard for the law. Opposition figures had also been in regular, though secret, contact with the security forces ("Sluzhba Bespeky Ukrayiny," referred to as the SBU) prior to the demonstrations, primarily through Oleh Rybachuk, to persuade them not to use force against the opposition. Wilson notes that the SBU was in fact split between professional and more political officers, and that one faction remained neutral while the other actively helped Yushchenko's staff by providing documents from Yanukovych headquarters detailing plans for election fraud.[125] The head of the SBU is credited with helping to call off the mobilization of the Ministry of the Interior's special forces discussed earlier,[126] and some members of the security forces joined the opposition's leaders on the stage on the Maidan.[127]

Any option the regime had of using force against the demonstrators, short of bringing in the military, which remained neutral, virtually evaporated once the crowds swelled to an estimated 100,000 on the first day, to half a million three days later, and eventually to approximately one million citizens. As the slogan adopted by the protestors, "Together We Are Many" (*Razom nas bahato*), indicated, the regime could arrest several thousand demonstrators, and had on previous occasions, but it could not arrest hundreds of thousands. The opposition's quiet efforts to build links to the military at the regional level, which began in late 2002, paid off in the fall of 2004, as midlevel officers made informal agreements with their friends in the opposition not to use force against the demonstrators. They also agreed to step in to stop any violence by the police or special forces that the regime might initiate should it occur.[128] Interviews with senior Western diplomats and Our Ukraine officials indicate that these agreements were critical, in fact, on November 28, when the chief of staff of the army threatened to have unarmed soldiers stand between the demonstrators and the special forces of the Ministry of the Interior after the

[125] Wilson, *Ukraine's Orange Revolution*, 98; Anika Locke Binnendijk and Ivan Marovic, "Power and Persuasion: Nonviolent Strategies to Influence State Security Forces in Serbia (2000) and Ukraine (2004)," *Communist and Post-Communist Studies* 39:3 (September 2006), 422–425.

[126] Binnendijk and Marovic, "Power and Persuasion," 424.

[127] See C. J. Chivers, "How Top Spies in Ukraine Changed the Nation's Path," *New York Times*, January 17, 2005, http://www.nytimes.com/2005/01/17/international/europe/17ukraine.html.

[128] Binnendijk and Marovic, "Power and Persuasion," 418–419.

latter had been ordered to mobilize.[129] In addition to the role of agreements, contacts, and pressure, the opposition also very consciously used its numbers to influence the forces of order. Although the opposition was less successful in contacting or influencing the special forces of the Interior Ministry who were brought in from the eastern regions of the country and had less certainty about what they would do in November 2004, the rapid growth in numbers of protestors itself helped to influence the outcome, for, as noted earlier, it became clear very soon that there was no way to peacefully disperse such a large crowd.[130]

The final actor that proved important to the success of the Orange Revolution was the Supreme Court. By holding that the second round was invalid due to massive fraud, the Court allowed it to be rerun. This step provided the legal framework for holding another round of voting, which led to Yushchenko's victory. Speaker of Parliament Volodymyr Lytvyn also played a key role in the resolution of the crisis by acting as an arbiter between the Yushchenko and Yanukovych camps and, in December, pushing through a package of compromises that reconstituted the Central Election Commission and revised other portions of the electoral code designed to reduce fraud in return for reducing the powers of the presidency. This agreement, in turn, allowed the third round of elections called for by the Supreme Court to be held. Reflecting on his role in an interview in June 2007, Lytvyn stated,

> It sometimes occurs that you cannot stand against a process, you can only lead it. A given situation has to be taken as a given; there couldn't have been any other decision to take. The masses of people were for the idea of a victory for Yushchenko and under pressure of these circumstances, a decision had to be taken not lightly but politically. The Ukrainian legal system does not allow for a third round.... we understood that the mass of people would not accept any other resolution. In principle, I wouldn't have done a third round: it was quite evident what the result would be.... democratic procedures required new elections.... Parliament and the Supreme Court decided the fate of the presidential election in Ukraine.[131]

OUTSIDE ACTORS: ANOTHER "ENGINEERED" REVOLUTION?

As in the other cases we examine in this volume, regime spokesmen in Ukraine accused the West of interfering in Ukraine's internal affairs and plotting to bring down the regime prior to Yushchenko's victory and continued to claim that he had won due largely to the actions of outside actors after the 2004 elections.[132] These and similar accusations paralleled those used by incumbents in

---

[129] Ibid., 419.
[130] Ibid., 425–429.
[131] Interview with Volodymyr Lytvyn, Kyiv, June 12, 2007.
[132] See Oleksandr Sushko and Olena Prystayko, "Western Influence," in *Revolution in Orange: The Origins of Ukraine's Democratic Breakthrough*, ed. Anders Åslund and Michael McFaul (Washington, DC: Carnegie Endowment for International Peace, 2006), 125–143, for an overview of these arguments and Western actions.

Slovakia and Serbia, as well as in Georgia. While it is clear that the Orange Revolution was not in fact engineered from outside, external actors did, as in the earlier cases we have discussed, contribute in very important ways to the victory of the opposition in 2004.

As we noted earlier, a good deal of the funding for the activities of Pora and the protests in Kyiv after the second round came from domestic Ukrainian sources, including small and medium-sized businessmen.[133] But Western actors contributed to the victory of the opposition in many ways. These included democracy-building assistance for party development, long-term support for the development of civil society, support for election-related informational and monitoring activities, high-level signaling and mediation, and, as in the case of Serbia and Georgia, facilitating contacts between graduates of earlier successes and Ukrainian groups.[134]

The role of outside actors is perhaps particularly evident in the case of the NGO community. Ukrainian civic organizations were the beneficiaries of a long process of civil society building support by NED, USAID, and various U.S. and European foundations beginning in the early 1990s. The Razumkov Center, for example, whose surveys provided valuable information on citizens' perspectives and the likelihood that they would engage in protest, and some of whose analysts worked on the strategy of Yushchenko's campaign, received approximately $1 million in 2004.[135] Brian Mefford, of IRI in Kyiv, noted in an interview in 2007 when asked about the U.S. contribution to the success of the Orange Revolution, "The 11 years prior to (2004) made the difference. You can't pull off an event of that magnitude without preparation."[136] He also pointed to the impact of leadership training for the leaders of civil society groups and political parties, noting that between 2002 and 2006, over eighty members of parliament, including Yulia Tymoshenko and President Yushchenko, had participated in IRI's training programs.[137]

Outside actors also supported the development and deployment of exit polls and other election-related activities. These included the poll conducted under the auspices of the Democratic Initiatives Foundation, which proved to be critical in allowing the opposition and NGO leaders to document the fraud in the second round, as well as other forms of election-related technical assistance. Oleksandr Sushko, director, and Olena Prystayko, project director, of the Center for Peace, Conversion and Foreign Policy of Ukraine, a research center in Kyiv, note that donors including the International Renaissance Foundation (Soros in Ukraine), NED, and USAID gave a total of more than $2.8 million

[133] Interview with Valeriy Chaly, Kyiv, June 14, 2007.
[134] Interviews with Nadia Diuk, Washington, DC, March 2008; and Brian Mefford, Kyiv, June 12, 2007. International Republican Institute, Annual Report, 2005, http://www.iri.org/pdfs/AR2005.pdf.
[135] Interview with Valeriy Chaly, Kyiv, June 14, 2007.
[136] Interviews with Brian Mefford, Kyiv, June 12, 2007; and Larry Garber, Washington, DC, April 9, 2010.
[137] Interview with Brian Mefford, Kyiv, June 12, 2007.

for activities related to the 2004 election. In line with the EU's policy of working through the governments of countries receiving assistance, the European Commission gave one million Euros to the Central Election Committee of Ukraine and sponsored other technical assistance projects to train both election observers and commission members; USAID also signed an agreement in 2004 with the Central Election Commission to train commission members and assist civic groups in monitoring the election.

International actors also supported and trained both domestic and international election observers. The OSCE, ODIHR, NATO, the Council of Europe's PACE program, and the European Parliament sent 650 observers for the first round as part of their combined International Election Observation Mission, 650 for the second round, and 1,367 for the rerun of the second round. Together with official observers from other countries and from international organizations, there were a total of 2,455 international observers for the first round and 13,644 for the rerun of the second round, one of the largest observation missions to date. By comparison, the OSCE sent 258 observers to Serbia in 2004 and 511 to Georgia in 2003. Freedom House and NDI sent an additional 1,000 observers after the Supreme Court's decision about the third round.[138] George Soros also provided support for election-monitoring activities, including those organized by the Committee of Voters.[139]

Finally, Western political leaders signaled their interest in free and fair elections both well in advance of and during the 2004 elections and played an important role in mediating between the regime and the opposition in 2004. Former secretary of state Madeleine Albright and former president Bush were among those who made trips to Ukraine to emphasize the importance of the 2004 elections for Ukraine's future and its integration into the Euro-Atlantic world.[140] President Bush sent a letter to Kuchma urging respect for free elections and threatening a review of U.S.–Ukrainian relations should the election be marred; he also sent Senator Richard Lugar as his personal representative to observe the second round.[141] Lugar and Secretary of State Colin Powell denounced the results of the flawed second round shortly after it happened.[142] EU officials also reiterated their interest in free and fair elections prior to the 2004 vote. New postcommunist members of the EU, including Poland, Lithuania, and Slovakia, took a particularly active role in calling for free and fair elections and sending election observers.[143] Boris Tarasiuk, then foreign

---

[138] Interview with Juhani Grossman, Kyiv, June 13, 2007.

[139] OSCE, "Final Report on the 2004 Presidential Election in Ukraine," May 11, 2005, http://www.osce.org/item/14224.html; interview with Jaroslavl Prytula, Lviv, August 3, 2005.

[140] See Sushko and Prystayko, "Western Influence," 129–134.

[141] Ibid., 133.

[142] Ibid., 134; see also "Text: Colin Powell Statement," *BBC News*, November 24, 2004, http://news.bbc.co.uk/2/hi/europe/4040177.stm; and "Remarks by United States Senator Richard Lugar on the Ukrainian Presidential Elections," Kiev, Ukraine, November 22, 2004, http://www.globalsecurity.org/wmd/library/news/ukraine/ukraine-041122-lugar.htm.

[143] Sushko and Prystayko, "Western Influence," 131.

minister of Ukraine, noted in a June 2007 interview that the success of the opposition in 2004 would have been impossible without outside support. Kuchma, he noted, paid attention to major actors in the international community, particularly Washington, and took any criticism into account, despite his authoritarian rule in Ukraine.[144]

The presidents of Poland and Lithuania, Alexander Kwasniewski and Valdas Adamkus, respectively, as well as the EU's Javier Solana and OSCE Secretary General Jan Kubis, played important roles in negotiating the end of the crisis during the protests after the second round. Oleh Rybachuk, then one of the Yushchenko campaign's top strategists and managers, in fact argued in an interview in 2009 that this intervention was the critical factor that prevented bloodshed on the Maidan.[145] Meeting with Yushchenko, Yanukovych, Kuchma, and Lytvyn, these actors helped negotiate an agreement by all sides not to use force that facilitated the peaceful resolution of the crisis by establishing the basis for further negotiations that led to the decision by the parliament in early December to rerun the second round.[146]

As in Serbia and Georgia, outside actors from the West also played another important role, that is, facilitating contact with "graduates" of earlier successes. Contact between NGO activists from Slovakia and Serbia, in particular, began soon after 1998 and 2000, respectively.[147] Slovak activists from organizations such as Civic Eye (Občianské oko) and think tanks such as the Institute for Public Affairs (IVO) were soon joined by those who had been active in Rock the Vote as well as by Otpor activists. As we discussed earlier in this chapter, links between some of these groups and Pora, especially through training camps and the sharing of Slovak experiences, encouraged the unification of activities of the NGO sector. The sharing of strategies and tactics learned from these experiences, as well as the experience in Georgia that we discuss in the next chapter, was also facilitated by meetings of activists from throughout the region held in Bratislava and elsewhere.

Pora leaders evaluated these contacts very positively. Volodymyr Horbach, for example, noting that the Serbian and Georgian examples were important and that Pora activists, in contrast to many people in Ukraine, believed that it would be possible to have an electoral breakthrough in Ukraine, stated that from the very beginning, the mission of the campaign and the emotional, social, and psychological grounds for it were the most important elements of the Serbian and Georgian experiences:

> We only had to use the tools sufficiently.... At the regional seminar in Novi
> Sad, an Otpor leader spent lots of time trying to persuade us that it was

---

[144] Interview with Boris Tarasiuk, Kyiv, June 13, 2007.

[145] Interview with Oleh Rybachuk, Washington, DC, February 26, 2009.

[146] Sushko and Prystayko, "Western Influence," 139–140; interview with Volodymyr Lytvyn, Kyiv, June 12, 2007.

[147] Sharon L. Wolchik and Ryszard Zięba, "Ukraine's Relations with the Visegrad Countries," in *Ukraine: The Search for a National Identity*, ed. Sharon L. Wolchik and Vladimir Aleksandrovich Zviglianich (Lanham, MD: Rowman & Littlefield, 2000), 133–164.

possible.... live people shared their own experiences, not so much to teach technologies that they had used but to share their experiences. When the time came, we didn't look (these) up in notebooks, but we had an idea about how it happened elsewhere and we did it our own way.[148]

Other activists, including leaders of Znayu, however, argued that the experiences of outsiders were not useful, as it was necessary to take Ukraine's own conditions into account in devising strategies and activities.[149] Some party and NGO activists, particularly those outside the capital, also downplayed the impact of outside experiences.[150] Miroslav Soldat, the manager of Yushchenko's campaign staff for the Lviv region, was more positive, noting that many of the techniques discussed in the seminars were well prepared and useful. Soldat also emphasized the need to adapt techniques to Ukrainian conditions: "Each territory had its own situation.... you must go from what works in the particular situation. You can use [techniques discussed by outside experts] but you must adapt them. Western Ukraine is different from Eastern Ukraine."[151]

Activists in Ukraine identified two additional roles of outside actors. The first was to serve as an inspiration, an "idea of the good that one could look up to."[152] The second was to keep the world's attention focused on Ukraine to both constrain the government's actions and encourage the protestors. In the words on one participant, who argued that the protests would not have succeeded without the actions of outside actors, the attention the world media gave to the protests "gave us a sense that we were not alone or abandoned by the world.... it gave us the strength to stay on the Maidan and also helped to prevent the use of violence [against the demonstrators]."[153] At the same time, it is clear that the role of outside actors and outside experiences was most evident and proved most useful in the capital and among the leaders of both the opposition and NGO sectors. As Bogdan Ben noted, "Maybe they used these experiences in central headquarters, but we didn't use it in our region."[154] And it is likely that most ordinary citizens who voted and participated in the protests knew little if anything about the contribution of graduates of other successful uses of the electoral model to the strategies of the NGO community and the opposition.[155]

[148] Interview with Volodymyr Horbach, Kyiv, June 12, 2007.
[149] Interviews with Dmytro Potekhin, Kyiv, June 13, 2007; and Kataryna Botanova, Kyiv, June 13, 2007.
[150] Interviews with Bogdan Ben, Lviv, August 2005.
[151] Ibid.
[152] Interview with Volodymyr Horbach, Kyiv, June 12, 2007.
[153] Interview with Volodymyr Horbach, Kyiv, June 12, 2007; see also McFaul, "Ukraine Imports Democracy," for a discussion of the impact of outside actors in providing ideas and pressure on the regimes.
[154] Interview with Bogdan Ben, Lviv, August 2005.
[155] For an analysis that stresses the role of people power from the bottom up, see Jane L. Curry and Doris Goedl, "Together We Are Strong: The People's Revolutions from the Bottom Up," unpublished manuscript.

In addition to these actors, we must also consider the actions of another outside actor that was not relevant in the other cases we have discussed so far, that is, Russia. Russia's goal in the 2004 elections was to see the perpetuation of the existing regime. However, not only did Russian leaders' support of Victor Yanukovych fail to achieve that result, it backfired. Seen by many analysts as an attempt to reassert Russia's dominance within its former empire, Russia's interference in the election took numerous forms, including overt support for Yanukovych, beginning in July 2004, and the loan of some of Russia's "political technologists," or campaign and public relations experts, to his campaign.[156] They also included efforts to emphasize the East–West regional divide in Ukraine and demonstrate the advantages of closer relations with Russia by means of economic concessions that favored Ukraine,[157] as well as funds for Yanukovytch. Estimates of the amount of money Russia spent on the elections in Ukraine vary widely, from the modest $5–10 million that Russian consultants claim was spent on the campaign to a figure of $300–900 million.[158] While it is impossible to resolve this debate, it is clear that funding for the campaign was one of Russia's main tools during this election. Russia also contributed funds to allow the regime to enact a dramatic increase in pensions prior to the election, and a major parade extolling Russian–Ukrainian relations was held in Kyiv several weeks before the first round of the election.

Vladimir Putin's October visit to Ukraine on the eve of the first round and his meeting with Yanukovych and Kuchma in Crimea prior to the second round were additional tools used, in the first case, to try to sway voters and, in the second, to urge the regime to use all its forces to make sure the vote favored Yanukovych in the second round.[159] Putin also attempted to legitimate the results of the fraudulent second round by congratulating Yanukovych on his victory – but before the official vote tabulation had even been announced. Russia also participated in the mediation effort during the protests. However, the Russian representative's insistence on the validity of the fraudulent second round clearly had little influence on the outcome.

CONCLUSION

In many respects, the breakthrough election that took place in Ukraine in 2004 resembled the Yugoslav presidential election that had occurred four years earlier. At the most general level, we find in both cases a long-term

---

[156] See Nikolai Petrov and Andrei Ryabov, "Russia's Role in the Orange Revolution," in *Revolution in Orange: The Origins of Ukraine's Democratic Breakthrough*, ed. Anders Åslund and Michael McFaul (Washington, DC: Carnegie Endowment for International Peace, 2006), 145–164; and Taras Kuzio, "Russian Policy toward Ukraine during Elections," *Demokratizatsiya* 13:4 (Fall 2005), 491–517.

[157] See Petrov and Ryabov, "Russia's Role in the Orange Revolution," 158–159.

[158] Ibid.

[159] Ibid., 157.

pattern of incumbent regimes resorting more and more frequently to violent actions in order to remain in power and a shorter-term development involving the adoption by opposition parties and civil society groups of innovative electoral strategies that made them far more effective than in the past at mobilizing popular support – both during the election and after the incumbent regime tried to steal the election. These similarities recognized, however, it is important to note that the Ukrainian electoral turnaround had several distinctive aspects, including the important roles played by Russia, business leaders, and the Supreme Court and the rapid dissolution of the regime's control over the media. At the same time, while external support for free and fair elections in Ukraine as well as for civil society groups was very influential, it was not premised – as in Serbia, in particular, but also in Croatia and Slovakia – on the goal of removing the incumbent from power, or on preventing his chosen successor from taking office. Free and fair elections, therefore, constituted the core U.S. goal in the Ukrainian presidential elections in 2004 and was not combined with the more ambitious mission of regime change, as in the other three countries. As we will discover in the next chapter, Ukraine was not the only case where the success of the opposition took the United States by surprise.

6

Georgia and Kyrgyzstan

Fraudulent Parliamentary Elections, Mass Protests, and Presidential Abdications

> The Yugoslav scenario was played out here.
>
> Eduard Shevardnadze[1]
>
> The United States did not get what it wanted in either Kyrgyzstan or Georgia.
>
> Isa Gambar[2]

In the last three chapters, we analyzed electoral breakthroughs from 1998 to 2004 in Slovakia and Croatia (Chapter 3), Serbia (Chapter 4), and Ukraine (Chapter 5). Although there were many differences among these electoral episodes, especially with respect to regime contexts and the role of popular protests in the transitions from one government to another, these elections nonetheless shared one common characteristic. The transfer of power took place for the simple reason that the democratic opposition won the elections and was able, as a result, to form a government, as in Slovakia, or win the presidential office, as in Croatia, Serbia, and Ukraine.

In this chapter, we compare the final two elections in the postcommunist region that led to the removal of authoritarian leaders from office: the November 2003 election in Georgia and the March 2005 election in Kyrgyzstan. The logic of pairing these two cases is, first, that these countries were removed in geographical terms from the hothouse atmosphere supporting democratic change as a result of the shared borders among Slovakia, Croatia, Serbia, and Ukraine. Second, the elections in Georgia and Kyrgyzstan were for the parliament, not for the presidency, the latter a post in both countries that is very powerful and directly elected. The next presidential elections were scheduled for 2005 in Georgia, where term limits would have required Shevardnadze

Our thanks to Anna Dolidze for reviewing this chapter and to Igor Logvinenko for carrying out interviews on our behalf in Kyrgyzstan.

[1] Quoted in Zurab Karumidze and James V. Wertsch, eds., *Enough! The Rose Revolution in the Republic of Georgia, 2003* (New York: Nova Science Publishers, 2005), 30.

[2] Interview in Baku, March 7, 2007.

to step down, and later in 2005 in Kyrgyzstan, where term limits were also in place. As a result, although the 2003 and 2005 parliamentary elections in Georgia and Kyrgyzstan, respectively, led to the removal of authoritarian presidents from office – events that followed on the heels of public protests in both cases – they achieved this outcome by extra-constitutional means. Parliamentary contests in both places served as pretexts for regime change – though pretexts that were aided, no doubt, by the potentially lame-duck status of presidential incumbents.[3]

We will devote most of this chapter to analyzing events in Georgia – a case that figures prominently throughout this book. As we will discover, while President Eduard Shevardnadze, like Milošević in Serbia, had been very successful in weathering a number of storms during his tenure in Georgia, his hold on power – in contrast to what happened in Serbia – was declining in quite visible ways by 2003. Thus, the opposition's use of some innovative electoral practices and the ambitions of Mikheil Saakashvili, the leader of the opposition, were easily sufficient to exploit the expanding opportunities for leadership change as a consequence of fraudulent parliamentary elections, a lame-duck president, and political protests.

We then turn to the events in Kyrgyzstan. Here, the dynamic took a different form. The electoral innovations that were characteristic of electoral turnovers in the earlier cases (including Georgia) were less in evidence in that country. Moreover, there was no opposition leader equal in power or ambitions to Saakashvili. However, two developments, peculiar to Kyrgyzstan, led Askar Akaev, the long-serving president, to abdicate. One was the fact that parliamentary election results had played into long-standing resentments in the South against the North by undermining existing patronage networks; as a result, the elections unleashed protests in the South that eventually moved to the capital, Bishkek. The other is ironic. Akaev was in some ways too studious an observer of the color revolutions in Georgia and Ukraine. Thus, rather than riding out the challenges posed by protests far smaller in size than those in our other cases, he assumed that they presented a substantial threat, panicked, and fled first to Uzbekistan and then to Moscow.[4] In this sense, demonstration effects played an unusually powerful role in the Kyrgyzstan electoral dynamic.

SOVIET AND GEORGIAN DISINTEGRATION

Following his rise to power in 1985, Mikhail Gorbachev introduced an extraordinarily ambitious reform agenda that included deregulation of both politics and economics in the Soviet Union, deregulation as well of the Soviet bloc, and the construction of an alliance between the Soviet Union, on the one

[3] Henry Hale, "Regime Cycles, Democracy, Autocracy and Revolution in Post-Soviet Eurasia," *World Politics* 58:1 (October 2005), 133–165.
[4] Interview with Li Lifan, Ithaca, NY, April 28, 2009.

hand, and, on the other, the West and reform-minded groups located within the Soviet Union and in Central and Eastern Europe. These innovations, however, did not have the expected effects of removing significant domestic and international barriers to change and laying the groundwork, as a result, for a renewed societal and party commitment to the Soviet experiment and a turnaround in Soviet economic performance. Instead, beginning in 1987, the Soviet Union and Central and Eastern Europe experienced a conjoined chain of events that began with a sharp decline in Moscow's ability to control political and economic developments within the republics that made up the ethnofederal Soviet state and in the Soviet bloc, and that then continued with a proliferation of civil society groups that called into question the right and capacity of the Communist Party to monopolize politics and economics. This dynamic fed in turn into nationalist mobilizations that simultaneously challenged Moscow's control at home and in the Soviet bloc and the existing borders of the Soviet as well as the Yugoslav and Czechoslovak states.[5] As a result, the regionwide hegemony of the Communist Party ended, and the Soviet Union, like Czechoslovakia and Yugoslavia, dissolved into its republican parts.

These dramatic developments played out in different ways in the republics that constituted the Soviet Union. The transitions from communism and from membership in the Soviet federal state went relatively smoothly, for example, in the Baltic republics, largely because of a mutually supportive agenda involving independent statehood, the establishment of capitalism and democracy, and membership in European institutions. By contrast, the road to statehood, regime change, and recalibration of identities and external alliances proved to be far more difficult in other parts of the Soviet federation, such as Georgia. As Jonathan Wheatley has argued, Georgian politics during this formative period involved a "bitter fight over the carcass of the Soviet state."[6] In the process, as Ronald Suny has noted: "Tragically, Georgians made political choices that deepened social and ethnic divisions."[7]

Thus, from 1987 to the formal end of the Soviet state on December 31, 1991, Georgia experienced an incendiary mix of large-scale nationalist demonstrations that built on earlier rounds of such protests during the Soviet period

---

[5] Valerie Bunce, *Subversive Institutions: The Design and the Destruction of Socialism and the State* (Cambridge: Cambridge University Press, 1999); Mark Beissinger, *Nationalist Mobilization and the Collapse of the Soviet State* (Cambridge: Cambridge University Press, 2002).

[6] Jonathan Wheatley, *Georgia from National Awakening to Rose Revolution: Delayed Transition in the Former Soviet Union* (Aldershot, UK; Burlington, VT: Ashgate, 2005), 34. Stephen Jones makes a persuasive case, however, that analysts have exaggerated the importance of nationalism in the Georgian conflicts accompanying the transition to statehood and the consensus among Georgians about the definition of the Georgian nation. See his *Georgia: A Political History* (London: I. B. Taurus, 2011), forthcoming.

[7] Ronald Suny, *The Making of the Georgian Nation* (Bloomington: Indiana University Press, 1994), 318.

beginning in 1976. These mobilizations converged not just on calls for independence from the Soviet Union, but also on the construction of a "Georgia for Georgians." Not surprisingly, the increasingly exclusivist Georgian nationalism and the loss of Moscow's protection from Georgian domination led to growing discomfort among minority communities and their political leaders. Fears about Georgian nationalism were particularly pronounced in Abkhazia and South Ossetia, two minority-defined subunits of the Georgian ethnofederation. At stake, for example, was the erasure of the linguistic and institutional autonomy of minority regions that the Soviet experiment had constructed. These developments were compounded by the disintegration of Communist Party control in the Georgian republic, as the party fell on the wrong side of the national question when responding to public demonstrations in Georgia during the Soviet period and then invited Soviet troops to use force against popular demonstrations in support of Georgian independence in April 1989.[8] Thus, in the fluid institutional landscape of Georgia in the second half of the 1980s and the early 1990s, majority nationalism fed minority nationalism, and vice versa. As a result, radicals within each camp took power, the democratic agenda and its supporters were sidelined, and conflicts between the two sets of nationalist players escalated.[9]

Zviad Gamsakhurdia, a longtime Georgian nationalist who made his opposition to both minorities and democracy clear in his rhetoric and the policies he advocated and implemented, contributed to the chaos of Georgia's transition from 1987 to 1992 and consolidated his personal power as a result of it. After serving as a nationalist leader and then as a parliamentarian, Gamsakhurdia became the head of a newly elected parliament in 1990 after an election, in which more than one hundred parties participated, that produced considerable overrepresentation of Georgians. After banning Georgian participation in the March 1991 Soviet referendum on the future of the USSR, while supporting a simultaneous referendum on independence in Georgia that passed easily (with minority communities participating in the former, but boycotting the latter), Gamsakhurdia was elected president of the country with 90 percent of the vote – that is, ironically, with a level of popular support similar to that enjoyed earlier by his enemies, the communists. Minority groups, again, opposed and often boycotted the election. His rule, in combination with the dissolution of the Soviet state, led to further escalation of conflicts between the Georgian state and minority regions and to political polarization as well between and among nationalists, the democratic opposition, and the

[8] Valerie Bunce, *Minority Politics in Ethnofederal States: Cooperation, Autonomy or Secession?* Einaudi Center for International Studies, Cornell University, Working Paper Series 08–07, July 2007; interview with Alexander Rondeli, Tbilisi, October 14, 2005; interview with Archil Gegeshidze, Tbilisi, October 17, 2005.

[9] Wheatley, *Georgia from National Awakening to Rose Revolution*, 35–74; Valerie Bunce and Stephen Watts, "Managing Diversity and Sustaining Democracy in the Postcommunist World," in *Sustainable Peace: Power and Democracy after Civil Wars*, ed. Philip Roeder and Donald Rothchild (Ithaca, NY: Cornell University Press, 2005): 133–158.

military.[10] In January 1992, Gamsakurdia was removed from power by a military coup d' etat – less than a year after his election as president.

Two months later, Eduard Shevardnadze returned to a Georgia ruled by a military junta and in the midst of one separatist war and on the brink of another. From 1972 to 1985, Shevardnadze had served as the first party secretary of Georgia. From 1985 to 1990, he had worked closely with Gorbachev as the foreign minister of the Soviet Union. Thus, Shevardnadze was in a unique position to head an interim government and establish some order in Georgia because of his past record in the republic and his ties to both Moscow and the West. The former was important because Georgia abutted the Russian Federation, and Russia had played a key role in supporting demands for autonomy in Abkhazia and South Ossetia; the latter was critical because of the need to counter Moscow's influence by attracting Western support for building a new state and regime in Georgia.

Shevardnadze pushed immediately for a reassertion of Georgian state control over Abkhazia and South Ossetia. However, both actions failed. Peace agreements that ended the wars placed Russian and OSCE troops in the two regions, and Abkhazia and South Ossetia, like other autonomous areas in the former communist world, such as Kosovo, Nagorno-Karabagh, and Transniestr, that had been the sites of secessionist-related wars, were transformed into frozen conflicts, proto-states occupying a halfway house between independent statehood and continued membership in their former states.[11]

---

[10] See, especially, Jones, *Georgia: A Political History*, Chs. 1–3. Also see Robert English, "Georgia: A Brief History," *New York Review of Books* 55:17 (November 6, 2008), 21–23; Svante Cornell, *Small Nations and Great Powers: A Study of Ethnopolitical Conflict in the Caucasus* (Richmond, Surrey, England: Curzon, 2001); Svante Cornell, "Autonomy as a Source of Conflict: Caucasian Conflicts in Theoretical Perspective," *World Politics* 54:2 (January 2002), 245–276; Monica Toft, *The Geography of Ethnic Violence: Identity, Interests, and the Indivisibility of Territory* (Princeton, NJ: Princeton University Press, 2003); Ronald Grigor Suny, *The Making of the Georgian Nation*; Ronald Grigor Suny, "The Emergence of Political Society in Georgia," in *Transcaucasia, Nationalism and Social Change, Essays in the History of Armenia, Azerbaijan and Georgia*, ed. Ronald Grigor Suny (Ann Arbor: University of Michigan Press, 1996), 109–140; Ronald Grigor Suny, "On the Road to Independence: Cultural Cohesion and Ethnic Revival in a Multinational Society," in *Transcaucasia, Nationalism and Social Change*, 377–400; Catherine Dale, "Abkhazia and Southern Ossetia: Dynamics of the Conflicts," in *Conflicts in the Caucasus*, ed. Pavel Baev and Ole Berthelsen (Oslo: International Peace Research Institute, 1996), 13–26; Charles King, "Post-Postcommunism: Transition, Comparison, and the End of 'Eastern Europe'," *World Politics* 53:1 (October 2000), 143–172; Charles King, "Misreading or Misleading? Four Myths about Democratization in Post-Soviet Georgia," unpublished manuscript, Georgetown University, 2001; Georgi Derluguian, *The Forgotten Abkhazia*, Program on New Approaches to Russian Security, Council on Foreign Relations, Working Paper Series, no. 18 (January 2001); Bunce, "Minority Politics in Ethnofederal States."

[11] See Jones, *Georgia: A Political History*, Chapter 4; Julie George, *The Politics of Ethnic Separatism in Russia and Georgia* (New York: Palgrave MacMillan, 2009); Julie George, "The Dangers of Reform: State-Building and National Minorities in Georgia," *Central Asian Survey* 28:2 (June 2009), 135–154. In addition, these conclusions were informed by interviews conducted with Alexander Rondeli, Tbilisi, October 14, 2005, and Archil Gegeshidze, Tbilisi, October 17, 2005.

Despite this outcome, however, Shevardnadze was, by all accounts, extremely successful in stabilizing Georgia. He did so by weaving together complex domestic and international coalitions that did not alter the status quo so much as reduce the destabilizing effects of weak political and economic institutions, contested borders, divergent agendas among key players, and a difficult geopolitical location that was too close to Moscow and too far from the West. He made, in short, the best of a bad situation. Archil Gegeshidze's circumspect summary of center-regional politics during the Shevardnadze era – that "conflicts frozen are better than conflicts unfrozen" – can be applied more generally to the coalitional politics of Shevardnadze's rule.[12] While a superb balancer, however, Shevardnadze was not a policy maker, a democratizer, or, more generally, an innovative leader with a vision.[13] Georgians admired his skills, which is why they nicknamed him "the Fox." However, they held limited personal affection for him.[14]

The regime that took shape under the leadership of Shevardnadze, therefore, was a classic example of a mixed regime. It combined the familiar characteristics of criminalized networks, extensive corruption (in which Shevardnadze also participated), ad hoc advisory councils and other informal governing institutions, and a powerful presidency with, at the same time, a liberal constitution (passed in 1995 and silent on the issue of the secessionist regions) and democratic decorations, such as competitive elections and relatively open media, that had the dual effect of dividing the democratic opposition while appeasing the West. His approach to state building was also a patchwork of compromises. Although he constructed a party, the Citizen's Union of Georgia, that helped institutionalize his powers, his control over Georgia was quite uneven. This was not just because of clan politics and the absence of much of a state outside the capital, but also because of his tolerance for considerable autonomy and personalized authoritarian rule in Adjaria, the presence of Russian peace-keeping troops within Georgia, and the freezing of conflicts within largely independent Abkhazia and South Ossetia.[15] Like leaders in most mixed regimes, therefore, Shevardnadze was unable to deliver much in the way of public services to the population. Thus, while less authoritarian than Serbia under Milošević and more consistently allied with the

---

[12] Interview with Archil Gegeshidze, Tbilisi, October 17, 2005.

[13] Interview with Mark Mullen, Tbilisi, October 14, 2005; and see, for example, King, "Misreading or Misleading?"; Anatol Lieven, "Georgia: A Failing State?," *Eurasia Insight*, February 5, 2001, from *Johnson's Russia List*, no. 5077, February 7, 2001; Stephen Jones, "Georgia: The Trauma of Statehood," in *New States, New Politics: Building the Post-Soviet Nations*, ed. Ian Bremer and Ray Taras (Cambridge: Cambridge University Press, 1997), 505–546; Thomas Goltz, "Georgia on the Brink." *Perspectives* 11:3 (January–February 2001), 1–8.

[14] Interview with Levan Ramashvili, Tbilisi, October 13, 2005.

[15] David Darchiashvili and Gigi Tevzadze, *Discussion Paper 9: Building Democracy in Georgia: Ethnic Conflicts and Breakaway Regions in Georgia*, International Institute for Democracy and Electoral Assistance (IDEA) Building Democracy in Georgia Discussion Paper no. 9 (May 2003).

West than either Serbia or Ukraine in the years before their electoral break-throughs, the Shevardnadze regime had neither the will nor the institutional wherewithal to be very democratic. In fact, none of the elections that were held during Shevardnadze's tenure or, for that matter, the elections that were held at the end of the Soviet period met international standards for being free and fair.[16] As Charles King summarized the regime several years prior to the Rose Revolution: "It is a pluralist, but not a democratic system, with a state whose existence is precarious at best, and one whose trajectory in democratization, government reform, and observance of basic human rights has been largely negative."[17]

REGIME DECLINE

Beginning in 1998, a series of developments took place in Georgia that sig-naled a weakening of the Shevardnadze regime.[18] In 1998, the economic crisis in Russia, which served as Georgia's primary trade partner and its primary energy provider, put an end to the brief Georgian economic recovery and highlighted the need for major political as well as economic reforms, espe-cially given the refusal of the International Monetary Fund to bail Georgia out of the crisis. For many of the political experts and democracy activists we interviewed in Georgia, this crisis was a turning point for the regime.[19] Shevardnadze responded by sacking the government (new parliamentary elec-tions that produced strong support for the CUG were held in 1998), giving verbal support for reform, and forming a new government that brought in a talented group of younger politicians and specialists. These shifts contributed to his reelection as president in 2000 – though this outcome also reflected

[16] See, especially, Tamar Zhvania, *Parallel Vote Tabulation (PVT) run by ISFED during Georgia's November 2, 2003 Parliamentary Elections*, International Society for Fair Elections and Democracy (ISFED) summary document (Tbilisi, Georgia, 2003).

[17] King, "Post-Postcommunism," 23.

[18] For excellent treatments of these developments, and of the Rose revolution itself, see Jones, *Georgia: A Political History*, Chs. 4 and 5; Giorgi Kandelaki, *Georgia's Rose Revolution: A Participant's Perspective*, United States Institute for Peace Special Report, Vol. 167, (Washington, DC: United States Institute of Peace, 2006); Jaba Devdariani, *Discussion Paper 11: The Impact of International Assistance on Georgia*, International IDEA, Building Democracy in Georgia Discussion Paper no. 11 (May 2003), http://www.idea.int/publications/georgia/upload/Book-11_scr.pdf; Cory Welt, "Regime Weakness and Electoral Breakthrough in Georgia," in *Democracy and Authoritarianism in the Postcommunist World*, ed. Valerie Bunce, Michael McFaul, and Kathryn Stoner-Weiss (Cambridge: Cambridge University Press, 2009), 155–188; Karumiże and Wertsch, eds., *Enough! The Rose Revolution in the Republic of Georgia*, 2003; Wheatley, *Georgia from National Awakening to Rose Revolution*; Barbara Christophe, *Understanding Politics in Georgia*, DEMSTAR Research Report No. 22 (November 2004); David Usupashvili, *Discussion Paper 1: An Analysis of the Presidential and Parliamentary Elections in Georgia: A Case Study, November, 2003 – March, 2004*, International IDEA Election Assessment in the South Caucasus (2003–04) (April 2004).

[19] Interviews with Giorgi Meladze, Tbilisi, October 13, 2005, and with Alexander Rondeli, Tbilisi, October 14, 2005.

electoral fraud and the absence of viable alternatives. However, it also became evident at that time that Shevardnadze was not committed to major reforms, since they demanded that he replace personalized rule, backroom deals, and criminalization of the economy – all of which weakened the state and undermined democracy – with stronger, transparent and accountable political and economic institutions, which would have undermined both his power and its coalitional base. The mixed character of the regime and the weakness of the state, in short, while undercutting his ability to institutionalize his powers, also served as the foundation of his rule.[20] Thus, he had few incentives to change the situation.[21]

From 2000 to 2003, both domestic and international support for the Shevardnadze regime declined. On the international side, George Soros (beginning in 2001), Richard Miles, the U.S. ambassador to Georgia, and close friends of the George W. Bush administration, such as James Baker, the former U.S. secretary of state, made it increasingly clear to the Shevardnadze regime that Georgia needed to show more democratic progress. While they did not go so far as to mount a concerted attempt to work with local groups to remove him from power through electoral means (as the United States did in Serbia), in large measure because they assumed that Shevardnadze would leave office in 2005 (because of term limits and indications that he was ready and willing to retire), his Western supporters were nonetheless signaling to both the regime and the opposition that Georgia needed to begin preparation for a more democratic post-Shevardnadze future.[22] These signals – though relatively subtle and not very consistent – energized both the NGO community and what became the major party of the opposition forces, the National Movement.[23]

At the same time, especially given rising corruption, backtracking on reform, fraudulent elections, the unresolved status of the minority regions, and the inability of the state to deliver basic services, Georgian citizens began to withdraw their support from Shevardnadze and recognize the need for a more activist regime bound by the rule of law. It was time, in short, to move on from an agenda of stabilization and a leader increasingly "out of touch"[24] to one that featured a more engaged leader who focused on policies and made governmental performance a priority.[25] Just as influential was an

---

[20] See, especially, King, "Post-Postcommunism."

[21] Interview with Alexandre Kukhianidze, Tbilisi, October 14, 2009.

[22] Lincoln Abraham Mitchell, *Uncertain Democracy: U.S. Foreign Policy and Georgia's Rose Revolution* (Philadelphia: University of Pennsylvania Press, 2009); and interview with Richard Miles, the U.S. ambassador to Georgia from 2002 to 2003, Washington, DC, September 25, 2009.

[23] Interview with Mark Mullen, Tbilisi, October 14, 2005.

[24] To quote from an interview with Giorgi Meladze, Tbilisi, October 13, 2005.

[25] Marina Muskhelishvili, *Constitutional Changes in Georgia*, International IDEA Policy Papers (2004), at http://www.idea.int/conflict/cb/upload/CBPGeorgiaMarina.pdf; Marina Muskhelishvili and Luiza Arutiunova, *Political Perceptions of Georgia's Population*, International IDEA Policy Papers (2004), at http://www.idea.int/europe_cis/

emotional shift. As Giorgi Nizharadze summarized the situation in the interview we conducted with him: Georgians had become increasingly "bored" with Shevardnadze and were seeking alternative leaders.[26]

Thus, what we find in Georgia from 2001 to 2003 is a theme similar to what we saw in the cases of the Milošević regime in Serbia and, for that matter, the protests that ended communism in Central and Eastern Europe: Georgians wanted to move away from their communist past and establish closer connections to Europe.[27] However, at the same time, it must be noted that Georgians' understandings of politics and their definition of their goals for the future were far from consensual. As Luiza Arutiunova and Marina Muskhelishvili have persuasively argued, discourses in Georgia prior to the Rose Revolution could be divided into four camps, depending upon support for tradition versus change and informal processes versus the rule of law.[28] Criticisms of Shevardnadze, therefore, did not converge on the goals of political change and instituting the rule of law – though both themes figured prominently in the important work done by the Georgian Young Lawyers Association, especially its defense of legally bounded politics and the independence of civil society.[29]

Third, there was a series of key political developments, beginning in 2000, that advertised the growing weakness of the regime. In 2000, Shevardnadze's party, the CUG, began to disintegrate, and in 2001 he resigned as the head of the party. In 2001, student-led protests, which took both the opposition and the government by surprise, stopped Shevardnadze's attempt to crack down on the independent television station, Rustavi-2.[30] These demonstrations were then followed by a new round in June 2003 that targeted the government's resistance to reform of a corrupt, politically slanted, and decidedly nontransparent electoral commission. The first demonstration, especially since it was successful and broke with a pattern of relative popular passivity, led to a resignation of the government and defections from Shevardnadze's coalition in parliament (a process that had actually begun in 2000). Perhaps most importantly, these protests led Mikheil Saakashvili, the minister of justice, to leave the government and defect to the opposition. Saakashvili, of course, became the leader of the 2003 challenge to Shevardnadze.[31]

These defections, moreover, were encouraged by the circulation of public opinion polls supported by Western democracy promoters, such as the

upload/Political%20Perceptions%20of%20Georgia%27s%20Population%20-%20 Eng%20chanegd.pdf.

[26] Interview with Giorgi Nizharadze, Tbilisi, October 16, 2005.

[27] Interview with Giorgi Meladze, Tbilisi, October 13, 2005.

[28] Muskhelishvili and Arutiunova, *Political Perceptions of Georgia's Population*.

[29] Discussions with Anna Dolidze, Ithaca, NY, June 9, 2009.

[30] Interview with Tinatin Khidasheli, Tbilisi, October 17, 2005; see Muskhelishvili, *Constitutional Changes in Georgia*, on the favorable ratings by Georgians of the trustworthiness of the media.

[31] Interviews with Tinatin Khidasheli and David Usupashvili, headquarters of the Republican Party, Tbilisi, October 17, 2005.

National Democratic Institute, that showed a significant decline in public support for Shevardnadze and by the circulation by ISFED (the International Society for Elections and Democracy) of information providing proof of falsified recent elections.[32] As a result, beginning in 2000, new parties began to form. In the local elections that took place in 2002, the democratic opposition did extremely well. Saakashvili was elected the mayor of Tbilisi after running an energetic campaign and enjoying strong support in the city council. Here, the parallels with Serbia are inescapable, given the role of the 1996 local elections in paving the way for the defeat of Milošević in 2000 and the election in 1996 of Zoran Djindjic, who served for two years as the prime minister of Serbia before he was assassinated, as the mayor of Belgrade. Finally, there were indications that Shevardnadze was becoming very isolated and more politically desperate. Both weaknesses were illustrated for all to see as a result of his failed take-over of Rustavi-2 and his failed attempt to push through amendments to the constitution that made it harder for opposition parties to win seats in the parliament. In addition, we also see in the years leading up to the Rose Revolution the formation of ever-changing coalitions around Shevardnadze that, in Corey Welt's terms, increasingly took the form of "a hodge-podge of marginal players."[33] Indeed, Shevardnadze came to rely more and more on Aslan Abashidze, the autocrat ruling Adjaria, to help him steal elections – as he was to do for a final time following the 2003 parliamentary elections.

Finally, because of greater domestic stability, a relatively liberal constitution, and the marginalization of the "Zviadists," the second half of the 1990s witnessed a reassertion of Georgian civil society – a development that was also assisted by the priority that U.S. democracy assistance placed on Georgia (as on Armenia), the emphasis that U.S. democracy and governance assistance placed in particular on support of civil society, and the role of the Open Society Institute in providing funding of an unusually wide range of associations through its small-grant competitions.[34] For example, it has been estimated that by 2000 there were 3,000 registered civil society organizations in Georgia, with both the United States and the Open Society Institute (which came to Georgia in 1994) providing significant support. It was also during the early years of the Shevardnadze regime that one of the most influential civil society organizations in the Rose Revolution – the Liberty Institute – was founded by two journalists.

[32] Interview with Giorgi Nizharadze, Tbilisi, October 16, 2005.

[33] Welt, "Regime Weakness," 5.

[34] Interviews with John Wright, Tbilisi, October 18, 2005; David Darchiashvili, Tbilisi, October 15, 2005; also see King, "Post-Postcommunism"; Welt, "Regime Weakness"; Jones, "Georgia: The Trauma of Statehood," 505–546; Jones, *Georgia: A Political History*; Stephen Jones, "Georgia's 'Rose Revolution' of 2003: A Forceful Peace," in *Civil Resistance and Power Politics: The Experience of Non-violent Action from Gandhi to the Present*, ed. Adam Roberts and Timothy Garton Ash (Oxford: Oxford University Press, 2009), 317–334; and Wheatley, *Georgia from National Awakening to Rose Revolution*.

However, it is very easy to overestimate the size and vibrancy of Georgian civil society, especially if we make a great deal of the protests, unusual at the time, of Georgians during the Soviet period; compare Georgia to its neighbors in the Caucasus; and extrapolate backward from the energetic activity of civil society groups during and immediately after the 2003 parliamentary elections.[35] It is true that a comparison of various ratings of civil society development seems to indicate a relatively strong civil society, especially when Serbia is brought in for comparison. For example, the Nations in Transit score (which range from 1 to 7, with seven being very weak civil society and 1 very strong) for civil society development in Georgia on the eve of the removal of Shevardnadze from office was 4.00, whereas the comparable figure for Serbia (1999) was 5.25, and the USAID measure of NGO sustainability (based on the same 1 to 7 scale) showed a score of 4.2 in Georgia in 2002 and 5.4 in Serbia in 1999.

However, these static figures overlook trends in civil society development in Georgia that remind us that, while the regime was weakening in certain ways, civil society was not in a position to rush in to fill the political vacuum. For example, if we focus on trends in NGO sustainability in Georgia and Serbia, we in fact find similar longer-term stories. Thus, just as Serbia deteriorated from a score of 4.8 to 5.4 from 1997 to 1999, as we would expect as a result of Milošević's crackdown, so Georgia also showed a decline in the years leading to its electoral breakthrough, moving from a score of 3.4 in 1998 (which is the first available rating) to 4.0 in 2000 and to 4.2 in 2002. These trends, moreover, reflected the reality on the ground.[36] As Giorgi Nizharadze and Tinatin Khidasheli both commented in their interviews with us, most of the civil society activity in Georgia could be reduced to two key players: the Liberty Institute and the Georgian Young Lawyers Association.[37] Civil society, in short, was more bluff than substance, though Saakashvili, far more than Shevardnadze, tended to believe the bluff.[38] More generally, as Stephen Jones has succinctly cautioned, "The Georgian Third Sector was elitist and weak; it had poor representation in the provinces, was dependent on Western funding, and its penetration of Georgian society was shallow."[39] It was for precisely these reasons that the Open Society Institute organized a trip of Georgian civil society leaders to New York in 2002.[40]

---

[35] Interviews with Armineh Arakelian, Yerevan, March 13, 2007, and Tbilisi, October 21, 2005.

[36] See, especially, Jones, "Georgia's Rose Revolution"; Ghia Nodia, *Civil Society Development in Georgia: Achievements and Challenges*, Caucasus Institute for Peace, Democracy and Development: Citizens Advocate Program Policy Paper (Tbilisi, 2005).

[37] Interviews with Giorgi Nizharadze, Tbilisi, October 16, 2005; Tinatin Khidasheli, Tbilisi, October 17, 2005.

[38] Interview with Tinatin Khidasheli, Tbilisi, October 17, 2005.

[39] Jones, *Georgia: A Political History*, Chapter 6; 18, 14; also see Nodia, "Civil Society Development in Georgia."

[40] Interview with David Darchiashvili, Tbilisi, October 15, 2005.

Taken together, the developments from 1998 onward in Georgia, therefore, present a mixed picture insofar as the defeat of the Shevardnadze regime was concerned. Although the regime was weakening, according to some important indicators, it was not clear by 2002 or 2003 that the opposition, which had grown in size but which was far from united, would be able to mount a strong challenge to Shevardnadze. This was especially unlikely if he kept with his past practice of stealing elections and if citizens kept with their past practice of letting Shevardnadze get away with it.[41] If the ability of publics to surmount the obstacles to collective action was unknown (as it was in all of our cases, in fact), so was the extent of the commitment of international democracy promoters to free and fair elections. For example, when James Baker, representing the Bush administration, came to Tbilisi in the summer of 2003 to press for electoral reforms, Shevardnadze was able to nod his approval and leave the far-from-transparent electoral commission largely intact.[42] Finally, there was little evidence that the opposition would unite, that civil society groups would focus on elections as a site for regime change, or that the two groups would form a close working relationship. In fact, unlike the situation in Serbia, in particular, Georgia demonstrated few precedents for any of these developments.

Thus, it is important to recognize that, while the regime was more vulnerable than it had been in the past, this did not necessarily translate in automatic fashion into its departure from power – especially in the context of parliamentary elections. Moreover, as Corey Welt has argued, what remained unclear in Georgia, especially given the large number of fraudulent elections in the past combined with the unwillingness of citizens to protest and the linkage in the early years of the transition between societal mobilizations and political violence, was whether citizens would in fact contest fraudulent elections by taking to the streets.[43] While the same problem presented itself in Serbia and Ukraine, as we saw in Chapters 4 and 5, there were some important differences between these cases and the situation in Georgia. In some respects, the Georgian case for electoral turnover was the weakest of the three. For example, popular protests were a more common feature of Serbian politics during the 1990s; Georgia, unlike Serbia, had never experienced election-related demonstrations; and Milošević, unlike Shevardnadze, was on the ballot. However, in other respects, Georgia was ripe for electoral change. Defections from the ruling circle prior to the pivotal election were far more extensive in Georgia than in Ukraine and Serbia, and there was no equivalent in Serbia or Ukraine of the disintegration of Shevardnadze's ruling party, the CUG.

[41] Eric Miller, "Georgia's New Start," *Problems of Post-Communism* 51:2 (April 2004), 12–21; Wheatley, *Georgia from National Awakening to Rose Revolution*; Peter Baker, "Tbilisi's 'Revolution of Roses' Mentored by Serbian Activists," *Washington Post*, November 25, 2003, page A22, http://www.washingtonpost.com/ac2/wp-dyn/A11577–2003Nov24?language=printer.

[42] See Mitchell, *Uncertain Democracy*.

[43] Welt, "Regime Weakness"; Interview with Gvantsa Liparteliani, Tbilisi, October 13, 2005.

ELECTORAL STRATEGIES OF THE OPPOSITION

From 2002 to 2003, however, detailed planning for political change tipped the balance in Georgia, and the obstacles for regime change were surmounted.[44] A key part of this story was "going international," as Giorgi Meladze put it – a strategy that was necessitated by the fact that Georgia was bounded on the north by Russia and on the south by two relatively authoritarian regimes. In January 2003, the Open Society Institute supported meetings between the Serbian opposition and the Serbian youth movement, Otpor, on the one hand, and the Georgian opposition, on the other. According to Ivan Marović, one of the founders of Otpor, a phone call from Tbilisi came out of the blue in mid-2002 asking for assistance in the defeat of Shevardnadze.[45] This led to a series of exchanges between the Georgians and the Serbian activists, sometimes also involving Slovak democratic activists, that began in January 2003 and that were facilitated by the Open Society Institute. Marović and Slobodan Djinović, also a leader of Otpor, played particularly important roles in these exchanges.[46] These meetings involved pep talks to the Georgian opposition, the sharing of experiences, and the transferring from Serbia and Slovakia to Georgia of the electoral strategies that had proven quite effective in weakening incumbent regimes and strengthening opposition forces.[47]

One consequence of these meetings was that Otpor, the Serbian youth movement, served as the template for the founding, the flat organizational structure, and the creative activities of Kmara ("Enough," a name borrowed directly from Otpor's campaign slogan), the Georgian youth organization that was formally founded in April 2003 following student protests in the previous month organized in part by the Liberty Institute.[48] While Kmara was not as large as Otpor and was formed much later relative to the date of the pivotal election, it nonetheless had roots going back to student activism in 2000 and played an important – though not decisive – role in the 2003 election.[49] For example, Kmara, together with the Liberty Institute,

[44] Megan Chabalowski, *Lessons for the Future of Civic Resistance: Georgia and Ukraine*, Peace Brief, United States Institute of Peace, 2005, http://www.usip.org/resources/lessons-future-civic-resistance-georgia-and-ukraine.

[45] Interview with Ivan Marović, Washington, DC, October 14, 2004.

[46] Interviews with Giorgi Meladze, Tbilisi, October 13, 2005; Gvantsa Liparteliani, Tbilisi, October 13, 2005.

[47] Wheatley, *Georgia from National Awakening to Rose Revolution*; Miller, "Georgia's New Start"; see interviews with James Baker, Mikheil Saakashvili, and Richard Miles in Karumiże and Wertsch, *Enough!*.

[48] Interviews with Tea Tutberidze, Tbilisi, October 13, 2005; Giorgi Meladze, Tbilisi, October 13, 2005; and Gvantsa Liparteliani, Tbilisi, October 13, 2005; also see Mitchell, *Uncertain Democracy*.

[49] Giorgi Kandelaki and Giorgi Meladze, "Enough! Kmara and the Rose Revolution," in *Reclaiming Democracy: Civil Society and Electoral Change in Central and Eastern Europe*, ed. Joerg Forbrig and Pavol Demeš (Washington, DC: German Marshall Fund, 2007), 101–125.

held summer camps in 2003 and various seminars that trained approximately 1,000 students in protest and electoral techniques.[50] Kmara not only worked in the campaign, supported turnout on election day (in part by traveling throughout Georgia with megaphones on top of cars), and participated in the protests after the election, but also formed close collaborative relations with ISFED, the Liberty Institute, and Saakashvili's National Movement. In close association with ISFED, Kmara helped prepare and implement a parallel vote tabulation based on the Serbian model that used voter signatures at the precinct level to generate a tabulation of the overall vote. Along with ISFED, Kmara also monitored voter registration, voter lists, and the construction of ballot boxes at the local level, as the usual practice of the regime was to eliminate opposition voters from the rolls and stuff ballots. As Tea Tutberidze recalled, Kmara, in conjunction with ISFED, also made a repeated point of announcing to citizens before and during the election that "We are watching violations."[51]

Like Otpor as well, Kmara courted the support of the police before the election by, for instance, coordinating "happenings" in front of police stations across Georgia and using the same arguments as Otpor activists when interacting with the police. Thus, they used such phrases as "We are on your side" and "The regime is not your fault."[52] Finally and more generally, Kmara also helped, along with ISFED, to propagate such new ideas and new actions in Georgian politics as citizenship rights (which had also been the interest of the Georgian Young Lawyers Association), exit polls (which had been used unevenly in some earlier elections), and democracy as direct participation in the political process by ordinary citizens and civil society groups.[53]

Serbian activists, moreover, provided the opposition and civil society groups with two films: a training film, which Giorgi Meladze (a member of the Liberty Institute) referred to as an "Otpor promotional movie," and *Bringing Down a Dictator* by the U.S. filmmaker Steve York, which chronicled, through interviews with participants and other footage, the events that had taken place in Serbia during and immediately after the 2000 elections. The latter film was shown twice on Georgian television before the 2003 election, and both films were, according to Meladze, very influential.[54]

Finally, Otpor activists in conjunction with those in other Serbian-based civil society organizations, such as CeSID (the Center for Elections and

[50] Interview with Gvantsa Liparteliani, Tbilisi, October 13, 2005; and see Giorgi Meladze, "Civil Society: A Second Chance for Post-Soviet Democracy: A Eurasianet Commentary," *Eurasianet*, September 6, 2005, http://www.eurasianet.org/departments/civilsociety/articles/eav090605.shtml.

[51] Interview with Andro Gigauri, Tbilisi, March 8, 2007; interview with Tamara Zhvania, Tbilisi, October 18, 2005.

[52] Interview with Tea Tutberidze, Tbilisi, October 13, 2005.

[53] Interview with Giorgi Nizharadze, Tbilisi, October 16, 2005.

[54] Interview with Giorgi Meladze, Tbilisi, October 13, 2005; but Muskhelishvili was less convinced of this.

Democracy), shared their experiences with finding ways to encourage the opposition to form a united front, running ambitious nationwide political campaigns, and using the media to undercut the regime (which was easier in Georgia, given the more open media and high levels of trust in the media).[55] CeSID's work in Georgia began in the fall of 2002, as the Open Society Institute provided opportunities for training in public opinion polling, getting out the vote, parallel vote tabulation, election monitoring, and rapid tabulation and then public announcements of the "real" vote.[56] Otpor also provided a model for building the institutional capacity of organizations, such as ISFED and Kmara, that worked closely together to register voters, oversee the construction of voter lists, get out the vote, and train internal vote monitors while reaching out to the international community to provide a network of monitors as well (which was a luxury the Serbian activists had not had in 2000).[57] In addition, Serbian activists emphasized the importance of focusing the campaign on core issues – which Georgian activists did by emphasizing the themes that Shevardnadze was responsible for Georgia's problems and that he would steal the election.[58]

Serbian activists also focused on the importance of peaceful resistance to the regime, the necessity of establishing collaborative ties (and a division of labor) among civil society organizations and the opposition, and, finally, especially important in the event of protests, establishing linkages with the military and the police (with the latter particularly receptive, given the absence of any paychecks for several months prior to the 2003 election). However, while all this was helpful, perhaps most important was the simple message that the Serbs could communicate by way of their own deeds – that is, their success in defeating a long-serving dictator with deep roots in the communist era. This was a particularly important message in the Georgian context.[59]

The United States Agency for International Development (USAID) funded such important organizations as ISFED, the Eurasia Foundation, Horizonty, the International Republican Institute, and the National Democratic Institute, and through the work of these organizations made significant contributions to political change in Georgia.[60] Moreover, USAID (and the Open Society Institute) provided a safety net for the "best and the brightest" in Georgian society, and the United States was particularly good at using back channels to reach politicians.[61] Considerable credit for the Georgian breakthrough,

---

[55] See Muskhelishvili, "Constitutional Changes in Georgia"; Muskhelishvili and Arutiunova, "Political Perceptions of Georgia's Population."

[56] Interview with Marko Blagojević, Belgrade, April 11, 2005.

[57] Interview with Mark Mullen, Tbilisi, October 14, 2005; interview with Nino Kobakidze, Tbilisi, October 19, 2005; interview with Tea Tutberidze, Tbilisi, October 13, 2005; interviews with Tamar Zhvania, Tbilisi, October 18, 2005.

[58] Interview with Giorgi Meladze, Tbilisi, October 13, 2005.

[59] Ibid.

[60] See interview with Strobe Talbott in Karumiże; and Wertsch, *Enough!*, 83–86.

[61] Interview with Mark Mullen, Tbilisi, October 14, 2005.

however, needs to be given to the Open Society Institute, which, in comparison to USAID, spent much less money, operated without the burden of large-scale and relatively rigid strategic plans, and targeted a much wider range of democracy-related activities. The Open Society Institute also gave Georgians numerous opportunities to learn how the Third Sector operated, because employees were all drawn from the local population, and multiple rounds of the open (small) grant competition helped Georgians organize, define their goals, and establish collaborative ties with one another.[62] The ability to move quickly was critical in the Georgian context, because getting rid of Shevardnadze was less about governance and capacity building, which was a major concern of USAID (and especially of the European Union), than about short-term politics.[63] Though less important than the US government and the Open Society Institute, other international actors, such as the European Union and the British Department of International Development, were also active. Unlike the situation in Ukraine, the OSCE did not play a very important role in Georgia.[64] Without minimizing the importance of the contributions of international democracy promoters, we would nonetheless conclude, as we did for Serbia and Ukraine, that the electoral project was a highly collaborative venture that was locally crafted, but internationally assisted.[65]

What is distinctive about the Georgian situation in 2003, however, is the fact that the 2003 election was a parliamentary contest and that many of the preparations by the opposition, civil society groups, and especially the international community were carried out on the assumption that the 2003 election was a trial run for the presidential elections scheduled for the spring of 2005. Thus, the U.S. ambassador, Richard Miles (who had also served as the chief of mission in Belgrade from 1996 to 1999 and as the first U.S. ambassador to independent Azerbaijan), the U.S. democracy promotion community in Georgia and in Washington, and the Open Society Institute did not envision these innovations in electoral politics to be anything more than laying the groundwork for an eventual transition out of the Shevardnadze era – a turnover in power that they welcomed, but only if it took place in ways that maintained political stability while investing in a more authentic democracy in Georgia.[66] In fact, this was also the view of many Georgian activists, including members of various opposition parties and even Saakashvili's party, the National Movement, that had formed in 2001.

However, all of these actors were proven wrong. In the 2003 election, Saakashvili ran an extraordinarily effective U.S.-style campaign that generated substantial political support, while the parties still associated with the

[62] Interview with David Darchiashvili, Tbilisi, October 15, 2005.

[63] Interview with Mark Mullen, Tbilisi, October 14, 2005.

[64] Interview with David Kostelancik, Washington, DC, November 16, 2006.

[65] As also argued by Meladze, interview in Tbilisi, October 13, 2005; and see Devdariani, *Discussion Paper 11: The Impact of International Assistance on Georgia.*

[66] Mitchell, *Uncertain Democracy.*

regime, along with Shevardnadze himself, hardly bothered to campaign. The behavior of the incumbent in 2003 was in fact the norm. Shevardnadze, unlike Milošević and, for that matter, Kuchma in Ukraine and Mečiar in Slovakia, had never been interested in elections, which he saw as a sideshow.[67] This is one reason why, in Ambassador Richard Miles' framing, the elections in 2003 were "massively flawed."[68] At the same time, turnout was very high in the Georgian election. This was in part because of Saakashvili's campaigning prowess, but it also reflected the energetic work of civil society organizations such as the Liberty Institute, the Georgian Young Lawyer's Association, Kmara, and ISFED.[69] Election monitoring also paid off when Western concerns about the quality of the elections were voiced and when local observers, in combination with exit polls (which were quickly released), were quickly able to generate electoral results that contrasted with the tabulations eventually provided by the regime. As in Serbia and Ukraine, therefore, it was not just that the two sets of results diverged; it was also that citizens believed the numbers provided and the concerns about voting practices voiced by the opposition and Georgian civil society organizations.

However, there were important differences between the Georgian electoral dynamic, on the one hand, and the breakthrough elections that took place in Serbia in 2000 and in Ukraine in 2004, on the other. One was that it was actually through the postelection demonstrations more than through either preparations for the election or the campaign itself that unity of the opposition was forged and a broad spectrum of Georgians, including not just civil society organizations and the opposition, but also representatives of the economic and cultural elite, managed to join forces.[70] In this sense, some of the electoral strategies that were implemented in Serbia and Ukraine early in the process were implemented more gradually in Georgia, and they were more dependent upon establishing the existence of electoral fraud.

Second, in contrast to Serbia, but much like what occurred in Ukraine, opposition groups and civil society organizations planned the demonstrations before election day, on the assumption that they would be necessary.[71] At the same time, however, the demonstrations themselves were smaller and much more episodic in Georgia in comparison to the very large but brief demonstrations in Serbia and the very large and more prolonged protests that took place in Ukraine. As Cory Welt has observed, while there were several

---

[67] Interview with Alexander Rondeli, Tbilisi, October 14, 2005.

[68] Interview with Richard Miles in Karumiže and Wertsch, *Enough!*, 73.

[69] Interviews with Tea Tutberidze, Tbilisi, October 13, 2005; Giorgi Meladze, Tbilisi, October 13, 2005; Gvanca Liparteliani, Tbilisi, October 13, 2005; Levan Ramishvili, Tbilisi, October 13, 2005; and Tinatin Khidasheli, Tbilisi, October 17, 2005.

[70] Mitchell, *Uncertain Democracy*, Chapter 3; Welt, "Regime Weakness"; Jones, "Georgia's Rose Revolution"; Wheatley, *Georgia from National Awakening to Rose Revolution*; Karumiže and Wertsch, *Enough!*

[71] Interviews with Tea Tutberidze, Tbilisi, October 13, 2005; Giorgi Meladze, Tbilisi, October 13, 2005.

large-scale demonstrations involving 20,000 or so demonstrators at the beginning of the mobilization and similar, if not larger, numbers on the final two days of the regime, "on ten of the twenty-one days between the election and Shevardnadze's resignation, there were no demonstrations to speak of. On eight days, the number of demonstrators may not have exceeded 5,000."[72] This pattern may very well have reflected the understandable ambivalence Georgians had about popular protests as a consequence of the very high price they had paid for taking to the streets in large numbers in the late 1980s and early 1990s.

Finally, while the opposition and civil society organizations in Serbia were far from certain that the police and the military would defect from the Milošević regime, and while there was somewhat more certainty about this issue in Ukraine, given early signaling, participants in and leaders of the demonstrations in Georgia seem to have been more confident about their personal security.[73] This was in part because the Shevardnadze regime, in contrast to the Milošević and Kuchma regimes, had made the fatal mistake of not paying the police for several months.

The final distinction we can draw is between removing presidents through presidential elections, as in Serbia and Ukraine, and forcing them to leave office after a parliamentary election, as in Georgia. What is clear from the interviews we conducted is that no one expected Saakashvili to use the large protests on November 22 – weeks after the election was over – to enter the first session of the new parliament and present Shevardnadze with a letter of resignation to be signed. The linkage between parliamentary elections and removal of the president, in short, seems to have been drawn by Saakashvili, rather than through deliberations carried on within the leadership stratum. Thus, as Gvantsa Liparteliani put it in her interview: "We expected the November 2003 elections to be defining, but not the end of the Shevardnadze era."[74] Saakashvili, however, had the idea, the widespread popularity, and the "impulsive personality" to make this happen.[75] Thus, it is not surprising that he won the presidential election early the following year with a vote total that came close to Soviet-era standards; that he quickly likened himself to Kemal Ataturk and claimed the need to impose a modernizing agenda on Georgia, as Ataturk had done in Turkey following the collapse of the Ottoman Empire; and that some analysts have summarized his approach to winning and exercising

---

[72] Welt, "Regime Weakness," p. 14.

[73] See, especially, interviews with Gvantsa Liparteliani, Tbilisi, October 13, 2005; Keti Nozadze, Tbilisi, conversations from October 14–18, 2005; Tea Tutberidze, Tbilisi, October 13, 2005; and Mark Mullen, Tbilisi, October 14, 2005. However, Richard Miles, the ambassador to Georgia at the time of the "Rose Revolution" (which had been named, in fact, by Mark Mullen), was less confident that the security forces would stand on the sidelines during the protests. Interview with Richard Miles, Washington, DC, September 25, 2009.

[74] Interview with Gvantsa Liparteliani, Tbilisi, October 13, 2005.

[75] Saakashvili's impulsive tendencies were noted by Richard Miles in the interview we conducted with him in Washington, DC, September 25, 2009.

power as typically Jacobin.[76] It was precisely concerns about rash behavior and his inability to listen, coupled with his tendency to engage in flamboyant political actions and his ability to draw large crowds with his gift for oratory, which made the U.S. Department of State, including the ambassador to Georgia at the time, nervous from the start about how Saakashvili would behave as president of Georgia.[77] Saakashvili, moreover, suffered from what David Usupashvili (a former ally and current head of the Republican Party in Georgia) described in his interview as a fundamental problem in Georgian politics – the inability of political leaders to distinguish between the competition for power built into democratic politics and politics as confrontation with the enemy.[78]

At the same time, in forcing Shevardnadze to leave office prematurely, Saakashvili and his allies managed to continue an unfortunate tradition in post-Soviet Georgian politics. Here, we refer to a recurring dynamic wherein power is seized through extra-constitutional means, citizens then rally around the new leader, and elections are finally held to legitimate the transfer of office. Losers then depart from the political game rather than remaining in the political arena and forming an opposition party. As a result, political power is consolidated and at the same time liberated from competitive pressures until the next round of extra-legal transitions in leadership takes place.[79]

THE 2005 ELECTION IN KYRGYZSTAN[80]

We can now turn to the second electoral breakthrough of interest in this chapter: the 2005 election in Kyrgyzstan. This was, as of this writing, the last successful example of an electoral removal of an authoritarian leader from office in a mixed regime in the postcommunist region. It was also a dynamic that shared two key characteristics with the Georgian case. One was that popular protests following the election served as the pretext for removing from office a long-serving leader, one who was not on the ballot because the elections were for the parliament, not for the presidential office. In fact, Akaev had been in power for fifteen years, having become president of Kyrgyzstan while

---

[76] Interview with Marina Mukhelishvili, Tbilisi, October 15, 2005; interview with David Usupashvili, Tbilisi, October 19, 2005; but see Ghia Nodia, "Georgian President's Record Mixed When Judged Against Ambitious Goals," *Radio Free Europe / Radio Liberty*, January 24, 2009.

[77] Interview with Mark Mullen, Tbilisi, October 14, 2005; Mitchell, *Uncertain Democracy*.

[78] Interview with David Usupashvili, Tbilisi, October 19, 2005. Also see Stephen Jones, *Georgia: A Political History*.

[79] Interview with Marina Muskhelishvili, Tbilisi, October 15, 2005. As Stephen Jones has argued, this dynamic has made Georgian political dynamics unusually dependent on the role of political leaders. See his *Georgia: A Political History*.

[80] We thank Igor Logvinenko for his valuable assistance in helping us reconstruct the "Tulip Revolution" in Kyrgyzstan. The interviews cited in this discussion (with the exception of interviews with Marko Blagojević in Belgrade and Amy Schultz in Baku) were conducted by Logvinenko in Bishkek in December 2007 and January 2008.

Shevardnadze was still the foreign minister of the USSR. The other similarity was that Akaev, like Shevardnadze, was scheduled to leave the presidency, because of term limits, in a subsequent election – in this case, in a matter of months, since the presidential election was expected to be scheduled during the fall of 2005. However, when facing demonstrations that were motivated by local elite anger regarding unexpected and unwelcome electoral defeats in the South and that eventually spread northward to the capital, Akaev responded not by waiting them out, but rather by quickly vacating his office and leaving the country.[81] As Amy Schultz, the director of the National Democratic Institute in Kyrgyzstan at the time these events took place, summarized what happened from February through March 2005: "The issue in Kyrgyzstan was not whether the elections were free and fair, but, rather, anger on the part of local elites, especially in the south of the country, about their candidates losing office."[82]

Her characterization of what happened in Kyrgyzstan reminds us that there is in fact only a superficial resemblance between the 2005 election in that country and the other cases of interest in this book that involved confrontations with authoritarian leaders at the polls and in the streets.[83] Thus, while protests in Kyrgyzstan originated, as in Georgia, Ukraine, and Serbia, in anger directed at the regime as a result of being denied the fruits of electoral victory, the individuals who took the lead in these protests and the sources of their anger were very different. In particular, unlike our other cases, the protests in Kyrgyzstan did not begin in the capital, and they were not started by opposition party candidates and their followers who were upset about electoral irregularities. Instead, they were led by disgruntled leaders of local networks in the South of the country who had assumed a guaranteed reelection, but who instead lost power and therefore plunder. Moreover, participants were unusually diverse with respect to their socioeconomic profiles, and largely rural citizens dominated the ranks of protesters.[84] What made the opposition and protesters angry, in short, was the violation of the assumption, built upon

---

[81] Interview with Li Lifan, Ithaca, NY, April 28, 2009.

[82] Interview with Amy Schultz, Baku, Azerbaijan, March 6, 2007.

[83] Also see Scott Radnitz, "What Really Happened in Kyrgyzstan?," *Journal of Democracy*, 17:2 (April 2006), 132–146; Scott Radnitz, "A Horse of a Different Color: Revolution and Regression in Kyrgyzstan," in *Waves and Troughs of Post-Communist Reform*, ed. Valerie Bunce, Michael McFaul, and Kathryn Stoner-Weiss (Cambridge: Cambridge University Press, 2009), 300–324; Matthew Fuhrmann, "A Tale of Two Social Capitals: Revolutionary Collective Action in Kyrgyzstan," *Problems of Post-Communism* 53:6 (2007), 16–29; Erica Marat, *The Tulip Revolution: Kyrgyzstan One Year After* (Washington, DC: Jamestown Foundation, 2006); Aleksandr Knyazev, *Gosudarstvennyi perevorot: 24 Marta 2005g v Kirgizii* (Moscow: Europa, 2005); Kathleen Collins, *Clan Politics and Regime Transitions in Central Asia* (Cambridge: Cambridge University Press, 2006); A. K., Kyzybaev, B. O. Orunbekov, L. A. Rud', G. Asanova, and Bolotkanov, eds., *Eldik Revolutsiya, 24-mart 2005 – Narodnaya Revoliutsiya* (Bishkek: Uckhun, 2006).

[84] Fuhrmann, "A Tale of Two Social Capitals"; Radnitz, "What Really Happened in Kyrgyzstan?".

multiple fraudulent electoral contests in the past and the personal networks that supported Akaev's rule, that the purpose of elections was to maintain the status quo, not to break with it. Thus, for the protesters in Kyrgyzstan, the problem with the 2005 parliamentary election was that there was too much, rather than too little, competition. In fact, while both of Akaev's children ran for a seat in parliament in 2005, only one was elected outright in the first round.

THE AKAEV REGIME

In Kyrgyzstan, Gorbachev's reforms and the dramatic changes they unleashed within the Soviet Union in the second half of the 1980s had the consequence in 1990 of bringing a noncommunist to power: Askar Akayev, who was a physicist and chair of the Kyrgyz Academy of Sciences. Thus, unlike all of its Central Asian neighbors and in fact most of the Soviet successor states, the Kyrgyz transition from communism produced a sharp break with Communist Party rule – a dynamic we also saw in Georgia, Armenia, and Azerbaijan early in the transition, and that in Eastern and Central Europe was usually associated (except in Croatia) with a rapid transition to democracy.[85] In addition, there were two other aspects of the early years of its transition that were distinctive to Kyrgyzstan: the opposition of Akaev and most elites and citizens in the country to the dissolution of the Soviet Union, and the absence, related in part to that opposition and to the lack of subunits based upon minority communities, of nationalist mobilizations accompanying the formation of a new state and regime. Akaev, therefore, did not ride a wave of nationalist fervor to power, unlike Gamsakhurdia in Georgia, Ter-Petrossian in Armenia, and Tudjman in Croatia. At the same time, unlike these other leaders, Akaev was allied with reform forces in Moscow – especially Andrei Sakharov and his parliamentary group.

Akaev, therefore, occupied an unusual political space that made him a good compromise candidate in the elections that took place in the Kyrgyz Supreme Soviet in 1990.[86] He had public stature, but he was neither a communist nor a bureaucrat and therefore separate and separable from the regime. At the same time, he was popular with liberals and with Russians within Kyrgyzstan and in Moscow. Finally, he was not a nationalist, and he supported the Soviet Union. He also had another advantage rooted in how politics and economics in Kyrgyzstan had worked during the Soviet period. He was from the North and the capital, whereas his communist predecessor was from the South.

[85] See, for example, Valerie Bunce, "The Political Economy of Postsocialism," *Slavic Review* 58:4 (Fall 1999), 756–793; Michael McFaul, "The Fourth Wave of Democracy and Dictatorship: Noncooperative Transitions in the Postcommunist World," *World Politics* 54:2 (January 2002), 756–793; and M. Steven Fish, "Democratization's Prerequisites." *Post-Soviet Affairs* 14:3 (July–September 1998), 212–247.

[86] John Anderson, *Kyrgyzstan: Central Asia's Island of Democracy?* (Amsterdam: Harwood, 1999).

It was this cleavage, best understood as the spatial translation of how interests and coalitions were organized from the grassroots upward within the country, that structured social and therefore political networks and that had succeeded in erecting powerful obstacles to political and economic change during the Soviet period. These networks, moreover, became if anything more important over time. While the policy of stability in cadres during the Brezhnev era (1964 to 1982) had locked in such networks in Kyrgyzstan as elsewhere throughout the Soviet Union (but especially in Central Asia and the Caucasus), the costs of the economic transition, once communism and the Soviet state had passed from the scene, made people even more dependent on their personal connections.[87]

Akaev began his rule as a liberal reformer – an approach to governance that made a great deal of political sense in a new and very poor state that lacked, unlike its neighbors, energy reserves. Thus, Akaev carried out ambitious economic reforms that broke up collective farms and encouraged rapid expansion of the private sector. He also carried out a liberalization of the political system that in the early 1990s involved weakening the power of the presidency to the benefit of the parliament and placing considerable power in localities rather than in Bishkek, the capital. Not surprisingly, these moves were viewed with considerable favor by the International Monetary Fund, which was strongly influenced at the time by the reigning ideology of the "Washington consensus." As a consequence, the IMF was quick to provide a sizeable package of support to Kyrgyzstan in 1994. Not surprisingly, Akaev was also very popular with the U.S. government, which appreciated his commitments to liberalization.

How deep Akaev's commitments to democracy and capitalism ran, however, was another story. On the one hand, embracing this agenda was a very good way to gather resources abroad. As Kumar Bekbolotov observed in an interview, "Democracy was understood to be the main export commodity of Kyrgyzstan."[88] On the other hand, these resources came with certain costs attached – which Shevardnadze also had discovered in Georgia as a result of his alliance with the West. These included, for example, the proliferation of largely Western-supported non-governmental organizations that eventually numbered one thousand or so by the early 2000s and that pushed in most cases for reforms of the economy, the political system, and social policy.[89] Moreover, as was typical of the postcommunist world, ambitious economic reforms translated in the first half of the 1990s into an economic slowdown, rising unemployment, the expansion of socioeconomic inequalities, and the retreat of the Soviet-era welfare state. As the result of the combination of a more active and organized civil society, the social capital that developed

---

[87] Collins, *Clan Politics*; Kelly McMann, *Economic Autonomy and Democracy: Hybrid Regimes in Russia and Kyrgyzstan* (Cambridge: Cambridge University Press, 2006).

[88] Interview with Kumar Bekbolotov, conducted by Igor Logvinenko, Bishkek, January, 2008.

[89] See Radnitz, "A Horse of a Different Color," note 12; and see Kelly M. McMann, "The Civic Realm in Kyrgyzstan," in *The Transformation of Central Asia*, ed. Pauline Jones Luong (Ithaca, NY: Cornell University Press, 2003).

from traditional networks,[90] and democratic change with increasing economic stress, Akaev faced growing threats to his power. Just as citizens were increasingly dependent on informal networks, the same was the case for Akaev. As Azamat Temirkulov, an assistant professor at American University–Central Asia, observed in an interview, "The state became weak and unreliable, so guarantees vanished. In Kyrgyzstan, as well as many other places, informal solidarity among friends, relatives and neighbors (*'tuganchylyk'* as it is called in Kyrgyz) became a substitute for what was previously provided for by the state. Employment opportunities were distributed along these lines."[91]

A turning point was reached in 1994. In that year, Akaev ran into serious conflicts with the communist deputies in the parliament, and he began to use a series of constitutional referenda (which he largely wrote himself, though appearing to be responding to a more open drafting process) to reconcentrate power in the presidential office. The 1995 parliamentary elections also showed that whatever interest Akaev had had in free and fair elections was now gone, and the referenda held in 1994, 1996, 1998, and 2003 demonstrated his growing commitment to an expansion of presidential powers.[92] In the second half of the 1990s and thereafter, he harassed the opposition and the media and introduced legislation that made it much harder for the Third Sector to operate. For example, before the 2000 presidential elections, Akaev jailed opposition candidates, and in 2002 he used violence against demonstrators.[93] Finally, he used his office to enrich his family and friends. For example, Akaev's older brother and two sisters-in-law were on the public payroll, and his son (like Robert Kocharian's son in Armenia) was able to monopolize the cell phone business in the country.

Akaev, of course, was hardly alone in his corrupt practices. Many politicians in Kyrgyzstan entered politics in order to protect, expand, and distribute economic resources, jobs, and the like. As the former prime minister, Tursunbek Chingishev (whom Akaev fired), publicly stated: *"Tol'ko duraki ne voruyut"* ("Only fools don't steal").[94] However, this "octopus of corruption," as Zamira Sadykova, the editor of *Res Republica*, put it in her congressional testimony, had one consequence that worked against Akaev's ability to maintain power. Over time, the pacts upon which Akaev's rule depended became more and more expensive to maintain.[95]

---

[90] Fuhrmann, "A Tale of Two Social Capitals."

[91] Interviewed with Azamat Temirkulov in Bishkek conducted by Igor Logvinenko, January 2008.

[92] Anderson, *Kyrgyzstan: Central Asia's Island of Democracy?*; interview with Kumar Bekbolotov, conducted by Igor Logvinenko, Bishkek, January, 2008.

[93] Marat, *The Tulip Revolution.*

[94] Interview with Shairbek Juraev, conducted by Igor Logvinenko, Bishkek, January 2008.

[95] As Zamira Sadykova, the editor of *Res Republica*, put it in her congressional testimony – see Commission on Security and Cooperation in Europe, "Kyrgyzstan's Revolution: Causes and Consequences," Hearing Before the Commission, 109th Congress, First Session, April 7, 2005, 3; Collins, *Clan Politics.*

Thus, beginning in the mid-1990s, the Akaev regime became more authoritarian, more corrupt, more strapped for money and support, and less interested in transparent politics and procedures. These trends translated, predictably, into a less secure civil society, an embattled opposition, and a more nervous regime. Akaev regularly fired people and used the Central Election Commission and trumped-up charges to stop individuals from running for office. He also relied on fraudulent elections, which from 1994 onward were based heavily on what Noor Borbieva has termed "conspicuous and free voting buying."[96] This led the liberals to begin to desert him and to defections from the ruling circle, including some key members of parliament and the former internal affairs minister, Felix Kulov. It also led to growing concerns about the regime on the part of his international supporters, such as the United States.

At the same time, throughout the 1990s and beyond, the opposition continued to be very fragmented.[97] The problem was not just the costs of operating in what Scott Radnitz has characterized as a classic competitive authoritarian regime, but also the failure of the opposition, as in so many of the postcommunist countries, to define itself in policy terms rather than in terms of power or personalities and to reach out to publics and members of civil society organizations.[98] Like the Serbian opposition during much of the 1990s, therefore, "posturing" was preferred over the politics of winning support and building winning coalitions.

Thus, by 1998 the "island of democracy" in Central Asia reverted to the Freedom House scores typical of its Central Asian neighbors, and in the same year Kyrgyzstan's government defaulted on two international loan payments. In some ways, this "regression to the regional political mean" was not surprising. As Bermet Tursunkulova commented in an interview, "It's important to recall that Kyrgyzstan was surrounded by fairly authoritarian states, and so there was little pressure to remain democratic. In this sense, 'authoritarian diffusion' played a role with time. Also, while many top officials were noncommunists, most of the midlevel elites remained ex-communist, and old habits die hard."[99] Growing authoritarianism was followed in turn by mounting defections from Akaev's ruling group, including the former internal affairs minister, Felix Kulov, and Danyan Usenov, a member of parliament and wealthy businessman.[100] Finally, corruption was exacting a toll. By 2000 the public debt of Kyrgyzstan was greater than its GDP.[101]

---

[96] See, especially, Noor O'Neill Borbieva, "Development in the Kyrgyz Republic: Exchange, Communal Networks, and the Foreign Presence," (Ph.D. dissertation, Harvard University, 2007); interview with Shairbek Juraev, conducted by Igor Logvinenko, Bishkek, January 2008.

[97] Marat, *The Tulip Revolution*; Radnitz, "A Horse of a Different Color."

[98] Radnitz, "A Horse of a Different Color"; interview with Amy Schultz, Baku, March 6, 2007; also see Borbieva, "Development in the Kyrgyz Republic," Chapter 7.

[99] Interview with Bermet Tursunkulova, conducted by Igor Logvinenko, Bishkek, January 2008.

[100] Radnitz, "A Horse of a Different Color."

[101] Ibid., 6.

ENDGAME

Akaev managed to survive the 2000 presidential election – by blocking strong candidates from running, buying votes, and using the Central Election Commission to control voter lists, voting procedures, and tabulation of the results. However, by the 2005 election there were three developments that made the president of Kyrgyzstan more vulnerable – though he was not on the ballot, since this was a parliamentary election, and though few expected that the election would serve as an occasion for him to be overthrown.

First, there were the ambiguities surrounding Akaev's political future. He had already amended the constitution to allow him to run for a third term in 2000 – an action that alienated many people, including those who thought they would gain improved access to power and money after Akaev departed from the presidency. The question then became what he would do in the fall of 2005, when he was once again scheduled to finish his final term. On the one hand, because of his past willingness to reach, whenever it was necessary for him to stay in power, into his "grab bag of dirty tricks,"[102] members of the opposition, individuals tied to Akaev, and ordinary citizens assumed that in 2005 Akaev would find a way to prolong his rule once again. This only made people more eager to get rid of him. On the other hand, because he might step down in the fall of 2005, he was a potential lame-duck president and thus one who had declining resources available to distribute to his clients.[103] Like the other interpretations of Akaev's future, this one carried the same implication: it was time for counterelites to begin jockeying for political power.

There were also growing international pressures for free and fair elections in Kyrgyzstan. Thus, the United States signaled clearly its dissatisfaction with the election process, and it invested heavily in improvements in the electoral procedures to be used in the 2005 parliamentary elections.[104] Mike Stone, a project director for Freedom House, was involved in this process, as were the U.S. ambassador, Steven Young, and Brian Kemple, a lawyer who was working with the Kyrgyz government on a project on legal reform supported by USAID.[105] While these actions played a role in the confrontations with Akaev that played out in March 2005, their direct impact on these events was nonetheless limited – because corrupt electoral procedures were deeply rooted in Kyrgyz society and eminently rational; because Kyrgyz citizens were and remained demobilized and cynical;[106] and because civil society organizations

---

[102] To borrow from Kimmage, Commission on Security and Cooperation in Europe, "Kyrgyzstan's Revolution: Causes and Consequences," 10.

[103] Hale, "Regime Cycles."

[104] Borbieva, "Development in the Kyrgyz Republic," Chapter 7.

[105] Richard Spencer, "Quiet American behind Tulip Revolution," *Telegraph*, April 2, 2005, http://www.telegraph.co.uk/news/worldnews/asia/kyrgyzstan/1486983/Quiet-American-behind-tulip-revolution.html.

[106] Borbieva, "Development in the Kyrgyz Republic."

in Kyrgyzstan were more reactive than active with respect to the protests that brought Akaev down. Moreover, the key issue that mobilized protests in 2005 was not electoral irregularities and the defeat of the opposition so much as the defeat of powerful network bosses.

However, the indirect effects of U.S. actions were nonetheless important – in particular, U.S. withdrawal of support for Akaev as well as the sheer amount of attention the United States paid to the 2005 election. Here, it is interesting to note the parallels with Georgia. For the United States, this election was a "practice run" for the coming presidential election, as the parliamentary elections in Georgia in 2003 had been, and the engagement of the United States in the election and its barrage of criticisms about the quality of elections in the country (as in Georgia) communicated the key message that the U.S. alliance with the president was on the verge of becoming history.

The precedents set by the Orange Revolution in Ukraine and the Rose Revolution in Georgia also undercut Akaev. Oddly enough, Askar Akaev himself highlighted the importance of these confrontations with dictators in the post-Soviet neighborhood by complaining about the proliferation of pro-democracy organizations in Kyrgyzstan and then publishing a book in January 2005 that went to great lengths to show why such a revolution would never come to Kyrgyzstan.[107] Shevardnadze's loss of power and the defeat of Yanukovych in Ukraine were also directly connected to developments in Kyrgyzstan. For example, CeSID (the Center for Elections and Democracy) in Serbia, which had played such a critical role in the defeat of Milošević, was involved in training individuals to do similar electoral work in Kyrgyzstan. Kel-Kel, a student group founded on the eve of the 2005 election that served as a counter to the "official" youth movement formed by Akaev, modeled itself directly on Kmara in Georgia and Pora in Ukraine, and some members of Kel-Kel had been on the Maidan in Ukraine during the 2004 protests.[108]

Finally, in 2003 Akaev, after carrying out a series of discussions with a wide variety of groups in the country and then, typically, following up these exchanges by doing exactly what he wanted, introduced some constitutional changes that, among other things, made it harder for the opposition to compete for power. The referendum on these changes passed. However, this development led many active members of the government to take increasingly public stances in opposition to Akaev. At the same time, an opposition angry about the constitutional changes and the procedures Akaev had used to craft and pass them, but heartened by divisions within Akaev's circle, launched "a flurry of new party formation and coalition-building [activities]."[109] For example, Roza Otunbaeva, a former foreign minister and ambassador who

---

[107] Fuhrmann, "A Tale of Two Social Capitals."
[108] Interview with Marko Blagojević, Belgrade, April 11, 2005.
[109] Radnitz, "What Really Happened in Kyrgyzstan?".

returned to Kyrgyzstan after serving as a diplomat in Sukhumi (the capital of Abkhazia, a secessionist region in Georgia), founded a new party, Ata-Jurt ("Fatherland"). This party then joined with others to form the People's Movement of Kyrgyzstan (NDK), with Otunbaeva and Karmanbek Bakiev, a former prime minister, serving as coleaders. What was striking about this party is that it transcended the North–South divide. However, another major opposition figure, Felix Kulov, failed to join the effort. Just as important is the fact that Akayev formed a party, Alga, only in 2005.

All of these developments paved the way for the events of February through March 2005. In the first round of the elections that took place on February 27, 400 candidates ran for 75 seats in the newly defined single-chamber parliament. These elections were monitored by 695 international and 2,000 local observers. Only thirty-five candidates won outright, and a second round of elections was planned for March 13. Among those scheduled to run in the second round were several major opposition candidates.

Small-scale protests had already broken out in the South in response to the removal of favored candidates from the ballot on the eve of the election, and further protests broke out after the election on March 3 because of anger, again in the South, over the defeat of their patrons. In an interview, Azamat Temirkulov (an assistant professor at American University in Bishkek) noted that this was when the slogan "Akaev Go!" started to appear.[110] From March 4 through March 8, protesters, who by some accounts were joined by members of organized crime, took over the building of the regional administration in Jalalabad. Soon thereafter the protests began to spread to Osh and other parts of the South. These protests gained supporters and established control over Jalalabad and Osh by early March. At this point, however, civil society organizations and the opposition were isolated from one another and on the sidelines, and most of the participants were poor people from small towns and villages.[111] This was, in short, very different from what we saw in Serbia, Ukraine, and even Georgia, that is, well-organized, urban-based protest movements led by a united opposition that collaborated with civil society groups and that had obvious and well-known leaders. Instead, as Scott Radnitz has argued, the dynamic in Kyrgyzstan was largely ad hoc and unplanned: "The protagonists had not previously organized as a party, advocated no ideology, and did not initially intend to overthrow Akaev."[112]

On March 10, the opposition announced the creation of a Coordination Committee that demanded the resignation of Akaev, new presidential elections, and annulment of the parliamentary elections. On March 13, the second round of the elections took place, and, while some opposition leaders won

[110] Interview with Azamat Temirkulov, conducted by Igor Logvinenko, Bishkek, January 2008.

[111] Fuhrmann, "A Tale of Two Social Capitals"; Radnitz, "A Horse of a Different Color."

[112] Radnitz, "A Horse of a Different Color," 4.

their districts, the opposition still denounced the results as falsified. From that point until March 20, the demonstrators repelled the police, took over much of the south of the country, and began to focus on Bishkek. The "power ministries" then began to stop taking Akaev's orders.[113] On March 22, the new parliament convened with only two-thirds of the deputies swearing allegiance to the constitution. Akaev addressed the deputies, noting that the color revolutions ..." are actually overthrows of the state (and) exceed the limits of the boundaries of the law."[114] On March 24, with half the country controlled by the opposition, over ten thousand protestors gathered in Bishkek, some under the control of the opposition and others not. The crowd then broke into the White House (where Akaev lived and where the presidential office was located), and Akaev fled to Uzbekistan and then to Russia. What had begun a month earlier as scattered protests had evolved relatively quickly into a coup d'etat. However, in many ways the challenge to Akaev's power was less direct than what we saw in Georgia in the sense that "nobody seized power in Kyrgyzstan. It was abandoned...."[115]

CONCLUSIONS

The electoral turnovers that took place in Georgia in 2003 and Kyrgyzstan in 2005 resembled in some ways the electoral breakthroughs that took place in Ukraine in 2004 and Serbia in 2000. Most obviously, we find in all four cases relatively authoritarian regimes, attempts by incumbents to steal elections, and significant post-election protests. However, it was precisely because of their common but distinctive qualities that we paired Georgia and Kyrgyzstan in one chapter. First, in some respects, these two cases provide stronger support than all the others analyzed in this book for the structural argument that regimes lose power when their institutional, economic, and international supports erode.[116] However, just as distinctive to the two elections of interest in this chapter is the fact that they were for parliament, not for the presidency. Nonetheless, these elections had the consequence of ending the Akaev and Shevardnadze eras. In this sense, the power of the regime was eroding, yet power was also seized.

How important were these differences between Georgia and Kygyzstan, on the one hand, and the earlier cases of electoral breakthroughs, on the other?

---

[113] Interview with Aleksander Knyazev in Knyazev, *Gosudarstvennyi perevorot*, 103.
[114] Quoted in Knyazev, *Gosudarstvennyi perevorot*, 103–104.
[115] Samira Sadykova, testimony before Congress, Commission on Security and Cooperation in Europe, "Kyrgyzstan's Revolution: Causes and Consequences," 4.
[116] See, especially, Steven Levitsky and Lucan Way, *Competitive Authoritarianism: Hybrid Regimes after the Cold War* (Cambridge: Cambridge University Press, 2010); Lucan Way, "The 'Real' Causes of the Color Revolutions," *Journal of Democracy* 19:3 (July 2008), 55–69; and the response by Valerie Bunce and Sharon L. Wolchik, "Getting Real about Real Causes," *Journal of Democracy* 20:1 (January 2009), 69–73.

In the next chapter, we provide more evidence to address this question by broadening our investigation to include five more elections – in Armenia, Azerbaijan, and Belarus from 2003 to 2008 – where oppositions mounted major challenges to authoritarian rule. Some of these elections were for the presidency and some (in presidential systems) were for parliament. However, in every case the opposition failed to prevail.

7

Failed Cases

Azerbaijan, Armenia, and Belarus

Each year I read Gene Sharp[s' book] and try to apply the techniques.... If we didn't have a sense of humor our situation would be tragic.

Isa Gambar[1]

The regime that planned an "elegant" victory has been exposed as nothing other than a fraud. The mask of legitimacy has slipped off.

Alexander Milinkevich[2]

When we [the Armenian diaspora] came to Armenia after the collapse of communism in order to help build a prosperous democracy, we did not expect to find such a "Soviet" country.

Alex Sadar[3]

In the preceding four chapters, we analyzed cases in which efforts to use elections to unseat authoritarian rulers succeeded. In this chapter we examine elections in which opposition parties and NGOs sought to use elections to depose authoritarian leaders but failed. We selected these "failed cases," which occurred in Azerbaijan, Armenia, and Belarus from 2003 to 2008, for analysis because they introduce variation in electoral outcomes while holding constant some important influences on electoral results. In particular, like the elections that led to turnover, these five elections took place in mixed regimes located in the postcommunist region. Moreover, despite the failure to replace authoritarian leaders with the opposition, all of these elections featured, like our successful cases, a united opposition. Finally, as in Serbia, Georgia, Ukraine, and Kyrgyzstan, significant public protests broke out in Armenia, Azerbaijan, and Belarus in response to electoral fraud.

[1] Interview with Isa Gambar, Baku, March 7, 2007.
[2] Alyaksandr Milinkevich, "Forward," in *Prospects for Democracy in Belarus*, ed. Joerg Forbrig, David R. Marples, and Pavol Demeš (Washington, DC: German Marshall Fund of the United States and the Heinrich Böll Stiftung, 2006), 9.
[3] Interview with Alex Sadar, Yerevan, March 14, 2007.

AZERBAIJAN, 2005 AND 2003

The 2005 parliamentary elections in Azerbaijan were contested by an opposition that was more united than it had been previously. Both the opposition and the regime were influenced by developments in Georgia and Ukraine, as were external actors, who called for free and fair elections but, in most cases, did not really want to see a "color revolution" take place in Azerbaijan. These elections thus consolidated the regime of Ilham Aliyev, who had come to power in the flawed presidential elections of 2003.

The Regime

As in some of our successful cases, Azerbaijan experienced a period of democratic political life immediately after the fall of the Soviet Union. This interlude, however, in which the opposition leader Ebulfez Elchibey was elected in what were generally recognized as free and fair elections in 1992, was brief, primarily because Elchibey was weakened by the conflict with Armenia in Nagorno-Karabagh, a largely Armenian enclave located within the borders of Azerbaijan. The domestic disorder that resulted from Elchibey's chaotic governing style, violent conflicts between Azeris and Armenians in Nagorno-Karabagh and in other parts of Azerbaijan, and the destabilizing interactions between nationalists in Armenia and in Azerbaijan also undermined Elchibey's government.[4] In 1993 Heydar Aliyev, the leader of Azerbaijan during the last years of communism who had also served on the all-union Politburo of the Soviet Union, came back to power by organizing a coup against Elchibey after Azerbaijan's defeat in Nagorno-Karabagh. This defeat, which resulted in the loss of 16 percent of Azerbaijan's territory to Armenia and the influx of 700,000 refugees from the area, colored and continues to color political life in Azerbaijan and was used very adeptly to justify the need for a strong government. Thus, in addition to using material incentives to reward its supporters and maintain their loyalty, as well as coercion against the opposition, the regime also used normative incentives – in this case, the call to Azeri patriotism – to preempt calls for change.[5]

By exploiting anger over these losses and skillfully using patronage coupled with coercion, Heydar Aliyev created a regime that was extremely effective in dividing and weakening any opposition and demobilizing the population and that became increasingly repressive over time. Able to rely on oil revenues, his government oversaw a complicated system of patronage networks that

---

[4] These difficulties were noted by the U.S. ambassador to Azerbaijan, Richard Miles, interview, Washington, DC, September 25, 2009.

[5] For a discussion of the use of these incentives under communism, see Zvi Y. Gitelman, "Power and Authority in Eastern Europe," in *Change in Communist Systems*, ed. Chalmers Johnson (Stanford, CA: Stanford University Press, 1970), 235–264.

controlled most of Azerbaijan's wealth, including privatized state enterprises, new businesses, and oil and gas resources.[6]

The government of Ilham Aliyev, who was elected president in 2003 when his father fell gravely ill, was less secure than that of his father. Ilham, who had studied in Moscow and taught at the Moscow Institute of International Relations, created the same patronage networks around himself, but had relatively little time to consolidate his power before the 2005 elections. Despite his talk of the need to cooperate with NATO and the EU and to enact economic reform, Ilham disappointed hopes that the regime would become more moderate and instead continued many of his father's practices, including his strategy of rule. International assessments of the degree of democratization, such as Freedom House rankings, in fact found that Azerbaijan had regressed on all measures except corruption, which remained the same (and consistently high), between 2003 and 2005. The country's overall ranking fell from "partly free" to "not free."[7]

Like the other semi-authoritarian leaders we discuss in this chapter, Ilham was a very diligent steward of his regime. Like his father, he benefited from his control over most of the country's considerable economic resources, which were closely intertwined with patronage networks based on familial and regional affiliations. A nearly classic resource-rich country, Azerbaijan experienced very positive trends in economic performance prior to the 2003 and 2005 elections. In 2003, 50 percent of the country's growth in exports and 90 percent of its exports came from oil and gas.[8] Coupled with the fact that 30 percent of the country's inhabitants were dependent on the government for employment and the very tight connections between politics and economics,[9] these resources gave the regime ample tools to maintain its power. Aliyev also benefited from ongoing popular resentment of the country's

[6] See, for example, Oksan Bayulgen, *Foreign Investment and Political Regimes: The Oil Sector in Azerbaijan, Russia, and Norway* (Cambridge: Cambridge University Press, 2010), and Pauline Jones Luong and Erika Weinthal, *Oil Is Not a Curse: Ownership Structure and Institutions in Soviet Successor States* (Cambridge: Cambridge University Press, 2010), Chapters 1, 2, 7, and 9.

[7] See Anar M. Valiyev, "Parliamentary Elections in Azerbaijan: A Failed Revolution," *Problems of Postcommunism* 53:3 (May–June 2006), 17–35, Table 2, for these scores from 1996 to 2005.

[8] Energy Information Administration, "Azerbaijan: Background," U.S. Department of Energy, http://www.eia.doe.gov/cabs/Azerbaijan/Background.html. See also Thad Dunning, *Crude Democracy: Natural Resource Wealth and Political Regimes* (Cambridge: Cambridge University Press, 2008).

[9] Valerie Bunce and Sharon Wolchik, *Azerbaijan's 2005 Parliamentary Elections: A Failed Attempt at Transition*, CDDRL Working Paper No. 89, Center for Democracy, Development and the Rule of Law, Freeman Spogli Institute for International Studies, Stanford University (September 2008). See also Oksan Bayulgen, *Foreign Investment and Political Regimes: The Oil Sector in Azerbaijan, Russia and Norway* (Cambridge: Cambridge University Press, 2010).

defeat in Nagorno-Karabagh as well as from his tight control over the military and police forces.

Opponents argue that the power of the Aliyev regime rests on a set of intertwined hierarchies. These include a regional hierarchy of Azeris from Armenia and Nakhchivan, and a hierarchy centered on the Aliyev family. State positions are filled as the result of bribery, which links officials or their proxies at various levels. Opposition activists argue that it is this feature of the regime that holds the system together. Because those involved in these networks, which reach down to the lower layers of the apparatus and permeate all sectors of the economy, realize that all will lose if the regime changes, they unite to resist pressure to change or threats to the regime.[10] Corruption is also rampant, as is evident in the fact that Transparency International ranked Azerbaijan 137th of 159 countries in 2005.[11]

These tools, as well as Aliyev's willingness to use force against his opponents, made it very difficult for the opposition to organize, unify, or reach larger groups of citizens. Evident in the beating and arrest of Isa Gambar, an opposition candidate for president in 2003 who had been speaker of parliament under Elchibey, and numerous other opposition leaders after the 2003 elections, Aliyev's determination to neutralize threats to his power was also clear in his preemptive moves against any of his associates who could be seen as potential rivals.[12]

At the same time, there was some ground prior to the 2005 elections to think that a challenge to Aliyev might succeed. Despite the phenomenal growth in GDP in the early 2000s, nearly 30 percent of the population continued to live in poverty, 8 percent in severe poverty.[13] A number of political factors also made Ilham's regime less secure than that of his father. His links to the patronage networks his father had created were more recent and thus less secure. He also appeared to be somewhat more concerned about maintaining friendly relations with the West. Although, as we discuss more fully later, external pressure on Azerbaijan to hold truly free and fair elections was far less evident than in several of the successful cases we have discussed, Ilham also did make some (largely cosmetic) concessions to international pressure by making some changes in the Election Code prior to the 2005 elections.[14]

At the same time, as the 2005 election approached, Aliyev renewed his efforts to intimidate his opponents and preempt any challenges. In October 2005, the regime prevented the return to Azerbaijan of Rasul Guliyev, a

---

[10] Interview with Baheddin Heziyev, conducted by Sara Rzayeva, Baku, January 8, 2006.

[11] Transparency International Corruption Perception Index (2005), http://www.transparency. org/news_room/latest_news/press_releases/2005/cpi_2005_18_10_05.

[12] Bunce and Wolchik, *Azerbaijan's 2005 Parliamentary Elections.*

[13] Ibid.

[14] Organization for Security and Cooperation in Europe, Venice Commission, "Final Opinion on the Amendments to the Election Code of the Republic of Azerbaijan," Opinion No. 336/2005 (Warsaw/Strasbourg, October 25, 2005), 2, http://www.osce.org/documents/ odihr/2005/11/16895_en.pdf.

former speaker of parliament, widely seen as someone who could appeal both to dissatisfied elements in the networks supporting the president and to certain elements of the opposition. The government also made every effort to promote internal cleavages within the opposition.[15]

Aliyev also took action against mass mobilization by the opposition, even going so far as to have police officers confiscate orange material in shopping centers in Baku in order to prevent the opposition, which had chosen orange as the color of its campaign in reference to the Orange Revolution in Ukraine, from using it.[16] Youth activists, including Ruslan Bashirli, the leader of Yeni Fikir, were detained and accused of working with the Armenian intelligence services. The government broke up meetings organized by opposition candidates and beat and arrested opposition supporters who tried to hold a rally in Baku in October prior to the election.[17]

In contrast to the situation in several of the successful cases we have discussed, in which the security forces either remained neutral or sided with opposition protestors after the crucial elections, in Azerbaijan the security forces remained loyal to the regime. Given their behavior in suppressing protests and opposition meetings, it is clear that no agreement was reached with the opposition concerning neutrality.

The Opposition Unifies

As in many of the cases in which democratizing elections succeeded in ousting semi-authoritarian leaders, the attempt by the opposition to use the 2005 elections to defeat Ilham Aliyev was preceded by earlier attempts. In the 2003 election, the opposition considered running a single candidate. However, seven candidates from opposition parties eventually ran for president in addition to Heydar and Ilham Aliyev, who ran for the same office from the same party, with the slogan "Two Candidates, One Campaign."[18] Leaders of several opposition parties met in London but decided not to run a single candidate. Rather, they agreed to support the candidate who garnered the most votes in what they anticipated would be the second round of the election. In the end, there was no second round, and Ilham was the winner in elections that were widely condemned as not meeting the standards of the international community.

---

[15] Khadija Ismayilova, "Azerbaijan Opposition Comes under Fire," *EurasiaNet*, September 6, 2005, http://www.eurasianet.org/departments/insight/articles/eav090605.shtml.

[16] Larissa Momryk, "Azerbaijan through Western Eyes," *Ukrainian Weekly*, January 8, 2006, No. 2, News and Views section, 8.

[17] Valiyev, "Parliamentary Elections in Azerbaijan," 25.

[18] See *EurasiaNet*, "Election Watch: BBC Monitoring Guide to the Azeri Presidential Elections," October 15, 2003, http://www.eurasianet.org/election2003/azer_bbc_report.shtml; and Human Rights Watch, *Azerbaijan: Presidential Elections 2003: Obstruction of Opposition Rallies*, Human Rights Watch Briefing Paper (October 13, 2003), http://www.hrw.org/en/reports/2003/10/13/azerbaijan-presidential-elections-2003.

As it would in 2005, the Aliyev regime used intimidation and force against opposition leaders. Rallies and meetings with voters on the outskirts of Baku were broken up, and on several occasions police and other regime supporters (described frequently as "athletically built people" in civilian clothes) clashed with opposition supporters. Widespread interference with the efforts of opposition leaders to post their materials or meet with voters continued throughout the campaign.[19]

Immediately after the 2003 election, a planned march and peaceful protest organized by opposition leaders led to violent clashes between police and opposition supporters in which many citizens were injured. The violence was in turn used by the regime as an excuse for a massive crackdown on the opposition and the arrest of many opposition leaders. In addition to the 196 protestors who were arrested immediately, over 600 supporters of the opposition were arrested in the following two months, and over 100 were imprisoned after unfair trials. Human rights groups documented police torture of those detained.[20] Although the detainees and political prisoners were eventually released, the restrictions on public activity by the opposition remained in effect until the approach of the 2005 election.

In its efforts to unify for the 2005 elections, the Azeri opposition had in fact a number of advantages not available to leaders in the other countries we examine in this chapter. One was the country's previous democratic experience. As Azeris proudly pointed out, Azerbaijan was a parliamentary republic during its brief period of independence from 1918 to 1920. Although this fledgling government was quickly conquered by the Red Army, its multiparty system, civil and political liberties, and national as opposed to religious orientation are a legacy that democrats in Azerbaijan cherish.[21] As noted earlier, the country also experienced a brief period after the end of the Soviet Union in 1991 that raised hopes that democratic politics would take root,[22] hopes that were soon dashed by Hejdar Alieyev's extra-legal seizure of power. Despite the

---

[19] See *EurasiaNet*, "Election Watch"; and Human Rights Watch, "Azerbaijan: Government Launches Crackdown after Election, Hundreds of Opposition Members Arrested," *Human Rights News*, October 22, 2003, http://www.hrw.org/en/news/2003/10/21/azerbaijan-government-launches-crackdown. Similar observations about harassment of the opposition during both the 2003 and 2005 elections were made by Dallas Frohrib, Baku, March 6, 2007; Isa Gambar Baku, March 7, 2007; Fuad Mustafayev, Baku, March 5, 2007; and Amy Schultz, Baku, March 6, 2007, in the interviews we conducted with them.

[20] International Press Institute, "2003 World Press Freedom Review: Azerbaijan," http://www.freemedia.at/cms/ipi/freedom_detail.html?country=/KW0001/KW0003/KW0049/&year=2003; Human Rights Watch, "Azerbaijan Police Violence Marks Election Campaign, Prospects for Free Elections in Doubt," *Human Rights News*, October 2005, http://www.hrw.org/english/docs/2005/10/04/azerba11819.htm.

[21] See Leila Alieva, "Azerbaijan's Frustrating Elections," *Journal of Democracy* 17:2 (April 2006), 147–160.

[22] See Valiyev, "Parliamentary Elections in Azerbaijan"; and Audrey L. Alstadt, "Azerbaijan's Struggle toward Democracy," in *Conflict, Cleavage, and Change in Central Asia and the Caucasus*, ed. Karen Dawisha and Bruce Parrott (Cambridge: Cambridge University Press, 1997).

fact that it soon became clear that Azerbaijan's brief democratic legacy would have little impact on postcommunist politics, several of the opposition parties formed at that time and some of their leaders remain active in politics.

Despite their experience and the courage they displayed in the face of repression and violence, few of the opposition leaders were charismatic, and there was no single leader who could unify the opposition and serve as a symbol of the movement for change in 2003 or 2005.[23] Many of the leaders of the political opposition had been active in politics for some time and were thus either linked to the loss of Nagorno-Karabagh or tarred by their association, however brief, with the regime of Heydar Aliyev.[24] As the result of both regime pressure and personal inclination, most confined their activities to the capital most of the time.

Despite the handicaps under which they worked, opposition leaders took steps to unify in order to contest the 2005 elections. Inspired by the events in Georgia and Ukraine, Isa Gambar and other opposition leaders joined forces in 2005 in the Azadliq alliance, which included Gambar's Musavat Party, the Popular Front Party of Azerbaijan led by Ali Karimli, and the Democratic Party of Azerbaijan. The Yeni Siyaset or New Policy bloc brought together the National Independence Party, the Social Democratic Party, the Intelligentsia Movement, and Ali Masimov, the prime minister under Elchibey. The Liberal Party of Azerbaijan led by Lala Shovket also fielded candidates. The opposition coalitions were formed well ahead of the elections. Parties in the coalitions had cooperated on short-term, smaller-scale acts in the past, but never to the extent they did in 2005, when each bloc/coalition put forward common parliamentary candidates.

Despite their unity, the opposition blocs had neither the resources nor the opportunity to mount a large-scale get-out-the-vote campaign. In addition to limitations imposed by the regime, a reluctance to engage in many of the techniques counseled by outside experts on party development and voter mobilization, such as door-to-door campaigning, canvassing, and personal contact with voters and potential supporters, also limited the opposition's reach.[25]

Often harassed, and operating from rundown offices on the outskirts of the capital or in borrowed quarters, opposition political leaders were generally able to organize meetings of their members and supporters, publish and circulate opposition newspapers, and meet with foreigners. In the course of the 2005 campaign, both the Azadliq and the YeS coalitions held meetings with thousands of voters in the countryside.[26] However, their main base of support

---

[23] Michael Mainville, "In Azerbaijan, Political and Economic Issues Heat Up," *The New York Sun*, August 11, 2005, http://www.nysun.com/foreign/in-azerbaijan-political-and-economic-issues-heat/18468/.

[24] See Bunce and Wolchik, *Azerbaijan's 2005 Parliamentary Elections*, for more information on the Azeri leaders.

[25] Interview, NDI representative, Baku, March 2007.

[26] Interviews with Ali Karimli, conducted by Sara Rzayeva, Baku, January 13, 2006; and with Ali Aliyev, conducted by Sara Rzayeva Baku, January 11, 2006.

was in the capital, where it was much more difficult for the regime to apply surveillance techniques than in smaller towns and villages.[27]

To reach voters, opposition and NGO activists employed many of the same techniques used in other attempts to unseat autocrats by means of elections. Some of these, such as the orange T-shirts and orange flags, were taken directly from the Ukrainian experience. Parties also sold or distributed other resistance symbols, such as badges and bandanas with YeS and Azadliq symbols.[28] These do not appear to have been as ubiquitous in Azerbaijan as in Serbia, Ukraine, Georgia, or Slovakia; however, they played an important role in spreading awareness of the opposition campaign and gaining new supporters. Some of the posters were in English and addressed the U.S. president: "Help us, Mr. Bush!"; "Mr. Bush, do not lose a friendly Muslim country!"[29]

In June 2005, the government yielded to international pressure after it had violently suppressed a peaceful demonstration on May 21 and once again allowed the opposition to organize a rally in the Baku suburbs, the first officially permitted opposition demonstration since the 2003 elections. But, although the government allowed this rally, it continued to harass opposition leaders and supporters during authorized rallies and brutally broke up another demonstration in September 2005.[30] The opposition was generally permitted to organize such events only outside of city centers for a few hours.

Opposition leaders abided by these restrictions when they organized peaceful protests outside of Baku shortly after the November 2005 elections, which drew 20,000 and later 30,000 people.[31] However, participants in authorized demonstrations also suffered intimidation and, on occasion, beatings and detention, as on November 26, 2005, when Lala Shovket and Ali Karimli called on citizens at an approved protest in Baku to remain where they were after the end of the approved time period. This demonstration was brutally repressed by the police, and numerous demonstrators were injured.[32]

---

[27] Interviews with Ali Karimli, conducted by Sara Rzayeva, Baku, January 13, 2006; and with Ali Masimov, conducted by Sara Rzayeva Baku, January 18, 2006. Also see Rufat Abbasov and Mina Muradova, "Azerbaijan: Television Is a Campaign Battleground," _EurasiaNet_, October 28, 2005, http://www.eurasianet.org/departments/civilsociety/articles/eav102805a. shtml.

[28] Interviews with lower-level Azadliq bloc members, conducted by Sara Rzayeva, Baku, January 9, 2006, and January 12, 2006.

[29] C. J. Chivers, "Crowd Protests Fraud in Azerbaijan Vote," _The New York Times_, November 10, 2005, http://www.nytimes.com/2005/11/10/international/asia/10azerbaijan.html.

[30] Larissa Momryk, "Azerbaijan through Western Eyes," 8; Khadija Ismayilova and Shahin Abbasov, "Azerbaijan's Political Temperature Rises as Parliamentary Election Campaign Looms," _Eurasia Insight_, May 23, 2005, http://www.eurasianet.org/departments/insight/ articles/eav052305.shtml; Freedom House, "Country Report – Azerbaijan, Civil Liberties" (2006), http://www.freedomhouse.org/template.cfm?ccrcountry=110&ccrpage=31&edition =7&page=140&section=74.

[31] Momryk, "Azerbaijan through Western Eyes."

[32] See Alieva, "Azerbaijan's Frustrating Elections."

NGOs and the Media

Numerous NGOs, most supported by outside funding, participated in voter education and get-out-the-vote campaigns. Two coalitions of NGOs, as well as some individual organizations, observed the elections. The first, the Election Monitoring Center, united 14 NGOs and sent 2,315 observers to 124 of the 125 electoral districts. The second, the Coordinative Advisory Council for Free and Fair Elections (CACFFE), which was comprised of 48 NGOs, sent out 2,237 observers to 80 districts. Both organizations recorded enough falsifications to conclude that a revote was needed.[33] Prior to the election, numerous NGOs, with the help of outside funding, worked to increase voter awareness, improve the quality of party platforms and election monitoring, and monitor the media.[34]

Several youth organizations were active in the elections. One of the most important was Yeni Fikir ("New Thinking"), founded in April 2004. Drawing their inspiration from youth organizations in countries that had experienced democratizing elections, Yeni Fikir activists trained citizens for nonviolent conflict and tried to emulate successful get-out-the-vote campaigns elsewhere.[35] A number of other youth organizations, including Magam ("Moment," also translated as "It's Time"), Dalga, ("Wave"), and Yokh ("No"), were also active, despite harassment by the regime.[36] Magam launched its activities in April 2005 with a translation of Gene Sharp's 1993 book, *From Dictatorship to Democracy*, which all four youth organizations actively disseminated.[37]

Aside from Yeni Fikir, which was closely linked to the opposition leader Ali Karimli of the Popular Front, and Dalga, which may have had links to some pro-government youth organizations, the other youth organizations were nonpartisan pro-democracy groups. As a member of Magam put it: "For us, it does not matter who is in power – [the governing] Yeni Azerbaijan Party or the opposition. We are for establishing rule of law in society, where all citizens, without any exclusion, have equal rights."[38] Hampered by the regime's

---

[33] Alieva, "Azerbaijan's Frustrating Elections," 153–154.

[34] See National Endowment for Democracy, "Eurasia Program Highlights" (2005), http://www.ned.org/grants/05programs/highlights-eurasia05.html; Open Society Institute – Assistance Foundation (OSI – AF), *Reports on Progress of Election Program* (Baku, Azerbaijan, August 5, 2005), http://www.osi-az.org/election.shtml; the Ankara Center for Turkish Policy Studies / International Crisis Group (Ankara, Turquía), *Azerbaijan's 2005 Elections: Lost Opportunity*, Crisis Group Europe Briefing No. 40 (November 21, 2005), 5, http://www.caei.com.ar/es/programas/cei/P09.pdf.

[35] Interviews in Baku, March 7, 2007, with three members of Yeni Fikir (the names have been withheld from the list in Appendix A in order to protect their identities).

[36] Khadija Ismayilova and Shahin Abbasov, "Young Activists Poised to Assume Higher Political Profile in Azerbaijan," *EurasiaNet*, June 14, 2005, http://www.eurasianet.org/departments/insight/articles/eav061405.shtml.

[37] Ismayilova and Abbasov, "Young Activists."

[38] As cited in Mina Muradova and Rufat Abbasov, "Youth Groups in Azerbaijan Encounter Difficulties during Run-up to Parliamentary Elections," *EurasiaNet*, November 3, 2005, http://www.eurasianet.org/departments/insight/articlles/eav 1103035b.shtml.

repression, the expulsion of members from university, and the arrest of leaders, these organizations did not succeed in increasing turnout, which dropped to 46 percent, according to official results.[39]

Although the government remained in firm control of the broadcast media as well as numerous daily papers, the opposition had access to several print outlets. The opposition paper *Yeni Musavat*, in fact, had the largest daily circulation (14,350) in 2003, a figure nearly twice that of the two state newspapers. *Azadliq*, another opposition outlet, had a daily circulation of 5,610.[40] However, most Azeris got information about politics from the broadcast media, which were firmly under the control of the regime.[41] Given the low levels of internet and cell phone use, and regime interference, these technologies were not key parts of the opposition's strategy.

The Role of Outside Actors

Numerous international actors influenced or attempted to influence the outcome of the 2003 and 2005 elections in Azerbaijan. These included Russia; the United States and other Western governments; the Organization for Security and Cooperation in Europe and other international election monitoring bodies; and U. S. and other Western NGOs. Activists and "graduates" of previous democratizing elections attempted to share their experiences and tactics, and the example of successful popular mobilizations elsewhere in the postcommunist region was an important inspiration for the opposition. Multinational corporations, by their investments, also played a role, albeit indirectly.

Despite its backing of Armenia in the conflict in Nagorno-Karabagh, Russia was an important player in Azerbaijan. Although the country's first two post-Soviet leaders had refused to become part of the Commonwealth of Independent States, Heydar Aliyev brought Azerbaijan into that group. All of the opposition leaders we interviewed as well as independent experts agreed that Russia had a strong interest in the maintenance of Ilham Aliyev's regime, which defends and balances Russia's interest against Western influence in the country.[42] Opposition leaders are convinced that Russia provided diplomatic

[39] Alieva, "Azerbaijan's Frustrating Elections." See also Muradova and Abbasov, "Youth Groups"; Khadija Ismayilova, "Youth Activists in Azerbaijan Say They Are Being Targeted by Government," *EurasiaNet*, October 20, 2005, http://www.eurasianet.org/departments/insight/articles/eavo92005.shtml; Rufat Abbasov and Mina Muradova, "Azerbaijan Hunger Strikes: Opposition of the Future?," *EurasiaNet*, January 30, 2006, http://www.eurasianet.org/departments/civilsociety/articles/eavo13006.shtml.

[40] Ilgar Khudiyev, "Coverage of the 2003 Post-Election Protests in Azerbaijan: Impact of Media Ownership on Objectivity" (M.A. thesis, The Manship School of Mass Communication, Louisiana State University, 2005), http://etd.lsu.edu/docs/available/etd-11152005–113447/unrestricted/Khudiyev_thesis.pdf.

[41] Liz Fuller, "Azerbaijan: Authorities Intensify Pressures on Independent Media," *Radio Free Europe Radio Liberty*, November 29, 2006, http://www.rferl.org/content/article/1073092.html.

[42] Interviews with Ali Karimli, conducted by Sara Rzayeva, Baku, January 13, 2006; Lala Shovket, conducted by Sara Rzayeva, Baku, January 13, 2006; Ali Aliyev, conducted by Sara

and unofficial support to the Aliyev government in falsifying the elections and suppressing mass protests.[43] These claims are supported by the CIS monitoring team's report and the subsequent strengthening of relations between the two countries.[44]

Numerous outside observers monitored the 2003 and 2005 elections.[45] In 2005, an International Election Observation Mission (IEOM), which included representatives from the OSCE, the Council of Europe, the European Parliament, and NATO's Parliamentary Assembly, observed the elections. The IEOM mission report noted that the progress made compared to previous elections, as in the area of candidate registration, was undermined by government interference in campaigning, media bias that favored pro-government candidates, and significant deficiencies in tabulating election results.[46] OSCE/ODIHR observers noted some improvement over the previous elections but reported significant irregularities in 13 percent of polling stations observed and concluded that the elections overall did not meet OSCE and other international standards for democratic elections.[47]

IFES, IRI, and other international NGOs also trained domestic election monitors. As the result of a last-minute decision by Aliyev, NGO activists and some youth leaders were able to act as election observers. Domestic election monitors also documented numerous violations of proper procedure, complaints that eventually led to new elections in a few constituencies.[48] Russia and other members of the CIS sent a monitoring mission that concluded that the elections had respected Azerbaijani law and would strengthen democracy in the country.[49] Three outside organizations conducted exit polls in Azerbaijan in 2005. However, the results of these polls, which in two cases appear to have been paid for by the government, were flawed and of little use.

Rzayeva, Baku, January 11, 2006; and Khaleddin Ibrahimli, conducted by Sara Rzayeva, Baku, January 10, 2006.

[43] Interviews with Ali Karimli, conducted by Sara Rzayeva, Baku, January 13, 2006; Lala Shovket, conducted by Sara Rzayeva, Baku, January 13, 2006; Ali Aliyev, conducted by Sara Rzayeva, Baku, January 2006; Khaleddin Ibrahimli, conducted by Sara Rzayeva, Baku, January 10, 2006.

[44] See Robert Parsons, "Analysis: Putin Seeks to Draw Azerbaijan Back into Russian Orbit," *Radio Free Europe Radio Liberty*, February 21, 2006, http://www.rferl.org/featuresarticle/2006/02/0335ec2e-489b-4be6-b5f0-f52d0c96226b.html.

[45] International Election Observation Mission, "Parliamentary Election, Republic of Azerbaijan, 6 November 2005: Statement of Preliminary Findings and Conclusions," November 7, 2005, http://www.osce.org/documents/odihr/2005/11/16889_en.pdf.

[46] Organization for Security and Cooperation in Europe, Office for Democratic Institutions and Human Rights, *Republic of Azerbaijan: Parliamentary Elections 6 November 2005, OSCE/ODIHR Election Observation Mission Final Report*, (February 1, 2006), 2–3, http://www.osce.org/documents/odihr/2006/02/17923_en.pdf.

[47] Ibid.

[48] See Alieva, "Azerbaijan's Frustrating Elections"; and Valiyev, "Parliamentary Elections in Azerbaijan."

[49] International Crisis Group, *Azerbaijan's 2005 Elections: Lost Opportunity*, ICG Europe Briefing No. 30 (November 21, 2005), 18.

In addition to providing election observers and training monitors, outside actors also provided funds to support the development of democracy and free elections. Azerbaijan received democracy and governance assistance from USAID,[50] for example, to fund programs to strengthen political parties, provide voter education, and support independent media as well as anticorruption and rule-of-law programs. USAID also provided broadcast transmitters to seven regional TV stations.[51] In 2005, USAID projects included training for representatives of political parties and domestic observers; a pilot exit poll during the municipal elections; and a national exit poll during the legislative elections. The EU included Azerbaijan in the European Neighborhood Policy in 2004 and began negotiating an action plan in 2005. Numerous private and semigovernmental foundations, including Soros, IFES, NDI, and IRI, also were active in 2005, when they funded voter information and get-out-the-vote activities.[52] Many of the programs of private, semiofficial organizations focused on civil society and the NGO sector.[53]

As in previous elections, Western governments, including the United States, urged the Azeri government to take steps to ensure free and fair elections in 2005. President Bush's statement during a May 2005 visit to Georgia – "Now, across the Caucasus, in Central Asia and the broader Middle East, we see the same desire for liberty burning in the hearts of young people. They are demanding their freedom – and *they will have it*"[54] – was believed by many in Azerbaijan to be a signal to the Azeri government that it must hold free and fair elections.[55] Madeline Albright in a summer 2005 visit brought a similar message.[56] At the same time, the United States did not support a change of regime in Azerbaijan. Instead, as Ambassador Reno Harnish noted in July 2005, Washington was conducting talks with the authorities and the opposition to promote a "new, evolutionary model of political change" that would allow the opposition to hold up to a third of the seats in parliament and involve cooperation between opposition deputies and the more liberal members of the YAP as a way to gradually liberalize without triggering a conservative counterreaction.[57] These talks did not produce any concrete results.

[50] World Bank, World Development Indicators, WDI online database, www.worldbank. org/data.
[51] USAID, Country Profile: Azerbaijan, January 2007.
[52] See Bunce and Wolchik, *Azerbaijan's 2005 Parliamentary Elections*; and IRI activity report, January 2006.
[53] Open Society Institute Azerbaijan Foundation website, www.osi.az.
[54] Cited in Haroutiun Khachatrian and Alman Mir-Ismail, "Sizing Up the 'Bush Effect' in Azerbaijan and Armenia," *EurasiaNet*, June 9, 2005, http://www.eurasianet.org/departments/ insight/articles/eav060905.shtml.
[55] Khachatrian and Mir-Ismail, "Sizing Up the 'Bush Effect.'"
[56] Antoine Blua, "Azerbaijan: West Maintaining Strong Pressure for Democratic Ballot," *Radio Free Europe Radio Liberty*, July 13, 2005, http://www.rferl.org/featuresarticle/2005/ 07/2ddd2753-76f1-449c-96a1-c05483654efd.html.
[57] Liz Fuller, "Azerbaijan: Will the Real Closet Liberals Please Stand Up?," *Eurasia Insight*, July 24, 2005, http://www.eurasianet.org/departments/insight/articles/pp072405.shtml.

Despite the strong statements of U.S. officials, the actual pressure exerted on the government by the United States and other outside actors appears to have been minimal. In May, the Aliyev government acknowledged certain mistakes in the conduct of elections and proposed steps to overcome problems resulting from a "post-Soviet mentality." In October, the government lifted the ban on NGOs with substantial foreign support and removed limitations on domestic election observers in order to comply with external demands. However, these measures had little impact on the elections.

Evident in evaluations of the elections afterward, this approach reflects the unwillingness of the United States and its allies to rock the boat in Azerbaijan, given strategic and energy considerations. Thus, the U.S. statement termed the elections "an improvement over previous elections in some areas," although, as the OSCE observed, they "did not meet a number of international standards."[58] There was no U.S. reaction to the violent suppression of mass protests after the falsification of the elections.[59] A statement made to us by a U.S. embassy official in an interview in Baku captured the U.S. perspective well: "Why should we want a change of regime in Azerbaijan? The Aliyev government has been a good ally to the United States."[60]

Azeri opposition leaders protested the lack of a promised "harsh response" to the falsification of the election results, which they attributed to the U.S. need for oil and the country's proximity to Iran.[61] Lala Shovket publicly asked a reporter for the *New York Times*, "Why is freedom and democracy not a top priority in Azerbaijan? ... Is it because we are not Christian? ... Or is it because we have oil?"[62] Clearly, both economic and strategic considerations, including Azerbaijan's location, trumped U.S. support for democracy and human rights in Azerbaijan.

EU officials, such as the Commissioner of External Relations Benita Ferrero-Waldner, also called for free and fair elections prior to the 2005 elections.

---

[58] United States Department of State, Adam Ereli, deputy spokesman, "Press Statement: Azerbaijan Parliamentary Elections," Press Statement No. 2005/1047 (Washington, DC: November 7, 2005), http://2001–2009.state.gov/r/pa/prs/ps/2005/56574.htm.

[59] United States Department of State, Sean McCormack, spokesman, "Press Statement: Azerbaijan Elections," Press Statement No. 2005/1128 (Washington, DC: December 2, 2005), http://2001–2009.state.gov/r/pa/prs/ps/2005/57599.htm.

[60] Interview with U.S. embassy official, Baku, March 2007.

[61] Interviews with Ali Karimli, conducted by Sara Rzayeva, Baku, January 13, 2006; Lala Shovket, conducted by Sara Rzayeva, Baku, January 13, 2006; Ali Aliyev, conducted by Sara Rzayeva, Baku, January 11, 2006; and Khaleddin Ibrahimli, conducted by Sara Rzayeva, Baku, January 10, 2006. Also see Rovshan Ismayilov, "Azerbaijan Opposition Charges U.S. with 'Double Standards'," *EurasiaNet*, December 6, 2005, http://www.eurasianet.org/departments/insight/articles/cav/20705.shtml.

[62] C. J. Chivers, "Police Break Up Peaceful Demonstration in Azerbaijan," *New York Times*, November 27, 2005, http://www.nytimes.com/2005/11/27/international/asia/27azer.html?scp=1&sq=CJ%20Chivers,%20%93Police%20Break%20Up%20Peaceful%20Demonstration%20in%20Azerbaijan,%94%20New%20York%20Times,%20November%2027,%202005&st=cse.

However, the EU presidency issued a muted reaction to the vote itself, noting some improvement since the 2003 presidential elections but continued problems in the counting of votes and interference in the voting process. In contrast to the role that the prospect of EU membership played in increasing support for the opposition in Slovakia in 1998, the EU was not in a position to offer incentives in order to influence events in Azerbaijan.

The efforts of outside NGOs and graduates of earlier democratizing elections to support democracy in Azerbaijan were limited, in large part due to restrictions on the activities of NGOs with foreign funding and government action to prevent them from entering Azerbaijan. Thus, although it is clear that the Orange and Rose Revolutions had an impact on the strategies of several opposition groups and youth organizations, whose leaders explicitly looked to those examples as inspiration,[63] the regime was quite effective in limiting their actual presence in and impact on Azerbaijan. For instance, Pora activists from Ukraine attempted to come to Azerbaijan to train Yeni Fikir supporters, only to be turned away at the border by the authorities. Other "graduates" of successful attempts to use elections to democratize, such as the Slovaks and Serbs, appear to have had little interest in developments in Azerbaijan.

THE ARMENIAN ELECTIONS OF 2003 AND 2008

Efforts to use elections to unseat an authoritarian leader also failed in Armenia in 2003 and 2008. In 2003, the regime used widespread fraud, as well as intimidation of and violence against the opposition, to ensure the reelection of President Robert Kocharian. In 2008, in elections that the international community once again judged to have fallen far short of democratic standards, similar tactics were used to achieve the victory of Kocharian's chosen successor, Serzh Sarkesian. The authorities also used force against demonstrators who were protesting the stolen elections in both cases.

The Regime

As in Azerbaijan, Armenia experienced a relatively free election in September 1991, when Levon Ter-Petrossian, who had come to prominence during the Gorbachev period as the leader of the opposition, was elected president. Petrossian's victory was marred, however, by the war in Nagorno-Karabagh, which, though widely perceived as an Armenian victory, was extremely costly in Armenia. After his narrow re-election in 1996 as a result of manipulation by the security forces and his subsequent resignation in 1998, Robert Kocharian, previously president of Nagorno-Karabagh and prime minister, was elected president in elections that the OSCE also judged to be "neither

---

[63] Interview with Yeni Fikir activists, Baku, March 2007; activists estimated that "80%" of their knowledge came from Pora via one of their members who had experience in Ukraine.

free nor fair."[64] In a clear parallel to the situation in Azerbaijan, the war and later frozen conflict in Nagorno-Karabagh pervaded all aspects of public life in Armenia and continued to influence politics as well as economic development and foreign policy.

After his election in 1998, Kocharian consolidated his hold over the security forces and the military, which became staunch supporters of his regime.[65] Although not formally a member of any political party, he controlled the three-party coalition government. More importantly, he presided over a network, many of whose members originally came from Nagorno-Karabagh, that controlled much of the country's wealth.[66]

On the eve of the 2003 elections, Kocharian's position appeared to be relatively secure. The Armenian economy, after its disastrous performance immediately following the breakup of the Soviet Union, during the war in Nagorno-Karabagh, and after a major earthquake, experienced the highest growth rate of all former Soviet republics in 2003, when GDP grew by over 13 percent.[67] However, as in Azerbaijan, this economic boom brought little benefit to most of the population, as more than half (55 percent) lived in poverty, 23 percent in extreme poverty.[68] In surveys conducted in 2003, 50 percent of respondents reported that their families had not benefited from the economic boom. The real unemployment rate was estimated to be approximately 25 percent in 2003.[69]

Much of Armenia's economic life was dominated by large businessmen with links to politically important figures, including, most prominently, Robert Kocharian. Having amassed massive fortunes and enjoying in many cases near or actual monopolies in their sectors, they controlled sections of the capital and developed patron–client relationships with citizens who lived in those areas. Kocharian's relatives were also heavily involved in the business sector. Economic and political life in Armenia is also influenced by labor migration and remittances. An estimated one-third of the total population work abroad, many in Russia, Ukraine, and Turkey, as well as in Central Europe.[70] The diaspora in the United States, Europe, and Russia also exerts

[64] Freedom House Report on Armenia, 1998, as cited in International Crisis Group, *Armenia: Internal Instability Ahead*, International Crisis Group Europe Report (ICG) No. 158, 18d (October 2004), 3, 70.

[65] See International Crisis Group Europe, *Armenia: Internal Instability Ahead*.

[66] See International Crisis Group, *Armenia: Internal Instability Ahead*, for a discussion of these groups; see also Vahe Sahakyan and Arthur Atanesyan, "Democratization in Armenia: Some Trends of Political Culture and Behavior," *Demokratizatsiya* 14:3 (Summer 2006), 347–354.

[67] World Bank Data and Statistics: Armenia, http://go.worldbank.org/3BUAXEQYY0.

[68] World Bank Poverty Assessment of Armenia 2003, as cited in International Crisis Group, *Armenia: Internal Instability Ahead*, 19; see also ibid.

[69] *United Nations Development Assistance Framework 2005–2009: Armenia* (Erevan: United Nations, UNDAF, 2003), http://europeandcis.undp.org/home/ ... /F729FE0A-F203-1EE9-BB1CF2E8873B6008.

[70] "Armenia Seeks to Boost Population," *BBC News*, February 21, 2007, http://news.bbc.co.uk/2/hi/europe/6382703.stm.

considerable influence on politics in Armenia. Several diaspora leaders have been active politically.[71]

In a mirror image of what occurs in Azerbaijan, the Armenian regime uses the threat of renewed violence or Azeri aggression in Nagorno-Karabagh as a tool to justify its rule. As in Azerbaijan, Armenian leaders have also pointed to the alleged chaos in Georgia following Shevardnadze's ouster to discredit any attempt to produce a similar "electoral revolution" in Armenia. The echoing of this view of events in Georgia by students and opposition figures as well as by regime supporters indicates how successful the regime has been in propagating this view.

The government also controlled most of the broadcast media. In April 2002 two independent television stations, A1+ and Noyan Tapan, lost their frequencies when the National Council on Television and Radio refused to reissue their licenses.[72] The approximately fifteen major newspapers continued to have greater freedom, although most were controlled by political parties or wealthy individuals. Low journalistic standards and the fact that 85 percent of the population rely on TV for information, owing to the high cost of newspapers and poor distribution networks, limited the influence of the print media.[73] Attacks against independent journalists and pressure on opposition newspapers increased after April 2003, when libel was made a criminal offense. In the 2008 elections, the media, particularly the broadcast media, clearly favored Sarkisian.[74]

The Kocharian regime also relied on the selective use of coercion and intimidation to keep the population in line and prevent the opposition from coalescing and gaining support. Thus, the government routinely arrested opposition activists prior to elections and used force against independent and opposition election monitors in both 2003 and 2008.[75] Sporadic violence – including arson at several of Ter-Petrossian's regional headquarters, the throwing of a rock at Ter-Petrossian, and the beating of election observers – marred the

---

[71] See International Crisis Group, *Armenia: Internal Instability Ahead*, for a brief discussion of tensions and different perspectives among the diasporas – Armenians from Armenia proper and those from Nagorno-Karabagh.

[72] Committee to Protect Journalists, "Attacks on the Press 2003: Armenia," Committee to Protect Journalists, March 11, 2004, at http://cpj.org/2004/03/attacks-on-the-press-2003-armenia.php; and International Crisis Group, *Armenia: Internal Instability Ahead*, 15.

[73] International Crisis Group, *Armenia: Internal Instability Ahead*; and M. Kurchivan, "The Armenian Media in Context: Soviet Heritage, the Politics of Transition, and the Rule of Law, *Democratizatsiya* 14:2 (Spring 2006), 268. See also Karen Andreasyan, "Media Landscape – Armenia," European Journalism Center, http://www.ejc.net/media_landscape/article/armenia/.

[74] See International Crisis Group, *Armenia: Picking up the Pieces*, ICG Europe Briefing No. 48 (April 8, 2008), 11, 14–15.

[75] See Human Rights Watch, "Armenia: Election Marred by Intimidation, Ballot Stuffing," March 6, 2003, http://www.hrw.org/en/news/2003/03/06/armenia-election-marred-intimidation-ballot-stuff.

election campaign in 2008.[76] The regime also used violence against the peaceful demonstrations that the opposition organized in June 2004 to call for the referendum the Constitutional Court had recommended after the flawed 2003 presidential elections. Large numbers of opposition supporters were arrested, and the demonstrators were violently dispersed.[77]

The Opposition

As is typical of mixed regimes, the political opposition in Armenia was extraordinarily fragmented for much of the 1990s. Subject to violence and divided by family loyalties, opposition leaders also had different positions on critical public issues.[78] Most had very little credibility with the public on the eve of the 2003 elections, when many citizens believed that these leaders were far more interested in gaining or regaining power for their own private economic ends than in serving the public.[79] Public opinion polls in August 2006 and January 2008, funded by USAID and sponsored by IRI, found that few Armenians believed that the elections would be free and fair.[80]

Initial plans by sixteen parties to propose a single candidate in the 2003 elections failed due to the inability to agree on a single candidate.[81] Nonetheless, there was some cooperation among opposition forces. As the candidate of the Justice Bloc composed of nine parties, Stepan Demirchian gained 32.5 percent of the vote.[82] Aram Sarkisian, the leader of the Republic Party, then withdrew in favor of Demirchian in the second round. The parties in the Justice Bloc, as well as the National Unity Party (AMK), which gained 17.3 percent of the vote, collaborated in boycotting parliament and organizing protests.[83]

In contrast to the energetic face-to-face tactics used by opposition candidates in our successful cases, opposition candidates in 2003 conducted campaigns that

---

[76] See International Crisis Group, *Armenia: Picking up the Pieces*, 11–12; see also Human Rights Watch, "Armenia: Violence at Polling Stations Mars Elections," February 22, 2008, http://www.hrw.org/en/news/2008/02/20/armenia-violence-polling-stations-mars-elections.

[77] Ibid.

[78] See International Crisis Group, *Armenia: Internal Instability Ahead*, 11–13, for a brief discussion of the most important clans and opposition parties.

[79] Ibid., 11.

[80] See International Republican Institute, "Armenian National Voters Study," August 2006, http://www.iri.org/sites/default/files/2006%20August%20Survey%20of%20Armenian%20 Public%20Opinion,%20July%2031-August%2010,%202006.pdf; International Republican Institute, "Armenian National Voters Study," January 13–20, 2008, http://www.iri.org/ sites/default/files/2008%20February%2015%20Survey%20of%20Armenian%20Public%20 Opinion,%20January%2013–20,%202008.pdf.

[81] See Aghassi Yesayan, *Discussion Paper 1 – An Analysis of the 2003 Presidential and Parliamentary Elections in Armenia* (Stockholm: International IDEA, 2004).

[82] Ibid., 11.

[83] Asbed Kotchikian, "Politics in Armenia: A Thorny 'Revolution' in the Making?," Groong/ Armenia News Network, April 5, 2004, http://groong.usc.edu/ro/ro-20040405.html; see also International Crisis Group, *Armenia: Internal Instability Ahead*.

were very similar to that of the incumbent and relied on traditional rallies and the little state television time they could afford. Independent monitoring agencies found that media coverage was heavily biased in favor of the incumbent. Private media typically favored one or another of the opposition candidates.[84]

Demichian challenged the results of the second round of the elections in the Constitutional Court. Nullifying the results in forty polling stations, the Court called for the legislature and president to hold a "referendum of confidence" within a year. When this step was not taken, the opposition organized protests to call for the referendum and Kocharian's resignation. International pressure on the regime after its use of violence to disperse the demonstrations and arrests of opposition leaders led to discussions with the opposition, but the referendum was never held.[85]

In the 2008 elections, former president Ter-Petrossian, who had himself engaged in widespread irregularities during the 1996 election and had been forced out of office in part because of his plan to negotiate a settlement with Azerbaijan in Nagorno-Karabagh, emerged as the main candidate to oppose Kocharian's handpicked successor, then Prime Minister Serzh Sarkisian. The emergence of Ter-Petrossian, who had withdrawn from active participation in politics after his resignation in 1998, was somewhat unexpected and complicated the opposition's strategy in 2008.

Civil Society

By 2003, over 3,500 NGOs were officially registered by Armenian authorities, roughly two-thirds of which were actively carrying out projects. However, few of these engaged in advocacy, and Armenian civil society on the whole was disengaged from the political sphere.[86] Several NGOs, such as the Helsinki Committee of Armenia and It's Your Choice, gained valuable political experience in 2003, when they ran large domestic election-monitoring and voter-education campaigns. Two mass campaigns, using the slogans "Stand by Your Vote" and "Defend Your Vote," rallied small numbers of opposition members to contest voter fraud and irregularities.[87] Groups such as the Yerevan

[84] Yesayan, *An Analysis of the 2003 Presidential and Parliamentary Elections in Armenia*, 14.

[85] Human Rights Watch, *Democracy on Rocky Ground: Armenia's Disputed 2008 Presidential Election, Post-Election Violence, and the One-Sided Pursuit of Accountability*, Human Rights Watch Report Number 1-56432-444-3 (February 2009), 11, at http://www.hrw.org/sites/default/files/reports/armenia0209web.pdf and http://www.hrw.org/en/reports/2009/02/25/democracy-rocky-ground-0.

[86] United States Agency for International Development, Bureau for Europe and Eurasia, Office of Democracy, Governance and Social Transition, "Armenia," in *The 2003 NGO Sustainability Index for Central and Eastern Europe and Eurasia*, seventh edition (June 2004), ed. Todd Anderson and Jennifer Stuart (Washington, DC: United States Agency for International Development, Bureau for Europe and Eurasia, Office of Democracy, Governance and Social Transition, June 2004), 22–25, http://www.usaid.gov/locations/europe_eurasia/dem_gov/ngoindex/2003/.

[87] Armine Ishkanian, *Democracy Building in Post-Soviet Armenia* (London: Routledge, 2008), 36–38.

Press Club and the Caucasus Media Institute monitored election coverage and candidate air time, skills that would later be used in 2008.

In 2008, Armenian NGOs were very active in the election campaign.[88] Although Armenian civil society remained quite weak during the periods between major election cycles, the prospect of challenging the ruling party energized a broad swath of NGOs across the country in 2008. A joint project funded by USAID, the Helsinki Committee of Armenia, and the Urban Foundation for Sustainable Development trained domestic election-monitoring teams and offered legal support to those witnessing violations of election law, for example.[89] NGOs also organized activities for minorities and the elderly in order to increase voter turnout.[90] Groups including E-Channel and Meltex Ltd, with funding from NED, attempted to undermine the state's stranglehold on broadcasting by creating alternative independent media outlets to disseminate news and information.[91] A nonpartisan youth group, Sksela ("It Has Started"), also staged provocative street events to try to increase interest in the elections among young people.[92] In contrast to the next case we will examine, however, regional actors, such as Slovak, Serbian, Georgian, and Ukrainian democratic activists, were not actively involved in working with either civil society or opposition political leaders in Armenia.

Protesting Another Fraudulent Election

As in June 2004, when the referendum on the government and president recommended by the Constitutional Court after the flawed 2003 elections was not held, protestors took to the streets after the 2008 presidential election to protest fraud and call for new elections. Ter-Petrossian, whom official results claimed received 21.5 percent of the vote compared to the 52.8 percent Sarkisian received, led around-the-clock protests in Yerevan to call for nullification of the election. These protests – which drew approximately 15,000 people, lasted

---

[88] United States Agency for International Development, Bureau for Europe and Eurasia, Office of Democracy, Governance and Social Transition, "Armenia," *The 2008 NGO Sustainability Index for Central and Eastern Europe and Eurasia*, twelth edition (June 2009), United States Agency for International Development, Bureau for Europe and Eurasia, Office of Democracy, Governance and Social Transition (Washington, DC: United States Agency for International Development, Bureau for Europe and Eurasia, Office of Democracy, Governance and Social Transition, June 2009), 52, http://www.usaid.gov/locations/europe_eurasia/dem_gov/ngoindex/2008/.

[89] Helsinki Committee of Armenia and Urban Foundation for Sustainable Development, *Youth Will Not Tolerate Fraud for the Sake of Its Future*, Report on Joint Project of Helsinki Committee of Armenia and Urban Foundation for Sustainable Development (March 26, 2008), at http://www.armhels.org/DownloadFile/122eng-Presidential_elections-2008.pdf.

[90] "Presidential Election Grants," Counterpart International, Civic Advocacy Project Support Program – Armenia, http://www.counterpart.am/en/?nid=240.

[91] From NED annual reports for the years 2000–2005, available at http://www.ned.org/publications/publications.html.

[92] Yigal Schleifer, "No Rock the Vote for Armenian Youth," *EurasiaNet*, February 18, 2008, at http://www.eurasianet.org/armenia08/news/021808b.shtml.

for 12 days, and included a tent city and marches past parliament – were brutally broken up by the police and troops of the Interior Ministry. Eight people died in the confrontation, and over 400 were wounded. Protestors, who formed barricades with buses and cars, threw Molotov cocktails at members of the security forces, who came in tanks and armored personnel carriers to break up the demonstrations. In the wake of the protests, Kocharian declared a twenty-day state of emergency that suspended most civil rights and allowed the government to assume extraordinary powers to restore order.[93] The regime arrested numerous opposition figures and placed Ter-Petrossian under house arrest.[94] Several officials previously loyal to the regime were also arrested after siding with the protestors. A number of other officials, including members of parties in the government coalition and the deputy speaker of parliament, also sided with the opposition.[95]

The Role of Outside Actors

As in the other cases we have examined, international organizations, the United States, the EU, other European governments, and Russia played a role in the 2003 and 2008 elections. OSCE/ODIHR and PACE sent 233 observers for the first round and 193 for the second in 2003.[96] In 2008, 333 short-term observers from 42 OSCE countries were deployed for the 2008 elections.[97] The CSCE (later OSCE) reports on both the presidential and parliamentary elections in 2003 and the presidential election in 2008 stated that they had failed to meet international standards for free and fair elections.[98] In 2008, the

---

[93] "Eight Reported Killed in Armenia after Clashes between Police, Protesters," *EurasiaNet*, March 1, 2008, at http://www.eurasianet.org/departments/insight/articles/pp030208.shtml.

[94] See "Armenia: Eight Killed after Clashes between Police, Protesters," *Radio Free Europe/Radio Liberty*, March 2, 2008, http://www.rferl.org/articleprintview/10795674.html.

[95] Marianna Grigoryan and Gayane Abrahamyan, "Deputy Parliamentary Speaker Resigns, Defections to Ter-Petrossian Continue," *EurasiaNet*, February 22, 2008, http://www.eurasianet.org/armenia09/news/022208.shtml. See also Human Rights Watch, *Democracy on Rocky Ground*.

[96] OSCE, Office for Democratic Institutions and Human Rights, *Presidential Election, 19 February and 5 March 2003, Republic of Armenia, OSCE /ODIHR Final Report* (Warsaw: OSCE, Office for Democratic Institutions and Human Rights, March 23, 2003), 2, http://www.osce.org/documents/odihr/2003/04/1203_en.pdf.

[97] OSCE, Office for Democratic Institutions and Human Rights, *Final Report on the 19 February 2008 Presidential Election in Armenia, OSCE/ODIHR Election Observation Mission Final Report, February 19, 2008* (Warsaw: OSCE, Office for Democratic Institutions and Human Rights, May 30, 2008), http://www.osce.org/odihr-elections/documents.html?lsi=true&limit=10&grp=222.

[98] Commission on Security and Cooperation in Europe, *Report on the 2003 Presidential and Parliamentary Elections in Armenia, Prepared for the 108th Congress Second Session* (Washington, DC: 2004), http://csce.gov/index.cfm?FuseAction=ContentRecords. ViewDetail&ContentRecord_id=334&Region_id=89&Issue_id=0&ContentType=G&ContentRecordType=G&CFID=32523783&CFTOKEN=27153712; OSCE, Office for Democratic Institutions and Human Rights, *Final Report on the 19 February 2008 Presidential Election in Armenia.*

OSCE judged that the election was "administered mostly in line with OSCE and Council of Europe commitments and standards." However, it also criticized numerous aspects of the process, including the fairness of press coverage, the incumbent's use of his office for campaign purposes, the lack of attention to the opposition's election observers' complaints, flawed vote counting at 16 percent of the polling stations, and the use of violence against opposition leaders and supporters.[99]

The United States has been strongly committed to assisting democratic development in Armenia since the Soviet Union dissolved and Armenia became an independent state. Between 1992 and 2004, U.S. aid to Armenia amounted to $87.71 million in total democracy assistance, or $2.03 per capita. During that period, $10.42 million was spent directly on elections. U.S. assistance amounted to $75.5 million, including $13.5 million in democracy assistance, in 2005,[100] with an additional $6 million going to the Armenian government to ensure free and fair elections in 2007 and 2008.[101] More illuminating is what these figures suggest about U.S. priorities, once we convert the numbers into per capita outlays and add a comparative perspective. USAID democracy and governance assistance to Armenia on a per capita basis was *greater* than that extended to any of the successful cases of electoral breakthroughs we have examined, whether we highlight the five-year or two-year period leading up to the particular election of interest. Indeed, on a per capita basis, Armenia ranks as the top recipient of USAID democracy and governance support in the postcommunist region from 1992 (the first year of statehood) to 2004.[102] Armenia was also chosen to participate in the Millennium Challenge Campaign in 2005, and a Millennium Challenge Corporation Compact for Armenia in the amount of $235.65 million was signed in Washington in March 2006. Disbursement of the money was to depend on improvement in the quality of the 2007 and 2008 elections.[103] In light of the results of the 2008 elections and the violence against protestors, the United States threatened to freeze an $11.3 million installment, equal to the amount received as of December 2007.[104] However, no funding was actually cut until June 2009,

---

[99] Gayano Abrahamyan and Elizabeth Owen, "International Observers: Armenia's Vote Passes the Mark," *EurasiaNet*, February 20, 2008, http://www.eurasianet.org/armenia09/news/o2208a.shtml.

[100] United States Agency for International Development, "Budget Justification to the Congress Fiscal Year 2007: Europe & Eurasia: Armenia", 2007, http://www.usaid.gov/policy/budget/cbj2007/ee/am.html.

[101] Anna Saghabalian, "U.S. Offers $6 Million Election-Related Assistance to Armenia," *Radio Free Europe, Radio Liberty*, October 27, 2005, http://www.armenialiberty.org/articleprintview/1579016.html.

[102] While Bosnia has received more support since 1995, and earlier Macedonia received more assistance, both of these cases are exceptional because of their ties to the war in Bosnia Herzegovina, which ended in 1995.

[103] Julie Corwin, "U.S.: Financial Aid Ready to Flow to Armenia," *Radio Free Europe/ Radio Liberty*, March 28, 2006, http://www.rferl.org/content/article/1067156.html.

[104] "U.S. Threatens to Freeze Aid to Armenia," *Radio Free Europe/ Radio Liberty*, March 13, 2008, http://www.armenialiberty.org/articleprintview/1593860.html; Ruben Meloyan,

when the Obama administration axed a road construction project totaling $67 million due to concerns over the pace of democratization in the country.[105]

Despite the high level of democracy assistance it had provided, the United States did not actively support regime change in Armenia but rather focused on the need for free and fair elections. In the words of a U.S. embassy official interviewed in Yerevan in March 2006, "We are here for the process, not the outcome." The same official noted that the United States was interested not in an electoral revolution in Armenia, but rather in an "Apricot evolution."[106] Similarly, although U.S. officials, including U.S. Ambassador John Evans, discussed the need for improved democratic performance prior to the 2008 elections, U.S. reaction to the violent crackdown on protests that killed at least eight people and the imposition of a state of emergency after the elections was mild. The U.S. Department of State issued a statement condemning the violence on March 1.[107] However, little else came out of the State Department until June 2008, when Assistant Secretary for European and Eurasian Affairs Daniel Fried noted claims of ballot stuffing, vote buying, intimidation and even beatings of poll workers and proxies, and other irregularities, as well as harassment of OSCE election monitors, and lamented the crackdown on the opposition and suppression of independent media.[108] The Armenian diaspora in the United States was also muted in its critique of the election and subsequent violence.

In Armenia, then, the transnational networks that provided technical know-how and strategies to the opposition and NGO communities, as well as the high-level pressure on the regime from outside governments evident in our successful cases, were lacking. And despite the high level of U.S. support for civil society and democracy assistance, the United States did not actively support regime change in Armenia, but rather encouraged a gradual evolution that would eventually result in some sort of power sharing between the regime and the opposition.

BELARUS IN 2006

The final case we consider in this chapter is the 2006 presidential election in Belarus. Like Armenia and Azerbaijan, Belarus gained independence as

"Freeze on U.S. Aid to Armenia 'Very Real'," *Radio Free Europe/ Radio Liberty*, March 28, 2008, http://www.armenialiberty.og/articlepinrview/1594158.html.

[105] Joshua Kucera, "Armenia: Washington Cuts Millennium Challenge Funding," *EurasiaNet*, June 17, 2009, http://www.eurasianet.org/departments/insightb/articles/eav061809a.shtml.

[106] Interview with Gavin Helf, Yerevan, March 9, 2007, and March 10, 2007.

[107] Joshua Kucera, "Armenia: Washington Cuts Millennium Challenge Funding."

[108] Daniel Fried, "State's Fried Remarks on Situation in South Caucasus Region: Fried Discusses Democracy and Conflict in Armenia, Azerbaijan, Georgia, June 19, 2008," transcript of Daniel Fried, assistant secretary for European and Eurasian affairs, statement before the House Foreign Affairs Committee, Washington, DC, June 18, 2008, http://www.america.gov/st/texttrans-english/2008/June/20080619105352xjsnommiso.4269831.html.

the result of the break-up of the Soviet Union in 1991. However, in contrast to both Armenia and Azerbaijan, there was no break with Communist Party rule. Unlike Azerbaijan, where energy revenues gave the regime vast resources to use to secure its power, or Armenia, where the regime survived the 1990s despite a devastating earthquake and severe economic crises, Lukashenka's regime weathered some initial economic difficulties associated with the breakup of the Soviet state, but later benefited from relatively positive economic developments.

Like Alieyev and Kocharian, Lukashenka, a former collective farm head and parliamentarian, proved to be an active and engaged steward of his rule. After winning a landslide victory by using an anticorruption campaign during a period of economic crisis in the relatively free and fair presidential elections of 1994, he quickly and successfully gained control of the state administration, media, and economy. He also moved steadily to restrict the freedom of action of institutions, such as the Constitutional Court and parliament, that resisted his efforts to increase the powers of the presidency and limit the ability of opposition leaders to challenge his power.[109]

The regime also resorted to coercion and murder. As the 2001 presidential election approached, several prominent and promising opposition political leaders disappeared. When an investigation of these disappearances led to the arrest of an official in a secret police unit, Lukashenka interfered to free him and replaced the prosecutor general in charge of the investigation with the supervisor of the unit allegedly involved.[110]

Lukashenka also benefited in both 2001 and 2006 from a certain degree of popular support. Polls taken in 2001 indicate that Lukashenka would have won the presidency even without resorting to manipulation and fraud. Although his popularity declined in 2003, it rose again as a result of increases in wages in the state sector in 2003 and 2004. Independent pollsters estimated after the 2006 elections that he had, in fact, won over 60 percent of the vote.[111]

Much of Lukashenka's popularity derived from the image he cultivated as a leader who had prevented Belarus from experiencing the corruption and economic crises that have plagued many postcommunist states, as well as from generally positive economic trends.[112] Public opinion polls found, for example, that many of those polled between 2003 and 2005 felt that their economic situation had improved. Although the proportion of respondents polled in 2006 who considered the quality of life in Belarus to be very bad was higher than those who judged it to be quite or very good (25 percent compared

---

[109] Vitali Silitski, "Preempting Democracy: The Case of Belarus," *Journal of Democracy* 16:4 (October 2005), 83–97.

[110] Silitski, "Preempting Democracy," 88–89.

[111] Ibid., 91.

[112] Lukashenka claimed to have successfully limited the role of corruption, but Belarus ranked number 151 out of 163 in Transparency International's "Corruption Perception Index" in 2006. See http://www.transparency.org/policy_research/surveys_indices/cpi/2006, accessed October 1, 2009.

to 18 percent), the majority of respondents (57.6 percent) considered it to be moderate.[113] Plans to vote, as well as support for Lukashenka, were highest among those who considered the quality of life to be good. The general quality of life, prices, health care, and jobs were seen as far more important than democracy, independence, corruption, and other issues. Growing optimism about the economic situation between 2004 and 2006 was one of the main reasons for the increase in Lukashenka's popularity from 47.7 percent to 58.6 percent between October 2004 and March 2006.[114]

THE 2001 PRESIDENTIAL ELECTIONS: DRESS REHEARSAL

As in our successful cases, the opposition's attempt to oust Lukashenka in the presidential elections in 2006 built on a previously unsuccessful attempt in the 2001 presidential elections. In 2001, the political opposition, with the support of numerous actors in the international community, attempted to emulate many of the strategies and tactics used in other postcommunist countries in which oppositions and NGO communities had succeeded in ousting semi-autocratic rulers. This effort to borrow from successful experiences was very explicit in Belarus and involved attempts to create a united political opposition and a get-out-the-vote campaign by NGO activists. It also – as in Serbia and Slovakia, in particular – was supported by outside actors who provided funding for NGO activities and training for political party leaders, as well as clear signaling at the leadership level about the importance of free and fair elections and sanctions against Belarus for violating international norms.[115]

Nonetheless, given his high level of control over the state apparatus, the election process, the media, and the economy, as well as a certain degree of popularity, Lukashenka easily won the elections. He also easily outmaneuvered the opposition in the 2004 parliamentary elections, which were marred by serious irregularities.[116]

The 2006 Presidential Elections

Lukashenka's actions to prevent a "color revolution" in Belarus were given added impetus by the victories of the opposition in Georgia in 2003 and

---

[113] Oleg Manaev, "Recent Trends in Belarusian Public Opinion," in *Prospects for Democracy in Belarus*, ed. Joerg Forbrig, David R. Marples, and Pavol Demeš (Washington, DC: German Marshall Fund of the United States and the Heinrich Böll Stiftung, 2006), 38.

[114] Manaev, "Recent Trends in Belarusian Public Opinion," 40.

[115] Rodger Potocki, "Dark Days in Belarus," *Journal of Democracy* 13:4 (October 2002), 144–166.

[116] See OSCE, Office for Democratic Institutions and Human Rights, *Republic of Belarus: Parliamentary Elections 17 October 2004, OSCE/ODIHR Election Observation Mission Final Report*, OHDIR.GAL/100/04 (Warsaw: OSCE, Office for Democratic Institutions and Human Rights, December 9, 2004), http://www.osce.org/documents/odihr/2004/12/3961_en.pdf.

Ukraine in 2004. In a clear example of learning by autocrats, the regime took additional steps to consolidate its power, demobilize and handicap the political opposition, hamstring the NGO sector, and keep voters from supporting alternatives.[117] Moving the elections from their scheduled date in July to March 19 was one of the first steps Lukashenka took to ensure his victory. In addition to limiting the time available to the opposition to organize, this change also reduced the likelihood of protest owing to the usually inclement weather in Belarus at that time. Lukashenka also used his control of the electoral process to pack the territorial and central electoral commissions with his supporters.

In addition to restrictions on the activities of NGOs and other measures to reduce the space available to civil society groups and opposition political parties to operate,[118] and the imprisonment of numerous NGO organizers, Lukashenka took preemptive steps against possible challengers from within his own circle, including the head of the KGB, who had met with protestors after the October 17, 2004, referendum.[119] He also increased pensions and state salaries and gave particular attention to securing his hold over the security forces and instructing them on how to meet expected challenges by the opposition.[120] Like the leaders in Armenia and Azerbaijan, Lukashenka used his control of the media not only to foster a positive image of himself but also to discredit the so-called color revolutions by portraying them as chaotic exercises organized by foreigners.[121]

[117] See Silitski, "Preempting Democracy"; and Vitali Silitski, "Belarus: Learning from Defeat," *Journal of Democracy* 17:4 (October 2006), 138–152; see also Vitali Silitski, "Signs of Hope Rather than a Color Revolution," in *Prospects for Democracy in Belarus*, ed. Joerg Forbrig, David R. Marples, and Pavol Demeš (Washington, DC: German Marshall Fund of the United States and the Heinrich Böll Stiftung, 2006), 20–28; David R. Marples, "Color Revolutions: The Belarus Case," *Communist and Post-Communist Studies* 39:3 (September 2006), 351–364; Grigory Ioffe, "Unfinished Nation-Building in Belarus and the 2006 Presidential Election," *Eurasian Geography and Economics* 48:1 (January–February 2007), 37–58; David R. Marples, "Elections and Nation-Building in Belarus: A Comment on Ioffe," *Eurasian Geography and Economics* 48:1 (January–February 2007), 59–67; and Grigory Ioffe, "Nation-Building in Belarus: A Rebuttal," *Eurasian Geography and Economics* 48:1 (January–February 2007), 68–72.

[118] See Silitski, "Preempting Democracy"; Pontis Foundation, *Anti-Revolution Legislation in Belarus: State is Good, Non-State is Illegal*, legal memorandum by the Pontis Foundation's Institute for Civic Diplomacy, Bratislava, December 22, 2005, http://www.nadaciapontis.sk/tmp/asset_cache/link/0000014889/Legal%20Memo%20on%20Anti%20Revolution%20Legislation%20of%20Belarus.pdf.

[119] Silitski, "Preempting Democracy," 94.

[120] See Kiryl Paznyak, "Lukashenka Mobilizes Uniformed Services," Election in Belarus 2006 Presidential Elections BelePAN Special Project, *BelePAN*, March 3, 2006, http://en.belaruselections.info/archive/2006/analytics/0022984/.

[121] Silitski, "Belarus: Learning from Defeat"; and David R. Marples, "The Presidential Election Campaign: An Analysis," in *Prospects for Democracy in Belarus*, ed. Joerg Forbrig, David R. Marples, and Pavol Demeš (Washington, DC: German Marshall Fund of the United States and the Heinrich Böll Stiftung, 2006), 95–102.

The Political Opposition Unifies

As in 2001, efforts by the opposition to unify around a single candidate were complicated by the wide variety of positions represented in the opposition, personal rivalries and ambitions, and the lack of a coherent common platform. Nonetheless, opposition forces were more unified in 2006 than previously. In contrast to 2001, when nearly a dozen candidates opposed Lukashenka, in 2006 most opposition parties supported one of two candidates, Alexander Milinkevich or Alexander Kazulin.[122]

Most opposition activists supported Milinkevich, who narrowly won in a second round of voting by the 800-member Congress of Democratic Forces that the "Five Plus" coalition of parties and NGOs had agreed would choose the opposition's single candidate.[123] Milinkevich's main opponent at the congress, Anatol Liabedzka, agreed to support Milinkevich's United Democratic Forces coalition. This effort to run a single opposition candidate built on earlier attempts at coordination that dated back to 1999, when a number of parties and several civic groups and trade unions had cooperated in a council organized by the OSCE Advisory and Monitoring Group in Belarus and the Bloc of Five Parties, which campaigned together in the 2004 parliamentary elections.[124]

Despite continued tensions within the opposition and the shortening of the campaign, Milinkevich and his supporters launched an energetic campaign to increase their visibility at the national level. Alexander Kazulin, initially suspected of being a pseudo-candidate to draw support away from Milinkevich,[125] used every opportunity to criticize Lukashenka and appeared with Milinkevich in the final days of the campaign. The ability of these two candidates to get their message to the public in light of their very limited access to the media depended heavily on use of the internet and efforts to take the campaign to the voters.[126]

---

[122] Valery Karbalevich, "Parties Demonstrate Their Capacity," Election in Belarus 2006 Presidential Elections BelePAN Special Project, *BelePAN*, February 9, 2006, http://en.belaruselections.info/archive/2006/analytics/0022976/.

[123] Silitski, "Belarus: Learning from Defeat," 141.

[124] David Marples and Uladzimir Padhol, "The Democratic Political Opposition," in *Prospects for Democracy in Belarus*, ed. Joerg Forbrig, David R. Marples, and Pavol Demeš (Washington, D.C.: German Marshall Fund of the United States and the Heinrich Böll Stiftung, 2006), 53–54; see Marples and Padhol, 47–56, for a detailed account of the political parties in Belarus and attempts at cooperation.

[125] See Center for Political Education (Minsk) Commissioned by Pontis Foundation's Institute for Civic Diplomacy (Bratislava), Slovakia-Belarus Task Force, *Belarus before Election: David against Goliath*, March 13, 2006, for an analysis that adheres to this view, http://www.nadaciapontis.sk/tmp/asset_cache/link/0000014859/Belarus%20Before%20Election_David%20against%20Goliath.pdf.

[126] Valentinas Mite, "Belarus: Opposition Politicians Embrace Internet, Despite Digital Divide," *Radio Free Europe/Radio Liberty*, February 7, 2006, http://www.rferl.org/content/Article/1065515.html; Steven Lee Myers, "Bringing Down Europe's Last Ex-Soviet Dictator," *The New York Times*, February 26, 2009, http://query.nytimes.com/gst/fullpage.html?res=9C02E0DA113EF935A15751C0A9609C8B63&sec=&spon=&pagewanted=6.

In contrast to Lukashenka, who, though he did not conduct a very active campaign, stressed the economic benefits his regime had brought and the advantages of political stability, the opposition's message focused on democracy and freedom. Unfortunately, as several independent surveys indicated, economic issues topped the list of most citizens' concerns. A poll conducted in January 2006, for example, found that 81 percent of respondents fully and 16 percent partly identified promises to guarantee decent living standards as the most important characteristic of an ideal presidential candidate. The proportion of those who ranked willingness to strengthen the development of democracy as most important was considerably lower (51 percent fully and 36 percent partly).[127]

Civil Society Disarmed

The ability of civil society and monitoring groups to participate in the 2006 elections was greatly hampered by the requirement that all organizations officially register and provide information on their members, as well as by harassment of NGO leaders and activists.[128] Legal restrictions on the ability of NGOs to accept funding from outside organizations and to organize training of their members further limited the ability of civil society groups to organize get-out-the-vote campaigns and prepare for postelection protests. As in Russia and Azerbaijan, the regime also sought to drain support away from legitimate NGOs by establishing similar organizations loyal to Lukashenka. The extent of pressure on civil society can be judged by the fact that the authorities closed over 100 NGOs between 2001 and the 2006 elections.[129]

As the 2006 elections approached, leaders of several NGOs were arrested and imprisoned. Leaders of the youth organizations Zubr ("Bison") and Young Front were particular targets, as these groups were seen as likely organizers of vote monitoring and postelection protest.[130] Zubr, which was founded in January 2001, explicitly drew on Otpor's example and its focus on nonviolent resistance and also was in close contact with individuals active in the OK'98 campaign in Slovakia.[131] Young Front, founded in 1993, was the youth group

[127] Pontis Foundation and Institute for Public Affairs, *Belarus Public Opinion Survey by the Slovakia-Belarus Task Force*, February 21, 2006, 5, at http://www.nadaciapontis. sk/tmp/asset_cache/link/0000014925/Pontis_IVO%20Polling%20Memo_Feb%2022% 202006x.pdf.

[128] See Andrei Sannikov and Inna Kuley, "Civil Society and the Struggle for Freedom," in *Prospects for Democracy in Belarus*, ed. Joerg Forbrig, David R. Marples, and Pavol Demeš, (Washington, DC: German Marshall Fund of the United States and the Heinrich Böll Stiftung, 2006), 57–64, for an overview of civic organizations in Belarus.

[129] Sannikov and Kuley, "Civil Society and the Struggle for Freedom," 58–59.

[130] Marples, "Color Revolutions: The Belarus Case."

[131] Vlad Kobets, "Zubr and the Fight against Europe's Last Dictatorship," Denmark: YES (Young Europeans for Security), February 27, 2005, http://www.yes-dk.dk/YES/index.php? option=content&task=view&id=145&Itemid=169.

most recognized by young people surveyed by Pontis in 2006.[132] In contrast to the situation in Serbia, Ukraine, and Georgia, where young people played key roles in the ouster of semi-authoritarian leaders, given the restrictions noted earlier, and the fact that known activists generally were expelled from university, if not beaten or arrested, it proved difficult to mobilize young people as well as other groups of citizens to protest.[133] A study conducted for Pontis in 2006 found that, although some young people had become radicalized, many had bought into the vision of Belarus presented by the regime.[134] At the same time, young people founded a number of NGOs, and youth were at the forefront of the protests that developed after the fraudulent elections.

Despite these restrictions, numerous NGOs worked with the Milinkevich campaign to collect signatures, publicize his candidacy, and get out the vote. Echoing tactics used in some of our successful cases, NGO leaders organized the Khopits ("Enough") campaign in 2006, which launched a so-called secret information war to spread oppositional information across the country.[135] Similarly, the Assembly of Pro-Democracy NGOs, which worked with Slovaks active in the Slovak-Belarus Task Force of the Pontis Foundation in Bratislava, the successor to the foundation that had distributed U.S. funding for and helped plan and organize OK'98 in Slovakia, organized a series of regional meetings to try to stimulate activities by NGOs outside Minsk. Established in 1997 and led mainly by leaders of the opposition Belarus Popular Front, the Assembly worked to unite the efforts of 250 NGOs. NGO leaders also met in Lviv in July 2005 to devise a strategy for the upcoming elections. At this meeting, Slovak participants note, it was clear that NGO activists lacked faith in the opposition. It was also evident that there was no unifying strategy and no clear vision of what to do.

The lack of unity in the NGO sector was reflected in the disparate activities that NGOs organized as the elections approached. Activists involved in the Za Svabodu ("For Freedom") campaign organized a rock concert just before the elections that drew approximately 10,000 people and also were active in the tent city set up in Minsk to protest the fraudulent elections.[136] Other civil society groups and individuals supported the second opposition candidate,

[132] Pontis Foundation, *Young People in Belarus: Next and/or the L. Generations; A Survey on Post-Election Development of the Youth Movement in Belarus* (Bratislava: Pontis Foundation, 2007), http://pdc.ceu.hu/archive/00003658/01/youth_survey.pdf.

[133] Marples, "Color Revolutions: The Belarus Case," 359; Olena Nikolayenko, *Youth Movements in Post-Communist Societies: A Model of Nonviolent Resistance*, CDDRL Working Paper No. 114, Center for Democracy, Development and the Rule of Law, Freeman Spogli Institute for International Studies, Stanford University (June 2009).

[134] Marples, "Color Revolutions: The Belarus Case," 359.

[135] Myers, "Bringing Down Europe's Last Ex-Soviet Dictator."

[136] Sannikov and Kuley, "Civil Society and the Struggle for Freedom," 60; see also "Dispatches from Minsk," in *Prospects for Democracy in Belarus*, ed. Joerg Forbrig, David R. Marples, and Pavol Demeš, (Washington, DC: German Marshall Fund of the United States and the Heinrich Böll Stiftung, 2006), 105–106, for an eyewitness account of the concert and other opposition activities.

Kazulin, and attempted to organize domestic election monitors similar to those active in 2004.[137] The arrest of the leaders of the unregistered "Partnership" association that had coordinated domestic monitors in previous elections in late February, however, prevented the group from fielding observers, though several NGOs did place a small number of independent observers, as did the two opposition candidates.[138]

Activists involved in Zubr, We Remember, and Charter 97 (which echoed in name a dissident organization, Charter 77, active in Czechoslovakia during the communist era) organized the Jeans Solidarity Campaign, also known as Solidarity 16. Originally founded to protest the beating of a Zubr youth activist when he used his denim shirt as a flag at a demonstration to commemorate the disappearance of two opposition figures,[139] the campaign used blue jeans and other denim clothing as symbols of an alternative lifestyle and commitment to democratic values. Activists organized events such as the Jeans Festival in September 2006, where 10,000 young activists wore blue jeans in Bangalore Square in Minsk, and, in 2006, supported the opposition.

In our successful cases, many NGO activists were ambivalent about whether NGOs should become involved in political matters. In Slovakia, in particular, leaders of the NGO campaigns in fact took great pains to insist that they were political but not partisan, although in fact their activities clearly favored the opposition. In Belarus, leaders of NGOs had no such qualms about being politically active or openly supporting the opposition against Lukashenka, and Milinkevich's campaign relied heavily on the activists, networks, and other resources of the NGO sector. Milinkevich's status as a long-term NGO activist prior to his selection as the opposition's joint candidate facilitated the close cooperation that developed between NGOs and the political opposition, as did the authorities' persecution of both.[140] However, in contrast to our successful cases, in Belarus NGOs were not able to organize exit polls or parallel vote tabulation. The regime also shut down efforts to provide domestic election observers and expelled members of some monitoring teams from abroad.[141]

In another contrast to all of our successful cases, where there were at least some independent media organs that remained and were available to the

[137] Sannikov and Kuley, "Civil Society and the Struggle for Freedom," 60.
[138] See OSCE, Office for Democratic Institutions and Human Rights, *Republic of Belarus: Presidential Election 19 March 2006, OSCE/ODIHR Election Observation Mission Report* (Warsaw: OSCE, Office for Democratic Institutions and Human Rights, June 7, 2006), 20, http://www.osce.org/documents/odihr/2006/06/19393_en.pdf.
[139] Sannikov and Kuley, "Civil Society and the Struggle for Freedom," 60–61; see www.solidarity16.org for information on this campaign.
[140] See Pontis Foundation, Institute for Civic Diplomacy, *Civil Society Monitoring Update*, March 13, 2006, for a brief overview of the activities of these and other civil society groups. See www.solidarity16.org; www.xopic.info; and www.za-svabodu.org for additional details.
[141] See "Belarus Expels Election Observers," *BBC News*, March 15, 2006, http://news.bbc.co.uk/go/pr/fr/-/2/hi/europe/4807756.stm.

opposition and NGO communities (though least so in Serbia and Ukraine, and even less so in Armenia and Azerbaijan), in Belarus the regime controlled virtually all available standard media outlets. Lukashenka closed down more than fifty independent newspapers. The few that continued to exist faced the need to self-censor in order to survive and did not present a clear opposition message.[142] Using the media-monitoring methodology developed by the Slovak NGO MEMO 98 to monitor electronic and print media in Belarus prior to the 2006 elections, the Belarusian Association of Journalists found, not surprisingly, that state media focused almost exclusively on presenting positive images of Lukashenka.[143] Thus, to an even greater extent than in Serbia under Milošević, the opposition had to get its message to the public without relying on the broadcast or regular print media.

Given this requirement, the opposition and NGO communities relied heavily on the internet as well as on cell phones to organize their campaigns and, after the election, the protest in Minsk. Activists also used these tools to organize new forms of protest, including flash mobs, after the election.[144] However, although internet use increased significantly in Belarus in the 2000s, by 2003 only approximately 17 percent of the population had access to the internet, the technology that was, in the view of the Pontis Foundation's Slovak-Belarus Task Force, "virtually the only source of information about ongoing political developments" in the course of the 2006 elections and protests.[145]

NGO activists and opposition candidates were also prevented from using the posters, stickers, and graffiti that were common features of the opposition campaigns in our successful cases. Although Lukashenka announced that he would not campaign, the regime made good use of the new national colors he adopted in opposition to the traditional Belarusian flag as well as posters with slogans supporting his candidacy with references to an abundant economy and political continuity.[146] Opposition posters, stickers, and grafitti declaring Dosta! ("Enough!") or supporting change were frequently torn down or painted over by the regime. As one observer noted, "Campaign efforts by the democratic opposition were similarly subtle. Only very occasionally did one find campaign activists handing out leaflets, independent newspapers, or election programs. Usually, they lurked by the metro stations, almost in hiding, only briefly coming out when a larger crowd of passengers disembarked."[147]

The authorities' control of the media and continued harassment of its opponents also meant that the various campaigns by NGOs reached relatively small portions of the population. As a report by the Pontis Foundation in Bratislava noted,

[142] Sannikov and Kuley, "Civil Society and the Struggle for Freedom," 59.
[143] Pontis Foundation, *Civil Society Monitoring Update*, March 13, 2006.
[144] Vitali Silitski, "Signs of Hope Rather Than a Color Revolution," 24; Nikolayenko, *Youth Movements in Post-Communist Societies.*
[145] Pontis Foundation, *Belarus Public Opinion Survey*, 8.
[146] "Dispatches from Minsk," 102.
[147] Ibid., 103.

reported campaign activities of NGOs are simply in contradiction with monitoring reports by independent international experts traveling to Belarus, who saw no stickers, newspapers or any other campaign materials on the streets throughout the campaign period, and also with the figures of public opinion surveys of the Pontis Foundation regarding perception of civil society activities from February and March 2006.[148]

Protest in Minsk

To the surprise of many Belarusians as well as international actors, the blatant fraud evident in the official announcement that Lukashenka had won 83 percent of the vote set off a wave of protests in 2006. These included an unprecedented demonstration by approximately 20,000 people in Minsk on election night, as well as a short-lived tent city (modeled on the 2004 protests in neighboring Ukraine). Far smaller in scale than those that took place in Serbia, Georgia, and Ukraine, these protests were initially tolerated by the regime. However, five days after the tent city was set up, authorities sealed off the square where the demonstrations were being held and arrested all of the (mainly young) residents. Although the closing of the tent city took place largely peacefully, on March 25 riot police brutally dispersed a march of 10,000 people, led by Alexander Kazulin, to the detention center where the protestors were being held. Kazulin was badly beaten and again arrested.[149] Popular response to the demonstrations was muted. Surveys conducted in January 2006 found that only 16 percent of respondents expected mass protests if the elections were fraudulent, and only 28 percent felt that it was right for NGOs to mobilize people to protest in such a case.[150] Polls conducted after the protests by the Independent Institute for Socio-Economic and Political Studies found that 20.4 percent of those surveyed approved of the postelection protests; 45.9 percent disapproved.[151]

In addition to their size, these protests differed in an even more important way from such actions in our successful cases. Alexander Milinkevitch had called on citizens of Minsk to await the results of the election outside their homes the night of March 19, but stopped short of calling for protests. As Silitski notes,

> The demonstrations were in fact impromptu, largely organized on the fly by the more radical among the younger activists. With little in the way of planning or coordination between civil society radical and opposition leaders, who were clearly unprepared to deal with the unexpectedly large crowds

[148] Pontis Foundation, *Soberness and Dilemmas*, Pontis Foundation Belarus Brief (March 30, 2006), 4.

[149] Silitski, "Belarus: Learning from Defeat," 145; see also OSCE, Office for Democratic Institutions and Human Rights, *Republic of Belarus: Presidential Election 19 March 2006*; Marples, "The Presidential Election Campaign," 99–100; "Dispatches from Minsk."

[150] Pontis Foundation and Institute for Public Affairs, *Belarus Public Opinion Survey*, February 21, 2006, 7.

[151] Silitski, "Belarus: Learning from Defeat," 145.

on election night and were further taken aback by the youngsters' erection
of the tent city, the protests ended as they began – as spontaneous, poorly
organized, ill-provided, dissident-like actions.[152]

Thus, in contrast to the careful planning and coordination of protests in
our successful cases, the opposition neither worked with civil society activists
ahead of time nor agreed on how to deal with the protests once they began.
Given their limited size, the lack of interest in the protest on the part of the
majority of citizens, even in Minsk, and the willingness of the regime to use
force against the protestors, it is not surprising that they did not succeed in
bringing about a new election or a change in regime.[153]

Outside Actors

As in most of the other elections we have analyzed, international organizations
sent monitors to observe the elections. The OSCE/ODIHR mission concluded
that the elections "failed to meet OSCE standards for democratic elections"
despite the fact that voters were presented with genuine choices in the four
candidates that ran.[154] Not surprisingly, a CIS observation team concluded
that the elections were "free, open, and transparent."[155] This judgment was
echoed by the Russian foreign ministry, although both statements noted some
deficiencies in the process.[156]

In contrast to the relatively hands-off approach of the United States and
other outside actors toward the regimes in Azerbaijan and Armenia, the U.S.
and European actors actively supported forces promoting regime change in
Belarus in 2006. This support was evident in both rhetoric and practical support for the opposition and for the development of civil society. EU policies
toward Belarus reflected the isolation of Belarus within Europe and in international institutions. The only country in Europe not a member of the Council
of Europe, Belarus suffered a suspension of talks with the EU concerning a
partnership and cooperation agreement following the November 1997 referendum that increased Lukashenka's power. The EU also froze most aid to

---

[152] Ibid., 146; Nikolayenko, *Youth Movements in Post-Communist Societies.*
[153] A very similar dynamic took place during the 2010 presidential election in Belarus. See
Michael Schwirtz, "After Elections in Belarus, Riot Police Attck Opposition," *New York
Times*, December 20, 2010, p. A6.
[154] Alina Belskaya, "International Responses to the Presidential Elections in Belarus," in
Prospects for Democracy in Belarus, ed. Joerg Forbrig, David R. Marples, and Pavol Demeš
(Washington, DC: German Marshall Fund of the United States and the Heinrich Böll
Stiftung, 2006), 140–141; see OSCE, Office for Democratic Institutions and Human Rights,
Republic of Belarus: Presidential Election 19 March 2006, for the mission's detailed report
on the shortcomings in the election.
[155] Belskaya, "International Responses to the Presidential Elections in Belarus"; OSCE, Office
for Democratic Institutions and Human Rights, *Republic of Belarus: Presidential Election
19 March 2006*, 141.
[156] Ibid.

the country and banned top officials from the EU in 1998.[157] Just prior to the March 2006 presidential elections the EU allocated two million Euros to support independent media in Belarus and initiated a daily radio broadcast from Lithuania.[158] Individual European countries also provided financial assistance to Belarus. However, as Kristi Raik, a Finnish researcher, notes, although the EU has been the largest single donor to Belarus (222 million euros from 1991 to 2005), very little (5 percent) of this aid went to civil society.[159] In 2005, for example, only five million of the total twelve million euros of EU aid went to strengthen civil society groups, democracy, human rights, and diversity.[160] As significantly, only two million euros each year were used for independent grants. The remaining aid went through the TACIS program, which gave the government a role in the selection of recipients.[161]

EU officials signaled strong interest in free and fair elections in Belarus in 2006, when EU External Affairs Commissioner Benita Ferrero-Walder threatened Belarus with stiffer travel bans and a freeze on assets if the vote was rigged.[162] The EU Parliament's Ad Hoc Delegation noted that the regime's arrests, crackdowns, restrictions, and refusal to allow EU observers "have clearly demonstrated that the conduct of the electoral campaign in Belarus was anything but fair and democratic."[163] EU officials also welcomed the mass demonstrations that followed the fraudulent elections; condemned the elections as not having met the required international standards of free, fair, equal, accountable, and transparent elections; and expressed solidarity with Milinkevich and Kazulin. In April, they implemented sanctions against Lukashenka and others responsible for violating electoral standards and initiating the crackdown against the opposition, including a travel ban and a freezing of their assets.[164] In 2009 the EU would partially rescind these sanctions in return for the freeing of a number of political prisoners.

[157] Thomas Ambrosio, "The Political Success of Russia-Belarus Relations: Insulating Minsk from a Color Revolution," *Demokratizatsiya* 14:3 (Summer 2006), 407–434.

[158] "EU Launches Broadcasts to Belarus," *BBC News*, February 26, 2006, http://newsvote.bbc.co.uk/mpapps/pagetools/print/news.bbc.co.uk/2/hi/Europe/4753772.stm.

[159] Kristi Raik, "Making Civil Society Support Central to EU Democracy Assistance," in *Prospects for Democracy in Belarus*, ed. Joerg Forbrig, David R. Marples, and Pavol Demeš (Washington, DC: German Marshall Fund of the United States and the Heinrich Böll Stiftung, 2006), 170.

[160] Pontis Foundation/Institute for Civic Diplomacy, *EU Democracy Assistance to Belarus: How to Make Small Improvements Larger and More Systematic?*, Policy Brief, Pontis Foundation/Institute for Civic Diplomacy (March 24, 2005).

[161] Ibid.

[162] "EU Threatens Belarus with Sanctions," *Radio Free Europe/Radio Liberty*, March 10, 2006, http://origin.rferl.org/content/article/1066578.html.

[163] European Parliament Ad Hoc Delegation to the Presidential Elections in Belarus, "Statement by the Ad Hoc Delegation to the Presidential Election in Belarus on 20 March 2006."

[164] "Political and Legal Foundations of EU-Belarus Relations," European Commission, External Relations, http://ec.europa.eu/external_relations/belarus/pdf/political_legal_foundations_en.pdf.

   U.S. officials also vigorously signaled their interest in free and fair elections in Belarus prior to the 2006 elections. U.S. Secretary of State Condoleeza Rice termed Lukashenka's Belarus the last dictatorship in Europe in 2005[165] and, together with then President Bush, supported the opposition rhetorically prior to the 2006 presidential elections.[166] In October 2004, the Belarus Democracy Act imposed sanctions on Belarus and provided funding for democratically oriented opposition groups.[167] This act was reauthorized after the March 2006 elections, which U.S. State Department officials, in a statement issued the day after the election, refused to consider legitimate.[168] Deputy Assistant Secretary of State for European and Eurasian Affairs David J. Kramer echoed these sentiments: "To say we were disappointed by the March 19 process would be an understatement. The election did not reflect the expression of the will of the people. Therefore, the results cannot be accepted as legitimate."[169] The 2006 act called for the release of political prisoners, refuted the results of the presidential elections, and extended funding for democratically oriented groups – including youth groups, independent trade unions, human rights groups, democratic political parties, and independent media – through 2008. It also denied the senior leaders of Belarus and their families entry to the United States and forbade the extension of loans, credits, and financial assistance to Belarus.[170] Foundations such as NED and GMFUS, and USAID also supported the opposition and NGO communities in Belarus.

   Thus, Western actors clearly made Lukashenka's defeat a higher priority than the defeat of autocrats in Azerbaijan or Armenia. However, it is important to remember that, despite the efforts Western actors made to call for free and fair elections, urge moderation on the regime, and support the development of civil society and the opposition, in fact the United States and Europe had few tools to exert leverage on Lukashenka. Although Belarus's trade with the EU has grown significantly since 2001,[171] the ability of Russian leaders to provide economic benefits, including cheap energy, to Belarus, and the close identification many Belarusians feel with Russia as well as their ambivalence

---

[165] George Gedda, "Calling for 'Change' in Belarus, Rice Meets with Dissidents," Associated Press, April 21, 2005.

[166] Ambrosio, "The Political Success of Russia-Belarus Relations," 417, 418.

[167] Charter 97, "Belarus Democracy Act Full Text: Belarus Democracy Act of 2004, 108th Congress," October 27, 2004, http://charter97.org/eng/news/2004/10/27/act/.

[168] Belskaya, "International Responses to the Presidential Elections in Belarus," 144.

[169] David Kramer, "A Transatlantic Approach to Democracy in Belarus," in *Prospects for Democracy in Belarus*, ed. Joerg Forbrig, David R. Marples, and Pavol Demeš (Washington, DC: German Marshall Fund of the United States and the Heinrich Böll Stiftung, 2006), 153.

[170] Charter 97, "Belarus Democracy Act Full Text: Belarus Democracy Act of 2004."

[171] Slovak-Belarus Task Force, *Dependence of Belarusian Economy on Trading with Western European Countries and USA*, Policy Paper, Belarus Brief (September 2005), http://www.nadaciapontis.sk/tmp/asset_cache/link/0000014892/Policy%20Paper_Belarus%20Economic%20Dependancy.pdf.

toward Europe,[172] all limited the options available to the West to have an impact on the conduct of the elections.

In contrast to the limited tools available to the United States and other Western actors, Russia was an active and energetic supporter of the Lukashenka regime. Although Russian-Belarusian relations subsequently cooled to some degree, during the period preceding the 2006 elections Russian leaders actively supported Lukashenka's regime by providing economic subsidies and favorable trade arrangements, as well as by political and diplomatic means. Putin supported Lukashenka in the 2001 elections, and Russian officials judged this election, as well as the parliamentary elections of 2004 and the 2006 presidential elections, to be free and fair.[173] Russia's ability to influence developments in Belarus was facilitated by popular attitudes, which favored close relations with Russia.[174]

CONCLUSION

In Armenia, Azerbaijan, and Belarus, the opposition as well as their outside supporters and the NGO communities hoped that they, like their counterparts in our breakthrough cases, could use elections to end authoritarian rule. Despite the ability of oppositions to form united fronts in the 2003 and 2008 elections in Armenia, the 2003 and 2005 elections in Azerbaijan, and the 2006 election in Belarus, and despite significant postelection protests in all five of these contests, however, the oppositions failed in their quest. Authoritarian incumbents or their anointed successors won the elections in all three cases.

In the next part of the book, we combine our analytical narratives of electoral struggles in order to answer two questions. First, why were oppositions able to win office in some mixed regimes in the postcommunist region, but not in others? Here, we will assess the impact of three sets of factors on election results: long-term trends, short-term developments, and international diffusion dynamics. Second, what difference did these electoral outcomes make with respect to democratic change after the elections, and what factors account for these differences?

---

[172] See Stephen White, Julia Korosteleva, and Ian McAllister, "A Wider Europe? The View from Russia, Belarus and Ukraine," *Journal of Common Market Studies* 46:2 (March, 2008), 219–241, for the results of public opinion polling on these issues.

[173] Ambrosio, "The Political Success of Russia-Belarus Relations," 418–419.

[174] Manaev, "Recent Trends in Belarusian Public Opinion," 41.

PART III

COMPARATIVE ANALYSES

8

Explaining Divergent Electoral Outcomes

Regime Strength, International Democracy Assistance, and Electoral Dynamics

> There are two keys to making challenges to dictators work: belief and planning.
> Giorgi Meladze[1]

> People wanted change more than they wanted specific candidates or parties. The opposition represented a mechanism for change.
> Robert Benjamin[2]

In Part II, we presented a series of case studies of the regimes and the pivotal elections that serve as the focus of this book. Our goal in all of these analytical narratives was the same: to trace what happened during these electoral confrontations with authoritarian rule and to situate these elections in turn in a broader economic and political, domestic and international context. The story that emerged in those five chapters was a far-from-uniform account of what happened before and during these electoral contests. This is the case whether we focus on all of our case studies or divide them into two groups, depending upon whether oppositions succeeded or failed to win elections and take office.

In this section of the book, we shift our focus from description to explanation. Thus, we merge our nine countries and eleven elections, compare them to one another, and draw some conclusions about the sources of electoral continuity and change in mixed regimes in the postcommunist world. In practice, this means working through the three sets of hypotheses we presented in Chapter 2. We will begin this process by evaluating the role of structural and institutional factors versus shorter-term influences on electoral outcomes. As we will discover, it is the latter set of influences that have the more consistent and therefore more powerful impact on electoral outcomes. In particular, whether regimes are strong or weak or more or less democratic are

[1] Interview with Giorgi Meladze, Tbilisi, October 13, 2005.
[2] Interview with Robert Benjamin, Washington, DC, April 9, 2010.

less important considerations than whether oppositions and their allies run
ambitious or lackluster political campaigns.

REGIME VULNERABILITY AND ELECTORAL CONTINUITY AND CHANGE

In Chapter 2, we argued that there are two schools of thought with respect
to the issue of what drives regime change. One is the "regime vulnerability"
school, which looks backward from the electoral context and focuses on how
long-term political and economic trends shape the regime's capacity to defend
itself in the election and, therefore, to remain in power. The key insight here
is that some regimes are ready to exit, because of how they have evolved and
their institutional configurations, whereas others are not. The second group
of hypotheses, which belongs to the "regime defeat" school, places more
emphasis on shorter-term dynamics, such as, in our case, characteristics of
the elections themselves – in particular, how variations in types of elections
and electoral dynamics influence the resources and strategies of the regime
and its allies versus the opposition and its allies. The assumption here is that
elections are important sites, at least potentially, for political change, and that
even vulnerable regimes must nonetheless be defeated before they leave power.
Thus, while the first approach is long-term and structural, the second is short-
term and recognizes the potential impact of agency.

In Table 8.1, we begin our assessment of the first group of hypotheses by
using Nations in Transit scores to compare trends in democratic development
in our nine countries during the two years leading up to their pivotal elections.
These scores evaluate democratic performance in general and in the specific
areas of civil society, media independence, electoral procedures, and levels of
corruption. They also conform well to the trends we have discussed in our
case studies. There are several patterns in the table that need to be highlighted.
One is the fact that, as elaborated in our case studies, the mixed regimes that
served as sites for significant electoral challenges to authoritarian rule featured very different mixtures of authoritarian and democratic elements. Thus,
as column two (the democracy score) summarizes, our cases run the gamut
from relatively democratic Slovakia to the very harsh regime environment of
Belarus, with Croatia and Georgia situated somewhat closer to Slovakia, and
Serbia, Kyrgyzstan, Armenia, and Azerbaijan closer to Belarus. Second, if we
compare the scores of the first and the second group of countries listed in
Table 8.1, we discover significantly greater variation among the cases where
electoral turnover took place (Croatia, Georgia, Kyrgyzstan, Serbia, Slovakia,
and Ukraine) than among the cases where oppositions failed in their quest to
win power (Armenia, Azerbaijan, and Belarus). For example, for the turnover cases, the score for electoral procedures (column four) ranges from 3.75
to 6.00, whereas for the elections that led to electoral continuity, the scores
range from 5.50 to 6.88. Third, the scores across the board reported for Serbia
and Kyrgyzstan, in particular, indicate that oppositions have managed to win

TABLE 8.1. *Nations in Transit trends. The numbers reported in this table are averages of scores for the two years preceding the election. For example, for Armenia in the 2003 election, the scores are an average of 2001 and 2002.*

Country	Election	DS[a]	CS	IM	EP	Corruption
Croatia	2000	−4.36	3.50	4.88	4.25	5.25[b]
Georgia	2003	−4.46	4.00	3.68	4.75	5.38
Kyrgyzstan	2005	−5.67	4.50	6.00	6.00	6.00
Serbia[c]	2000	−5.67	5.18	5.13	5.25	6.25
Slovakia[d]	1998	−3.80	3.25	4.25	3.75	N/A
Ukraine	2004	−4.82	3.68	5.50	4.25	5.88
Armenia	2003	+4.83	3.50	4.75	5.50	5.75
Armenia	2008	−5.68	3.50	5.68	5.75	5.75
Azerbaijan	2003	−5.59	4.50	5.68	5.75	6.25
Azerbaijan	2005	−5.55	4.48	5.68	5.88	6.25
Belarus[e]	2006	−6.59	6.75	6.75	6.88	5.89

[a] The + or − in this column refers to whether the average score for the two years preceding the election represented an improvement or a decline in democratic performance in comparison to the previous three years.
[b] Scores for 2000/1999. Scores for 1998 not available.
[c] Score for 1999/2000. Score for 1998 not available.
[d] Score for 1997. Scores for 1996 not available.
[e] The scores for the postelection period include only results from 2007, as the scores for 2008 are not yet available.
Notes: DS = Democracy Score; CS = Civil Society; IM = Independent Media; VA = Voice and Accountability; EP = Electoral Process.
Sources: Freedom House, *Nations in Transit* (New York: Freedom House, 2007, 2006, 2005, 2004, 2003, 2002, 2001, 2000, 1998, 1997).
Note on methodology: Nations in Transit's Democracy scores are an average of political rights and civil liberties scores; 7 indicates most repressive and 1 indicates most free. Remaining scores are based on the same range.

power even in relatively authoritarian political settings. Just as instructive is the fact that these two regimes are comparable in their democratic deficits to Armenia and Azerbaijan, where oppositions failed to defeat authoritarian incumbents. For example, Serbia and Kyrgyzstan have overall democracy and corruption scores that are equal to those of Armenia and Azerbaijan (see columns two and six), and Serbia and Kyrgyzstan have worse civil society scores (see column three) in the two years leading up to the 2000 election than those reported for Armenia and Azerbaijan.

Finally, the plus or minus signs that precede the overall democracy scores reported in column two remind us of an important trend that appeared repeatedly in our case studies. Virtually all of our elections (Armenia in 2003 is the only exception), whether they broke with or maintained authoritarian rule, took place following several years of growing authoritarianism. In fact, democratic deterioration in these countries took many forms, such as increasingly opaque and irregular political procedures and legal changes that made it harder for the Third Sector to operate and for the opposition to compete for power; expansion of presidential powers (or the power of the prime minister, as in the Slovak case); reduction in the power of the parliament and the political autonomy of the courts; and harassment of the media and the opposition. Moreover, as our case studies made clear, regimes in both the "successful" and the "failed" camps used violence against their opponents – for example, the murder of the editor of the opposition magazine, *Monitor*, in Azerbajan in 2005; the murder and beheading of a journalist critical of the Kuchma regime in Ukraine in 2000, along with the poisoning of Viktor Yushchenko, the opposition's candidate for president in the 2004 election; and the kidnapping of the adult son of President Kováč and the firebombing of the car of the investigator assigned to the case in Slovakia. The most dramatic example of a regime becoming increasingly violent, however, is Serbia – one of our successful cases of electoral change. From 1998 to 2000, there were at least twenty political murders that were linked to the Milošević regime.[3]

Thus, the trends in political violence and political repression, coupled with the scores reported in Table 8.1, lead to a surprising finding. Variations in electoral outcomes do not seem to be explained by variations in how democratic mixed regimes are or, consequently, by the extent to which regimes narrow or widen opportunities for democratic change.[4] This finding has several important theoretical implications. First, it calls into question the validity of two equally compelling but opposing political scenarios about the impact of regime repression that we laid out in Chapter 2. On the one hand, democratic improvements would seem to create additional space for opposition challenges and enhanced incentives for the opposition to unite and run a strong campaign as a result of having less fear about political reprisals and greater optimism about winning *and* being able to take office. By contrast, crackdowns, one can suggest, would have the opposite effects of narrowing the room for competition, generating pessimism about the prospects for change, and ruling out, because of their likely costs, defections from the regime, as expressed through the voting behavior of the citizenry and/or actions taken by members of the regime's inner circle that would signal a change of heart and interests. Interestingly enough, it is precisely this line of argument that surfaced repeatedly in a roundtable discussion, organized by Andrew Bennett and Taline Sanassarian of the National Democratic Institute in Armenia, that we had with leaders of opposition parties.[5] As one party leader complained, and the thirteen or so other leaders in the room immediately responded by nodding

---

[3] As reported by Gabriel Partos, "Serb Killings Linked to Corrupt Government," *BBC News: Europe*, April 26, 2000, http://news.bbc.co.uk/1/hi/world/Europe/727052.stm.

[4] See Nicolas Van de Walle, "Meet the New Boss: Same as the Old Boss: The Evolution of Political Clientelism in Africa," in *Patrons, Clients and Policies: Patterns of Democratic Accountability and Political Competition*, ed. Herbert Kitschelt and Steven I. Wilkinson (Cambridge: Cambridge University Press, 2007), 50–67.

[5] Roundtable held March 12, 2007. Our thanks to Andrew Bennett and Taline Sanassarian, NDI, for putting together this event.

their heads in full agreement: "Look, the problem is very simple. We cannot win elections. The regime makes this impossible, and there is nothing we can do about it." From this vantage point (which had the advantage, among other things, of locating the blame for opposition defeats outside the room, rather than within it), it was the absence of any meaningful space for political competition that foreclosed the possibility of electoral change. What is striking about the data reported in Chapter 1, however, is that the very same argument could have been made by party leaders in Georgia, Ukraine, and especially Serbia on the eve of their electoral breakthroughs.

On the other hand, the overlap in democracy scores between our two sets of regimes in Table 8.1 also calls into question an equally plausible, but opposing, scenario. Regimes that rely on increasingly authoritarian practices can encourage allies of the regime and citizens to defect to the opposition, not just out of anger, but also out of what we would characterize, building on the commentary of many activists we interviewed in Slovakia, Serbia, Georgia, and Ukraine, as a "despotism dilemma."[6] Growing repression can in fact signal regime weakness, rather than strength. Repression can indicate to oppositions and other observers that the regime has been forced to take desperate measures in order to forestall its loss of power. At the same time, such actions can lead citizens, oppositions, and even regime allies to feel that the regime has gone too far. While this argument, like the earlier line of thinking, emerged repeatedly in the interviews we conducted, it is very hard to operationalize in a precise way. Moreover, it fails in any event to demonstrate a consistent relationship with electoral outcomes. That recognized, however, this argument could help account for one similarity that spans half of our successful cases and all of our failed ones – that is, significant postelection protests. At the very least, such protests indicate widespread recognition of electoral fraud and, more surprisingly, a willingness to take to the streets to express anger about stolen elections.

The rather modest correlation in Table 8.1 between levels of democratic development and opposition success in winning power also challenges another common argument that often functions as an assumption – that is, that oppositions will necessarily be weaker in repressive regimes than in more open ones. As we discussed in Chapter 4, the Serbian case provides perhaps the strongest refutation of this argument. Throughout the 1990s, despite the increasingly heavy hand of the Milošević regime, we find clear evidence of a relatively active civil society and a rich array of opposition parties that participated in the twelve elections that took place during that decade. Moreover, as we also noted in that chapter, elections in Serbia became more competitive over time in

---

[6] See, especially, Ronald Francisco, "The Dictator's Dilemma," paper prepared for the conference Repression and Mobilization: What do We Know and Where Do We Go from Here?, University of Maryland, June 21–24, 2001; Ronald Wintrobe, "Dictatorship: Analytical Approaches," in *The Oxford Handbook of Comparative Politics*, ed. Carles Boix and Susan C. Stokes (Oxford: Oxford University Press, 2007), 363–396; interview with Nenad Konstantinović, Belgrade, April 15, 2005.

spite of the fact that the regime became more repressive and more willing and able to engage in electoral fraud. What explains this seemingly contradictory pattern? One contributing factor was the foundation for pluralism laid during the communist era, when Serbia was a key site within the Yugoslav federation for spirited debates about economic and political reforms, popular protests (especially during the first half of the 1980s), and industrial strikes. Another factor was the role of the wars that accompanied the breakup of the Yugoslav state in generating a strong antiwar movement in Serbia, especially in the capital, Belgrade. Here, we must remember that, while Milošević kept winning elections, he and his allies never drew significant support in Belgrade – even when he began in the second half of the 1990s to go to extremes to manipulate election results. We are suggesting, therefore, that historical legacies can intervene to the point where they can place regime and opposition development on separate tracks.

POLITICAL PLURALISM AND ECONOMIC PERFORMANCE

In Table 8.2, we introduce some new indicators developed by USAID and the World Bank that target the extent to which the media, nongovernmental organizations, the legal system, and various aspects of political participation and influence conform to democratic standards, and we add to these measures several indicators we constructed ourselves regarding trends in political protests and rates of leadership turnover. The picture that emerges in columns two through five of this table is similar, not surprisingly, to what we discovered in Table 8.1. Thus, while we find significant cross-national variation within our category of successful defeats of authoritarian leaders in such areas as NGO sustainability and the rule of law, we find somewhat less variation in these areas in our group of failed attempts to defeat authoritarian leaders. However, the variation in both groups of countries is large, and there is again significant overlap between our two sets of cases. Georgia, Ukraine, and especially Kyrgyzstan and Serbia feature scores similar to those registered by Armenia, Azerbaijan, and Belarus.

Second, in the last two columns in the table (patterns of political protest and changes in governments over the course of the transition) we find strikingly similar scores within and across our two sets of countries. For example, despite significant political constraints on such activities, major protests took place in Armenia, Croatia, Georgia, Slovakia, and Serbia during the communist era. Moreover, the collapse of communism and the dissolution of the Soviet, Yugoslav, and Czechoslovak states were accompanied by large-scale popular mobilizations in Armenia, Azerbaijan, Croatia, Georgia, Serbia, Slovakia, and Ukraine. Finally, in most of our cases (Belarus and Serbia are the only exceptions), the Communist Party lost the first competitive election – an outcome that, interestingly enough, was usually associated elsewhere in the postcommunist region with subsequent improvements in democratic

TABLE 8.2. *Trends in political pluralism*

Country	Election	NGO Sustainability	Media Sustainability	Rule of Law	Voice and Accountability	Political Protests[a]	Governmental Turnover[b]
Croatia	2000	4.7	na	-0.16	-0.29	Medium*	No
Georgia	2003	4.2	1.71	-1.25	-0.58	Medium	Yes
Kyrgyzstan	2005	4.2	1.74	-0.82	-0.96	Low	No
Serbia	2000	5.4	na	-1.29	-1.11	High*	No
Slovakia	1998	na	na	+0.21	+0.28	Low	Yes
Ukraine	2004	3.9	1.96	-0.86	-0.66	Medium	No
Armenia	2003	4.2	1.71	-0.46	-0.52	Low	Yes
Armenia	2008	4.0	1.6	-0.51	-0.59	High*	No
Azerbaijan	2003	5.2	1.76	-0.88	-0.82	Medium	Yes
Azerbaijan	2005	4.9	1.81	-0.83	-0.85	High*	No
Belarus	2006	5.8	0.66	-1.09	-1.66	Low*	No

[a] In this column we provide a rough measure of the frequency and size of popular protests against the regime in the five years preceding the election of interest. The asterisks in the column represent the existence of a precedent of popular protests associated with fraudulent elections.

[b] By governmental turnover, we refer to a simple contrast between countries when oppositions have formed governments or occupied the presidency and countries where they have not.

Notes: All data are for the year prior to the contested election, except for Croatia (1998) and Slovakia (1996).

Sources: Daniel Kaufmann, Aart Kraay, and Massimo Mastruzzi, *Governance Matters VIII: Aggregate and Individual Governance Indicators, 1996–2008* (June 29, 2009). World Bank Policy Research Working Paper No. 4978, http://ssrn.com/abstract=1424591 and http://go.worldbank.org/ATJXPHZMH0; U.S. Agency for International Development, *2007 NGO Sustainability Index for Central and Eastern Europe and Eurasia 11th Edition* (June 2008), http://www.usaid.gov/locations/europe_eurasia/dem_gov/ngoindex/2007); and International Research and Exchange Board (IREX), *Media Sustainability Index, Europe and Eurasia*, 2001, 2002, 2003, 2004, 2005, and 2006/2007, http://www.irex.org/programs/MSI_EUR/index.asp#cc.

Note on methodology: Voice and Accountability and Rule of Law scores are measured on a scale of +2.5 to –2.5. Higher scores correspond to better governance. NGO Sustainability is rated on a scale of 1 to 7; 7 indicates a low or poor level of development and 1 indicates a very advanced NGO sector. The Media Sustainability index is based on a scale from 1 to 5, where scores of 0–1 indicate an unsustainable, unfree press; 1–2 indicates an unsustainable mixed system; 2–3 indicates near sustainability; and 3–4 indicates a sustainable press. The index was first compiled in 2001; data for Croatia, Serbia, and Slovakia were thus unavailable.

performance.[7] Thus, neither a tradition of protest nor turnovers in governing parties and leaders differentiate well between elections where oppositions succeeded in winning power and elections where they failed to do so.

Our two groups of elections are also similar in another way – that is, in whether a precedent had been established for linking fraudulent elections and antiregime mobilizations (see column six in Table 8.2). In theory, such a precedent could play opposing roles – building a base for subsequent efforts or, conversely, leaving oppositions and ordinary citizens too discouraged to return to the streets. Here, it is striking that in the mid-1990s such demonstrations occurred in Croatia and Serbia following local elections that the regimes attempted to nullify, and protests also broke out following the 2001 presidential election in Belarus and the 2003 elections in Armenia and Azerbaijan. While the case studies of Slovakia, Croatia, Serbia, Georgia, and Ukraine provide evidence that oppositions drew useful lessons from previous confrontations with the regime, however, the same does not seem to have been the case for their counterparts in Armenia, Azerbaijan, and Belarus. At the very least, therefore, it is important to recognize that dress rehearsals involving postelection mobilizations against the regime did not necessarily lay the groundwork for a future victory by the opposition.

Before we leave the political factors highlighted in Table 8.2, however, we should note that there is a related factor that is not reported in Table 8.2, but that distinguishes well between our two sets of elections: outcomes of local elections in the five years prior to the elections of interest in this study. While opposition parties had made local inroads into the regime's political monopoly in all of the successful cases, except in Kyrgyzstan, they had not done so during the same period in Armenia, Azerbaijan, or Belarus. We will devote more discussion to this factor later in this chapter when we address opposition electoral strategies.[8]

We can now turn to the economic basis of regime capacity (see Table 8.3). Here, we find once again that our cases exhibit significant variation – in this case, in such important areas as gross domestic product per capita and rates of economic growth, unemployment, and inflation. For example, at the time of their pivotal elections, the Croatian economy was six times larger on a per capita basis than the Georgian or Armenian economy (see column two in Table 8.3). Second, while there seems to be no relationship between economic development and electoral outcomes, there are some differences between our two groups of elections with respect to economic growth (see column three). Once again, the group of successful electoral challenges to authoritarian rule

---

[7] See, for example, Valerie Bunce, "Sequencing Political and Economic Reforms," in *East-Central European Economies in Transition*, ed. John Hardt and Richard Kaufman (Washington, DC: Joint Economic Committee, Congress of the United States, 1994), 46–63; and M. Steven Fish, "Democratization's Prerequisites," *Post-Soviet Affairs* 14:3 (July–September 1998), 212–247.

[8] Also see Beatriz Magaloni, *Voting for Autocracy: Hegemonic Party Survival and Its Demise in Mexico* (Cambridge: Cambridge University Press, 2006), 89, on the Mexican case.

TABLE 8.3. *Economic performance one year before each election*

Country	Election	GDP Per Capita ($)	GDP Growth (%)	Inflation (%)	Unemployment (%)
Croatia	2000	4371	−0.9	4	13.5
Georgia	2003	741	5.5	6	11.9
Kyrgyzstan	2005	434.5	7.0	5	9.3
Serbia	2000	2319	−1.8	na	25.5
Slovakia	1998	3935	4.6	5	11.8
Ukraine	2004	1053.3	9.6	8	3.6
Armenia	2003	740.3	13.2	2	10.8
Armenia	2008	1112.8	13.4	5	7.4
Azerbaijan	2003	760.5	10.6	3	1.4
Azerbaijan	2005	1050.9	10.2	8	1.4
Belarus	2006	3098.3	9.4	19	1.5

Note: All the data are for the year prior to the contested election.
Sources: European Bank for Reconstruction and Development, "Economic Statistics and Growth," www.ebrd.com/country/sector/econo/stats/index.htm. World Bank Key Development Data and Statistics, http://go.worldbank.org/1SF48T40L0.

shows greater variation than the cases of electoral continuity. For example, while Croatia and Serbia registered a mild economic contraction in 1999, Kyrgyzstan and Ukraine grew by 7.0 percent and 9.6 percent, respectively, on the eve of the Tulip and Orange Revolutions. The overall record of economic performance in the year preceding the pivotal elections in Armenia, Azerbaijan, and Belarus was consistently strong. Thus, while helpful to the survival of the regime, strong economic performance carries no political guarantees.[9]

The relationship between economic performance and electoral outcomes, however, is muddied even further when we extend our assessment to include longer-term economic and electoral trends. For example, Ukraine, like Russia, experienced an economic collapse throughout the 1990s that reflected both the close ties between the two economies and the costs of partial reform.[10] However, while the Communist Party split, elections were competitive, and new parties and leaders came to power during the 1990s, these developments did not result from a strong opposition movement or produce an empowerment of democratic forces. It was only during the Kuchma regime that any growth was registered in the Ukrainian economy, and the highest level of

[9] See Robin Shephard, "The Economy and Democratic Change: The Missing Link?," in *Reclaiming Democracy: Civil Society and Electoral Change in Central and Eastern Europe*, ed. Joerg Forbrig and Pavol Demeš (Washington, DC: German Marshall Fund, 2007). However, see Magaloni, *Voting for Autocracy*, especially 13, 84–85, and Chapter 7 for evidence about the lagged effects of declining economic performance in Mexico during the rule of the PRI and, more generally, in what she terms "hegemonic-party" regimes.

[10] See Joel Hellman, "Winners Take All: The Politics of Partial Reform in Postcommunist Transitions," *World Politics* 50:2 (January 1998), 203–234.

growth occurred in the year before the Orange Revolution.[11] A similar economic pattern, moreover, appears in Georgia, Kyrgyzstan, and even in Serbia (despite the negative growth rate that appears in Table 8.3), where leaders survived significant downturns only to be forced to leave office when the economy was in fact on an upswing, albeit one that reflected, especially in Georgia and Serbia, what happens after an economy has bottomed out. By contrast, in Armenia and Azerbaijan, which, like Serbia and Ukraine, experienced dramatic economic deterioration during the 1990s (reflecting the costs of war in Nagorno-Karabagh and additionally, in Armenia, a disastrous earthquake and unfortunate linkages to the Russian economy), turnovers in government did accompany economic decline, and these turnovers came to a halt when the so-called Karabagh clan and the Aliyev family succeeded in consolidating their control over Armenia and Azerbaijan, respectively.

REGIME CAPACITY

In Table 8.4, we complete our assessment of factors that were in place prior to the elections we examine by focusing on a final set of political and economic indicators of regime strength, each of which, we admit, is less than ideal. Here, we find, first, remarkable variation among our nine countries with respect to the ability of authoritarian leaders to institutionalize their powers – for example, the extent of presidential powers (column 2), the founding of a strong ruling party (column 5), and rates of defection from the ruling party and/or inner circle (column 6).[12] Variation in these areas, however, does not correlate with differences in electoral outcomes. For example, to focus on two of the "failed" cases: while Lukashenka inherited a strong Communist Party and then invested further in the party as an instrument of his personal power, neither Kocharian nor Sarkisian are connected to the Communist Party in Armenia (which found itself on the wrong side of the national question at the end of the Soviet period and thereby lost power). Moreover, neither the former nor the current Armenian president seems to have built the formidable party machine that we find in Belarus.[13] To provide another example of the

---

[11] Robin Shephard, "The Economy and Democratic Change."
[12] On the importance of political parties in the durability of authoritarian rule, see, especially, Magaloni, *Voting for Autocracy*; Benjamin Smith, "Life of the Party: The Origins of Regime Breakdown and Persistence under Single-Party Rule," *World Politics* 57:3 (Spring 2005), 421–451; Lucan Way, "Ukraine's Orange Revolution: Kuchma's Failed Authoritarianism," *Journal of Democracy* 16:2 (April 2005), 131–145; Lucan Way, "Authoritarian State Building and the Sources of Regime Competitiveness in the Fourth Wave: The Cases of Belarus, Moldova, Russia, and Ukraine," *World Politics* 57:2 (January 2005), 231–261; Eva Bellin, "The Robustness of Authoritarianism in the Middle East," *Comparative Politics* 36:2 (January 2004), 139–157; Barbara Geddes, "Authoritarian Breakdown: Empirical Testing of a Game Theoretic Argument," paper presented at the annual meeting of the American Political Science Association, Atlanta, GA, September 1, 1999.
[13] Vitali Silitski, "Contagion Deterred: Preemptive Authoritarianism in the Former Soviet Union," in *Democracy and Authoritarianism in the Postcommunist World*, ed. Valerie

TABLE 8.4. *Regime capacity on the eve of elections*

Country	Election	Presidential Power[a]	Divided Opposition Pattern[b]	Regime Durability[c]	Ruling Party Strength[d]	Defections[e]	Secession of Regions[f]	Size of Public Sector[g]
Croatia	2000	9	Usually	High	Medium	Low	No	40
Georgia	2003	13	Usually	Medium	Medium	High	Yes	35
Kyrgyzstan	2005	16	Usually	High	Medium	High	No	25
Serbia	2000	na	Usually	High	High	High	Yes	Na
Slovakia	1998	4	Usually	Medium	Medium	Low	No	25
Ukraine	2004	13	Usually	High	High	High	No	35
Armenia	2003	16	Usually	Medium	Medium	Low	Yes	30
Armenia	2008							25
Azerbaijan	2003	18	Usually	Medium	High	High	Yes	40
Azerbaijan	2005							40
Belarus	2006	21	Usually	Medium	High	High	No	75

[a] The higher the number, the greater the presidential power for 1990 to 2002. These data were provided to the authors by Timothy Frye, and they are drawn from the Timothy Frye, Joel Hellman, and Joshua Tucker Political Data Base. Presidential powers increased from 1990 to the electoral period of interest in Armenia, Belarus, Georgia, Kyrgyzstan, Serbia (Bunce and Wolchik estimation), and Ukraine.

[b] The issue is whether there was any precedent of opposition unity in earlier elections. In every case, there was – whether in local contests (as in Croatia, Georgia, Serbia, and Ukraine) or in national contests (as in Slovakia, Armenia, Azerbaijan, and Belarus).

[c] This column highlights a contrast between a history of turnover in leaders and governing coalitions (as in Georgia, Slovakia, Armenia, Azerbaijan, and Belarus, where there was the Communist Party in 1994) versus rule by a single leader and party during the entire postcommunist period (as in Croatia, Serbia, and Ukraine).

[d] The "Medium" score in this column reflects cases where the ruling party was a loose-knit coalition that did not institutionalize the leader's power (as in Slovakia and Armenia) or where a once well-institutionalized party disintegrated before the key election (as in Croatia and Georgia). A "High" score indicates strong institutionalization evident up to the election.

[e] A "Low" defection rate means few defections from the ruling circle before the pivotal election and a "High" rate signifies many defections to the opposition of key actors associated with the regime.

[f] This column refers to the existence of ongoing conflicts between secessionist regions and the state.

[g] This is the percentage of GDP produced by the state-owned sector.

Source: European Bank for Reconstruction and Development, "Economic Statistics and Growth," www.ebrd.com/country/sector/econo/stats/index.htm. European Bank for Reconstruction and Development, "Structural Change Indicators," www.ebrd.com/pages/research/economics/data/macro.shtml#structural.

overlap between our two categories with respect to the institutionalization of the autocrat's power: while governing parties turned over with some frequency in Azerbaijan, Slovakia, and Ukraine over the course of the transition, and there was a single turnover in party power in Georgia and Armenia, the same party remained in power throughout the transition from communism in Belarus, Croatia, Kyrgyzstan, and Serbia.

At the same time, and just as puzzling, we see little variation both across and within our categories with respect to another widely used explanation of regime change – that is, precedents for opposition cohesion (see column three).[14] Thus, just as there had been experiments in forging a united opposition in earlier elections (usually at the local level) in most of the cases where democratizing elections eventually occurred (Kyrgyzstan is the sole exception), so in Armenia, Azerbaijan, and Belarus we find in fact multiple experiments by the opposition with forming united fronts to compete for power in national elections.

Even when we combine all of our measures of regime capacity, we are still unable to differentiate very well between our two sets of cases. For example, Belarus, a failed transition from authoritarian rule, and Serbia, a successful challenge to authoritarian rule (and one that, by all accounts – but not included in the data used in Table 8.4 – combined, in part because of continuity in Communist Party rule and the necessity of a wartime economy, considerable centralization of power and a very large public sector), stand out in Table 8.4 as being relatively strong regimes. This is far from surprising, because in both of these countries (and in Ukraine) communists or former communists succeeded in staying in power throughout the transition. In addition, as column two in Table 8.4 indicates, presidential power scores in Armenia, Azerbaijan, and Kyrgyzstan are not appreciably lower than what we find in Belarus and Serbia, and the scores for presidential power in Georgia and Ukraine on the eve of their breakthrough elections are not significantly different, in turn, from these cases.[15]

While it is true that the regimes where challenges to authoritarian rule did not succeed tend to be stronger on the whole than the other regimes, it is also

---

Bunce, Michael McFaul, and Kathryn Stoner-Weiss (Cambridge: Cambridge University Press, 2009), 274–299; Vitali Silitski, "What Are We Trying to Explain?," *Journal of Democracy* 20:1 (January 2009), 86–89; interview with Armineh Arakelian, Yerevan, March 13, 2007; interview with Andrew Bennett, Yerevan, March 12, 2007; interview with Chedomir Flego, Yerevan, March 14, 2007; interview with Gavin Helf, Yerevan, March 9 and 10, 2007; interview with Alex Sadar, Yerevan, March 14, 2007.

[14] At first glance, the Serbian case would appear to be miscoded. However, our interest here is in defections that took place prior to the election and that, as a result, signaled regime weakness and reshaped the strategies of key players. In Serbia, the key defections took place only after the contrast between the regime's tabulation of the vote and that of the opposition and its allies was made public in September 2000. Defection, in short, was tied to electoral outcomes, rather than preceding the contest for the presidency.

[15] On Belarus, see, especially, David Marples, *Belarus: A Denationalized Nation: Postcommunist States and Nations* (Amsterdam: Harwood Academic, 1999).

the case that the capacity of leaders in the "failed group" to control politics and economics is both greater and less than it would seem from Table 8.4, once we shift our attention from Belarus to Armenia and Azerbaijan. On the one hand, while the public sectors in both Armenia and Azerbaijan are relatively small, these figures do not tell a full story of the economic resources available to these regimes. For example, the leaders of Azerbaijan have access to significant energy rents, and both regimes (like Belarus, Georgia, Kyrgyzstan, Serbia, and Ukraine) score exceptionally high on various corruption indices. On the other hand, Armenia and Azerbaijan have been locked in a territorial dispute over Nagorno-Karabagh for twenty years. In both cases, this conflict over a sizeable portion of Azerbaijan's territory generated large-scale public protests early in the transition and led to the removal of incumbent leaders. Moreover, in comparison to Belarus, leaders in both Armenia and Azerbaijan have faced more frequent and larger public protests. For instance, in 2003 in Azerbaijan, an estimated thirty thousand citizens participated in the demonstrations that followed the November election.[16] At the same time, Azerbaijan has had five leaders since it began its transition to statehood; these turnovers have not been responses to term limits (as in Armenia), and alternations in power in that country (unlike the situation in Armenia) have been between the opposition and the former communists. Finally, one leader of the opposition in Azerbaijan, Lala Shovket, was a minister in Heydar Aliyev's government, but eventually defected and formed an opposition party in order to oppose Heydar's son and the current president, Ilham Aliyev.[17] Thus, to reinforce an earlier point: it would be wrong to assume that even regimes that are very powerful on paper have had the luxury of being able to insulate themselves from serious challenges to their survival.

We also discover the most variation along these diverse dimensions of regime capacity within the first group of regimes listed in Table 8.4. This pattern reinforces our earlier finding that successful electoral challenges to authoritarian rule in the postcommunist region have occurred in quite varying political and economic contexts. This is the case whether we focus on long-term political trends, such as patterns over time in defections from the ruling circle, regime durability, and internal and external conflicts, or on institutional and structural characteristics, such as presidential power and the size of the public sector. The regimes in Croatia, Georgia, Kyrgyzstan, Serbia, Slovakia, and Ukraine, in short, varied substantially from one another.

The Case against Structural and Institutional Accounts

The pattern of scores reported in Tables 8.1 through 8.4 counsels a shift in focus from the structural and institutional backdrop of these elections to the

---

[16] Robert Parsons,"Analysis: Putin Seeks to Draw Azerbaijan Back into Russian Orbit," *Radio Free Europe Radio Liberty* (February 21, 2006), http://www.rferl.org/featuresarticle/2006/02/0335ec2e-489b-4be6-b5f0-f52d0c96226b.html.

[17] Interview with Lala Shovket, Baku, March 5, 2007.

nature of the elections themselves. Such a shift makes particular sense given the failure of many of these "pre-election" factors to differentiate clearly between our two sets of cases, and given as well the repeating pattern of considerable economic and political variation among the regimes that served as sites for successful electoral challenges to authoritarian rule. It is precisely such a combination of findings that leaves considerable room for the impact of more short-term influences.

However, there are two other reasons to look more closely at elections. One is the nature of mixed regimes. Such regimes are vulnerable to leadership and party turnover for the simple reason that they hold regular and competitive elections. Here, the problem is not just the opportunities for electoral change that such regimes provide; it is also the visible tensions they generate between real and "fake"[18] democracy, especially in the region of concern in this study, where such contrasts were a fact of daily life during the communist era, as well as the source of many jokes. In addition, mixed regimes are unusually vulnerable in comparison to other types of regimes, because they typically exhibit a syndrome composed of weak state institutions (in part because of problems with consolidating borders and integrating nations), high levels of corruption, and fluctuations over time in their mixtures of authoritarian and democratic politics.[19]

Despite these problems, however, mixed regimes are in fact relatively durable, because the very ways in which these regimes operate – by design and by accident – undermine the ability of oppositions to mount effective electoral challenges. Here, we refer in part to the obvious point that such regimes are often in a position to defend themselves through control of the media, parliaments, the courts, and elections; harassment of the opposition and civil society groups; and interventions that fragment oppositions and keep them isolated from civil society groups. There are, however, two other less widely recognized aspects of mixed regimes that undermine opposition effectiveness.

One is particularly noticeable in the postcommunist world. In that setting, the deeply penetrative character of the communist experience and its classless legacies, together with the costs of partial economic reforms, translate into an unusually fluid party system. Parties, moreover, exist relatively independent of social cleavages, and they are often dominated by political leaders who have little interest in intraparty democracy, bargaining and compromise, campaigning for votes, or using public opinion polls as indicators of popular preferences and guidelines for campaign promises. As a result, opposition politics in the mixed regimes in this region tends to be long on sweeping pronouncements

---

[18] Andrew Wilson, *Virtual Politics: Faking Democracy in the Post-Soviet World* (New Haven, CT: Yale University Press, 2005).

[19] See, for example, David Epstein, Robert Bates, Jack Goldstone, Ida Kristensen, and Sharyn O"Halloran, "Democratic Transitions," *American Journal of Political Science* 50:3 (2006), 551–569; and Philip G. Roessler and Marc M. Howard, "Post-Cold-War Political Regimes: When Do Elections Matter?," in *Democratization by Elections: A New Mode of Transition?* ed. Staffan Lindberg (Baltimore: Johns Hopkins University Press, 2009).

and short on policy details.[20] The familiar representational and policy-making functions of political parties, therefore, are little in evidence in mixed regimes in the postcommunist world.

This mind-set was well articulated in an interview we conducted with Lala Shovket, the leader of the Liberal Party, who was a rare example of an opposition candidate who won office in the 2005 parliamentary elections in Azerbaijan.[21] As she argued quite forcefully: "My party stands on principle, and that meant that, while I won a seat, my conscience required me to register my dissatisfaction with the regime by boycotting parliament." She then very quickly dismissed with a wave of her hand our question about whether boycotting was fair to the citizens who voted for her and who likely expected, if she won, that she would represent them. Soon thereafter, she said she might "get around to returning to parliament at some point."[22]

It is very easy to fault the opposition for its failings. However, in the rush by both analysts and local and international democracy activists to point the finger of blame at the opposition, a more fundamental constraint on opposition development, one built into the very nature of mixed regimes, has been overlooked. Because of their fluid political characteristics – given weak institutions, ever-changing rules of the political game, and incomplete and often biased information about the "true" opinions of the public and the "true" state of the regime's power – mixed regimes, especially where elections are rigged, present oppositions with a set of unusually diverse, difficult, and therefore divisive strategic choices. As our case studies in Part II pointed out, the opposition in each of our nine countries confronted these choices in every election, and they responded, not surprisingly, in different ways at different times.

There was another complication common to many countries in the postcommunist world, including most of those analyzed in this book. Because of past territorial disputes and costly mobilizations associated with state formation, leaders of many of our mixed regimes had based their rule on appeals to nationalism and political order.[23] This was especially the case in Croatia,

---

[20] This was a common theme in the interviews we conducted with party leaders and international democracy promoters in Washington, DC, and in Armenia, Azerbaijan, Georgia, and Serbia. See, for example, interviews with Daniel Calingaert, Washington, DC, July 19, 2005; Lala Shovket, Baku, March 5, 2007; Dallas Frohrib, Baku, March 6, 2007; Amy Schultz, Baku, March 6, 2007; Raffi Hovhannisyan, Yerevan, March 9, 2007; Andrew Bennett, Yerevan, March 12, 2007; Aleksandr Iskandaryan, Yerevan, March 13, 2007; Alex Sadar, Yerevan, March 14, 2007; Chedomir Flego, Yerevan, March 14, 2007; Suzana Grubjesic, Belgrade, April 12, 2005; Sonja Licht, Belgrade, April 12, 2005; David Usupashvili, Tbilisi, Georgia, October 19, 2005; Amineh Arakelian, Tbilisi, October 21, 2005; Nadia Diuk, Washington, DC, April 2, 2010; Larry Garber, Washington, DC, April 9, 2010; and Robert Benjamin, Washington, DC, April 9, 2010.

[21] Interview at Lala Shovket's headquarters on the far outskirts (like the other opposition parties) of Baku, March 5, 2007.

[22] Interview with Lala Shovket, Baku, March 5, 2007.

[23] The logic of the argument here is drawn from two sources, as well as a number of our interviews. See Marc Hetherington and Jonathan Weiler, *Divided We Stand: Polarization,*

Serbia, Georgia, Armenia, and Azerbaijan. Such appeals crowd out other concerns, especially those related to social and economic reforms as well as priorities emphasizing the need for a more democratic politics, that might serve as a basis for challenging the regime. In addition, they delegitimize calls for change, since such appeals can be quickly characterized as unpatriotic in a time of heightened concern about the security of the nation, and they divide and demobilize opposition groups and ordinary citizens who would normally embrace change-oriented agendas. Thus, oppositions have little room for political or policy maneuver, since they must always parade their nationalist credentials. This is especially true when, as in Armenia, Azerbaijan, Georgia, and Slovakia, earlier governments had lost power because they had lost territory or taken too accommodating a position on controversial issues associated with nation and territory.

These understandable constraints on the development of effective oppositions, coupled with repeated failures by the opposition to win office, had powerful effects, not surprisingly, on how citizens in mixed regimes viewed the regime, the opposition, and elections. From their vantage point, voting – both in general and for the opposition in particular – was a waste of time, because the regime could and would manipulate the results in its favor. Just as importantly, the opposition was not only unlikely to win, but also, due to its sorry record of squabbling, collaboration with the regime, boycotting elections, and the like, unworthy of support.[24] These effects make it very hard for oppositions to mount successful challenges in mixed regimes, even when the regime is widely disliked and perceived to be vulnerable. For example, as

---

Authoritarianism, and the Contemporary Political Divide (Cambridge: Cambridge University Press, 2009); and V. P. Gagnon, *The Myth of Ethnic War: Serbia and Croatia in the 1990s* (Ithaca, NY: Cornell University Press, 2004). In addition, this interpretation was also offered, for example, by Andrew Bennett, interview in Yerevan, Armenia, March 12, 2007; Dallas Frohrib, Baku, March 6, 2007; Amy Schultz, Baku, March 6, 2007; Gavin Helf, Yerevan, March 9, 2007; Gregory Koldys, Yerevan, March 9, 2007; Daniel M. Renna, Yerevan, March 9, 2007; Giorgi Nizharadze, Tbilisi, October 16, 2005; and Alexander Rondeli, Tbilisi, October 14, 2005.

[24] For example, surveys in Azerbaijan show that, while citizens have a number of grievances against the regime, they are even more dissatisfied with the opposition (interview with Amy Schultz, Baku, March 6, 2007). For detailed evidence on public concerns about the opposition in Serbia, see Jasna Milošević Djordjević, "Činioci izborne apstinencije u Srbiji," in *Političke stranke u Srbiji. Struktura I funkcionisanje*, ed. Zoran Lutovac (Beograd: Friedrich Ebert Stiftung/Institut društvenih nauka, 2005), 139–156; Dušan Pavlović, "Polarizacija stranačkog sistema nakon 2000. godine," in *Političke stranke u Srbiji. Struktura I funkcionisanje*, ed. Zoran Lutovac (Beograd: Friedrich Ebert Stiftung/Institut društvenih nauka, 2005) 157–169; Srećko Mihailović, "Political Formulae for the Perseverance and Change of Regime in Serbia," in *Revolution and Order: Serbia after October 2005*, ed. Ivana Spasić and Milan Subotić (Belgrade: Institute for Philosophy and Social Theory, 2001), 59–72; and Vladimir Ilić, "Otpor!," in *Or Beyond Politics*. (Belgrade: Helsinki Committee for Human Rights in Serbia, 2001). These arguments were also made in interviews conducted in Belgrade with three specialists on public opinion: Srdjan Bogosavljević, April 13, 2005; Milan Nikolić, April 12, 2005; and Marko Blagojević, April 11, 2005.

Donald Blessington, the director of IFES (the International Foundation for Electoral Systems) in Azerbaijan, noted, while the ruling party in that country, YAP (the New Azerbaijan Party), was, according to a poll carried out by the International Republican Institute, very unpopular, the opposition parties were even more unpopular.[25] In fact, popular sentiments are unusually hard to decipher in such political settings, especially in the more authoritarian variants, because public opinion polls are infrequent, often unreliable, and/ or limited in their circulation, and because publics respond to stolen elections by participating less and less over time in the electoral process. As a result, electoral outcomes, already manipulated in many cases by the regime, have a pronounced tendency over time to underrepresent the size of regime opposition and to overrepresent regime supporters and "acquiescers." All this means that oppositions in such contexts might be in a position to gain from a weakening regime, but only if – and this is a big if – they are able at the same time to convince publics to vote, to vote for them, and, if necessary, to defend their choices in the streets. This is a very tall order.

This discussion carries an important implication that refocuses our attention on variations in electoral dynamics. Structural (and many historical institutional) accounts of political struggles between regimes and oppositions in authoritarian contexts tend to be based on two core assumptions: that there are only two players in the game, and that (in zero-sum fashion) a decline in regime popularity leads necessarily to an expansion in opposition support.[26] However, if oppositions are unpopular as well, this transfer of political support will not necessarily take place. Citizens do not have to support anyone, especially since they do not have to vote. Moreover, they are not required to take to the streets after fraudulent elections.

Microanalytical accounts of these struggles also share this zero-sum understanding of citizen preferences and behaviors, though adding the collective action problem to the equation and arguing, at least in the case of what they term the "color revolutions," that fraudulent elections have characteristics that facilitate popular mobilization on behalf of the opposition.[27] However, these analyses are no more successful than the others in explaining why the political contest narrows to these two options and why, if it does, publics are willing and able to transfer their support to the opposition and, what is more (especially in view of the fact that all the elections in this study featured more than two candidates), to some opposition groups in particular. Moreover, there are

---

[25] Interview with Daniel Blessington, Baku, March 5, 2007.
[26] Way, "Authoritarian State Building"; Lucan Way, "The Real Causes of the Color Revolutions," *Journal of Democracy* 19:3 (July 2008), 55–69.
[27] Joshua A. Tucker, "Enough! Electoral Fraud, Collective Action Problems, and the Second Wave of Post-Communist Democratic Revolutions," *Perspectives on Politics* 5:3 (September 2007), 535–551; Mark R. Thompson and Philipp Kuntz, "Stolen Elections: The Case of the Serbian October," *Journal of Democracy* 15:4 (October 2004), 159–172; Philipp Kuntz and Mark Thompson, "More than Just the Final Straw: Stolen Elections as Revolutionary Triggers," *Comparative Politics* 41:3 (April 2009), 253–272.

two other problems with studies that focus on collective action issues. One is that only some fraudulent elections prompt popular protests. For example, one can contrast the elections in Azerbaijan in 2003 and 2005 with those held in 2007. In the first two cases, popular protests followed the election, whereas in the third instance they failed to materialize. This is despite the obvious point that everyone knew in 2007, as their behavior in the earlier two elections indicated, that Aliyev had stolen elections. The other problem in collective action studies is that protests are one thing, and the transfer of political power is another – a point that was brought home by our comparison of Armenia, Azerbaijan, and Belarus in Chapter 7. In this sense, even if we assume that fraudulent elections help citizens surmount collective action problems (though the relationship between these two factors is obviously uneven), we cannot then take the further step of arguing that such protests necessarily achieve their political objectives.

VARIATIONS AMONG THE ELECTIONS

Several of the hypotheses discussed in Chapter 2 that could logically differentiate among elections – such as whether the incumbent is on the ballot and whether the election took place at a time when the leader's control over patronage was in seeming decline – fail to differentiate clearly between our two groups of elections. For example, despite their contrasting results, the presidential elections in Armenia in 2008, in Ukraine in 2004, and in Croatia in 2000 shared the commonality of not having an incumbent president on the ballot – because of term limits in the first two cases and because of the death of the incumbent in the third case. Moreover, the Georgian elections in 2003 and the elections in Kyrgyzstan in 2005, like the elections in Azerbaijan in 2005 and in Armenia in 2003, were parliamentary contests where, because the systems were presidential, incumbent presidents were not on the ballot. The distinction between incumbents up for reelection and the absence of what could be termed incumbent effects, therefore, fails to differentiate between our two sets of electoral outcomes.

At the same time, our cases call into question arguments about the incentives for continuation of regime support as a result of continuity in patronage opportunities versus the possibility of changes in those opportunities. On the one hand, there was a question of approaching term limits in Georgia, where Shevardnadze's term in office was to end in 2005, and in Kyrgyzstan, where Akaev's term was due to end in the fall of 2005. The problem here, however, is that, especially for Akaev, there were reasons to doubt that term limits would actually be respected in view of his past behavior. Moreover, each of these leaders faced significant divisions within his ruling party, which would have made appointment of a reliable successor very difficult. On the other hand, if the key issue is precisely disarray in the ruling party, and thus an unraveling of reliable patronage networks, along with approaching term limits, then how can we explain the defeat of Milošević in Serbia in 2000? Milošević had shown himself to be quite adept at getting around the problem of term limits and at maintaining his control over a well-organized and long-ruling party.

At this point, then, we need to confront the cases where term limits had a history of being respected and where the election required a transition from an authoritarian incumbent to his chosen successor. Here, we find not just Armenia in 2008 but also Ukraine in 2004. In both cases, the incumbent and his chosen successor – that is, Kocharian/Sarkisian and Kuchma/Yanukovych, respectively – were closely tied to one another, and there was little reason to assume that either the Karabagh or the Kuchma "clan" (as they are widely characterized) would be in a poor position to keep the faucet of patronage flowing. However, while massive protests in Ukraine led to the Orange Revolution, large-scale protests in Armenia following the 2008 presidential election led to violent crackdowns and the passing of power from Kocharian to his longtime ally and leader of the wars in Nagorno-Karabagh, Serzh Sarkisian.

Another distinction among elections that we drew in Chapter 2 was between a united and a divided opposition running for office – a distinction that is repeatedly drawn in the literature on oppositions and transitions to democracy. The importance of a united opposition is its efficiency in concentrating votes; the signals it sends to voters regarding the opposition's rejection of earlier divisive actions and its ability to govern effectively; and the constraints it places on such well-practiced regime tactics as cracking down on the opposition and various divide-and–rule strategies. Moreover, external democracy promoters are much more willing to invest in oppositions that seem serious about trying to win office – for instance, by coalescing with one another – than in those that are not.[28] However, precisely because of the "silver bullet" character of this variable, we controlled for the influence of this factor by limiting our comparison to elections that featured a united opposition. Not surprisingly, therefore, the unity of the opposition is unable to differentiate between electoral continuity and turnover.

The distinction between free and fair elections, on the one hand, and fraudulent elections, on the other, with the latter posited to mobilize publics against the regime and thereby to increase opportunities for regime change, also blurs, rather than sharpens, the contrast between our two sets of cases. First, while it is true that all of the fraudulent elections in this study prompted significant popular protests, it is also true – and this is far from accidental, since this factor served as yet another control in this study – that these protests were followed in some cases by continuity in authoritarian rule and in others by the empowerment of the democratic opposition. Moreover, it is also true, as we discussed in Chapters 4 through 7, that earlier fraudulent elections in the more authoritarian countries in our group led in some cases to popular protests, as

---

[28] See, especially, Marc Morjé Howard and Philip G. Roessler, "Liberalizing Electoral Outcomes in Competitive Authoritarian Regimes," *American Journal of Political Science* 50:2 (April 2006), 362–368; and Lincoln Abraham Mitchell, *Uncertain Democracy: U.S. Foreign Policy and Georgia's Rose Revolution* (Philadelphia: University of Pennsylvania Press, 2009).

TABLE 8.5. *U.S. democracy assistance*

Country	Total Democracy and Governance (DG) Assistance per Capita ($)[a]	Average DG Assistance per Capita ($) for Five Years Prior to Election	Average DG Assistance per Capita ($) for Two Years Prior to Election	Percentage Change in DG Assistance[b]	Percentage Growth in Electoral Assistance[c]
Croatia	1.29	1.69	1.82	−54.5%	+1.3%
Georgia	1.24	2.52	2.23	+41.5%	+172%
Serbia	3.15	0.77	1.28	+340%	+111%
Slovakia	0.44	0.86	1.13	−20.5%	+12.8%
Ukraine	0.30	0.44	0.47	+40.7%	+145%
Armenia	2.03	3.69	3.58	(2003) +19.0%	(2003) −35.4%
Azerbaijan	0.51	1.09	0.87	(2003) +2.9%	(2003) +54.3%
Belarus	0.22	na	na	na	na

[a] These data are calculated from the dataset. The years are 1990–2004.

[b] This is the percentage change in overall DG assistance during the two years prior to the pivotal election. For Armenia and Azerbaijan, the two electoral episodes are averaged.

[c] This is the percentage change in solely electoral assistance during the two years prior to the pivotal election. For Armenia and Azerbaijan, the two electoral episodes are averaged.

Source: Steven Finkel, Andrew T. Green, Aníbal Pérez-Liñán, and Mitchell Seligson, *Democracy Assistance Project, Phase II Project Dataset (1990–2004)* of the project "Cross-National Research on USAID's Democracy and Governance Programs," http://www.pitt.edu/~politics/democracy/democracy.html.

in Belarus in 2001 and Serbia throughout the 1990s, and in others failed to do so, as in Georgia in 2000, Ukraine in 1999, and Azerbaijan in 2007.

International Democracy Assistance

We now turn to an evaluation of the impact of international democracy assistance. In Table 8.5, we apply a variety of measures of USAID democracy and governance assistance to our nine countries.[29] First, as columns one through three indicate, all of the countries in this study received significant amounts of democratic assistance. Second, the United States favored some of our countries over others, but not in a pattern that suggests a key role for the United States in the electoral breakthroughs. Thus, if we focus on the entire time span for which reliable data are available (1990 to 2004), we find, first, that on a per capita basis, Croatia, Georgia, and especially Serbia and Armenia received

[29] We focus on the United States for two reasons. First, there are no reliable comparable data on assistance provided by private foundations and the European Union. Second, our interviews with both European and American democracy promoters and local participants in these elections in Armenia, Azerbaijan, Croatia, Georgia, Serbia, Slovakia, and Ukraine converged on the argument that the key international player was the United States, with the Europeans playing a more critical role in Slovakia and Ukraine.

the most aid, whereas far less support was provided to Slovakia, Ukraine, Azerbaijan, and Belarus (see column one). If we focus our attention on trends during the five years leading up to the elections (column two), we discover that Georgia and Armenia are favored, and that in the two years preceding the elections, Armenia, Georgia, and Croatia received more overall support than any of the other countries listed in this table. Also striking is the huge jump in democracy and governance assistance, evident in column four of Table 8.5, which was provided to Serbia before the 2000 elections. This is hardly surprising, given the shift in U.S. foreign policy in 1999 from tolerating the Milošević regime to forming a group within the White House focused on the task of ending that regime. Finally, while electoral assistance grew substantially in Serbia, Georgia, Azerbaijan, and Ukraine before the elections that took place from 2000 to 2004, its growth rate was far more modest in Croatia and Slovakia.[30]

The low correlation between U.S. financial support of democratic development and variations in electoral outcomes, therefore, casts some doubt on the argument that the United States engineered electoral change in postcommunist Europe and Eurasia.[31] This conclusion is not surprising in view of the literature on international democracy assistance. It is also far from surprising given the perspectives on the impact of this aid offered in the interviews we conducted with leaders of the opposition and civil society groups and with members of the international democracy assistance community, including the National Democratic Institute, the International Republican Institute, the National Endowment for Democracy, Freedom House, the European Union, IDEA (the International Institute for Democracy and Electoral Assistance), IFES (the International Foundation for Election Systems), the Open Society Institute, the Charles Stewart Mott Foundation, Rockefeller Brothers, the German Marshall Fund of the United States, and the International Center for Non-violent Conflict.[32] Two sets of observations by members of these groups

---

[30] U.S. support for free and fair elections also increased substantially in Kyrgyzstan in 2005. See Noor Borbieva, "Development in the Kyrgyz Republic: Exchange, Communal Networks, and the Foreign Presence" (Ph.D. dissertation, Harvard University, 2007), Chapter 7.

[31] See, especially, Aleksandr Knyazev, *Gosudarstvennyi perevorot: 24 Marta 2005g v Kirgizii* (Moscow: Europa, 2005).

[32] Interviews with Lindsay Lloyd, Washington, DC, November 16, 2006; Andrew Bennett, Yerevan, March 12, 2007; Aleksandr Iskandaryan, Yerevan, March 13, 2007; Alex Sadar, Yerevan, March 14, 2007; Chedomir Flego, Yerevan, March 14, 2007; Daniel Renna, Yerevan, March 9, 2007; Keneshbek Sainazarov, Yerevan, March 14, 2007; Daniel Blessington, Baku, March 5, 2007; Dallas Frohrib, Baku, March 6, 2007; Amy Schultz, Baku, March 6, 2007; Fuad Suyleymanov, Baku, March 5, 2007; Armineh Arakelian, Tbilisi, October 21, 2005; David Darchiashvili, Tbilisi, October 15, 2005; Mike Kelleher, Tbilisi, October 19, 2005; Mark Mullen, Tbilisi, October 14, 2005; John Wright, Tbilisi, October 18, 2005; Adriana Lazinica, Belgrade, April 15, 2005; Mike Staresinic, Belgrade, April 15, 2005; Gregory Simpson, Belgrade, April 13, 2005; Mitchell, *Uncertain Democracy*; and National Research Councils of the National Academies, Committee on Evaluation of USAID Democracy Assistance Programs, *Improving Democracy Assistance: Building Knowledge through Evaluations and Research* (Washington, DC: National Academies Press, 2008).

and organizations stand out. One is that the international democracy assistance community uses a "scattergun" approach to supporting democratic change. This is in part because of a lack of coordination among organizations and individuals, even when they are funded by the same source. However, it also reflects a lack of agreement – and relatively vague and untested theories – about the kinds of investments that are most likely to support democratic progress.[33]

The other common theme that emerged in our interviews is that, in comparison to development assistance (which has a much longer history and is far more deeply embedded in American foreign policy), democracy aid is a much more modest operation – which is one reason why the growth of such assistance could be so dramatic, as in the cases of Georgia, Serbia, and Ukraine in columns four and five in Table 8.5. For instance, democracy and governance assistance has never constituted more than 10 percent of the USAID budget, and electoral assistance in turn has never exceeded 10 percent of overall democracy aid.[34]

We also need to be very careful about using the economic data reported in Table 8.5 as a representative summary of U.S. involvement in electoral change in the postcommunist region. One problem is that these data are biased in favor of those cases, as discussed in earlier chapters, in which private foundations and the EU, while collaborating with the United States, assumed major responsibilities for supporting electoral change – for instance, Slovakia, Croatia, and Belarus. Another is that international democracy assistance is always a collaborative effort with local actors, and it always rests on such admittedly contradictory considerations as the access the regime allows (which is a particular problem in Belarus), the needs of local actors because of constraints on democratic change, and the existing capacity of opposition parties and civil society groups. Thus, for example, the United States can try to compensate for local democratic deficits or define its role as one of merely "topping off" extensive local capacities for change. Moreover, some interventions can be critical but cheap, such as (in the cases of Croatia, Georgia, Serbia, Slovakia, and Ukraine) supplying several plane or train tickets to support a sharing of electoral strategies between "graduates" of successful electoral breakthroughs and opposition groups hoping and planning to emulate them. This approach to democratic change was particularly popular among members of the National Democratic Institute, who had begun to use international "learning delegations" following the defeat of Marcos in the Philippines in 1986.[35]

[33] See, especially, Andrew Ng, "Accompanying the King: Building a Democratic Governance State in Morocco" (honors thesis, Department of Government, Cornell University, April 16, 2007); and National Research Council, *Improving Democracy Assistance.*

[34] Mitchell, *Uncertain Democracy.*

[35] Interview with Larry Garber, Washington, DC, April 9, 2010; interview with Kenneth Wollack, Washington, DC, May 12, 2010; interview with Roger Potocki, Washington, DC, May 7, 2010.

However, there is a final consideration. External interventions in democratic development abroad vary for two simple reasons. One is that different goals drive U.S. foreign policy, and the other is that the goals and capacities of opposition groups on the ground also vary. Here, we can draw a simple distinction between two approaches to international electoral assistance. One is support for free and fair elections. This can include money and technical advice; pressure on regimes to improve their electoral procedures; linkages between development aid and electoral performance; and public criticism by U.S. officials (and other players, such as the OSCE and heads of European governments and the EU) of the quality of the election. In addition, the United States and European governments can, in the face of popular protests against rigged elections, make it clear that they share this reading of the conduct of the elections. The other approach marries support for free and fair elections with a more radical goal: regime change. Thus, the United States alone or in collaboration with private foundations, the EU, and European governments can express strong opposition to a regime and provide generous resources in support of not just improvements in the quality of the election, but also the development of an alternative media, the use of public opinion and exit polls, and the widespread circulation of sophisticated campaign literature. More generally, international actors can invest heavily in the political and economic capacity of the opposition and supportive groups. It is this approach, of course, that comes closest to the "international cabal" interpretation offered by Russian and other observers.[36]

Serbia, Slovakia, and Croatia, however, are the *only* examples in our group in which this more ambitious scenario played out, and even in those instances, it would be wrong, as we explained in Chapters 3 and 4, to summarize what transpired as a simple case – reminiscent of the Cold War and the U.S. toppling of governments in Iran, Guatemala and Chile – of the United States forcing regime change. This is because in the case of democracy assistance the United States did not act alone, but rather in close collaboration with a large group of local players, along with other international democracy promoters based in the West and in the postcommunist region itself. The victory of the opposition in the Slovak, Serbian, and Croatian elections, moreover, reflected to a significant extent the difficult, time-consuming, and often "gutsy" actions of oppositions, civil society groups, and ordinary citizens in these countries.

However, our other cases of electoral turnover (Georgia, Ukraine, and Kyrgyzstan) fall into the first category – that is, U.S. support for free and fair elections. Here, we can provide four brief examples, each of which testifies to the importance of focusing on the details of both U.S. electoral assistance and

---

[36] Knyazev, *Gosudarstvennyi perevorot*; and see the quotations offered by Bertil Nygren, "The Beauty and the Beast: When Electoral Democracy Hit Eurasia," unpublished manuscript, 2005; see also Donnacha Ó Beacháin, "Roses and Tulips: Dynamics of Regime Change in Georgia and Krygyzstan," *Journal of Communist and Transition Studies* 25:2–3 (June–September 2009), 199–226, on variations in the role of the West in seeking electoral turnovers.

the resources and goals of opposition forces. The first two are taken from our successful group of cases and the latter two from our failed group.

In Ukraine, the United States was very quick (along with the presidents of both Lithuania and Poland, but not the EU) to register its considerable disappointment with the quality of the first round of the 2004 presidential election and, thus, the official results, and to signal as well – though for the first time since the beginning of the election season – its strong support of Viktor Yushchenko, the leader of the opposition, and his allies camping on the Maidan. U.S. reactions, in this regard, were very different from those of Putin and the Russian leadership, who rushed to congratulate their candidate, Yanukovych, even before the official election results were announced. Thus, while the United States had initially focused on the relatively modest goal of supporting improved electoral procedures in Ukraine, it took a more active position after the fraudulent presidential election of 2004. Why the United States did so reflected the intersection of three aspects of the Ukrainian election. It combined, in particular, a presidential contest and, thus, a legitimate transfer of presidential power (unlike Georgia or Kyrgyzstan) with hard evidence (drawn not just from extensive vote monitoring but also from decisions taken by the Supreme Court of Ukraine) of massive electoral fraud and a likely victory by Yushchenko (evidence that was less available for, say, Armenia in 2008).

Georgia represents another variant. During the summer of 2003, there was a visit with Shevardnadze by James Baker, the former secretary of state, a close friend of the Bush family, a personal friend of the Georgian president, and, not incidentally, the head in 2000 of the Republican challenge in the battle over how to count the deeply flawed Florida ballots in the U.S. presidential election. There is no small irony in the fact that Baker's mission was to convince Shevardnadze to clean up the abysmal quality of Georgian elections. However, Shevardnadze made a series of promises he never kept, and the United States government, still relatively blind to the poor economic and political performance of the regime and to Shevardnadze's unpopularity and, at the same time, uncertain about Saakashvili, remained supportive of Shevardnadze (though George Soros, also a friend of Shevardnadze, was far more critical). Thus, while recognizing the problems with the Georgian elections, the United States did not register the kind of dissatisfaction it was to display in Ukraine a year later. If the alliance with Shevardnadze was one reason, so was the fact that the Georgian elections were for the parliament, and the primary concern of the United States was with the 2003 elections as a preparation for the presidential election scheduled for 2005. While the United States had provided significant electoral support as well as long-term support for Georgian civil society (as Table 8.5 illustrates), it did not do so because of any strong commitment to regime change, especially one that took place after a parliamentary election.[37]

---

[37] See, especially, Mitchell, *Uncertain Democracy.*

As in Georgia, so in Armenia the United States had made a significant long-term investment in democratic development. Moreover, also as in Georgia, there was a correlation, ironically, between trends in democracy assistance and trends in authoritarianism. However, the United States was not as close to the Kocharian regime, although the Armenian diaspora located in the United States was relatively tolerant of the democratic deficits of the homeland. The protests that broke out in 2003 took leaders in the United States by surprise, but the United States continued its policy of providing substantial electoral and civil society support. In the 2007 parliamentary elections, the United States assumed that improved electoral procedures constituted the first stage in improving the quality of the presidential elections that were to follow in 2008. This was a prediction that turned out to be quite off the mark, especially in view of not only the large-scale protests that broke out after that election, but also the violence the Kocharian regime used against the protesters. Despite the fact that infrastructure support through the Millennium Challenge Account was linked to electoral performance, the United States decided to dilute the standard by settling for "improved" electoral procedures over evidence of fully free and fair elections.[38] Armenia, therefore, was a case that combined, like Georgia, substantial assistance and agnosticism with respect to the question of leadership turnover. However, in Georgia there was a turnover, while in Armenia there was not.

Finally, there is the case of Azerbaijan. Here, the United States did provide more overall assistance on a per capita basis than it did to Slovakia and Ukraine and provided reasonable financial support as well for free and fair elections. Moreover, the United States, as evidenced by a visit by Madeline Albright and calls for improved electoral practices by the U.S. ambassador, Reno Harnish, and the Office for Democratic Institutions and Human Rights (which is part of the Organization for Security and Cooperation in Europe), publicly urged the regime to reform the Central Electoral Commission. These actions, however, had more impact on the opposition than they had on the regime, on U.S. policy in general toward the regime, or on U.S. reactions to the elections. In particular, U.S. support for free and fair elections – along with the powerful precedents established in Ukraine and Georgia, also post-Soviet states, of using elections to remove authoritarians from office – led opposition leaders and their followers in Azerbaijan to assume that the United States would stand with them.[39] Isa Gambar, the leader of the Musavat Party and earlier the leader of the parliament when the opposition was in power in Azerbaijan,

---

[38] Roundtable discussion with various political, cultural, and development officers at the American embassy in Yerevan, Armenia, March 9, 2007. Also see Vahe Sahakyan and Arthur Atanesyan, "Democratization in Armenia: Some Trends of Political Culture and Behavior," *Demokratizatsiya* 14:3 (Summer 2006), 347–354; and International Republican Institute, "Armenia Voter Study: Armenia National Voter Study," November 10–16, 2006, http://www.iri.org/sites/default/files/2006%20November%20Survey%20of%20Armenian%20Public%20Opinion,%20November%2010-19,%202006.pdf.

[39] Valerie Bunce and Sharon L. Wolchik, "Azerbaijan's 2005 Parliamentary Elections: A Failed Attempt at Transition," paper prepared for the workshop, Workshop on External Influences

made precisely this argument in his interview with us. He also pointed out that he had been in Ukraine during the Orange Revolution, and that he was in regular contact with the then president of Ukraine, Viktor Yushchenko. That his office sported many mementos of the Orange Revolution made his observations, as well as the details he was able to provide, very convincing.[40]

What Gambar and other opposition leaders in Azerbaijan did not fully understand in the 2003 and 2005 contests was that the United States was not a reliable political ally. This is because of Azerbaijan's energy resources (including gas as well as oil), its access through the Caspian Sea to the energy reserves of Central Asia, and, more generally, its strategic geopolitical location as a result of its borders with Iran, Armenia, Georgia, and Russia. Thus, if the United States values democracy, it also places a premium on political stability in Azerbaijan – a priority that compromised its follow-through on electoral reform.[41]

Thus, like the patterns exhibited in Table 8.5, so more nuanced treatments of U.S. democracy and governance assistance do not seem to account very well for variations in electoral outcomes. The United States did not make regime change a priority in most cases, though when it did, one leader, Lukashenka of Belarus, was able nonetheless to prevail. At the same time, the goal of regime change was not a necessary condition for electoral turnover to occur. In fact, the electoral shifts in Georgia, Ukraine, and Kyrgyzstan all took the United States by surprise.

Electoral Innovations

We can now turn to the final hypothesis we will examine in this chapter: the distinction between the relatively passive campaigns that oppositions typically run in mixed regimes and campaigns that break the mold be being creative and ambitious. The essence of this contrast has been captured well by Pavol Demeš, a Slovak NGO leader who is now European director of the German Marshall Fund of the United States. As he argued in an interview we conducted with him, there are two key ingredients to successfully unseating authoritarian leaders: one is hope, or the belief that it can be done, and the other is organization (or a strategy) to bring it about.[42]

Belief refers to moving from a well-established norm – that is, pessimism about the chances of defeating the incumbent – to a more optimistic scenario for the future among opposition groups, civil society organizations, and ordinary citizens. Such optimism is in turn linked to a series of interrelated, onerous, and often mundane election-related tasks that in quite deliberate and

---

on Democratic Transitions, Center on Democracy, Development and the Rule of Law, Stanford University, October 2008.

[40] Interview with Isa Gambar, Baku, March 7, 2007.

[41] Interview with a Department of State official conducted at the American embassy in Baku, March 9, 2007.

[42] Interview with Pavol Demeš, Washington, DC, December 1999.

creative fashion maximize the chances for an opposition victory. These strategies include, for example, not just forging a unified opposition that puts forward a single candidate, but combining this with ambitious, nationwide campaigns by the opposition; the collection and distribution of public opinion data that candidates then use to frame their appeals; and orchestration of energetic voter registration and turnout drives. Strategic innovation also includes the formation of youth movements that support political change through elections; close collaboration with civil society organizations; and creation of new organizations that have the resources in terms of money, people, and training sessions to carry out internal election monitoring, last-minute voter turnout campaigns, exit polls, and, where necessary because of electoral fraud, parallel vote tabulation and postelection protests.

In Table 8.6, we apply this list of activities to our two sets of elections. Here, we find for the first time in this chapter a sharply-etched contrast between the elections that took place in Slovakia, Croatia, Georgia, Ukraine, and Kyrgyzstan from 1998 to 2005 and the elections that were held from 2003 to 2008 in Armenia, Azerbaijan, and Belarus. Thus, while all the electoral breakthroughs feature extraordinary efforts to win power on the part of oppositions and their domestic and international allies (though this generalization applies less well to Kyrgyzstan), the elections in Armenia, Azerbaijan, and Belarus, although featuring a united opposition and producing significant protests, did not exhibit a similar utilization by the opposition of such sophisticated electoral strategies.[43] This conclusion, moreover, is further supported by two other differences between our cases. One is that, despite opposition cohesion in all of the presidential contests, there were in fact more candidates in the failed than in the successful electoral challenges to authoritarian rule. The other is that the difference between high- and low-energy contests translated into differences in electoral turnout – with high turnout, we must remember, testifying to the key role of youth movements and local electoral-focused civil society groups in getting alienated segments of the population to cast their votes. This dynamic was particularly important in Slovakia, Croatia, Serbia, and Georgia. For example, turnout in Croatia moved from 68.8 percent in 1995 to 76.5 percent in 2000 and in Yugoslavia (Serbia) from 65 percent to 71 percent. By contrast, it is telling that turnout in Azerbaijan fell from 68 percent in 2003 to 40.5 percent in 2005.

What makes this contrast between hard-fought and elaborately planned electoral challenges to authoritarian rule and "politics as usual" even more compelling as an explanation of electoral stability and change are two more considerations. First, the defining characteristics of the successful elections as detailed in Table 8.6 were distinctive to them in comparison to earlier contests

---

[43] Scott Radnitz, "A Horse of a Different Color: Revolution and Regression in Kyrgyzstan," in *Waves and Troughs of Post-Communist Reform*, ed. Valerie Bunce, Michael McFaul, and Kathryn Stoner-Weiss (Cambridge: Cambridge University Press, 2009), 300–324; see also Borbieva, "Development in the Kyrgyz Republic."

TABLE 8.6. *Electoral strategies: oppositions and civil society groups*

Country	Unity of Opposition	Ambitious Campaigns[a]	Voter Registration Drives[b]	Voter Turnout Drives[b]	Pressures on Election Commissions[c]	Collaboration among Civil Society, Youth Movements, and Opposition	Public Opinion Polls[d]	Exit Polls[b]	Parallel Voter Tabulation[b]
Croatia	+	+	+	+	+	+	+	+	+
Georgia	+	+	+	+	+	+	+	+	+
Kyrgyzstan	+	+	-	-	+	+	+	°	-
Serbia	+	+	+	+	+	+	+	+	+
Slovakia	+	+	+	+	+	+	+	+	+
Ukraine	+	+	+	+	+	+	+	+	+
Armenia	+	-	-	-	+	-	-	+	-
Azerbaijan	+	-	-	-	-	-	-	°	-
Belarus	+	-	-	-	-	-	-	-	-

[a] This includes nationwide campaigns and extensive use of the media and distribution of campaign literature.

[b] These were typically carried out by local (but often internationally funded) civil society organizations such as the Liberty Institute and Kmara in Georgia and Otpor, CeSID, and Izlaz in Serbia.

[c] This was largely done by the U.S. government and the OSCE.

[d] Such polls were typically collaborative efforts by local experts and organizations such as IRI and NDI.

° In Serbia, exit polls were not allowed, and in Azerbaijan in 2005 they were severely flawed, in part because of regime involvement. See Khadija Ismayilova, "Azerbaijan: Debate over Exit Polls Threatens Confidence in Election Results," Oct. 5, 2005, http://www.eurasianet.org/departments/insight/articles/eav100505.shtml. In Armenia, exit polls (conducted by a British firm) were used in 2008. See Emil Danielyan, "Armenia: Planned Presidential Poll Causes Controversy," January 7, 2008, http://www.eurasianet.org/departments/insight/articles/eav010708.shtml, and "Exit Poll Gives Sarkisian Victory in Armenian Election," February 18, 2008, www.alernet.org/thenews/newsdesk/L199517.html.

Sources: Interviews. See Appendix.

in the same countries. While bits and pieces of this ensemble of electoral strategies appeared earlier, such as some use of vote monitoring, public opinion polls, and, in a few cases, exit polls, most of the ensemble that came together in the successful elections constituted fully new and fully coordinated additions to the previous electoral repertoire of oppositions and civil society groups. It was precisely this contrast that emerged, for instance, in our case studies of Slovakia, Serbia, Ukraine, and Georgia. For example, in Serbia prior to 2000 the opposition had never run a nationwide campaign; the opposition usually ignored opinion polls and had virtually no contact with civil society organizations, especially outside the capital and the larger cities; and civil society organizations were in turn alienated from the opposition and felt that their role should be an apolitical one, which meant separation from opposition parties. In addition, national-level electoral contests had never engaged young people or featured street theater, marches, rallies, posters, platform statements, parallel vote tabulation, internal election monitoring, voter registration drives, and voter turnout campaigns. All this is not to mention another key feature of the Serbian and Ukrainian political dynamic – attempts by young people and leaders of the opposition, who anticipated the need for protests after the election in order to ensure a transfer of office, to win over the police and the military. These wide-ranging activities were unprecedented, largely because of how much coordination they required and how demanding they were in general, especially in the context of highly repressive regimes, which, among other things, in the Serbian case did not allow external vote monitoring.

THE ENDOGENEITY CHALLENGE

Our central conclusion in this chapter is that variation in electoral results can be explained by whether oppositions adopted the electoral model. When they did, they won power. It could be countered, however, that the relationship between implementation of the electoral model and electoral outcomes is endogenous. Thus, the question before us is whether the electoral model is the cause of the opposition's success, as we have argued, or whether adoption of this model reflects the impact of other factors, such as the vulnerability of the regime, which expands opportunities for electoral turnover, gives the opposition strong incentives to mount an ambitious electoral campaign, and encourages the international community to support the opposition both in words and by the transfer of significant resources. This is precisely the kind of structural argument that Steven Levitsky and Lucan Way make, for example, in their comparative study of the rise and evolution of competitive authoritarian regimes.[44]

We are not persuaded, however, by this rival interpretation of the sources of electoral stability and change. First, as we demonstrated earlier in this chapter,

---

[44] Steven Levitsky and Lucan Way, *Competitive Authoritarianism: Hybrid Regimes after the Cold War* (Cambridge: Cambridge University Press, 2010).

a variety of political and economic indicators of regime context and regime strength fail to account in a systematic way for electoral outcomes. Thus, in direct contrast to the claim about endogeneity, oppositions in our cases were in fact no more likely to adopt the electoral model when the regime was more vulnerable – for example, when economic performance plummeted, when the regime was more open, when there was a history of governmental turnover and popular protests, or when the United States made regime change a priority and/or provided substantial democracy and governance assistance – than when the regime was, by these and other measures, in a more secure position. This conclusion holds even when we focus our attention on two factors that are often used to indicate regime weakness and to explain regime collapse and regime transition – that is, the defection of elites from the ruling circle and the defection, in particular, of the police, the security forces, and the military. On the one hand, the ruling party in Georgia disintegrated prior to the 2003 election, and both Saakashvili of Georgia and Yushchenko of Ukraine, the victorious presidential candidates of the opposition in these two countries, had once been part of the Georgian and Ukrainian governments. On the other hand, there were no significant defections from the Socialist Party in Serbia leading up to the 2000 election. Even more important, our interviews with members of the opposition and civil society groups stressed time and again the fact that no one within the community of democratic activists in Serbia, Kyrgyzstan, Georgia, or Ukraine knew beforehand how the police, the internal security forces, and the military would respond to stolen elections and the popular protests that followed. In addition, no one felt that he or she could predict with any certainty how the other pillars of these regimes would react once the dual election results were announced – for example, the Orthodox Church (which defected in Serbia, but not in Georgia), the media (which defected in Ukraine, but not in Serbia), and the Constitutional Court (which defected in Ukraine, but not in Serbia). Even if we could establish a clear pattern of defections, moreover, we would still face a problem with attributing too much explanatory power to this variable. Because defections came so late in many of our cases, it is hard to argue that they were a cause of regime change. Instead, they were an important component of the regime transition dynamic itself. In this sense, defection rates suffer from serious endogeneity problems. We have also argued throughout this book that mixed regimes are fluid formations that send out contradictory and ever-changing signals. This means that it is very hard for citizens and opposition groups to read the strength of a mixed regime and to adjust their behavior accordingly. At the same time, regimes that straddle democracy and dictatorship provide very poor information about the extent of public support for the regime and opposition groups. The political "fog" in which everyone operates, therefore, means that electoral outcomes are unlikely to be driven by contrasting takes – and relatively consensual ones, at that – on the regime's future. Moreover, even small variations in how opposition leaders read regimes can make a big difference. To provide one example: in our interviews, some opposition leaders saw regime vulnerability as a good reason for collaborative ventures, largely because they assumed that they needed every vote they could get, whereas others, operating on the basis of a somewhat more optimistic reading of their electoral prospects, felt that collaboration was a bad idea, because it would force them to share the spoils of victory.

A third problem with the endogeneity critique of the electoral model claim is that, if citizens reject the regime, it does not automatically – or, indeed, even usually – follow that they will then embrace the opposition. As we have noted throughout this book, the inability of the opposition to win elections and the way the opposition had conducted itself often meant that citizens in mixed regimes disliked the opposition and doubted that it either could or should win office. Thus, authoritarian leaders often maintain power in mixed regimes not because they are popular, powerful or a combination of the two, but rather because they benefit from the absence of viable political alternatives.

This leads to a final reason why the concern about endogeneity is misplaced. The electoral model performs a variety of distinctive functions that can be considered prerequisites for an opposition victory. For example, it is telling that most of the breakthrough elections were very close and that they were decided, as a result, by the votes of young people who had not participated in elections in the past and older people who were alienated from the regime. It was precisely these two constituencies that were targeted in voter registration and turnout drives. More generally, a major function of the electoral model is to redistribute critical resources from the regime to the opposition. This is accomplished by activities that advertise the deficiencies of the regime, convince publics that change is possible and that their participation is necessary to make it happen, and transform a once discredited and weak opposition into an effective contender for political power. These are changes that structural factors, for reasons that we have already noted, cannot accomplish.

These contributions of the electoral model, plus its capacity to mobilize and organize large-scale popular protests when elections are rigged, also help explain why the police and security forces failed to defend the regimes in Georgia, Serbia, Kyrgyzstan, and Ukraine. While it is true that in the final analysis the defection of these groups from the regime was decisive, it is also true that these key defections are hard to imagine in the absence of growing evidence, courtesy of the model, that the regime was weak and corrupt and that the opposition had significant support. In our view, therefore, the electoral model stands by itself as a factor explaining electoral stability and change.

CONCLUSIONS

The purpose of this chapter has been to merge the eleven elections that have served as the focus of the case studies presented in Chapters 3 through 7 in order to test two sets of hypotheses developed in Chapter 2 about why elections in mixed regimes would be more or less likely to lead to the empowerment of the democratic opposition. We began our assessment by examining the impact of factors that tap important aspects of the regime context and the strength of the government and the opposition on the eve of the elections – for example, economic development and growth, the strength of civil society, long-term trends in popular protests and turnover in governments, and defections from the ruling circle. As we discovered, none of these variables seem to differentiate well between electoral continuity and turnover. In this sense, the vulnerability of mixed regimes did not tell us very much about the likelihood of opposition victories.

These findings led us to compare electoral episodes. Here, we found that, while many of the distinctions among elections were as unhelpful as our structural variables, one factor provided a clear line of demarcation between our two sets of elections. The key issue was whether the opposition, in collaboration with civil society groups and regional and Western-based democracy activists, used an ensemble of sophisticated, intricately planned, and historically unprecedented electoral strategies to win office, or whether opposition parties and candidates worked separately and settled for a more passive approach to contesting the election. Thus, the key was not simply unifying the opposition, but also running ambitious political campaigns, orchestrating elaborate voter registration and voter turnout drives, and putting in place electoral monitoring procedures that in combination made oppositions more effective and more politically attractive to voters. These electoral innovations – which we summarized by the term "the electoral model" – created a widespread sense that victory was possible and made it much harder, as a result, for the regime to win the election or to remain in office after it had lost. The successful defeat of authoritarian rulers, therefore, while exploiting regime vulnerability in certain ways (such as the most general one, the regime's toleration of competition), rested in both more or less vulnerable and more or less democratic regimes on the deployment of a set of new, well-planned, detailed, and sometimes dangerous strategies for winning political power.

This conclusion, however, introduces several new issues that need to be addressed before we can be confident that we have a satisfactory explanation of electoral continuity and change in mixed regimes. One is explaining why these strategies in particular proved to be so politically effective. Put differently: what functions did they serve? Another is why the opposition adopted these strategies while the regime failed to do so. Yet another question is why this particular set of strategies was adopted and, as Table 8.6 reminds us, adopted by so many oppositions in the region. Finally, as Armenia, Azerbaijan, and Belarus remind us, and as earlier elections in our turnover cases also testify, not all the oppositions in the region ran such ambitious campaigns. The puzzle here is: why not?

In Chapters 9 and 10, we provide answers to each of these questions. As we will discover, the key insight is the important role in electoral outcomes in mixed regimes of the cross-national diffusion of an innovative tool kit of electoral strategies and techniques, the electoral model.

9

The Electoral Model

Evolution and Elements

> Politics is the art of getting people to vote for you. It's applicable all over the world. If it wasn't, I wouldn't have a job.
>
> David Dettman, political consultant who worked
> on party development in Ukraine and then
> in Baghdad, Tikrit, and Hilla, Iraq[1]

> The citizen is not a constant political actor.
>
> Gabriel Almond and Sidney Verba[2]

In the previous chapter, we compared our eleven elections in order to assess a series of hypotheses about why oppositions in mixed regimes would succeed or fail in their quest to win power. We concluded that the vulnerability of the regime on the eve of the elections was less helpful in explaining electoral results than what happened *during* the elections. In particular, the key distinction that emerged was whether oppositions and their allies ran ambitious or modest political campaigns. Thus, oppositions won when they took such innovative actions as forming collaborative ties with each other; running creative, nationwide campaigns; carrying out significant voter registration and turnout drives; and making use, where possible, of international and domestic vote monitoring, professional exit polls, and parallel vote tabulation. While the oppositions in Slovakia, Croatia, Serbia, Georgia, and Ukraine used these and other innovative strategies when they ran for office, their counterparts in Armenia, Azerbaijan, and Belarus took only a few of these crucial steps – for example, forming in every case an opposition bloc.

The purpose of this chapter is to step back from these findings and focus our attention on this ensemble of electoral strategies – which we term the

---

[1] George Packer, *The Assassin's Gate: America in Iraq* (New York: Farrar, Straus and Giroux, 2005), 410.

[2] Gabriel Almond and Sidney Verba, *The Civil Culture: Political Attitudes and Democracy in Five Nations* (Princeton, NJ: Princeton University Press, 1963), 347.

electoral model.[3] While the goal of this model is simple, its implementation is in fact devilishly difficult – as we saw in Chapters 3 through 7. Part of the problem is purely political – for example, how to level a political playing field in mixed regimes where authoritarian incumbents have significant resources at their disposal to win elections, and how to get citizens who are skeptical about the prospects for political change and alienated from the regime, and often from the opposition, to go to the trouble of registering to vote, supporting the opposition, and, if necessary, taking to the streets to defend the opposition's victory in the event that the regime refuses to abide by the election results.[4] There is another aspect of the electoral model that motivates, but also complicates, its implementation. As Robert Pastor has astutely observed, "At one and the same time, elections are both the supreme political act and a complicated administrative exercise."[5] Energy and creativity, in short, are not enough. Attention to the technical side of elections is also critical.

We begin our discussion of the electoral model by laying out the premises underlying it and identifying its core components. We then discuss the evolution of this approach to democratic change – a discussion that helps us gain insight into the global origins and reach of this collection of electoral strategies. The chapter closes with an evaluation of the many benefits of using the electoral model to defeat authoritarian leaders or their anointed successors.

DEMOCRATIZING ELECTIONS: PREMISES

The electoral model is based upon two simple but powerful premises. One is that elections provide ideal sites for democratic change. It has often been observed, as we argued in the first chapter, that democracy should not be reduced to elections, and that democratization has many requirements aside from the holding of regular and competitive elections. We agree with this observation, but recognize at the same time that democratic progress is strongly associated with the electoral calendar.[6]

---

[3] The term "model" has been used in a variety of ways. We use this term in accordance with its definition in dictionaries; that is, "a standard or example for imitation or comparison." See http://dictionary.reference.com/browse/model.

[4] Interview with Kenneth Wollack, Washington, DC, May 12, 2010.

[5] Robert Pastor, "A Brief History of Electoral Commissions," in *The Self-Restraining State: Power and Accountability in New Democracies*, ed. Andreas Schedler, Larry Diamond, and Marc F. Plattner (Boulder, CO: Lynne Rienner Publishers, 1999), 75.

[6] Emily Beaulieu and Susan D. Hyde, "In the Shadow of Democracy Promotion: Strategic Manipulation, International Observers, and Election Boycotts," *Comparative Political Studies* 42:3 (March 2009), 392–415; Jan Teorell and Axel Hadenius, "Elections as Levers of Democracy: A Global Inquiry," in *Democratization by Elections: A New Mode of Transition?*, ed. Staffan Lindberg (Baltimore: Johns Hopkins University Press, 2009), 77–100; Stephen Levitsky and Lucan Way, "Competitive Authoritarian Regimes: The Evolution of Post-Soviet Competitive Authoritarianism 1992–2005," paper presented at the Conference on Postcommunist Resilience, Dartmouth University, May 25–26, 2007; and Valerie Bunce and Sharon L. Wolchik, "Mixed Regimes in Postcommunist Eurasia: Tipping Democratic and Tipping Authoritarian," in *Hybrid Regimes: International Anchoring and Domestic Dynamics in Post-Soviet States*, ed. Elena Barcani (Florence, Italy: European Press Academic Publishing, 2010), 57–86.

Elections are in a position to have these effects for several reasons. One is that both elections and international election monitoring have become ubiquitous.[7] For example, it has been estimated that by 2002 only 8 countries out of more than 190 in the world had failed to hold national elections, and that by 2004 nearly 80 percent of all elections held outside Western democracies were internationally observed.[8] Elections are also a core focus of U.S. democracy assistance. Despite the small size of this category within the overall allocation for democracy assistance in the USAID budget (usually around 5 percent),[9] electoral support is in fact more strongly associated statistically with improvements in democratic performance than investments in civil society, rule of law, and democratic institutions.[10] Third, elections have the advantage (which we will elaborate later) of being short-term political events that provide optimal conditions for citizen mobilization.[11] As Tea Tutberidze, a member of the Liberty Institute in Georgia and an activist in the 2003 election that ended the Shevardnadze era, succinctly observed in our interview with her, "It is easier to motivate protests when there are elections."[12] Finally, elections are viewed by citizens, especially in new democracies, as a defining feature of the democratic experience.[13]

[7] Susan Hyde, "Observing Norms: Explaining the Causes and Consequences of Internationally Monitored Elections" (Ph.D. dissertation, Department of Political Science, University of California San Diego, 2006); Eric C. Bjornlund, *Beyond Free and Fair: Monitoring Elections and Building Democracy* (Washington, DC: Woodrow Wilson Center Press, 2004); Judith Kelley, "Assessing the Complex Evolution of Norms: The Rise of International Election Monitoring," *International Organization* 62:2 (April 2008), 221–255.

[8] Beaulieu and Hyde, "In the Shadow of Democracy Promotion"; Hyde, "Observing Norms."

[9] See Lincoln Abraham Mitchell, *Uncertain Democracy: U.S. Foreign Policy and Georgia's Rose Revolution* (Philadelphia: University of Pennsylvania Press, 2009).

[10] Steven F. Finkel, Aníbal Pérez-Liñán, Mitchell A. Seligson, and Dinorah Azpuru, *Effects of US Foreign Assistance on Democracy Building: Results of a Cross-National Quantitative Study*, Final Report, USAID, Version No. 34 (January 12, 2006), http://www.usaid.gov/our_work/democracy_and_governance/publications/pdfs/impact_of_democracy_assistance.pdf; Steven E. Finkel, Aníbal Pérez-Liñán, and Mitchell Seligson, "The Effects of U.S. Foreign Assistance on Democracy Building," *World Politics* 59:3 (April 2007), 404–439.

[11] See, especially, Doug McAdam, Sidney Tarrow, and Charles Tilly, "Comparative Perspectives on Contentious Politics," in *Comparative Politics: Rationality, Culture, and Structure*, 2nd edition, ed. Mark Irving Lichbach and Alan S. Zuckerman (Cambridge: Cambridge University Press, 2009), 260–290, on "temporal cueing;" Doug McAdam and Sidney Tarrow, "Ballots and Barricades: On the Reciprocal Relationship between Elections and Social Movements," paper presented at the conference Hot Models and Hard Conflicts: The Agenda of Comparative Political Science in the 21st Century, a symposium in honor of Hanspeter Kriesi, Center for Comparative and International Studies (CIS), Zurich, Switzerland, June, 26, 2009; Guillermo Trejo, "The Political Foundations of Ethnic Mobilization and Territorial Conflict in Mexico, 1975–2000," in *Federalism and Territorial Cleavages*, ed. Ugo Amoretti and Nancy Bermeo (Baltimore: Johns Hopkins University Press, 2004), 355–386.

[12] Interview with Tea Tutberidze, Tbilisi, October 13, 2005.

[13] Robert Mattes and Michael Bratton, "Learning about Democracy in Africa: Awareness, Performance and Experience," *American Journal of Political Science* 51:1 (January 2007), 192–217; Russell J. Dalton, Doh L. Shin, and Willy Jou, *Popular Conceptions of the Meaning of Democracy: Democratic Understanding in Unlikely Places*, Center for the

Indeed, the close linkage in the public mind between elections and democracy is a major reason why even leaders in communist regimes, in search of domestic legitimacy and concerned with identifying mechanisms to pressure local elites to improve the delivery of public goods, often held elections and introduced electoral reforms.[14] This association is also why elections have become a fixture in other types of authoritarian regimes[15] and why, at the same time, accusations of electoral fraud have been so successful in stimulating public protests.[16] For example, Robert Pastor has identified eighty-one cases of mass protests against electoral fraud during the 1990s – a dynamic that has continued in more recent years not just in Armenia, Azerbaijan, Belarus, Georgia, Kyrgyzstan, Serbia, and Ukraine, but also in Ethiopia, Ghana, the Ivory Coast, Kenya, Mexico, Nicaragua, Peru, Togo, Zimbabwe, and, most recently, Iran.[17]

Study of Democracy Paper, University of California at Irvine (May 18, 2007), at http://escholarship.org/uc/item/2j74b860; but see Frederick Charles Schaffer, *Democracy in Translation: Understanding Politics in an Unfamiliar Culture* (Ithaca, NY: Cornell University Press, 1998).

[14] Barnabas Racz, "Political Participation and Developed Socialism: The Hungarian Elections of 1985," *Soviet Studies* 39:1 (January 1987), 40–62; Victor Zaslavsky and Robert Brym, "The Functions of Elections in the USSR," *Soviet Studies* 30:3 (July 1978), 362–371.

[15] Ellen Lust Okar, "Divided They Rule: The Management and Manipulation of Political Opposition," *Comparative Politics* 36:2 (January 2004), 159–179; Ellen Lust Okar, "Elections under Authoritarianism: Preliminary Lessons from Jordan," unpublished paper, Department of Political Science, Yale University, 2005; Ellen Lust Okar, "Opposition and Economic Crises in Jordan and Morocco," in *Authoritarianism in the Middle East: Regimes and Resistance*, ed. Marsha Pripstein Posusney and Michelle Penner Angriste (Boulder, CO: Lynne Rienner Publishers, 2005), 143–168; Ellen Lust Okar, "Legislative Elections in Hegemonic Authoritarian Regimes: Competitive Clientelism and Resistance to Democratization," in *Democratization by Elections: A New Mode of Transition?*, ed. Staffan Lindberg (Baltimore: Johns Hopkins University Press, 2009), 226–245; Lisa Blaydes, "Authoritarian Elections and Elite Management: Theory and Evidence from Egypt," unpublished manuscript, April 2008; Jennifer Gandhi, and Ellen Lust Okar, "Elections under Authoritarianism," *Annual Review of Political Science* 12 (2009), 403–422.

[16] Joshua A. Tucker, "Enough! Electoral Fraud, Collective Action Problems, and the Second Wave of Post-Communist Democratic Revolutions," *Perspectives on Politics* 5:3 (September 2007), 535–551; Mark R. Thompson and Philipp Kuntz, "Stolen Elections: The Case of the Serbian October," *Journal of Democracy* 15:4 (2004), 159–172; Philipp Kuntz and Mark R. Thompson, "More than Just the Final Straw: Stolen Elections as Revolutionary Triggers," *Comparative Politics* 41:3 (April 2009), 253–272; and Pastor, "A Brief History of Electoral Commissions."

[17] See, for example, Michael Kamber, "In an Untamed Tide of Violence, Bystanders Die," *New York Times*, May 5, 2005, at www.nytimes.com/2005/05/05/international/africa/05togo. html; Michael Wines, "Grass-Roots Effort Aims to Upend Mugabe in Zimbabwe," *New York Times*, March 27, 2005, at www.nytimes.com/2005/03/27/international/27zimbabwe.html. The Kenyan presidential election in late December 2007 and the violent protests that followed remind us, however, that fraudulent elections can be used for a variety of political purposes. In this case, it was not just that both the incumbent and the challenger tried to steal the election; it was also that there appeared to be preparations to use accusations of electoral fraud in order to carry out ethnic cleansing.

This fact leads to the second premise underlying the electoral model. While elections can function as agents of democratic change, their capacity to play this role is quite limited in mixed regimes. Put simply: it is extremely hard to defeat authoritarian leaders. While leaders in such regimes are vulnerable for the simple reason that "it is difficult to strike a balance between the regime's substantive authoritarian characteristics and its procedural democratic ones,"[18] authoritarian incumbents nonetheless enjoy, we must remember, considerable advantages when competing for power against opposition forces.[19] As a result, oppositions cannot succeed in winning power unless they pay considerable attention to both the political and the technical side of elections.[20] The obstacles in the way of defeating incumbent authoritarians also mean that electoral success depends upon careful planning and long-term learning. Success may seem both sudden and fortuitous, as Robert Benjamin argued in the interview we conducted with him, but it is usually a product of careful attention to details, coordination, and lessons culled from past failures.[21]

Just as critical in surmounting the obstacles to an opposition victory is using the occasion of an election to bring together diverse constituencies that can unite, at the least, in their support of free and fair elections and, at most, around changes in political leadership and policy. Here, we do not refer just to the unity of the opposition – which will be discussed in greater detail later. We also refer to a larger process: the formation of transnational networks that include local oppositions and civil society groups, along with electoral activists from the region and international democracy promoters. As with most cases of large-scale and successful social movements, as McAdam, Tarrow, and Tilly have persuasively argued, brokerage is vital: the forging of social connections among previously unlinked persons or sites.[22] Such coalitions – or what are also called networks – have three benefits: they encourage the opposition to reach out to new constituencies and gather new ideas and strategies; they provide new resources to the opposition; and they boost the confidence of the opposition. In all of these cases, we must note, the international

---

[18] Thompson and Kuntz, "Stolen Elections."

[19] See, for instance, Marsha Pripstein Posusney, "Enduring Authoritarianism: Middle East Lessons for Comparative Theory," *Comparative Politics* 36:2 (January 2004), 127–138; Ellen Lust Okar, "Divided They Rule"; Henry Hale, "Regime Cycles, Democracy, Autocracy and Revolution in Post-Soviet Eurasia," *World Politics* 58:1 (October 2005), 133–165; Henry Hale, "Democracy or Autocracy on the March? The Colored Revolutions as Normal Dynamics of Patronal Presidentialism," *Communist and Postcommunist Studies* 39:3 (September 2006), 305–329; Lucan Way, "Authoritarian State Building and the Sources of Regime Competitiveness in the Fourth Wave: The Cases of Belarus, Moldova, Russia, and Ukraine," *World Politics* 57:2 (January 2005), 231–261.

[20] Larry Diamond, "Thinking about Hybrid Regimes," *Journal of Democracy* 13:2 (April 2002), 24.

[21] Interview with Robert Benjamin, Washington, DC, April 9, 2010. Kenneth Wollack, for example, quoted a member of the Chilean opposition: "Even if we lose, nothing will be the same." Interview with Kenneth Wollack, Washington, DC, May 12, 2010.

[22] McAdam, Tarrow, and Tilly, "Comparative Perspectives on Contentious Politics."

community plays a role. As Pavol Demeš and Joerg Forbrig have observed about the "color revolutions" in postcommunist Europe and Eurasia: for the opposition "an important part of the learning process was interaction with international partners."[23]

OPPOSITION UNITY

What are the main components of the electoral model? The first, which has received a good deal of attention from scholars interested in why authoritarian leaders sometimes lose power, is the formation of a unified democratic opposition.[24] Thus, a major goal of the transnational network supporting democratic change and free and fair elections is encouraging a fragmented opposition – which is the norm in mixed regimes – to work together to win political power. Oppositions can join forces, for instance, by pooling resources, forming formal alliances, and/or agreeing on common candidates to run for parliament or a common candidate to run for president. Such collaborative ventures are critical for several reasons. Most obviously, they reduce the number of wasted votes. Less obviously, as John Crist and his associates have observed "successful coalition-building shows opponents, potential supporters, and outside observers that the movement has momentum."[25] Collaboration, therefore, sends out a clear signal that the opposition is serious about contesting power, and that it has the commitment and the political skills to form an effective government. This is a message, moreover, that reaches beyond the borders of the state. Just as it helps persuade skeptical citizens and civil society groups to take a chance on the opposition, so it encourages external democracy activists to make free and fair elections – and sometimes support for the opposition, in particular – a high priority.[26]

[23] Pavol Demeš and Joerg Forbrig, "Civic Action and Democratic Power Shifts: On Strategies and Resources," in *Reclaiming Democracy: Civil Society and Electoral Change in Central and Eastern Europe*, ed. Joerg Forbrig and Pavol Demeš (Washington, DC: German Marshall Fund, 2007), 177; Ray Jennings, *Serbia's Bulldozer Revolution: Evaluating Internal and External Factors in the Successful Democratic Breakthrough in Serbia*, CDDRL Working Paper No. 105, Center on Democracy, Development and the Rule of Law, Freeman Spogli Institute for International Studies, Stanford University (March 2009).

[24] See, especially, Vladimir Gelman, "Political Opposition in Russia: A Dying Species?," *Post-Soviet Affairs* 21:3 (July–September 2005), 237–238; Nicolas Van de Walle, *Why Do Oppositions Coalesce in Electoral Autocracies?*, Einaudi Center for International Studies Working Paper Series, No. 01–05, Cornell University (August 2005); Nicolas Van de Walle, "Tipping Games: When Do Opposition Parties Coalesce?," in *Electoral Authoritarianism: The Dynamics of Unfree Competition*, ed. Andreas Schedler (Boulder, CO: Lynne Rienner Publishers, 2006), 77–94; Marc Morjé Howard and Philip G. Roessler, "Liberalizing Electoral Outcomes in Competitive Authoritarian Regimes," *American Journal of Political Science* 50:2 (April 2006), 362–368.

[25] John T. Crist, Harriet Hentges, Daniel Paul Serwer, and United States Institute of Peace, *Strategic Nonviolent Conflict: Lessons from the Past, Ideas for the Future*, Special Report Vol. 87 (Washington, DC: United States Institute of Peace, 2002), 6.

[26] Mitchell, *Uncertain Democracy*.

The role of opposition unity in democratic change, however, is more complicated than many analysts have recognized. One issue is methodological. Does the unification of the opposition lead to the defeat of dictators (which is the usual interpretation), or do the enhanced prospects for future success – prompted, for example, by crises in authoritarian rule – create the necessary incentives for collaboration among opposition groups?[27] Another problem is that we in fact know very little in a detailed empirical sense about why oppositions resist cooperation (aside from the familiar commentaries in the media about conflicts over personality and policy) and, thus, the circumstances that might encourage them to change direction and work together. Most studies of oppositions are either profiles of how specific oppositions behave in a given country or, more commonly, analyses that rely on deductive reasoning to draw generalizations.[28]

The interviews we conducted with opposition leaders, international democracy promoters, and leaders of civil society organizations active in Armenia, Azerbaijan, Belarus, Croatia, Georgia, Romania, Serbia, Slovakia, and Ukraine revealed that the formation of a unified opposition is the most difficult piece of the electoral model to put into place.[29] This is hardly surprising. For example, in the 2003 Armenian elections, more than one hundred parties were registered – which works out to roughly one party per twenty thousand people.[30] Thus, oppositions in the postcommunist world, as in other regions where competitive politics is relatively new, tend to be extremely fragmented. This fragmentation often persists even in the face of the familiar and understandable pattern, over the course of repeated elections, of smaller parties either disappearing or merging in response to accumulated failures to win seats.[31] At the same time, as political developments in Georgia after 2003, in Ukraine after 2004, and in Serbia after 2000 remind us, cooperation, even when it produces political payoffs, can nonetheless be fleeting. After winning through unity, opposition parties can very quickly return to old habits and go their separate ways – which was also true, we must remember, of the large united fronts in the Baltic states, Poland, East Germany, Czechoslovakia,

---

[27] Van de Walle, "Tipping Games"; Nicolas van de Walle, "Meet the New Boss: Same as the Old Boss: The Evolution of Political Clientelism in Africa," in *Patrons, Clients and Policies: Patterns of Democratic Accountability and Political Competition*, ed. Herbert Kitschelt and Steven I. Wilkinson (Cambridge: Cambridge University Press, 2007), 50–67.

[28] An exception to this generalization is Kenneth F. Greene, *Why Dominant Parties Lose: Mexico's Democracy in Comparative Perspective* (Cambridge: Cambridge University Press, 2007).

[29] Interviews with Kenneth Wollack, Washington DC, May 12, 2010; Robert Benjamin, Washington, DC, April 9, 2010; Barbara Haig, Washington, DC, May 14, 2010; and Carl Gershman, Washington, DC, May 14, 2010.

[30] Hyde, "Observing Norms."

[31] Karen Dawisha and Stephen Deets, "Political Learning in Post-Communist Elections," *East European Politics and Societies* 20:4 (November 1, 2006), 691–728; Jack Bielasiak, "Party Competition in Emerging Democracies: Representation and Effectiveness in Post-Communism and Beyond," *Democratization* 12:3 (June 2005), 331–356.

and Slovenia that brought down communism and won the first competitive elections after communism. Indeed, at least some of the reasons behind these dynamics were the same. While a common enemy helped unify both the communist and the postcommunist opposition, success in defeating that enemy removed some of the incentives to cooperate, especially when the issue on the table shifted from bringing down the old regime to jockeying for position and payoffs in the new one. These divisions, moreover, grew out of continuing tensions among members of the coalition, which the united opposition fought hard to hide from the electorate in Serbia, Georgia, and Ukraine, in particular.[32]

We also discovered from our interviews that, while a number of factors seem to have influenced the decision to collaborate, expectations about the political vulnerability of the incumbent – that is, the endogeneity argument sketched earlier – played a relatively minor role. Instead, collaboration seemed to grow out of lessons drawn from earlier experiments in cooperation, usually in local elections; broad recognition, based upon data provided by pollsters, that one opposition candidate in particular was more popular with voters than others and, therefore, the opposition's "best hope"; and considerable pressures exerted on opposition leaders by youth organizations and, more generally, by transnational democracy assistance networks to pool resources, candidates, and campaigns. Indeed, in many of the interviews we conducted with members of the international democracy assistance community, the common refrain was their frustration with repeated attempts to help heal divisions among opposition parties.[33] This argument was also put particularly forcefully by Isa Gambar, the leader of the Musavat Party in Azerbaijan.[34]

There are two critical implications we can draw from the significant role of external agents in these processes. One is that, while authoritarian leaders were viewed as vulnerable (as they had been viewed in the past as well), they were hardly seen, especially in light of their often long tenure in office and the lengths to which they were willing to go to remain in power, as "pushovers." Thus, the assumption was that victory was far from guaranteed, and that collaboration had the possible – but only possible – effect of improving prospects

---

[32] Mitchell, *Uncertain Democracy*; interviews with Nenad Konstantinović, Belgrade, April 15, 2005; Florian Bieber, Belgrade, April 10, 2005; Marko Blagojević, Belgrade, April 11, 2005; Suzana Grubješić, Belgrade, April 11, 2005; Mark Mullen, Tbilisi, October 14, 2005; and Marina Muskhelishvili, Tbilisi, October 15, 2005.

[33] Interviews with Daniel Calingaert, Washington, DC, July 19, 2005; Ivan Vejvoda, Belgrade, April 11, 2005; Gregory Simpson, Belgrade, April 13, 2005; Mike Staresinic, Belgrade, April 15, 2005; Mark Mullen, Tbilisi, October 14, 2005; Andrew Bennett, Yerevan, March 12, 2007; Chedomir Flego, Yerevan, March 14, 2007; Alex Sadar, Yerevan, March 14, 2007; Keneshbek Sainazarov, Yerevan, March 14, 2007; Gavin Helf, Yerevan, March 9 and 10, 2007; Amy Schultz, Baku, March 6, 2007; Daniel Blessington, Baku, March 5, 2007; and Dallas Frohrib, Baku, March 6, 2007.

[34] Interview in Baku, March 7, 2007.

for success. The other is that the international community in particular was signaling through the attention it gave to the opposition that it supported a strong electoral challenge to authoritarians. This message was particularly important in Serbia, where the West had ignored the success of the opposition in coming together (which is what its name, "Zajedno," meant) in 1996–97 to compete in local elections, to win many important posts, and to launch large protests for close to three months in response to Milošević's refusal to let the opposition take office.[35]

Several other themes that developed in our interviews were just as revealing about opposition politics. One is the fact that opposition leaders had very different readings of the vulnerability of the regime and their prospects for winning power. Some saw the regime as becoming more and more vulnerable, but others were more skeptical, in part because of inaccurate forecasts in the past. This is far from surprising, because the power of mixed regimes in fact is very hard to read. For example, repression sends a dual message – either that the leader is worried or that he is supremely confident. Moreover, a careful tracing of defections from the ruling circle (see Chapters 3 through 8) shows that even these commonly used indicators of regime weakness often appear very late in confrontations between the regime and the opposition. Thus, they are as often a part of the change dynamic itself as precursors of political change.

At the same time, as we discovered in our interviews, some opposition leaders made very different calculations, even when they assumed expanded opportunities for winning power. Some said that this was a good reason to collaborate – for instance, in order to share the benefits of ruling while increasing the probability that winning would actually occur. However, others said the opposite, that is, that going it alone would be best because winning without the burdens of a large coalition would translate after the election into easier allocation of jobs, fewer interests to represent, and a more durable government.[36] Finally, while there is certainly evidence that a unified opposition improves the prospects for the defeat of authoritarian leaders, the fact is that unity carries no political guarantees. There are degrees of unity; dictators can still win elections irrespective of opposition cohesion, as we discovered in the cases of Armenia, Azerbaijan, and Belarus (see Chapter 7); and dictators can lose but still find ways to steal elections. Under any of these conditions, the result is the same: authoritarian leaders stay in office, and oppositions remain on the sidelines. What all this seems to suggest is that, while unity of the opposition is important, so are a number of other factors that, not accidentally, are also built into the electoral model.

[35] Mladen Lazić and Liljana Nikolić, *Protest in Belgrade: Winter of Discontent* (Budapest: Central European University Press, 1999).

[36] See Jennifer Gandhi, *Political Institutions under Dictatorship* (Cambridge: Cambridge University Press, 2008), for a similar argument, albeit one that focuses on variations in presidential resources.

ELECTORAL PROCEDURES AND CIVIL SOCIETY

The electoral approach also targets formal procedures, with an overarching goal of improving their quality and the transparency of elections. In most mixed regimes, there are electoral commissions that oversee the electoral process. However, it is often the case that a significant portion of the members of these electoral commissions are appointed and thereby controlled by the incumbent regime, and these biases, plus legal loopholes and purposefully careless or inaccurate monitoring, often translate into politically skewed processes of candidate selection, voter registration, construction of the final voter list, and, of course, tabulation of the vote. In addition, it is not unusual for oppositions to be harassed during the campaign and for election-day procedures to be adopted that make it easy to buy votes, steal votes, block votes, and, most commonly, generate extra ballots to ensure the success of incumbents and their allies.[37]

To counteract these problems, incumbent regimes are frequently pressured by influential international actors prior to the election to reform both the institutions governing elections and actual voting procedures. For example, as our case studies indicated, the U.S. government made this a high priority in nearly all of the elections of interest in this book, whether incumbents or their anointed successors ultimately won or lost the contest.[38] Oppositions had other international allies as well. Backed by such organizations as IDEA (the International Institute for Democracy and Electoral Assistance), IFES (the International Foundation for Electoral Systems), and ODIHR (the Office for Democratic Institutions and Human Rights), domestic oppositions, along with local nongovernmental organizations, were in a position in many cases to keep the pressure on the regime over the course of the election.

Campaign processes are also a core priority. A key concern here is encouraging the opposition to run ambitious and well-organized campaigns that

---

[37] On how these processes work, see, especially, Larry Garber and Glenn Cowan, "The Virtues of Parallel Vote Tabulations," *Journal of Democracy* 4:2 (April 1993), 95–107; Hyde, "Observing Norms"; Bjornlund, *Beyond Free and Fair*; Haroutiun Khachatrian, "Armenia: Not Sizzling, but Fizzling Out," *Transitions Online*, December 19, 2005, 1–2; Vahe Sahakyan and Arthur Atanesyan, "Democratization in Armenia: Some Trends of Political Culture and Behavior," *Demokratizatsiya* 14:3 (Summer 2006), 347–354; roundtable at the U.S. embassy in Yerevan, March 9, 2007; Emil Danielyan, "The West: Sponsoring without Monitoring?," *Transitions on Line*, December 13, 2005; Haroutium Khachatrian, "Armenia: A Guinness-Fuelled Vote?" *Transitions Online*, December 1, 2005; Brian Whitmore, "Armenia: Parliamentary Vote Sets Scene for 2008 Presidential Race," *Radio Free Europe/Radio Liberty*, May 11, 2007; and "OSCE Chairman Visits Azerbaijan: Peace Head Stresses that Azerbaijan Ballot Must be Democratic," *Radio Free Europe/Radio Liberty Newsletter*, 9:168 (September 6, 2005), www.rferl.org/newsline/2005/09/060905.asp?po=y; Sabrina Tavernise, "Protesters and Police Clash as Armenia Unrest Grows," *New York Times*, March 2, 2008, www.nytimes.com/2008/03/02/world/europe/02 armenia.html.

[38] See, especially, Noor Borbieva, "Development in the Kyrgyz Republic: Exchange, Communal Networks and the Foreign Presence" (Ph.D. dissertation, Harvard University, 2007).

highlight the costs of keeping the government in power and that bring opposition leaders into direct contact with both new voters and citizens outside the capital and major cities. Another task is to increase both voter registration and turnout – processes that require a huge effort. In the absence of such increases, for example, it is likely that Vladimír Mečiar, Slobodan Milošević, and Viktor Yanukovych – and not the opposition candidates – would have won the elections in Slovakia, Serbia, and Ukraine in 1998, 2000, and 2004, respectively. We draw this conclusion for the simple but telling reason that each of these contests was extremely close.[39] Thus, turnout, especially of opposition supporters (who are often younger or first-time voters), may well have made all the difference.

Campaigns to increase citizen engagement often used unorthodox techniques, such as bus tours and marches, along with more familiar mechanisms that were nonetheless new to these contexts, such as citizen meetings with candidates and door-to-door canvassing. Youth groups also played a critical role. For example, they drew upon street theater, satire, and ridicule to delegitimize the incumbent regime and catch the attention of voters. They, along with other groups, also frequently used rock concerts and the media to energize voters and make participation in elections "fun and not just a duty," in the words of several participants in OK'98 in Slovakia. These activities, along with the widespread use of slogans, placards, stickers, hats, and T-shirts, were part of an effort to project a positive message in order to overcome the passivity and apathy of citizens who had come to believe that their votes did not matter. As is the case with the unification of the opposition, these activities created a climate of optimism supporting the ideas that votes count and that change was possible.[40]

Put more generally, activation of civil society is a key element of the electoral model. This is largely because of the benefits a robust civil society brings to democratic development. As Pavol Demeš and Joerg Forbrig have noted, "Civil society organizations play an indispensable role for the vibrancy of democracy. Among other functions, they sensitize society to pressing domestic and international issues, build cohesion within communities, help citizens to articulate their beliefs and interests, exercise control over those holding power and provide public services."[41] In all of our successful cases of electoral defeat of authoritarian leaders or their designated successors, nongovernmental organizations, including both established groups that were the result in many cases of sustained U.S. and Western European support for civil society development, and new groups – including youth groups, such as Otpor in

---

[39] As we discussed in Chapter 3, Mečiar's party in fact won the most votes in Slovakia in 1998; however, he was unable to form a coalition, and the opposition coalition thus formed the government.

[40] See, especially, Peter Novotný and Balász Jarábik, *Voter Education and Mobilization Campaigns* (Washington, DC: Freedom House, 2004).

[41] Demeš and Forbrig, "Civic Action and Democratic Power Shifts."

Serbia, Kmara in Georgia, and Pora in Ukraine – and organizations formed specifically to engage in election-related activities – such as monitoring the media, election monitoring, informing citizens of their rights and about issues in the campaign, and getting out the vote – have been critical.

The level of prior organization of the third sector, as well as the degree of cooperation within the third sector and between civil society organizations and the political opposition, varied in the cases we are analyzing in this book.[42] However, it is fair to say that civil society groups were important to the success of efforts to oust authoritarian leaders in all of our cases (though less so in Kyrgyzstan), and that implementation of the electoral model in particular played a key role in bringing civil society groups and the opposition together. In the absence of these strategic innovations and, for that matter, a transnational democracy assistance community pressing for such cooperation, civil society groups and opposition parties had at best informal and episodic ties. This reflected in part the isolation of the opposition and in part a set of values held by many activists in nongovernmental organizations that usually defined their mandates in quite apolitical terms and that included distrust of partisan politics and political leaders of all stripes.

Aside from these core features, however, electoral efforts can include a remarkable range of activities, depending upon regime context. For example, the opposition and its allies can exploit media openings and institutional loopholes. The more open media in Georgia is an example of the first, and the relatively independent role of the Supreme Court in Ukraine in calling for new elections in 2004 is an example of the second. Implementation of the electoral model can also include, when local circumstances permit, the use of exit polls, parallel vote tabulation, and external (in addition to internal) election monitoring – as ways of reducing the possibility of both voter harassment and fraudulent election results.[43] Where stolen elections are a distinct possibility, moreover, the electoral approach can include, as we argued in Chapters 4 through 6, opposition contacts with security forces before and during the elections, and preparations for the possibility of mass protests as a way to force authoritarians to accept defeat and transfer political power.

These preparations can, as in the Ukrainian case, include arrangements to provide food and shelter, as well as communication, during lengthy protests. More frequently, they include the training of activists in the techniques of civil disobedience and nonviolent conflict. Seminars and summer training camps

---

[42] Nicklaus Laverty, "The Problem of Lasting Change: Civil Society and the Colored Revolutions in Georgia and Ukraine," *Demokratizatsiya* 16:2 (Spring 2008), 143–162.

[43] On how parallel vote tabulation works, see Garber and Cowan, "The Virtues of Parallel Vote Tabulations." The key point is not that individual votes are recounted, but rather that efforts are made to generate the number of ballots cast versus the number of ballots that are reported in the official results. Part of the issue here is access and privacy concerns, but the other part is the fact that most elections are stolen by adding ballots. In addition, see Peter Novotný, "The Backlash against Election Monitoring: How the Profession Can Respond," lecture presented at the National Endowment for Democracy, Washington, DC, January 28, 2010.

(such as those held in Budapest in the case of Serbia and in the case of Georgia in both Bratislava and Belgrade), as well as the production of brochures and booklets outlining these techniques, are often used.

POLITICS AS USUAL

To those of us who live in well-established democratic systems, many of these activities appear to be little more than electoral "politics as usual." However, for citizens living in the many regimes in the world headed by authoritarian leaders who manipulate electoral procedures and results, the electoral model of democratization represents a *significant* departure from the way elections have traditionally been conducted. Indeed, the very purpose of the model is to surmount common obstacles to free and fair elections and to the full engagement of citizens in shaping – indeed, choosing – their political future.[44] These obstacles include, for example, the very success leaders in mixed regimes have had with respect to dividing, marginalizing, demobilizing, and co-opting the opposition. During elections, moreover, authoritarian leaders and their allies regularly harass the opposition; monopolize the media and sources of campaign funding; prevent campaign rallies or break them up; confuse voters by creating fake parties and running candidates with the same names as opposition candidates (a common strategy in Azerbaijan); and control electoral procedures, including not just the construction of voter lists but also candidate registration and vote tabulation.

Moreover, as already noted, citizens in many mixed regimes have become quite disenchanted with opposition parties. As a result, it is very tempting for citizens to become political bystanders, caught between a regime they do not like and an opposition that holds little appeal. In many cases, citizens are also affected – as are oppositions – by the sheer durability and draconian actions of authoritarian rulers. Why go to the trouble – and, in some settings, why take the personal risk – of registering to vote, going to rallies, volunteering for political work, voting, or, for that matter, defending the vote in the streets if the regime is willing to use force to protect itself and, in any event, would never be willing to give up power?

The electoral model, therefore, is a sophisticated instrument designed to surmount the formidable obstacles that mixed regimes erect to prevent challengers from being effective and therefore fully competitive. The model breaks with past practices by communicating an important message: ordinary citizens and opposition groups can make democratic change happen by using the opportunities provided by elections to translate their subversive political dreams into concrete political actions. Given the political drama they provide, massive get-out-the-vote campaigns and, particularly, mass street demonstrations, these elections are also good vehicles to engage the attention of external

---

[44] Tucker, "Enough!"; Sidney G. Tarrow, *The New Transnational Activism* (Cambridge: Cambridge University Press, 2005).

supporters of democracy who, if not already involved, can be drawn in to urge the regime to respect electoral results and encourage the autocrat to step down. Indeed, that is precisely how the United States became involved in electoral change – as we will see later in the case of the Philippines and then Chile during the Reagan administration.

INVENTING THE MODEL

The electoral model did not originate in the postcommunist region, and it took shape through a series of dress rehearsals. We can begin the story of how this package of electoral innovations was constructed by noting some relatively long-term domestic and international developments that helped pave the way for this approach to winning elections. One key contributor was the global spread of democratic governance that began in the mid-1970s. As the Third Wave of democratization progressed from its origins in southern Europe and Latin America in the 1970s to other parts of the world, it generated several important insights about how transitions from dictatorship to democracy take place – insights that influenced not just scholarly work, but also the thinking and actions of policy makers, international democracy promoters, and even local political activists. One revelation involved recasting democratization as a process of regime change that could happen quickly rather than slowly and that could be fashioned by the targeted actions of a set of political players that included not just regime and opposition leaders, but also citizens and the international democracy assistance community.[45] To borrow from Guiseppe Di Palma, democracy could be crafted.[46]

The other lesson culled from the Third Wave was that if democratization could be quick and crafted, then elections were ideally suited to serve as key sites for democratic change.[47] We have already explained why this is the case.

---

[45] See, for example, Giuseppe Di Palma, *To Craft Democracies: An Essay on Democratic Transitions* (Berkeley: University of California Press, 1990); Guillermo A. O'Donnell, Philippe C. Schmitter, and Laurence Whitehead, *Transitions from Authoritarian Rule: Comparative Perspectives* (Baltimore: Johns Hopkins University Press, 1988); Lawrence Whitehead, "Three International Dimensions of Democratization," in *The International Dimensions of Democratization: Europe and the Americas*, ed. Laurence Whitehead (Oxford: Oxford University Press, 2001), 3–25; Valerie Bunce, "Rethinking Recent Democratization: Lessons from the Postcommunist Experience," *World Politics* 55:2 (January 2003), 167–192; Peter Ackerman and Jack Duvall, *A Force More Powerful: A Century of Nonviolent Conflict*, 1st Palgrave paperback edition (New York: St. Martin's Press, 2000); Kurt Schock, "Nonviolent Action and Its Misconceptions: Insights for Social Scientists," *PS: Political Science and Politics* 36:4 (October 2003), 705–712; and Milada Anna Vachudova, *Europe Undivided: Democracy, Leverage, and Integration after Communism* (Oxford: Oxford University Press, 2005).

[46] Di Palma, *To Craft Democracies*.

[47] Staffan Lindberg, *Democracy and Elections in Africa* (Baltimore: Johns Hopkins University Press, 2006); Staffan Lindberg, ed., *Democratization by Elections: A New Mode of Transition?* (Baltimore: Johns Hopkins University Press, 2009); Leslie Anderson and Lawrence C. Dodd, *Learning Democracy: Citizen Engagement and Electoral Choice in Nicaragua, 1990–2001* (Chicago: University of Chicago Press, 2005).

Perhaps the most surprising reason is the rise and then spread of international election monitoring, despite the fact that such monitoring violates state sovereignty and can pose serious threats to authoritarian control.[48] While the first example of "outsiders" monitoring elections in other countries took place in the early years of the twentieth century when the United States was involved in election monitoring (by invitation) in Central America, it was really only in the 1980s that international election monitoring started to become a fixture of electoral life around the world.[49]

The spread of international election monitoring reflected in turn other developments, such as the proliferation of nongovernmental organizations beginning in the second half of the 1980s, many of which were involved in improving the quality of elections. Also influential was the growing involvement of both Western governments and the United Nations in peacekeeping operations, most of which involved election management, and the changing priorities of international organizations, which involved in particular an expanding commitment to free and fair elections.[50] As a result, by the second half of the 1990s, there were a large number of organizations involved in election monitoring. These included the Organization of American States, the European Union, the Organization for Security and Cooperation in Europe (and its electoral wing, ODIHR), IFES, and, on the U.S. domestic side, the Carter Center, together with the government-funded National Endowment for Democracy, the National Democratic Institute, and the International Republican Institute.[51] All of these organizations benefited in turn from growing domestic and international expertise with respect to public opinion polling, political campaigns, and the conduct of free and fair elections, as well as the invention of techniques to ensure fair elections such as parallel vote tabulation.[52] Also important – and distinctive to the United States as compared to Western Europe – was the fact that both NDI and IRI had a number of people on their staffs with personal experience in either working in U.S. elections or serving on the staffs of state- or national-level politicians. The growing influence of

---

[48] Hyde, "Observing Norms"; Arturo Santa Cruz, *International Election Monitoring, Sovereignty, and the Western Hemisphere Idea: The Emergence of an International Norm.* (New York: Routledge, 2005); Bjornlund, *Beyond Free and Fair*; Kelley, "Assessing the Complex Evolution of Norms."

[49] See, especially, Paul Drake, "From Good Men to Good Neighbors, 1912–1932," in *Exporting Democracy: The U.S. and Latin America*, ed. Abraham Lowenthal (Baltimore: Johns Hopkins University Press, 1991), 3–40; Santa Cruz, *International Election Monitoring*; Bjornlund, *Beyond Free and Fair*; Kelley, "Assessing the Complex Evolution of Norms."

[50] See, for example, Jon C. Pevehouse, *Democracy from Above: Regional Organizations and Democratization* (Cambridge: Cambridge University Press, 2005); Jon C. Pevehouse, "Democracy from the Outside-In? International Organizations and Democratization," *International Organization* 56:3 (Summer 2002), 515–549; Pastor, "A Brief History of Electoral Commissions"; Pastor, "The Third Dimension of Accountability."

[51] See, for example, Bjornlund, *Beyond Free and Fair*, Chapter 2; Pevehouse, *Democracy from Above*; Pevehouse, "Democracy from the Outside-In?"; and Vachudová, *Europe Undivided*.

[52] See note 46 to this chapter.

approaches to political change in nondemocratic settings that rested upon the
use of planned and highly strategic challenges by citizens to the right and
capacity of oppressive regimes to rule them – an approach that played a central
and eventually successful role in defeating communist domination in Central
and Eastern Europe – was also helpful.[53]

Thus, lessons drawn from the Third Wave and changes in international
politics converged to focus external democracy assistance on elections (as well
as on other areas, such as civil society development) in countries that tolerated
some degree of political competition. While a review of these developments
captures important influences on the development of the electoral model, specific events on the ground are equally if not more important. The electoral
model was an instrument shaped by creative and hard-working oppositions,
civil society organizations, ordinary citizens, and international democracy
promoters.

EARLY EXPERIMENTS

As with all innovations, political or otherwise, the origins of the electoral
model are hard to nail down.[54] However, it is fair to argue that this ensemble of
electoral strategies made its first appearance in the presidential election in the
Philippines in 1986 and in the presidential plebiscite held in Chile in 1988.[55] In
both the election in the Philippines and the Chilean referendum, incumbents
assumed that these political exercises were "rigged rituals" that would deliver
easy victories. They thought so because the election and the plebiscite were

---

[53] See Ackerman and Duvall, *A Force More Powerful*; and Kurt Schock, "Nonviolent Action
and Its Misconceptions: Insights for Social Scientists," *PS: Political Science and Politics*
36:4 (October 2003): 705–712. On the role of the National Endowment for Democracy, the
AFL–CIO, and other public and private organizations based in the United States in supporting Solidarity in the 1980s, see Gregory F. Domber, "Supporting the Revolution: America,
Democracy, and the End of the Cold War in Poland, 1981–1989" (Ph.D. dissertation,
Department of History, The George Washington University, Washington, DC, January
2008).

[54] See, especially, interview with Patrick Merloe, Washington, DC, April 30, 2009.

[55] See, for example, Ackerman and Duvall, *A Force More Powerful*, Chapters 7 and 10; Garber and
Cowan, "The Virtues of Parallel Vote Tabulations"; Mary Racelis, "New Visions and Strong
Actions: Civil Society in the Philippines," in *Civil Society Aid and Democracy Promotion*,
ed. Marina Ottaway and Thomas Carothers (Washington, DC: Carnegie Endowment, 2000),
159–190; Mark Thompson, *The Anti-Marcos Struggle: Personalistic Rule and Democratic
Transition in the Philippines* (New Haven, CT: Yale University Press, 1995); Jason Brownlee,
Authoritarianism in an Age of Democratization (Cambridge: Cambridge University Press,
2007), Chapter 3; Bjornlund, *Beyond Free and Fair*; David Altman, Sergio Toro, and
Rafael Piñeiro, *International Influences on Democratic Transitions: The Successful Case
of Chile*, CDDRL Working Paper No. 86, Center for Democracy, Development and the Rule
of Law, Freeman Spogli Institute for International Studies, Stanford University (July 2008);
and interviews with Patrick Merloe, Washington, DC, April 30, 2009; Scott Carpenter,
Washington, DC, April 9, 2009; Kenneth Wollack, Washington, DC, May 12, 2010; and
Harry Barnes, Philadelphia, February 24, 2007.

both announced suddenly, with the assumption that the opposition would not have time to prepare and certainly not enough time to coalesce in a common cause. This was in fact precisely the logic – and just as flawed – of the communists in Poland when they suddenly called for semi-competitive elections in June 1989 and, much later, of Milošević in 2000.

Local opponents of each of the two regimes, however, did come together, and they were aided by an international democracy assistance community that was largely, we must recognize, still in formation. In this sense, the relationship between international and local democracy activists in the second half of the 1980s is best understood as a two-way street. Just as oppositions in the Philippines and Chile were recipients of democracy assistance from abroad, so they played a tutorial role in helping the emerging international democracy assistance community define its goals and strategies. At the same time, the oppositions also drew upon their earlier experiences and, especially in the Chilean case, upon precedents set elsewhere. Here, we refer in the case of the Philippines to the important insights the opposition gained as a result of their experiences in the 1978 presidential election and the 1984 congressional election, the latter of which provided NAMFREL (the National Citizen's Movement for Free Elections) its first opportunity to mobilize substantial numbers of volunteers to oversee elections.[56] With respect to external precedents, we refer in the case of Chile to the powerful influence of two surprising developments – the defeat of Marcos in the Philippines in 1986 (two years before the Chilean referendum) and the defeat of the military in the rigged 1980 plebiscite in Uruguay.[57] More generally, what we find in both countries are extraordinarily ambitious campaigns to register voters and get out the vote (for example, through the Crusade for Citizen Participation in Chile); to monitor the quality of the elections; and to educate voters about regime abuses and the importance of seizing the political moment to reject the regime, in the Chilean case (the plebiscite offered no alternative candidate), or to support the Acquino–Laurel ticket in the Philippines. What emerged in both political struggles, in short, were the core components of the electoral model of democratization. However, it was in the Philippines that the model was first developed and applied and registered its first success.

Also critical in these two episodes (as it was to be in others) was the willingness of the United States, despite its long alliance with both Marcos and Pinochet, to support the opposition. In Chile, the United States signaled this support before and during the plebiscite, whereas in the Philippines U.S. support for the opposition took shape only when it became clear that the

---

[56] See, especially, Bjornlund, *Beyond Free and Fair*, 209–210. NAMFREL, in fact, dates back to the 1950s and, according to one of our interviewees, received funding in its early years from the Central Intelligence Agency. Interview with Larry Garber, Washington, DC, April 9, 2010.

[57] Altman, Toro, and Piñeiro, "International Influences on Democratic Transitions." The assertiveness of U.S. ambassadors was also important. Interview with Robert Benjamin, Washington, DC, April 9, 2010.

opposition had won, that Marcos was trying to steal the election, that large numbers of Filipinos would remain on the streets until the opposition's victory was recognized, and that pressure from the United States, as a result, would be decisive in resolving the crisis and getting Marcos to leave office. Here, we must keep in mind that these confrontations between dictators and opposition took place in the second half of the 1980s. This was a time when regimes tended to be either democratic or autocratic and when democracy assistance, while beginning to play a role in U.S. foreign policy, was still competing with far older and more entrenched Cold War priorities that included U.S. support of anticommunist dictators such as Pinochet and Marcos.[58]

The sequence of events in the Philippines and Chile, precisely because of the trailblazing role of these elections with respect to their success in challenging dictators *and* their influence on U.S. foreign policy, was somewhat different from what transpired later on in the postcommunist world. In particular, in these two electoral confrontations between regime and opposition, developments on the ground – that is, clear evidence of declining support for the dictator, visible violations of free and fair elections, and a large and well-organized democratic opposition positioned to challenge dictatorial power – played a key role in building the case in Washington for a shift in U.S. foreign policy in the direction of keeping dictators at some distance and supporting democracy in general and free and fair elections in particular. However, it is also important to recognize that Washington was already relatively receptive to these arguments, given, for example, the legacy of President Carter's support for human rights and the growing discomfort in Congress with U.S. relations with dictators such as Pinochet. (U.S. military and economic support of the Chilean regime in fact had started to decline in 1981.) Perhaps most important, however, was President Reagan's strong interest in supporting democratic change abroad. This was articulated clearly, for example, in his 1982 speech to the British House of Commons and evidenced as well in his decision to found (in collaboration with the U.S. Congress) the National Endowment for Democracy and its related organizations, the International Republican Institute and the National Democratic Institute for Foreign Affairs.

Indeed, the interaction among "new thinking" (to borrow from Gorbachev) about U.S. foreign policy in Washington, longer-term support of the Chilean opposition by both European- and U.S.-based private and public organizations,

---

[58] See, especially, Altman, Toro, and Piñeiro, "International Influences on Democratic Transitions"; A. David Adesnik and Sunhyuk Kim, *If at First You Don't Succeed: The Puzzle of South Korea's Democratic Transition*, CDDRL Working Paper No. 83, Center for Democracy, Development and the Rule of Law, Freeman Spogli Institute for International Studies, Stanford University (July 2008); Kristina Kaush and Richard Youngs, *Algeria: Democratic Transition Case Study*, CDDRL Working Paper No. 84, Center for Democracy, Development and the Rule of Law, Freeman Spogli Institute for International Studies, Stanford University (August 2008); and interviews with Harry Barnes, Philadelphia, February 24, 2007; and Robert Gelbard, Ithaca, NY, March 1, 2007. We would also like to thank David Adesnik for the observations he shared with us in March 2009 at the Center for Democracy, Development and the Rule of Law at Stanford University.

and the fast-moving events in the Philippines and Chile was a major theme in the interviews we conducted with both ambassadors and administration officials connected with these two pivotal electoral episodes.[59] For example, Robert Gelbard, who was a member of the National Security Council at the time, argued that pressures from the U.S. ambassadors to these two countries, as well as from officials of the National Endowment for Democracy – especially those from the National Democratic Institute, who were in close touch with the Chilean opposition – played a critical role in sensitizing President Reagan and his Secretary of State, George Schultz, to the need to withdraw support from dictators and side with democrats.[60] Just as important is another consideration: the powerful impact of the Philippines on the Chilean opposition, influence facilitated not just by the "distant" appeal of a successful precedent, but also by the role of the National Endowment for Democracy and especially the National Democratic Institute in bringing members of the opposition from Chile and the Philippines together.[61] These meetings were instructive in and of themselves, and they also set a precedent, especially in the case of NDI, for using "learning delegations" to transfer innovative electoral procedures across national boundaries. Just as remarkable was another precedent: the United States provided support to the Chilean opposition before and during the plebiscite and, in the Philippines, facilitated the departure of Marcos from office.[62]

While both Marcos and Pinochet lost their elections (though Pinochet stayed in power for two more years), the road to democracy in both countries was far from trouble-free. However, by most accounts, a corner was turned – a corner that was the result, it must be recognized, of hard work not just during the election, but also years before that. These elections, in short, conform well to our definition of democratizing elections as events that expand opportunities for democratic change. Another remarkable aspect of these two electoral confrontations was the fact that NED was at the same time providing similar levels of support to Poland in its struggle against communist rule. While the desire to provide "equal" support to struggles against very different forms of authoritarianism prompted these decisions, this "even-handed" approach to democracy promotion had the important consequence of linking these two regional theaters of political mobilization against authoritarianism and thereby encouraging a pooling of ideas, strategies, and even international participants. In fact, it was precisely these ties, as Daniel Serwer, who at that time headed a study group on the Balkans at the U.S. Institute of Peace, explained in an interview with us, that served as the basis for discussions at the U.S. Institute of Peace about how both the earlier struggles

---

[59] Altman, Toro, and Piñeiro, "International Influences on Democratic Transitions."
[60] Interview with Robert Gelbard, Ithaca, NY, March 1, 2007.
[61] We thank Patrick Merloe, Larry Garber, and Kenneth Wollack for this information. We are also grateful for information about these linkages provided by Kurt Weyland.
[62] Our thanks to Kurt Weyland for sharing this information with us, and to Robert Gelbard, Kenneth Wollack, and Ambassador Harry Barnes for sharing their experiences.

against communism and those against Pinochet could inform the development of successful approaches to ridding Serbia of Milošević.[63] Yet another critical consequence of what transpired in the Philippines and Chile, however, was that citizens were willing and able (like the opposition) to take the election seriously, rather than ignore it; to express their true political preferences, despite the danger in many cases of doing so; and, in the Philippines, to carry out sustained protests that succeeded in ending the Marcos era.

What we saw, in short, was a new model of regime change that transformed elections in authoritarian settings into genuinely competitive processes that expanded opportunities for democratic change. This approach to removing authoritarian leaders from office then moved to other parts of the world, such as Nicaragua, Indonesia, Ghana, Panama, and Zimbabwe.[64] One of the most interesting cases was the Nicaraguan election of 1990, as the Sandinistas, fearing fraud, but supremely confident of their public support, welcomed international election monitors – who then ended up certifying the victory of the opposition.[65] Just as interesting is the fact that the Sandinistas accepted this judgment, as did, for example, the losers many years later in pivotal elections that took place not just in Slovakia and Croatia from 1998 to 2000, but also in Romania in 1996 and Bulgaria in 1997. In the latter two cases, the communists lost power, and the elections served as a turning point in democratic development.[66] However, in Serbia in 2000 (as in the Philippines and Indonesia before it), the election was immediately followed by popular protests to support an electorally mandated transfer of political power in the face of attempts by the incumbents to falsify the election results – a dynamic that also materialized in Georgia in 2003 and Ukraine in 2004.

MOVING TO THE POSTCOMMUNIST REGION

The electoral model made its first appearance in the postcommunist region very soon after the collapse of communism – in the 1990 Bulgarian elections.[67]

---

[63] As Daniel Serwer explained to us in an interview, Washington, DC, November 17, 2006.

[64] Interview with Patrick Merloe, Washington, DC, April 30, 2009; interview with Scott Carpenter, Washington, DC, April 9, 2009; also see Todd A. Eisenstadt, "Off the Streets and into the Courtrooms: Resolving Post-Election Conflicts in Mexico," in *The Self-Restraining State: Power and Accountability in New Democracies*, ed. Andreas Schedler, Larry Diamond, and Marc F. Plattner (Boulder, CO: Lynne Rienner Publishers, 1999), 83–104; Edward Aspinall and Marcus Meitzner, *From Silkworms to Bungled Bailout: International Influences on the 1998 Regime Change in Indonesia*, CDDRL Working Paper No. 85, Center for Democracy, Development, and the Rule of Law, Freeman Spogli Institute for International Studies, Stanford University (July 2008); Pastor, "The Third Dimension of Accountability"; and Bjornlund, *Beyond Free and Fair.*

[65] For a longer-term view of the Nicaraguan case, see Anderson and Dodd, *Learning Democracy.*

[66] See, especially, Nassya Kralevska-Owens, *Communism versus Democracy* (Ithaca, NY: Cornell University Press, 2010); and Venelin Ganev, *Preying on the State: The Transformation of Bulgaria after 1989* (Ithaca, NY: Cornell University Press, 2007).

[67] Interview with Patrick Merloe, Washington, DC, April 30, 2009; interview with Scott Carpenter, Washington, DC, April 9, 2009; and discussion with Peter Novotný, Washington,

The National Endowment for Democracy (NED), the National Democratic Institute for Foreign Affairs (NDI), and the National Republican Institute for Foreign Affairs (as it was called at that time, before it changed its name a few years later to the International Republican Institute or IRI) all worked very closely with Bulgarian officials in order to ensure that the first competitive election in Bulgaria since 1931 would meet international democratic standards. On the face of it, it is surprising that the June 1990 Bulgarian election elicited so much interest among U.S. democracy promoters. It seems to have done so for two reasons. One was that the Bulgarian election came at the end of a run of founding elections in Central and Eastern Europe that had engaged the interest of the U.S. democracy assistance community in particular. The United States, in short, already had some experience in the region and had established an institutional presence. At the same time, in the view of international democracy promoters who were involved in the region at this time, Bulgaria resembled, far more than any other regime in the postcommunist area, the situation in the Philippines and Chile in the 1980s. In particular, the perception was that the regime was mixed because it combined rule by authoritarians with electoral competition, and that the opposition was resourceful but faced an uphill struggle. Thus, the electoral model could make a difference. Moreover, Bulgarian civil society – in particular, student and labor organizations – and the opposition expressed strong interest in receiving international democracy aid.[68] Thus, in addition to providing support for free and fair elections, NED and especially IRI and NDI helped develop new civil society organizations, such as the Bulgarian Association for Fair Elections (BAFE), and worked closely with the very fragmented and, of course, inexperienced opposition in Bulgaria. For example, they encouraged opposition parties to work together; NDI brought members of NAMFREL to Bulgaria to share their experiences; and NDI and IRI organized the first parallel vote tabulation in the region following the collapse of communism.

However, much to the surprise of everyone, the Bulgarian Socialist Party (the successor to the communists) managed to squeak out a victory. This outcome carries two important lessons for this study. One is that the former communists (and other authoritarians) do have support in some countries in the postcommunist region, particularly in places where, as in Bulgaria, the communists had relatively deep historical roots and had demonstrated important policy achievements over the course of their rule. At the same time, the

DC, February 24, 2010. Also see the National Republican Institute for International Affairs and the National Democratic Institute for International Affairs, *The June 1990 Elections in Bulgaria*, International Delegation Report, Washington, DC, (1990); and Larry Garber, "Bulgaria: June 10, 1990," in *The New Democratic Frontier: A Country by Country Report on Elections in Central and Eastern Europe*, ed. Larry Garber and Eric Bjornlund (Washington, DC: National Democratic Institute, 1992), 135–160.

[68] Interviews with Larry Garber, Washington, DC, April 9, 2010; Patrick Merloe, Washington, DC, April 30, 2009; and Scott Carpenter, Washington, DC, April 9, 2009. In addition, see National Republican Institute for International Affairs and the National Democratic Institute for International Affairs, *The June 1990 Elections in Bulgaria*.

1990 Bulgarian election demonstrates that the electoral model does not always translate into an opposition victory – though it certainly made the election closer than it would otherwise have been.

What also facilitated the transfer of the electoral model from Latin America and southeast Asia to southeastern Europe was the evident appeal of a successful application of the model elsewhere. These positive precedents were especially attractive to oppositions that were seeking, we must remember, not just more democracy (whether in name only or in reality), but also political power. This is a major reason why student organizations, opposition parties, and labor organizations in Bulgaria all reached out to NED, IRI, and especially NDI for help in the early spring of 1990. More generally, the regionwide collapse of communist regimes in Europe and Eurasia had left in its wake a large number of new regimes with political profiles that were potentially ripe for the application of the electoral model.

This potential was only enhanced by the international context of postcommunist transitions. Here, we refer, first, to the centrality of the postcommunist region to democracy assistance efforts on the part of the United States and, for that matter, the European Union.[69] This focus on the postcommunist region in particular is important, not just because the world's remaining superpower made democratic change in the postcommunist region a priority, but also because the United States was then very popular in a part of the world that had long been dominated by the Soviet Union. The priority that the United States attached to democratic change in the postcommunist world also made it very easy to connect – in terms of both the actual people involved and the policies associated with electoral challenges to authoritarian rule – what had taken place in such countries as Chile, the Philippines, and Nicaragua, on the one hand (where the United States, we must remember, was quite involved), and what could happen in Central and Eastern Europe. Indeed, it was striking in our interviews how much personnel overlap there was between the Americans involved in Chile and the Philippines, on the one hand, and in the Serbian struggle against Milošević, on the other. These electoral episodes, we must remember, were more than a decade apart.[70]

The overlap in the kinds of electoral strategies that were put forward and in the people who participated in these electoral confrontations reflected the impact of three factors. One was that many people who had worked in programs that supported opposition politics in Central and Eastern Europe during the communist era had taken positions with the newly created NED, IRI, and NDI in Latin America and in Southeast Asia. Once the Cold War ended, many of these people were transferred in turn to the newest and most rapidly expanding theater for international democracy

---

[69] Valerie Bunce and Sharon L. Wolchik, "Favorable Conditions and Electoral Revolutions," *Journal of Democracy* 17:4 (October 2006), 5–18.

[70] Interviews with Daniel Serwer, Washington, DC, November 17, 2006; Harry Barnes, Philadelphia, February 24, 2007; Robert Gelbard, Ithaca, NY, March 1, 2007; and Patrick Merloe, Washington, DC, April 30, 2009.

assistance: postcommunist Europe and Eurasia. Second, assisting Polish dissidents who were struggling against communism was an important focus of NED's work soon after its founding in late 1983. Indeed, because Solidarity was a trade union (although workers, ironically, did not constitute a majority of its membership), its continuing struggles with Polish authorities in the 1980s were of considerable interest to the AFL–CIO and its affiliated NGO, the Free Trade Union Institute, which became a core grantee of NED. Finally, many members of the State Department and especially the United States Institute of Peace (which had been founded by Congress in 1984) viewed the struggles between oppositions and authoritarian rulers in mixed regimes in the postcommunist world through the lenses not just of the electoral defeats of authoritarian rulers in other parts of the world, but also of the earlier struggles against communism in general and in particular the rise of Solidarity in Poland in 1980.[71]

What made it even easier to connect these seemingly very different theaters of political action was what many analysts saw as the postcommunist region's strong potential for democracy – for example, unusually high rates of literacy, proximity to the West, and the incentives of European Union membership.[72] However, perhaps the most important consideration was the power of diffusion – an argument that we will address in greater detail in the next chapter. As the rapid-fire collapse of communism from 1987 to 1991 reminds us, the region that was called the Soviet Union and Eastern Europe during the Cold War period seems to be a part of the world that is unusually prone to diffusion effects.[73] Thus, democratic change in one country in this region held the

[71] Interviews with Scott Carpenter, Washington, DC, April 9, 2009; Daniel Serwer, Washington, DC, November 17, 2006; Robert Gelbard, Ithaca, NY, March 1, 2007; and Patrick Merloe, Washington, DC, April 30, 2009; and see Dombar, "Supporting the Revolution." While it is not surprising that the fall of communism influenced thinking about democratization through elections in the same region, it is much more surprising, as Daniel Serwer noted in our interview with him, that the events of 1989 were used to inform discussions about the American invasion of Iraq. There are few parallels between Central and Eastern Europe at that time and Iraq in 2002–03, particularly for the one case that received the most attention – Poland, one of the most homogeneous countries in the world, an old state (though interrupted by partition), and a remarkably well-defined nation that spent enormous time protesting against both imperial and authoritarian rule.

[72] Bunce and Wolchik, "Favorable Conditions and Electoral Revolutions"; Steven Levitsky and Lucan Way, "Linkage and Leverage: How Do International Factors Change Domestic Balances of Power?," in *Electoral Authoritarianism: The Dynamics of Unfree Competition*, ed. Andreas Schedler (Boulder, CO: Lynne Rienner Publishers, 2006), 199–216, and their concepts of linkage and leverage; Vachudová, *Europe Undivided*.

[73] Bunce and Wolchik, "Favorable Conditions and Electoral Revolutions"; Valerie Bunce and Sharon L. Wolchik, "Debating the Color Revolutions: Getting Real about Real Causes," *Journal of Democracy* 20:1 (January 2009), 5–19; Valerie Bunce and Sharon Wolchik, "Defining and Domesticating the Electoral Model: A Comparison of Slovakia and Serbia," in *Democracy and Authoritarianism in the Postcommunist World*, ed. Valerie Bunce, Michael McFaul, and Kathryn Stoner-Weiss (Cambridge: Cambridge University Press, 2009), 134–154; Valerie Bunce and Sharon L. Wolchik, "A Regional Tradition: The Diffusion of Democratic Change under Communism and Postcommunism," in *Democracy and Authoritarianism in*

promise of spreading to other countries in the region. In fact, some studies of the diffusion of democracy have concluded that cross-national patterns of democratic change evidence strong neighborhood effects.[74] What is significant for our purposes about this argument is that in the postcommunist region, this could happen not just because of some relatively vague theories about democratic dominoes, but also for more "practical" reasons. Small states situated next to one another, some of which had in fact recently been members of the same state and, for that matter, empire, feature unusually dense cultural, political, and social ties and, thus, pronounced propensities to monitor each other and learn from one another. Moreover, small, contiguous, similar, and interactive states make it extremely easy for oppositions, civil society organizations, and indeed international democracy promoters to move around, meet, compare notes, share strategies, found organizations, and organize movements. Slovakia, Croatia, Serbia, Ukraine, and, for that matter, Bulgaria and Romania, which had experienced breakthrough elections in 1996 and 1997 and which influenced Slovak NGO and opposition politics in the struggle against Mečiar, were all neighbors. Just as relevant to diffusion dynamics were two other facts: that U.S. democracy promoters had regional offices that facilitated movement among these states, and that U.S. ambassadors, such as William Montgomery and Richard Miles, had been posted in several states in the region (in the first case, Bulgaria and Croatia, in the second, Bulgaria, Serbia, and Georgia).

Thus, this group of countries seems to have functioned as a particularly effective hothouse for developing, applying, and sharing innovative strategies of electoral change. It is not surprising, therefore, how interconnected democracy activists from these countries were during the first decade of postcommunism (and in many cases during communism) and, going a step further, how interconnected many political turning points in these countries were as well in terms of timing and participants. Here, we refer to such important events as the 1990 election in Bulgaria, the 1996 to 1997 local elections and protests in Serbia, the 1996 election in Romania, the 1997 election in Bulgaria, and, thereafter, the wave of electoral change that we have dated in this book as beginning in 1998 in Slovakia. Thus, demonstration effects, dense personal ties, and collaborative protests explain why this part of the postcommunist region was where the wave

    the Postcommunist World, ed. Valerie Bunce, Michael McFaul, and Kathryn Stoner-Weiss (Cambridge: Cambridge University Press, 2009), 30–58.

[74] See Daniel Brinks and Michael Coppedge, "Diffusion Is No Illusion: Neighbor Emulation in the Third Wave of Democracy," *Comparative Political Studies* 39:4 (May 1, 2006), 463–489; Kristian Skrede Gleditsch and Michael D. Ward, "Diffusion and the International Context of Democratization," *International Organization* 60:4 (October 2006), 911–933; Barbara Wejnert, "Diffusion, Development, and Democracy, 1800–1999," *American Sociological Review* 70:1 (February 2005), 53–81; and John O'Loughlin, Michael D. Ward, Corey L. Lofdahl, Jordin S. Cohen, David S. Brown, David Reilly, Kristian S. Gleditsch, and Michael Shin, "The Diffusion of Democracy, 1946–1994," *Annals of the Association of American Geographers* 88:4 (December 1998), 545–574.

of electoral turnovers began, and why it was in Slovakia, Croatia, Serbia, and Ukraine – and not in the more geographically removed countries of Georgia or Kyrgyzstan – that electoral turnover had the strongest impact on democratic development (as we will discuss in Chapter 11).

THE BENEFITS OF THE ELECTORAL APPROACH

As we have argued earlier, popular challenges to authoritarian rule are hard to mount, even in mixed regimes and even with the help of international democracy promoters.[75] However, the electoral model is well designed to ease many of these limitations on democratic change. One reason is the focus on elections.

Elections are helpful in part because they are events. It is far from accidental, for example, that many, if not most, cases of mass protests, while foreshadowed no doubt by a variety of longer-term developments, are precipitated by dramatic events – for example, the sudden increase in prices that prompted protests in Poland in 1970 and 1976 and the firing of a highly respected activist worker, Anna Walentinowicz, in the Gdansk shipyards in 1980 that quickly led to the formation of Solidarity.[76] Events can be powerful instigators of public action, because they affect many people in the same way at the same time, and they serve as summaries of what is wrong or indefensible. As Peter Ackerman and Jack Duvall have noted regarding the election in Ukraine in 2004, "The breakpoint was reached because the people decided that enough was enough. The Orange Revolution was an existential response to the crooked oligarchy and rigged politics orchestrated by President Leonid Kuchma, who ignored political rights and tyrannized independent media."[77] The slogans of the opposition and of youth groups in particular in Serbia, Georgia, and Ukraine reflected the same sentiment.

Elections, moreover, can be catalytic events. They take place within a circumscribed period of time; they carry expectations about increased political engagement; they address directly the distribution of political power; and they have visible political results – which everyone learns about at the same time and which serve as a concise summation of both where things stand and where they are likely to go. Elections are also unique schools for democracy,

[75] See, for example, Grigore Pop-Eleches and Graeme H. Robertson, "Elections, Information, and Political Change in the Post-Cold War World," unpublished paper, December 2009.

[76] See, for example, the following books on Solidarity: David Ost, *Solidarity and the Politics of Anti-Politics: Opposition and Reform in Poland since 1968* (Philadelphia: Temple University Press, 1990); Jan Kubik, *The Power of Symbols against the Symbols of Power: The Rise of Solidarity and the Fall of State Socialism in Poland* (College Park: Pennsylvania State University Press, 1994); Roman Laba, *The Roots of Solidarity: A Political Sociology of Poland's Working-Class Democratization* (Princeton, NJ: Princeton University Press, 1991); and Shana Penn, *Solidarity's Secret: The Women Who Defeated Communism in Poland* (Ann Arbor: University of Michigan Press, 2005).

[77] Peter Ackerman and Jack DuVall, "The Secret to Success in Ukraine," *International Herald Tribune*, December 28, 2004.

because they involve political debate and participation, assessments of regime performance, and choice of representatives. Elections can also be times set aside for citizens to ponder their values, interests, and goals.

In addition, elections are announced ahead of time, and they involve specific tasks. These characteristics are highly beneficial for collective action – for several reasons. One is that activities associated with elections are both familiar and relatively easy to define, and they lend themselves to planning. Another is that there are common demands on everyone during electoral periods, and these demands are calibrated by a common electoral calendar. At the same time, elections are unusual in allocating political power and yet resting – sometimes only in theory – on peaceful adjudication of conflicting preferences. Here, it is important to remember that a nonviolent movement against a dictator cannot be effective, as Jack Duvall notes, "unless it is driven by a strategy to take power."[78] Finally, elections link actions to outcomes, and these outcomes provide not just a tally of the votes, but also a visible verdict on such critical questions as the size of regime support, the very right of the regime to rule, and, more generally, the quality of democratic life. Indeed, for precisely these reasons, changes in the frequency and size of mass mobilization over time tend to show electoral cycle effects,[79] and fraudulent elections seem to be unusually good at bringing people out onto the streets.[80] In the latter case, for example, stolen elections focus discontent and thereby create a large and outraged "community of robbed voters."[81]

Whether the many benefits of elections for mobilization of public demands for democracy will be realized, however, as we saw in Chapter 7 and as we have also seen most recently in the Iranian presidential elections of 2009, depends to a significant extent on whether oppositions and their allies deploy the kinds of sophisticated strategies that we have termed the electoral model. Even then, of course, there are no guarantees – as the Bulgarian opposition learned in the 1990 election. However, in the absence of such strategies, it is hard to imagine an opposition victory in a mixed regime.

Not all elections, by any means, are high-octane events. Whether they are depends upon the commitment by citizens, the opposition, and civil society groups to carry out the tasks associated with the electoral model. Elections provide only an opportunity for change – an opportunity that must be consciously seized through such unglamorous and sometimes dangerous activities as registering to vote, serving as political volunteers, attending rallies, voting, and, if necessary, taking to the streets to defend the electoral results. One remarkable feature of electoral breakthroughs is that the very activities that

---

[78] Jack Duvall, "Liberation without War," *Sojourners Magazine*, February 2004, p. 3, www.sojo.net/index/cfm?action:magazine.article.

[79] Guillermo Trejo, "The Political Foundations of Ethnic Mobilization"; McAdam and Tarrow, "Ballots and Barricades."

[80] Thompson and Kuntz, "Stolen Elections"; Kuntz and Thompson, "More than Just the Final Straw"; Thompson, *The Anti-Marcos Struggle*; Tucker, "Enough!"

[81] Thompson and Kuntz, "Stolen Elections."

engage citizens in democratic politics and enhance the prospects, as a result, for success in defeating autocrats often produce in their wake feelings of heady optimism – what some participants in these processes have termed "a winning atmosphere."[82] They also empower citizens who become less and less willing to tolerate the politics of the past, where the political playing field was uneven and where authoritarians were allowed to remain in office.

The electoral approach and its ability to stimulate, organize, and channel demands, therefore, carries many advantages with respect to the role of citizens in democratic change. However, there are two other advantages. One is modularity.[83] The electoral model consists of a remarkably clear set of interrelated tasks; takes advantage of the fact that elections are regular, common, and familiar events; and is relatively easy, as a result, to transfer from one political setting to another – not just because it is an appealing political precedent, but also because of transnational networks supporting democratic change through elections. This is a major reason, of course, why we see such a long history of pivotal elections – as we discussed in our overview of the development of the electoral model earlier in this chapter.

Mixed regimes and the constraints they place on democratic development are also important considerations. When dictatorships weaken, struggles for democracy are often diverted by conflicts focused on the definition of the nation and the boundaries of the state.[84] As a result, it is far from accidental that mixed regimes are often located in states weakened by tensions between majorities and minorities.[85] It was precisely these tensions, for example, that divided the liberal opposition in Slovakia, Serbia, Georgia, and Ukraine in the early years of the transition.[86] As a result of its emphasis on defeating dictators

---

[82] Crist, Hentges, Serwer, and United States Institute of Peace, "Strategic Nonviolent Conflict."

[83] However, as we discovered in Chapter 7, the very characteristics of the electoral approach that make it so supportive of democratic change – for example, that elections take place within a circumscribed period of time and that the package of election-related tasks is so modular – also make it very easy for authoritarians, minding their power, to erect blockades against the electoral threat. See Mark Beissinger, "Structure and Example in Modular Political Phenomena: The Diffusion of Bulldozer/Rose/Orange/Tulip Revolutions," *Perspectives on Politics* 5:2 (June 2007), 259–276; Vitali Silitski, "The Long Road from Tyranny: Post-Communist Authoritarianism and Struggle for Democracy in Serbia and Belarus," unpublished manuscript, 2005; Vitali Silitski, "Is the Age of Post-Soviet Electoral Revolutions Over?," *Democracy at Large* 1:4 (September 2005), 8–10; Vitali Silitski, "Different Authoritarianisms: Distinct Patterns of Electoral Change," in *Reclaiming Democracy: Civil Society and Electoral Change in Central and Eastern Europe*, ed. Joerg Forbrig and Pavol Demeš (Bratislava: German Marshall Fund, 2007), 155–173; and Regine A. Spector and Andrej Krickovic, "The Anti-Revolutionary Toolkit," unpublished manuscript, University of California, Berkeley, Department of Political Science and Institute for International Studies, March 7, 2007.

[84] See Valerie Bunce, "The National Idea: Imperial Legacies and Post-Communist Pathways in Eastern Europe," *East European Politics and Societies* 19:3 (Summer 2005), 406–442.

[85] See David L. Epstein, Robert Bates, Jack Goldstone, Ida Kristensen, and Sharyn O'Halloran, "Democratic Transitions," *American Journal of Political Science* 50:3 (July 2006), 551–569.

[86] See, for example, Zsuzsa Csergo, *Talk of the Nation: Language and Conflict in Romania and Slovakia* (Ithaca, NY: Cornell University Press, 2007); and Kevin Deegan-Krause, *Elected*

and ending their divisive politics, building a more authentic and inclusive democracy, and constructing, as a result, a more legitimate state, the electoral model can help soften conflicts between majorities and minorities and thereby depoliticize the citizenship and boundary issues that for so long have kept authoritarians in power and divided democrats in mixed regimes.[87] As Pavol Demeš and Joerg Forbrig have argued in their comparative study of civic campaigns that have contributed to electoral breakthroughs: "Throughout these campaigns a new form of patriotism, based on proud, active citizenship, rather than the aggressive populist nationalism of the regimes, emerged."[88]

OTHER BENEFICIARIES

Thus far, our assessment of the benefits of the electoral model has focused primarily on mass publics. However, the electoral approach is also beneficial for other players involved in democratic change. For example, the electoral model is distinctive in building bridges between political parties and civil society organizations, and it leaves behind some important organizations that continue to invest in the quality of elections – for instance, CeSID (the Center for Free Elections and Democracy) in Serbia.[89] At the same time, one of the strengths of this model with respect to the opposition is that it invests in democratic development by building on the power of self-interest. Finally, and usually overlooked, the electoral model also helps the international democracy assistance community overcome some of its built-in limitations. First, the electoral model allows international democracy promoters to be both effective and legitimate, because this approach to democratic change softens the familiar tension between supporting regime change – which has the problem of constituting a major violation of state sovereignty, while pursuing policies that bear a distressing resemblance to Cold War practices – and taking the far more defensible position of providing help for free and fair elections. In fact, as we argued in the last chapter, members of the international democracy assistance community do not usually pursue a project of regime change through elections. Thus, the U.S. and European commitment to turnover in governing parties and political leaders in Slovakia in 1998 and Croatia and Serbia in 2000 was the exception, not the rule.[90]

Affinities: Democracy and Party Competition in Slovakia and the Czech Republic (Stanford, CA: Stanford University Press, 2006).

[87] See, especially, V. P. Gagnon, *The Myth of Ethnic War: Serbia and Croatia in the 1990s* (Ithaca, NY: Cornell University Press, 2004).

[88] Demeš and Forbrig, "Civic Action and Democratic Power Shifts," 185.

[89] Thomas Carothers, "The End of the Transition Paradigm," *Journal of Democracy* 13:1 (January 2002), 5–21.

[90] See Carl Gershman and Michael Allen, "The Assault on Democracy Assistance," *Journal of Democracy* 17:2 (April 2006), 36–51; Walt Bogdanich and Jenny Nordberg, "Democracy Undone: Back Channels versus Policy; Mixed U.S. Signals Helped Tilt Haiti toward Chaos," *New York Times*, January 29, 2006.

Moreover, unlike so many tasks associated with building democracy, the actions associated with improving the quality of elections – helping them to be, in short, more free and fair – are relatively easy to specify, to carry out (if local conditions permit), and to measure with respect to success and failure, improvements and retrogression. This is in contrast to other types of assistance, such as the rule of law or development of parties and parliaments, where it is much harder to demonstrate the value-added effects of assistance efforts. If funding for such programs is to continue, demonstrating impact is a bureaucratic necessity, and it can also help counter the familiar critique that international democracy assistance lacks accountability, largely because external actors do not have to live with the results of their interventions.[91]

In addition, it is important to realize that many of the individuals involved in democracy assistance – especially those working for the National Democratic Institute and the International Republican Institute – have had considerable experience with elections, whether as public officials or as members of their staffs in Washington or in the states. They are very different in this sense from their European counterparts. They are less likely, as a result, to make mistakes when working in this area – in contrast to, say, other types of democracy assistance, such as support of civil society, governance, and the rule of law. In fact, it can be argued that while many aspects of democratic development must necessarily be sensitive to local conditions, cultures, and needs, and that external actors make many mistakes because of their inability to take local conditions into account, elections have fewer constraints in this regard. The way one wins elections in the United States can be more easily transferred to other competitive political settings than the way one, say, forms committees in Congress, drafts legislation, or builds political parties. This does not mean, of course, that campaign issues, party platforms, and other important details of electoral politics would be or could be the same. But it does mean that there is, at the most general level, a tried-and-true formula for making strong bids to win political power.

Perhaps the most important benefit of the electoral model – and one that international democracy promoters are very quick to recognize themselves – is that it helps them solve their own collective action problems. As our interviews in Washington and in Baku, Belgrade, Bratislava, Kyiv, Lviv, Tbilisi, Yerevan, London, and Zagreb repeatedly brought home, the international democracy assistance community is not really a community, if by "community" we mean shared membership in a group that pursues common goals and engages in regular interactions defined by a set of shared and often overlapping tasks. In practice, international democracy promoters on the ground – even if they are

---

[91] See Benedict Anderson, *Long-distance Nationalism: World Capitalism and the Rise of Identity Politics* (Berkeley: Center for German and European Studies, University of California, 1992); and National Research Councils of the National Academies, Committee on Evaluation of USAID Democracy Assistance Programs, *Improving Democracy Assistance: Building Knowledge through Evaluations and Research* (Washington, DC: National Academies Press, 2008).

from the same country – pursue quite different tasks, often work alone, and often fail to coordinate their actions.[92]

By focusing attention on elections and delineating specific tasks to be performed, the electoral model invests in a more (but far from fully) collaborative and coordinated process of international democracy assistance. This occurs largely because of the nature of elections and the electoral model. Also important is the familiarity with elections, and the excitement that comes when elections are called and opportunities for change present themselves. As James C. O'Brien, who served in the State Department as the leader of the Washington side of the campaign against Milošević, stated in an interview with us: "We were at a loss about how to bring down Milošević. But then he called early elections and suddenly we had a chance to mount a focused campaign against him."[93] For all these reasons, at least some of the built-in inefficiencies of international assistance are less pronounced if we focus on elections and the international democracy promotion apparatus.[94]

CONCLUSIONS

The purpose of this chapter has been to lay out the key components of the electoral model, identify its origins and geographical spread, and assess its ability to override many of the constraints on electoral change in mixed regimes. Rather than summarize our discussion, let us highlight two core observations that frame our discussion. One is that the electoral model is a remarkably efficient approach to defeating authoritarian leaders in mixed regimes, because it is well positioned to exploit opportunities for democratic change while surmounting many of the obstacles to such change. The other observation is more theoretical. The electoral model reminds us, like our case studies, that agency played a prominent role in shaping who won and who lost these elections. Authoritarian leaders do not vacate office simply because they have grown increasingly weak as a result of long-term political and economic trends. While these factors no doubt play some role, they must be combined with other influences, the most important of which is ambitious campaigns run by opposition parties and their allies. However, while individual and group

---

[92] Interviews with Adriana Lazinica, Belgrade, April 15, 2005; Gregory Simpson, Belgrade, April 13, 2005; Mike Staresinic, Belgrade, April 15, 2005; Patrick Merloe, Washington, DC, April 30, 2009; Lindsay Lloyd, Washington, DC, November 16, 2006; Scott Carpenter, Washington, DC, April 9, 2009; Amy Schultz, Baku, March 6, 2007; Dallas Frohrib, Baku, March 6, 2007; Chedomir Flego, Yerevan, March 14, 2007; Armineh Arakelian, Yerevan, March 13, 2007; Alex Sadar, Yerevan, March 14, 2007; Andrew Bennett, Yerevan, March 12, 2007; Gavin Helf, Yerevan, March 9 and 10, 2007; and Taline Sanassarian, Yerevan, March 13, 2007; and see Jeffrey Kopstein, "The Transatlantic Divide over Democracy Promotion," *The Washington Quarterly* 29:2 (Spring 2006), 85–98; National Research Councils, *Improving Democracy Assistance*; and Mitchell, *Uncertain Democracy*.

[93] Interview with James C. O'Brien, Washington, DC, November 16, 2006.

[94] William Easterly, "The Cartel of Good Intentions: The Problem with Bureaucracy in Foreign Aid," *Journal of Policy Reform* 5:4 (December 2002), 223–250.

actions are critical to electoral outcomes and thereby point to the impact of agency, these actions, we must remember, involve careful implementation of a detailed list of specific and interrelated activities. Thus, agency in our case says more about the role of planning, coordination, and hard work, and about the importance of transnational networks, than about the more accidental and chaotic processes and the impact of a handful of people that are so often associated with arguments that emphasize agency.

10

The Cross-National Diffusion of Democratizing Elections

> My Croatian friends should look at the [Slovak] election and learn from our mistakes.
>
> Vladimír Mečiar[1]

> Diffusion is the process whereby past events make future events more likely.
>
> Pamela Oliver and David Meyers[2]

In the previous two chapters, we presented three arguments. First, oppositions have won power in mixed regimes in postcommunist Europe and Eurasia when they and their allies have mounted innovative and sophisticated campaigns for political office. Second, the electoral model is vital to the success of the opposition, because it is very effective at getting citizens to vote, support the opposition, and, if necessary, defend their choices in the streets. Finally, this model did not originate in the postcommunist region. Its origins can be found, instead, in the United States, where it became standard operating procedure in national and state elections, and in the Philippines and Chile, where it played a key role in ending authoritarian rule during the second half of the 1980s.

The purpose of this chapter is to build on these arguments by switching our approach from one that treats the elections of interest in this book as separate events to one that analyzes them as related developments. We are interested, therefore, in the question of whether the cross-national diffusion of the electoral model explains why oppositions won or lost and why there were so many electoral turnovers in the postcommunist region in such a short period of time.

---

[1] Quoted in Marko Fukić and Željko Čapin, "Vladimir Mečiar, bivši premijer Republike Slovačke: Hrvatski prijatelji voci izbora mogu učiti na našim pogreškama," *Večernji list*, November 17, 1999, p. 17.

[2] Pamela E. Oliver and Daniel J. Myers, "Networks, Diffusion, and Cycles of Collective Action," in *Social Movement Analysis: The Network Perspective*, ed. Mario Diani and Doug McAdam (Oxford: Oxford University Press, 2003), 174.

BURDEN OF PROOF

Our assessment of diffusion in this chapter proceeds from the assumption that any case in support of diffusion requires a substantial burden of proof. This is, first, because it is insufficient, despite the claims made in many studies of diffusion, to demonstrate simply that similar innovations were adopted in multiple locales within a circumscribed period of time. Instead, other kinds of evidence must also be brought to the table that account for gaps in the cross-national transmission of an innovation, identify the drivers of diffusion, and eliminate competing explanations.[3] Moreover, it is extremely important to specify the innovation that is moving among sites and to separate it from its consequences – standards that many studies of the diffusion of democracy, for example, fail to meet.[4] At the same time, it is important to keep in mind that there are sizeable barriers to cross-national diffusion, if only because, as Margaret Keck and Kathryn Sikkink note, "sovereignty is eroded only in clearly delimited circumstances."[5] This leads us to a final consideration that takes us back to the innovation of interest in this book, the electoral model. Innovations are far less likely to travel across state boundaries when they threaten the prevailing distribution of political and economic power. In these circumstances, incumbent elites and their domestic and international allies stand as unusually resolute guardians of the status quo. Just as they monitor closely developments in their own countries that might undermine their privileged position, so they pay close attention to developments in their regional neighborhood that hold open the possibility of doing the same.

With these issues in mind, we can now turn to our evaluation of diffusion dynamics in the spread of electoral change in the postcommunist region. We begin our assessment by turning briefly to the literature on diffusion and

[3] Valerie Bunce and Sharon Wolchik, "International Diffusion and Postcommunist Electoral Revolutions," *Communist and Post-Communist Studies* 39:3 (September 2006), 283–304; Valerie Bunce and Sharon Wolchik, "Transnational Networks, Diffusion Dynamics, and Electoral Change in the Postcommunist World," in *The Diffusion of Social Movements*, ed. Rebecca Kolins Givan, Sarah A. Soule, and Kenneth M. Roberts (Cambridge: Cambridge University Press, 2010), 140–162; Wade Jacoby, "Inspiration, Coalition and Substitution: External Influences on Postcommunist Transformations," *World Politics* 58:4 (July 2006), 623–651; Wade Jacoby, *The Enlargement of the European Union and NATO: Ordering from the Menu in Central Europe* (Cambridge: Cambridge University Press, 2004); Everett Rogers, *Diffusion of Innovations* (New York: Free Press, 1996); Johanna Bockman and Gil Eyal, "Eastern Europe as a Laboratory for Economic Knowledge: The Transnational Roots of Neoliberalism," *The American Journal of Sociology* 108:2 (September 2002), 310–352.

[4] Daniel Brinks and Michael Coppedge, "Diffusion Is No Illusion: Neighbor Emulation in the Third Wave of Democracy," *Comparative Political Studies* 39:4 (May 1, 2006), 463–489; Kristian Skrede Gleditsch and Michael D. Ward, "Diffusion and the International Context of Democratization," *International Organization* 60:4 (October 2006), 911–933.

[5] Margaret E. Keck and Kathryn Sikkink, *Activists beyond Borders: Advocacy Networks in International Politics* (Ithaca, NY: Cornell University Press, 1998), 212.

providing some definitions, generalizations about its key characteristics, and competing theories about its underlying causes.[6]

DIFFUSION: DEFINITIONS AND PATTERNS

Diffusion can be defined as a process whereby new ideas, institutions, policies, models, or repertoires of behavior spread geographically from a core site to new sites, whether within a given state (as when the movement of new policies invented in one political subunit spreads to other subunits within a polity) or across states (as with the spread, for example, of public sector downsizing or nongovernmental organizations).[7] Diffusion, therefore, implies, on the one hand, a specific constellation of actions that represent a significant departure from previous practices and, on the other, a transfer of the innovation within a limited time span from the site of origin to new settings.

Diffusion has been associated in a number of studies with some distinctive patterns that will prove helpful in our assessment of electoral change. One is that planning often plays a critical role in both introducing innovation and its diffusion. Innovations, in short, are usually more deeply rooted and more carefully crafted than they appear. At the same time, they are also less original than they seem. While "newness" is central to the idea of innovation, innovation nonetheless owes at least some of its originality to past developments – in

---

[6] Doug McAdam and Dieter Rucht, "The Cross-National Diffusion of Movement Ideas," *The Annals of the American Academy of Political and Social Science* 528:1 (July 2003), 56–74; David Strang and Sarah A. Soule, "Diffusion in Organizations and Social Movements: From Hybrid Corn to Poison Pills," *Annual Review of Sociology* 24:1 (August 1998), 265–290.

[7] See, for example, the pioneering work of Jack Walker, "The Diffusion of Innovation among the American States," *The American Political Science Review* 63:3 (September 1969); and Zvi Gitelman, *The Diffusion of Political Innovation: From Eastern Europe to the Soviet Union* (Beverly Hills: Sage Publications, 1972); along with Peter Ackerman and Jack DuVall, *A Force More Powerful: A Century of Nonviolent Conflict* (New York: St. Martin's Press, 2000); Doug McAdam and Dieter Rucht, "The Cross-National Diffusion of Movement Ideas"; Strang and Soule, "Diffusion in Organizations"; Sada Aksartova, "Civil Society Promotion or Global Organizational Diffusion? U.S. Civil Society Assistance for the FSU," paper presented at the Eastern Sociological Society, Washington, DC, May 17–20, 2005; Chang Kil Lee and David Strang, "The International Diffusion of Public-Sector Downsizing: Network Emulation and Theory-Driven Learning," *International Organization* 60:4 (October 2006), 883–909; Mark Beissinger, *Nationalist Mobilization and the Collapse of the Soviet State* (Cambridge: Cambridge University Press, 2002); Daniel Brinks and Michael Coppedge, "Diffusion Is No Illusion"; John Markoff, *Waves of Democracy: Social Movements and Political Change* (Thousand Oaks, CA: Pine Forge Press, 1996); Sidney G. Tarrow, *The New Transnational Activism* (Cambridge: Cambridge University Press, 2005); Sidney Tarrow and Donatella della Porta, "Globalization, Complex Internationalism and Transnational Contention," in *Transnational Protest and Global Activism*, ed. Donatella della Porta and Sidney Tarrow (Lanham, MD: Rowman and Littlefield, 2005), 227–246; Doug McAdam, Sidney G. Tarrow, and Charles Tilly, *Dynamics of Contention* (Cambridge: Cambridge University Press, 2001); and Mario Diani and Doug McAdam, eds., *Social Movements and Networks: Relational Approaches to Collective Action* (Oxford: Oxford University Press, 2003).

several ways. One is that there are usually some dress rehearsals, with elements of the innovation serving as a source of experimentation. The other is that, even before they embark on their cross-national journey, innovations have themselves usually been the product of diffusion. Here, we are reminded of our discussion in the last chapter, where we laid out the invention of the electoral model in the Philippines and its transfer to Chile. Implied in the argument that diffusion itself contributes to innovations that are then subject to diffusion is the importance of not just continuing and creative interactions among importers and exporters and the important lessons that have been culled from each round of electoral change, but also changes in "the political opportunity structure" that create space for mobilization and the facilitating role of transnational actors.[8]

Most studies of diffusion also emphasize the importance of regional effects in the movement of innovations. The argument here is that, all else being equal, innovations are more likely to travel to neighboring locales than to far-flung settings, largely because proximity increases the probability of knowledge about changes that have occurred outside the borders of the state, while increasing the likelihood that similar opportunities and needs will encourage the drawing of analogies and "structural facilitation."[9] The key issue, therefore, is the intersection between information and commonalities that reflect the shared cultures, history, and political, economic, and social systems that are characteristic, for example, of subunits located within the same state or in states sharing the same region. However, diffusion can also take place in less geographically compact centers of activity, especially when similar opportunities for change present themselves and when the innovation is perceived to be both successful and resonant with the values and interests of local constituencies. These are precisely the reasons why, for instance, we find similar opposition strategies in the Philippines and Chile in 1986 and 1988 and why oppositions in such diverse contexts as Ethiopia, Guinea, Iran, the Ivory Coast, Kenya, Lebanon, Mexico, Peru, Togo, Venezuela, and Zimbabwe have been quick to embrace at least some parts of the electoral model.

Another aspect of diffusion that bears highlighting is the fact that both the innovation itself and its processes of transmission tend to change in response to variations in local conditions. For example, there are understandable amendments in the innovation that occur as a result of different readings of what needs to be done; differences in the goals and capacities

---

[8] See, especially, Sidney Tarrow, *Power in Movement: Social Movements and Contentious Politics* (Cambridge: Cambridge University Press, 1998); and Sidney Tarrow, "From Lumping to Splitting: Specifying Globalization and Resistance," in *Globalization and Resistance: Transnational Dimensions of Social Movements*, ed. Jackie Smith and Hank Johnston (Lanham, MD: Rowman and Littlefield, 2003), 229–250; Keck and Sikkink, *Activists beyond Borders*; Diani and McAdam, eds., *Social Movements and Networks*; Oliver and Myers, "Networks, Diffusion, and Cycles"; and McAdam, Tilly, and Tarrow, *Dynamics of Contention*.

[9] Drawing on Beissinger, *Nationalist Mobilization*.

of constituencies affected both positively and negatively by the innovation; changes in the availability and the resources of international allies supporting local adoption of the innovation; and cross-national variations in opportunity structures.[10] One implication of these arguments is that, while the claim of the cross-national diffusion of innovation rests upon the existence of similar developments, these developments can have – and usually do have – different consequences. For example, as we will argue in the next chapter, electoral turnovers meant different things in different countries.

The uneven character of democratic development after these elections also reminds us that international precedents provide important lessons not just to would-be adopters, but also to would-be resisters. The diffusion of innovation, therefore, always involves political struggle, and analyses that presume otherwise often understate the resistance to change. Analysts also tend to ignore the questions of why there are gaps in the spread of innovation and why diffusion comes to an end.[11] In addition, as the tragic example of the protests and ethnic cleansing that followed the Kenyan presidential election in late 2007 reminds us, innovations, such as the electoral model, can be used for a variety of purposes apart from the struggle to carry out free and fair elections. Thus, built into the diffusion project are significant variations – in the content of the innovation, its purposes, and its consequences, as well as in rates of adoption across time and space.[12]

Finally, the diffusion of innovation seems to follow a relatively predictable cycle. As Mark Beissinger has summarized in his study of the nationalist protests that led to the dissolution of the Soviet Union, early innovators – or what he calls "early risers" – had the disadvantage of limited precedents for their actions, but the considerable advantage of structural conditions that helped "embolden" challengers to the status quo to move in new directions.[13] This is precisely why, when communism began to unravel in the Soviet Union, for example, activists in the Baltic republics from 1987 to 1988 were able to reframe their identities and invent new forms of participation, which then combined

---

[10] See Tarrow, *Power in Movement*; and Tarrow, "From Lumping to Splitting."

[11] See, especially, Jacoby, *The Enlargement of the European Union and NATO*; Jacoby, "Inspiration, Coalition and Substitution: External Influences on Postcommunist Transformations;" and Beate Sissenich, *Building States without Society: European Union Enlargement and the Transfer of EU Social Policy to Poland and Hungary* (Lanham, MD: Lexington Books, 2007).

[12] The Moldovan election in 2004 provides yet another variant on this dynamic. Fearing a "color revolution," the incumbent, Vladimir Voronin, moved away from his alliance with Russia in order to weaken the democratic opposition and, as a result, won reelection. See Menno Fenger, "The Diffusion of Revolutions: Comparing Recent Regime Turnovers in Five Post-Communist Countries," *Demokratizatsiya* 15:1 (Winter 2007), 5–27; and Valerie Bunce and Sharon L. Wolchik, "Mixed Regimes in Postcommunist Eurasia: Tipping Democratic and Tipping Authoritarian," in *Hybrid Regimes: International Anchoring and Domestic Dynamics in Post-Soviet States*, ed. Elena Barcani (Florence, Italy: European Press Academic Publishing, 2010), 57–86.

[13] Beissinger, *Nationalist Mobilization*.

to form innovative responses to the status quo that were then available for subsequent diffusion to other geographic locales. They also benefited from what can be termed "mini-innovations," such as smaller-scale protests, street theater, and marches, which in other contexts and times, such as in Poland in the 1980s, had contributed key elements to the eventual mobilization package.[14] However, as anti-regime protests merged with antistate protests and the combination of the two spread outside its founding core through a "mimetic process" that meant that "protest makers [did] ... not have to reinvent the wheel at each place and in each conflict,"[15] the weightings of structural support for change versus demonstration effects shifted. While the cross-national impact of precedents in the neighborhood increased, it was simultaneously joined by weaker and weaker local structural support for change. Put simply, the image of positive outcomes began to outrace both local capabilities and careful preparations.

SUPPORTIVE FACTORS

How do we know when diffusion has taken place? We would argue that a two-stage explanation is required. First, central to establishing diffusion is uncovering a particular pattern of change wherein similar innovations appear in staggered fashion in multiple locales. Such a pattern, however, is only suggestive of diffusion, especially in the absence of alternative explanations and evidence delineating the how and why of cross-national transmission. Here, we can offer one telling historical example that highlights why the identification of underlying causes is so important. Was the rise of communism throughout Eastern Europe (minus Greece) and in China following the end of World War II a case of the cross-national diffusion of the communist model? It is certainly true that, on the face of it, the spread of communism looks very much like diffusion. The victory of communism involved a dramatic and distinctive political and economic departure from earlier regimes in these countries; the regimes that arose were remarkably similar to one another (though they later diverged); and the rise of communist regimes took place through a process that was lagged in time, yet clustered in terms of geography (with the exception of China). However, there is a dearth of evidence supporting the existence of transnational transmission – which is crucial to diffusion – in the rise of these communist regimes from 1944 to 1949. Instead, the victory of communist parties in most of Central and Eastern Europe reflected the Soviet Union's imposition of its model – though using variable methods, under variable international conditions, and with varying degrees of local support.[16] At the same

---

[14] Kenney, *A Carnival of Revolution: Central Europe, 1989* (Princeton, NJ: Princeton University Press, 2003); and Nils R. Muiznieks, "The Influence of the Baltic Popular Movements on the Process of Soviet Disintegration," *Europe-Asia Studies* 47:1 (January 1995), 3–25.

[15] McAdam and Rucht, "The Cross-National Diffusion of Movement Ideas," 58.

[16] See, for example, R. V. Burks, *The Dynamics of Communism in Eastern Europe* (Princeton, NJ: Princeton University Press, 1961); Zbigniew K. Brzezinski, *The Soviet Bloc: Unity and*

time, in the two cases where communism was "homegrown" and less affected by Soviet interventions – that is, in Yugoslavia and China – the case for diffusion is just as weak. Instead, in both countries communism grew out of similar, but parallel, developments: the collapse of the old order in wartime and the ability of communist movements to emerge victorious after the war as a result of their ability – as opposed to that of other forces – to defend the homeland against foreign occupation.

COMPETING EXPLANATIONS

What this example suggests is that diffusion can be an illusion (to borrow from Brinks and Coppedge)[17] when a cross-national pattern of similar changes reflects in practice a largely vertical process involving either similar responses to common conditions or international orchestration of such changes. The key question, as a result, centers on establishing the *horizontal* foundations of the diffusion story, that is, the factors that encourage the cross-national transmission of innovation.

Studies of diffusion have offered widely varying accounts of the dynamics supporting the cross-national movement of innovation.[18] In our view, this thicket of competing explanations can be pruned back to reveal three different lines of argument. One is that diffusion can occur because the model itself is unusually amenable to cross-national applications. This can be because the model is easy to transport; because it is widely viewed as successful; because it resonates with the interests and values of large constituencies in a range of

---

Conflict (Boston: Harvard University Press, 1967); Charles Gati, *Failed Illusions: Moscow, Washington, Budapest, and the 1956 Hungarian Revolt* (Stanford, CA: Stanford University Press, 2006); Charles Gati, *Hungary and the Soviet Bloc* (Durham, NC: Duke University Press, 1986); and Mark Kramer, "The Dynamics of Contagion in the Communist Bloc and the Impact on Regime Survival," paper presented at the Conference on Postcommunist Resilience, Dartmouth University, May 25–26, 2007.

17 Brinks and Coppedge, "Diffusion Is No Illusion."

18 See, for instance, Tarrow, *The New Transnational Activism*; Mark Beissinger, "Promoting Democracy: Is Exporting Revolution a Constructive Strategy?," *Dissent* 53:1 (Winter 2006), 18–24; John K. Glenn, *Framing Democracy: Civil Society and Civic Movements in Eastern Europe* (Stanford, CA: Stanford University Press, 2001); Johanna Bockman and Gil Eyal, "Eastern Europe as a Laboratory for Economic Knowledge: The Transnational Roots of Neoliberalism"; Strang and Soule, "Diffusion in Organizations and Social Movements"; Aksartova, "Civil Society Promotion or Global Organizational Diffusion?"; Rogers, *Diffusion of Innovation*; Lee and Strang, "The International Diffusion of Public-Sector Downsizing"; Gleditsch and Ward, "Diffusion and the International Context of Democratization"; Beth Simmons, Frank Dobbin, and Geoffrey Garrett, eds., *The Global Diffusion of Markets and Democracy* (Cambridge: Cambridge University Press, 2008); Beth Simmons and Zachary Elkins, "The Globalization of Liberalization: Policy Diffusion in the International Political Economy," *American Political Science Review* 98:1 (February 2004), 171–189; and Zachary Elkins and Beth Simmons, "On Waves, Clusters, and Diffusion: A Conceptual Framework," *The Annals of the American Academy of Political and Social Science* 589 (March 2005), 33–51.

countries; and/or because it is well suited to exploit opportunities for change. Perhaps the most important consideration with respect to the innovation, however, is the multiplier effects associated with the accumulation of appealing dress rehearsals. As Mark Beissinger has explained, "The successful example of early risers disrupts the compliance systems facing other groups, lowering some of the obstacles that subsequent mobilizers must surmount in order to embolden supporters."[19]

The second explanation for diffusion is the presence of similar local conditions in the "sending" and "receiving" sites (though the trick here, we must remember, is establishing similarities that support cross-national adoption but that fail, at the same time, to reduce adoption of similar innovations to parallel responses to similar local needs, opportunities, and ideas). These conditions can be either relatively fixed – for example, similarities in political, economic, and social regimes and the hierarchies, needs, and capacities they generate – or relatively short-term – for instance, political or economic crises, cross-national commonalities in the availability of new resources, or a sharp decline in the power and cohesion of coalitions supporting the status quo.[20] While many accounts of diffusion stress objective similarities, perceptions of similarities on the part of key actors also play a role.[21] As Doug McAdam and Dieter Rucht have observed, "Consistent with the general thrust of diffusion theory, adopters must identify at some minimal level with transmitters if diffusion is to occur."[22]

Finally, the diffusion of innovation can occur because of the existence of transnational networks committed to the spread of the model from one site to others. These networks typically bring together both domestic and international actors who share the same concerns and goals and who – as a result of repeated interactions over time, the forging of connections among nonrelational players, and the provision of new resources – devise a common approach.[23] However, it is important to recognize that these actors may want the same outcome for different reasons, reasons that become far more apparent after the innovation is imported. Moreover, just as local actors may seek international allies, the reverse can also happen, with the result that the two sets of players find collaboration beneficial and converge on a common approach that in some instances can solidify into a playbook that can be applied and exported.[24]

---

[19] Beissinger, *Nationalist Mobilization*, 159.

[20] Steven Levitsky and Lucan Way, *Competitive Authoritarianism: The Origins and Evolution of Hybrid Regimes in the Post-Cold War Era* (Cambridge: Cambridge University Press, 2010); Henry Hale, "Regime Cycles, Democracy, Autocracy and Revolution in Post-Soviet Eurasia," *World Politics* 58:1 (October 2005), 133–165; Henry Hale, "Divided We Stand," *World Politics* 56:2 (January 2004), 165–193.

[21] See, especially, McAdam, Tarrow, and Tilly, *Dynamics of Contention*; and Charles Tilly and Sidney Tarrow, *Contentious Politics* (Boulder, CO: Paradigm Publishers, 2007).

[22] McAdam and Rucht, "The Cross-National Diffusion of Movement Ideas," 63.

[23] And see Tilly and Tarrow, *Contentious Politics*.

[24] See Tarrow, *The New Transnational Activism*; and Keck and Sikkink, *Activists beyond Borders*.

All three of these explanations – that is, the nature of the innovation itself, similarities in local conditions, and transnational networks – address the "why" question by specifying sets of factors that facilitate the cross-national spread of innovations. However, it is the final influence that speaks most directly to the "who" and the "how" issues, that is, the role of individuals, embedded in networks, who transport innovative and tried ideas to new settings, while capitalizing on the contributions to diffusion of playbooks, positive precedents, and similar contexts. Just as these explanations tend to overlap and interact, as well as to compete with one another, so they can be combined to construct a useful hypothesis. It can be argued that diffusion is more likely to occur when more of these factors are in place. The presence of more, rather than fewer, supportive factors, moreover, would seem to be particularly important when the innovation in question, like the electoral model, is one that takes on the prevailing power structures.

PATTERNS OF DIFFUSION

The case studies presented in Chapters 3 through 6 and our comparison in Chapter 8 of successful and failed electoral attempts to remove authoritarian leaders from office together provide strong evidence that the electoral shifts that occurred in the postcommunist region from 1996 to 2005 followed a pattern consistent with a diffusion model of cross-national change. What we see, in particular, are breakthrough elections that took place in lagged fashion across a large group of countries located within the same region, where some of the countries bordered upon one another (Georgia and Kyrgyzstan are the only exceptions). Moreover, the contexts within which these elections took place were roughly similar in two respects: all of these countries were once republics embedded in larger communist states, and they all straddled democracy and authoritarianism after independence. There is also little doubt that all the breakthrough elections were innovative events, because they marked a sharp departure from the political past – in three ways. One is that the elections of interest had outcomes quite different from those of prior elections – though the opposition in Slovakia had occupied office briefly in the past. Another is that the victory of the opposition contributed to improved democratic performance – though to quite varying degrees, as we will elaborate further in the next chapter. Finally and most importantly, electoral turnover was based in all cases (though least so in Kyrgyzstan) on deployment of the electoral model (see Chapters 8 and 9).

If the electoral model made it much harder for the regime to continue governing and much easier for the opposition to win power, it also provided the latter with an insurance policy of sorts. As we saw in Ukraine, in particular, the many thousands of Western electoral observers were encouraged to voice strong concerns about the regime's electoral management because they saw firsthand that the election was neither free nor fair. Moreover, they saw that the opposition was strongly committed to winning office and had run a strong campaign, and that there was a sharp contrast between the regime's calculation of the vote and that of the opposition (as a result of both exit polls and parallel vote tabulation, often carried out via collaboration between local and Western polling organizations). At the same time, implementation of the electoral model involved the construction of a series of organizations that had as their missions running sophisticated political campaigns, linking the opposition with civil society, encouraging voter registration and turnout, and promoting free and fair elections. These organizations, in turn, were in a strong position to respond quickly and effectively to last-minute challenges. Most obviously, these organizations served as a base for popular protests when, as in Georgia, Serbia, and Ukraine, in particular, the regime tried to steal the election – for example, by claiming in a two-round presidential election system that a second round was required or by claiming an outright victory. Less obviously, these organizations had the volunteers, the coordinative capacity, and the data to respond effectively and quickly on election day to patterns of voter turnout that worked against a possible victory by the opposition.[25]

Thus, what we find in the case of our breakthrough elections is a classic diffusion pattern. Moreover, the case for diffusion rests not just on the general pattern of electoral breakthroughs and the striking similarities in the electoral tool kits deployed by the opposition and its allies or the fact that this was the first time, in every case, that this distinctive package of strategies was used. It is also that we find among our successful cases of electoral breakthroughs a striking "redundancy" in stylistic flourishes, ranging from the extensive use of marches and street theater and the creation of youth groups to the adoption of similar symbols (such as specific colors and the clenched fist) and slogans, as we have discussed in the last chapter.

Also resonant with the literature on diffusion is the fact that these breakthrough elections involved modifications of the innovation in response to local conditions. For example, once the struggle moved to more authoritarian political settings, popular protests became necessary for postelection transfers of political power to the opposition. At the same time, the spread of the electoral model is typical of diffusion dynamics in other ways, including, for instance, the role of earlier, but partial, experiments and the importance of planning.

Finally, we also find a familiar diffusion cycle at work. As the wave moved, it entered more difficult terrain for democratic change. Just as the regime context for these electoral struggles shifted from less to more authoritarian, so, not surprisingly, more extreme measures were needed in order for oppositions to win power and take office. Take, for example, the contrast between Slovakia, where the model was first fully elaborated and implemented, and Kyrgyzstan, where the departure of Akaev (who was not even on the ballot in this parliamentary election) spoke directly to the triumph

---

[25] Interview with Marko Blagojević, Belgrade, April 11, 2005.

of demonstration effects over planning.[26] If precedents outran planning, however, as we argued in detail in Chapter 6, so defenders of the status quo, especially as the cases of successful electoral breakthroughs accumulated, became more and more committed to preempting electoral challenges in their own countries.

Indeed, it was precisely for both of these reasons, along with a thinning of the transnational network that carried the electoral model from place to place, that oppositions in Armenia, Azerbaijan, and Belarus failed to win office in the elections that took place in these countries from 2003 to 2008. All of these elections took place, we must remember, toward the end of the wave of electoral breakthroughs. Moreover, as we set out in more detail in Chapters 7 and 8, in all three cases, just as the opposition parties failed to deploy all the components of the electoral model (though they did unify), so authoritarian incumbents remained vigilant guardians of their powers – in striking contrast, for instance, to Shevardnadze in Georgia. Kocharian, Aliyev, and Lukashenka were able to stave off strong electoral challenges and popular protests after the elections because they combined the techniques that regimes in Serbia, Georgia, and Ukraine had used, but to no avail, in 2000, 2003, and 2004, respectively, such as resisting international pressures to improve electoral procedures, harassing the opposition and civil society groups, and stealing the elections, with new measures implemented during and after the elections that assured their continuing control over the media, the security forces, political institutions such as the parliament and the courts, and, finally, public spaces. What we find, in short, is learning on the part of some authoritarian incumbents. For example, just as all three leaders prevented extensive vote monitoring, so Aliyev in Azerbaijan in 2003 and 2005 and Lukashenka in Belarus in 2006 (and in 2001) allowed protests to take place following the elections, but were careful to block off important sections of the capital from the demonstrators. Thus, the electoral model failed to diffuse to Armenia, Azerbaijan, and Belarus in part because of regime actions, but also, it must be emphasized, because of inaction on the part of local democracy activists and, in the case of Armenia and Azerbaijan, lack of clear international support for a change of regime.

DEBATING DIFFUSION

The wave of democratizing elections in the postcommunist region, along with the geographical limits of that wave, therefore, conforms closely to scholarly understandings of international diffusion dynamics. This conclusion is

---

[26] See, especially, Scott Radnitz, "What Really Happened in Kyrgyzstan?," *Journal of Democracy* 17:2 (April 2006) 132–146; and Scott Radnitz, "A Horse of a Different Color: Revolution and Regression in Kyrgyzstan," in *Democracy and Authoritarianism in the Postcommunist World*, ed. Valerie Bunce, Michael McFaul, and Kathryn Stoner-Weiss (Cambridge: Cambridge University Press, 2010), 300–324.

particularly compelling because it applies to both the serial adoptions of the electoral model in Slovakia, Croatia, Serbia, Georgia, Ukraine, and Kyrgyzstan and to holdouts to the transmission of this model, as in Armenia, Azerbaijan, and Belarus. In some respects, this conclusion about the role of diffusion in these elections is not surprising. Postcommunist Europe and Eurasia is a region of the world unusually rich in examples of the cross-national spread of political change.[27] That the spread of democracy, more generally, seems to be a process that takes place within regions is another reason to be confident about interpreting the spread of the electoral model and, with that, electoral turnover as a diffusion dynamic.[28]

At the same time, however, there are compelling reasons to question the interpretation of diffusion. As we argued in earlier chapters, there are formidable behavioral and structural obstacles in mixed regimes in particular to the cross-national movement of democratic change. For example, such regimes tend to produce fragmented oppositions; leaders in such regimes have considerable resources at their disposal with which to woo and demobilize citizens while blocking challenges to their power; and such regimes often have powerful international allies (such as Russia in the cases of both Armenia and Belarus, and, as we suggested earlier in this book, the United States, ironically, in the case of Azerbaijan). What makes the strategies of authoritarians so effective, we must remember, is the nature of elections. Because they are scheduled in advance, take place during a prescribed period of time, and feature a relatively predictable set of activities, elections are well suited to become prime targets for preemptive strikes by powerful actors. In this sense, while ideal in some respects for challenging dictatorial rule (as we argued in the previous chapter), the electoral model also carries with it some distinct advantages for authoritarians intent on defending their powers. Moreover, in mixed-regime settings, such as Russia under Putin, for example, dictators can be relatively popular – though the real distribution of both public sentiment and the stability of the coalitions surrounding the leader are unknown. At the same time, the norm in such polities is for citizens to be demobilized for the simple reason that regime policies, the sheer durability of the regime, and the nature of the opposition itself have converged to make mobilization against the regime a very difficult and seemingly futile activity. While repression plays a role in sidelining citizens, so does widespread suspicion of the opposition. In this sense, electoral continuity in mixed regimes reflects the fact that both sides in the struggle for power are culpable.

---

[27] See, for instance, Gitelman, "The Diffusion of Political Innovation."

[28] Gleditsch and Ward, "Diffusion and the International Context of Democratization"; Brinks and Coppedge, "Diffusion Is No Illusion"; Harvey Starr and Christina Lindborg, "Democratic Dominoes Revisited: The Hazards of Governmental Transitions, 1974–1996," *Journal of Conflict Resolution* 47:4 (August 2003), 490–519; Barbara Wejnert, "Diffusion, Development, and Democracy, 1800–1999," *American Sociological Review* 70:1 (February 2005), 53–81; Markoff, *Waves of Democracy.*

COMPETING INTERPRETATIONS

These behavioral and structural constraints can be joined, moreover, with another reason to doubt diffusion. There is a distinct possibility that other factors, aside from those encouraging cross-national transmission, produced the diffusion-like pattern of democratizing elections. Here, we refer to the alternative scenarios, noted earlier, of either similar local conditions giving rise to similar innovative reactions or powerful international actors orchestrating similar innovations in a group of countries within the same region. In fact, our discussion in Chapter 2 and in the case study chapters provided some evidence in support of alternative accounts. Thus, common features shared by mixed regimes could have been responsible for giving rise to similar kinds of electoral challenges, especially given the learning that could come from repeated elections in which the opposition lost. The wave of electoral change from 1998 to 2005 could also reflect the considerable commitment on the part of the United States to promoting democracy in the postcommunist region in particular and its preoccupation with elections as both key indicators of, and gateways for, democratic development.

In our view, neither interpretation fits the facts on the ground. First, as we argued in earlier chapters, there is little doubt that the vulnerability of the regime played a role in each of our elections. For example, incumbent regimes in Armenia, Azerbaijan, and Belarus all featured relatively strong economic performance on the eve of their elections, and leaders in these three countries had been, on the whole, more successful than their counterparts in the other cases in institutionalizing their power and thereby controlling such gatekeepers of the regime as the military, the police, and the media.[29] At the same time, we do not find a pattern in the failed cases, as we do in the successful ones (except in Kyrgyzstan), of oppositions building a case for public support by winning power at the local level before mounting major challenges to authoritarian rule at the national level.

However, this line of argument can go only so far. One problem is that in three of our cases of electoral change (Croatia, Slovakia, and Ukraine), the economy was in fact on the upswing. Moreover, in many of the breakthrough cases, including Serbia, Georgia, and Ukraine, earlier elections had delivered a victory to the incumbents, yet had taken place in disastrous economic circumstances. Finally, while it is true that Armenia, Azerbaijan, and Belarus were more authoritarian at the time of their key elections than, say, Slovakia, the regime contrast between our two sets of elections blurs once we add Croatia, Serbia, Georgia, Ukraine, and Kyrgyzstan to the comparison. Thus, it would be hard to explain contrasting electoral results by simply referring to regime context or trends in politics and economics.

---

[29] See, especially, Vitali Silitski's comparison of Serbia and Belarus in Vitali Silitski, "The Long Road from Tyranny: Post-Communist Authoritarianism and Struggle for Democracy in Serbia and Belarus," unpublished manuscript, 2005.

A structural explanation that posits the possibility of similar conditions giving rise to similar electoral results also has little to say about the distinctive characteristics of the pivotal elections themselves, that is, the unprecedented willingness and ability of oppositions, the third sector, and ordinary citizens to seize the opportunities provided by regime decline and, at the same time, their adoption of one approach in particular to winning power – an approach that had not been deployed in the past. As we have argued throughout this book, there was a widespread perception in *all* of these countries that the government in power was invincible. This is because of its sheer duration in most cases, despite the challenges, for example, of lost wars, cascading corruption, and economic decline; because the opposition in *every* case had a long record of fragmentation, incompetence, collusion with the regime, and indifference toward voters; and because publics were suspicious of the opposition and doubtful of their own ability to make political change happen. Moreover, political habits die hard. The clear lesson of the many elections that preceded the breakthrough contests was that the opposition would fail and complain, while authoritarians would remain in power, and that all this would occur even in the face of both public protests and concerns expressed by the international community about the quality of elections.

Thus, what all of our breakthrough elections shared, to repeat our key finding in Chapter 8, was the implementation of the electoral model, a model explicitly designed to surmount the behavioral and structural constraints on electoral change. As a result, while structural considerations played a role in the democratizing elections, they cannot explain the timing of the electoral breakthroughs, their success, or the cross-national commonalities among the distinctively innovative strategies upon which these electoral successes rested. It is also hard to imagine how each of these oppositions – who were, after all, not very experienced in electoral politics – would be able to invent such an innovative portfolio of strategies for winning power – and, what is more, the same portfolio.

U.S. ORCHESTRATION

This leads to the second alternative to diffusion – that is, the role of the United States in engineering democratizing elections throughout the postcommunist region.[30] The argument here is that the United States, backed or assisted by

---

[30] And see Graeme Marche Herd, "Colorful Revolutions and the CIS," *Problems of Postcommunism* 52:2 (April 2005), 3–18; Bertil Nygren, "The Beauty and the Beast: When Electoral Democracy Hit Eurasia," unpublished manuscript, 2005; Vitali Silitski, "Different Authoritarianisms: Distinct Patterns of Electoral Change," in *Reclaiming Democracy: Civil Society and Electoral Change in Central and Eastern Europe*, ed. Joerg Forbrig and Pavol Demeš (Washington, DC: German Marshall Fund, 2007), 155–173; Aleksandr Knyazev, *Gosudarstvennyi Perevorot: 24 Marta 2005g v Kirgizii* (Moscow: Europa, 2005); and Fukić and Čapin, "Vladimir Mečiar, bivši premijer Republike Slovačke: Hrvatski prijatelji voci izbora mogu učiti na našim pogreškama."

the EU, the OSCE, and a variety of foundations, provided the funding and the infrastructure necessary to defeat authoritarian leaders in Croatia, Georgia, Kyrgyzstan, Serbia, Slovakia, and Ukraine. This support was vital to electoral success because it gave the opposition not just the ideas, the money, and the organizational tools to be victorious in the electoral contest, but also the promise of future support, should the opposition win power. From this perspective, one could reexamine the data we have presented to argue that, just as common strategies for defeating authoritarian leaders across our six cases could very well testify to the power of a single outside player – or international alliance of players – to dictate a specific approach to winning elections, so lags in adoption of this model could merely reflect variations in the attention span of U.S. democracy promoters and in the political opportunities presented by cross-national electoral calendars.

Does this interpretation have merit? In some ways, it is persuasive. As we argued in earlier chapters, there is little doubt that the United States has been very supportive of democratization through free and fair elections, that the United States has favored the postcommunist region over other parts of the world in its global efforts to support democratic development, and that significant U.S. democracy assistance was extended to all of the six countries that served as sites for democratizing elections.[31] However, it would be a serious mistake to leap from the observation that the United States contributed to democratic development in our six countries to the conclusion that U.S. democratic assistance was responsible for "producing" each of our electoral breakthroughs.

One problem with such an interpretation emerged in earlier chapters where we emphasized the decentralized and often disorganized character of U.S. democracy promotion efforts; the limited and sometimes perverse consequences of U.S. assistance; and the uneven commitment of the United States to democratic development, given shifting geographic priorities and equally shifting calculations with respect to the relationship between democracy promotion and the pursuit of the national interest.[32] Even more pertinent to an

---

[31] See Chapter 3 of this volume; and Valerie J. Bunce and Sharon L. Wolchik, "International Diffusion and Postcommunist Electoral Revolutions."

[32] Lincoln Abraham Mitchell, *Uncertain Democracy: U.S. Foreign Policy and Georgia's Rose Revolution* (Philadelphia: University of Pennsylvania Press, 2009); Noor O'Neill Borbieva, "Development in the Kyrgyz Republic: Exchange, Communal Networks, and the Foreign Presence" (Ph.D. dissertation, Harvard University, 2007); interviews in Armenia with Chedomir Flego, Yerevan, March 14, 2007; Alex Sadar, Yerevan, March 14, 2007; Gavin Help, Yerevan, March 9 and 10, 2007; Armineh Arakelian, Yerevan, March 13, 2007; Andrew Bennett, Yerevan, March 12, 2007; and Taline Sanassarian, Yerevan, March 13, 2007; interviews in Azerbaijan with Dallas Frohrib, Baku, March 6, 2007; Isa Gambar, Baku, March 7, 2007; and Amy Schultz, Baku, March 6, 2007; interviews in Georgia with David Darchiashvili, Tbilisi, October 15, 2005; Andro Gigauri, Tbilisi, March 8, 2007; Mike Kelleher, Tbilisi, October 19, 2005; Mark Mullen, Tbilisi, October 14, 2005; and Giorgi Meladze, Tbilisi, October 13, 2005; and interviews in Serbia with Marko Blagojević, Belgrade, April 11, 2005; and Ivan Vejvoda, Belgrade, April 11, 2005; as well as interviews about Serbia with Gregory

assessment of the U.S. impact on our electoral episodes is the *record* of U.S. electoral interventions in the postcommunist region from 1998 to 2008. First, as we will elaborate later in this chapter, the United States did not act alone. It was an important member of a democracy promotion network that, among other things, supported free and fair elections and democratic change. Second, as we detailed in Chapter 8, there is little correlation between the extent of U.S. commitment to electoral change (as measured by money spent and policy priorities) and electoral results. Third, the record shows that U.S. support for electoral change has been inconsistent in another way: reactions by the U.S. government to flawed elections in the postcommunist region. While the United States was quick to respond to the Ukrainian crisis, for example, it had earlier overlooked irregularities in the Russian presidential election of 1996, and it continued to do the same during the Putin era when electoral practices had become increasingly problematic.[33] Perhaps more telling is the fact that the United States has even looked the other way when large-scale protests break out in response to stolen elections – as in Serbia in 1996, Azerbaijan in 2003 and 2005, and Armenia in 2003 and 2008. Finally, there are limits to U.S. influence. Even when the United States has made the defeat of dictators a priority and even when it has formed coalitions with other Western actors to support such an outcome, electoral interventions have sometimes failed. Here, the case of Belarus stands out.

However, there is a more general consideration that casts doubt on the argument that the United States orchestrated electoral change in postcommunist Europe and Eurasia. As Bockman and Eyal have argued in their careful study of the rise of neoliberal orthodoxy in Central and Eastern Europe, it is both patronizing and inaccurate to assume that changes that shift policies and politics in the region in a more Western-oriented direction are sudden developments that necessarily reflect the ability of powerful outside actors to orchestrate new behaviors on the part of less powerful actors.[34] Just as repeated interactions between Western and "Eastern" economists during the Cold War laid the basis for the rise of neoliberal policies in postcommunist Europe and in the process generated transnational networks supporting such ideas and anticipating regime change, so the electoral breakthroughs we have analyzed in this book were in many respects long in the making and in every instance a product of local struggles and transnational collaborations. While power asymmetries exist, therefore, they do not reach the level of substituting external influences for local ideas and efforts.

Does the failure of a U.S.-centric explanation, along with the earlier one tying similar conditions to similar responses, mean, however, that an interpretation of diffusion "wins," in effect, by process of elimination? The hundreds

---

Simpson, Charlottesville, VA, November 9, 2007; Daniel Calingaert, Washington, DC, July 19, 2005; and James C. O'Brien, Washington, DC, November 16, 2006.

[33] See Steven M. Fish, *Democracy Derailed in Russia: The Failure of Open Politics* (Cambridge: Cambridge University Press, 2005).

[34] Bockman and Eyal, "Eastern Europe as a Laboratory."

of interviews we conducted and the mountains of electoral materials we analyzed all point to a more positive, rather than reactive, line of argument. In
particular, as the case studies in Part II of this book illustrate, the wave of
electoral change in the postcommunist region was in fact driven by the very
same mechanisms that we identified earlier in this chapter in our review of the
literature on international diffusion. Thus, democratizing elections were able
to move throughout this region because of the nature of the electoral model,
similar conditions in multiple locales, and expanding and assertive transnational networks. What we had earlier summarized as competing explanations,
in short, are better understood as cumulative influences.

THE BENEFITS OF THE ELECTORAL MODEL

The electoral model had three advantages. One was the fact that the model
made it harder for the regime to protect itself. Another was that these electoral
strategies enabled the opposition to become a more capable competitor for
political power. Finally, the model helped the international democracy assistance community become a more effective contributor to democratic change.

The modular character of the electoral model – that is, its tidy "to do" list
of concrete actions – and regularities in the electoral cycle in mixed regimes
also meant that this innovation, more than most, was unusually amenable to
transplantation.[35] In addition, what facilitated its travels around the region
was its strong record of success in defeating authoritarian leaders, and the
distinctive ability of these electoral strategies to exploit the opportunities for
political change provided not just by regular electoral contests, but also by
the contradictions in mixed regimes between constraints on competition, on
the one hand, and, on the other, the widespread reading of elections as a
time reserved for choice and regime evaluation and as the foundation for the
regime's claim to being a democracy.[36] The electoral model also had another
advantage insofar as diffusion is concerned: it played directly to the self-
interest of unsuccessful oppositions and angry publics.

Perhaps the most important reason why this ensemble of electoral strategies was so well suited for cross-national diffusion was that it went far toward
solving the coordination problems that had long bedeviled attempts by domestic and international supporters of democracy to carry out democratic change.
Thus, for fragmented oppositions, the model provided what they had been

---

[35] And see Mark Beissinger, "Structure and Example in Modular Political Phenomena: The
Diffusion of Bulldozer/Rose/Orange/Tulip Revolutions," *Perspectives on Politics* 5:2
(June 2007), 259–276; Sidney Tarrow, *Power in Movement*; and Sidney Tarrow, *The New
Transnational Activism*.

[36] And see Andreas Schedler, *Electoral Authoritarianism: The Dynamics of Unfree Competition*
(Boulder, CO: Lynne Rienner Publishers, 2006); and Andreas Schedler, "Sources of
Competition under Electoral Authoritarianism," in *Democratization by Elections: A New
Mode of Transition?*, ed. Staffan Lindberg (Baltimore: Johns Hopkins University Press,
2009), 179–201.

missing: optimism about victory and identification of a direct tie between that victory and collaboration among parties in candidate selection and campaign efforts. For citizens, who had long been demobilized and divided, the electoral model made it easier to believe that voting mattered, that the opposition was worthy of support, that the opposition could win, and, finally, that the opposition could take office. At the same time, the contributions of the electoral model both to more energetic campaigns that were carried out throughout the country and to more transparency in both the media and electoral procedures made it easier for citizens to sense where others stood and to act in concert. Finally, among international democracy promoters, where parallel play was often the norm, coordination was facilitated, because the goals of the model were simple and clear and associated with specific actions. Moreover, just as elections occur within a finite span of time and lend themselves to both planning and short-term targeted actions, so they produce quick and clear measures of success or failure – a rarity in the democracy assistance business.

It was precisely these assets of the electoral model that provided strong incentives for oppositions in other countries to follow the lead of their counterparts in neighboring states where successful electoral breakthroughs had been carried out. In this sense, demonstration effects and ease of cross-national transfer went hand in hand.

SIMILAR CONDITIONS: OBJECTIVE AND SUBJECTIVE SIMILARITIES

It is true that the fall of communism and communist states produced in its wake a region that was far more poorly structured than in the past to support the cross-national transmission of political or economic change. In particular, regimes varied more from one another after communism, and state-building and nation-building projects dictated a hardening of boundaries between states in the region. However, the potential of the postcommunist region for diffusion was greater than these developments imply. First, there was a very clear regional pattern associated with democratic change. Thus, the best predictor of democratization was whether the communists – that is, the authoritarians – lost the first competitive elections.[37] Electoral turnover, in short, was vital to democratic development – a lesson that was not lost on oppositions. Second, after communism we find a proliferation of mixed regimes throughout the region. These regimes shared not just the defining characteristics of electoral competition and authoritarian politics, but also, in most cases, cultural diversity, new statehood, and poor economic performance.

---

[37] Valerie Bunce, "Sequencing Political and Economic Reforms," in *East-Central European Economies in Transition*, ed. John Hardt and Richard Kaufman (Washington, DC: Joint Economic Committee, 1994), 46–63; Valerie Bunce, "Rethinking Recent Democratization: Lessons from the Postcommunist Experience," *World Politics* 55:2 (January 2003), 167–192; and M. Steven Fish, "Democratization's Prerequisites," *Post-Soviet Affairs* 14 (July–September 1998), 212–247.

The similarities we have outlined, however, are all objective in nature. While these commonalities encouraged citizens and oppositions, along with their international allies, to recycle successful electoral precedents in the neighborhood, they hardly guaranteed that emulation would take place, especially given variations in regime contexts as a result of varying mixes of democracy and dictatorship. This fact leads to a second aspect of similarity that played a vital role in transplantation: a widespread assumption shared by those who had already carried out such challenges, those who wanted to follow in their footsteps, and Western democracy promoters that there were in fact fundamental similarities among the mixed regimes in the region that could support the diffusion of democratizing elections. In our interviews, this assumption – that is, the subjective side of the similarities among contexts – surfaced repeatedly and without prompting on our part.[38]

This development took us by surprise because of two widely recognized divides in this region. One is the distinction between Central and Eastern Europe, on the one hand, and the former Soviet Union, on the other, reflecting, for example, differences in the duration and the depth of the communist experience. As Aleksandr Iskandaryan, the director of the Caucasus Media Institute in Yerevan, Armenia, cautioned in response to hearing a summary of our project: "You cannot compare us with Serbia, because the post-Soviet space is completely different from the Balkans."[39] In this sense, the electoral model "jumped" several of the areas within this region when it moved from Central and Eastern Europe to the former Soviet Union.

The other divide is more familiar. In this region of the world, as in others, ordinary citizens, political activists, and intellectuals are quick to point out the uniqueness of their nation. Such beliefs, moreover, are especially pronounced in situations where, as in most of our cases, statehood is recent and the product of political struggles against colonial domination – whether the empire in question was a larger state, such as the Soviet Union, Yugoslavia, or Czechoslovakia, or the somewhat more typical imperial structure represented by the Soviet bloc. It is precisely here where we confront a major deterrent to diffusion: the capacity of nationalism to draw boundaries among people because of its inherent exclusionary claims.[40] Here, it is important to

---

[38] Joerg Forbrig and Pavol Demeš, eds., *Reclaiming Democracy: Civil Society and Electoral Change in Central and Eastern Europe* (Washington, DC: German Marshall Fund, 2007); Giorgi Kandelaki, and United States Institute of Peace, *Georgia's Rose Revolution: A Participant's Perspective*, United States Institute of Peace Special Report Vol. 167 (Washington, DC: United States Institute of Peace, 2006); interviews with Pavol Demeš, Bratislava and Washington, 1998–2007; Milan Nič, Bratislava, June 2005; Dušan Ondrušek, Bratislava, June 2005; Sonja Licht, Belgrade, April 12, 2005; Ivan Marović, Belgrade, April 14, 2005; Srdja Popovic, Oxford, March 2007; Vesna Pusić, Zagreb, May 15, 2005; Ivan Krastev, Berlin, July 27, 2005; Tamara Zhvania, Tbilisi, October 18, 2005; Ghia Nodia, Tbilisi, October 18, 2005; and Joldon Kutmanaliev, Bishkek, January, 2008.

[39] Interview with Aleksandr Iskandaryan, Yerevan, March 13, 2007.

[40] Anthony W. Marx, *Faith in Nation: Exclusionary Origins of Nationalism* (Oxford: Oxford University Press, 2003).

remember that in the countries of interest in this study, a relatively common political scenario was for authoritarian leaders to justify their powers by playing up the distinctiveness of the nation in order to harden newly established state boundaries while in the process weakening the opposition by encouraging them to divide, defect, and demobilize, rather than unite, expand in size, and participate.[41]

What repeatedly surfaced in our interviews, however, was the fact that in the minds of many opposition leaders, political activists, and intellectuals, the claim to national distinctiveness was placed alongside a series of other arguments that recognized many similarities among states in the region that supported diffusion. One was that, just as communism had produced similar political and economic contexts, so leaving communism successfully seemed to have a common set of preconditions. While recognizing that certain legacies and situations made the break with communism easier or more difficult, this "to do" list was understood nonetheless to be applicable across the region. Thus, it was widely assumed that a successful break with communism required the expansion of civil society as well as more focused anti-regime movements that brought together disparate oppositions, civil society organizations, and ordinary citizens; exploitation of opportunities for change as a result of both divisions among the elites and changes in the international system that weakened authoritarians; and the breakdown of compliance systems as citizens moved from being passive observers to active participants. It was also assumed that trial runs contributed to future success, given the clear pattern in this region of failed challenges to authoritarian rule preceding successful ones. As a result, it was assumed that valuable lessons could be culled from earlier confrontations with the regime.

This understanding of how authoritarianism could be challenged was not just well known to and widely discussed by political activists throughout the region, but also had the additional and obvious selling point of having succeeded in many instances in bringing down communism. It was also assumed that these actions were amenable to recycling, with some amendments, to the new conditions presented by the rise of mixed regimes and the opportunities for change presented by semicompetitive elections. In this sense, while everyone recognized differences between 1989 and the wave of electoral change in the years that followed with respect to the nature of the regimes in power, the available sites for challenging those in power, and the forms of mass mobilization required to defeat dictators, they also saw significant continuity across the two democratizing episodes in what successful anti-regime projects entailed.[42]

---

[41] See, especially, V. P. Gagnon, *The Myth of Ethnic War: Serbia and Croatia in the 1990s* (Ithaca, NY: Cornell University Press, 2004).

[42] Valerie Bunce and Sharon L. Wolchik, "A Regional Tradition: The Diffusion of Democratic Change under Communism and Postcommunism," in *Democracy and Authoritarianism in the Postcommunist World*, ed. Valerie Bunce, Michael McFaul, and Kathryn Stoner-Weiss (Cambridge: Cambridge University Press, 2009), 30–58.

As a result, just as both older and newer activists, members of civil society organizations, and leaders of the opposition all learned from one another, even when their interactions crossed national boundaries, so, more generally, the dissident past – which was, we must remember, a dissident but not a distant past – carried several powerful lessons. One was that opposition to the regime could succeed, and another was that there were clear benefits to be gained from sharing strategies across national boundaries and across mobilizing episodes when the common motivation was one of defeating authoritarian leaders, whether in the streets, at the bargaining table, or at the polls.[43]

What further facilitated this perception of similarities across both time and space was continuity in dissident communities. Some of the very people who had been, for example, in Charter 77 in Czechoslovakia or in the "islands of creative deviance" that existed in Slovakia during the communist period later participated in the struggle against Mečiar in Slovakia and contributed as well to the electoral defeats of dictators in Croatia and Serbia. Similarly, many of the most important dissidents in Serbia, whose activities dated back to the struggles for political liberalization of Yugoslavia in the 1970s and 1980s and the antiwar movement of the 1990s, played key roles in the defeat of Milošević. Of course, they did not act alone. One of the striking commonalities in virtually all of our cases, as we highlighted in Chapters 3 through 6, was the rise of a new generation of young activists who played a key role in carrying out various tasks stipulated by the electoral model and thereby contributing to the defeat of authoritarian leaders. These youth movements were particularly important in Slovakia, Croatia, Serbia, and Ukraine, though they were also present in Georgia and, to a lesser extent, Kyrgyzstan (and to an even lesser extent in Azerbaijan). Many of these activists, moreover, were quick to share their experiences with other young people in the region, which, as our interviews also suggested, sometimes had the important effect of pumping life into a pessimistic opposition worn out by years of unsuccessful political struggle.[44]

SELF-INTEREST

We would be remiss in our discussion of perceived similarities and their support for a sharing of ideas and experiences, however, if we did not recognize, once again, the power of self-interest. As our interviews with political activists in Slovakia, Ukraine, Georgia, Serbia, and Croatia revealed, self-interest did not just alert these people to the political possibilities presented by the electoral model and its successes. It also nudged oppositions in the direction of reconstructing readings of their own situations and scenarios for the future that were in closer alignment with what had transpired during elections in other countries in the region where authoritarian leaders had been defeated. Self-interest,

---

[43] And see Kenney, *A Carnival of Revolution*, on Solidarity and regional outreach during the 1980s.

[44] Interviews with Sonja Licht, Belgrade, April 12, 2005; and Vesna Pešić, Belgrade, April 14, 2005.

in short, played two keys roles. It blurred the lines between countries where democratizing elections had taken place and other countries in the region, and it replaced pessimistic and divisive views of the future with more optimistic, consensual, and energizing scenarios. With respect to the latter: what opposition would not like to win power? What opposition would not like a playbook that showed how to accomplish that? And, therefore, what opposition would not appreciate precedents showing that there were clear payoffs for implementing the electoral model?

Self-interest also motivated the behaviors of exporters, as well as importers, of the electoral model. Fresh from victory, activists were eager to keep using the weapons they had so carefully acquired, and they also thought that the longer-term success of their electoral breakthroughs would be secured by supporting similar developments in neighboring countries. This was a particularly powerful argument in the cases of Slovakia, Croatia, Serbia, and Ukraine (and in the earlier cases of Bulgaria and Romania), where shared borders, with their potential for compromising democratic breakthroughs in the neighborhood, placed a premium on a collective democratic effort. In many ways, this was a lesson that was also a holdover from the communist-era experience, when both dissent and then crackdowns on political protests were developments that tended to cluster among states in the region. Moreover, this was the message implied in the founding of the European Coal and Steel Community, the rise of the European Community and then Union, and the expansion of the EU to include not just the new democracies of southern Europe, but also those of Eastern and Central Europe. By connecting new democracies to more established ones, it was assumed that the larger and expanding democratic project was made more secure, with the very logic of European collaboration in support of the postwar German democratic experiment the founding precedent.

Regional outreach was also facilitated by the changing nature of democracy assistance in the region. Membership in the EU in 2004 carried with it for Slovaks, Czechs, Poles, and Hungarians in particular a transition from being the recipients of democracy aid to becoming donors – and donors that could draw upon not just significant funding, but also the considerable expertise they had accumulated in their struggles against authoritarianism in the communist and later the postcommunist world.[45] Discussions within the European Union to focus assistance on a group of countries that border the expanded EU – which eventually culminated in the European Neighborhood Policy – supported this process.[46] As a result, over the past few years more informal

[45] See, especially, Tsveta Petrova, "From Recipients to Donors: New Europe Promotes Democracy in the Neighborhood" (Ph.D. dissertation, Department of Government, Cornell University, August 2010).

[46] Sabine Fisher, "The EU's Strategy of 'New Neighborhood' and Its Impact on International Relations of the Former Soviet Union," paper presented at the annual meeting of the International Studies Association, Honolulu, March 1–5, 2005; Judith Kelley, "New Wine in Old Wineskins: Promoting Political Reforms through the New European Neighborhood Policy," *Journal of Common Market Studies* 44:1 (March 2006), 29–55.

ties among the mixed and more democratic regimes in the region have taken a more institutionalized – and, one could argue, quietly subversive – turn.

Self-interest also played a role in a more narrowly defined sense. With the decline in the outside funding for NGOs that often accompanied successful breakthroughs, many of the NGOs that had played an important role in bringing about democratic change faced the question of how to ensure their continued existence. Sharing their experiences and providing training for democratic activists in other countries gave these NGOs a renewed mission and sources of funding by the international community.

TRANSNATIONAL NETWORKS

Our analysis thus far has contained clear hints of a third factor central to the cross-national diffusion of democratizing elections: an array of domestic and international actors who played the multiple and equally critical roles of defining, applying, exporting, and importing the electoral model. Like our discussion of both the electoral model and similar conditions, this third factor straddles the divide between structure and agency in diffusion dynamics. On the one hand, individuals served as conscious conduits; on the other hand, they formed collaborative ties that gave diffusion an organizational base, complete with a mission; well-specified sites for action; coalitions founded on a common set of values, interests, and activities; and memberships that were at the same time durable and expanding. What we find, in short, is a network composed of an assembly of transnational actors promoting the diffusion of electoral change through implementation of the electoral model.

Who joined this network? There was a dizzying array of individuals and groups involved; our list of the individuals we interviewed and their organizational affiliations in the Appendix provides a representative sample. On the Western side, members included U.S. ambassadors and other embassy personnel, along with U.S. government-supported democracy promoters (Freedom House, the National Endowment for Democracy, the United States Institute of Peace, the International Foundation for Electoral Systems, the American Center for International Labor Solidarity, the International Republican Institute, and the National Democratic Institute for International Affairs, as well as USAID); U.S.-based foundations (especially the Open Society Institute, Rockefeller Brothers, the Charles Stewart Mott Foundation, and the German Marshall Fund of the United States); the European Union and organizations associated with the Council of Europe (for instance, OSCE); and European-based foundations, sometimes cross-national in composition and sometimes based in individual countries (such as the Pontis Foundation, the International Institute for Democracy and Electoral Assistance, the Westminster Foundation, and the German party foundations). On the domestic side, members included leaders of opposition parties and movements, along with civil society activists, most of whose organizations were funded in part by the West. While some of these organizations had been in existence for some time (such as the Georgian

Young Lawyers' Association and the Liberty Institute in Georgia), others were created with some eye on the goal of defeating dictators and implementing aspects of the electoral model (such as the Center for Elections and Democracy in Serbia and the various youth organizations, such as Otpor in Serbia, Kmara in Georgia, Pora in Ukraine, and, to a lesser extent, Kel-Kel in Kyrgyzstan).

However, there was a third group that has received far less attention, but that played a vital role: loose-knit coalitions and sometimes organizations composed of graduates of successful electoral breakthroughs who shared their experiences with players abroad who wanted to copy their strategies and their success. As the model moved from place to place, this group expanded. It began in response to the Bulgarian election in 1990; expanded through inter-actions among Serbian, Bulgarian, Romanian, and Slovak activists from 1996 to 1998; and beginning in 2000 reached out to Croatian and Serbian and then Georgian and Ukrainian activists.[47] Even Polish democracy promoters joined the project, drawing upon their experiences under communism and benefiting from their transition from being the recipients of democracy aid to becoming donors and, after 2004, their accession to the European Union. This transition was also critical for Slovak democracy promoters, who became quite involved like their Polish counterparts in Ukraine as well as in Croatia, Serbia, Belarus, and Uzbekistan.[48]

What did these various players do? They all played multiple roles in putting into place the ingredients required for successful electoral challenges to dicta-torial rule. For example, they worked together to organize voter registration and turnout drives; to found organizations that were capable of collecting systematic information about the electorate and its concerns and that engaged in various forms of electoral mobilization and monitoring (including public opinion polls, exit polls, and parallel vote tabulation); and to bring civil soci-ety groups into closer relations with one another and with opposition parties. They also helped opposition parties to develop both an organizational and a personnel presence outside the large cities; to identify issues of importance to the electorate and to develop campaign literature that resonated with these concerns; and, more generally, to expand their interactions with the electorate while encouraging a pooling of candidates and a coordination of campaign efforts. In addition, these transnational groups pressured regimes to make voter lists, vote tabulation, and their political and economic records more transparent, and they provided quick and critical reactions to specific moves by the regime to control the media and harass the opposition and their sup-porters. Finally, the local implementation and cross-national transfer of the electoral model benefited greatly from the funding that the Western-based democracy promotion community provided and from the technical assistance that it, along with local graduates, made available.

---

[47] Interviews with Giorgi Meladze, Tbilisi, October 13, 2005; Ivan Marović, Washington, DC, October 4, 2004; and Ivan Krastev, Berlin, July 27, 2005.

[48] See, especially, Petrova, "From Recipients to Donors."

While the structure of this network was in fact relatively flat and while most activities were collaborative ventures, there was, nonetheless, a rough division of labor. The U.S. democracy promotion community (especially the National Democratic Institute, the International Republican Institute, Freedom House, the Open Society Institute, Mott and Rockefeller Brothers, as well as the German Marshall Fund of the United States) played a key role in bringing groups together, such as the opposition itself and regional and local activists; in transferring electoral technology and campaign strategies; and in providing resources for campaign literature, public opinion polls, civil society organizations, and an independent media. They also, together with the Europeans, added substantial international weight to local pressures on regimes to "clean up their electoral act." The United States also often worked closely with the Europeans on party development and electoral monitoring.

At the same time, the regional "graduates" were widely viewed by activists on the ground as key sources of valuable information about useful strategies for combating regime repression and winning power. As one Kmara activist in Georgia remarked: "Apart from specific techniques on how to stage a nonviolent campaign, what we really learned from the Serbs was the importance of creating a sense of moral superiority over the autocratic regime."[49] Precisely because they had been in the trenches, veterans of earlier successful struggles testified to what was politically possible.[50] They also built bridges between older opposition groups and newer ones. Their outsider yet insider status placed them in an ideal position to override generational differences, much as the outsider status of external democracy promoters had placed them in an ideal position to forge ties between once conflicting opposition parties.[51]

However, work on the ground – that is, the actual implementation of the electoral model and its modification in keeping with local circumstances – was carried out by local activists, whether members of movements, parties, or civil society organizations. Much of what they accomplished was either tedious or dangerous. Without their engagement and hard work, the electoral model would never have moved from being an abstract and appealing idea to being manifested in specific actions that succeeded in defeating dictators.

---

[49] Kandelaki, *Georgia's Rose Revolution*, 4.

[50] Similar observations were also made by Vesna Pusić, Zagreb, May 15, 2005; Tinatin Khidasheli, Tbilisi, October 17, 2005; Gvantsa Liparteliani, Tbilisi, October 13, 2005; Levan Ramishvili, Tbilisi, October 13, 2005; and Giorgi Meladze, Tbilisi, October 13, 2005.

[51] See, especially, interviews with Patrick Merloe, Washington, DC, April 30, 2009; and Scott Carpenter, Washington, DC, April 9, 2009. This was also critical in the case of Chile from 1988 through 1990, when the National Democratic Institute in particular was successful in bringing together the once implacable foes, the Christian Democrats and the Socialists, in order to win the 1990 election and thereby bring the Pinochet era to an end. See also David Altman, Sergio Toro, and Rafael Piñeiro, *International Influences on Democratic Transitions: The Successful Case of Chile*, CDDRL Working Paper No. 86, Center for Democracy, Development and the Rule of Law, Freeman Spogli Institute for International Studies, Stanford University (July 2008), http://cddrl.stanford.edu/publications/international_influences_on_democratic_transitions_the_successful_case_of_chile/ .

When we stand back from this description of the network, several aspects stand out. One is the importance of planning – rather than, say, diffusion that results from "uncoordinated interdependence."[52] Such planning was necessary, given, for example, the details and the difficulties involved in forming effective oppositions that would participate in elections, rather than boycott them, and succeed in mounting effective campaigns. Moreover, planning was required to convince voters to register, vote, support the opposition, and demand that their votes count; to win the election while gathering the data necessary to demonstrate that victory and while convincing voters at the same time that the opposition tally was more accurate than the "official" version; and to prepare themselves and their fellow citizens for the possibility that victory would not lead to taking office. While the United States, as already noted, did not orchestrate these electoral challenges to authoritarian rule, these challenges were nonetheless well orchestrated. Thus, these regimes did not collapse of their own weight, but were defeated.

Also critical to the dynamic was the existence of practice runs with earlier elections, particularly at the local level (as in Slovakia, Croatia, Serbia, Georgia, and Ukraine); prior rounds of political protest; invigoration of divided and dispirited dissident networks; and even earlier experiences with public opinion polling, election monitoring, and exit polls (all of which, for example, were already in place in Bulgaria, Romania, Slovakia, and Georgia). But when all is said and done, the key element was the existence of transnational coalitions that were particularly vibrant, flexible, persistent, and, it must be said, geographically expansive, if not restless, in the postcommunist region. If electoral challenges to authoritarian rule were a moving target, given the timing of elections and changing political opportunities, so were the people who promoted the electoral model as a regionwide political weapon.

Finally, we need to return to an earlier point – the importance of common perceptions and common identities in motivating the network. There was a deep-seated belief shared by activists throughout the region that the struggle for democracy in countries that fell short of democratic standards in the postcommunist region was in large measure the *same* struggle. Illiberal leaders and their allies, it was widely assumed, used similar strategies, in part because of their experiences under communism (where there were also, we must remember, regular elections), and in part because they had committed similar transgressions and provided, as a result, similar opportunities for political change.

Thus, for "graduates" of successful applications of the electoral model, the assumption was that their experiences were relevant to oppositions in neighboring countries where such changes were also needed.[53] Just as interesting

[52] Elkins and Simmons, "On Waves, Clusters, and Diffusion."
[53] Giorgi Meladze, "Civil Society: A Second Chance for Post-Soviet Democracy: A EurasiaNet Commentary," *EurasiaNet*, September 6, 2005, http://www.eurasianet.org/departments/ civilsociety/articles/eav090605.shtml; interview with Giorgi Meladze, Tbilisi, October 13, 2005.

was a strong belief that they had a responsibility to share their insights about effective strategies for political change through elections and later through other mechanisms, such as assistance in the development of more robust local governments and civil society. The activities of the Pontis Foundation in Bratislava in training democratic activists in Belarus, Ukraine, and even Uzbekistan are a case in point.[54] As with the political opposition, the participation in these efforts on the part of some of the veterans of successful struggles elsewhere also stemmed to some degree from self-interest, since, as we have noted earlier, such activities were one way to get continued support from governments and foundations that no longer supported activities in their countries once they were firmly on a democratic path. But these activities also stemmed from the belief, noted earlier, that their democracy would not be safe until it was embedded in a larger democratic community.

Importers of these strategies, moreover, also assumed that they could and should model themselves after the successful local cases – albeit recognizing the importance of modifications based upon local conditions. Again, in the interviews we conducted it was frequently observed that, while local conditions and local struggles were both distinctive and important, knowing that it had been done elsewhere successfully and learning from participants about how it had been done – in short, both precedent and emulation – were critical to the decision to try to defeat authoritarian leaders and to a careful implementation of the electoral model. From the vantage point of local activists, therefore, electoral breakthroughs elsewhere contributed optimism and energy and, because of shared information, strategies as well. Indeed, far more than the Americans or the Europeans, the "graduates" of electoral breakthroughs were judged to be the most important contributors to successful electoral change in other countries.[55]

CONCLUSIONS

In this chapter, we have argued that the geography of opposition victories in mixed regimes in postcommunist Europe and Eurasia can be explained by the cross-national diffusion of the electoral model. We drew this conclusion because of the pattern of similarities among these victories, along with the failure of competing hypotheses to explain this pattern. Just as important was

---

[54] Interview with Milan Nič, Belgrade, April 13, 2005.

[55] See, for example, Giorgi Meladze, "Emerging Democracies Not Reliant on the West," Comments/Letters, FT.com, June 29, 2005, www.news.ft.com/cms/s/sc16dcc8-e83b-11 d9–9786–00000e2511c8.html; Jaba Devdariani, "The Impact of International Assistance," International IDEA Building Democracy in Georgia Discussion Paper 11 (May 2003), http://www.idea.int/publications/georgia/upload/Book-11_scr.pdf; and Giorgi Kandelaki, "An Inside Look at Georgia's 'Rose Revolution,' or How I Became a Revolutionary," *Scholar Forum: The Journal of the Open Society Institute's Network Scholarship Program*, Regional Focus the Caucasus 9 (Fall 2004), 3–5, http://www.soros.org/initiatives/scholarship/articles_publications/publications/sforum9_20050705/sf9_20050705.pdf.

our ability to point to the role of three mechanisms driving the cross-national transfer of the electoral model. First, the model itself was quite amenable to import and export, because it was successful, featured a concrete list of tasks, and tapped directly into the self-interest of oppositions. Second, there were both objective and subjective similarities between the "sending" and "receiving" countries. Finally, central to cross-national transmission was the hard work of a transnational network, co-organized by foundations located in the West and organizations funded by the United States and by European countries, regional democracy promoters, and local oppositions and nongovernmental organizations. It was this community that fashioned, applied, and exported the model.

These conclusions have several important implications for how we have understood international diffusion, U.S. democracy assistance, and comparative methods. First, a strong case in support of the cross-national spread of democracy depends not just on establishing patterns of change that are consistent with the idea of diffusion, but also on carrying out a series of other tasks that are often left for future research – for example, disentangling cause and effect and thereby specifying clearly the particular innovation that is supporting democratic change; eliminating competing hypotheses; and identifying the factors that are responsible for the transfer of the innovation from one site to others. These issues in turn suggest that it is very hard to establish the diffusion of democracy or of other innovations without knowing a great deal about what is happening on the ground.

Second, by concluding that multiple factors played a role in the spread of the electoral model, we parted company with many analysts who place a premium in their studies of diffusion on choosing among competing explanations of why and how innovations move across locales.[56] Our decision to embrace a three-part explanation, however, did not reflect resistance on our part to taking a stance on this question. Rather, in our view, characteristics of the model itself, similar conditions, and transnational networks were all necessary for the simple reason that the spread of deeply subversive innovations,

---

[56] For competing perspectives on diffusion, see Jacoby, *The Enlargement of the European Union and NATO* and "Inspiration, Coalition and Substitution"; Strang and Soule, "Diffusion in Organizations and Social Movements"; Lee and Strang, "The International Diffusion of Public-Sector Downsizing"; Tarrow, *The New Transnational Activism*; Bockman and Eyal, "Eastern Europe as a Laboratory"; Glenn, *Framing Democracy*; McAdam, Tarrow, and Tilly, *Dynamics of Contention*; Elkins and Simmons, "On Waves, Clusters, and Diffusion"; Simmons and Elkins, "The Globalization of Liberalization"; Beissinger, *Nationalist Mobilization*; Beissinger, "Promoting Democracy" and "Structure and Example"; Maryjane Osa, "Mobilization Structures and Cycles of Protest: Post-Stalinist Contention in Poland, 1954–9," *Mobilization* 6:2 (Fall 2001), 211–231; Muiznieks, "The Influence of the Baltic Popular Movements on the Process of Soviet Disintegration"; Mario Diani, "Introduction: Social Movements, Contentious Actions and Social Networks: From 'Metaphor' to Substance?", in *Social Movement Analysis: The Network Perspective*, ed. Mario Diani and Doug McAdam (Oxford: Oxford University Press, 2003), 1–20; and McAdam and Rucht, "The Cross-National Diffusion."

such as electoral strategies that threaten to end authoritarian regimes, has unusually stiff requirements.

Third, the analysis in this chapter also diverges in many respects from studies of U.S. democracy assistance. Rather than focusing on the goals driving U.S. foreign policy, aggregated actions and outcomes, and the politics of either the donor community or the recipients of aid, we have addressed instead specific goals, policies, processes, and players, including local oppositions and civil society groups, on the one hand, and both regional and Western democracy promoters, on the other. Such a focus allows us to move from a general discussion of the costs and benefits, opportunities, and limitations of U.S. democracy assistance to a more fine-grained set of arguments identifying the conditions under which such assistance can play an important and positive role. Thus, U.S. participation in the diffusion dynamic was important, but not decisive. It was important not because the United States was so powerful and acted alone, but rather because U.S. goals were both precise and modest; because the United States focused on what it knows best and what is perhaps most easily transferred to foreign settings (that is, how to win elections); and because the United States worked in close collaboration with others who also brought distinctive skills to the table and who had the additional advantages of being experts in fighting authoritarianism and having direct stakes in electoral outcomes.

This leads to a final implication – in this case, a methodological one. It is traditional in comparative and international politics to draw a clear line between approaches that assume that cases are separate from one another and approaches that assume that they are related. We would argue, however, that at least in the case of explaining electoral outcomes in mixed regimes, these two sets of assumptions – and the kinds of analyses they support – can be treated as complementary, rather than competing or mutually exclusive, modes of explanation. Thus, it was the comparisons among our elections that uncovered the importance of the electoral model and the likely relevance of diffusion dynamics in the spread of electoral change in postcommunist Europe and Eurasia. Second, the similarities and the differences among our elections and the regimes in which they took place played the vital role of helping us test hypotheses about factors influencing both electoral outcomes and receptivity to diffusion dynamics. Each approach, in short, provided important pieces to the puzzle of why authoritarian leaders in mixed regimes win or lose elections.

II

After the Elections

Explaining Divergent Regime Trajectories

> You go to democracy with the country you have, not the one you wish you had.
>
> Thomas Friedman[1]

> These breakthrough elections in the postcommunist region were not just important in and of themselves; they were also the beginning of a longer-term process of democratization through institutional change.
>
> Kenneth Wollack[2]

In the previous chapters, the puzzle of interest was explaining variations in electoral outcomes in mixed regimes located in postcommunist Europe and Eurasia. As we discovered, the contrast between the norm in mixed polities – that is, continuity in authoritarian rule – and the exception – that is, electoral victories by the opposition – reflected the extent to which oppositions and their allies were willing and able to implement a set of innovative electoral strategies that made them far more effective at winning power. Although struggles between oppositions and regimes in each country played a role in this process, so did international diffusion – in devising, implementing, and transferring this model of winning power.

This chapter shifts our attention from the causes of electoral stability and change to the consequences. Our interest, therefore, is in treating these elections not as a dependent variable, but rather as an independent one. Put simply: how much of a difference did these elections make? We address this issue by carrying out two types of comparisons that focus on political and economic developments after the elections: among the countries where electoral breakthroughs took place, and between this group of elections and those where oppositions failed to win power. We draw three conclusions. First, the elections did make a difference by contributing to democratic progress in a variety of areas. There are good reasons, therefore, to term these elections,

---

[1] Thomas Friedman, "The Country We've Got," *New York Times*, January 6, 2005, A27.
[2] Interview with Kenneth Wollack, Washington, DC, May 12, 2010.

as we have done throughout this study, democratizing events. Second, this difference is particularly evident if we compare these cases to those in which turnover did not occur. While almost all of our elections were preceded by the similar pattern of deepening authoritarianism, this trend continues in cases where elections maintained the status quo but is interrupted in cases where turnover took place. In this sense, breakthrough elections invested in democracy in both a negative and a positive sense. Thus, they both reversed authoritarian trends and contributed to democratic development. Third, within the group of countries that experienced electoral turnover, however, we find variable consequences, reflecting in large measure four factors: 1) the position of the country in the diffusion wave; 2) the international position of the country and the commitment of Western governments to integration; 3) the strength of civil society prior to the elections; and 4) the nature of the election and transition, that is, an orderly process versus an elite coup. We conclude with a discussion of what our findings have to say about theories of democratization and the study of social movements and contentious politics and the implications of our assessment for practitioners involved in elaborating and carrying out democracy assistance strategies and activities.

WHAT DIFFERENCE DID SUCCESS MAKE?

We now turn to one of the central questions of our project: that is, what difference did the use of elections to oust autocrats, which created democratic openings in countries where these efforts succeeded, make over time? Did the victory of the opposition matter, and, if so, how? Numerous observers of political developments in our successful cases have noted the problems that have occurred since the change of regime. Thus, analysts have pointed to the conflict among leaders in Ukraine that brought about a seeming defeat of the Orange Coalition in the 2006 parliamentary elections that brought Yushchenko's former rival to the position of prime minister, and the near armed conflict in early 2007 between the supporters of Yushchenko and Yanukovych over issues related to control of the Ministry of the Interior. They have also commented on the early elections in 2007 that, contrary to the expectations of many key actors, led to the resurrection of the Orange Coalition, only to be followed by open acrimony between the country's two top leaders and the victory of Yanukovych in the 2010 presidential elections.[3] Numerous commentators have also focused on the antidemocratic measures against the opposition and the media, as well as against protestors, that Saakashvili has taken in Georgia,[4] and argued in the case of Kyrgyzstan that the 2005 changes merely brought

---

[3] See Mark Kramer, "Ukraine's Orange Evolution," *Current History* 107:707 (March 2008), 112–118; and Nathaniel Copsey, "The Ukrainian Parliamentary Elections of 2007," *Journal of Communist Studies & Transition Politics* 24:2 (June 2008), 297–309.

[4] See Pamela Jawad, *Democratic Consolidation in Georgia after the "Rose Revolution,"* Peace Research Institute Frankfurt (PRIF) Report 73 (Frankfurt am Main: Peace Research Institute Frankfurt, 2005), http://www.hsfk.de/fileadmin/downloads/prif73.pdf; Lincoln Abraham

to power a different group of authoritarian leaders who did little to reintro-duce democratic political life in that country, a view that was validated by the ouster of the Bakiev government after massive protests and riots in 2010.[5]

We have several responses to these pessimistic portrayals of political developments following victories by the oppositions in Georgia, Ukraine, Kyrgyzstan, and other countries in the postcommunist region. First, it is important to recognize that, if these countries were ideally configured to support democratic progress, autocrats would never have won and exercised power after the collapse of communism. Thus, it is important to keep in mind that mixed regimes exist for a reason, and the struggle for democracy in such contexts is precisely that – a struggle, and one that does not go away because oppositions finally win power (and, we must remember, with narrow victories in most cases). The standard for assessment, therefore, should not be, say, Poland or Hungary in the 1990s, let alone today. Second, the data on politi-cal performance following the electoral breakthroughs do not for the most part support these pessimistic readings. With the partial exception of Georgia and the greater exception of Kyrgyzstan, these elections *did* make a demo-cratic difference. If we look at Figure 11.1, which presents several of the usual scores used by Freedom House, there is little doubt that in most of these cases,

Mitchell, *Uncertain Democracy: U.S. Foreign Policy and Georgia's Rose Revolution* (Philadelphia: University of Pennsylvania Press, 2008); Liz Fuller, "Georgia: Is the Country Becoming Progressively Less Democratic?," *Radio Free Europe/Radio Liberty* (June 29, 2005); Robert Parsons, "Georgia: Analyst Ghia Nodia Assesses Saakashvili's Attempts to Transform Country," *Radio Free Europe / Radio Liberty* (June 15, 2005); Laurence Broers, "After the 'Revolution': Civil Society and the Challenges of Consolidating Democracy in Georgia," *Central Asian Survey* 24:3 (September 2005), 333–350; Julie A. George, "Minority Political Inclusion in Mikheil Saakashvili's Georgia," *Europe-Asia Studies* 60:7 (November 2008), 1151–1175; Nana Sumbadze, "Saakashvili in the Public Eye: What Public Opinion Polls Tell Us," *Central Asian Survey* 28:2 (June 2009), 185–197; Alexandre Kukhianidze, "Corruption and Organized Crime in Georgia before and after the 'Rose Revolution'," *Central Asian Survey* 28:2 (June 2009), 215–234; Stephen F. Jones, "Introduction: Georgia's Domestic Front," *Central Asian Survey* 28:2 (June 2009), 93–98; Cory Welt, "Still Staging Democracy: Contestation and Conciliation in Postwar Georgia," *Demokratizatsiya* 17:3 (2009), 196–227; Svante E. Cornell and Niklas Nilsson, "Georgian Politics since the August 2008 War," *Demokratizatsiya* 17:3 (Summer 2009), 251–268; Charles H. Fairbanks, Jr., "Georgia's Soviet Legacy," *Journal of Democracy* 21:1 (January 2010), 144–151; Lionel Beehner, "Letter from Tbilisi: Georgia's Confidence Game," *Foreign Affairs* online, 11 August 2009, http://www.foreignaffairs.com/features/letters/letter-from-tbilisi-georgias-confidence-game.

[5] See the following on Kyrgyzstan: Peter Sinnott, "Kyrgyzstan: A Political Overview," *American Foreign Policy Interests* 29:6 (November 2007), 427–436; Alexander Cooley, "U.S. Bases and Democratization in Central Asia," *Orbis* 52:1 (January 2008), 65–90; Maija Paasiaro, "Home-grown Strategies for Greater Agency: Reassessing the Outcome of Civil Society Strengthening in Post-Soviet Kyrgyzstan," *Central Asian Survey* 28:1 (March 2009), 59–77; Erica Marat, *The Tulip Revolution: Kyrgyzstan One Year After* (Washington, DC: Jamestown Foundation, 2006), also available electronically at http://www.jamestown.org/uploads/media/Jamestown-TulipRevolution.pdf; James Traub, "It's Not Too Late to Save Kyrgyzstan," *Foreign Policy*, June 22, 2010, at http://www.foreignpolicy.com/articles/2010/06/22/its_not_too_late_to_save_kyrgyzstan_by_james_traub?page=0,1&sms_ss=email.

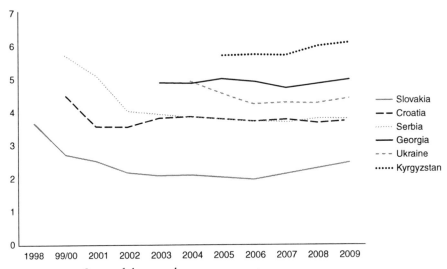

FIGURE 11.1. Successful cases: democracy scores.
Source: Freedom House's *Nations in Transit*, 1997 to 2009.

political life was more open, the opposition had more room to operate, and civil society and a free media had better opportunities to develop than before the events, despite a slight worsening in democracy scores in most countries in the last few years.

The impact of the successful use of elections to oust autocrats is more clearly illustrated by comparing the results for the countries in Figure 11.1, where the autocrat was ousted, to those in Figure 11.2, where efforts to use elections to unseat incumbents were made, but failed. As Figure 11.2 illustrates, in all of the unsuccessful cases, democracy scores have become slightly or significantly worse over time, although in the case of Belarus, there was a slight improvement between 2008 and 2009.

The impact of electoral turnover in stopping growing authoritarianism is even more evident if we look at trends in three postcommunist countries where there was no attempt to use elections to oust authoritarian leaders – Russia, Moldova, and Kazakhstan, where the trend over time is also negative. (See Figure 11.3.) Thus, in all of our successful cases, electoral turnover stopped, temporarily at least, a slide toward increasing authoritarianism, although the impact was more dramatic in some than in others.

This impact of the elections we have examined is not often noted in discussions of problems in democratic development, but it bears emphasizing. Although we agree with those who argue that elections by themselves are not enough to bring about democratic development, and although an electoral breakthrough is not a guarantee against backsliding in some areas afterward, we would nonetheless conclude that electoral turnover in mixed regimes significantly expands opportunities for democratic progress. In the absence of turnover, moreover, authoritarian politics invariably prevails.

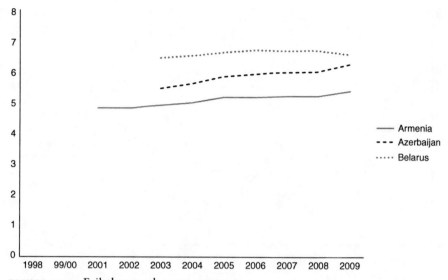

FIGURE 11.2. Failed cases: democracy scores.
Source: Freedom House's *Nations in Transit*, 1998 to 2009.

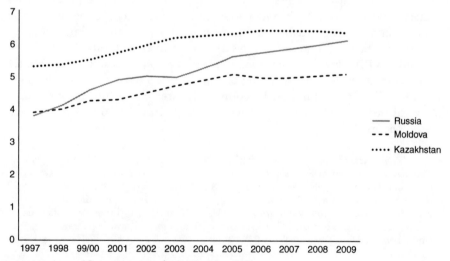

FIGURE 11.3. Non-attempts: democracy scores.
Source: Freedom House's *Nations in Transit*, 1997 to 2009.

VARIATION AMONG SUCCESSFUL CASES

If we look at the successful cases again, there are several patterns that stand out. The first pattern, which occurred in Slovakia, where the election ended a pattern of de-democratization (see Figure 11.4), saw fairly dramatic,

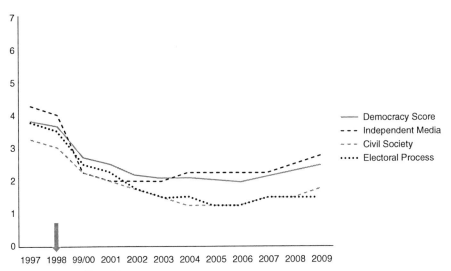

FIGURE 11.4. Slovakia.

Source: Freedom House's *Nations in Transit*, 1997 to 2009.

rapid, and sustained progress on all scores, including electoral process, civil society, and the overall democracy score. In Slovakia, the victory of the opposition was followed by a rapid return to a fully functioning democracy that restarted economic reforms and saw Slovakia admitted to both the EU and NATO. Slovakia continued to score well on all counts, particularly until 2007, when Robert Fico's victory in the 2006 parliamentary elections caused a slight worsening of the country's scores on all dimensions except electoral process, where scores remained stable from 2006 to 2009 after a slight increase.[6]

---

[6] See Karen Henderson, "The Slovak Republic: Explaining Defects in Democracy," *Democratization* 11:5 (December 2004), 133–155; Grigorij Mesežnikov, Miroslav Kollár, and Tom Nicholson, eds., *Slovakia 2002: A Global Report on the State of Society* (Bratislava: Institute for Public Affairs, 2003); Grigorij Mesežnikov, ed., *Slovakia after the Elections: Public Opinion, Political Players, Media* (Bratislava: Institute for Public Affairs, 2003); Kevin Deegan Krause, "Slovakia's Second Transition," *Journal of Democracy*, 14:2 (April 2003), 65–79; Tim Haughton, "'We'll Finish What We've Started': The 2002 Slovak Parliamentary Elections," *Journal of Communist Studies and Transition Politics* 19:4 (December 2003), 65–90; Katarína Mathernová and Juraj Renčko, "'Reformology': The Case of Slovakia," *Orbis* 50:4 (September 2006), 629–640; Geoffrey Pridham, "Coalition Behavior in New Democracies of Central and Eastern Europe: The Case of Slovakia," *Journal of Communist Studies & Transition Politics* 18:2 (June 2002), 75–102; Tim Haughton and Marek Rybář, "All Right Now? Explaining Successes and Failures of the Slovak Centre-Right," *Journal of Communist Studies & Transition Politics* 20:3 (September 2004), 115–132; Tim Haughton and Marek Rybář, "A Change of Direction: The 2006 Parliamentary Elections and Party Politics in Slovakia," *Journal of Communist Studies & Transition Politics* 24:2 (June 2008), 232–255; Mathew Rhodes, "Slovakia after Mečiar: A Midterm Report," *Problems of Post-Communism* 48:4 (July–August 2001), 3–13.

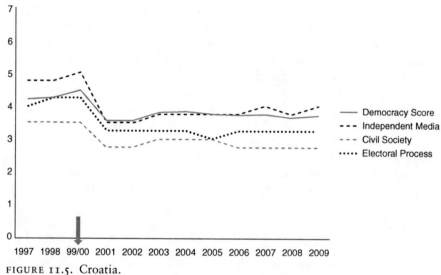

FIGURE 11.5. Croatia.
Source: Freedom House's *Nations in Transit*, 1997 to 2009.

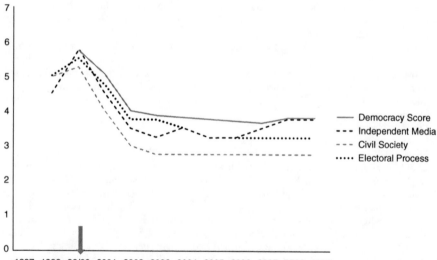

FIGURE 11.6. Serbia.
Source: Freedom House's *Nations in Transit*, 1997 to 2009.

The pattern in Croatia and Serbia (Figures 11.5 and 11.6) is similar, with steady improvement on most scores.[7] Democratic progress is particularly

---

[7] Works on Croatia after the elections include Alex J. Bellamy, "Croatia after Tudjman," *Problems of Post-Communism* 48:5 (September 2001), 18–31; Matthew Longo, "The HDZ's

dramatic in Serbia, where it resulted in a very rapid drop, not to the Slovak level, but from very unfavorable scores prior to Milošević's ouster.[8]

Despite the numerous critiques of Yushchenko and other leaders of the Orange Revolution,[9] there was also significant improvement in Ukraine, as is evident in Figure 11.7. Compared to the previous three countries, progress has not been as dramatic or steady, but Ukraine clearly scores better overall than it did prior to the Orange Revolution, and political life is far more competitive, with greater freedom of the press and more room for civil society than under Kuchma. The victory of Yanukovych in the 2010 presidential election has been taken by some as an indication of the failure of the Orange Revolution and as likely to undermine democracy in Ukraine.[10] We, on the contrary, along with numerous other observers, view this election, in which the outcome was

Embattled Mandate: Divergent Leadership, Divided Electorate, 2003–2006," *Problems of Post-Communism* 53:3 (May 2006), 36–43; Siniša Kušić, "Croatia: Advancing Political and Economic Transformation," *Journal of Southeast European & Black Sea Studies* 6:1 (March 2006), 65–81; and Elizabeth Pond, *Endgame in the Balkans: Regime Change, European Style* (Washington, DC: Brookings Institution Press, 2006). See the following literature on Serbia after Milošević: Judy Batt, *The Question of Serbia* (Paris: European Union Institute for Security Studies, 2005); Boris Begović and Boško Mijatović, *Four Years of Transition in Serbia* (Belgrade: Center for Liberal-Democratic Studies, 2005); Maurizio Massari, "Do All Roads Lead to Brussels? Analysis of the Different Trajectories of Croatia, Serbia-Montenegro and Bosnia-Herzegovina," *Cambridge Review of International Affairs* 18:2 (July 2005), 259–273; Sabrina P. Ramet, "The Denial Syndrome and Its Consequences: Serbian Political Culture since 2000," *Communist & Post-Communist Studies* 40:1 (March 2007), 41–58; Wolfgang Petritsch, Goran Svilanović, and Christophe Solioz, eds., *Serbia Matters: Domestic Reforms and European Integration* (Baden-Baden: Nomos Verlagsgesellschaft, 2009); Darina Malova and Peter Uče, "Slovakia," *European Journal of Political Research* 48:7/8 (November–December 2009), 1100–1105.

[8] But see Timothy Edmunds, "Illiberal Resilience in Serbia," *Journal of Democracy* 20:1 (January 2009), 128–141, for a more pessimistic view.

[9] See Taras Kuzio, "The Orange Revolution at the Crossroads," *Demokratizatsiya* 14:4 (Fall 2006), 477–493; Paul D'Anieri, "What Has Changed in Ukrainian Politics? Assessing the Implications of the Orange Revolution," *Problems of Post-Communism* 52:5 (2005), 82–91; Geir Flikke, "Pacts, Parties and Elite Struggle: Ukraine's Troubled Post-Orange Transition," *Europe-Asia Studies* 60:3 (May 2008), 375–396; Paweł Wołowski, "Ukrainian Politics after the Orange Revolution: How Far from Democratic Consolidation?," in *Chaillot Paper no 108, Ukraine: Quo vadis*, ed. Sabine Fischer (Paris: EU Institute for Security Studies, February 2008), 25–53, at http://www.iss.europa.eu/uploads/media/cp108.pdf; Politics Division, Ukrainian Center for Independent Political Research, *Political Risks and Political Stability in Ukraine*, UCIPR Document on Political Risk Assessment (May 2009), at http://www.ucipr. kiev.ua/files/books/Political_risks_May2009e.pdf; Anders Aslund, *How Ukraine Became a Market Economy and Democracy* (Washington, DC: Peterson Institute for International Economics, March 2009), especially Chapters 8 and 9; Paul Kubicek, "Problems of Post-post-communism: Ukraine after the Orange Revolution," *Democratization* 16:2 (April 2009), 323–343; Adrian Karatnycky and Alexander J. Motyl, "The Key to Kiev," *Foreign Affairs* 88:3 (May–June 2009), 106–120. Many of the essays in Juliane Besters-Dilger, ed., *Ukraine on Its Way to Europe: Interim Results of the Orange Revolution* (Frankfurt: Peter Lang, 2009), also highlight problematic aspects of post-2004 political developments in Ukraine.

[10] Alexander J. Motyl, "Ukrainian Blues," *Foreign Affairs* 89:4 (July–August 2010), 125–136.

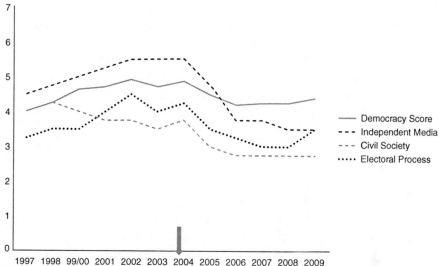

FIGURE 11.7. Ukraine.

Source: Freedom House's *Nations in Transit*, 1997 to 2009.

uncertain until the election itself, as an illustration of how the political climate has changed in Ukraine. The openness of the media and the ability of NGOs to function without harassment by the government are further examples of the impact of the 2004 elections, at least to date.[11]

When we turn to Georgia, the picture is considerably more mixed (see Figure 11.8): the overall democracy score in fact worsens, and the scores for

---

[11] See Gerhard Simon, "After the Orange Revolution: The Rocky Road to Democracy," in *Ukraine on Its Way to Europe: Interim Results of the Orange Revolution*, ed. Juliane Besters-Dilger (Frankfurt: Peter Lang, 2009), 13–26. Lucan Way, "Burnt Orange: What Ukraine's Presidential Election Means for Democracy," *Foreign Affairs*, February 4, 2010, at http://www.foreignaffairs.com/articles/65954/lucan-way/burnt-orange, agrees that Ukraine is a "functioning democracy," but warns of the potential for serious instability irrespective of the outcome of the 2010 elections. See Samuel Charap, "Seeing Orange: Why a Ukraine without Viktor Yushchenko Might Be in a Better Position to Cooperate with the West," *Foreign Policy*, January 18, 2010, at http://www.foreignpolicy.com/articles/2010/01/18/seeing_orange; Christian Caryl, "Yanukovych Won: Get Over It," *Foreign Policy*, February 8, 2010, at http://www.foreignpolicy.com/articles/2010/02/08/yanukovich_won_get_over_it; David J. Kramer, "The Revolution Is Dead, Long Live the Revolution," *Foreign Policy*, February 8, 2010, at http://www.foreignpolicy.com/articles/2010/02/08/why_the_orange_revolution_didnt_just_die; David J. Kramer, Mark Cunningham, and Pavol Demeš, *Ukraine: Democracy in Progress*, German Marshall Fund of the United States Focus on Ukraine (January 19, 2010), http://www.gmfus.org/galleries/ct_publication_attachments/GMF_UkraineSeries_KramerCunningham.pdf; and David J. Kramer, *Ukraine's Post-Election 'To-Do' List*, German Marshall Fund of the United States Focus on Ukraine (February 11, 2010), http://www.gmfus.org/galleries/ct_publication_attachments/GMF_UkraineSeries_KramerToDoList.pdf;jsessionid=aet2Hpf npRL4QIoxEL.

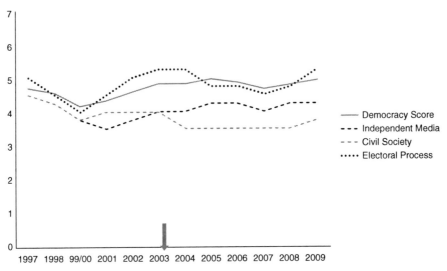

FIGURE 11.8. Georgia.

Source: Freedom House's *Nations in Transit*, 1997 to 2009.

independent media and the electoral process worsen more dramatically, particularly after 2007. The main bright spot in Georgia, in addition to the fact
that the Rose Revolution stopped a movement toward greater authoritarianism between 2001 and 2003 in all areas except independent media, is in the
area of civil society, where the score improved after 2003 and remained stable
until 2009, when it worsened slightly. Georgia has also made some progress
in the areas of corruption and the rule of law, in addition to implementing
significant educational reforms.

Finally, in the case of Kyrgyzstan, there was a small improvement in the
independent media score, which did not last, and in the overall democracy
score, which also did not last, but virtually no change in the civil society score
until 2009, when it worsened, and a deterioration in the area of electoral
process between 2005 and 2009 (see Figure 11.9). This pattern, as we have
argued in previous chapters, is very consistent with other diffusion dynamics
in cases where the innovation being diffused is diluted, in effect, the further
it travels and where, due to less propitious conditions, diffusion results in
less change.

Although we cannot go into detail concerning subscores across countries,
there is one area that merits special mention, and that is corruption. One of
the main reasons for Ukraine's recent democracy scores, for example, is the
fact that its corruption score has been and continues to be high, as does its
score on national governance. As Figure 11.10 illustrates, this pattern has been
true in all of the successful cases, with the exception of Slovakia, where the
corruption score is lower than in all of the other cases. The corruption scores
in Serbia and Georgia improved significantly immediately after the ousters of

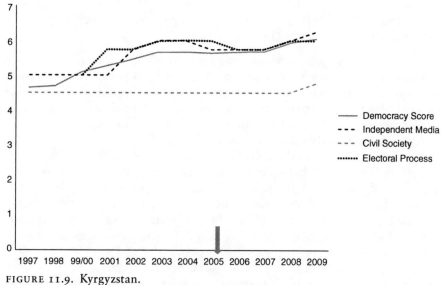

FIGURE 11.9. Kyrgyzstan.
Source: Freedom House's *Nations in Transit*, 1997 to 2009.

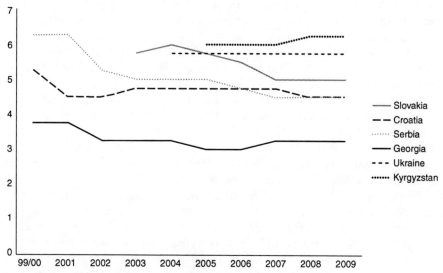

FIGURE 11.10. Successful cases: corruption.
Source: Freedom House's *Nations in Transit*, 1997 to 2009.

Milošević and Shevardnadze, respectively. However, both countries started at such a high level that the improved score is still relatively high, as are the scores of all of the other countries studied. Corruption, as we noted earlier in the book, is a serious problem in mixed regimes in particular.

EXPLAINING DIFFERING DEVELOPMENTS AFTER SUCCESSFUL
OUSTERS OF AUTHORITARIAN LEADERS

Looking at our successful cases only, we are left with the question of why some
of these events led to smoother movement toward a consolidated democracy
than others. In order to answer this question, we examined several possible
explanations for the variation in outcomes, many of which failed to differentiate between our successful and unsuccessful cases or to shed much light on
different patterns within the first group.

The first of these was the context, or degree of democratic development,
evident in the country before the opposition victory, and thus the point of
political and economic departure. We examined this factor in two ways. First,
we looked at the overall democracy scores used to construct the graphs we have
discussed earlier in this chapter. From this perspective, it is clear that the starting point did set the parameters of what happened after the opposition won.
The critical elections we have examined thus served to end de-democratization
(Slovakia), end authoritarian rule (Croatia, Serbia, Ukraine, and Georgia),
and begin a transition to democracy (Kyrgyzstan). However, the starting
point, measured here by the country's democracy score prior to the critical
elections, tells us surprisingly little about the degree of change, as measured
by the gain score, or the difference between the average of scores for the two
years preceding the critical elections and 2008. This measure, in fact, disad-
vantages countries, such as Slovakia, that had better democracy scores at the
outset, as they had less far to go. However, as Table 11.1, which provides the
gain score in column one illustrates, gain scores do show a great deal of variation across our successful cases. Thus, the highest gains in democracy scores
occurred in Serbia, where the regime was far from democratic, and Slovakia,
which had experienced a period of de-democratization immediately prior to
the 1998 elections. We have also included our failed cases in Table 11.1; here
it is interesting that the degree of change, in a negative direction, in Georgia
and Kyrgyzstan was relatively similar to that which occurred in Armenia in
2008 and in Azerbaijan in both elections of interest.

The second factor that we examined was the degree of Western assistance: did the process work better where the U.S. and other Western actors
supportive of democracy provided more assistance? In Chapter 8, we concluded that U.S. assistance did not differentiate well between our successful and unsuccessful cases. Here, we are interested in whether variations in
U.S. assistance can explain differences among our successful cases.[12] As Table
8.5 in Chapter 8 demonstrated, however, patterns of U.S. democracy aid do
not account for the contrast between Georgia and Kyrgyzstan, on the one
hand, and Croatia, Serbia, Slovakia, and Ukraine, on the other. For example,

---

[12] We restrict our focus to U.S. government aid, because there is a comprehensive data set available for this type of assistance. The same cannot be said for democracy and governance aid
provided by U.S. foundations or European governmental or private agencies.

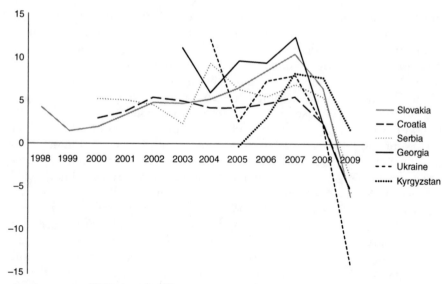

FIGURE 11.11. GDP growth (%).
Notes: Data for 2008 are estimates. Data for 2009 are projections.
Source: European Bank for Reconstruction and Development, "Growth in Real GDP," October 2009.

contrasting postelection political trajectories do not seem to reflect differences in such areas as per capita outlays on Democracy and Governance; the percentage change in Democracy and Governance assistance for two years prior to the election; or the percentage growth in electoral assistance during the same period. Nor does lengthening the time period change the picture: we also looked at these figures for five years prior to the pivotal elections to see if the time period chosen would affect our conclusions, but, in fact, it does not. Thus, although U.S. assistance was important in many ways, including supporting the development of civil society and funding activities that let graduates of earlier successes share their experiences and strategies with others, its level was not the main factor affecting success.

Third, we looked at economic performance. Our hypothesis was that since, as ample survey data demonstrate, many people in this region associate democracy with an improved material standard of living and since, other things being equal, it is clearly easier to introduce significant political and economic reforms in an era of growth than in one of increasing scarcity, improved economic performance should go along with or facilitate improvements in democracy. As Figure 11.11 illustrates, it is difficult to discern such a pattern: in fact, it is difficult to discern *any* pattern here. Kyrgyzstan, which had a negative growth rate in 2005, experienced the greatest growth in GDP prior to the global economic crisis of 2008 and 2009. Slovakia also experienced a clear upward trend, and Croatia's economic performance generally improved prior to the general downturn in 2008, but both Georgia and Ukraine experienced fairly radical ups and downs. In Serbia, economic performance reflects more erratic political developments after 2000. As the graph illustrates, the economies of all of these countries suffered greatly in the late 2000s, and all but Kyrgyzstan in fact experienced declines in GDP.

Finally, we looked at the impact of continued unity or fragmentation of the political elite. We used two indicators: 1) the continuation of the coalition in power and 2) the defection of significant numbers of leaders. In fact, this factor had little relationship to the scores we have been examining. If we look at the first dimension, the coalition that won the parliamentary elections or supported the victor in the presidential elections was reelected in the next elections in Slovakia and Serbia, but not in Croatia or Ukraine. In Georgia and Kyrgyzstan, Saakashvili and Bakiev and their supporters won handily in the 2008 and 2007 elections, and both were subsequently elected president by huge margins. Incumbents or their designated successors won easily in the cases where efforts to use the model failed or where efforts were not made. Continuity of leadership made little systematic difference, then, and the difference it did make was not in the expected direction. This is an important finding, as commentators frequently view disunity among the victors and later political conflict as signs that democracy is not doing well. We would argue the reverse: high levels of competition in fact strengthen, rather than diminish, democratic development. With regard to the second indicator, there were frequent defections from the winning coalition in all of the successful cases we studied. Thus, we would reject the argument that there were clear costs attached to the ephemeral nature of opposition unity. Indeed, it can be argued that postelection divisions of the opposition make two important contributions to democratic change: they make it harder for a new political monopoly to form, and they contribute to the development of the political party system.

If these factors do not explain the difference among our successful cases, what does? We now turn to four factors that do appear to have had important effects. These include the position of the country in the diffusion wave, the international position of the country involved, the strength of civil society prior to the elections, and the nature of the transition itself. First, let us reiterate: if we see these events as part of a diffusion process – the tendency for less success as we go further down the wave, where conditions are generally less favorable than in what Mark Beissinger calls the "early risers" – then the pattern is fairly consistent with what we would expect. Later in the wave, conditions were less propitious, there was less planning and organization by the opposition and civil society, and incumbents and their allies had greater warning, although there is little evidence that Shevardnadze in particular made use of being forewarned. But diffusion dynamics alone do not explain the different outcomes in Georgia and Ukraine, for example.

The second factor that differentiates between our two groups of successful cases is the international position/orientation of the country. Proximity to

Europe or, more broadly, the strength of the commitment of other democratic governments to integrate the country into European or Euroatlantic institutions, has often been identified as key to post-turnover outcomes[13] and does, in fact, help differentiate between our two groups. The influence of this factor, which Lucan Way and Steven Levitsky have noted in their analysis of the strong effects of linkage and leverage, is clearest in the case of Slovakia, where a desire not to be excluded from the golden circle of Central European countries by Mečiar's policies was clearly one – although, as we have argued, only one – of the factors that led people to support the opposition in 1998.[14] This factor also has been related to democratic gains in Croatia, even under the governments of Tudjman's successors, who came back to power in the elections after 2000, and also, one could argue, in Serbia, as evident in the choice made by a majority of the Serbian electorate in the 2008 election (and in earlier elections following the defeat of Milošević in 2000) to reject the focus on nationalism and the loss of Kosovo – the position taken, for example, by the Radical Party and its leader, Tomislav Nikolić – and support pro-EU integration parties surrounding the incumbent president, Boris Tadić. The position of Europe and the United States toward the integration of Ukraine and, particularly after the August 2008 war with Russia, Georgia, has been far more ambiguous. Although the United States supported Kyrgyzstan as an island of democracy in Central Asia soon after the demise of the USSR, and although the United States has a military base there, there was little talk of further integration, even prior to the overthrow of the Bakiev government and the ethnic and regionally based unrest in that country in 2010. This difference highlights the important role that potential membership in the EU and NATO has played in influencing political development in the region as a whole. It also raises a critical question, which is how Europe and the United States can support democratic change without the incentives that EU and NATO membership offer. It is also interesting that the three countries in which opposition

---

[13] Milada Anna Vachudová, *Europe Undivided: Democracy, Leverage, and Integration after Communism* (Oxford and New York: Oxford University Press, 2005); Jeffrey S. Kopstein and David A. Reilly, "Geographic Diffusion and the Transformation of the Postcommunist World," *World Politics* 53:1 (Oct, 2000), 1–37; Jeffrey Kopstein, "The Transatlantic Divide over Democracy Promotion," *The Washington Quarterly* 29:2 (Spring 2006), 85–98; Kataryna Wolczuk, "Implementation without Coordination: The Impact of EU Conditionality on Ukraine under the European Neighbourhood Policy," *Europe-Asia Studies* 61:2 (March 2009), 187–211; Richard Youngs, "'A Door Neither Closed nor Open': EU Policy Towards Ukraine during and since the Orange Revolution," *International Politics* 46:4 (July 2009), 358–375. But see also Tim Haughton and Marek Rybář, "A Tool in the Tolbox: Assessing the Impact of EU Membership on Party Politics in Slovakia," *Journal of Communist Studies and Transition Politics* 25:4 (December 2009), 540–563.

[14] See Lucan A. Way and Steven Levitsky, "Linkage, Leverage and the Postcommunist Divide," *East European Politics and Societies* 21:1 (2007), 48–66. Way and Levitsky argue that the international context of hybrid regimes has powerful effects on their political trajectories. For example, democratic progress is more likely when there are dense ties between these regimes and the West (linkage) and when these regimes are vulnerable to Western political and economic pressures (leverage).

TABLE 11.1. *Nations in Transit trends. (The assessments in this table are two-year averages of performance. For example, for Armenia in 2003, the scores are an average of 2001 and 2002.)*

Country	Election	DS[a]	CS	IM	EP	Corruption	Postelection Trend[b]
Croatia	2000	−4.36	3.50	4.88	4.25	5.25[c]	+1.18
Georgia	2003	−4.46	4.00	3.68	4.75	5.38	−0.44
Kyrgyzstan	2005	−5.67	4.50	6.00	6.00	6.00	−0.29
Serbia[d]	2000	−5.67	5.18	5.13	5.25	6.25	+1.14
Slovakia[e]	1998	−3.80	3.25	4.25	3.75	N/A	+1.09
Ukraine	2004	−4.82	3.68	5.50	4.25	5.88	+0.48
Armenia	2003	+4.83	3.50	4.75	5.50	5.75	−0.16
Armenia	2008	−5.68	3.50	5.68	5.75	5.75	na
Azerbaijan	2003	−5.59	4.50	5.68	5.75	6.25	−0.16
Azerbaijan	2005	−5.55	4.48	5.68	5.88	6.25	−0.45
Belarus[f]	2006	−6.59	6.75	6.75	6.88	5.89	−0.09

[a] The + or − in this column refers to whether the average score for the two years preceding the election represented an improvement or a decline in democratic performance in comparison to the previous three years.

[b] The purpose of this column is to provide a brief summary of democratic developments after the election.

[c] Scores for 1999/2000. Scores for 1998 not available.

[d] Score for 1999/2000. Score for 1998 not available.

[e] Score for 1997. Scores for 1996 not available.

[f] The scores for the postelection period include only results from 2007, as the scores for 2008 are not yet available.

Note: DS - Democracy Score; CS - Civil Society; IM - Independent Media; EP - Electoral Process.

Source: Freedom House, *Nations in Transit*, http://www.Freedomhouse.org/uploads/nit/2008/Tables-WBB.pdf.

victories have had least impact were parts of the former Soviet Union and are still seen by some as being in Russia's sphere of influence. The three cases, however, have different orientations toward Russia (Kyrgyszstan under Bakiev was somewhat pro-Russian, though its relations with the Russian leadership deteriorated over the course of his tenure; Georgia, especially after the 2008 war, is anti-Russian; and Ukraine falls somewhere in the middle), which do not parallel the degree of or lack of democratic development.

The third factor that influences democratic progress after the elections is the level of development of civil society prior to the critical elections. If we look again at Table 11.1, which provides Freedom House scores for civil society sustainability, there is some support for the expected relationship between a strong and vigorous civil society prior to the elections and movement toward democracy afterwards, but not as much as one might want. Slovakia, for example, is a very good case in this respect, as is Croatia, as in both countries civil society, in part as the result of longer-term support for the development of the third sector, was well-developed. This factor, which affected the ability of opposition elites to mobilize popular support during the critical elections, was also important in Serbia, where, despite the high negative score regarding civil society sustainability that reflected Milošević's increasing repression prior to the 2000 elections, remnants of the vigorous NGO sector and independent think tanks that had developed in Yugoslavia under communism, as well as the antiwar movement that the wars in Yugoslavia provoked, provided a basis for resisting Milošević's effort to totally control public debate and information. In Ukraine, nearly a decade of Western support for grassroots organizations throughout the country paid off when the political opposition decided to make common cause in 2004 and, in contrast to the 2002 elections – in which their victory in the proportionally elected half of parliament had been stolen by Kuchma's manipulations and the victory of his forces in the half elected by majority – also worked with the NGO sector to mobilize voters and plan for and direct mass protest.

As Table 11.1 illustrates, scores for civil society sustainability were lower in Georgia and Kyrgyzstan. The tendency of Georgians soon after the end of communism to protest and take to the streets has sometimes been seen as an indicator of a high level of civic consciousness on the part of the population. We would argue, though, that it is important to distinguish between the ability of citizens to be mobilized and civil society. In the Georgian case, in fact, despite the activities of outside funders and NGO activists, civil society was relatively weak prior to 2003, and there were relatively few NGOs that engaged in advocacy. Also, in contrast to the situation in Slovakia, Croatia, and Serbia, in particular, but also in Ukraine to a large extent, where most NGO leaders consciously decided to stay out of the newly formed government and continue their roles as watchdogs of partisan politicians, in Georgia many of the most important civic leaders joined the government, only to leave it in disillusionment, in some cases, after clashes with Mikheil Saakashvili. In Kyrgyzstan, traditional local-level groups and those centered around individual candidates were more important actors than the relatively few civil society groups, including KelKel, the youth organization modeled on Otpor, Kmara, and Pora, which had very few adherents. Thus, the development of civil society over the long term is an important factor in determining what democratizing elections will actually bring.

The final factor that distinguishes among the two groups – that is, those where democratic development has progressed, albeit unevenly and in fits and starts, on the one hand, and Georgia and Kyrgyzstan, where there was less change after the breakthrough election and more backsliding, on the other – is the nature of the election or transition itself. In those cases in which democratic development has proceeded furthest, the incumbents who were replaced were in fact up for election, and the elections, although rigged to some degree in favor of the regime, were part of an orderly process of change. In Georgia and Kyrgyzstan, by contrast, the incumbent who was replaced was not up for election. In fact, many local and international actors involved in supporting the development of civil society in Georgia have argued in effect that the "revolution" was premature in the sense that the parliamentary elections were understood to be a prelude to, or practice run for, the presidential elections to follow.[15] Shevardnadze's departure, according to this scenario, was also premature, as it thrust the opposition, which was still divided on many issues, into power without sufficient planning or consensus. Similarly, in Kyrgyzstan, the abrupt departure of Akaev created a political vacuum that was filled by a coalition that formed not before the election in order to orchestrate an opposition victory but after his departure in order to divide up the spoils. In both cases, then, although to a more extreme degree in Kyrgyzstan, the consensus-building work involved in creating a united opposition coalition was absent, as was a deliberate strategy to involve civil society groups. Perhaps more importantly, in both cases we see elite orchestrated coups that, although they took place in the context of parliamentary elections, were extra-legal seizures of power that did not use democratic methods to achieve democratic outcomes. This method was costly because it reinforced the view that politics is about winning power by whatever means and did not, as opposition campaigns supported by civil society did in our other successful cases, invest in democratic development. In Georgia, one could argue that Saakashvili merely repeated Shevardnadze's earlier pattern of winning power and then holding elections, which he won by a landslide. In Kyrgyzstan, Akaev's probably premature abdication opened the way for a process of elite turnover that merely perpetuated much of the old system of (as Scott Radnitz terms it) localism and clientelism, but with a new leader, who himself was eventually ousted by popular protests, albeit protests not connected to an election.[16] The landslide "victories" of Saakashvili and Bakiev in subsequent presidential elections, compared to the narrow victories of oppositions in the other critical elections we have examined and the fact that some of them lost in subsequent elections, reaffirm a very old argument in democratic theory. Competition is better than consolidation of power, even when competition leads to acrimonious politics and fragile, and therefore ineffective, governments.

IMPLICATIONS FOR DEMOCRATIZATION

What does this exploration tell us, then, about the role of elections in democratization, and what do these results have to say to those involved in a practical

---

[15] Interview with Richard Miles, U.S. ambassador to Georgia, 2003–05, Silver Spring, MD, September 25, 2009. See, especially, Mitchell, *Uncertain Democracy.* Similar arguments about the costs of a premature challenge to the rule of an incumbent autocrat were made in other interviews conducted with respect to the Georgian election of 2003 with Anna Dolidze, Ithaca, NY, June 9, 2009; Armineh Arakelian, Tbilisi, October 21, 2005; Marina Muskhelishvili, Tbilisi, October 15, 2005; and David Usupashvili, Tbilisi, October 19, 2005; and, for the case of Kyrgyzstan in 2005, in interviews with Shairbek Juraev, Bishkek, January 2008; Li Lifan, Ithaca, NY, April 28, 2009; and Amy Schultz, Baku, March 6, 2007.

[16] Scott Radnitz, "What Really Happened in Kyrgyzstan?," *Journal of Democracy* 17:2 (April 2006), 132–146; Scott Radnitz, "A Horse of a Different Color: Revolution and Regression in Kyrgyzstan," in *Democracy and Authoritarianism in the Postcommunist World,* ed. Valerie Bunce, Michael McFaul, and Kathryn Stoner-Weiss (Cambridge: Cambridge University Press, 2009), 300–324.

way in democracy assistance? In the first area, they very clearly demonstrate the point made by many participants in a recent project on democratizing elections organized by Staffan Lindberg at the University of Florida,[17] concerning the impact of elections on democratization. Can elections be considered, in addition to elite pacting and mass demonstrations not related to elections, as a mode of democratic transition? Based on our research, our answer would be: yes, but it depends. First, it is clearly easier to create a democratic opening by using elections than it is to produce a fully functioning democracy. But that is also true, of course, of other methods of transition, including pacting and mass protest unrelated to elections. It is also true, as the quotation from Thomas Friedman at the beginning of this chapter notes, that some countries have more potential, given, for example, their geopolitical location or the strength of civil society, to exploit the opportunities for democratic change provided by electoral turnover. Given the impact of semi-authoritarian rule and the many problems faced by most of the countries where these elections occurred, it is not surprising that some of them have struggled.

Where, then, can an electoral strategy have the best chance of success? Our results suggest that such elections will be more likely to lead to democratic development after the ouster of authoritarian leaders in contexts where civil society is strong and where the process comes about as the result of coordinated planning over an extended period by an opposition that has had time to come to at least temporary agreement on the division of responsibilities and goals of the government-to-be. As the victory of Viktor Yanukovych in Ukraine's parliamentary elections a scant two years after the Orange Revolution and his victory in the 2010 presidential elections – as well as the election of Robert Fico in Slovakia eight years after Mečiar was ousted – illustrate, even then there are likely to be setbacks. However, at the same time, such "setbacks," which reflect important political cleavages and policy differences that are expressed in high levels of interparty competition, are certainly preferable to the postelection dynamics in Georgia and Kyrgyzstan, where each of the leaders who succeeded the autocrat won the presidential election that followed his parliamentary road to power by an extraordinarily large margin and then used that victory to consolidate his power to the detriment of both democratic progress and the development of a strong opposition. This observation is an important counterpoint to the frequently heard tendency to characterize Ukraine – where there are deep and ongoing cleavages within what were once the "orange" forces, as well as with other elites – as approaching the status of a failed state, and to the argument that Serbia is not a fit applicant for EU membership because of the support given to the far right Radical Party. We are not ignoring the importance of these factors or the difficulties they create for governmental efficiency or even popular support of political leaders and political institutions. But despite these difficulties, there is no doubt that,

---

[17] Staffan Lindberg, ed., *Democratiztion by Elections: A New Mode of Transition?* (Baltimore: Johns Hopkins University Press, 2009).

compared to Georgia and Kyrgyzstan, political life in these countries is far more pluralistic than in countries where there are no effective oppositions to serve as a check on the power of new elites. Moreover, there is something to be said for the fact that the highly competitive elections that have taken place in Croatia, Serbia, Slovakia, and Ukraine reflect the diversity of public opinion in those countries that thereby informs foreign and domestic policy.

To summarize, then, the chances for sustained movement toward democracy appear to be better in situations in which the ground has been prepared by the development of civil society; the old elites are not ousted in an extra-legal, extra-constitutional way; and the new leaders are constrained in their powers by small rather than large electoral mandates. In other words, competition, the rule of law, and a well-developed civil society are always advantageous for democratic progress.

We conclude this chapter with somewhat of a paradox. Given the importance of supportive local conditions and the high cost of failure, as well as learning by authoritarians, it may be tempting to conclude that the current strategy some actors have espoused, that of renouncing "revolutionary" change through support of democratizing elections in favor of gradual or "evolutionary" change, is wise. But here we must remember the finding of a recent study that most authoritarian regimes are replaced not by democratic regimes but by other authoritarian regimes.[18] We should also remember that – in the postcommunist world, at least – democratizing elections have been the *only* way that semi-authoritarian regimes have been replaced by more open, competitive political systems.

---

[18] Axel Hadenius and Jan Teorell, "Pathways from Authoritarianism," *Journal of Democracy* 18:1 (January 2007), 143–156; Lindberg, *Democratization by Elections*.

12

Conclusions

Democratizing Elections, International Diffusion, and U.S. Democracy Assistance

Democracy is not the voting, it's the counting.

Tom Stoppard[1]

It is a good thing that U.S. democracy assistance is so chaotic. Otherwise, people might see it as a plot.

Nino Kobakhidze[2]

Why do authoritarian leaders lose elections? This question is important for three reasons. First, regimes that combine authoritarian politics with electoral competition have proliferated over the course of the global wave of democratization. For example, these hybrid political systems have been estimated to comprise between one-fourth and one-fifth of all regimes that currently exist in the world.[3] Second, elections have a habit of foreshadowing important changes in politics. The rise, consolidation, and termination of both democracy and dictatorship, for instance, seem to be very sensitive to the electoral calendar.[4] Finally, because incumbents have more resources than their

---

[1] Quoted in Thomas Friedman, "Bullets and Barrels," *New York Times*, June 21, 2009, 8.
[2] Interview with Nino Kobakhidze, Tbilisi, October 19, 2005.
[3] Larry Diamond, "Thinking about Hybrid Regimes," *Journal of Democracy* 13:2 (April 2002), 21–35; Andreas Schedler, "The Nested Game of Democratization by Elections," *International Political Science Review / Revue Internationale De Science Politique* 23:1 (January 2002), 103–122; Philip G. Roessler, and Marc Morjé Howard, "Post-Cold-War Political Regimes: When Do Elections Matter?," in *Democratization by Elections: A New Mode of Transition*, ed. Staffan Lindberg (Baltimore: Johns Hopkins University Press, 2009), 101–127.
[4] Jan Teorell and Axel Hadenius, "Elections as Levers of Democracy: A Global Inquiry," in *Democratization by Elections: A New Mode of Transition*, ed. Staffan Lindberg (Baltimore: Johns Hopkins University Press, 2009), 77–100; Staffan I. Lindberg, *Democracy and Elections in Africa* (Baltimore: Johns Hopkins University Press, 2006); Valerie Bunce, "Sequencing Political and Economic Reforms," in *East-Central European Economies in Transition*, ed. John Hardt and Richard Kaufman (Washington, DC: Joint Economic Committee, 1994), 46–63; M. Steven Fish, "Democratization's Prerequisites," *Post-Soviet Affairs* 14:3 (July–September 1998), 212–247; Nancy Bermeo, *Ordinary People in Extraordinary Times: The Citizenry and the Breakdown of Democracy* (Princeton, NJ: Princeton University Press, 2003).

opponents in mixed regimes, electoral turnovers in such political settings are rare events.[5] The norm of continuity in leadership has led some analysts to characterize elections in these political contexts not as a constraint on what authoritarian leaders can do, but rather "as a means by which dictators hold on to power."[6]

The purpose of this book has been to address the puzzle of electoral turnover in mixed regimes by comparing two sets of elections that took place in postcommunist Europe and Eurasia from 1998 to 2008. In the first set, we placed six elections that had the similar and surprising outcome of producing a victory for the opposition over the authoritarian incumbent or his designated successor. The cases here included Slovakia (1998), Croatia and Serbia (2000), Georgia (2003), Ukraine (2004), and Kyrgyzstan (2005).[7] The second set, by contrast, consisted of five elections that produced continuity in authoritarian rule, that is, in Armenia (2003 and 2008), Azerbaijan (2003 and 2005), and Belarus (2006). What made this comparison so illuminating for our purposes, aside from the contrast in election results, were the many similarities between our two groups of regimes and elections. For example, all of these regimes are located in new states that were formed in the early 1990s as a consequence of the collapse of Communist Party hegemony and the accompanying dissolution of the Soviet, Yugoslav, and Czechoslovak states. Just as important is the fact that all of the elections featured a united opposition, and most of them were rigged and prompted large-scale postelection popular protests. These are

---

[5] Marc Morjé Howard and Philip G. Roessler, "Liberalizing Electoral Outcomes in Competitive Authoritarian Regimes," *American Journal of Political Science* 50:2 (April 2006), 362–368; Roessler and Howard, "Post-Cold-War Political Regimes"; Grigore Pop-Eleches and Graeme Robertson, "Elections, Information and Liberalization in the Post–Cold War Era," unpublished manuscript, Princeton University and the University of North Carolina, 2009; Andreas Schedler, "Sources of Competition under Electoral Authoritarianism," in *Democratization by Elections: A New Mode of Transitions?*, ed. Staffan Lindberg (Baltimore: Johns Hopkins University Press, 2009), 179–201; Andreas Schedler, *Electoral Authoritarianism: The Dynamics of Unfree Competition* (Boulder, CO: Lynne Rienner Publishers, 2006); and see Kristin McKie, "The Politics of Adopting Term Limits in Sub-Saharan Africa," paper presented at the annual meeting of the American Political Science Association, Boston, MA, August 29, 2008, on the impact of term limits.

[6] Jennifer Gandhi and Ellen Lust Okar, "Elections under Authoritarianism," *Annual Review of Political Science* 12 (June 2009), 404.

[7] This wave of electoral change was followed by a wave of studies of the "color revolutions." See, for example, Michael McFaul, "Transitions from Postcommunism," *Journal of Democracy* 16:3 (July 2005), 5–19; Joerg Forbrig and Pavol Demeš, eds., *Reclaiming Democracy: Civil Society and Electoral Change in Central and Eastern Europe* (Bratislava: German Marshall Fund of the United States, 2007); Taras Kuzio, ed., "Democratic Revolutions in Post-Communist States," special issue of *Communist and Postcommunist Studies* 39:3 (September 2006); Menno Fenger, "The Diffusion of Revolutions: Comparing Recent Regime Turnovers in Five Post-Communist Countries," *Demokratizatsiya* 15:1 (Winter 2007), 5–28; Mark Beissinger, "Structure and Example in Modular Political Phenomena: The Diffusion of Bulldozer/Rose/Orange/Tulip Revolutions," *Perspectives on Politics* 5:2 (June 2007), 259–276; Joshua Tucker, "Enough! Electoral Fraud Collective Action Problems and Post-Communist Colored Revolutions," *Perspectives on Politics* 5:3 (September 2007), 537–553.

characteristics that, according to some recent studies, should have made the opposition a more formidable political opponent.[8]

In the course of testing a number of hypotheses in order to explain why electoral results diverged, we addressed some other issues of considerable interest to specialists in comparative and international politics. One was whether these elections were related to one another through a process of international diffusion. This possibility was suggested by recent findings regarding the spread of democracy as a diffusion dynamic and by the fact that our electoral breakthroughs followed a pattern consistent with a role for cross-national diffusion – for example, the clustering of these electoral turnovers across time and space.[9] A related question that we examined was the impact of outside actors on these electoral confrontations between authoritarian incumbents

[8] Nicolas Van de Walle, "Meet the New Boss: Same as the Old Boss: The Evolution of Political Clientelism in Africa," in *Patrons, Clients and Policies: Patterns of Democratic Accountability and Political Competition*, ed. Herbert Kitschelt and Steven I. Wilkinson (Cambridge: Cambridge University Press, 2007), 50–67; Nicolas Van de Walle, *Why Do Oppositions Coalesce in Electoral Autocracies?*, Einaudi Center for International Studies Working Paper Series, No. 01–05, Cornell University, August 2005; Nicolas Van de Walle, "Tipping Games: When Do Opposition Parties Coalesce?," in *Electoral Authoritarianism: The Dynamics of Unfree Competition*, ed. Andreas Schedler (Boulder, CO: Lynne Rienner Publishers, 2006), 77–94; Howard and Roessler, "Liberalizing Electoral Outcomes in Competitive Authoritarian Regimes"; Mark R. Thompson and Philipp Kuntz, "Stolen Elections: The Case of the Serbian October," *Journal of Democracy* 15:4 (October 2004): 159–172; Tucker, "Enough!"

[9] Pam Oliver and Dan Myers, "Network Diffusion and Cycles of Collective Action," in *Social Movements and Networks: Relational Approaches to Collective Action*, ed. Mario Diani and Doug McAdam (Oxford: Oxford University Press, 2003), 173–203; Doug McAdam and Dieter Rucht, "The Cross-National Diffusion of Movement Ideas," *The Annals of the American Academy of Political and Social Science* 528:1 (July 2003), 56–74; David Strang and Sarah A. Soule, "Diffusion in Organizations and Social Movements: From Hybrid Corn to Poison Pills," *Annual Review of Sociology* 24:1 (August 1998), 265–290; Mark Beissinger, *Nationalist Mobilization and the Collapse of the Soviet State* (Cambridge: Cambridge University Press, 2002); Wade Jacoby, "Inspiration, Coalition and Substitution: External Influences on Postcommunist Transformations," *World Politics* 58:4 (July 2006), 623–651; Everett Rogers, *Diffusion of Innovations* (New York: Free Press, 1996); Beth Simmons and Zachary Elkins, "The Globalization of Liberalization: Policy Diffusion in the International Political Economy," *American Political Science Review* 98:1 (February 2004), 171–189; Zachary Elkins and Beth Simmons, "On Waves, Clusters, and Diffusion: A Conceptual Framework," *The Annals of the American Academy of Political and Social Science* 598 (March 2005), 33–51; Beth Simmons, Frank Dobbin, and Geoffrey Garrett, *The Global Diffusion of Markets and Democracy* (Cambridge: Cambridge University Press, 2008); Daniel Brinks and Michael Coppedge, "Diffusion Is No Illusion: Neighbor Emulation in the Third Wave of Democracy," *Comparative Political Studies* 39:4 (May 1, 2006), 463–489; Kristian Skrede Gleditsch and Michael D. Ward, "Diffusion and the International Context of Democratization," *International Organization* 60:4 (October 2006), 911–933; Kurt Weyland, "The Diffusion of Revolution: '1848' in Europe and Latin America," *International Organization* 63:3 (Summer 2009), 391–423; Kurt Weyland, "Diffusion Dynamics in European and Latin American Democratization," paper presented at the 105th annual meeting of the American Political Science Association, Toronto, September 3–6, 2009; and Scott Mainwaring and Aníbal Pérez-Liñán, "International Factors and Regime Change in Latin America, 1945–2005," paper presented at the 105th annual meeting of the American Political Science Association, Toronto, September 3–6, 2009.

and opposition groups. Here, we were particularly interested in the role of the U.S. democracy assistance community, although we also examined the influence of the European Union and European governments and foundations.[10]

[10] See, for example, Gordon Crawford, *Foreign Aid and Political Reform: A Comparative Analysis of Democracy Assistance and Conditionality* (Basingstoke, UK: Palgrave, 2001); Eric C. Bjornlund, *Beyond Free and Fair: Monitoring Elections and Building Democracy* (Washington, DC: Woodrow Wilson Center Press, 2004); Jon C. Pevehouse, *Democracy from Above: Regional Organizations and Democratization* (Cambridge: Cambridge University Press, 2005); Thomas Carothers, "The End of the Transition Paradigm," *Journal of Democracy* 13:1 (January 2002), 5–21; Thomas Carothers, *Critical Missions: Essays on Democracy Promotion* (Washington, DC: Carnegie Endowment for International Peace, 2004); Thomas Carothers, *Aiding Democracy Abroad: The Learning Curve* (Washington, DC: Carnegie Endowment for International Peace, 1999); Michael Cox, G. John Ikenberry, and Takashi Inoguchi, *American Democracy Promotion: Impulses, Strategies, and Impacts* (Oxford: Oxford University Press, 2000); Richard Youngs, *International Democracy and the West: The Roles of Governments, Civil Society, and Multinational Business* (Oxford: Oxford University Press, 2004); Gideon Rose, "Democracy Promotion and American Foreign Policy: A Review Essay," *International Security* 25:3 (Winter 2000), 186–203; Scott Mainwaring and Aníbal Pérez-Liñán, *Why Regions of the World Are Important: Regional Specificities and Region-Wide Diffusion of Democracy,* Kellogg Institute, University of Notre Dame, Working Paper 322 (October 2005); Ronald Haly Linden, *Norms and Nannies: The Impact of International Organizations on the Central and East European States* (Lanham, MD: Rowman & Littlefield Publishers, 2002); Stephen Knack, "Does Foreign Aid Promote Democracy?," *International Studies Quarterly* 48:1 (March 2004), 251–266; Wade Jacoby, *The Enlargement of the European Union and NATO: Ordering from the Menu in Central Europe* (Cambridge: Cambridge University Press, 2004); Anna Milada Vachudová, *Europe Undivided: Democracy, Leverage, and Integration after Communism* (Oxford: Oxford University Press, 2005); Steven F. Finkel, Aníbal Pérez-Liñán, Mitchell A. Seligson, and Dinorah Azpuru, *Effects of U.S. Foreign Assistance on Democracy Building: Results of a Cross-National Quantitative Study, Final Report,* USAID (January 12, 2006), http://www.usaid.gov/ourwork/democracyandgovernance/publications/pdfs/impactof-democracyassistance.pdf; Ralph Morris Goldman and William A. Douglas, *Promoting Democracy: Opportunities and Issues: Democracy in the World* (New York: Praeger, 1988); Peter J. Schraeder, *Exporting Democracy: Rhetoric vs. Reality* (Boulder, CO: Lynne Rienner Publishers, 2002); and Michael Mandelbaum, "Foreign Policy as Social Work," *Foreign Affairs* 75:1 (January–February 1996). See also detailed case studies of democracy promotion in one country: Walt Bogdanich and Jenny Nordberg, "Democracy Undone: Back Channels versus Policy; Mixed U.S. Signals Helped Tilt Haiti toward Chaos," *New York Times,* January 29, 2006, http://www.nytimes.com/2006/01/29/international/americas/29haiti.html; David Backer and David Carroll, "NGOs and Constructive Engagement: Promoting Civil Society, Good Governance and Rule of Law in Liberia," *International Politics* 38:1 (March 2001), 1–26; Andrew Ng, "Accompanying the King: Building a Democratic Governance State in Morocco" (honors thesis, Department of Government, Cornell University, April 16, 2007). But see Laurence Whitehead, *The International Dimensions of Democratization: Europe and the Americas* (Oxford: Oxford University Press, 1996) for a longer-term perspective. Also see Strobe Talbott, "Democracy and the National Interest," *Foreign Affairs* 75:6 (November–December 1996), 47–63; Jaba Devdariani, *The Impact of International Assistance on Georgia,* International Institute for Democracy and Electoral Assistance (IDEA) Building Democracy in Georgia Discussion Paper no. 11 (May 2003), http://www.idea.int/publications/georgia/upload/Book-11_scr.pdf; Jonathan Monten, "The Roots of the Bush Doctrine," *International Security* 29:4 (Spring 2005), 112–156; and Eric Hershberg,

Finally, we analyzed variations in the longer-term consequences of these elections. Why was democratic progress greater in some countries that experienced electoral turnover than in others, and what political difference did it make that oppositions won or lost elections?

Difficult questions such as these demand detailed data and diverse approaches. With respect to the first issue: we gathered a wide range of information, including over two hundred interviews conducted with local and international participants in our eleven elections. We then assembled this information in several different ways in order to shed light on the key factors shaping electoral outcomes. Thus, in Part II of the book we presented analytical narratives of what happened in each of our countries and elections, whereas in Part III we merged our cases. In practice, the latter meant first treating our elections as separate events and using controlled comparisons among them to test the impact of structural, institutional, and short-term factors. We then proceeded from the opposite premise that they were related to one another and evaluated the extent to which international diffusion affected whether oppositions lost or won elections.

NEGATIVE FINDINGS: STRUCTURAL AND INSTITUTIONAL FACTORS

What did we discover? We can begin our summary by noting briefly some of the hypotheses that we were able to reject. Perhaps the most surprising negative finding in this study was that familiar indicators of the strength of the regime versus that of the opposition on the eve of the election – in particular, the political character of the regime itself and long-term trends in economic and political performance – failed to account in a consistent way for variations in electoral outcomes. For example, while it is true (as one would expect) that all of the failures to dislodge authoritarian leaders took place in relatively authoritarian regimes, it is also the case that many opposition victories were registered in regimes that were just as authoritarian. At the same time, there was significant overlap between our two sets of elections with respect to trends in such areas as economic performance and the frequency of governmental turnovers and anti-regime protests.[11] These findings do not, of

"Democracy Promotion in Latin America," *Democracy and Society* 4:2 (Spring 2007), 3–5. On the role of international influences on democratic change, see, for instance, Guillermo A. O'Donnell, Philippe C. Schmitter, and Laurence Whitehead, *Transitions from Authoritarian Rule: Comparative Perspectives* (Baltimore: Johns Hopkins University Press, 1988); Laurence Whitehead, "Three International Dimensions of Democratization," in *The International Dimensions of Democratization: Europe and the Americas*, ed. Laurence Whitehead (Oxford: Oxford University Press, 2001), 3–25; Youngs, *International Democracy and the West*; and Jan Zielonka, *Democratic Consolidation in Eastern Europe* (Oxford: Oxford University Press, 2001).

[11] Lucan Way, "The Real Causes of the Color Revolutions," *Journal of Democracy* 19:3 (July 2008), 55–69; Valerie Bunce and Sharon L. Wolchik, "Debating the Color Revolutions: Getting Real about 'Real Causes,'" *Journal of Democracy* 20:1 (January 2009), 69–73; Steven

course, challenge the fact that some political settings are more supportive of opposition victories than others, or that extreme degrees of political repression foreclose the possibility of an opposition electoral victory. However, what we would argue is that the structural and institutional parameters on political change are surprisingly elastic in mixed regimes.

Two other negative findings were also unexpected. One was that liberalization of politics in the years leading up to the pivotal elections had *no* relationship to the success of electoral challenges mounted by the opposition. Indeed, virtually all of the elections, whether producing continuity in or a break with authoritarian rule, were preceded by a period of growing authoritarianism.[12] We also failed to find, even when expanding our study to include earlier electoral confrontations between the regime and the opposition in our nine countries, the expected role for unity of the opposition, electoral fraud, or popular protests following the election. None of these developments correlated very well with opposition victories.[13]

THE ELECTORAL MODEL

By contrast, explanatory factors of a more short-term character that focused on the dynamics of the elections emerged as being more influential. In particular, what proved to be decisive in distinguishing between opposition victory and defeat was whether oppositions and their allies ran sophisticated and energetic political campaigns. When they did, they succeeded in taking office – either immediately after the election or, where incumbents or their chosen successors attempted to steal the election, following popular protests.

What did this ensemble of innovative electoral strategies – which we have termed the electoral model – mean in practice? Included in this tool kit was, first, the formation of a united front among major opposition parties. In addition, for the opposition the electoral model included such activities as

Levitsky and Lucan A. Way, "Competitive Authoritarian Regimes: The Evolution of Post-Soviet Competitive Authoritarianism 1992–2005," paper presented at the conference Why Communism Didn't Collapse: Understanding Regime Resilience in China, Vietnam, Laos, North Korea and Cuba, Dartmouth College, Hannover, NY, May 25–26, 2007; Jason Brownlee, *Authoritarianism in an Age of Democratization* (Cambridge: Cambridge University Press, 2007); Steven Levitsky and Lucan Way, *Competitive Authoritarianism: Hybrid Regimes after the Cold War* (Cambridge: Cambridge University Press, 2010).

[12] Wayne Francisco, "After the Massacre: Mobilization in the Wake of Harsh Repression," *Mobilization: An International Journal* 9:2 (January 2004), 107–126. Also see Sidney Tarrow, *Power in Movement: Social Movements and Contentious Politics* (Cambridge: Cambridge University Press, 1998). However, it is important to recognize at the same time that growing authoritarianism did correlate with propensity to protest – as we saw not just in Serbia, Georgia, Ukraine, and Kyrgyzstan, but also in Armenia, Azerbaijan, and Belarus.

[13] Tucker, "Enough!"; Van de Walle, "Meet the New Boss: Same as the Old Boss"; Van de Walle, "Why Do Oppositions Coalesce in Electoral Autocracies?"; Van de Walle, "Tipping Games: When Do Opposition Parties Coalesce?"; Howard and Roessler, "Liberalizing Electoral Outcomes in Competitive Authoritarian Regimes"; Mark R. Thompson and Philipp Kuntz, "Stolen Elections."

mounting large-scale voter registration and turnout drives; carrying out creative and ambitious nationwide campaigns; and collaborating closely with civil
society groups, including youth organizations, women's organizations, and
organizations devoted to organizing and analyzing the elections and the electorate. The electoral model also made extensive use of cultural events such
as rock concerts, marches, and even bicycle tours to increase public interest
in the election, and of the media, public opinion polls, exit polls, and external and internal vote monitoring and parallel vote tabulation. When combined, these wide-ranging and interrelated activities put in place all the pieces
that were required for an opposition victory. To put the issue succinctly: these
strategies highlighted the costs of continuing the regime in office and demonstrated the credibility of the opposition. As a result, citizens became more
optimistic about the possibilities for political change; they were more willing
to vote; and they were more ready to throw their support to the opposition. In
more authoritarian regimes, moreover, these critical shifts in the perceptions,
preferences, and behaviors of ordinary citizens, when joined with the contrast
between the official vote tally and the real results of the election, provided the
necessary conditions for large-scale public protests that succeeded in forcing a
transfer of power to the victorious opposition.

Thus, the electoral model solved long-standing coordination and collective
action problems.[14] In this sense, the most important impact of the electoral
model was to level the political playing field in mixed regimes by empowering
the opposition and its supporters. However, this conclusion introduces an obvious question. What explains the failure of authoritarian incumbents or their
anointed successors to adopt the electoral model as well? After all, they had a
lot to lose by allowing the opposition to run a more sophisticated campaign.
Our response to this question is twofold. First, authoritarian incumbents or
their chosen successors were prisoners of their previous successes. Why go
to the trouble of doing something different, especially since elections could
always be stolen at the last minute? Second, authoritarian incumbents paid a
steep price for their isolation – from information about the real distribution of
their political support within the population (votes, for instance, were a poor
guide, since opponents of the regime tended not to vote); from the international democracy assistance community, which provided detailed information
about how campaigns could be run and elections won; and, more generally,
from the cross-national diffusion dynamic described earlier that brought the
electoral model to oppositions in these countries, but not to authoritarian
incumbents. The fact is that the electoral model was a foreign import, and
there was a good reason for this. Elections were too new to these countries to
have spawned such an elaborate and sophisticated ensemble of electoral strategies. Thus, while commanding impressive resources in most respects, authoritarian leaders were in fact disadvantaged in one area vital to their tenure.

---

[14] Our thanks to David Patel for drawing the important distinction between coordination and
collective action.

They did not understand what they needed to do to fend off strong electoral challenges to their power. Indeed, they mistakenly assumed that, as in the past, the opposition would be divided, weak, and unpopular.

International Diffusion

It was far from accidental that the electoral model was adopted by opposition groups in so many countries in postcommunist Europe and Eurasia within such a brief span of time. The wave of electoral breakthroughs reflected, in particular, a two-stage diffusion dynamic that we have traced through the more than 200 interviews we conducted with participants in this process. The first stage involved a cross-regional transfer of innovative electoral strategies from the Philippines and Chile, where oppositions had mounted successful challenges to authoritarian rule in the second half of the 1980s, to Bulgaria in 1990, where competitive elections were being held for the first time since World War II. A number of factors facilitated the transfer of electoral strategies from Latin America and Southeast Asia to the postcommunist region. One was that members of the International Republican Institute and especially the National Democratic Institute had become convinced that democratic change was well served by bringing opposition groups (including political parties and civil society associations) that had successfully challenged authoritarian rule to meet with similar groups in other countries that wanted to accomplish the same objective. These "learning delegations," as Larry Garber characterized them, were efficient mechanisms for passing on useful political strategies, and they also flattened the hierarchical relationship between the international democracy assistance community and local democratic activists.[15]

Second, Bulgaria was chosen as the focus of such activities in 1990 because the new regime in power was relatively open, yet widely perceived by local and international democracy activists as likely to move in a decidedly more authoritarian direction if the Bulgarian Socialist Party won the election.[16] Finally, democratic change both in Latin America and in Central and Eastern Europe had been a high priority for the National Endowment for Democracy, the International Republican Institute (as it came to be called), the National Democratic Institute, the Free Trade Union Institute, and Freedom House since their founding in 1983. This is why, for example, we see so much personnel overlap between activists who had been involved in Latin America in the 1980s and the activists who played key roles in the postcommunist transitions in the 1990s.

The second stage of the diffusion process concentrated on regimes within the postcommunist region. Here, the Slovak case looms large. It was in that

---

[15] Interview with Larry Garber, Washington, DC, April 9, 2010.
[16] Interviews with Patrick Merloe, Washington, DC, April 30, 2009; Larry Garber, Washington, DC, April 9, 2010; Kenneth Wollack, Washington, DC, May 12, 2010; and Thomas Melia, Washington, DC, April 12, 2010.

country's 1998 election where we find the first full application in the postcommunist region of the electoral model as described earlier in this chapter, and the first case as well of this model succeeding in its mission to replace authoritarians with democrats. The Slovak approach to defeating authoritarian leaders was then transferred in quite deliberate fashion to oppositions and their allies in Croatia, Serbia, Georgia, Ukraine, and, to a lesser extent, Kyrgyzstan from 2000 to 2005. Three mechanisms were responsible for the cross-national transfer of the electoral model within postcommunist Europe and Eurasia. One was the portability of the model and its widespread appeal because of its success and its ability to provide efficient solutions to many problems that had long prevented oppositions from winning power. A second driver of diffusion was the existence of an assumption shared by both exporters and importers of the model that it was widely applicable (with some tinkering) to many other regimes in the postcommunist region. Finally, the model was transferred to new sites because of the hard work of transnational networks that defined, shared, amended, and implemented the model. Members of this transnational network included groups funded by USAID and private foundations, U.S. ambassadors and their staffs, and European-based public and private democracy assistance organizations. In addition, local oppositions and civil society groups played a key role, as did another less widely recognized set of players: political activists from neighboring countries in the postcommunist region who had been successful in mounting electoral challenges to authoritarian rule.

The spread of the electoral model was also typical of diffusion dynamics in several other respects. One was that the cycle of adoption moved from using elements of the model and then putting together a well-rounded tool kit for domestic use and international export to modifying this ensemble of strategies in response to new environments that were much less hospitable to electoral change. That is why, for example, we see the addition of postelection popular protests in the final four cases of electoral turnover. Another pattern that we found in our cases and that is typical of the way diffusion works, particularly when the innovation of interest is (as ours was) very threatening to the prevailing distribution of money and power, is a thinning of transnational networks as they spread out from their original site of operation to more far-flung locales over the course of the wave. This development, plus the growing awareness among authoritarian leaders that they needed to take strong actions to defend themselves from electoral challenges and the tendency of oppositions, witnessing the wave in their neighborhood, to underestimate what they needed to do to make it happen in their own countries, explains the geographical and temporal limits of the spread of the diffusion dynamic.

INTERNATIONAL DEMOCRACY ASSISTANCE

Our analysis of electoral stability and change also generated insights about how international democracy assistance works and its role in electoral stability and change in postcommunist Europe and Eurasia. Here, three conclusions stand out. One is that international democracy assistance is, in practice, a relatively chaotic process.[17] The field itself is very crowded because of the involvement of so many governments and private foundations, along with the vast array of civil society groups they support. In addition, priorities on the ground and in the home organizations shift rapidly; there is no consensus about the kinds of activities that contribute to democratic progress; and there is limited capacity to evaluate the impact of interventions. Moreover, especially in the case of the United States, the process is very decentralized, and turnover rates of members of the U.S. democracy assistance community are extremely high.[18] As a consequence, despite what happened with respect to the elections analyzed in this book, lack of coordination among the Western foundations and governments involved in democracy assistance is the norm.

Second, contrary to the assumptions underlying the very use of the term "exporting democracy," the relationship between donors and recipients – at least in the cases of interest in this study – is neither as hierarchical nor as unidirectional as many critical accounts assume. Thus, just as donors do not always dictate what recipients can and should do, so donors often learn from recipients.[19] Transnational networks that bring together local, regional, and Western activists in a common cause serve as the key players in international democracy assistance.

---

[17] See, especially, National Research Councils of the National Academies, Committee on Evaluation of USAID Democracy Assistance Programs, *Improving Democracy Assistance: Building Knowledge through Evaluations and Research* (Washington, DC: National Academies Press, 2008).

[18] Finkel et al., "Effects of US Foreign Assistance on Democracy Building"; Lincoln Abraham Mitchell, *Uncertain Democracy: U.S. Foreign Policy and Georgia's Rose Revolution* (Philadelphia: University of Pennsylvania Press, 2009); National Research Councils of the National Academies, Committee on Evaluation of USAID Democracy Assistance Programs, *Improving Democracy Assistance*; Erzsebet Fazekas, "Exporting Ideas for Institution-Building: U.S. Foundation Grant-Making for Civil Society Development in Postcommunist Hungary, 1989–2004," paper presented at the annual meeting of the American Association for the Advancement of Slavic Studies, November 14–18, 2007; Andrew Green, "Democracy and Donor Funding: Patterns and Trends," *Eastern European Studies Newsletter*, Woodrow Wilson Center for International Scholars (September–October, 2007), 5–11; Devdariani, *The Impact of International Assistance on Georgia*; Carothers, "The End of the Transition Paradigm"; Carothers, *Critical Missions*; Carothers, *Aiding Democracy Abroad*; Thomas Carothers, "Misunderstanding Gradualism," *Journal of Democracy* 18:3 (July 2007), 18–22; Thomas Carothers, "The 'Sequencing' Fallacy," *Journal of Democracy* 18:1 (January 2007), 12–27. Moreover, as Florian Bieber has suggested in a personal exchange, European democracy promoters tend to be professional bureaucrats who are committed primarily to capacity building and who have a well-defined and relatively apolitical portfolio of tasks that they apply wherever they serve. This is in sharp contrast to many of their American counterparts, who have greater room to maneuver in the field and who more often come from backgrounds in the political world.

[19] See Diamond, "Thinking about Hybrid Regimes"; but see Beate Sissenich, *Building States without Society: European Union Enlargement and the Transfer of EU Social Policy to Poland and Hungary* (Lanham, MD: Lexington Books, 2007), especially on the asymmetries built into certain aspects of EU expansion.

Finally, in the particular case of the elections of interest in this study, while a number of international actors played important roles, it was the United States that in fact dominated the field, though always in collaboration, we must emphasize, with other actors, local and international. Here, we refer, for example, to U.S.-based foundations, such as the Open Society, the Charles Stuart Mott foundation, Rockefeller Brothers, and the German Marshall Fund of the United States, as well as to U.S. government–funded actors, such as the United States Institute of Peace and especially the National Endowment for Democracy, the International Republican Institute, the National Democratic Institute, and Freedom House. The role of the United States in these electoral struggles grew in part out of U.S. foreign policy priorities. The United States became involved in democracy assistance in the postcommunist world before other international players, and USAID outlays on democracy and governance favored the postcommunist region in the 1990s in particular.[20]

While money matters, however, so does the fact that the United States took a distinctive approach to democracy assistance that was particularly critical in influencing electoral outcomes. Thus, as we discovered through our interviews and analysis of relevant documents, the United States specialized in five areas of assistance: 1) extending financial and technical support for free and fair elections, including putting pressure on regimes to improve their electoral procedures and providing support for exit polls and parallel vote tabulation, along with civil society organizations that were involved in voter registration and turnout drives; 2) supporting greater engagement in politics and policy by such underrepresented and demobilized groups as women, minorities, and citizens located in smaller towns and rural areas; 3) working with the opposition parties to encourage them to collaborate with each other and to reach out to civil society groups; 4) assisting in the development, transfer, and implementation of the electoral model; and 5) providing sizeable long-term support for civil society.[21]

At the same time, as local participants in these elections emphasized repeatedly in interviews with us, the United States was far more "nimble" than the Europeans, who were less concerned with the politics of the moment and far more committed to longer-term capacity building. U.S. assistance also was more likely to involve civil society groups directly, while European assistance, particularly through the EU, focused more on aid to government organizations or, as in the case of aid to civil society, had to be channeled through the government. Part of the reason for this difference was the strong interest of the United States in elections – what Kenneth Wollack characterized as "the heart of the country's political process."[22] But part of it was also the decentralized

---

[20] As calculated from Finkel et al., "Effects of U.S. Foreign Assistance on Democracy Building," 28, 32. Also see Valerie Bunce and Sharon L. Wolchik, "Favorable Conditions and Electoral Revolutions," *Journal of Democracy* 17:4 (October 2006): 5–18.

[21] We especially thank Barbara Haig, Carl Gershman, and Kenneth Wollack for defining these activities.

[22] Interview with Kenneth Wollack, Washington, DC, May 12, 2010.

character of U.S. democracy assistance, and part too the differences in the professional backgrounds of individuals involved in democracy assistance. While the Europeans were largely bureaucrats by training and experience, the Americans had prior histories in U.S. politics – in Washington and in the states. Finally, the United States was important for the simple reason that it is the most powerful country in the international system. As a result, it mattered to the political calculations of local players when the United States signaled strong interest in the conduct of elections, when it withdrew support from authoritarian incumbents, and when it engaged in all the other activities highlighted earlier.

POSTELECTION TRAJECTORIES

This observation leads to our final set of conclusions: patterns of democratic progress after successful and failed attempts to defeat authoritarian rulers. While all of the successful breakthroughs produced a democratic opening, if only because they removed authoritarian leaders from office and led to a more competitive politics, they varied nonetheless in whether these opportunities translated into significant or limited democratic development after the opposition took power. Thus, while Croatia and Serbia made virtual leaps from dictatorship to democracy, democracy returned to Slovakia, and Ukraine made significant steps in becoming more democratic, the outcomes in Georgia and especially in Kyrgyzstan were far more mixed.

This contrast reflected three factors in particular: long-term trends in the development of civil society; variations in whether the elections had led to a constitutional transition in leadership or one that forced sitting presidents, even though they were not up for reelection, to vacate office; and electoral mandates. Thus, it is striking that, of the successful cases of electoral turnover, it is only in Georgia and Kyrgyzstan that we find extra-legal removals of authoritarians from office by the opposition and a draining of what had already been a small and fragile civil society as a result (especially in Georgia) of activists joining the new government. These two cases also stand out because of the one-sided electoral victories in the presidential elections that followed the parliamentary elections that had served as pretexts for leadership change. Landslide victories gave the new leaders of Georgia and Kyrgyzstan the luxury – unlike their counterparts of Serbia, Georgia, Ukraine, Croatia, Bulgaria, and Slovakia – of ruling without much opposition.

In this sense, the continuing political struggles between authoritarian and democratic forces in Serbia and Ukraine – which have led many analysts to question how much the pivotal elections contributed to democratic change – have been a blessing insofar as democratic change is concerned.[23] While both

[23] Theodor Tudoroiu, "Rose, Orange and Tulip: The Failed Post-Soviet Revolutions," *Communist and Postcommunist Studies* 40:3 (September 2007), 315–342; but see Lucia Kureková, "Electoral Revolutions and their Socio-Economic Impact: Bulgaria and Slovakia

Viktor Yushchenko, who lost the presidency in the 2010 election, and Boris Tadić, who was elected and then reelected president of Serbia in 2004 and 2008, respectively, were very constrained in their actions by oppositions on the left and on the right, they were at the same time blocked, unlike their counterparts in Georgia and Kyrgyzstan, from becoming increasingly autocratic over time or recycling the patronage networks left behind by their predecessors. Moreover, competitive politics in Ukraine and Serbia, as in Croatia and Slovakia after their electoral breakthroughs, is rooted in policy differences among relatively well-defined political parties. As a result, although they are still fluid in many respects, and although new parties enter and old parties exit the political scene between elections, the party systems in these countries are far more institutionalized and more supportive of democracy than the party systems – or, more accurately, the loose-knit patronage-based networks arrayed around specific leaders – that we find in Georgia and Kyrgyzstan.

While the political trajectories of the breakthrough cases varied, however, the postelection experiences of the failed attempts to remove authoritarians from office were remarkably similar. Fraudulent elections, followed by popular protests, led to growing authoritarianism in Armenia, Azerbaijan, and Belarus. What we have seen, therefore, is a deepening of earlier political trends favoring authoritarian politics – in sharp contrast, in most of our successful cases, to a sharp break with similar pre-election trends. Thus, regimes that were similar at the time of the pivotal elections – politics in Serbia, Georgia, Ukraine, and Kyrgyzstan was as repressive, we must remember, as politics in Armenia and Azerbaijan in particular – began to diverge from one another following the elections of concern in this book.

This contrast, especially when combined with similarities between regime trends in Armenia, Azerbaijan, and Belarus, on the one hand, and in Russia and Kazakhstan, on the other, which also began the transition as mixed systems but did not feature the syndrome of opposition cohesion and postelection protests after manipulated elections, led us to draw another conclusion. In the absence of electoral breakthroughs, there seems to be little to stop mixed regimes in this part of the world from tilting in an increasingly authoritarian direction over time. In fact, the growing pessimism among many analysts over the past few years about the future of democracy is based in large measure on one regional trend: growing authoritarianism in postcommunist Eurasia.[24]

Thus, electoral turnovers in mixed regimes matter for two reasons. More than any other factor, they are likely to improve democratic performance, and – again, more than any other factor – they play a key role in reversing an ongoing slide into increasingly repressive politics. However, there is

in Comparative Perspective" (master's thesis, Department of International Relations and European Studies, Central European University, Budapest, 2006), for a more nuanced assessment.

[24] See, especially, Thomas Carothers, *Stepping Back from Democratic Pessimism*, Carnegie Endowment for International Peace, Democracy and Rule of Law Program, Paper no. 99 (February 2009).

another implication that we can draw from our analysis of postelection political trends. There are extremely high stakes attached to launching popular protests in response to fraudulent elections. If the demonstrations succeed, democratic progress is likely to follow. However, if they fail, the regime invariably becomes more repressive.

In the remainder of this chapter, we return to the theoretical debates we outlined in Chapter 1 and draw some implications from our findings. We begin with the issue of mixed regimes and their potential for democratic change.

Mixed Regimes

Are authoritarian leaders in mixed regimes weak or strong? Our analysis supports both points of view. On the one hand, authoritarian leaders emerge in this study as relatively powerful. Even when they are vulnerable according to a variety of measures, they can withstand the challenge of even united oppositions and popular protests. Moreover, our finding about the electoral model suggests that unseating authoritarian leaders requires enormous effort.

On the other hand, while we discovered significant constraints on the ability of oppositions to win elections, we also found evidence suggesting that in some respects analysts have overestimated the freedom to maneuver of authoritarian leaders in regimes featuring competition for political power. Here, we would question the recent trend in the study of authoritarianism that emphasizes how powerful authoritarian leaders are as a result, for example, of political repression and the economic tools they have at their disposal and the role of even seemingly democratic institutions in enhancing their ability to monopolize politics.[25] In response, we would draw attention, on the basis of the behavior of authoritarian incumbents or their anointed successors in Serbia, Georgia, Kyrgyzstan, and Ukraine, to several important facts on the ground. One is the cost for their own political survival of resorting to more authoritarian practices over time, and the other is the cost of unchallenged rule. In the first instance, in the cases of Serbia, Ukraine, and Georgia in particular, despotism was widely interpreted by democratic activists and ordinary citizens as a sign of desperation. Thus, the leader was seen as more, not less, vulnerable.

We can also point to some of the costs attached to what appears to be political invincibility. These costs are particularly high when the duration of authoritarian rule has been built upon repeated successes by the leader in defeating challenges to his power – from oppositions and from actions

---

[25] Ellen Lust Okar, "Divided They Rule: The Management and Manipulation of Political Opposition," *Comparative Politics* 36:2 (January 2004), 159–179; Gandhi and Lust Okar, "Elections under Authoritarianism"; Lisa Blaydes, "Authoritarian Elections and Elite Management: Theory and Evidence from Egypt," unpublished manuscript, April 2008; Jennifer Gandhi and Adam Przeworski, "Cooperation, Cooptation, and Rebellion under Dictatorships," *Economics & Politics* 18:1 (March 2006), 1–26; Brownlee, *Authoritarianism in an Age of Democratization*.

taken by the international community. Thus, long-serving leaders, such as Milošević, Kuchma, Shevardnadze, and Akaev (at least before protesters appeared in Bishkek), assumed that the behavior of the opposition, civil society groups, ordinary citizens, Western governments, and the international democracy assistance community would not change. In this sense, leaders can be punished for relying too much on past precedents.

Thus, while we are sympathetic to the arguments that students of democratization have been biased as a result of their selective attention to indicators of democratic development and their pronounced tendency to ignore alternative interpretations, we think that the decision to counter these problems by focusing on the many ways authoritarian leaders are strong, creative, resilient, and the like suffers from serious biases as well.[26] If nothing else, these assumptions about the power of authoritarians are problematic in view of our limited knowledge about politics within the palace, the tendency to project onto the present and into the future the resilience of authoritarian rule in the past, and, finally, the puzzling belief, contrary to the way politics often works, that politicians can control what happens after they introduce changes, including seemingly democratic reforms, that they see as serving their interests. We argue this, not just because of the data presented in this book, but also because of our professional resumes. Before we analyzed transitions to democracy and mixed regimes in the postcommunist region, we were students of communism.

Moreover, if transitology suffered in its early development from a research design that often involved looking only at cases of successful transitions from authoritarian rule, then students of authoritarianism sometimes suffer from looking only at long-standing authoritarian polities, such as those in the Middle East or in China (a communist regime, we must note, that is still less long-lived than its Soviet counterpart). The tendency to predict durable authoritarianism is also a reaction to studies of the Middle East and China in the 1990s that wrestled repeatedly, because of the events of 1989 and the global wave of democratization, with the possibility of democratic change.

The role of different area studies in supporting very different expectations about the power of autocrats and the potential for democratic change leads to another insight about mixed regimes. Whether autocrats in mixed regimes are presumed by scholars to be vulnerable or powerful, careless or calculating, may depend on how the mixed regimes came into existence. While in the Middle East, for example, regimes that feature authoritarian leaders but competitive politics arose as part of a continuing state and

---

[26] Lisa Anderson, "Searching Where the Light Shines: Studying Democratization in the Middle East," *Annual Review of Political Science* 9 (June 2006), 189–214; Eva Bellin, "The Robustness of Authoritarianism in the Middle East," *Comparative Politics* 36:2 (January 2004), 139–157; Jason Brownlee, "Low Tide after the Third Wave: Exploring Politics under Authoritarianism," *Comparative Politics* 34:4 (July 2002), 477–498. Also see David Shambaugh, *China's Communist Party: Atrophy and Adaptation* (Berkeley: University of California Press, 2008).

authoritarian political project, the formation of mixed regimes in the post-communist region followed dramatic political and economic ruptures. As a consequence, while mixed regimes in many regions of the world grew out of decisions by autocrats to implement certain types of political reforms, mixed regimes in the postcommunist region in particular grew out of a rough balance of power between two sets of players. One was discredited authoritarian incumbents, who were intent on maintaining power in the new domestic and international circumstances they confronted, and the other was the opposition, which was often divided and inexperienced but empowered, at least potentially, by the same new circumstances. Balancing and bargaining between authoritarians and democrats in a time of regime and state transition, therefore, produced a very different type of mixed regime – and one where authoritarians were likely more constrained – than a dynamic involving a sprinkling of the polity by well-ensconced leaders with some carefully selected democratic decorations.

Whether such democratic decorations actually contribute to democratic development, however, may very well depend not so much on the institutional and structural vulnerability of the regime as on the willingness and capacity of oppositions and their allies to exploit openings provided by the combination of authoritarian rule and electoral competition for office. Thus, we would also question the tendency in more structural accounts of political change in mixed systems to argue that the key issue insofar as regime change is concerned is whether the regime is in decline as a result of structural considerations.[27] Weak regimes can survive for a very long time, especially if there are few alternatives on the horizon and if they are supported by outside actors. In addition, many of the structural weaknesses of the regimes analyzed in this book were evident in many of the elections that preceded those that led to opposition victories. Finally, it is telling that, despite all the hard work of oppositions and their allies in the successful cases, victories were usually razor-thin. If the regime was ready to fall and everyone knew it, why were the votes so close?

Finally, this study counsels us to rethink how we conceptualize regimes that combine authoritarian and democratic elements. In particular, we are skeptical about the value and validity of placing too much emphasis on the "regime-ness" of these political formations. This is a practice that is implied,

---

[27] See, for example, Lucan Way, "Authoritarian State-Building and the Sources of Regime Competitiveness in the Fourth Wave: The Cases of Belarus, Moldova, Russia and Ukraine," *World Politics* 57:2 (January 2005), 231–261; Way, "The Real Causes of the Color Revolutions"; Levitsky and Way, *Competitive Authoritarianism*; and Brownlee, *Authoritarianism in an Age of Democracy*. In some other work, however, both Brownlee and Way seemed to give more explanatory power to agency and processes, such as elections. See, for example, Lucan Way, "Deer in Headlights: Authoritarian Skill and Regime Trajectories after the Cold War," paper presented at the Conference on Central Asia and Sub-Saharan Africa, Cornell University, September 26–28, 2008; and Jason Brownlee, "Harbingers of Change: Competitive Elections before the End of Authoritarianism," in *Democratization by Elections: A New Mode of Transition?*, ed. Staffan Lindberg (Baltimore: Johns Hopkins University Press, 2009), 128–147.

for example, in the preoccupation with giving various names to these regimes, drawing increasingly fine-grained distinctions among them, and treating them as political outcomes equal to those polities that are fully democratic or authoritarian and therefore amenable to comparison to them in the quest to identify the causes behind divergent regime pathways.[28] The very act of calling them "regimes" and freezing them in time suggests a certain jelling of their characteristics and the parameters on how they will evolve in the future. However, both implications are countered not just by the trends toward and away from democracy and authoritarianism that we have analyzed in this book, but also by the finding in the literature that such regimes are, quite simply, unusually resistant to "staying put."

Elections and Democratization

As we noted in the introductory chapters of this book, while some scholars see elections as sites that merely register long-term political and economic developments, other scholars give elections causal import in their own right and argue, as a result, that elections can be considered a mode of regime transition.[29] This study provides strong support for the second characterization, while recognizing, like Andreas Schedler, that elections have contingent effects.[30] For example, it is striking that the elections of interest in this book had very different outcomes, despite similarities in regime points of departure. Also notable are the facts that the contrast in these electoral outcomes reflected differences in electoral efforts on the part of the opposition and their allies, and that political developments after the pivotal elections widened the regime gap between the countries where oppositions won power and those where they did not.

[28] Valerie Bunce, *Subversive Institutions: The Design and the Destruction of Socialism and the State* (Cambridge: Cambridge University Press, 1999); Michael McFaul, "The Fourth Wave of Democracy and Dictatorship: Noncooperative Transitions in the Postcommunist World," *World Politics* 54:2 (January 2002), 212–244; Marina Ottaway, *Democracy Challenged: The Rise of Semi-Authoritarianism* (Washington, DC: Carnegie Endowment for International Peace, 2003); Diamond, "Thinking about Hybrid Regimes"; Levitsky and Way, *Competitive Authoritarianism*.

[29] Compare, for example, Brownlee, *Authoritarianism in an Age of Democratization*, to Staffan I. Lindberg, "The Surprising Significance of African Elections," *Journal of Democracy*, 17:1 (January 2006), 139–151; Staffan Lindberg, ed., *Democratization by Elections: A New Mode of Transition?* (Baltimore: Johns Hopkins University Press, 2009); Teorell and Hadenius, "Elections as Levers"; Tucker, "Enough!"; and Valerie Bunce, "Reflections on Elections," *Newsletter of the Comparative Politics Section of the American Political Science Association* 19 (Fall 2008), 1–5. For a distinction between electoral processes and leadership turnover as influences on policy innovation, see Valerie Bunce, *Do New Leaders Make a Difference? Executive Succession and Public Policy under Capitalism and Socialism* (Princeton, NJ: Princeton University Press, 1981).

[30] Andreas Schedler, "The Contingent Power of Authoritarian Elections," in Staffan Lindberg, ed., *Democratization by Elections: A New Mode of Transition?* (Baltimore: Johns Hopkins University Press, 2009), 291–313.

As with other, more commonly discussed modes of transition from authoritarianism to democracy, such as mass protests unrelated to elections and elite pacting, then, democratizing elections do not necessarily lead to the consolidation of democracy. Like protests and pacting, electoral breakthroughs can be followed not just by democratic progress, but also by democratic backsliding or even breakdowns. But these possibilities do not negate the importance of the fact that elections in semi-authoritarian regimes often play the role of creating an opening for a transition to democracy. It is precisely for these reasons that we have used the term "democratizing elections" throughout this book.

But these conclusions lead to an obvious question: what is it about elections that expands the potential for democratic change? Most obviously, elections can remove key obstacles to democratic progress in mixed regimes by removing authoritarian leaders from office and thereby, albeit to varying degrees, disassembling patronage networks and the security forces that backed them, redefining international alliances, and bringing new voters and groups into politics and bringing their interests into the policy calculus of governments.[31] However, whether they set in motion this train of important developments depends, as we have seen, on how oppositions and their allies campaign for power and the impact of their efforts on electoral outcomes.

It is here that we need to recognize the contributions of the electoral model to democratic development. At the most general level, the electoral model exploits the fact that elections are regular and well-defined events in terms of their beginnings and endings, and that they combine high stakes, expectations of popular participation, and widely visible political outcomes. Elections, therefore, are uniquely energizing events.[32] More specifically, the electoral model creates a new type of election by helping solve the collective action and coordination problems that not only prevent ordinary citizens, opposition parties, and civil society groups from embracing the same cause and taking concerted action to further their common agenda, but also inhibit international democracy promoters, who suffer as well from difficulties in defining a common mission and working together to achieve shared goals. The deployment of the electoral model can surmount these problems because elections can serve as focal points for action. The model, moreover, specifies what needs to be done while communicating a distinctive message – that change is possible, especially when everyone works together to make it happen.

---

[31] Interview with Larry Garber, Washington, DC, April 9, 2010.

[32] Doug McAdam and Sidney Tarrow, "Ballots and Barricades: On the Reciprocal Relationship between Elections and Social Movements," paper presented at the conference Hot Models and Hard Conflicts: The Agenda of Comparative Political Science in the 21st Century, a symposium in honor of Hanspeter Kriesi, Center for Comparative and International Studies (CIS), Zurich, Switzerland, June 26, 2009; Guillermo Trejo, "The Political Foundations of Ethnic Mobilization and Territorial Conflict in Mexico, 1975–2000," in *Federalism and Territorial Cleavages*, ed. Ugo Amoretti and Nancy Bermeo (Baltimore: Johns Hopkins University Press, 2004), 355–386.

But do these arguments about electoral efforts, in conjunction with the limited impact of structural and institutional factors, mean that our explanation of variations in electoral outcomes can be reduced to the powerful effects of agency? On the one hand, this is precisely what we are arguing in the sense that the election-related activities of individuals made all the difference in who won and who lost. However, we would nonetheless caution strongly against reducing agency in this case – as the term has been used in so many other studies – to the ad hoc and last-minute actions of a handful of individuals. What is striking about these electoral efforts is that they were planned, widely and deeply collaborative, and quite task-oriented. They were also based upon a sophisticated and tested model that was invented outside the postcommunist region and then transferred, applied, and adapted to local conditions within that region by a large cast of players. While one could argue that the key in these elections was a short-term dynamic involving the actions of individuals, therefore, this did not mean that there was anything idiosyncratic, accidental, or individualistic about why, how, or where authoritarian rulers were defeated.

INTERNATIONAL DIFFUSION OF DEMOCRACY

This study also contributes to an area of growing interest in the study of democratization, that is, the impact of international influences on democratic change in general and, more specifically, the role of cross-national diffusion in the spread of democracy.[33] It is obvious from what we have argued in this book that we agree with the more recent position that the introduction and development of democracy, especially during the Third Wave, cannot be understood without reference to the influence of international actors, institutions, and norms. That recognized, however, it is also important to note that, while international actors were important in the electoral breakthroughs that took place in the postcommunist region from 1998 to 2005, they worked in conjunction with local actors who, in the final analysis, were the ones who carried out the tasks that led to the defeat of authoritarian rulers and the empowerment of the democratic opposition. In this sense, while international influences figured prominently in our study, so did domestic politics. Indeed, it was the electoral model that joined these two key arenas of democratic struggle.

[33] Barbara Wejnert, "Diffusion, Development, and Democracy, 1800–1999," *American Sociological Review* 70:1 (February 2005), 53–81; Mainwaring and Pérez-Liñán, "Why Regions of the World Are Important"; Brinks and Coppedge, "Diffusion Is No Illusion"; Gleditsch and Ward, "Diffusion and the International Context of Democratization"; Harvey Starr and Christina Lindborg, "Democratic Dominoes Revisited: The Hazards of Governmental Transitions, 1974–1996," *Journal of Conflict Resolution* 47:4 (August 2003), 490–519; John Markoff, *Waves of Democracy: Social Movements and Political Change* (Thousand Oaks, CA: Pine Forge Press, 1996); Pevehouse, *Democracy from Above*; Youngs, *International Democracy and the West*; Finkel et al., "Effects of U.S. Foreign Assistance on Democracy Building."

What also emerged in this study is the value of looking at democratization through the lens of international diffusion. Here, we would offer some suggestions. First, analysts of diffusion processes need to assume more of a burden of proof than they have in the past when claiming that similar developments in a group of cases in a relatively short span of time testify necessarily to the impact of international diffusion. As we argued in Chapters 9 and 10, what is often missing from studies of the diffusion of democracy in particular is clear specification of the innovation (and one not to be confused with similar outcomes) and mechanisms of cross-national transfer. For example, it is unhelpful to argue on behalf of the spread of democracy without specifying what exactly is being diffused – for example, democratic institutions, the idea of democracy, or specific modes of transition that can counter effectively the power of authoritarians and/or empower democrats. At the same time, without the specification of the mechanisms involved in the transfer of innovation among sites, the case for diffusion is necessarily weak.

This discussion of mechanisms leads in turn to another requirement in making a compelling case for diffusion: assessing alternative hypotheses to explain the clustered pattern of similar changes across time and space. For example, such patterns could reflect similar local conditions prompting similar responses or the role of powerful outside actors dictating similar changes in a group of weak countries. In either case, the cross-national similarities of interest would not reflect the work of diffusion dynamics.

Gaps in diffusion must be explained as well. It is striking how often analysts overlook the obvious fact that innovative precedents in the neighborhood do not just resonate with supporters of such changes in other sites, but also elicit fears on the part of actors in those other sites who find such changes threatening to their values and interests. Rather than being a nearly automatic and indeed bloodless process, which is the way it is often depicted, the cross-national spread of innovation usually involves fierce local struggles. This is particularly the case when a wave of adoptions has already taken place, and opponents of the innovation in neighboring sites have been amply forewarned and therefore forearmed. As a result, it is a mistake to restrict one's analytical focus to cases in which innovations have been adopted. Such an approach is particularly suspect on methodological grounds. As in comparative politics we cannot be secure in identifying causes in the absence of examining cases that vary in their outcomes, so we cannot nail down the drivers of diffusion, and thus the very fact that it has taken place, without confronting the issue of uneven adoption rates.

In this sense, there are in fact clear similarities between the more familiar methods used in comparative politics – that is, examining variable outcomes by selecting cases that are otherwise similar – and methods that should be used to analyze international diffusion. In fact, as we have argued in this book, the two approaches to political change can be seen as complimentary rather than conflicting. They feature a similar logic with respect to the optimal approach to identifying causality, and they can be partnered with one another to specify how, why, and where similar political changes take place. Just as our comparison of similarities and differences among our countries and elections helped us understand the importance of the electoral model, so the analysis of diffusion helped us explain the origins, modifications, and uneven spread of that model.

While the analysis we have presented in this book meets these standards for establishing the role of cross-national diffusion of innovation, it also reminds us of how rare diffusion must be in view of its formidable requirements. This insight, in turn, carries one final lesson for students of diffusion. It is very important to draw a distinction between innovations that amend the status quo and those that have the explicit purpose of subverting it. For the latter type of innovation, it is fair to argue that purposive and planned transmission plays an unusually important role, that the mechanisms driving diffusion are usually multiple in nature, and that the establishment of diffusion rests, even more than usual, on analyzing the process as it played out on the ground.[34]

TWO CHEERS FOR DEMOCRACY ASSISTANCE?

We can now conclude this book by addressing a final issue: the implications of this study for our understanding of the role of U.S. democracy assistance and for those involved in a practical way in that effort. We can begin by observing that U.S. democracy promotion is a very controversial enterprise. For example, in a recent survey carried out by the German Marshall Fund of the United States, less than half of all Americans said that they supported international democracy assistance programs. Sixty-four percent of Americans who identified with the Republican Party did so, but only thirty-five percent of Democratic Party identifiers took a similar position.[35] It is not surprising that people disagree about the value of U.S. support for democratic development abroad. Most obviously, the controversial wars in Iraq and Afghanistan have linked U.S. democracy assistance to military interventions and the escalation of violence in the countries where the U.S. has intervened. Second, even for the cases of interest in this book, the struggle for democratic change remains a largely domestic political project. Thus, international democracy assistance necessarily takes place at the margins, and it can only build upon, rather than substitute for, a domestic arena ripe for democratic development.[36]

Finally, the United States has no special claim to knowing how to promote democracy in other countries, as members of the U.S. democracy assistance community readily admitted in the interviews we conducted with them. While there is strong evidence that democracy is good in itself and has the additional

[34] Jacoby, "Inspiration, Coalition and Substitution."

[35] "German Marshall Fund Survey: Transatlantic Trends," German Marshall Fund of the United States, 2006, www.transatlantictrends.org.

[36] Carothers, "The End of the Transition Paradigm"; Carothers, *Critical Missions*; Carothers, *Aiding Democracy Abroad*; Carothers, "Misunderstanding Gradualism"; Carothers, "The 'Sequencing' Fallacy"; Mitchell, *Uncertain Democracy*.

advantages of promoting peaceful relations among states and enhancing the quality of human life, there is mixed evidence in support of the corollary argument that the United States, as a result, can and should promote democracy abroad. The problem with drawing such a conclusion is that U.S. commitment to democratic change has been inconsistent, even since the end of the Cold War. Equally telling is the fact that the evidence demonstrating the positive effects of U.S. democracy and governance assistance is uneven, as is the quality of such assessments.[37]

All of these concerns about the value and validity of U.S. democracy promotion have merit. However, many critiques of U.S. democracy assistance are very removed from what actually happens on the ground, and they rely

[37] The National Councils of the National Academies, Committee on Evaluation of USAID Democracy Assistance Programs, *Improving Democracy Assistance*; Finkel et al., "Effects of U.S. Foreign Assistance on Democracy Building"; Martha Finnemore, *The Purpose of Intervention: Changing Beliefs about the Use of Force* (Ithaca, NY: Cornell University Press, 2003); Devdariani, *The Impact of International Assistance on Georgia*; Paul Drake, "From Good Men to Good Neighbors, 1912–1932," in *Exporting Democracy: The U.S. and Latin America*, ed. Abraham Lowenthal (Baltimore: Johns Hopkins University Press, 1991), 3–40; Lise Rakner and Lars Svåsand, "The Politics of the Elections (or How Incumbents Remain in Office): The Cases of Malawi and Uganda," paper presented at the workshop Democratization by Elections?, University of Florida, Gainesville, November 30–December 2, 2007; Alexander Cooley, "Base Politics," *Foreign Affairs* 84:6 (November–December 2005), 79–92; Alexander Cooley, "U.S. Bases and Democratization in Central Asia," *Orbis* 52:1 (January 2008), 65–90; Alexander Cooley and James Ron, "The NGO Scramble: Organizational Insecurity and the Political Economy of Transnational Action," *International Security* 27:1 (Summer 2002), 5–39; Jeff Erlich, "Uzbekistan after the Backlash: How Can the U.S. Promote Democracy Where It Is Not Welcome?" (MA thesis, Global Master of Arts Program, Tufts University, Fletcher School, March 12, 2006); Sarah Elizabeth Mendelson and John K. Glenn, *The Power and Limits of NGOs: A Critical Look at Building Democracy in Eastern Europe and Eurasia* (New York: Columbia University Press, 2002); Lisa McIntosh Sundstrom, "Foreign Assistance, International Norms, and NGO Development: Lessons from the Russian Campaign," *International Organization* 59:2 (Spring 2005), 419–449; Sarah Mendelson and Theodore P. Gerber, "Local Activist Culture and Transnational Diffusion: An Experiment in Social Marketing among Human Rights Groups in Russia," unpublished manuscript, April 2005; Laurence Jarvik, "NGOs: A New Class in International Relations," *Orbis* 51:2 (Spring 2007), 217–238; Frederic Charles Schaffer, *The Hidden Costs of Clean Election Reforms* (Ithaca, NY: Cornell University Press, 2008); Frederick Charles Schaffer, *Democracy in Translation: Understanding Politics in an Unfamiliar Culture* (Ithaca, NY: Cornell University Press, 1998); Carothers, "Misunderstanding Gradualism"; Carothers, "The 'Sequencing' Fallacy"; Crawford, *Foreign Aid and Political Reform*; Kristina Kaush and Richard Youngs, *Algeria: Democratic Transition Case Study*, CDDRL Working Paper No. 84, Center for Democracy, Development and the Rule of Law, Freeman Spogli Institute for International Studies, Stanford University (August 2008); Bogdanich and Norberg, "Democracy Undone"; Sarah L. Henderson, "Selling Civil Society: Western Aid and the Nongovernmental Organization Sector in Russia," *Comparative Political Studies* 35:2 (March 2002), 139–167; Sarah L. Henderson, *Building Democracy in Contemporary Russia: Western Support for Grassroots Organizations* (Ithaca, NY: Cornell University Press, 2006); Janine R. Wedel, *Collision and Collusion: The Strange Case of Western Aid to Eastern Europe, 1989–1998* (New York: St. Martin's Press, 1998).

in many instances on only a few cases or on only one (often rare and far from representative) form of assistance, such as military intervention in Iraq.[38] At the same time, many critics wrongly assume that U.S. democracy assistance is engineered by Washington, and that it is an enterprise that involves clearly specified goals, a list of fixed activities, and considerable coordination among the actors involved. As Richard Miles, a former U.S. ambassador to Azerbaijan and Georgia and chief of mission in Yugoslavia, argued in the interview we conducted with him: "It is very unusual for the State Department to dictate specific development or democracy assistance programs to U.S. embassies. Instead, most decisions are made on the ground. Moreover, the flow of information between Washington and the field is primarily from the field to Washington rather than vice-versa."[39]

Many analysts also seem to assume that international democracy promoters work in isolation from local actors, are ignorant of local circumstances, and are in a position to dictate what happens. However, if, as in this study, we look at democracy assistance from the ground up (in the postcommunist region and in Washington), take into account the perspectives and actions of both donors and recipients, look at a variety of programs and players, and examine a range of cases where democracy assistance has been in play, we necessarily operate from a broader and deeper data base and on the basis of some very different assumptions.

All of these considerations lead us to draw more nuanced conclusions regarding such questions as the costs and benefits of, along with the limits on and possibilities for, U.S. support of democratic change abroad. Based on the electoral breakthroughs analyzed in this book, we would conclude that the United States can be, and in most of our successful cases was, an important and effective contributor to democratic change.

However, having made this broad claim, we must quickly amend it by recognizing that, as in the case of international diffusion, the devil is very much in the details. First, and most obviously, democracy assistance is only one, and often not the most important, aspect of U.S. foreign policy and actions in particular countries. As the lack of U.S. interest in assisting actors seeking to oust autocrats in Azerbaijan and Armenia illustrates, security and energy concerns (as in the first case) and U.S. domestic political considerations (as in the second) frequently trump the U.S. commitment to supporting movement

[38] Steve Watts, "Military Interventions and the Construction of Political Order," paper presented at the annual meeting of the American Political Science Association, Washington, DC, September 1–4, 2005; Mark Peceny, "Democracy Promotion and American Foreign Policy: Afghanistan, Iraq, and the Future," in *American Foreign Policy in a Globalized World*, ed. David Forsythe, Patrice McMahon, and Andrew Wedeman (New York: Routledge, 2006), 324–360; Mark Peceny, *Democracy at the Point of Bayonets* (University Park: Pennsylvania State University Press, 1999); Margaret G. Hermann and Charles Kegley, "The U.S. Use of Military Intervention to Promote Democracy: Evaluating the Record," *International Interactions* 24:2 (June 1998), 91–114.

[39] Interview with Richard Miles, Washington, DC, September 25, 2009.

toward democracy abroad. While the United States did not "engineer" any of the successful breakthroughs we analyzed, and U.S. commitment to regime change was not the determining factor, U.S. interest in an opposition victory clearly varied in the elections we examined.

Second, the standard used to assess U.S. influence on democratic development matters a great deal. If we argue that the United States can contribute to democratic change, we are not by any means asserting that the United States can, let alone should, "export" democracy, "create" a democracy, "guarantee" democratic progress in the future, or "construct" a full-scale democratic polity overnight. Instead, we are suggesting that the United States can take actions that expand *opportunities* for democratic development in other countries.[40] Whether these opportunities are seized, however, seems to depend largely on local political dynamics. U.S. democracy assistance, in short, contributes at the margins, and it is within these parameters that one should judge the impact of U.S. democracy assistance on democratic change and whether its effects are positive or negative.

In addition, as we have repeatedly emphasized throughout this book, the United States hardly acted alone in our electoral breakthroughs. Other international actors, including the EU, European governments, European and U.S. foundations, the Organization for Security and Cooperation in Europe, and regional graduates of these electoral breakthroughs, along with domestic actors – including opposition parties, civil society organizations, youth movements, and ordinary citizens – played a critical and, just as importantly, a deeply collaborative role in the defeat of authoritarian leaders. The effort, in short, was both cross-national and transnational – as we saw in Part II, where we provided a series of case studies, and in Part III, where we analyzed the impact of external democracy assistance on electoral stability and change and the role of international diffusion in these electoral face-offs between regimes and oppositions. The implication here is that if the United States acts alone, it will certainly fail, if not make matters worse.

We also need to unpack the United States as an international actor involved in these elections. Here, we refer, for example, to the role not just of specific U.S. administrations and the State Department, along with USAID and the groups it has funded – such as Freedom House, the United States Institute of Peace, the National Endowment for Democracy and its International Republican Institute and National Democratic Institute for Foreign Affairs, and the Free Trade Union Institute – but also of private foundations based in the United States, such as the Open Society Institute, Rockefeller Brothers, the Mott Foundation, and the German Marshall Fund of the United States. While often engaging in parallel play, these varied organizations and players nonetheless were able to come together in order to provide important assistance to local oppositions and their allies. But such assistance, as James O'Brien,

---

[40] Interviews with Barbara Haig, Washington, DC, May 14, 2010; Carl Gershman, Washington, DC, May 14, 2010; and Kenneth Wollack, Washington, DC, May 12, 2010.

the special envoy to the Balkans during the Clinton administration and the Washington-based director of the campaign to defeat Milošević, noted, merely "built on the plumbing of the past."[41] While elections provided an opportunity for creative and collaborative work among international democracy promoters in general and those in the United States in particular, therefore, local struggle and a ripening of local capacities for change were essential.

Finally, U.S. "success" in the specific way we have understood it was also based upon several other considerations that are often overlooked in debates about the value of international democracy assistance. One is that the focus of assistance in our cases was on countries that were situated between democracy and dictatorship. While not always halfway houses on the road to democracy, mixed regimes provide the raw material in general – and regular political and especially electoral opportunities in particular – for improved democratic performance. At the same time, the very nature of elections can enhance the prospects for oppositions, civil society groups, ordinary citizens, and international democracy promoters to work in concert, rather than separately, and to mobilize in support of democratic change, rather than remain in their usual roles as atomized political bystanders or political actors at war with one another. While many aspects of the U.S. experience may be of little help or relevance to other countries – for instance, the unusual character of the U.S. party system, federalism, and a presidential form of government that, for some reason, has not encouraged democratic breakdown in the United States as it has in other parts of the world – the U.S. experience with how elections can be won is very different. It is a model that travels relatively well, and it is a form of assistance that U.S. democracy promoters know well. The politics of getting out the vote, therefore, is less specific to individual countries than questions involving, say, the optimal design of political institutions and public policy.

The results of our research also have a great deal to say regarding the debate, which took place a few years ago and which is being repeated, although in somewhat different terms, today, concerning which strategy is likely to have the bigger payoff: long-term efforts to assist the development of civil society and the rule of law in semi-authoritarian regimes or an infusion of funding and training for the opposition and NGO communities "just in time," as it were – that is, in the context of an upcoming election. Clearly, as we have argued, the latter has had important payoffs in the short term. Thus, the electoral model can be very effective in getting citizens to vote and support the opposition and in creating, as a result, a democratic opening. And, as we have emphasized, such an opening is a necessary, though not sufficient, condition for further democratic progress. However, as the differing results after our breakthrough elections illustrate, long-term support for the development of civil society and the rule of law is also important, if success in removing authoritarian leaders is to translate into longer-term progress toward creating consolidated democratic systems. Thus, there is little to be gained from

[41] Interview with James C. O'Brien, Washington, DC, November 16, 2006.

forcing a choice between short-term and longer-term approaches to democracy assistance. The two approaches play critical and complementary roles.

What we are arguing, therefore, is that the United States has contributed in important ways to democratic development abroad. However, this has been the case only under the very special – indeed, stringent – conditions discussed here. Thus, we can conclude this study of democratizing elections, borrowing from Irving Kristol's characterization of capitalism and E. M. Forester's earlier characterization of democracy, by offering "two cheers" in support of U.S. democracy assistance.[42]

---

[42] Irving Kristol, *Two Cheers for Capitalism* (New York: New American Library, 1979). Kristol, in turn, borrowed his title from E. M. Forster, *Two Cheers for Democracy* (New York: Harcourt Brace Jovanovich, 1966). Our thanks to Marc Plattner for pointing this out.

Appendix

List of Interviews

ARMENIA

Armineh Arakelian, head of programme for Europe and the CIS for International IDEA (International Institute for Democracy and Electoral Assistance), Yerevan, March 13, 2007.

Andrew Bennett, country director, National Democratic Institute (NDI), Yerevan, March 12, 2007.

Tressa Rae Finnerty, cultural affairs officer, Embassy of the United States, Yerevan, March 9, 2007.

Chedomir Flego, chief of party, International Foundation for Electoral Assistance (IFES), Yerevan, March 14, 2007.

Gevorg Hakobyan, National Academy of Sciences, Armenia; youth NGO. Yerevan, March 14, 2007.

Aghasi Harutyunyan, student, Yerevan State University, Yerevan, March 10, 2007.

Gavin Helf, civil society advisor, United States Agency for International Development (USAID), Yerevan, March 9 and 10, 2007.

Aleksandr Iskandaryan, director, Caucasus Media Institute, Yerevan, March 13, 2007.

Gregory Koldys, senior democracy advisor, anti-corruption team leader, United States Agency for International Development (USAID), Yerevan, March 9, 2007.

Heghine Manasyan, director, Caucasus Research Resource Center–Armenia, Eurasia Foundation, Yerevan, March 12, 2007.

Hasmik Mikayelyan, cultural affairs assistant, embassy of the United States, Yerevan, March 10, 12, and 13, 2007.

Arsen Mkrtchyan, program officer, United Nations and European Union, Yerevan, March 11, 2007.

Valeri V. Poghossyan, member of the Constitutional Court and professor at Yerevan State Linguistic University, Yerevan, March 14, 2007.

Daniel Renna, political officer, embassy of the United States, Yerevan, March 9, 2007.

Alex Sadar, chief of party, United States Agency for International Development (USAID), implementing partner, Civic Advocacy Support Program, Yerevan, March 14, 2007.

Keneshbek Sainazarov, International Foundation for Electoral Assistance (IFES), Yerevan, March 14, 2007.

Taline Sanassarian, country director, National Democratic Institute (NDI), Yerevan, March 13, 2007.

Nver Sargsyan, programme associate, United Nations Development Programme (UNDP), Gender and Politics Program in Southern Caucasus, Yerevan, March 13, 2007.

George Zaricky, program officer, democratic governance, United States Agency for International Development (USAID), Yerevan, March 9, 2007.

AZERBAIJAN

Leila Alieva, president, Center for National and International Studies, Baku, March 5, 2007; Washington, DC, March 2008.

Ali Aliyev, chairman of the National Independence Party and a member of YeS's (New Policy) coordination council, interviewed in Baku by Sara Rzayeva, January 11, 2006.

Aida Badalova, president, Youth without Frontiers, Baku, March 6, 2007.

Daniel Blessington, country director, International Foundation for Electoral Assistance (IFES), Baku, March 5, 2007.

Mequam and Yeni Fekir, youth activists, Baku, March 7, 2007.

Dallas Frohrib, country director, International Republican Institute (IRI), Baku, March 6, 2007.

Isa Gambar, chairman, Musavat Party, Baku, March 7, 2007.

Peter Hauslohner, former United States Agency for International Development (USAID) contractor, Baku, March 5, 2007.

Baheddin Heziyev, one of the chief contributors to *Azadliq*, the newspaper of the Popular Front Party, and an active party member, interviewed in Baku by Sara Rzayeva, January 8, 2006.

Khaleddin Ibrahimli, director, Caucasian Research Center, professor of history at Azerbaijan University, and candidate for prime minister of the "Azadliq" bloc in the 2005 parliamentary elections, interviewed in Baku by Sara Rzayeva, January 10, 2006.

Ali Karimli, chairman, Popular Front Party of Azerbaijan (PFPA), interviewed in Baku by Sara Rzayeva, January 13, 2006.

Fuad Mustafayev, deputy chairman, Azerbaijan Popular Front Party, Baku, March 5, 2007.

Rebecca Naslund, political officer, embassy of the United States, Baku, March 7, 2007.

Marianna Nosa, contractor, United States Agency for International Development (USAID), Baku, March 5, 2007.

Joan Polaschik, first secretary, political and economic affairs, embassy of the United States, Baku, March 7, 2007.

Amy Schultz, country director, National Democratic Institute, Baku, March 6, 2007.

Lala Shovket, professor and chairperson of the National Unity Movement and the Liberal Party, March 5, 2007.

Fuad Suyleymanov, director of civil society programs, Open Society, Baku, March 5, 2007.

Samir Taghiyev, program manager, Eurasia Foundation, Baku, March 6, 2007.

BELARUS

Balázs Jarábik, senior program officer, Institute for Civic Diplomacy, Pontis Foundation, Kyiv, June 12, 2007.

Vladzimir Kobets, leader, Zubr, Kyiv, June 16, 2007.

Joanna Rohozinska, program officer, National Endowment for Democracy (NED), Washington, DC, February 18, 2009.

Milan Šagát, project manager, Pontis Foundation, Bratislava, June 5, 2007.

Vitali Silitski, Palo Alto, CA, and Washington, DC, numerous interviews, 2005–08.

Lenka Surotchak, director, Pontis Foundation, Bratislava, June 2005 and June 2007.

Larissa Titarenko, professor of sociology, Belarus State University, Ithaca, NY, April 2008.

BULGARIA

Avis Bohlen, U.S. ambassador to Bulgaria (1996–99), Washington, DC, November 15, 2006.

Scott Carpenter, co-director, Regional Office for Central and East European Affairs, (Bratislava), International Republican Institute (IRI), Washington, DC, April 9, 2009.

Ivan Krastev, director, Center for Liberal Strategies, Berlin, July 27, 2005.

Patrick Merloe, senior associate and director of electoral programs, National Democratic Institute (NDI), Washington, DC, April 30, 2009.

CROATIA

Jill Benderly, director, STAR Network of World Learning, Zagreb, May 15, 2005.

Ivan Grdešić, Croatian ambassador to the United States (2000–04), interviewed by Michael Varnum, Zagreb, May 21, 2005.

Marek Kapusta, campaign manager, Foundation for a Civil Society, Bratislava, May 2002.

Danielle Katunar, Ph.D. student, University of Zagreb, Zagreb, May 2005.

Vesna Pusić, member of parliament, Zagreb, May 15, 2005.

Alan Vojvodić, GONG activist, Zagreb, May 16, 2005.

GEORGIA

Armineh Arakelian, head of programme for Europe and the CIS, International IDEA (International Institute for Democracy and Electoral Assistance), Tbilisi, October 21, 2005.

Tsotni Bakaria, former colleague of Aslan Abashidze, the president of Adjaria, Washington, DC, September 2006.

Keti Bakradze, Office of Democracy and Governance, United States Agency for International Development (USAID), Tbilisi, March 8, 2007.

Guram Chikovani, rector, Tbilisi Institute of Asia and Africa, Tbilisi, October 17, 2005.

David Darchiashvili, executive director, Open Society Georgia Foundation (2004–08), Tbilisi, October 15, 2005.

Anna Dolidze, president, Georgian Young Lawyers' Association (2004–06), Ithaca, NY, June 9, 2009.

Archil Gegeshidze, senior fellow, Georgia Foundation for Strategic and International Studies, Tbilisi, October 17, 2005.

Andro Gigauri, project specialist, Office of Democracy and Governance, United States Agency for International Development (USAID), Tbilisi, March 8, 2007.

Mike Kelleher, country director, National Democratic Institute (NDI), Tbilisi, October 19, 2005.

Tinatin Khidasheli, president of the Georgian Young Lawyers' Association (1999–2001, 2003–04), Tbilisi, October 17, 2005.

Nino Kobakhidze, director's assistant, National Democratic Institute (NDI), Tbilisi, October 19, 2005.

Alexandre (Sasha) Kukhianidze, director, Georgian Office of the Transnational Crime and Corruption Center (based at American University), Tbilisi, October 14, 2007.

Gvantsa Liparteliani, Liberty Institute, Tbilisi, October 13, 2005.

Giorgi Meladze, Liberty Institute, Tbilisi, October 13, 2005.

Valeri Melikadze, economist, Tbilisi, October 18, 2005.

Richard Miles, U.S. ambassador to Georgia (2002–05), Silver Spring, MD, September 25, 2009.

Mark Mullen, director, National Democratic Institute (NDI) (1997–2003), Tbilisi, October 14, 2005.

Marina Muskhelishvili, analyst, Center for Social Studies, Tbilisi, October 15, 2005.

Giorgi Nizharadze, social research director, International Center on Conflict and Negotiation, Tbilisi, October 16, 2005.

Ghia Nodia, founder and chair, Caucasian Institute for Peace, Democracy and Development, political analyst and political scientist, Tbilisi, October 18, 2005.

Keti Nozadze, student and former member of Kmara, Tbilisi, October 14–18, 2005.

Vladimer Papava, economist, Philadelphia, February 24, 2007.

Levan Ramishvili, director, Liberty Institute, Tbilisi, October 13, 2005.

Alex Rondeli, president, Georgian Foundation for Strategic and International Studies. Tbilisi, October 14, 2005.

Tea Tutberidze, Liberty Institute, Tbilisi, October 13, 2005.

David Usupashvili, chairman, Republican Party, Tbilisi, October 19, 2005.

John Wright, European Center for Minority Issues, Tbilisi, October 18, 2005.

Tamara Zhvania, director, International Society for Fair Elections and Democracy, Tbilisi, October 18, 2005.

KYRGYZSTAN

Kumar Bekbolotov, Central Asia program director for the Institute for Women's Political Research (IWPR), interviewed in Bishkek by Igor Logvinenko, January 2008.

Noor Borbieva, anthopologist, Notre Dame, IN, April 23, 2008.

Judy Helme, medical attache, United States embassy (Bishkek, Kyrgystan), Washington, DC, February 2006.

Shairbek Juraev, assistant professor, American University–Central Asia, interviewed by Igor Logvinenko in Bishkek, January 2008.

Joldon Kutmanaliev, assistant professor, Bishkek Humanities University, interviewed by Igor Logvinenko in Bishkek, January 2008.

Li Lifan, associate professor and deputy secretary-general of the Center for Shanghai Cooperation Organization Studies, Shanghai Academy of Social Sciences, council member of Shanghai Society for Russia and Central Asia, China. Ithaca, NY, April 28, 2009.

Joanna Rohozinska, program officer, National Endowment for Democracy (NED), Washington, DC, February 18, 2009.

Keneshbek Sainazarov, country director, United States Agency for International Development (USAID) Quality Learning Project; former director of civic education and consultant in training for International

Foundation for Electoral Assistance (IFES), Armenia. Yerevan, March 13, 2007. Also interviewed by Igor Logvinenko on January 2008 in Bishkek.

Amy Schultz, former country director, National Democratic Institute (NDI), Baku, March 6, 2007.

Azamat Temirkulov, assistant professor, American University–Central Asia, interviewed by Igor Logvinenko, Bishkek, January 2008.

Bermet Tursunkulova, chair, International and Comparative Politics Department, American University–Central Asia, interviewed by Igor Logvinenko, January 2008.

SERBIA

Svetlana Adamović, associate professor, Faculty of Political Sciences, University of Belgrade, Belgrade, April 14, 2005.

Boris Begović, professor of economics at the School of Law at the University of Belgrade and vice president, Center for Liberal-Democratic Studies, Belgrade, April 15, 2005.

Florian Bieber, lecturer, Department of Politics and International Relations, University of Kent, Belgrade, April 10, 2005.

Marko Blagojević, director, Center for Elections and Democracy (CeSid), Belgrade, April 11, 2005.

Srdjan Bogosavljević, director, Strategic Marketing Research, Belgrade, April 13, 2005.

Daniel Calingaert, deputy director for Eastern Europe, International Republican Institute (IRI), Washington, DC, July 19, 2005.

Suzana Grubješić, founding member of the G17Plus, Belgrade, April 12, 2005.

Stephen B. Heintz, president, Rockefeller Brothers Fund, Belgrade, April 16, 2005.

Dušan Janjić, senior researcher, Institute for Social Sciences, Belgrade, and coordinator of the Forum for Ethnic Relations, Belgrade, April 11, 2005.

Nenad Konstantinović, Subotić-Homen Law Office and member of the Executive Committee of the Democratic Movement/Committee for Legal Issues, Belgrade, April 15, 2005.

Adriana Lazinica, senior program manager, United States Agency for International Development (USAID), Belgrade, April 15, 2005.

Sonja Licht, executive director and president, Fund for an Open Society in Yugoslavia (later Serbia) (1991–2003) and longtime civil society activist, Belgrade, April 12, 2005; Charlottesville, VA, November 9, 2007; and Philadelphia, February 23, 2007.

Ivan Marović, leader, Otpor, Washington, DC, October 14, 2004, and Belgrade, April 14, 2005.

Andrej Milivojević, member, Otpor, Berkeley, CA, February 14, 2007.

Anthony Monaghan, Office of Small Arms Control for the United Nations Development Programme (UNDP), Belgrade, April 12, 2005.

Milan Nič, development director, Pontis Foundation, Belgrade, April 13, 2005.

Milan Nikolić, director, Center for Policy Studies, Belgrade, April 12, 2005, and Charlottesville, VA, November 9, 2007.

James C. O'Brien, presidential envoy for the Balkans and senior advisor to Secretary of State Madeline K. Albright, United States Department of State; deputy director, Office of Policy Planning, United States Department of State, Washington, DC, November 16, 2006.

Dušan Pavlović, associate professor of Political Science, Department of Political Science, University of Belgrade. Belgrade, April 13 and 14, 2005.

Vesna Pešić, founder and director, Centre for Antiwar Action; founding member, Yugoslav Helsinki Committee (1985); founding member, Association for the Yugoslav Democratic Initiative (1989) and the Yugoslav European Movement (1991); president of the Civic Alliance of Serbia (1992–98); leader of the Coalition Zajedno (1993–97); founding member, Alliance for Change, Belgrade, April 14, 2005.

Srdja Popović, Otpor leader, Oxford, March, 2007.

Aaron Presnall, director, Jefferson Institute, Belgrade, April 9, 2005.

Biljana Presnall, director of finance, Jefferson Institute, Belgrade, April 9, 2005.

Daniel Serwer, vice president, Peace and Stability Operations, United States Institute of Peace (USIP), Washington, DC, November 17, 2006.

Steven Simic, consultant, Belgrade, April 13, 2005.

Gregory Simpson, country director, International Republican Institute (IRI), Belgrade, April 13, 2005; Charlottesville, November 9, 2007.

Vojislav Stanovčić, faculty of political sciences, University of Belgrade, Belgrade, April 14, 2005.

Mike Staresinic, Freedom House, Belgrade (1999–2000), Belgrade, April 15, 2005.

Marijana Trivunović, independent consultant, Open Society and United Nations, Belgrade, April 12, 2005.

J. Walter Veirs, program officer, Charles Stewart Mott Foundation, Belgrade, April 16, 2005.

Ivan Vejvoda, founding member, Belgrade Circle, and opposition intellectual, Belgrade, April 11, 2005.

Aleksandra Vesić, executive director, Balkan Communities Initiative Fund, (Belgrade Program for Political Distinctiveness), Belgrade, April 12, 2005.

SLOVAKIA

Martin Bútora, founder and president, Institute for Public Affairs (IVO), Bratislava and Washington, numerous discussions, 1995–2008.

Zora Bútorová, senior research fellow, Institute for Public Affairs (IVO); member of coordinating committee, OK'98, Bratislava and Washington, DC, numerous discussions, 1996–2009.

Pavol Demeš, executive director of the Slovak Academic Information Agency–Service Center for the Third Sector (SAIA-SCTS); head of the Third Sector Gremium; member of coordinating committee, OK'98, Bratislava and Washington DC, numerous interviews, 1991–2009.

Alexander Duleba, president, Slovak Foreign Policy Association, Bratislava, March 2000.

Ján Figel, state secretary of the Ministry of Foreign Affairs, Slovakia (1998–2002); member of the European Commission responsible for Education, Training, Culture and Youth, numerous interviews, Washington, DC, and Bratislava, 1995–2007.

Dr. Joerg Forbrig, program officer for Central and Eastern Europe, German Marshall Fund of the United States, Bratislava, June 2005.

Ol'ga Gyárfášová, senior research fellow, Institute for Public Affairs (IVO), Bratislava, Bratislava and Washington, DC, numerous discussions, 1999–2009.

Ralph Johnson, U.S. ambassador to Slovakia (1996–99); coordinator for U.S. assistance to Central and Eastern Europe, United States Department of State (1993–95), Bratislava, May 1998.

Marek Kapusta, Rock the Vote, Foundation for a Civil Society (Bratislava), Bratislava, May 1999 and March 2000.

Wendy Luers, founder and president, Foundation for a Civil Society, New York and Washington, DC, summer 1996 and April 2007.

Katerína Malíková, director, Slovak Foreign Aid Foundation, Bratislava, May 2005.

L'udmila Malíková, associate professor, Department of Political Science, Comenius University, Bratislava; director, Institute for Public Policy, Comenius University, Bratislava, Bratislava and Washington, DC, numerous discussions, 1999–2009.

Katarína Mathernová, former senior advisor to the deputy prime minister for economic affairs of Slovakia (1999–2002), Washington, DC, and Bratislava, numerous discussions, 1996–2008.

Grigoryi Mesežnikov, president, Institute for Public Affairs (IVO), Bratislava and Washington, DC, numerous discussions, 1996–2009.

František Mikloško, member of parliament, Christian Democratic Movement, Bratislava, June 7, 2007.

Marek Mračko, Open Eye and MEMO, Bratislava, May 1998 and March 2000.

László Nagy, chair, Committee on Human Rights, Slovak parliament; former head of the Hungarian Civic Party, Bratislava and Washington, DC, numerous discussions, 1990–2009.

Milan Nič, development director, Pontis Foundation, Bratislava, May 2005.

Dušan Ondrušek, Slovakia director, Partners for Democratic Change, Bratislava and Washington, DC, numerous discussions, 1993–2007.

Šarlota Pufflerová, president, Foundation for Minority Rights; spokesperson for OK'98, Bratislava and Washington, DC, numerous interviews, 1993–2009.

Iveta Radičová, analyst, SPACE, Bratislava, numerous discussions, 1990–2005.

Theodore Russell, U.S. ambassador to Slovakia (1993–96), Bratislava and Washington, DC, numerous discussions, 1990–2008.

František Šebej, former parliamentarian and member of the Committee on Foreign Relations, Slovak parliament; former deputy chairman of the Democratic Party in Slovakia, Bratislava and Washington, DC, May 1998 and May 2000.

Jan Surotchak, resident program director, Central and Eastern Europe, International Republican Institute (IRI); resident program officer, International Republican Institute (IRI), Bratislava, May 2005, June 2007, and June 2009.

Lenka Surotchak, president, Pontis Foundation, Bratislava, June 2007 and June 2009.

Soňa Szomolányi, professor of political science and head, Department of Political Science, Comenius University Bratislava, numerous discussions, 1996–2009.

Scott Thayer, deputy chief of mission, United States embassy, Bratislava, Washington, DC, and Bratislava, numerous discussions, 2004–2008.

UKRAINE

Bogdan Ben, Independent Ukrainian Youth Organization, Lviv, June 2005.

Roman Bezsmertnyi, chief of staff, Yushchenko's campaign, Nasha Ukraina, Kiev, June 15, 2007.

David Black, member of Democracy and Governance Section, United States Agency for International Development (USAID), Washington, DC, September 30, 2005.

Martha Bohachevsky-Chomiak, director, U.S. Fulbright Office, Kyiv, June 14, 2007.

Kataryna Botanova, journalist, Znaju, Kyiv, June 13, 2007.

Valeriy Chaly, deputy director, Razumkov Center, Kyiv, June 14, 2007.

Ross Chomiak, officer (retired), United States Agency for International Development (USAID), Kyiv, June 14, 2007.

Orest Danchewsky, Committee of Voters of Ukraine, Lviv, August 4, 2005.

Nadia Diuk, senior director for Europe and Eurasia, National Endowment for Democracy (NED), Washington, DC, February 2009.

Alexander Duleba, director, Slovak Foreign Policy Association, Bratislava, March 2000.

Juhani Grossman, senior program officer, Civic Participation in Elections in Ukraine, Freedom House, Kyiv, June 13, 2007.

Evhenyi Holovaka, Institute of Sociology, National Academy of Science, Ukraine, Kyiv, June 15, 2007.

Volodymyr Horbach, Yellow Pora adviser; historian; leader of Rukh, Kyiv, June 12, 2007.

Oleskandr Horin, ambassador extraordinary and plenipotentiary of Ukraine to the Republic of Singapore (2002–06), Kyiv, June 11, 2007.

Andriy Ignatev, Democratic Initiatives Foundation, Kyiv, June 15, 2007.

Balázs Jarábik, Pontis Foundation, Kyiv, June 12, 2007.

Marek Kapusta, project manager, Rock the Vote, Foundation for a Civil Society, Bratislava, March 2000.

Vladyslav Kaskiv, Yellow Pora, Kyiv, June 13, 2007.

Andriy Kohout, leader, Pora, Kyiv, June 14, 2007.

Vasil Kosiv, professor, Lviv Academy of Arts, Lviv, August 4, 2005.

Katarína Košťálová, director, Slovak Academic Information Agency–Service Center for the Third Sector (SAIA-SCTS), Bratislava, April 12, 2000.

Orysia Kulyk, U.S. Fulbright student, Kyiv, June 11, 2007.

Pavol Lukáč, Slovak Foreign Policy Association, Bratislava, March 2000.

Ihor Lylo, Reagan-Fascell Democracy Fellow, National Endowment for Democracy; radio journalist and director of political programming, Lviv Wave Radio station; assistant professor, Ivan Franko State National University, Lviv, Washington, DC, February 24, 2009.

Volodymyr Lytvyn, speaker, Ukrainian Parliament; member of parliament, Kyiv, June 12, 2007.

Brian Mefford, country director for Ukraine, International Republican Institute (IRI), Kyiv, June 12, 2007.

Mikola Mishenko, researcher, Institute of Psychology, Ukrainian National Academy of Science, Kyiv, June 12, 2007.

Yulia Mostovaya, editor, *Dzerkalo Tyzhnia/Zerkalo nedeli*, Kyiv, June 12 and 13, 2007.

Marek Mračko, Open Eye and MEMO, Bratislava, March 2000.

Alena Pániková, executive director, Open Society Foundation–Bratislava, Bratislava, March 2000.

Dmytro Potekhin, Znaju, Kyiv, June 13, 2007.

Jaroslavl Prytula, professor, Ivan Franko National University, Lviv, August 3, 2005.

Anatoliy Rachok, director general, Razumkov Centre, Kyiv, Kyiv, June 2007.

Mykola Rybachuk, leading Ukrainian intellectual, poet, and political analyst, Philadelphia, February 2007.

Oleh Rybachuk, head of the office of Prime Minister Yushchenko, 1999–2002; spokesman for Orange coalition; chief of staff, President Yushchenko, 2005–06, Washington, DC, February 26, 2009.

Eleanor Seats, member of Election Programs, United States Agency for International Development (USAID), Kyiv, Kyiv, June 17, 2007.

Victoria Sereda, professor of social and cultural studies, Ivan Franko National University, Lviv; NGO activist, Lviv, August 4, 2005.

Marisa Shukost, homemaker, wife of Greek Catholic priest, Smerechka, August 1, 2005.

Volodymyr Sivkovych, member of parliament, Party of Regions, Kyiv, June 11, 2006.

Miroslav Soldat, regional director for Lviv, Yushenko's campaign organization, Lviv, August 3, 2005.

Oleksandr Stegniy, Institute of Sociology, National Academy of Science, Ukraine, Kyiv, June 15, 2007.

Boris Tarasiuk, Ukrainian foreign minister (1998–2000, 2005–06), Kyiv, June 13, 2006.

MULTIPLE CASES

Harry Barnes, U.S. ambassador to Chile (1985–88), Philadelphia, February 24, 2007.

Robert Benjamin, senior associate and regional director for Central and Eastern Europe, National Democratic Institute (NDI), Washington, DC, April 9, 2010.

Scott Carpenter, co-director, Regional Office for Central and East European Affairs (Bratislava), International Republican Institute (IRI), Washington, DC, April 9, 2009.

Pavol Demeš, European director, German Marshall Fund of the United States, Washington, DC, Bratislava, and Philadelphia, numerous interviews, 1995–2009.

Nadia Diuk, senior director for Europe and Eurasia, National Endowment for Democracy, Washington, DC, April 2, 2010.

Larry Garber, expert consultant, United States Agency for International Development (USAID), Washington, DC, April 9, 2010.

Robert Gelbard, U.S. ambassador to Indonesia (1999–2001); President Clinton's special representative for the Balkans (1997–99); assistant secretary of state (1993–97), Ithaca, NY, March 1, 2007.

Carl Gershman, president, National Endowment for Democracy (NED), Washington, DC, May 14, 2010.

Barbara Haig, deputy to the president for policy and strategy, National Endowment for Democracy (NED), Washington, DC, May 14, 2010.

David Kostelancik, deputy director, Office of North Central Europe, Bureau of European and Eurasian Affairs, U.S. Department of State, (2005–07), Washington, DC, November 16, 2006.

Roland Kovats, director, Freedom House Europe, Budapest, May 24, 2006.

Lindsay Lloyd, program officer, International Republican Institute (IRI), Bratislava (1995–99); co-director of IRI's Regional Program for Central and Eastern Europe, Bratislava (1999–2002); regional director for Europe, International Republican Institute (IRI), Bratislava, April, 10, 2000; Washington, DC, November 16, 2006.

Patrick Merloe, senior associate and director of electoral programs, National Democratic Institute (NDI), Washington, DC, April 30, 2009.

Peter Novotný, director, Občianské oko, Washington, DC, February 24, 2010.

Roger Potocki, director for Europe and Eurasia, National Endowment for Democracy (NED), Washington, DC, May 7, 2010.

Joanna Rohozinska, program officer, National Endowment for Democracy (NED), Washington DC, February 18, 2009.

Daniel Serwer, vice president, peace and stability operations, United States Institute of Peace, Washington, DC, November 17, 2006.

Kenneth Wollack, president, National Democratic Institute (NDI), Washington, DC, May 12, 2010.

ROUNDTABLES

Baku, Azerbaijan, March 7, 2007: roundtable with leaders of NGOs in Azerbaijan. Included Anar Ahmadov, director, Caucasus Research Resource Center, Eurasia Foundation; Aida Badalova, president, Youth without Frontiers; Tabriz Jabbarov, Free Minds Association; Emin Milli, Alumni Network; and Parviz Bagirov, youth/education programs director, Open Society Institute-Assistance Foundation.

Belgrade, Serbia, April 13, 2005: organized by the Jefferson Institute (Aaron and Biljana Presnall). Ivana Spasić, associate professor, Department of Sociology, Faculty of Philosophy, University of Belgrade; Milan St. Protić, president of Defense (SDK Odbrana) and co-president of New Serbia, member of the main board of the Democratic Party of

Serbia (DSS), 1992–93, and former mayor of Belgrade (2000–01); and Dušan Pavlović, associate professor of political science, Department of Political Science, University of Belgrade.

Charlottesville, VA, November 9, 2007: organized by the Jefferson Institute (Aaron and Biljana Presnall). Gregory Simpson, former country director for Serbia, International Republican Institute (IRI); Sonja Licht, executive director and president, Fund for an Open Society in Yugoslavia (later Serbia), 1991–2003, and longtime civil society activist; Milan Nikolić, director, Center for Policy Studies; Aaron Presnall, director, Jefferson Institute; and Paul Shoup, professor emeritus of political science at the University of Virginia.

Yerevan, Armenia, March 9, 2007: roundtable with eight members of the USAID Democracy and Governance Team, American embassy.

Yerevan, Armenia, March 9, 2007: roundtable discussions with the Armenian Center for National and International Studies; Raffi Hovhannisyan, director, Armenian Center for National and International Studies.

Yerevan, Armenia, March 12, 2007: roundtable with political party leaders organized by the National Democratic Institute.

Yerevan, Armenia, March 12, 2007: roundtable at the Institute for Political Research (advisors to the president of Armenia). Hovhannes Asryan, director, Institute for Political Research; Ashot Yeghiazaryan; Hayk Demoyan; Igor Muradyan; Ruzanna Issaghulyan; Garnik Issagulyan, president's advisor on national security issues; and Levon Andreasyan, vice director, Institute of Political Research.

Index

CPSIA information can be obtained at www.ICGtesting.com
Printed in the USA
LVOW082337180113

316386LV00003B/4/P